Professional Ethics and Insignia

Second Edition

edited by
John Stierman
Kathleen E. Joswick
Jeanne Koekkoek Stierman
Roderick L. Sharpe

The Scarecrow Press, Inc.
Lanham, Maryland, and London
2000

SCARECROW PRESS, INC.

Published in the United States of America
by Scarecrow Press, Inc.
4720 Boston Way, Lanham, Maryland 20706
www.scarecrowpress.com

4 Pleydell Gardens, Folkestone
Kent CT20 2DN, England

Copyright © 2000 by John Stierman, Kathleen E. Joswick, Jeanne Koekkoek Stierman,
and Roderick L. Sharpe

British Library Cataloguing in Publication Information Available

Library of Congress Cataloging-in-Publication Data

Professional Ethics and insignia / edited by John P. Stierman . . . [et al.].
— 2nd ed.   p.   cm.
Rev. ed. of: Professional ethics and insignia / Jane Clapp. 1974.
Includes bibliographical references and index.
ISBN: 0-8108-3620-3 (alk. paper)
  1. Professional associations—United States—Directories. 2. Trade
associations—United States—Handbooks, manuals, etc. 3. Professional
associations—United States—Insignia. 4. Trade associations—United
States—Insignia. 5. Professionals ethics—United States. I. Stierman,
John P., 1959– II. Clapp, Jane. Professional ethics and insignia.
HD6504.A194   2000
061'.3—dc21   00-025108

♾™ The paper used in this publication meets the minimum requirements of
American National Standard for Information Sciences—Permanence of
Paper for Printed Library Materials, ANSI/NISO Z39.48–1992.
Manufactured in the United States of America.

Contents

Foreword . . . . *ix*

Preface . . . . *xi*

Organizations

AACE International 1

Academy of Management 3

Air and Waste Management Association, Inc. 8

Air Traffic Control Association 9

American Academy of Actuaries 10

American Academy of Dermatology 13

American Academy of Family Physicians 14

American Academy of Ophthalmology 14

American Academy of Optometry 16

American Academy of Orthopaedic Surgeons 17

American Academy of Otolaryngology—Head and Neck Surgery Foundation, Inc. 20

American Academy of Physician Assistants 21

American Advertising Federation 22

American Anthropological Association 22

American Arbitration Association 26

American Association for Marriage and Family Therapy 29

American Association for Public Opinion Research 34

American Association for Respiratory Care 35

American Association of Advertising Agencies 36

American Association of Airport Executives 37

American Association of Bioanalysts 38

American Association of Family and Consumer Sciences 38

American Association of Homes and Services for the Aging 40

American Association of Nurse Anesthetists 41

American Association of Oriental Medicine 43

American Association of Pastoral Counselors 43

American Association of School Administrators 47

American Association of University Professors 47

American Bar Association 49

American Bed and Breakfast Association 49

American Board of Opticianry / National Contact Lens Examiners 50

American Chemical Society 51

American College of Health Care Administrators 52

American College of Healthcare Executives 54

American College of Nurse-Midwives 56

American College of Obstetricians and Gynecologists 57

American College of Surgeons 60

American Congress on Surveying and Mapping 67

American Consulting Engineers Council 68

American Correctional Association 69

American Counseling Association 70

American Dance Therapy Association 84

American Dental Assistants Association 85

American Dental Association 86

American Dental Hygienists' Association 95

American Dietetic Association 98

American Federation of Musicians of the United States and Canada 100

American Federation of Police 101

American Federation of Teachers 102

American Health Care Association 103

American Health Information Management Association 105

American Historical Association 106

American Hospital Association 109

American Institute of Aeronautics and Astronautics 112

The American Institute of Architects 113

American Institute of Certified Planners 117

American Institute of Certified Public Accountants 119

American Institute of Chemical Engineers 122

The American Institute of Chemists 123

The American Institute of Professional Geologists 124

American Judicature Society 126

American League of Lobbyists 130

American Library Association 131

American Marketing Association 132

American Mathematical Society 133

American Medical Association 135

American Medical Technologists 136

American Mental Health Counselors Association 137

American Meteorological Society 145

American Nuclear Society 146

American Nurses Association 147

American Occupational Therapy Association, Inc. 154

American Optometric Association 155

American Osteopathic Association 157

American Pharmaceutical Association—Academy of Pharmacy Practice and Management 158

American Physical Society 159

American Physical Therapy Association 160

American Physiological Society 161

American Planning Association 163

American Podiatric Medical Association 165

American Political Science Association 168

American Psychiatric Association 175

American Psychoanalytic Association 180

American Psychological Association 182

American Psychological Society 197

American Purchasing Society, Inc. 198

American Society for Microbiology 198

American Society for Public Administration 199

American Society for Quality 200

American Society of Agronomy 201

American Society of Anesthesiologists 202

American Society of Appraisers 203

American Society of Association Executives 213

American Society of Civil Engineers 214

American Society of Health-System Pharmacists 217

American Society of Heating, Refrigerating, and Air-Conditioning Engineers 217

American Society of Interior Designers 217

American Society of Internal Medicine 219

American Society of Journalists and Authors 221

American Society of Landscape Architects 223

American Society of Mechanical Engineers 226

American Society of Newspaper Editors 226

American Society of Plastic and Reconstructive Surgeons 227

American Society of Safety Engineers 232

American Society of Transportation and Logistics, Inc. 232

American Society of Travel Agents 233

American Sociological Association 234

American Speech-Language-Hearing Association 246

American Statistical Association 248

American Urological Association 249

Appraisal Institute 250

Archaeological Institute of America 255

Associated Builders and Contractors 257

Association for Career and Technical Education 258

Association for Computing Machinery 259

Association for Investment Management & Research 263

Association of Clinical Research Professionals 266

Association of Consulting Chemists & Chemical Engineers 267

Association of Information Technology Professionals 267

Association of Management Consulting Firms 269

Association of Professional Genealogists 269

Association of Trial Lawyers of America 270

Board for Certification of Genealogists 271

Board of Certified Safety Professionals 272

Botanical Society of America 272

Certified Financial Planner Board of Standards 274

Chartered Property Casualty Underwriter Society 281

Child Welfare League of America 282

Clinical Social Work Federation 282

College of American Pathologists 289

Community Associations Institute 289

The Direct Marketing Association 289

Ecological Society of America 295

Entomological Society of America 297

Federal Bar Association 299

Financial Executives Institute 314

General Agents and Managers Association 314

Genetics Society of America 315

Guild of Prescription Opticians of America 317

Human Factors and Ergonomics Society 317

Industrial Designers Society of America 319

Institute for Certification of Computing Professionals 320

Institute of Certified Management Accountants 324

Institute of Electrical and Electronics Engineers 324

Institute of Industrial Engineers 325

Institute of Internal Auditors 325

Institute of Management Accountants 326

Institute of Management Consultants 328

Institute of Real Estate Management 329

International Association for Financial Planning 331

International Association of Administrative Professionals 333

International Association of Assessing Officers 335

International Association of Chiefs of Police 339

International Association of Clothing Designers and Executives 341

Contents

vii

International Association of Correctional Officers 341
International Association of Culinary Professionals 342
International Association of Fire Chiefs 343
International City/County Management Association 344
International Facility Management Association 344
International Fire Marshals Association 345
International Hearing Society 347
International Reading Association 350
Manufacturers' Agents National Association 351
Minerals, Metals & Materials Society 351
Modern Language Association 352
Music Teachers National Association 355
National Association for College Admission Counseling 356
National Association for Home Care 363
National Association of Alcoholism and Drug Abuse Counselors 366
National Association of Colleges and Employers 369
National Association of Counties 372
National Association of Credit Management 373
National Association of Emergency Medical Technicians 374
National Association of Environmental Professionals 375
National Association of Fire Investigators 376
National Association of Health Underwriters 377
National Association of Home Builders 377
National Association of Legal Assistants 378
National Association of Legal Secretaries 379
National Association of Life Underwriters 380
National Association of Performing Arts Managers and Agents 381
National Association of Professional Educators 384
National Association of Purchasing Management 385
National Association of REALTORS® 386
National Association of Social Workers 395
National Auctioneers Association 395
National Dance Association's National Registry of Dance Educators 397
National Education Association 398
National Environmental Health Association 399
National Federation of Interscholastic Coaches Association 400
National Genealogical Society 401
National Guild of Hypnotists 402
National Press Photographers Association 404
National Property Management Association 405
National Recreation and Park Association 405

National Registry of Environmental Professionals 406

National Sheriffs' Association 407

National Society of Accountants 408

National Society of Fund Raising Executives 408

National Society of Professional Engineers 410

National Society of Public Accountants 413

National Therapeutic Recreation Society 415

National Weather Association 417

National Writers Association 417

Professional Numismatists Guild, Inc. 418

Professional Photographers of America 420

Public Relations Society of America 420

Radio-Television News Directors Association 422

Radiological Society of North America 422

Society for Human Resource Management 422

Society for Technical Communication 423

Society of American Archivists 424

Society of American Foresters 425

Society of Financial Service Professionals 426

Society of Fire Protection Engineers 428

Society of Petroleum Engineers 430

Society of Professional Journalists 431

Society of Professionals in Dispute Resolution 432

Soil Science Society of America 434

Special Libraries Association 434

Wedding and Portrait Photographers International 435

The Wildlife Society 435

Cross-Index of Represented Professions *437*

About the Editors *445*

Foreword

Professional ethics have been the subject of increased attention and scrutiny in the past twenty-five years. Dramatic cases such as the Watergate scandal and the controversial activities of Dr. Kevorkian have prompted a closer examination of the responsibilities of traditional professions such as law and medicine.

In recent years, many occupational groups have attempted to "professionalize" by seeking elevation to the status of the professions. Although there is no generally accepted definition of what a profession is, there are characteristics found among the paradigms of professional occupations. These qualities include skill and specialized knowledge, often with a scholarly component, acquired through lengthy training and preparation and maintained by continued study and practice. Professional activity is complex, requiring not only specific knowledge, but also autonomy and discretion to exercise professional judgment and the employment of professional skills. Professions are typically committed, in some broad sense, to serve the welfare of society, a goal often pursued indirectly through service to clients. The relationship between the professions and the larger society can be understood as an implicit contract whereby professions are granted significant leeway in exchange for a commitment to society and an assurance of self-policing.

Codes of ethics can be viewed in this context. Members of professions or occupational groups seeking professional status often organize themselves into associations which aim at promoting autonomy and collegiality, at developing standards for training and competence, and at setting goals and principles for professional practice. Codes of ethical practices and responsibilities reflect the agreement among members of a profession on the goals and the standards of ethical conduct. Generally, the latter defines three types of ethical relationships for professionals: to their clients, to the public at large, and to the profession itself, including fellow professionals.

Ethical codes vary greatly in their quality and effectiveness. Some are properly accused of being self-serving and narrowly focused on matters such as conflicts of financial interests (like fee-splitting arrangements) among professional practitioners. However, the better ones can play a valuable role in elevating the quality of service by encouraging increased education and acquisition of skills and by expanding the self-understanding of the profession's roles and responsibilities. They can also provide effective self-regulation by establishing ethical conduct guidelines. Effective codes help professionals resist the pressure to behave unethically or to look the other way at such behavior by others. Professionals who work for large employers in bureaucratic settings such as government agencies or major corporations are particularly likely to benefit from such assistance.

This new edition of *Professional Ethics and Insignia* provides a wide array of ethical codes for examination and comparison. The editors chose to work with a broad definition of "profession," which enabled them to be more inclusive of emerging and aspiring professional groups. Yet, they were still able to exclude some occupations lacking the more salient traits that characterize professions. The editors relied on the various associations that represent the professional occupations to provide statements of the codes of ethics. It is apparent that the codes themselves have undergone revision in light of changing environments and other challenges facing professionals in their practice. The second edition will prove to be a valuable resource for its comprehensiveness and timeliness.

Mario Morelli, Ph.D.
Professor, Philosophy and Religious Studies
Western Illinois University

ix

Preface

Professional Ethics and Insignia (second edition) brings together the official codes of ethics or conduct from 222 organizations representing professions common in the United States. The original edition, compiled by Jane Clapp and published in 1974, filled an important need as a reference resource, but is now outdated. Although many professional organizations post their codes of conduct on their World Wide Web pages, this second print edition, like the first, offers easy comparison of the codes in different or related occupations, as well as ready access to an occupation's code without requiring knowledge of the professional associations that represent it. The editors expect that the second edition will continue to be useful to students, teachers of business and professional ethics, and to members of organizations in the process of defining and codifying their own standards of professional conduct. Likewise, licensing boards, litigators, researchers, disciplinary committees, and people seeking more information about careers will find the second edition valuable.

This edition of *Professional Ethics and Insignia*, however, differs from the first in several important ways. The number and identities of the occupations vary greatly from the first edition. In determining which professions to include, the editors used a broad definition of "professional," culling professions from Clapp's work and from several published registers of occupations. While adding professions that have risen to prominence in the past twenty-five years, they also eliminated some of the occupations that Clapp had included: most trades, labor unions, large classifications of government employees, and occupations requiring little specialized training. Once they identified appropriate professions, the editors searched for associations representing them. If the goals of the profession were exemplified by more than one association, the editors usually contacted the largest to supply the code of ethics. In many cases, however, the editors approached several associations for a single profession and chose codes from those supplied. Because the lists of occupations and associations were completely revamped, only one-third of

the codes in the first edition are included here in their current form; almost two-thirds were eliminated. The second edition added approximately 140 codes that were not in the first edition. Nonetheless, while more current and comprehensive than the first edition, this edition of *Professional Ethics and Insignia* is not definitive. More than one-half of the associations identified for this edition either did not have a code of ethics, were not willing to have their code reproduced here, or never responded to the inquiries about their organization. Because of these factors, some of the organizations included here represent a subset of the profession, rather than its primary agency; other recognized professions are not represented at all. This collection should be viewed as a sampling of professional codes of ethics.

The other differences from the first edition concern the format and the content of the entries. In this edition, codes of conduct appear in alphabetical order by the authoring association and the list of professions is in the index, with references to the associations. This format allows the associations to be cross-listed under more than one applicable profession. Because detailed information about each association is readily available elsewhere, only the association name, address, phone number, World Wide Web address, document title, and insignia are included. Since the primary purpose of this edition is to provide ready access to an extensive collection of codes of ethics, the histories, descriptions of the insignia, licensing requirements, professional designations, and bibliographies contained in the original work have been eliminated.

In all cases, the designated professional associations provided the ethical codes appearing here and retain all rights over the use and reproduction of all or parts of the codes. Each code is reprinted here according to the editorial house style of its issuing organization. For the sake of uniformity, the editors followed certain formatting conventions, but, for the most part, the titles of the documents, plus capitalizations and the use of boldface and italic print within the texts of the codes, follow the text supplied by the issuing association and represent its emphasis. There are no deletions, paraphrases, or editorial summaries. Occasionally, the editors added notes within an entry to describe the history of the code's development, to alert the reader to related documents published by the sponsoring association, or to explain the relationship between or among associations. These editorial notes, clearly marked as parenthetical statements, do not express an evaluation of the code or imply comprehensive documentation of the code's history. The dates the organization adopted and/or revised the code, when provided, follow the document titles. All addresses, phone numbers, and World Wide Web addresses are current through March, 2000. Readers are cautioned, however, that the fluid nature of the World Wide Web makes those addresses especially susceptible to change. Association emblems or insignias are included for those organizations that supplied them and gave permission to reprint them, but the reader should not infer that the lack of an insignia in the book means that the organization has none.

The editors extend their sincere thanks to the organizations that contributed their ethical codes to this project and to the association employees whose efficiency and diligence made the task of compiling the codes much easier. The editors are grateful also to the library student workers at Western Illinois University who assisted with typing, photocopying, filing, scanning, and proofreading: Sarah Brown, Jenifer Calvert, Melissa Castrey, Dianne Griswold, Amy Hevner, Brandi Kramer, Ben Lubinski, Anna Nelson, Pam Nichting, Mike Regan, and Kristin Walker. Finally, the editors thank Dr. Donna Goehner, dean of the library throughout most of this project, and other administrators at Western Illinois University who have included library faculty in the university's community of scholars, and who encourage and support their research.

AACE INTERNATIONAL (Association for the Advancement of Cost Engineering)

Address: 209 Prairie Avenue, #100
             Morgantown, WV 26501
Telephone: 304/296-8444 or 800/858-2678
WWW: www.aacei.org
Document: Canon of Ethics

INTRODUCTION
The AACE member, to uphold and advance the honor and dignity of Cost Engineering and the Cost Management profession and in keeping with the high standards of ethical conduct will (1) be honest and impartial and will serve employer, clients, and the public with devotion; (2) strive to increase the competence and prestige of their profession; and (3) will apply knowledge and skill to advance human welfare.

I. Relations With the Public
A. Members will hold paramount the safety, health, and welfare of the public, including that of future generations.

B. Members will endeavor to extend public knowledge and appreciation of cost engineering and cost management and its achievements, and will oppose any untrue, unsupported, or exaggerated statements regarding cost engineering and cost management.

C. Members will be dignified and modest, ever upholding the honor and dignity of their profession, and will refrain from self-laudatory advertising.

D. Members will express an opinion on a cost engineering or cost management subject only when it is founded on adequate knowledge and honest conviction.

E. On cost engineering or cost management matters, members will issue no statements, criticisms, or arguments that are inspired or paid for by an interested party or parties, unless they preface their comments by identifying themselves, by disclosing the identities of the party or parties on whose behalf they are speaking, and by revealing the existence of any pecuniary interest they may have in matters under discussion.

F. Members will approve or seal only those documents, reviewed or prepared by them, which are determined to be safe for public health and welfare in conformity with accepted cost engineering, cost management and economic standards.

G. Members whose judgment is overruled under circumstances where the safety, health, and welfare of the public are endangered shall inform their clients or employers, of the possible consequences.

H. Members will work through professional societies to encourage and support others who follow these concepts.

I. Members will work only with those who follow these concepts.

J. Members shall be objective and truthful in professional reports, statements, or testimony. They shall include all relevant and pertinent information in such reports, statements, and testimony.

II. Relations With Employers and Clients
A. Members will act in all matters as a faithful agent or trustee for each employer or client.

1

B. Members will act fairly and justly toward vendors and contractors and will not accept any commissions or allowances from vendors or contractors, directly or indirectly.

C. Members will inform their employer or client of financial interest in any potential vendor or contractor, or in any invention, machine, or apparatus that is involved in a project or work for either employer or client. Members will not allow such interest to affect any decisions regarding cost engineering or cost management services that they may be called upon to perform.

D. When, as a result of their studies, members believe a project(s) will not be successful, or if their cost engineering and cost management or economic judgment is overruled, they shall so advise their employer or client.

E. Members will undertake only those cost engineering and cost management assignments for which they are qualified. Members will engage or advise their employers or clients to engage specialists whenever their employer's or client's interests are served best by such an arrangement. Members will cooperate fully with specialists so engaged.

F. Members shall treat information coming to them in the course of their assignments as confidential and shall not use such information as a means of making personal profit if such action is adverse to the interests of their clients, the employers, or the public.

   1. Members will not disclose confidential information concerning the business affairs or technical processes of any present or former employer or client or bidder under evaluation, without consent, unless required by law.
   2. Members shall not reveal confidential information on a finding of any commission or board of which they are members, unless required by law.
   3. Members shall not duplicate for others, without express permission of the client(s), designs, calculations, sketches, etc., supplied to them by clients.
   4. Members shall not use confidential information coming to them in the course of their assignments as a means of making personal profit if such action is adverse to the interests of their clients, employers, or the public.

G. Members will not accept compensation—financial or otherwise—from more than one party for the same service or for other services pertaining to the same work, without consent of all interested parties.

H. Employed members will engage in supplementary employment or consulting practice only with the consent of their employer.

I. Members shall not use equipment, supplies, laboratory, or office facilities of their employers to carry on outside private practice without the consent of their employers.

J. Members shall not solicit a contract from a governmental body on which a principal officer or employee of their organization serves as a member.

K. The member shall act with fairness and justice to all parties when administering a construction (or other) contract.

L. Before undertaking work for others in which the member may make improvements, plans, designs, inventions, or records that may justify copyrights or patents, the member shall enter into a positive agreement regarding the rights of the respective parties.

M. Members shall admit and accept their own errors when proven wrong and refrain from distorting or altering the facts to justify their decisions.

N. Members shall not attempt to attract an employee from another employer by false or misleading representations.

O. Members shall act in professional matters for each employer or client as faithful agents or trustees and shall avoid conflicts of interest.

   1. Members shall avoid all known or potential conflicts of interest with their employers or clients and shall promptly inform their employers or clients of any business association, interests, or circumstances that could influence their judgment or the quality of their services.
   2. Members shall not solicit or accept gratuities, directly or indirectly, from contractors, their agents, or other parties dealing with their clients or employers in connection with work for which they are responsible.

III. Relations With other Professionals

A. Members will take care that credit for cost engineering and cost management work is given to those to whom credit is properly due.

B. Members will provide prospective employees with complete information on working conditions and their proposed status of employment. After employment begins, they will keep the employee informed of any changes in status and working conditions.

C. Members will uphold the principle of appropriate and adequate compensation for those engaged in cost engineering and cost management work, including those in subordinate capacities.

D. Members will endeavor to provide opportunity for the professional development and advancement of individuals in their employ or under their supervision.

E. Members will not attempt to supplant other cost engineers or cost management professionals in a particular employment after becoming aware that definite steps have been taken toward the others' employment or after they have been employed.

F. Members shall not maliciously or falsely, directly or indirectly, injure the professional reputation, prospects, practice, or employment of another, nor shall they indiscriminately criticize another's work. Proof that another cost professional has been unethical, illegal, or unfair in his/her practice shall be cause for advising the proper authority.

G. Members will not compete unfairly with other cost professionals.

H. Members will cooperate in advancing the cost engineering and cost management profession by interchanging information and experience with other cost professionals and students, by contributing to public communication media and to cost engineering, cost management and scientific societies and schools.

I. Members will not request, propose, or accept professional commissions on a contingent basis under circumstances that compromise their professional judgment.

J. Members will not falsify or permit misrepresentation of their own or their associates' academic or professional qualifications. They shall not misrepresent or exaggerate their degrees or responsibility in or for the subject matter of prior assignments. Brochures or other presentations incident to the solicitation of employment shall not misrepresent pertinent factors concerning employers, employees, associates, joint ventures, accomplishments, or membership in technical societies.

K. Members will prepare articles for the lay or technical press that are only factual, dignified, and free from ostentatious or laudatory implications. Such articles shall not imply credit to the cost professionals for other than their direct participation in the work described unless credit is given to others for their share of the work.

L. Members will not campaign, solicit support, or otherwise coerce other cost professionals to support their candidacy or the candidacy of a colleague for elective office in a technical association.

IV. Standards of Professional Performance

A. Members shall be dignified and modest in explaining their work and merit and will avoid any act tending to promote their own interests at the expense of the integrity, honor, and dignity of the profession.

B. Members, when serving as expert witnesses, shall express a cost engineering and cost management opinion only when it is founded upon adequate knowledge of the facts, upon a background of technical competence, and upon honest conviction.

C. Members shall continue their professional development throughout their careers and shall provide opportunities for the professional development of those cost professionals under their supervision.

1. Members should keep current in their specialty fields by engaging in professional practice, participating in continuing education courses, reading in the technical literature, and attending professional meetings and seminars.

2. Members should encourage their cost engineering and cost management employees to become certified at the earliest possible date.

3. Members should encourage their cost engineering and cost management employees to attend and present papers at professional and technical society meetings.

4. Members shall uphold the principle of mutually satisfying relationships between employers and employees with respect to terms of employment including professional grade descriptions, salary ranges, and fringe benefits.

© AACE International. Reprinted with permission.

ACADEMY OF MANAGEMENT

Address:	Pace University, PO Box 3020
	Briarcliff Manor, NY 10510-3020
Telephone:	914/923-2607
WWW:	www.aom.pace.edu
Document:	Academy of Management Code of
	Ethical Conduct (1995)

CREDO

We believe in discovering, sharing, and applying managerial knowledge.

PREAMBLE

Our professional goals are to enhance the learning of students, colleagues, and others and to improve the effectiveness of organizations through our teaching, research, and practice of management. We have five major responsibilities:

1. To our students—Relationships with students require respect, fairness, and caring, along with recognition of our commitment to the subject matter and to teaching excellence.
2. To managerial knowledge—Prudence in research design, human subject use, confidentiality, result reporting, and proper attribution of work is a necessity.
3. To the Academy of Management and the larger professional environment—Support of the Academy's mission and objectives, service to the Academy and our institutions, and the recognition of the dignity and personal worth of colleagues is required.
4. To both managers and the practice of management—Exchange of ideas and information between the academic and organizational communities is essential.
5. To all people with whom we live and work in the world community—Sensitivity to other people, to diverse cultures, to the needs of the poor and disadvantaged, to ethical issues, and to newly emerging ethical dilemmas is required.

STUDENT RELATIONSHIPS

In our roles as educators, the central principles that underlie appropriate student-educator relationships are professionalism, respect, fairness, and concern.

Striving for teaching excellence. It is the duty of Academy members who are educators to prepare themselves carefully. Maintenance of current knowledge in the field requires a broad understanding of management theories, research and practice, and use of current classroom materials. Educators should have or develop expertise in the areas in which they teach. Effective teaching requires sufficient time allocated to preparation, clear classroom communication, timely grading, and a willingness to provide an explanation of a student's grade. Educators should act as role models in their relationships. They should also sensitize students to the ethical dimensions of man-

agement. In addition, educators have an obligation to present material without conscious bias and to make their own relevant biases known to their students. Educators should attempt to evaluate their teaching through some appropriate outcome assessment method which goes beyond concept retention.

Showing respect for students. It is the duty of Academy members who are educators to show appropriate respect for students' feelings, interests, needs, contributions, and intellectual freedom. Students' right to privacy requires maintaining the confidentiality of academic records and private communications unless disclosure is mandated by law, institutional policy, or a morally compelling purpose. Educators must avoid manipulation, coercion, or exploitation of students (especially acts directed at securing monetary, ego, or sexual gratification) and should demonstrate a sensitivity to cultural and personal diversity by avoiding racial, sexual, religious, and ethnic discrimination.

Maintenance of objectivity and fairness. It is the duty of Academy members who are educators to treat students equitably. Fair treatment of students requires explicitly explaining and adhering to academic requirements or standards. Any subsequent change in these requirements or standards, either of the institution or in an individual course, should appropriately recognize the impact on students. Impartiality, objectivity, and fairness are required in all dealings with students. Examinations should be carefully prepared and written work graded in an impartial manner. Educators should scrupulously avoid entering any overly personal relationship or accepting any gift or favor that might influence, or appear to influence, an objective evaluation of a student's work. Appropriate evaluation of student performance requires test design, assignments, and testing conditions that minimize the possibility of academic misconduct. It is the educator's responsibility to pursue appropriate disciplinary action if necessary.

Counseling of students. It is the duty of Academy members to be helpful and sensitive in counseling students. When serving as academic advisors, members must be knowledgeable about academic requirements and should communicate these clearly and fully to advisees. Educators may play critical roles in a variety of counseling situations. This requires careful analysis of the student and the situation and calls for special expertise and competence. Counseling advice should be identified as an expression of the member's own opinion. Letters of recommendation require candor and fairness. Members should not make insupportable statements nor fail to disclose material facts.

ADVANCEMENT OF MANAGERIAL KNOWLEDGE

Research of Academy members should be done honestly, have a clear purpose, show respect for the rights of all individuals and organizations, efficiently use resources, and advance knowledge in the field.

Conducting and reporting. It is the duty of Academy members conducting research to design, implement, analyze, report, and present their findings rigorously. Research rigor includes careful design, execution, analysis, interpretation of results, and retention of data. Presentation of research should include a treatment of the data that is honest and that reveals both strengths and weaknesses of findings. When important alternate hypotheses or explanations exist, they should be noted and data that disconfirm hypotheses should be acknowledged. Authorship and credit should be shared in correct proportion to the various parties' contributions. Whether published or not, ideas or concepts derived from others should be acknowledged, as should advice and assistance received. Many management-related journals have policies prohibiting or restricting potential articles from being reviewed concurrently in other outlets. These policies should be closely observed or there should be explicit discussion with the relevant journal editors concerning the intended multiple submissions. More than one report of essentially the same data and results should not be published unless the reports are explicitly directed to different audiences through different types of outlets. When several separate but related reports result from a single study, the existence of the different reports should be made known to the relevant journal editors and the reports should reference each other. Reviewer comments should be considered thoughtfully before a manuscript is submitted to a different journal.

Participants. It is the duty of Academy members to preserve and protect the privacy, dignity, well-being, and freedom of research participants. This duty requires both careful research design and informed consent from all participants. Risks and the possibility of harm to research participants must be carefully considered, and to the extent possible, these must be minimized. When there is a degree of risk or potential harm inherent in the research, potential participants—organizations as well as individuals—

must be informed. Informed consent means explaining to potential participants the purposes and nature of the research so they can freely choose whether or not to become involved. Such explanations include warning of possible harm and providing explicit opportunities to refuse to participate and to terminate participation at any time. Because students and employees are particularly subject to possible coercion, even when unintended, special care must be taken in obtaining their informed consent. Third-party review is one means of protecting the interests of research participants. Research plans involving human participants should be reviewed by an appropriate third party such as a university human subjects committee or a focus group of potential participants. Questions regarding confidentiality or anonymity must be resolved between researcher and potential research participants, both individuals and organizations; if confidentiality or anonymity is requested, this must be honored. Deception should be minimized, and when necessary, the degree and effects must be mitigated as much as possible. Researchers should carefully weigh the gains achieved against the cost in human dignity. To the extent that concealment of deception is necessary, the researcher must provide a full and accurate explanation to participants at the conclusion of the study, including counseling, if appropriate.

Dissemination. It is the duty of journal editors and reviewers to exercise their position of privilege in a confidential, unbiased, prompt, constructive, and sensitive manner. They have a duty to judge manuscripts only on their scholarly merits. Conflicts of interest may arise when a reviewer is in basic disagreement with the research approach or the line of research represented by a manuscript. In such cases, a reviewer should consult with the journal editor to decide whether to accept or decline to review the manuscript. Protecting intellectual property is a responsibility of the reviewer and the editor. The content of a manuscript is the property of its authors. It is therefore inappropriate to use ideas or show another person a manuscript one has been asked to review, without the explicit permission of its authors. Advice regarding specific, limited aspects of the manuscript may be sought from qualified colleagues so long as the authors' intellectual property remains secure. Sharing of reviewing responsibilities is inappropriate. The review is the sole responsibility of the person to whom it was assigned by the journal editor. In particular, students and colleagues should not be asked to prepare reviews unless the journal's editor has given explicit approval. Anyone contributing to a review should receive formal recognition. Constructive review means providing critiques and comments in a spirit of collegiality with thoroughness, timeliness, compassion, and respect, and in ways intended to improve the quality of the manuscript.

Grants and contracts. It is the duty of Academy members to accurately represent themselves and their proposed projects and to manage those projects as promised. Representation means accurate disclosure of one's level of expertise and expected actual involvement, the outcomes that can be reasonably expected, the realistic funding level needed, and any potential conflicts of interest. Grant and contract management requires independence and objectivity such that one does not compromise one's responsibilities or create conflicts of interest. One must also manage time and budget responsibly and use the funds as promised unless permission is explicitly granted to do otherwise.

THE ACADEMY OF MANAGEMENT AND THE LARGER PROFESSIONAL ENVIRONMENT

The Mission Statement of the Academy describes member benefits and professional opportunities of members which impose corresponding duties and service responsibilities.

Sharing and dissemination of information. To encourage meaningful exchange, Academy members should foster a climate of free interchange and constructive criticism within the Academy and should be willing to share research findings and insights fully with other members.

Academy participation. The Academy is a voluntary association whose existence and operations are dependent on cooperation, involvement, and leadership from its members. Members should abide by the constitution, bylaws, policies, and codes of the Academy. Members should consider offering their time and talent to carry out activities necessary to maintain the Academy and its functions. Officers and members should fulfill their Academy obligations and responsibilities in a timely, diligent, and sensitive manner, without regard to friendships or personal gain. Members should honor all professional commitments, including presentation of accepted papers and participation in scheduled roles as chair, discussant, or panel member. If absence from a scheduled meeting is unavoidable, members must contact appropriate individuals and pursue suitable alternative arrange-

ments. One should consider the impact one's projects or activities may have on the integrity or reputation of the Academy, and one should not engage in such projects or activities that may have possible negative implications. Members should not imply that their work is sanctioned by the Academy unless an appropriate Academy body has specifically done so.

Commitment to professional standards of conducts. By this code, the Academy provides ongoing ethical guidance for its members. Members should work to raise the consciousness of other members concerning ethical responsibilities, and they should encourage acceptance of these responsibilities. Members should notify appropriate Academy officers or committees regarding the practices or actions of members they believe may violate Academy regulations or general standards of ethical conduct. In this manner, the aspirational and educational goals of this code are served through discussion of the ethical dilemmas and values of our profession.

Strengthening and renewal of the Academy. The Academy of Management must have continuous infusions of members and new points of view to remain viable and relevant as a professional association. Members may contribute by encouraging all eligible individuals to participate in the Academy and by assisting new and prospective members in developing their skills, knowledge, and understanding of their professional obligations.

The professional environment for many Academy members includes the university community. The central values that underlie appropriate university participation are understanding, involvement, respect, fairness, and the pursuit of knowledge.

Participation in university leadership. Professors should take an active interest in university governance. Professors should be aware of university policies that affect the dissemination of policies. Professors should endeavor to positively influence policies relating to the quality of education and service to students. Active organizational involvement requires exercise of personal voting rights and respect for such rights of others, without regard to rank or tenure. Professors should evaluate colleagues for purposes of promotion or tenure on the basis of appropriate academic criteria that is fairly weighted in accordance with standards understood by the faculty and the subject of evaluation. It is the duty of Academy members to treat their colleagues with respect and fairness. Members should safeguard confidential personnel matters and avoid disclosing opinions expressed, attribution of statements, voting behavior, and outcomes. Members should address misunderstandings and conflicts with those directly involved and avoid speculative criticism that might damage the reputations of individuals or groups. When speaking or acting outside their university roles, professors should avoid creating the impression that they are speaking or acting for the university or its administration. Professors should dispose of complimentary books requested from publishers by a manner other than sale.

All Academy members, whether affiliated with a university, business, governmental, service, or consulting organization have an obligation to interact with others in a professional manner.

Membership in the professional community. It is the duty of Academy members to interact with others in our community in a manner that recognizes individual dignity and merit. The responsible professional promotes and protects the rights of individuals without regard to race, color, religion, national origin, handicap, sex, sexual orientation, age, political beliefs, or academic ideology, and refrains from sexual harassment. In the spirit of intellectual inquiry, the professional should welcome suggestions and complaints openly without reprisal. Members should ensure that outside activities do not significantly diminish their availability and energy to meet their institutional obligations.

MANAGERS AND THE PRACTICE OF MANAGEMENT

Consulting with client organizations ("clients") has the potential for enriching the teaching and practice of management, for translating theory into practice, and for furthering research and community service. To maximize such potential benefits, it is essential that members who consult be guided by the ideals of competence, integrity, and objectivity.

Credentials and capabilities. It is the duty of consultants to represent their credentials and capabilities in an accurate and objective manner. Consultants shall accept only those assignments for which they have appropriate expertise. Consultants shall refrain from exaggerating their professional qualifications to secure prospective assignments. Consultants shall examine any factors (e.g., prior experience, capabilities, other commitments) that might limit their judgment or objectivity in carrying out an assignment. University endorsement of the consulting activities of Academy members should not be represented or implied to

potential clients unless the assignment is formally under university sponsorship or is so approved.

Obligations to clients. Consultants have a duty to fulfill their obligations to their present and prospective clients in a professionally responsible and timely manner. Consultants shall place the highest possible priority on their clients' interests. Consultants shall avoid or withdraw from situations in which their clients' interests come into serious conflict with their own. Consultants shall not serve two or more competing clients without the consent of all parties. Consultants shall fully inform their clients. This means presenting results or advice in an unbiased manner and discussing fully with the client the values, risks, and limitations of the recommendations.

Client Relations. Consultants must fulfill duties of confidentiality and efficiency as part of the relationship with their clients. Consultants shall maintain confidentiality with respect to their clients' identities and the assignments undertaken, unless granted permission by the client. Consultants should exercise concern for the protection of clients, employees, and other stakeholders by maintaining, in particular, appropriate confidentiality. Consultants shall not take personal or financial advantage of confidential information acquired as a result of their professional relationships, nor shall they provide the basis upon which others may take such advantage. Consultants should meet their time commitments, and they should conserve the resources that are utilized.

Remuneration. It is the duty of consultants to negotiate clear and mutually accepted remuneration agreements for their services. Consultants shall provide a realistic estimate of the fees to be charged in advance of assignments. Fees charged shall be commensurate with the services performed.

Societal responsibilities. Consultants have a duty to uphold the legal and moral obligations of the society in which they function. Consultants should report to the appropriate authorities any unlawful activities that may have been uncovered during the course of their consulting engagements, except where their functional professional code directs otherwise.

Students and employees. It is the duty of the consultant to safeguard the rights of students and employees when they are involved in consulting assignments. Consultants may involve students in work generated by consulting engagements, especially if such work possesses learning potential, but students must not be coerced into participation. When they are so involved, students, as well as employees, should be fairly compensated, and they should be made aware of the nature of the work they are doing.

THE WORLD COMMUNITY

As citizens of the world community, Academy members may have much to contribute in shaping global consciousness through their teaching, research, and service.

World view. Academy members have a duty to consider their responsibilities to the world community. In their role as educators, members of the Academy can play a vital role in encouraging a broader horizon for decision making by viewing issues from a multiplicity of perspectives, including the perspectives of those who are least advantaged. As researchers, members of the Academy should consider, where appropriate, increasing their exposure to other cultures via travel, study, and research. Where appropriate, the research might highlight the responsible stewardship of the earth's resources. In addition, members should take as a challenge the ongoing task of identifying evolving ethical issues by listening to those whose welfare is affected and by exploring the interaction of people and technology. In fulfilling their service responsibilities, members of the Academy should consider how they might lend their time and talent to enhance the world community through involvement in uncompensated public service.

SEXUAL HARASSMENT

The Academy of Management and its members are committed to providing academic environments that are free of sexual harassment and all forms of sexual intimidation and exploitation.

Sexual harassment consists of unwelcome sexual advances, requests for sexual favors, and other visual, verbal, or physical conduct of a sexual nature when:

1. It is implicitly or explicitly suggested that submission to or rejection of the conduct will be a factor in academic employment, admission, evaluation, or participation in an academic activity.
2. The conduct has the purpose or effect of interfering with an individual's academic or work performance, by creating an intimidating, hostile, offensive, or otherwise unacceptable educational or work environment.

The determination of what constitutes sexual harassment depends upon the specific facts and the context in which conduct occurs. Sexual harassment takes many forms: subtle and indirect or blatant and overt; conduct affecting an individual of the opposite or same sex; between peers or between individuals in a hierarchical relationship; between teacher and student. Regardless of the intentions or the actor, the key question is always whether the conduct is unwelcome to the individual to whom it is directed.

There are special risks in any consensual sexual or romantic relationship between individuals in inherently unequal positions (such as student and faculty, or junior and senior faculty). Relationships in which one party is in a position to review the work or influence the career of the other may constitute sexual harassment when that relationship gives undue access or advantage, restricts opportunities, or creates a hostile and unacceptable environment for others in the work or classroom environments. Furthermore, such relationships may be less consensual than the individual whose position confers power believes, because of the complex and subtle effects of that power. Moreover, circumstances may change and conduct that was previously welcome may become unwelcome. Even when both parties have consented at the outset to a romantic involvement, subsequent unwelcome conduct may constitute sexual harassment.

© Academy of Management. Reprinted with permission.

AIR & WASTE MANAGEMENT ASSOCIATION

Address:	One Gateway Center, Third Floor Pittsburgh, PA 15222
Telephone:	412/232-3444
WWW:	www.awma.org
Document:	Bylaws—Article XIV—Professional Practice—Sections 1–3

Section 1—Code of Ethics
That the responsibility of his or her chosen profession be maintained, it is the duty of every member:

a) To carry on his or her work in a spirit of fairness to all those with whom he or she comes in professional contact, including employees and contractors. This also includes fidelity to clients and employers, and devotion to high ideals of personal honor.

b) To refrain from associating with or allowing the use of his or her name by any enterprise of questionable character.

c) To treat as confidential, knowledge of the business affairs or technical processes of clients or employers when their interests require secrecy.

d) To inform a client or employer of any business connections, interests, or affiliations which might influence judgment or impair the disinterested quality of services.

e) To accept financial or other compensation for a particular service from one source only, except with the full knowledge and consent of all interested parties.

f) To advertise only in a dignified manner, to refrain from using improper or questionable methods for promoting professional work, and to decline to pay or to accept commissions for work secured by improper or questionable methods.

g) To refrain from using unfair means to win professional advancement, and to avoid unfairly injuring another person's chances to secure and hold employment.

h) To co-operate in advancing the profession of air pollution control and waste management by the interchange of general information and experience with fellow members; and by contributing to the work of other associations, schools of applied science, and the technical press.

i) To maintain interest in the public welfare and to be ready to apply his or her special knowledge, skill, and training in the public behalf for the use and benefit of mankind.

Section 2

In all professional or business relations the members of the Association shall be governed by the Code of Ethics above and by these Bylaws.

Section 3

Charges that any member has been guilty of violation of these Bylaws or of conduct unbecoming of a member shall be detailed in a letter addressed to the board and signed by not less than three (3) members. Any member who has been so charged or accused shall be entitled to a hearing before the Board, where the member may testify in his or her own defense. If two-thirds (2/3) of the Board vote that the member is guilty as charged, the member shall be expelled, immediately after such a vote, from the Association.

AIR TRAFFIC CONTROL ASSOCIATION, INC.

Address: 2300 Clarendon Boulevard, Suite 711 Arlington, VA 22201
Telephone: 703/522-5717
WWW: www.atca.org
Document: By-Laws—Article V.—Code of Ethics (1956. Most recently revised 1996.)

In order that the dignity and honor of the Air Traffic Control Profession may be upheld, that its sphere of usefulness and its benefits may be extended, and that members of this Association may be guided by the highest standards of integrity and fair dealing, whether as individuals or in association with others in the aviation industry, the Board of the Air Traffic Control Association has adopted the following Code of Ethics and Conduct for the guidance of the Association's membership:

1. Members will endeavor to keep abreast of scientific and technical developments within the profession, and will constantly strive for improvement.

2. Members will endeavor to contribute new knowledge to the Global Aviation System by making known to the aviation world any significant work, improvements or research accomplished.

3. Members will not engage in unfair competition with other members of their profession.

4. Members will not take credit for research or technical work done by others; and in publications or meetings, will attempt to give credit where due.

5. Members will, to the best of their ability, render instructions, advice, and other assistance to fellow members in the discharge of their professional service.

6. Members will base their professional practice on safe and sound principles.

7. Members will refuse to engage in practices which are generally recognized as being detrimental to the public welfare.

8. Members will make every effort to discourage sensationalism, exaggeration, and unwarranted statements concerning the field of their profession, and will refrain from making extravagant claims.

© Air Traffic Control Association, Inc. Reprinted with permission.

AMERICAN ACADEMY *of* ACTUARIES

AMERICAN ACADEMY OF ACTUARIES

Address: 1100 Seventeenth Street NW,
                Seventh Floor
                Washington, DC 20036
Telephone: 202/223-8196
WWW: www.actuary.org
Document: Code of Professional Conduct of the
                American Academy of Actuaries

(AAA's *Code of Professional Conduct* was developed for the actuarial profession in the United States. Other actuarial associations that subscribe to this code include the Society of Actuaries, the American Society of Pension Actuaries, the Casualty Actuarial Society, and the Conference of Consulting Actuaries. Representatives from all of these organizations served on a joint committee, The Actuarial Board for Counseling and Discipline, to develop this final document.—Eds.)

Preamble

The Precepts of this Code of Professional Conduct identify the professional and ethical standards with which an actuary must comply. The Annotations provide additional explanatory, educational and advisory material to members of the actuarial profession on how the Precepts are to be interpreted and applied. An actuary must be familiar with, and keep current with revisions to, the Code of Professional Conduct, its Precepts and Annotations.

Professional Integrity

PRECEPT 1. An actuary shall act honestly and in a manner to uphold the reputation of the actuarial profession and to fulfill the profession's responsibility to the public.

ANNOTATION 1-1. An actuary fulfills the profession's responsibility to the public through compliance with this Code, and by offering actuarial advice, recommendations and opinions that are the product of the actuary's exercise of professional judgment.

ANNOTATION 1-2. An actuary who pleads guilty to or is found guilty of any misdemeanor related to financial matters or any felony shall be presumed to have contravened Precept 1 of this Code, and shall be subject to the profession's counseling and discipline procedures.

ANNOTATION 1-3. An actuary shall not use a relationship with a third party to attempt to obtain illegal or materially improper treatment from such third party on behalf of a principal (i.e., present or prospective client or employer).

PRECEPT 2. An actuary shall perform professional services with integrity, skill and care.

ANNOTATION 2-1. "Professional services" refers to the rendering of advice, recommendations or opinions based upon actuarial considerations, and also includes other services provided to a principal (i.e., present or prospective client or employer) by one acting as an actuary.

Qualification Standards

PRECEPT 3. An actuary shall perform professional services only when the actuary is qualified to do so and meets applicable qualification standards.

ANNOTATION 3-1. It is the professional responsibility of the actuary to observe applicable qualification standards in the jurisdiction in which the actuary renders professional services, and to keep current regarding changes in these standards. For example, for practice in the United States, the Qualification Standards promulgated by the American Academy of Actuaries apply; for practice in Canada, the eligibility conditions promulgated by the Canadian Institute of Actuaries as set out in the Canadian Institute of Actuaries' bylaws apply.

Standards of Practice

PRECEPT 4. An actuary shall ensure that professional service performed by or under the direction of the actuary meet applicable standards of practice.

ANNOTATION 4-1. It is the professional responsibility of the actuary to observe applicable standards of practice in the jurisdiction in which the actuary renders professional services, and to keep current regarding changes in these standards. For example, for practice in the United States, the Standards of Practice promulgated by the Actuarial Standards Board apply; for practice in Canada, the Standards of Practice promulgated by the Canadian Institute of Actuaries apply.

ANNOTATION 4-2. Where there is a question regarding the applicability of a standard of practice, the professional judgment of the actuary, taking into account the applicable accepted principles of the actuarial practice, shall prevail.

Disclosure

PRECEPT 5. An actuary shall, in communicating professional findings, indicate clearly that the actuary is responsible for the findings.

ANNOTATION 5-1. An actuary who makes an actuarial communication should indicate clearly the extent to which the actuary or other source(s) are available to provide supplementary information and explanation.

ANNOTATION 5-2. An actuary who makes an actuarial communication assumes responsibility for it except to the extent the actuary disclaims responsibility by stating reliance on other sources. Reliance on other sources means making use of those sources without assuming responsibility therefore. A communication making use of such reliance should define the extent of reliance. An actuary may rely upon other sources for information except where limited or prohibited by applicable standards of practice.

ANNOTATION 5-3. Any written communication of professional findings must be signed with the name of the actuary who is responsible for it. The name of an organization with which the actuary is affiliated may be incorporated into the signature but the actuary's responsibilities and those of the organization are not affected by the form of the signature.

PRECEPT 6. An actuary shall, in communicating professional findings, identify the principal(s) (i.e., the client(s) or employer(s)) for whom such findings are made and shall describe the capacity in which the actuary serves.

PRECEPT 7. An actuary shall make full and timely disclosure to a principal (i.e., present or prospective client or employer) of the sources of all direct and indirect compensation that the actuary or the actuary's firm may receive in relation to an assignment for which the actuary provides professional services for that principal.

ANNOTATION 7-1. An actuary who is not financially and organizationally independent concerning any matter related to the subject of an actuarial communication should disclose to the principal any pertinent relationship which is not apparent.

ANNOTATION 7-2. "Indirect compensation" is any material consideration received from any source in relation to an assignment for which the actuary provides professional services, other than direct remuneration for those services.

ANNOTATION 7-3. Actuaries employed by firms which operate in multiple sites are subject to the requirement of disclosure of sources of compensation which the actuary's firm may receive in relation to professional services with respect to a specific assignment for that principal, regardless of the location in which such compensation is received.

Conflict of Interest

PRECEPT 8. An actuary shall not perform professional services involving an actual or potential conflict of interest unless:

a) the actuary's ability to act fairly is unimpaired; and

b) there has been disclosure of the conflict to all known direct users whose interests would be affected by the conflict; and

c) such known direct users have expressly agreed to the performance of the services by the actuary.

ANNOTATION 8-1. A "direct user" of an actuary's services is a principal (i.e.,. present or prospective client or employer) having the opportunity to select the actuary and able to communicate directly with the actuary about qualifications, work, and recommendations.

ANNOTATION 8-2. If the actuary is aware of any significant conflict between the interests of the direct user and the interests of another party relative to the actuary's work, the actuary should advise the direct user of the conflict. The actuary should also include appropriate qualifications or disclosures in any related actuarial communication.

Control of Work Product

PRECEPT 9. An actuary shall not perform professional services when the actuary has reason to believe that they may be used to mislead or to violate or evade the law.

ANNOTATION 9-1. Material prepared by an actuary may be used by another party in a way which may influence the actions of a third party. The actuary should recognize the risks of misquotation, misinterpretation or other misuse of such material and should take reasonable steps to ensure that the material is clear and presented fairly, and that the actuary is identified as responsible for the material as required by Precept 5 of this Code.

Confidentiality

PRECEPT 10. An actuary shall not disclose to another party any confidential information obtained through professional services performed for a principal (i.e., client or employer) unless authorized to do so by the principal or required to do so by law.

ANNOTATION 10-1. "Confidential information" refers to information not in the public domain of which the actuary becomes aware in conjunction with the rendering of professional services to a principal. It may include information of a proprietary nature, information which is legally restricted from circulation or information which the actuary has reason to believe that the principal would not wish to be divulged.

Courtesy and Cooperation

PRECEPT 11. An actuary shall perform professional services with courtesy and shall cooperate with others in the principal's (i.e., client's or employer's) interest.

ANNOTATION 11-1. Differences of opinion among actuaries may arise, particularly in choices of assumptions and methods. Discussions of such differences, whether directly between actuaries or in observations made to a principal by one actuary on the

work of another, should be conducted objectively and with courtesy.

ANNOTATION 11-2. An actuary in the course of an engagement or employment may encounter a situation such that the best interest of the principal would be served by the actuary's setting out an alternative opinion. Nothing in this Code should be construed as preventing the actuary from expressing such an alternative opinion to the principal.

ANNOTATION 11-3. A principal has an indisputable right to choose a professional advisor. An actuary may provide service to any principal who requests it even though such principal is being or has been served by another actuary in the same manner.

If an actuary is invited to advise a principal for whom the actuary knows or has reasonable grounds to believe that another actuary is already acting in a professional capacity with respect to the same matter or has recently so acted, it may be prudent to consult with the other actuary both to prepare adequately for the assignment and to make an informed judgment whether there are circumstances involving a potential violation of this Code which might affect acceptance of the assignment.

The prospective new or additional actuary should request the principal's consent to such consultation. When the principal has given consent, the original actuary may require reasonable compensation for the work required to assemble and transmit the relevant information such as pertinent data, work papers and documents. The actuary need not provide any items of a proprietary nature, such as computer programs.

Advertising

PRECEPT 12. An actuary shall not engage in any advertising or business solicitation activities with respect to professional services that the actuary knows or should know are false or misleading.

ANNOTATION 12-1. "Advertising" encompasses all communications by whatever medium, including oral communications, which may directly or indirectly influence any person or organization to decide whether there is a need for actuarial services or to select a specific person or firm to perform actuarial services.

Titles and Designations

PRECEPT 13. An actuary shall make use of membership titles and designations of an actuarial organization only in a manner that conforms to the practices authorized by that organization.

ANNOTATION 13-1. "Title" means any title conferred by an actuarial organization related to a specific position within that organization. "Designation" means a specific reference to membership status within an actuarial organization.

Collateral Obligations

PRECEPT 14. An actuary with knowledge of an apparent, unresolved material violation of this Code shall disclose such violation to the appropriate counseling and discipline body of the profession, except where the disclosure would divulge confidential information or be contrary to law.

ANNOTATION 14-1. A material violation of this code is one which is important, has influence or effect, or affects the merits of a situation, as opposed to one which is trivial, does not affect an outcome, or is one merely of form.

ANNOTATION 14-2. Except when an actuary is prohibited by law or while the actuary is acting in an adversarial environment involving another actuary or actuaries, when the actuary becomes aware of an apparent material violation of this Code, the actuary is required to undertake promptly the following course of action:

a) If appropriate, discuss the situation with the other actuary or actuaries and, if necessary, agree upon a course of action to ensure that the apparent violation is resolved;

b) If (a) is not appropriate or is not successful, bring the apparent violation to the attention of the appropriate investigatory body. For example, for violations of this Code arising out of practice in the United States, the actuary should refer the matter to the Actuarial Board for Counseling and Discipline; for violations of this Code arising out of practice in Canada, the actuary should follow procedures established by the Canadian Institute of Actuaries.

PRECEPT 15. An actuary or the actuary's representative shall respond promptly in writing to any letter received from a person duly authorized by the appropriate counseling and disciplinary body of the profession to obtain information or assistance regarding possible violations of this Code.

PRECEPT 16. An actuary shall abide by this Code of Professional conduct whenever providing professional services.

ANNOTATION 16-1. Laws and regulations may impose obligations upon the actuary. Where the requirements of law or regulation conflict with this Code, the requirements of law or regulation shall take precedence.

ANNOTATION 16-2. For professional services rendered in Canada, the Rules of the Canadian Institute of Actuaries apply.

© American Academy of Actuaries. Reprinted with permission.

AMERICAN ACADEMY OF DERMATOLOGY

Address: 930 North Meacham Road
Schaumburg, IL 60173
Telephone: 847/330-0230 or 888/462-3376
WWW: www.aad.org
Document: Ethics in Medical Practice,
With Special Reference to
Dermatology (1992)

(The AAD's *Ethics in Medical Practice, With Special Reference to Dermatology* includes the information found below as well as the following which are not reprinted here: American Medical Association's *Principles of Medical Ethics*, (see p. 00.), AAD's "Opinions on Specific Issues," such as "Disclosure of Conflict of Interest," "Advertising," "Patient Records," "Prescription and Sale of Drugs and Devices," "Relations with Colleagues," "Relations with Society and Specifically the Press," and "Doctor-Patient Relationships," and AAD's "Administrative Regulations."—Eds.)

The American Academy of Dermatology believes that to these principles (*Principles of Medical Ethics*) should be added the following *General Precepts* that identify other areas of concern:

1. Physicians should provide patients a reasonable explanation of the etiology, treatment and prognosis of their disease.
2. Physicians should practice a method of healing founded upon a scientific basis.

3. Having undertaken the care of a patient, a physician may not neglect the patient unless the physician has been discharged and may discontinue medical service only after giving adequate notice to the patient.

4. In the practice of medicine, physicians should receive remuneration for services personally rendered by them or by professionals under their supervision.

5. Physicians should endeavor to provide to their patients care of high quality and low cost. Financial remuneration should not be the motivating influence behind the type of medical management provided. Physicians' fees should be commensurate with services rendered, and physicians should neither pay nor receive commissions for the referral of patients.

6. Physicians should not dispense or supply drugs, remedies or appliances unless it is manifestly in the best interest of their patients, as emphasized in Resolution #154-AMA House of Delegates 1987: *The American Medical Association supports the physician's right to dispense drugs and devices when it is in the best interest of the patient and consistent with the AMA's ethical guidelines.*

7. Physicians should provide to the general public information necessary or helpful to select a qualified physician.

8. Physicians should not engage in advertising or other forms of solicitation that are false, fraudulent, deceptive, or misleading.

9. Physicians should recognize the necessity for communication and mutual respect between doctors in Academe and those in private practice, as well as between those in the same or in other specialties.

10. It is incumbent upon physicians to strive for an environment in which competent and affordable medical care is available to all regardless of age, sex, race, color, creed, infirmity or economic status.

© American Academy of Dermatology. Reprinted with permission.

AMERICAN ACADEMY OF FAMILY PHYSICIANS

Address: 11400 Tomahawk Creek Parkway
                Leawood, KS 66211-2672

Telephone: 913/906-6000 or 800/274-2237
WWW: www.aafp.org

The American Academy of Family Physicians subscribes to the same code of ethics as the American Medical Association. See p. 00.

 AMERICAN ACADEMY OF OPHTHALMOLOGY

AMERICAN ACADEMY OF OPHTHALMOLOGY

Address: 655 Beach Street, PO Box 7424
                San Francisco, CA 94120-7424
Telephone: 415/561-8500
WWW: www.eyenet.org
Document: Code of Ethics of the American
                Academy of Ophthalmology (1995)

(The AAO's *Code of Ethics* was drafted in the late 1970s. The *Code* went into effect in 1984. It is reviewed annually and updated as necessary with the membership voting on Ethics Committee-recommended revisions. In addition to the *Code*, the AAO has published the following which are not reprinted here: fourteen Advisory Opinions which amplify the rules of the *Code*, four Policy Statements, and two Information Statements. The Academy has also published a monograph on the subject of ethics and ophthalmology: *The Ethical Ophthalmologist: A Primer* (1993).—Eds.)

PREAMBLE
The Code of Ethics of the American Academy of Ophthalmology applies to the American Academy of Ophthalmology and to its Fellows and Members, and is enforceable by the American Academy of Ophthalmology.

A. PRINCIPLES OF ETHICS
The Principles of Ethics form the first part of this Code of Ethics. They are aspirational and inspirational model standards of exemplary professional conduct for all Fellows or Members of the Academy in any class of membership. They serve as goals for which Academy Fellows and Members should constantly strive. The Principles of Ethics are not enforceable.

1. Ethics in Ophthalmology. Ethics address conduct, and relate to what behavior is appropriate or inappropriate, as reasonably determined by the entity setting the ethical standards. An issue of ethics in ophthalmology is resolved by the determination that the best interests of patients are served.

2. Providing Ophthalmological Services. Ophthalmological services must be provided with compassion, respect for human dignity, honesty and integrity.

3. Competence of the Ophthalmologist. An ophthalmologist must maintain competence. Competence can never be totally comprehensive, and therefore must be supplemented by other colleagues when indicated. Competence involves technical ability, cognitive knowledge, and ethical concerns for the patient. Competence includes having adequate and proper knowledge to make a professionally appropriate and acceptable decision regarding the patient's management.

4. Communication with the Patient. Open communication with the patient is essential. Patient confidences must be safeguarded within the constraints of the law.

5. Fees for Ophthalmological Services. Fees for ophthalmological services must not exploit patients or others who pay for the services.

6. Corrective Action. If a member has a reasonable basis for believing that another person has deviated from professionally accepted standards in a manner that adversely affects patient care or from the Rules of Ethics, the member should attempt to prevent the continuation of this conduct. This is best done by communicating directly with the other person. When that action is ineffective or is not feasible, the member has a responsibility to refer the matter to the appropriate authorities and to cooperate with those authorities in their professional and legal efforts to prevent the continuation of the conduct.

7. An Ophthalmologist's Responsibility. It is the responsibility of an ophthalmologist to act in the best interest of the patient.

B. RULES OF ETHICS

The Rules of Ethics form the second part of this Code of Ethics. They are mandatory and descriptive standards of minimally acceptable professional conduct for all Fellows or Members of the Academy in any class of membership. The Rules of Ethics are enforceable.

1. Competence. An ophthalmologist is a physician who is educated and trained to provide medical and surgical care of the eyes and related structures. An ophthalmologist should perform only those procedures in which the ophthalmologist is competent by virtue of specific training or experience or is assisted by one who is. An ophthalmologist must not misrepresent credentials, training, experience, ability or results.

2. Informed Consent. The performance of medical or surgical procedures shall be preceded by appropriate informed consent.

3. Clinical Trials and Investigative Procedures. Use of clinical trials or investigative procedures shall be approved by adequate review mechanisms. Clinical trials and investigative procedures are those conducted to develop adequate information on which to base prognostic or therapeutic decisions or to determine etiology or pathogenesis, in circumstances in which insufficient information exists. Appropriate informed consent for these procedures must recognize their special nature and ramifications.

4. Other Opinions. The patient's request for additional opinions shall be respected. Consultation(s) shall be obtained if required by the condition.

5. The Impaired Ophthalmologist. A physically, mentally or emotionally impaired ophthalmologist should withdraw from those aspects of practice affected by the impairment. If an impaired ophthalmologist does not cease inappropriate behavior, it is the duty of other ophthalmologists who know of the impairment to take action to attempt to assure correction of the situation. This may involve a wide range of remedial actions.

6. Pretreatment Assessment. Treatment shall be recommended only after a careful consideration of the patient's physical, social, emotional and occupational needs. The ophthalmologist must evaluate the patient and assure that the evaluation accurately documents the ophthalmic findings and the indications for treatment. Recommendation of unnecessary treatment or withholding of necessary treatment is unethical.

7. Delegation of Services. Delegation is the use of auxiliary health care personnel to provide eye care services for which the ophthalmologist is responsible. An ophthalmologist must not delegate to an auxiliary those aspects of eye care within the unique competence of the ophthalmologist (which do not include those permitted by law to be performed by auxiliaries). When other aspects of eye care for which the ophthalmologist is responsible are delegated to an auxiliary, the auxiliary must be qualified and adequately supervised. An ophthalmologist may make different arrangements for the delegation of eye care in special circumstances, so long as the patient's welfare and rights are the primary considerations.

8. Postoperative Care. The providing of postoperative eye care until the patient has recovered is integral to patient management. The operating ophthalmologist should provide those aspects of postoperative eye care within the unique competence of the ophthalmologist (which do not include those permitted by law to be performed by auxiliaries). Otherwise, the operating ophthalmologist must make arrangements before surgery for referral of the patient to another ophthalmologist, with the patient's approval and that of the other ophthalmologist. The operating ophthalmologist may make different arrangements for the provision of those aspects of postoperative eye care within the unique competence of the ophthalmologist in special circumstances, such as emergencies or when no ophthalmologist is available, so long as the patient's welfare and rights are the primary considerations. Fees should reflect postoperative eye care arrangements with advance disclosure to the patient.

9. Medical and Surgical Procedures. An ophthalmologist must not misrepresent the service that is performed or the charges made for that service.

10. Procedures and Materials. Ophthalmologists should order only those laboratory procedures, optical devices or pharmacological agents that are in the best interest of the patient. Ordering unnecessary procedures or materials or withholding necessary procedures or materials is unethical.

11. Commercial Relationships. An ophthalmologist's clinical judgment and practice must not be affected by economic interest in, commitment to, or benefit from professionally related commercial enterprises.

12. Communications to Colleagues. Communications to colleagues must be accurate and truthful.

13. Communications to the Public. Communications to the public must be accurate. They must not convey false, untrue, deceptive, or misleading information through statements, testimonials, photographs, graphics or other means. They must not omit material information without which the communications would be deceptive. Communications must not appeal to an individual's anxiety in an excessive or unfair way; and they must not create unjustified expectations of results. If communications refer to benefits or other attributes of ophthalmic procedures that involve significant risks, realistic assessments of their safety and efficacy must also be included, as well as

the availability of alternatives and, where necessary to avoid deception, descriptions and/or assessments of the benefits or other attributes of those alternatives. Communications must not misrepresent an ophthalmologist's credentials, training, experience or ability, and must not contain material claims of superiority that cannot be substantiated. If a communication results from payment by an ophthalmologist, this must be disclosed unless the nature, format or medium makes it apparent.

14. Interrelations Between Ophthalmologists. Interrelations between ophthalmologists must be conducted in a manner that advances the best interests of the patient, including the sharing of relevant information.

15. Conflict of Interest. A conflict of interest exists when professional judgment concerning the well-being of the patient has a reasonable chance of being influenced by other interests of the provider. Disclosure of a conflict of interest is required in communications to patients, the public, and colleagues.

C. ADMINISTRATIVE PROCEDURES

(The Administrative Procedures of the AAO's Ethics Committee form the third part of the association's code of ethics. For more information regarding these procedures, contact the American Academy of Ophthalmology at the address listed above.)

© American Academy of Ophthalmology. Reprinted with permission.

AMERICAN ACADEMY OF OPTOMETRY

Address:	6110 Executive Boulevard, Suite 506 Rockville, MD 20852
Telephone:	301/984-1441
WWW:	www.aaopt.org
Document:	By-Laws — Article III — Standards of Conduct

(In addition to these *Standards*, the Academy also publishes "Interpretation of the *Standards of Conduct*, Article III, of the By-Laws of the American Academy of Optometry," which is not reprinted here.—Eds.)

Section 1. Members of the Academy shall be of good moral character and maintain the highest standards of the profession.

Section 2. Members of the American Academy of Optometry shall accept responsibility for the consequences of their acts, make every effort to insure that their services are used appropriately, and, when indicated, recommend alternate sources of care.

Section 3. Members of the American Academy of Optometry shall maintain the highest degree of professional competence by rendering services, using techniques, and providing opinions that meet the highest standards of practice.

Section 4. The moral, ethical, and legal standards of behavior of a member are a personal matter to the same degree as they are for any other citizen, except as they may compromise the fulfillment of a member's professional responsibilities.

Section 5. The professional standards of members of the Academy require that public statements, announcements and promotional activities not be deceptive, fraudulent, or misleading.

Section 6. Members of the Academy will at all times observe the principles of collegiality when communicating to, or about, other members.

© American Academy of Optometry. Reprinted with permission.

AMERICAN ACADEMY OF ORTHOPAEDIC SURGEONS

Address: 6300 North River Road
              Rosemont, IL 60018-4262

Telephone: 847/823-7186
WWW: www.aaos.org
Document: Code of Ethics for Orthopaedic
              Surgeons (1988. Most recently
              revised 1995.)

(The AAOS has a collection of documents relating to ethics at their WWW site. In addition to the *Principles of Medical Ethics* referred to in the "Preamble" below, the site includes "Opinion on Ethics" statements for a variety of situations. These publications are not reprinted here.—Eds.)

PREAMBLE

Concerns for the patient's welfare and the appropriate behavior of the physician are a part of the heritage of medicine originating with the Code of Hammurabi, a code of ethics dating from 2000 BC. Guidelines for ethical behavior must address the demands of contemporary orthopaedic practice. The American Academy of Orthopaedic Surgeons (Academy) developed *The Principles of Medical Ethics for the Orthopaedic Surgeon* and the *Code of Ethics for Orthopaedic Surgeons* primarily for the benefit of our patients and to serve as a guide to conduct in the physician-patient relationship. These documents are, in *Medical Ethics for* part, derived from the *Current Opinions of the Council on Ethical and Judicial Affairs* of the American Medical Association (AMA). Since the AMA document is necessarily broad, the Academy documents are directed to concerns of specific interest to orthopaedic surgeons. Orthopaedic surgeons are encouraged to refer to the *Current Opinions of the Council on Ethical and Judicial Affairs* of the AMA for guidance if the particular ethical matter at issue is not addressed in the Academy's *Principles of Medical Ethics for the Orthopaedic Surgeon* or *Code of Ethics*.

The Academy's *Principles of Medical Ethics for the Orthopaedic Surgeon* and *Code of Ethics* provide standards of conduct that define the essentials of honorable behavior for the orthopaedic surgeon. *The Principles of Medical Ethics for the Orthopaedic Surgeon* and *Code of Ethics*, while taking into account the legal requirements of medical practice, call for and espouse a standard of behavior that is higher than that required by the law.

Orthopaedic surgeons should recognize that they are role models for orthopaedic surgeons-in-training and other health care professionals and should by their deeds and actions comply with the Academy's *Principles of the Orthopaedic Surgeon* and *Code of Ethics*.

I. The Physician-Patient Relationship

I. A. The orthopaedic profession exists for the purpose of caring for the patient. The physician-patient relationship is the central focus of all ethical concerns.

I. B. The physician-patient relationship has a contractual basis and is based on confidentiality, trust, and honesty. Both the patient and the orthopaedic surgeon are free to enter or discontinue the relationship within any existing constraints of a contract with a third party. An orthopaedist has an obligation to render care only for those conditions that he or she is competent to treat. The orthopaedist shall not decline to accept patients solely on the basis of race, color, gender, sexual orientation, religion, or national origin or on any basis that would constitute illegal discrimination.

I. C. The orthopaedic surgeon may choose whom he or she will serve. An orthopaedic surgeon should render services to the best of his or her ability. Having undertaken the care of a patient, the orthopaedic surgeon may not neglect that person. Unless discharged by the patient, the orthopaedic surgeon may discontinue services only after giving adequate notice to the patient so that the patient can secure alternative care. Managed care agreements may contain provisions which alter the method by which patients are discharged. If the enrollment of a physician or patient is discontinued in a managed care plan, the physician will have an ethical responsibility to assist the patient in obtaining follow-up care. In this instance, the physician will be responsible to provide medically necessary care for the patient until appropriate referrals can be arranged.

I. D. When obtaining informed consent for treatment, the orthopaedic surgeon is obligated to present to the patient or to the person responsible for the patient, in understandable terms, pertinent medical facts and recommendations consistent with good medical practice. Such information should include alternative modes of treatment, the objectives, risks and possible complications of such treatment, and the complications and consequences of no treatment.

II. Personal Conduct

II. A. The orthopaedic surgeon should maintain a reputation for truth and honesty. In all professional conduct, the orthopaedic surgeon is expected to provide competent and compassionate patient care, exercise appropriate respect for other health care professionals, and maintain the patient's best interests as paramount.

II. B. The orthopaedic surgeon should conduct himself or herself morally and ethically, so as to merit the confidence of patients entrusted to the orthopaedic surgeon's care, rendering to each a full measure of service and devotion.

II. C. The orthopaedic surgeon should obey all laws, uphold the dignity and honor of the profession, and accept the profession's self-imposed discipline. Within legal and other constraints, if the orthopaedic surgeon has a reasonable basis for believing that a physician or other health care provider has been involved in any unethical or illegal activity, he or she should attempt to prevent the continuation of this activity by communicating with that person and/or identifying that person to a duly-constituted peer review authority or the appropriate regulatory agency. In addition, the orthopaedic surgeon should cooperate with peer review and other authorities in their professional and legal efforts to prevent the continuation of unethical or illegal conduct.

II. D. Because of the orthopaedic surgeon's responsibility for the patient's life and future welfare, substance abuse is a special threat that must be recognized and stopped. The orthopaedic surgeon must avoid substance abuse and, when necessary, seek rehabilitation. It is ethical for an orthopaedic surgeon to take actions to encourage colleagues who are chemically dependent to seek rehabilitation.

III. Conflicts of Interest

III. A. The practice of medicine inherently presents potential conflicts of interest. Whenever a conflict of interest arises, it must be resolved in the best interest of the patient. The orthopaedic surgeon should exercise all reasonable alternatives to ensure that the most appropriate care is provided to the patient. If the conflict of interest cannot be resolved, the orthopaedic surgeon should notify the patient of his or her intention to withdraw from the relationship.

III. B. If the orthopaedic surgeon has a financial or ownership interest in a durable medical goods provider, imaging center, surgery center or other health care facility where the orthopaedic surgeon's financial interest is not immediately obvious, the orthopaedic surgeon must disclose this interest to the patient. The orthopaedic surgeon has an obligation to know the applicable laws regarding physician ownership, compensation and control of these services and facilities.

III. C. When an orthopaedic surgeon receives anything of value, including royalties, from a manufacturer, the orthopaedic surgeon must disclose this fact to the patient. It is unethical for an orthopaedic surgeon to receive compensation (excluding royalties) from a manufacturer for using a particular device or medication. Reimbursement for administrative costs in conducting or participating in a scientifically sound research trial is acceptable.

III. D. An orthopaedic surgeon reporting on clinical research or experience with a given procedure or device must disclose any financial interest in that procedure or device if the orthopaedic surgeon or any institution with which that orthopaedic surgeon is connected has received anything of value from its inventor or manufacturer.

III. E. Except when inconsistent with applicable law, orthopaedic surgeons have a right to dispense medication, assistive devices, orthopaedic appliances, and similar related patient-care items, and to provide facilities and render services as long as their doing so provides a convenience or an accommodation to the patient without taking financial advantage of the patient. Ultimately, the patient must have the choice of accepting the dispensed medication or patient-care items or obtaining them outside the physician's office.

IV. Maintenance of Competence

IV. A. The orthopaedic surgeon must continually strive to maintain and improve medical knowledge and skill, and should make available to patients and colleagues the benefits of his or her professional attainments. Each orthopaedic surgeon should participate in continuing relevant medical educational activities.

V. Relationships With Orthopaedic Surgeons, Nurses, and Allied Health Personnel

V. A. Good relationships among physicians, nurses, and other health care professionals are essential for good patient care. The orthopaedic surgeon should promote the development of an expert health care team that will work together harmoniously to provide optimal patient care.

V. B. The professional conduct of the orthopaedic surgeon will be scrutinized by local professional associations, hospital(s), managed care organization(s), peer review committees, and state medical and/or licensing boards. These groups deserve the participation and cooperation of orthopaedic surgeons.

V. C. Orthopaedic surgeons are frequently called upon to provide expert medical testimony in courts of law.

In providing testimony, the orthopaedic surgeon should exercise extreme caution to ensure that the testimony provided is nonpartisan, scientifically correct, and clinically accurate. The orthopaedic surgeon should not testify concerning matters about which the orthopaedic surgeon is not knowledgeable. It is unethical for an orthopaedic surgeon to accept compensation that is contingent upon the outcome of litigation.

VI. Relationship to the Public

VI. A. The orthopaedic surgeon should not publicize himself or herself through any medium or form of public communication in an untruthful, misleading, or deceptive manner. Competition between and among surgeons and other health care practitioners is ethical and acceptable.

VI. B. Professional fees should be commensurate with the services provided. It is unethical for orthopaedic surgeons to bill individually for services that are properly considered a part of the "global service" package where defined, i.e., services that are a necessary part of the surgical procedure. It is unethical for orthopaedic surgeons to submit billing codes that reflect higher levels of service or complexity than those that were actually required. It is unethical for orthopaedic surgeons to charge for services not provided.

VI. C. Physicians should be encouraged to devote some time and work to provide care for individuals who have no means of paying.

VI. D. The orthopaedic surgeon may enter into a contractual relationship with a group, a prepaid practice plan, or a hospital. The physician has an obligation to serve as the patient's advocate and to ensure that the patient's welfare remains the paramount concern.

VII. General Principles of Care

VII. A. An orthopaedic surgeon should practice only within the scope of his or her personal education, training, and experience. If an orthopaedic surgeon contracts to provide comprehensive musculoskeletal care, then he or she has the obligation to ensure that appropriate care is provided in areas outside of his or her personal expertise.

VII. B. It is unethical to prescribe, provide, or seek compensation for unnecessary services or not to provide services that are medically necessary. It is unethical to prescribe controlled substances when they are not medically indicated. It is also unethical to prescribe substances for the sole purpose of enhancing athletic performance.

VII. C. The orthopaedic surgeon should not perform a surgical operation under circumstances in which the responsibility for diagnosis or care of the patient is delegated to another who is not qualified to undertake it.

VII. D. When a patient submits a proper request for records, the patient is entitled to a copy of such records as they pertain to that patient individually. Charges should be commensurate with the services provided to reproduce the medical records. Certain correspondence from insurance carriers or attorneys may call for conclusions on the part of the orthopaedic surgeon. As such, a reasonable fee for professional services is permissible.

VIII. Research and Academic Responsibilities

VIII. A. All research and academic activities must be conducted under conditions of full compliance with ethical, institutional, and government guidelines. Patients participating in research programs must have given full informed consent and retain the right to withdraw from the research protocol at any time.

VIII. B. Orthopaedic surgeons should not claim as their own intellectual property that which is not theirs. Plagiarism or the use of others' work without attribution is unethical.

VIII. C. The principal investigator of a scientific research project or clinical research project is responsible for proposing, designing, and reporting the research. The principal investigator may delegate portions of the work to other individuals, but this does not relieve the principal investigator of the responsibility for work conducted by the other individuals.

VIII. D. The principal investigator or senior author of a scientific report is responsible for ensuring that appropriate credit is given for contributions to the research described.

IX. Community Responsibility

IX. A. The honored ideals of the medical profession imply that the responsibility of the orthopaedic surgeon extends not only to the individual but also to society as a whole. Activities that have the purpose of improving the health and well-being of the patient and/or the community in a cost-effective way deserve the interest, support, and participation of the orthopaedic surgeon.

AMERICAN ACADEMY OF OTOLARYNGOLOGY— HEAD AND NECK SURGERY FOUNDATION, INC.

Address: One Prince Street
              Alexandria, VA 22314-3357
Telephone: 703/836-4444
WWW: www.entnet.org
Document: Code of Ethics (1987. Most recently
              revised 1995.)

Preamble

Physicians assume extraordinary responsibilities in the care of patients and in their relationships with other health care professionals. These responsibilities require the highest ethical standards of every physician. The American Academy of Otolaryngology— Head and Neck Surgery Foundation, Inc. promulgates the following Code of Ethics to be used as a standard of behavior for physicians in the performance of their duties and in the care of patients. These ethical principles should be aspired to by all Fellows and Members of the Academy. The Academy also endorses the principles of the American Medical Association's Code of Ethics:

Principles

1. The best interest of the patient must be the foremost concern of the physician in all circumstances.
2. The patient must be treated with competence, respect, dignity and honesty. Accepted principles of confidentiality must be respected.

3. The physician must maintain proficiency and competence in the administration of patient care through a process of continuing education.
4. Fees must be commensurate with the service rendered and the ability of the patient to pay.
5. The impaired physician must withdraw from practice until the impairment has been overcome.
6. Academy members should assist their colleagues with complying with these principles.

© American Academy of Otolaryngology—Head and Neck Surgery Foundation, Inc. Reprinted with permission.

AMERICAN ACADEMY OF PHYSICIAN ASSISTANTS

Address: 950 North Washington Street
              Alexandria, VA 22314-1552
Telephone: 703/836-2272
WWW: www.aapa.org
Document: Code of Ethics of the Physician
              Assistant Profession

The American Academy of Physician Assistants recognizes its responsibility to aid the profession in maintaining high standards in the provision of quality and accessible health care services. The following principles delineate the standards governing the conduct of physician assistants in their professional interactions with patients, colleagues, other health professionals and the general public. Realizing that no code can encompass all ethical responsibilities of the physician assistant, this enumeration of obligations in the Code of Ethics is not comprehensive and does not constitute a denial of the existence of other obligations, equally imperative, though not specifically mentioned.

Physician Assistants shall be committed to providing competent medical care, assuming as their primary responsibility the health, safety, welfare, and dignity of all humans.

Physician Assistants shall extend to each patient the full measure of their ability as dedicated, empathetic health care providers and shall assume responsibility for the skillful and proficient transactions of their professional duties.

Physician Assistants shall deliver needed health care services to health consumers without regard to sex, age, race, creed, socio-economic and political status.

Physician Assistants shall adhere to all state and federal laws governing informed consent concerning the patient's health care.

Physician Assistants shall seek consultation with their supervising physician, other health providers, or qualified professionals having special skills, knowledge or experience whenever the welfare of the patient will be safeguarded or advanced by such consultation. Supervision should include ongoing communication between the physician and the physician assistant regarding the care of all patients.

Physician Assistants shall take personal responsibility for being familiar with and adhering to all federal/state laws applicable to the practice of their profession.

Physician Assistants shall provide only those services for which they are qualified via education and/or experiences and by pertinent legal regulatory process.

Physician Assistants shall not misrepresent in any manner, either directly or indirectly, their skills, training, professional credentials, identity, or services.

Physician Assistants shall uphold the doctrine of confidentiality regarding privileged patient information, unless required to release such information by law or such information becomes necessary to protect the welfare of the patient or the community.

Physician Assistants shall strive to maintain and increase the quality of individual health care service through individual study and continuing education.

Physician Assistants shall have the duty to respect the law, to uphold the dignity of the physician assistant profession and to accept its ethical principles. The physician assistant shall not participate in or conceal any activity that will bring discredit or dishonor to the physician assistant profession and shall expose, without fear or favor, any illegal or unethical conduct in the medical profession.

Physician Assistants, ever cognizant of the needs of the community, shall use the knowledge and experience acquired as professionals to contribute to an improved community.

Physician Assistants shall place service before material gain and must carefully guard against conflicts of professional interest.

Physician Assistants shall strive to maintain a spirit of cooperation with their professional organization and the general public.

AMERICAN ADVERTISING FEDERATION
THE UNIFYING VOICE FOR ADVERTISING

AMERICAN ADVERTISING FEDERATION

Address: 1101 Vermont Avenue NW, Suite 500
              Washington, DC 20005-6306
Telephone: 202/898-0089
WWW: www.aaf.org
Document: The Advertising Principles of
              American Business (1984)

TRUTH
Advertising shall tell the truth, and shall reveal significant facts, the omission of which would mislead the public.

SUBSTANTIATION
Advertising claims shall be substantiated by evidence in possession of the advertiser and advertising agency, prior to making such claims.

COMPARISONS
Advertising shall refrain from making false, misleading, or unsubstantiated statements or claims about a competitor or his/her products or services.

BAIT ADVERTISING
Advertising shall not offer products or services for sale unless such offer constitutes a bona fide effort to sell the advertising products or services and is not a device to switch consumers to other goods or services, usually higher priced.

GUARANTEES AND WARRANTIES
Advertising of guarantees and warranties shall be explicit, with sufficient information to apprise consumers of their principal terms and limitations or, when space or time restrictions preclude such disclosures, the advertisement should clearly reveal where the full text of the guarantee or warranty can be examined before purchase.

PRICE CLAIMS
Advertising shall avoid price claims which are false or misleading, or saving claims which do not offer provable savings.

TESTIMONIALS
Advertising containing testimonials shall be limited to those of competent witnesses who are reflecting a real and honest opinion or experience.

TASTE AND DECENCY
Advertising shall be free of statements, illustrations or implications which are offensive to good taste or public decency.

AMERICAN ANTHROPOLOGICAL ASSOCIATION

Address: 4350 North Fairfax Drive, Suite 640
              Arlington, VA 22203-1620
Telephone: 703/528-1902

WWW: www.aaanet.org
Document: Code of Ethics of the American
         Anthropological Association (1997)

I. Preamble

Anthropological researchers, teachers and practitioners are members of many different communities, each with its own moral rules or codes of ethics. Anthropologists have moral obligations as members of other groups, such as the family, religion, and community, as well as the profession. They also have obligations to the scholarly discipline, to the wider society and culture, and to the human species, other species, and the environment. Furthermore, fieldworkers may develop close relationships with persons or animals with whom they work, generating an additional level of ethical considerations.

In a field of such complex involvements and obligations, it is inevitable that misunderstandings, conflicts, and the need to make choices among apparently incompatible values will arise. Anthropologists are responsible for grappling with such difficulties and struggling to resolve them in ways compatible with the principles stated here. The purpose of this Code is to foster discussion and education. The American Anthropological Association (AAA) does not adjudicate claims for unethical behavior.

The principles and guidelines in this Code provide the anthropologist with tools to engage in developing and maintaining an ethical framework for all anthropological work.

II. Introduction

Anthropology is a multidisciplinary field of science and scholarship, which includes the study of all aspects of humankind—archaeological, biological, linguistic and sociocultural. Anthropology has roots in the natural and social sciences and in the humanities, ranging in approach from basic to applied research and to scholarly interpretation.

As the principal organization representing the breadth of anthropology, the American Anthropological Association (AAA) starts from the position that generating and appropriately utilizing knowledge (i.e., publishing, teaching, developing programs, and informing policy) of the peoples of the world, past and present, is a worthy goal; that the generation of anthropological knowledge is a dynamic process using many different and ever-evolving approaches; and that for moral and practical reasons, the generation and utilization of knowledge should be achieved in an ethical manner.

The mission of American Anthropological Association is to advance all aspects of anthropological research and to foster dissemination of anthropological knowledge through publications, teaching, public education, and application. An important part of that mission is to help educate AAA members about ethical obligations and challenges involved in the generation, dissemination, and utilization of anthropological knowledge.

The purpose of this Code is to provide AAA members and other interested persons with guidelines for making ethical choices in the conduct of their anthropological work. Because anthropologists can find themselves in complex situations and subject to more than one code of ethics, the AAA Code of Ethics provides a framework, not an ironclad formula, for making decisions.

Persons using the Code as a guideline for making ethical choices or for teaching are encouraged to seek out illustrative examples and appropriate case studies to enrich their knowledge base.

Anthropologists have a duty to be informed about ethical codes relating to their work, and ought periodically to receive training on current research activities and ethical issues. In addition, departments offering anthropology degrees should include and require ethical training in their curriculums.

No code or set of guidelines can anticipate unique circumstances or direct actions in specific situations. The individual anthropologist must be willing to make carefully considered ethical choices and be prepared to make clear the assumptions, facts and issues on which those choices are based. These guidelines therefore address *general* contexts, priorities and relationships which should be considered in ethical decision making in anthropological work.

III. Research

In both proposing and carrying out research, anthropological researchers must be open about the purpose(s), potential impacts, and source(s) of support for research projects with funders, colleagues, persons studied or providing information, and with relevant parties affected by the research. Researchers must expect to utilize the results of their work in an appropriate fashion and disseminate the results through appropriate and timely activities. Research fulfilling these expectations is ethical, regardless of the source of funding (public or private) or purpose (i.e., "applied," "basic," "pure," or "proprietary").

Anthropological researchers should be alert to the danger of compromising anthropological ethics as a condition to engage in research, yet also be alert to proper demands of good citizenship or host-guest relations. Active contribution and leadership in seeking to shape public or private sector actions and policies may be as ethically justifiable as inaction, detachment, or noncooperation, depending on circumstances. Similar principles hold for anthropological researchers employed or otherwise affiliated with nonanthropological institutions, public institutions, or private enterprises.

A. Responsibility to people and animals with whom anthropological researchers work and whose lives and cultures they study.

1. Anthropological researchers have primary ethical obligations to the people, species, and materials they study and to the people with whom they work. These obligations can supersede the goal of seeking new knowledge, and can lead to decisions not to undertake or to discontinue a research project when the primary obligation conflicts with other responsibilities, such as those owed to sponsors or clients. These ethical obligations include:

   • To avoid harm or wrong, understanding that the development of knowledge can lead to change which may be positive or negative for the people or animals worked with or studied
   • To respect the well-being of humans and nonhuman primates
   • To work for the long-term conservation of the archaeological, fossil, and historical records
   • To consult actively with the affected individuals or group(s), with the goal of establishing a working relationship that can be beneficial to all parties involved

2. Anthropological researchers must do everything in their power to ensure that their research does not harm the safety, dignity, or privacy of the people with whom they work, conduct research, or perform other professional activities. Anthropological researchers working with animals must do everything in their power to ensure that the research does not harm the safety, psychological well-being or survival of the animals or species with which they work.

3. Anthropological researchers must determine in advance whether their hosts/providers of information wish to remain anonymous or receive recognition, and make every effort to comply with those wishes. Researchers must present to their research partici-

pants the possible impacts of the choices, and make clear that despite their best efforts, anonymity may be compromised or recognition fail to materialize.

4. Anthropological researchers should obtain in advance the informed consent of persons being studied, providing information, owning or controlling access to material being studied, or otherwise identified as having interests which might be impacted by the research. It is understood that the degree and breadth of informed consent required will depend on the nature of the project and may be affected by requirements of other codes, laws, and ethics of the country or community in which the research is pursued. Further, it is understood that the informed consent process is dynamic and continuous; the process should be initiated in the project design and continue through implementation by way of dialogue and negotiation with those studied. Researchers are responsible for identifying and complying with the various informed consent codes, laws and regulations affecting their projects. Informed consent, for the purposes of this code, does not necessarily imply or require a particular written or signed form. It is the quality of the consent, not the format, that is relevant.

5. Anthropological researchers who have developed close and enduring relationships (i.e., covenantal relationships) with either individual persons providing information or with hosts must adhere to the obligations of openness and informed consent, while carefully and respectfully negotiating the limits of the relationship.

6. While anthropologists may gain personally from their work, they must not exploit individuals, groups, animals, or cultural or biological materials. They should recognize their debt to the societies in which they work and their obligation to reciprocate with people studied in appropriate ways.

B. Responsibility to scholarship and science

1. Anthropological researchers must expect to encounter ethical dilemmas at every stage of their work, and must make good-faith efforts to identify potential ethical claims and conflicts in advance when preparing proposals and as projects proceed. A section raising and responding to potential ethical issues should be part of every research proposal.

2. Anthropological researchers bear responsibility for the integrity and reputation of their discipline, of scholarship, and of science. Thus, anthropological researchers are subject to the general moral

rules of scientific and scholarly conduct: they should not deceive or knowingly misrepresent (i.e., fabricate evidence, falsify, plagiarize), or attempt to prevent reporting of misconduct, or obstruct the scientific/scholarly research of others.

3. Anthropological researchers should do all they can to preserve opportunities for future fieldworkers to follow them to the field.

4. Anthropological researchers should utilize the results of their work in an appropriate fashion, and whenever possible disseminate their findings to the scientific and scholarly community.

5. Anthropological researchers should seriously consider all reasonable requests for access to their data and other research materials for purposes of research. They should also make every effort to insure preservation of their fieldwork data for use by posterity.

C. Responsibility to the public

1. Anthropological researchers should make the results of their research appropriately available to sponsors, students, decision makers, and other nonanthropologists. In so doing, they must be truthful; they are not only responsible for the factual content of their statements but also must consider carefully the social and political implications of the information they disseminate. They must do everything in their power to insure that such information is well understood, properly contextualized, and responsibly utilized. They should make clear the empirical bases upon which their reports stand, be candid about their qualifications and philosophical or political biases, and recognize and make clear the limits of anthropological expertise. At the same time, they must be alert to possible harm their information may cause people with whom they work or colleagues.

2. Anthropologists may choose to move beyond disseminating research results to a position of advocacy. This is an individual decision, but not an ethical responsibility.

IV. Teaching

Responsibility to students and trainees

While adhering to ethical and legal codes governing relations between teachers/mentors and students/trainees at their educational institutions or as members of wider organizations, anthropological teachers should be particularly sensitive to the ways such codes apply in their discipline (for example, when teaching involves close contact with students/trainees in field situations). Among the widely recognized precepts which anthropological teachers, like other teachers/mentors, should follow are:

1. Teachers/mentors should conduct their programs in ways that preclude discrimination on the basis of sex, marital status, "race," social class, political convictions, disability, religion, ethnic background, national origin, sexual orientation, age, or other criteria irrelevant to academic performance.

2. Teachers'/mentors' duties include continually striving to improve their teaching/training techniques; being available and responsive to student/trainee interests; counseling students/trainees realistically regarding career opportunities; conscientiously supervising, encouraging, and supporting students'/trainees' studies; being fair, prompt, and reliable in communicating evaluations; assisting students/trainees in securing research support; and helping students/trainees when they seek professional placement.

3. Teachers/mentors should impress upon students/trainees the ethical challenges involved in every phase of anthropological work; encourage them to reflect upon this and other codes; encourage dialogue with colleagues on ethical issues; and discourage participation in ethically questionable projects.

4. Teachers/mentors should publicly acknowledge student/trainee assistance in research and preparation of their work; give appropriate credit for coauthorship to students/trainees; encourage publication of worthy student/trainee papers; and compensate students/trainees justly for their participation in all professional activities.

5. Teachers/mentors should beware of the exploitation and serious conflicts of interest which may result if they engage in sexual relations with students/trainees. They must avoid sexual liaisons with students/trainees for whose education and professional training they are in any way responsible.

V. Application

1. The same ethical guidelines apply to all anthropological work. That is, in both proposing and carrying out research, anthropologists must be open with funders, colleagues, persons studied or providing information, and relevant parties affected by the work about the purpose(s), potential impacts, and source(s) of support for the work. Applied anthropologists must intend and expect to

utilize the results of their work appropriately (i.e., publication, teaching, program and policy development) within a reasonable time. In situations in which anthropological knowledge is applied, anthropologists bear the same responsibility to be open and candid about their skills and intentions, and monitor the effects of their work on all persons affected. Anthropologists may be involved in many types of work, frequently affecting individuals and groups with diverse and sometimes conflicting interests. The individual anthropologist must make carefully considered ethical choices and be prepared to make clear the assumptions, facts and issues on which those choices are based.

2. In all dealings with employers, persons hired to pursue anthropological research or apply anthropological knowledge should be honest about their qualifications, capabilities, and aims. Prior to making any professional commitments, they must review the purposes of prospective employers, taking into consideration the employer's past activities and future goals. In working for governmental agencies or private businesses, they should be especially careful not to promise or imply acceptance of conditions contrary to professional ethics or competing commitments.

3. Applied anthropologists, as any anthropologist, should be alert to the danger of compromising anthropological ethics as a condition for engaging in research or practice. They should also be alert to proper demands of hospitality, good citizenship and guest status. Proactive contribution and leadership in shaping public or private sector actions and policies may be as ethically justifiable as inaction, detachment, or noncooperation, depending on circumstances.

VI. Epilogue

Anthropological research, teaching, and application, like any human actions, pose choices for which anthropologists individually and collectively bear ethical responsibility. Since anthropologists are members of a variety of groups and subject to a variety of ethical codes, choices must sometimes be made not only between the varied obligations presented in this code but also between those of this code and those incurred in other statuses or roles. This statement does not dictate choice or propose sanctions. Rather, it is designed to promote discussion and provide general guidelines for ethically responsible decisions.

American Arbitration Association
Dispute Resolution Services Worldwide

AMERICAN ARBITRATION ASSOCIATION

Address: 335 Madison Avenue, 10th floor
             New York, NY 10017-4605
Telephone: 212/716-5800 or 800/778-7879
WWW: www.adr.org
Document: Model Standards of Conduct for
             Mediators (1994)

(AAA's *Model Standards of Conduct for Mediators* was prepared by a joint committee composed of two delegates from the American Arbitration Association, two from the Litigation Section and the Dispute Resolution Section of the American Bar Association, and two from the Society of Professionals in Dispute Resolution and approved by each body. In addition to the *Model Standards*, AAA has published the following which are not reprinted here: *Code of Ethics for Arbitrators in Commercial Disputes* and *Code of Professional Responsibility for Arbitrators of Labor-Management Disputes.*—Eds.)

Introductory Note

The initiative for these standards came from three professional groups: the American Arbitration Association, the American Bar Association, and the Society of Professionals in Dispute Resolution.

The purpose of this initiative was to develop a set of standards to serve as a general framework for the practice of mediation. The effort is a step in the development of the field and a tool to assist practitioners in it—a beginning, not an end. The model standards are intended to apply to all types of mediation. It is recognized, however, that in some cases the application of these standards may be affected by laws or contractual agreements.

Preface

The model standards of conduct for mediators are intended to perform three major functions: to serve as a guide for the conduct of mediators; to inform the mediating parties; and to promote public confidence in mediation as a process for resolving disputes. The standards draw on existing codes of conduct for mediators and take into account issues and problems that have surfaced in mediation practice. They are offered in the hope that they will serve an educational function and provide assistance to individuals, organizations, and institutions involved in mediation.

Mediation is a process in which an impartial third party—a mediator—facilitates the resolution of a dispute by promoting voluntary agreement (or "self-determination") by the parties to the dispute. A mediator facilitates communications, promotes understanding, focuses the parties on their interests, and seeks creative problem solving to enable the parties to reach their own agreement. These standards give meaning to this definition of mediation.

I. Self-Determination: *A Mediator Shall Recognize that Mediation is Based on the Principle of Self-Determination by the Parties.*

Self-determination is the fundamental principle of mediation. It requires that the mediation process rely upon the ability of the parties to reach a voluntary, uncoerced agreement. Any party may withdraw from mediation at any time.

COMMENTS:
- The mediator may provide information about the process, raise issues, and help parties explore options. The primary role of the mediator is to facilitate a voluntary resolution of a dispute. Parties shall be given the opportunity to consider all proposed options.
- A mediator cannot personally ensure that each party has made a fully informed choice to reach a particular agreement, but it is a good practice for the mediator to make the parties aware of the importance of consulting other professionals, where appropriate, to help them make informed decisions.

II. Impartiality: *A Mediator Shall Conduct the Mediation in an Impartial Manner.*

The concept of mediator impartiality is central to the mediation process. A mediator shall mediate only those matters in which she or he can remain impartial and evenhanded. If at any time the mediator is unable to conduct the process in an impartial manner, the mediator is obligated to withdraw.

COMMENTS:
- A mediator shall avoid conduct that gives the appearance of partiality toward one of the parties. The quality of the mediation process is enhanced when the parties have confidence in the impartiality of the mediator.
- When mediators are appointed by a court or institution, the appointing agency shall make reasonable efforts to ensure that mediators serve impartially.

- A mediator should guard against partiality or prejudice based on the parties' personal characteristics, background or performance at the mediation.

III. Conflicts of Interest: *A Mediator Shall Disclose all Actual and Potential Conflicts of Interest Reasonably Known to the Mediator. After Disclosure, the Mediator shall Decline to Mediate unless all Parties Choose to Retain the Mediator. The Need to Protect Against Conflicts of Interest also Governs Conduct that Occurs During and After the Mediation.*

A conflict of interest is a dealing or relationship that might create an impression of possible bias. The basic approach to questions of conflict of interest is consistent with the concept of self-determination. The mediator has a responsibility to disclose all actual and potential conflicts that are reasonably known to the mediator and could reasonably be seen as raising a question about impartiality. If all parties agree to mediate after being informed of conflicts, the mediator may proceed with the mediation. If, however, the conflict of interest casts serious doubt on the integrity of the process, the mediator shall decline to proceed.

A mediator must avoid the appearance of conflict of interest both during and after the mediation. Without the consent of all parties, a mediator shall not subsequently establish a professional relationship with one of the parties in a related matter, or in an unrelated matter under circumstances which would raise legitimate questions about the integrity of the mediation process.

COMMENTS:
- A mediator shall avoid conflicts of interest in recommending the services of other professionals. A mediator may make reference to professional referral services or associations which maintain rosters of qualified professionals.
- Potential conflicts of interest may arise between administrators of mediation programs and mediators and there may be strong pressures on the mediator to settle a particular case or cases. The mediator's commitment must be to the parties and the process. Pressure from outside of the mediation process should never influence the mediator to coerce parties to settle.

IV. Competence: *A Mediator Shall Mediate Only When the Mediator Has the Necessary Qualifications to Satisfy the Reasonable Expectations of the Parties.*

Any person may be selected as a mediator, provided that the parties are satisfied with the mediator's qualifications. Training and experience in mediation, however, are often necessary for effective mediation. A person who offers herself or himself as available to serve as a mediator gives parties and the public the expectation that she or he has the competency to mediate effectively. In court-connected or other forms of mandated mediation, it is essential that mediators assigned to the parties have the requisite training and experience.

COMMENTS:

- Mediators should have information available for the parties regarding their relevant training, education and experience.
- The requirements for appearing on a list of mediators must be made public and available to interested persons.
- When mediators are appointed by a court or institution, the appointing agency shall make reasonable efforts to ensure that each mediator is qualified for the particular mediation.

V. Confidentiality: *A Mediator Shall Maintain the Reasonable Expectations of the Parties with Regard to Confidentiality.*

The reasonable expectations of the parties with regard to confidentiality shall be met by the mediator. The parties' expectations of confidentiality depend on the circumstances of the mediation and any agreements they may make. The mediator shall not disclose any matter that a party expects to be confidential unless given permission by all parties or unless required by law or other public policy.

COMMENTS:

- The parties may make their own rules with respect to confidentiality, or the accepted practice of an individual mediator or institution may dictate a particular set of expectations. Since the parties' expectations regarding confidentiality are important, the mediator should discuss these expectations with the parties.
- If the mediator holds private sessions with a party, the nature of these sessions with regard to confidentiality should be discussed prior to undertaking such sessions.
- In order to protect the integrity of the mediation, a mediator should avoid communicating information about how the parties acted in the mediation process, the merits of the case, or settlement offers. The mediator may report, if required, whether parties appeared at a scheduled mediation.
- Where the parties have agreed that all or a portion of the information disclosed during a mediation is confidential, the parties' agreement should be respected by the mediator.
- Confidentiality should not be construed to limit or prohibit the effective monitoring, research, or evaluation of mediation programs by responsible persons. Under appropriate circumstances, researchers may be permitted to obtain access to statistical data and, with the permission of the parties, to individual case files, observations of live mediations, and interviews with participants.

VI. Quality of the Process: *A Mediator Shall Conduct the Mediation Fairly, Diligently, and in a Manner Consistent with the Principle of Self-Determination by the Parties.*

A mediator shall work to ensure a quality process and to encourage mutual respect among the parties. A quality process requires a commitment by the mediator to diligence and procedural fairness. There should be adequate opportunity for each party in the mediation to participate in the discussions. The parties decide when and under what conditions they will reach an agreement or terminate a mediation.

COMMENTS:

- A mediator may agree to mediate only when he or she is prepared to commit the attention essential to an effective mediation.
- Mediators should only accept cases when they can satisfy the reasonable expectations of the parties concerning the timing of the process. A mediator should not allow a mediation to be unduly delayed by the parties or their representatives.
- The presence or absence of persons at a mediation depends on the agreement of the parties and mediator. The parties and mediator may agree that others may be excluded from particular sessions or from the entire mediation process.
- The primary purpose of a mediator is to facilitate the parties' voluntary agreement. This role differs substantially from other professional-client relationships. Mixing the role of a mediator and the role of a professional advising a client is problematic, and mediators must strive to distinguish between the roles. A mediator should, therefore, refrain from providing professional advice. Where appropriate, a mediator should recommend that parties seek outside professional advice, or consider resolving their dispute through arbitration, counseling, neutral evaluation, or other processes. A mediator who undertakes, at the request of the parties, an additional dispute resolution role in the

same matter assumes increased responsibilities and obligations that may be governed by the standards of other professions.

- A mediator shall withdraw from a mediation when incapable of serving or when unable to remain impartial.
- A mediator shall withdraw from a mediation or postpone a session if the mediation is being used to further illegal conduct, or if a party is unable to participate due to drug, alcohol, or other physical or mental incapacity.
- Mediators should not permit their behavior in the mediation process to be guided by a desire for a high settlement rate.

VII. Advertising and Solicitation: *A Mediator Shall be Truthful in Advertising and Solicitation for Mediation.*

Advertising or any other communication with the public concerning services offered or regarding the education, training, and expertise of the mediator shall be truthful. Mediators shall refrain from promises and guarantees of results.

COMMENTS:

- It is imperative that communication with the public educate and instill confidence in the process.
- In an advertisement or other communication to the public, a mediator may make reference to meeting state, national, or private organization qualifications only if the entity referred to has a procedure for qualifying mediators and the mediator has been duly granted the requisite status.

VIII. Fees: *A Mediator Shall Fully Disclose and Explain the Basis of Compensation, Fees, and Charges to the Parties.*

The parties should be provided sufficient information about fees at the outset of a mediation to determine if they wish to retain the services of a mediator. If a mediator charges fees, the fees shall be reasonable, considering, among other things, the mediation service, the type and complexity of the matter, the expertise of the mediator, the time required, and the rates customary in the community. The better practice in reaching an understanding about fees is to set down the arrangements in a written agreement.

COMMENTS:

- A mediator who withdraws from a mediation should return any unearned fee to the parties.
- A mediator should not enter into a fee agreement which is contingent upon the result of the mediation or amount of the settlement.

- Co-mediators who share a fee should hold to standards of reasonableness in determining the allocation of fees.
- A mediator should not accept a fee for referral of a matter to another mediator or to any other person.

IX. Obligations to the Mediation Process: *Mediators Have a Duty to Improve the Practice of Mediation.*

COMMENTS:

- Mediators are regarded as knowledgeable in the process of mediation. They have an obligation to use their knowledge to help educate the public about mediation; to make mediation accessible to those who would like to use it; to correct abuses; and to improve their professional skills and abilities.

© American Arbitration Association. Reprinted with permission.

AMERICAN ASSOCIATION FOR MARRIAGE AND FAMILY THERAPY

Address:	1133 15th Street NW, Suite 300
	Washington, DC 20005-2710
Telephone:	202/452-0109
WWW:	www.aamft.org
Document:	AAMFT Code of Ethics (1991)

The Board of Directors of the American Association for Marriage and Family Therapy (AAMFT) hereby promulgates, pursuant to Article 2, Section 2.013 of the Association's Bylaws, the Revised AAMFT Code of Ethics, effective August 1, 1991.

The AAMFT Code of Ethics is binding on Members of AAMFT in all membership categories, AAMFT Approved Supervisors, and applicants for membership and the Approved Supervisor designation (hereafter, AAMFT Member).

If an AAMFT Member resigns in anticipation of, or during the course of an ethics investigation, the Ethics Committee will complete its investigation. Any publication of action taken by the Association will include the fact that the Member attempted to resign during the investigation.

Marriage and family therapists are strongly encouraged to report alleged unethical behavior of colleagues to appropriate professional associations and state regulatory bodies.

1. Responsibility to Clients

Marriage and family therapists advance the welfare of families and individuals. They respect the rights of those persons seeking their assistance, and make reasonable efforts to ensure that their services are used appropriately.

1.1 Marriage and family therapists do not discriminate against or refuse professional service to anyone on the basis of race, gender, religion, national origin, or sexual orientation.

1.2 Marriage and family therapists are aware of their influential position with respect to clients, and they avoid exploiting the trust and dependency of such persons. Therapists, therefore, make every effort to avoid dual relationships with clients that could impair professional judgment or increase the risk of exploitation. When a dual relationship cannot be avoided, therapists take appropriate professional precautions to ensure judgment is not impaired and no exploitation occurs. Examples of such dual relationships include, but are not limited to, business or close personal relationships with clients. Sexual intimacy with clients is prohibited. Sexual intimacy with former clients for two years following the termination of therapy is prohibited.

1.3 Marriage and family therapists do not use their professional relationships with clients to further their own interests.

1.4 Marriage and family therapists respect the right of clients to make decisions and help them to understand the consequences of these decisions. Therapists clearly advise a client that a decision on marital status is the responsibility of the client.

1.5 Marriage and family therapists continue therapeutic relationships only so long as it is reasonably clear that clients are benefiting from the relationship.

1.6 Marriage and family therapists assist persons in obtaining other therapeutic services if the therapist is unable or unwilling, for appropriate reasons, to provide professional help.

1.7 Marriage and family therapists do not abandon or neglect clients in treatment without making reasonable arrangements for the continuation of such treatment.

1.8 Marriage and family therapists obtain written informed consent from clients before videotaping, audiorecording, or permitting third party observation.

2. Confidentiality

Marriage and family therapists have unique confidentiality concerns because the client in a therapeutic relationship may be more than one person. Therapists respect and guard confidences of each individual client.

2.1 Marriage and family therapists may not disclose client confidences except: a) as mandated by law; b) to prevent a clear and immediate danger to a person or persons; c) where the therapist is a defendant in a civil, criminal, or disciplinary action arising from the therapy (in which case client confidences may be disclosed only in the course of that action); or d) if there is a waiver previously obtained in writing, and then such information may be revealed only in accordance with the terms of the waiver. In circumstances where more than one person in a family receives therapy, each such family member who is legally competent to execute a waiver must agree to the waiver required by subparagraph (d). Without such a waiver from each family member legally competent to execute a waiver, a therapist cannot disclose information received from any family member.

2.2 Marriage and family therapists use client and/or clinical materials in teaching, writing, and public presentations only if a written waiver has been obtained in accordance with Subprinciple 2.1(d), or when appropriate steps have been taken to protect client identity and confidentiality.

2.3 Marriage and family therapists store or dispose of client records in ways that maintain confidentiality.

3. Professional Competence and Integrity

Marriage and family therapists maintain high standards of professional competence and integrity.

3.1 Marriage and family therapists are in violation of this Code and subject to termination of membership or other appropriate action if they: a) are convicted of any felony; b) are convicted of a misdemeanor related to their qualifications or functions; c) engage in conduct which could lead to conviction of a felony, or a misdemeanor related to their qualifications or functions; d) are expelled from or disciplined by other professional organizations; e) have their licenses or certificates suspended or revoked or are otherwise disciplined by regulatory bodies; f) are no longer competent to practice marriage and family therapy because they are impaired due to physical or mental causes or the abuse of alcohol or other substances; or g) fail to cooperate with the Association at any point from the inception of an ethical complaint through the completion of all proceedings regarding that complaint.

3.2 Marriage and family therapists seek appropriate professional assistance for their personal problems or conflicts that may impair work performance or judgment.

3.3 Marriage and family therapists, as teachers, supervisors, and researchers, are dedicated to high standards of scholarship and present accurate information.

3.4 Marriage and family therapists remain abreast of new developments in family therapy knowledge and practice through educational activities.

3.5 Marriage and family therapists do not engage in sexual or other harassment or exploitation of clients, students, trainees, supervisees, employees, colleagues, research subjects, or actual or potential witnesses or complainants in investigations and ethical proceedings.

3.6 Marriage and family therapists do not diagnose, treat, or advise on problems outside the recognized boundaries of their competence.

3.7 Marriage and family therapists make efforts to prevent the distortion or misuse of their clinical and research findings.

3.8 Marriage and family therapists, because of their ability to influence and alter the lives of others, exercise special care when making public their professional recommendations and opinions through testimony or other public statements.

4. Responsibility to Students, Employees, and Supervisees

Marriage and family therapists do not exploit the trust and dependency of students, employees, and supervisees.

4.1 Marriage and family therapists are aware of their influential position with respect to students, employees, and supervisees, and they avoid exploiting the trust and dependency of such persons. Therapists, therefore, make every effort to avoid dual relationships that could impair professional judgment or increase the risk of exploitation. When a dual relationship cannot be avoided, therapists take appropriate professional precautions to ensure judgment is not impaired and no exploitation occurs. Examples of such dual relationships include, but are not limited to, business or close personal relationships with students, employees, or supervisees. Provision of therapy to students, employees, or supervisees is prohibited. Sexual intimacy with students or supervisees is prohibited.

4.2 Marriage and family therapists do not permit students, employees, or supervisees to perform or to hold themselves out as competent to perform professional services beyond their training, level of experience, and competence.

4.3 Marriage and family therapists do not disclose supervisee confidences except: a) as mandated by law; b) to prevent a clear and immediate danger to a person or persons; c) where the therapist is a defendant in a civil, criminal, or disciplinary action arising from the supervision (in which case supervisee confidences may be disclosed only in the course of that action); d) in educational or training settings where there are multiple supervisors, and then only to other professional colleagues who share responsibility for the training of the supervisee; or e) if there is a waiver previously obtained in writing, and then such information may be revealed only in accordance with the terms of the waiver.

5. Responsibility to Research Participants

Investigators respect the dignity and protect the welfare of participants in research and are aware of federal and state laws and regulations and professional standards governing the conduct of research.

5.1 Investigators are responsible for making careful examinations of ethical acceptability in planning studies. To the extent that services to research participants may be compromised by participation in research, investigators seek the ethical advice of qualified professionals not directly involved in the investigation and observe safeguards to protect the rights of research participants.

5.2 Investigators requesting participants' involvement in research inform them of all aspects of the research that might reasonably be expected to influence willingness to participate. Investigators are especially sensitive to the possibility of diminished consent when participants are also receiving clinical services, have impairments which limit understanding and/or communication, or when participants are children.

5.3 Investigators respect participants' freedom to decline participation in or to withdraw from a research study at any time. This obligation requires special thought and consideration when investigators or other members of the research team are in positions of authority or influence over participants. Marriage and family therapists, therefore, make every effort to avoid dual relationships with research participants that could impair professional judgment or increase the risk of exploitation.

5.4 Information obtained about a research participant during the course of an investigation is confidential unless there is a waiver previously obtained in writing. When the possibility exists that others, including family members, may obtain access to such information, this possibility, together with the plan for protecting confidentiality, is explained as part of the procedure for obtaining informed consent.

6. Responsibility to the Profession

Marriage and family therapists respect the rights and responsibilities of professional colleagues and participate in activities which advance the goals of the profession.

6.1 Marriage and family therapists remain accountable to the standards of the profession when acting as members or employees of organizations.

6.2 Marriage and family therapists assign publication credit to those who have contributed to a publication in proportion to their contributions and in accordance with customary professional publication practices.

6.3 Marriage and family therapists who are the authors of books or other materials that are published or distributed cite persons to whom credit for original ideas is due.

6.4 Marriage and family therapists who are the authors of books or other materials published or distributed by an organization take reasonable precautions to ensure that the organization promotes and advertises the materials accurately and factually.

6.5 Marriage and family therapists participate in activities that contribute to a better community and society, including devoting a portion of their professional activity to services for which there is little or no financial return.

6.6 Marriage and family therapists are concerned with developing laws and regulations pertaining to marriage and family therapy that serve the public interest, and with altering such laws and regulations that are not in the public interest.

6.7 Marriage and family therapists encourage public participation in the design and delivery of professional services and in the regulation of practitioners.

7. Financial Arrangements

Marriage and family therapists make financial arrangements with clients, third party payors, and supervisees that are reasonably understandable and conform to accepted professional practices.

7.1 Marriage and family therapists do not offer or accept payment for referrals.

7.2 Marriage and family therapists do not charge excessive fees for services.

7.3 Marriage and family therapists disclose their fees to clients and supervisees at the beginning of services.

7.4 Marriage and family therapists represent facts truthfully to clients, third party payors, and supervisees regarding services rendered.

8. Advertising

Marriage and family therapists engage in appropriate informational activities, including those that enable laypersons to choose professional services on an informed basis.

General Advertising

8.1 Marriage and family therapists accurately represent their competence, education, training, and experience relevant to their practice of marriage and family therapy.

8.2 Marriage and family therapists assure that advertisements and publications in any media (such as directories, announcements, business cards, newspapers, radio, television, and facsimiles) convey information that is necessary for the public to make an appropriate selection of professional services. Information could include: a) office information, such as name, address, telephone number, credit card acceptability, fees, languages spoken, and office hours; b) appropriate degrees, state licensure and/or certification, and AAMFT Clinical Member status; and c) description of practice. (For requirements for advertising under the AAMFT name, logo, and/or the abbreviated initials AAMFT, see Subprinciple 8.15, below).

8.3 Marriage and family therapists do not use a name which could mislead the public concerning the identity, responsibility, source, and status of those practicing under that name and do not hold themselves out as being partners or associates of a firm if they are not.

8.4 Marriage and family therapists do not use any professional identification (such as a business card, office sign, letterhead, or telephone or association directory listing) if it includes a statement or claim that is false, fraudulent, misleading, or deceptive. A statement is false, fraudulent, misleading, or deceptive if it a) contains a material misrepresentation of fact; b) fails to state any material fact necessary to make the statement, in light of all circumstances, not misleading; or c) is intended to or is likely to create an unjustified expectation.

8.5 Marriage and family therapists correct, wherever possible, false, misleading, or inaccurate information and representations made by others concerning the therapist's qualifications, services, or products.

8.6 Marriage and family therapists make certain that the qualifications of persons in their employ are represented in a manner that is not false, misleading, or deceptive.

8.7 Marriage and family therapists may represent themselves as specializing within a limited area of marriage and family therapy, but only if they have the education and supervised experience in settings which meet recognized professional standards to practice in that specialty area.

Advertising Using AAMFT Designations

8.8 The AAMFT designations of Clinical Member, Approved Supervisor, and Fellow may be used in public information or advertising materials only by persons holding such designations. Persons holding such designations may, for example, advertise in the following manner:
Jane Doe, Ph.D., a Clinical Member of the American Association for Marriage and Family Therapy. Alternately, the advertisement could read, *Jane Doe, Ph.D., AAMFT Clinical Member.*
John Doe, Ph.D., an Approved Supervisor of the American Association for Marriage and Family Therapy. Alternately, the advertisement could read, *John Doe, Ph.D., AAMFT Approved Supervisor.*
Jane Doe, Ph.D., a Fellow of the American Association for Marriage and Family Therapy. Alter-

nately, the advertisement could read, *Jane Doe, Ph.D., AAMFT Fellow.*
More than one designation may be used if held by the AAMFT Member.

8.9 Marriage and family therapists who hold the AAMFT Approved Supervisor or the Fellow designation may not represent the designation as an advanced clinical status.

8.10 Student, Associate, and Affiliate Members may not use their AAMFT membership status in public information or advertising materials. Such listings on professional resumes are not considered advertisements.

8.11 Persons applying for AAMFT membership may not list their application status on any resume or advertisement.

8.12 In conjunction with their AAMFT membership, marriage and family therapists claim as evidence of educational qualifications only those degrees a) from regionally accredited institutions or b) from institutions recognized by states which license or certify marriage and family therapists, but only if such state regulation is recognized by AAMFT.

8.13 Marriage and family therapists may not use the initials AAMFT following their name in the manner of an academic degree.

8.14 Marriage and family therapists may not use the AAMFT name, logo, and/or the abbreviated initials AAMFT or make any other such representation which would imply that they speak for or represent the Association. The Association is the sole owner of its name, logo, and the abbreviated initials AAMFT. Its committees and divisions, operating as such, may use the name, logo, and/or the abbreviated initials, AAMFT, in accordance with AAMFT policies.

8.15 Authorized advertisements of Clinical Members under the AAMFT name, logo, and/or the abbreviated initials AAMFT may include the following: the Clinical Member's name, degree, license or certificate held when required by state law, name of business, address, and telephone number. If a business is listed, it must follow, not precede the Clinical Member's name. Such listings may not include AAMFT offices held by the Clinical Member, nor any specializations, since such a listing under the AAMFT name, logo, and/or the abbreviated initials AAMFT would imply that this specialization has been credentialed by AAMFT.

8.16 Marriage and family therapists use their membership in AAMFT only in connection with their clinical and professional activities.

8.17 Only AAMFT divisions and programs accredited by the AAMFT Commission on Accreditation for Marriage and Family Therapy Education, not businesses nor organizations, may use any AAMFT-related designation or affiliation in public information or advertising materials, and then only in accordance with AAMFT policies.

8.18 Programs accredited by the AAMFT Commission on Accreditation for Marriage and Family Therapy Education may not use the AAMFT name, logo, and/or the abbreviated initials, AAMFT. Instead, they may have printed on their stationery and other appropriate materials a statement such as: *The* (name of program) *of the* (name of institution) *is accredited by the AAMFT Commission on Accreditation for Marriage and Family Therapy Education.*

8.19 Programs not accredited by the AAMFT Commission on Accreditation for Marriage and Family Therapy Education may not use the AAMFT name, logo, and/or the abbreviated initials, AAMFT. They may not state in printed program materials, program advertisements, and student advertisement that their courses and training opportunities are accepted by AAMFT to meet AAMFT membership requirements.

AMERICAN ASSOCIATION FOR PUBLIC OPINION RESEARCH

Address: 426 Thompson Street
               PO Box 1248
               Ann Arbor, MI 48106-1248
Telephone: 734/764-1555
WWW: www.aapor.org
Document: Code of Professional Ethics and
               Practices (1986)

We, the members of the American Association for Public for Opinion Research, subscribe to the principles expressed in the following code. Our goals are to support sound and ethical practice in the conduct of public opinion research and in the use of such research for policy and decision-making in the public and private sectors, as well as to improve public understanding of opinion research methods and the proper use of opinion research results.

We pledge ourselves to maintain high standards of scientific competence and integrity in conducting, analyzing, and reporting our work in our relations with survey respondents, with our clients, with those who eventually use the research for decision-making purposes, and with the general public. We further pledge ourselves to reject all tasks or assignments that would require activities inconsistent with the principles of this code.

THE CODE

I. Principles of Professional Practice in the Conduct of Our Work

A. We shall exercise due care in developing research designs and survey instruments, and in collecting, processing, and analyzing data, taking all reasonable steps to assure the reliability and validity of results.

  1. We shall recommend and employ only those tools and methods of analysis which, in our professional judgement, are well suited to the research problem at hand.

  2. We shall not select research tools and methods of analysis because of their capacity to yield misleading conclusions.

  3. We shall not knowingly make interpretations of research results, nor shall we tacitly permit interpretations that are inconsistent with the data available.

  4. We shall not knowingly imply that interpretations should be accorded greater confidence than the data actually warrant.

B. We shall describe our methods and findings accurately and in appropriate detail in all research reports, adhering to the standards for minimal disclosure specified in Section III.

C. If any of our work becomes the subject of a formal investigation of an alleged violation of this Code, undertaken with the approval of the AAPOR Executive Council, we shall provide additional information on the survey in such detail that a fellow survey practitioner would be able to conduct a professional evaluation of the survey.

II. Principles of Professional Responsibility in Our Dealings With People

A. The Public:

1. If we become aware of the appearance in public of serious distortions of our research, we shall publicly disclose what is required to correct these distortions, including, as appropriate, a statement to the public media, legislative body, regulatory agency, or other appropriate group, in or before which the distorted findings were presented.

B. Clients or Sponsors:

1. When undertaking work for a private client, we shall hold confidential all proprietary information obtained about the client and about the conduct and findings of the research undertaken for the client, except when the dissemination of the information is expressly authorized by the client, or when disclosure becomes necessary under terms of Section I-C or II-A of this Code.
2. We shall be mindful of the limitations of our techniques and capabilities and shall accept only those research assignments which we can reasonably expect to accomplish within these limitations.

C. The Profession:

1. We recognize our responsibility to contribute to the science of public opinion research and to disseminate as freely as possible the ideas and findings which emerge from our research.
2. We shall not cite our membership in the Association as evidence of professional competence, since the Association does not so certify any persons or organizations.

D. The Respondent:

1. We shall strive to avoid the use of practices or methods that may harm, humiliate, or seriously mislead survey respondents.
2. Unless the respondent waives confidentiality for specified uses, we shall hold as privileged and confidential all information that might identify a respondent with his or her responses. We shall also not disclose or use the names of respondents for non-research purposes unless the respondents grant us permission to do so.

III. Standard for Minimal Disclosure

Good professional practice imposes the obligation upon all public opinion researchers to include, in any report of research results, or to make available when that report is released, certain essential information about how the research was conducted. At a minimum, the following items should be disclosed:

1. Who sponsored the survey, and who conducted it.
2. The exact wording of questions asked, including the text of any preceding instruction or explanation to the interviewer or respondents that might reasonably be expected to affect the response.
3. A definition of the population under study, and a description of the sampling frame used to identify this population.
4. A description of the sample selection procedure, giving a clear indication of the method by which the respondents were selected by the researcher, or whether the respondents were entirely self-selected.
5. Size of samples and, if applicable, completion rates and information on eligibility criteria and screening procedures.
6. A discussion of the precision of the findings, including, if appropriate, estimates of sampling error, and a description of any weighting or estimating procedures used.
7. Which results are based on parts of the sample, rather than on the total sample.
8. Method, location, and dates of data collection.

© American Association for Public Opinion Research. Reprinted with permission.

AMERICAN ASSOCIATION FOR RESPIRATORY CARE

Address: 11030 Ables Lane
                Dallas, TX 75229-4593
Telephone: 972/243-2272
WWW: www.aarc.org
Document: AARC Statement of Ethics and
                Professional Conduct (1994)

In the conduct of their professional activities the Respiratory Care Practitioner shall be bound by the following ethical and professional principles. Respiratory Care Practitioners shall:

Demonstrate behavior that reflects integrity, supports objectivity, and fosters trust in the profession and its professionals.

Actively maintain and continually improve their professional competence, and represent it accurately.

Perform only those procedures or functions in which they are individually competent and which are within the scope of accepted and responsible practice.

Respect and protect the legal and personal rights of patients they treat, including the right to informed consent and refusal of treatment.

Divulge no confidential information regarding any patient or family unless disclosure is required for responsible performance of duty, or required by law.

Provide care without discrimination on any basis, with respect for the rights and dignity of all individuals.

Promote disease prevention and wellness.

Refuse to participate in illegal or unethical acts, and shall refuse to conceal illegal, unethical or incompetent acts of others.

Follow sound scientific procedures and ethical principles in research.

Comply with state or federal laws which govern and relate to their practice.

Avoid any form of conduct that creates a conflict of interest, and shall follow the principles of ethical business behavior.

Promote the positive evolution of the profession, and health care in general, through improvement of the access, efficacy, and cost of patient care.

Refrain from indiscriminate and unnecessary use of resources, both economic and natural, in their practice.

© American Association for Respiratory Care. Reprinted with permission.

AMERICAN ASSOCIATION OF ADVERTISING AGENCIES

Address: 405 Lexington Avenue, 18th Floor
            New York, NY 10174-1801

Telephone: 212/682-2500
WWW: www.aaaa.org
Document: Standards of Practice (1924. Most recently revised 1990.)

We hold that a responsibility of advertising agencies is to be a constructive force in business.

We hold that, to discharge this responsibility, advertising agencies must recognize an obligation, not only to their clients, but to the public, the media they employ, and to each other. As a business, the advertising agency must operate within the framework of competition. It is recognized that keen and vigorous competition, honestly conducted, is necessary to the growth and the health of American business. However, unethical competitive practices in the advertising agency business lead to financial waste, dilution of service, diversion of manpower, loss of prestige, and tend to weaken public confidence both in advertisements and in the institution of advertising.

We hold that the advertising agency should compete on merit and not by attempts at discrediting or disparaging a competitor agency, or its work, directly or by inference, or by circulating harmful rumors about another agency, or by making unwarranted claims of particular skill in judging or prejudging advertising copy.

To these ends, the American Association of Advertising Agencies has adopted the following *Creative Code* as being in the best interests of the public, the advertisers, the media, and the agencies themselves. The A.A.A.A. believes the Code's provisions serve as a guide to the kind of agency conduct that experience has shown to be wise, foresighted, and constructive. In accepting membership, an agency agrees to follow it.

Creative Code
We, the members of the American Association of Advertising Agencies, in addition to supporting and obeying the laws and legal regulations pertaining to advertising, undertake to extend and broaden the application of high ethical standards. Specifically, we will not knowingly create advertising that contains:

a. False or misleading statements or exaggerations, visual or verbal

b. Testimonials that do not reflect the real opinion of the individual(s) involved

c. Price claims that are misleading

d. Claims insufficiently supported or that distort the true meaning or practicable application of statements made by professional or scientific authority

e. Statements, suggestions, or pictures offensive to public decency or minority segments of the population.

We recognize that there are areas that are subject to honestly different interpretations and judgment. Nevertheless, we agree not to recommend to an advertiser, and to discourage the use of, advertising that is in poor or questionable taste or that is deliberately irritating through aural or visual content or presentation.

Comparative advertising shall be governed by the same standards of truthfulness, claim substantiation, tastefulness, etc., as apply to other types of advertising.

These Standards of Practice of the American Association of Advertising Agencies come from the belief that sound and ethical practice is good business. Confidence and respect are indispensable to success in a business embracing the many intangibles of agency service and involving relationships so dependent upon good faith.

Clear and willful violations of these Standards of Practice may be referred to the Board of Directors of the American Association of Advertising Agencies for appropriate action, including possible annulment of membership as provided by Article IV, Section 5, of the Constitution and By-Laws.

AMERICAN ASSOCIATION OF AIRPORT EXECUTIVES

Address: 601 Madison Street
                    Alexandria, VA 22314
Telephone: 703/824-0500
WWW: www.airportnet.org
Document: Code of Ethics (1988)

As a professional Airport Executive in the performance of my duties and responsibilities, I pledge to:

1. Be dedicated to the safe, efficient and economic operation of airports and the national air transportation system and believe that professional management is the method to achieve this objective.

2. Be dedicated to the highest ideals of honor and integrity in all public and personal relationships in order to earn and retain the respect and confidence of public officials, employees and the general public.

3. Refrain from participation in the election of the members of the employing governmental body and from all partisan political activities which would compromise the performance of a professional executive.

4. Resist any encroachment on professional responsibility and duties, believing that the executive should be free to carry out official policies without interference and handle each problem without discrimination on the basis of principle and justice.

5. Neither seek nor accept any favor of gift from persons or firms under which circumstances could be reasonably inferred that the favor would influence or compromise the executive or governing body.

6. Submit policy proposals to the employing governmental body and officials, provide them with facts and advice on matters of policy as a basis for making decisions and establishing airport goals, implement and execute policies adopted by the governing officials.

7. Recognize that elected and/or appointed officials are responsible for the establishment of airport policies and that policy execution is the responsibility of the airport executive.

8. Keep the community informed on airport affairs, encourage communication between the users, citizens and all public officials, emphasize friendly and courteous service to the public and constantly seek to improve the quality and public image of the airport executives.

9. Handle all personnel matters on the basis of merit in order that fairness and impartiality govern the executive's decision pertaining to appointments, salary adjustments, promotions and discipline.

10. Strive to continually improve professional competence and ability through education and research; and to encourage the professional development of associates and subordinates.

AMERICAN ASSOCIATION OF BIOANALYSTS

Address:	917 Locust Street, Suite 1100
	St. Louis, MO 63101-1419
Telephone:	314/241-1445
WWW:	www.aab.org
Document:	Code of Ethics

The American Association of Bioanalysts and its membership subscribe freely and without reservation to the premise that, in their capacity as competent and responsible bioanalysts, they must:

- Be aware of their responsibility for the health and welfare of the patient who depends upon their skills as bioanalysts;
- Protect and maintain the confidential nature of their reports, and reveal information concerning the patient to no one other than the referring physician;
- Support and participate in the scientific and academic programs of the Association in their continuing effort to enhance the profession;
- Uphold the welfare of their community and support its laws and institutions;
- Avoid and actively discourage all practices of a questionable legal or moral character.

© American Association of Bioanalysts. Reprinted with permission.

AMERICAN ASSOCIATION OF FAMILY AND CONSUMER SCIENCES

Address:	1555 King Street
	Alexandria, VA 22314-2752
Telephone:	703/706-4600
WWW:	www.aafcs.org
Document:	Code of Ethics (1996)

I. Preamble

These principles are intended to aid members of the American Association of Family and Consumer Sciences individually and collectively in maintaining a high level of ethical conduct. They are guidelines by which a member may determine the propriety of conduct in relationships with clients, with colleagues, with members of allied professions and with various publics.

A member of the family and consumer sciences profession and of the American Association of Family and Consumer Sciences shall:

1. Maintain the highest responsible standard of professional performance, upholding confidentiality and acting with intelligence, commitment, and enthusiasm.
2. Fulfill the obligation to continually upgrade and broaden personal professional competence.
3. Share professional competence with colleagues and clients, to enlarge and continue development of the profession.
4. Support the objectives of the American Association of Family and Consumer Sciences and contribute to its development through informed, active participation in its programs.
5. Advance public awareness and understanding of the profession.
6. Maintain a dedication of enhancing individual and family potential as a focus for professional efforts.

The mission of the American Association of Family and Consumer Sciences is to effect the optimal well-being of families and individuals by:

- Empowering members to act on continuing and emerging concerns;
- Focusing the expertise of members for action on critical issues;
- Assuming leadership among organizations with mutual purposes.

II. Statement of Principles of Professional Practice

Preamble

These Principles of Professional Practice guide American Association of Family and Consumer Sciences members in all categories: those Certified in Family and Consumer Sciences (CFCS); applicants for membership in the association; and applicants for the Certified in Family and Consumer Sciences designation. The Principles also provide members of the association with guidelines and descriptions of the actions required for ethical professional practice.

Professional Competence
AAFCS members base their competence on educational degrees earned from regionally accredited institutions and from training, experience, and certification programs recognized by AAFCS.

1. AAFCS members seek continuing education reflecting new expectations, procedures, and values.
2. AAFCS members assure accurate presentation of their work by organizations with whom they are affiliated.
3. AAFCS members identify themselves as Certified in Family and Consumer Sciences in cases in which this designation is consistent with the procedures and guidelines of the AAFCS Council for Certification. They may use the CFCS acronym in this identification and designation.
4. AAFCS members claim competence only in an area or areas for which they have education, training, and experience.
5. AAFCS members accurately present competencies of students, supervisors, colleagues, and others with whom they work.
6. AAFCS members practice within the law and within the recognized boundaries of their education, training, and experience.
7. AAFCS members verify the credentials of their employees and supervisees.
8. AAFCS members refrain from professional practice when impairment due to mental or physical causes, including chemical and alcohol abuse, affects professional competence. Members seek appropriate professional help for such impairments.

Respect for Diversity
AAFCS members respect differences in the abilities and needs of the people with whom they work.

1. AAFCS members recognize that differences exist among individuals and families and do not discriminate against or patronize others.
2. AAFCS members obtain education, training, and experience to provide competent services to persons of diverse background or persuasions.
3. AAFCS members conduct research relating to the uniqueness of individuals and families.

4. AAFCS members utilize and present subject matter in such a way as to recognize and develop appreciation of diversity.

Scholarship and Research
AAFCS members conduct, utilize, and report research using recognized research procedures and facilitate professional standards for the respective research foci.

1. AAFCS members secure review and approval of research designs by knowledgeable professionals consistent with standards used by institutional review boards.
2. AAFCS members, as part of their research efforts, secure review of research designs by knowledgeable professionals not directly involved in the investigation.
3. AAFCS members secure the informed consent of research participants based on disclosure of the research design and potentially harmful effects of participation. Investigators are especially sensitive to consent among at-risk and protected populations.
4. AAFCS members honor individuals' choice to decline participation or withdraw at any time from research studies.
5. AAFCS members acknowledge through publication credit and other avenues the efforts and contributions of others to research activities.
6. AAFCS members are obliged to take steps to ensure that their research findings are accurately and clearly understood by consumers.

Confidentiality
AAFCS members maintain and guard the confidentiality of persons with whom they have professional relationships.

Conflicts of Interest
AAFCS members avoid conflicting roles and take active steps to prevent and avoid exploitation of the individuals with whom they work.

1. AAFCS members assume responsibility for fair treatment of consumers, other professionals, individuals and/or families.
2. AAFCS members make financial arrangements with clients, third-party payers, and supervisees that conform to commonly accepted professional practices and that are easily understood by all populations served.
3. AAFCS members report truthfully all professional services rendered.

Responsibility to the Profession

AAFCS members support the objectives of the American Association of Family and Consumer Sciences and contribute to association roles and development through active, informed participation.

1. AAFCS members advance public awareness and understanding of the association and its mission.
2. AAFCS members respect the rights and responsibilities of peers.
3. AAFCS members devote time and energy to public policy issues and to the public good.
4. AAFCS members speak on behalf of the association in ways consistent with the directives and policies of the association Board of Directors.
5. AAFCS members utilize the American Association of Family and Consumer Sciences logo only in ways approved by the association Board of Directors.

© American Association of Family and Consumer Sciences. Reprinted with permission.

AMERICAN ASSOCIATION
OF HOMES AND SERVICES
FOR THE AGING

AMERICAN ASSOCIATION OF HOMES AND SERVICES FOR THE AGING

Address: 901 E Street NW, Suite 500
             Washington, DC 20004-2011
Telephone: 202/783-2242
WWW: www.aahsa.org
Document: AAHSA Membership Credo (1991)

As members of the American Association of Homes and Services for the Aging, we aspire to a set of values and beliefs that make up the membership credo.

Preamble

As members of AAHSA, we are not-for-profit or government-sponsored organizations dedicated to providing quality housing, health, community and related services to meet the needs of America's diverse aging population. We have distinct and charitable roots—ethnic, religious or fraternal—and serve individuals of diverse background and needs.

Values

As members, we aspire to a set of values in our relations with the older persons we serve, our governing boards and staff, volunteers, the communities in which we live and work, the government and other organizations.

Accountability: A responsibility to each of the groups we serve or with whom we have a relationship.

Benevolence: An understanding that to do good requires housing or caring for older persons in need.

Compassion: A commitment to providing a more meaningful life for all persons, allowing them to live full lives with dignity and self-respect.

Competency: A commitment to the highest standards of training, continuing education, research, fiscal management, leadership and operations.

Integrity: A commitment to honesty within our organization and in our relations with the larger community, as well as a respect for confidentiality.

Renewal: A recognition of both interdependency and group frailty that encourages us to reevaluate ourselves continuously.

Social responsibility: A commitment to non-discrimination and to equitable treatment for all.

Stewardship: A focus on providing the highest quality of care and on the responsible use of resources.

Beliefs

Based on these values, as members of AAHSA, we share a set of beliefs that affect how we relate to others.

The People We Serve

We believe that every person is unique, irreplaceable and has individual physical, psychological, spiritual and quality of life needs. To meet those needs, we:

• Promote an environment in which a person can live and die with dignity.
• Promote personal autonomy in everyday life.
• Involve the individuals we serve and their families in planning and services and provide for their input in the governance of the organization.
• Ensure that all individuals can voice their concerns or grievances in an organized or informal manner—without fear of reprisal.

Governing Boards

We believe that members of our governing boards should have diverse skills and talents. As the heart of the organization, the board should:

- Ensure that the mission is carried forward.
- Ensure that our finances are managed with diligence and prudence.
- Inspire ethical reflection and behavior in both management and in the care and service of the aging.

Staff

We believe that, because the work place is important to each staff member, we:

- Orient all staff to the organization's mission in serving the needs of the aging and to current law or regulation.
- Ensure that staff have the education and resources—human or otherwise—to achieve excellence on the job.
- Promote involvement and empowerment of all staff in decision-making.

Volunteers

We believe that volunteers enhance the quality of life for the individuals we serve and that volunteers work with the aging as much to receive as to give. In working with volunteers, we:

- Provide orientation and training so that each individual understands his or her role in the organization's mission.
- Recognize and support each individual and ensure that assignments enhance self-worth and the lives of those we serve.
- Encourage people of all ages to serve so that they understand the needs of the aging and how working with the aged can enrich their lives.

Communities

We believe that, as important community resources, we:

- Encourage continued attention to the environment.
- Encourage a commitment to community service, public education and voluntarism.
- Emphasize interrelations with the community both in our mission and operations.

Government

We believe that laws and regulations generally set forth minimum standards. We:

- Strive to go beyond those standards.
- Promote national, state and local standards that seek to improve the quality of health care, housing or services for the aging.

- Challenge those standards which are unreasonable, unethical or unfair.
- Participate regularly in national, state or local association advocacy activities on issues affecting the aging.

Other Organizations

We believe that not-for-profit organizations exist to fulfill the unmet needs of society, and we:

- Encourage the sharing of information with others.
- Interact with fairness and honesty and a sense of social responsibility.
- Demonstrate accountability through public communications and reports.

© American Association of Homes and Services for the Aging. Reprinted with permission.

AMERICAN ASSOCIATION OF NURSE ANESTHETISTS

Address: 222 South Prospect Avenue
              Park Ridge, IL 60068-4001
Telephone: 847/692-7050
WWW: www.aana.com
Document: Code of Ethics for the Certified
              Registered Nurse Anesthetist (1986.
              Most recently revised 1997.)

Preamble

Certified Registered Nurse Anesthetists practice nursing by providing anesthesia and anesthesia related services. They accept the responsibility conferred upon them by the state, the profession, and society. The American Association of Nurse Anesthetists has adopted this Code of Ethics to guide its members in fulfilling their obligation as professionals. Each member of the American Association of Nurse Anesthetists has a personal responsibility to uphold and adhere to these ethical standards.

1. Responsibility to Patients

Certified Registered Nurse Anesthetists (CRNAs) preserve human dignity, respect the moral and legal rights of health consumers, and support the safety and well being of the patient under their care.

1.1 The CRNA renders quality anesthesia care regardless of the patient's race, religion, age, sex, nationality, disability, social or economic status.

1.2 The CRNA protects the patient from harm and is an advocate for the patient's welfare.

1.3 The CRNA verifies that a valid anesthesia informed consent has been obtained from the patient or legal guardian as required by federal or state laws or institutional policy prior to rendering a service.

1.4 The CRNA avoids conflicts between his or her personal integrity and the patient's rights. In situations where the CRNA's personal convictions prohibit participation in a particular procedure, the CRNA refuses to participate or withdraws from the case provided that such refusal or withdrawal does not harm the patient or constitute a breach of duty.

1.5 The CRNA takes appropriate action to protect patients from healthcare providers who are incompetent, impaired, or engage in illegal or unethical practice.

1.6 The CRNA maintains confidentiality of patient information except in those rare events where accepted nursing practice demands otherwise.

1.7 The CRNA does not knowingly engage in deception in any form.

2. Competence

The scope of practice engaged in by the Certified Registered Nurse Anesthetist is within the individual competence of the CRNA. Each CRNA has the responsibility to maintain competency in practice.

2.1 The CRNA engages in lifelong, professional educational activities.

2.2 The CRNA participates in continuous quality improvement activities.

2.3 The practicing CRNA maintains his or her state license as a Registered Nurse, meets advanced practice statutory or regulatory requirements, if any, and maintains recertification as a CRNA.

3. Responsibilities as a Professional

Certified Registered Nurse Anesthetists are responsible and accountable for the services they render and the actions they take.

3.1 The CRNA, as an independently licensed professional, is responsible and accountable for judgments made and actions taken in his or her professional practice. Neither physician orders nor institutional policies relieve the CRNA of responsibility for his or her judgments made or actions taken.

3.2 The CRNA practices in accordance with the professional practice standards established by the profession.

3.3 The CRNA participates in activities that contribute to the ongoing development of the profession and its body of knowledge.

3.4 The CRNA is responsible and accountable for his or her conduct in maintaining the dignity and integrity of the profession.

3.5 The CRNA collaborates and cooperates with other health care providers involved in a patient's care.

3.6 The CRNA respects the expertise and responsibility of all healthcare providers involved in providing services to patients.

4. Responsibility to Society

Certified Registered Nurse Anesthetists collaborate with members of the health professions and other citizens in promoting community and national efforts to meet the health needs of the public.

5. Endorsement of Products and Services

Certified Registered Nurse Anesthetists endorse products and services only when personally satisfied with the product's or service's safety, effectiveness and quality. CRNAs do not state that the AANA has endorsed any product or service unless the Board of Directors of the American Association of Nurse Anesthetists has done so.

5.1 Any endorsement is truthful and based on factual evidence of efficacy.

5.2 A CRNA does not exploit his or her professional title and credentials for products or services which are related to his or her professional practice or expertise.

6. Research

Certified Registered Nurse Anesthetists protect the integrity of the research process and the reporting and publication of findings.

6.1 The CRNA evaluates research findings and incorporates them into practice as appropriate.

6.2 The CRNA conducts research projects according to accepted ethical research and reporting standards established by public law, institutional procedures, and the heath professions.

6.3 The CRNA protects the rights and well being of people and animals that serve as subjects in research.

6.4 The CRNA participates in research activities to improve practice, education, and public policy relative to health needs of diverse populations, the health workforce, the organization and administration of health systems, and health care delivery.

7. Business Practices

Certified Registered Nurse Anesthetists, regardless of practice arrangements or practice settings, maintain ethical business practices in dealing with patients, colleagues, institutions, and corporations.

7.1 The contractual obligations of a CRNA are consistent with the professional standards of practice and the laws and regulations pertaining to nurse anesthesia practice.

7.2 The CRNA will not participate in deceptive or fraudulent business practices.

© American Association of Nurse Anesthetists. Reprinted with permission.

AMERICAN ASSOCIATION OF ORIENTAL MEDICINE

Address:	433 Front Street
	Catasauqua, PA 18032
Telephone:	610/266-1433 or 888/500-7999
WWW:	aaom.org
Document:	AAOM Oriental Medicine Ethics Statement (1995)

The Oriental Medicine Practitioner's high and only mission is to restore the sick to health with a rapid, gentle, and permanent restoration of balance to the individual in the most reliable, efficient, and effective manner using the concepts of the unity of the body, mind, and spirit found in Oriental Medical philosophy.

To this end, the following is more specific:

- We will respect the rights, dignity, and individuality of each patient, strongly separating our professional practice of healing from any personal, religious, racial, or sexual considerations, referring out to another practitioner immediately should this become apparent.

- We will provide accurate information regarding professional education, training, experience, certification, and professional affiliation, working to increase skills to at least the equivalency of the rising standards of the profession by continuing education.

- We will keep accurate records and refer out to other health care modalities as indicated for the safety and well-being of the patient, not creating unwarranted expectations or treating excessively for personal gain, while exercising appropriate financial discretion in the treatment of indigent patients.

- We will treat our fellow Acupuncturists with dignity and respect in regard to their professional philosophy and work through our professional organizations or in a personal fashion to take action toward correcting what we consider to be unethical behavior prior to addressing that behavior in a public forum, while maintaining personal behavior which reflects well on the profession as a whole.

- We will promote responsibility to our patients by requiring necessary training by regulation to be able to make use of additional scope as practice acts are expanded or developed for our profession.

© American Association of Oriental Medicine. Reprinted with permission.

AMERICAN ASSOCIATION OF PASTORAL COUNSELORS

Address:	9504A Lee Highway
	Fairfax, VA 22031-2303
Telephone:	703/385-6967
WWW:	www.aapc.org
Document:	Code of Ethics (1994)

PRINCIPLE I—PROLOGUE

As members of the American Association of Pastoral Counselors, we are committed to the various theologies, traditions, and values of our faith communities and to the dignity and worth of each individual. We are dedicated to advancing the welfare of those who seek our assistance and to the maintenance of high standards of professional conduct and competence. We are accountable for our ministry whatever its setting. This accountability is expressed in relationships to clients, colleagues, students, our faith communities, and through the acceptance and practice of the principles and procedures of this Code of Ethics.

In order to uphold our standards, as members of AAPC we covenant to accept the following foundational premises:

A. To maintain responsible association with the faith group in which we have ecclesiastical standing.
B. To avoid discriminating against or refusing employment, educational opportunity or professional assistance to anyone on the basis of race, gender, sexual orientation, religion, or national origin; provided that nothing herein shall limit a member or center from utilizing religious requirements or exercising a religious preference in employment decisions.
C. To remain abreast of new developments in the field through both educational activities and clinical experience. We agree at all levels of membership to continue post-graduate education and professional growth including supervision, consultation, and active participation in the meetings and affairs of the Association.
D. To seek out and engage in collegial relationships, recognizing that isolation can lead to a loss of perspective and judgement.
E. To manage our personal lives in a healthful fashion and to seek appropriate assistance for our own personal problems or conflicts.
F. To diagnose or provide treatment only for those problems or issues that are within the reasonable boundaries of our competence.
G. To establish and maintain appropriate professional relationship boundaries.

PRINCIPLE II—PROFESSIONAL PRACTICES

In all professional matters members of AAPC maintain practices that protect the public and advance the profession.

A. We use our knowledge and professional associations for the benefit of the people we serve and not to secure unfair personal advantage.
B. We clearly represent our level of membership and limit our practice to that level.
C. Fees and financial arrangements, as with all contractual matters, are always discussed without hesitation or equivocation at the onset and are established in a straightforward, professional manner.
D. We are prepared to render service to individuals and communities in crisis without regard to financial remuneration when necessary.
E. We neither receive nor pay a commission for referral of a client.
F. We conduct our practice, agency, regional and Association fiscal affairs with due regard to recognized business and accounting procedures.
G. Upon the transfer of a pastoral counseling practice or the sale of real, personal, tangible or intangible property or assets used in such practice, the privacy and well being of the client shall be of primary concern.
   1. Client names and records shall be excluded from the transfer or sale.
   2. Any fees paid shall be for services rendered, consultation, equipment, real estate, and the name and logo of the counseling agency.
H. We are careful to represent facts truthfully to clients, referral sources, and third party payers regarding credentials and services rendered. We shall correct any misrepresentation of our professional qualifications or affiliations.
I. We do not malign colleagues or other professionals.

PRINCIPLE III—CLIENT RELATIONSHIPS

It is the responsibility of members of AAPC to maintain relationships with clients on a professional basis.

A. We do not abandon or neglect clients. If we are unable, or unwilling for appropriate reasons, to provide professional help or continue a professional relationship, every reasonable effort is made to arrange for continuation of treatment with another professional.
B. We make only realistic statements regarding the pastoral counseling process and its outcome.
C. We show sensitive regard for the moral, social, and religious standards of clients and communities. We avoid imposing our beliefs on others, although we may express them when appropriate in the pastoral counseling process.

D. Counseling relationships are continued only so long as it is reasonably clear that the clients are benefiting from the relationship.

E. We recognize the trust placed in and unique power of the therapeutic relationship. While acknowledging the complexity of some pastoral relationships, we avoid exploiting the trust and dependency of clients. We avoid those dual relationships with clients (e.g., business or close personal relationships) which could impair our professional judgement, compromise the integrity of the treatment, and/or use the relationship for our own gain.

F. We do not engage in harassment, abusive words or actions, or exploitative coercion of clients or former clients.

G. All forms of sexual behavior or harassment with clients are unethical, even when a client invites or consents to such behavior or involvement. Sexual behavior is defined as, but not limited to, all forms of overt and covert seductive speech, gestures, and behavior as well as physical contact of a sexual nature; harassment is defined as but not limited to, repeated comments, gestures or physical contacts of a sexual nature.

H. We recognize that the therapist/client relationship involves a power imbalance, the residual effects of which are operative following the termination of the therapy relationship. Therefore, all sexual behavior or harassment as defined in Principle III, G with former clients is unethical.

PRINCIPLE IV—CONFIDENTIALITY

As members of AAPC we respect the integrity and protect the welfare of all persons with whom we are working and have an obligation to safeguard information about them that has been obtained in the course of the counseling process.

A. All records kept on a client are stored or disposed of in a manner that assures security and confidentiality.

B. We treat all communications from clients with professional confidence.

C. Except in those situations where the identity of the client is necessary to the understanding of the case, we use only the first names of our clients when engaged in supervision or consultation. It is our responsibility to convey the importance of confidentiality to the supervisor/consultant; this is particularly important when the supervision is shared by other professionals, as in a supervisory group.

D. We do not disclose client confidences to anyone, except: as mandated by law; to prevent a clear and immediate danger to someone; in the course of a civil, criminal or disciplinary action arising from the counseling where the pastoral counselor is a defendant; for purposes of supervision or consultation; or by previously obtained written permission. In cases involving more than one person (as client) written permission must be obtained from all legally accountable persons who have been present during the counseling before any disclosure can be made.

E. We obtain informed written consent of clients before audio and/or video tape recording or permitting third party observation of their sessions.

F. We do not use these standards of confidentiality to avoid intervention when it is necessary, e.g., when there is evidence of abuse of minors, the elderly, the disabled, the physically or mentally incompetent.

G. When current or former clients are referred to in a publication, while teaching or in a public presentation, their identity is thoroughly disguised.

H. We as members of AAPC agree that as an express condition of our membership in the Association, Association ethics communications, files, investigative reports, and related records are strictly confidential and waive their right to use same in a court of law to advance any claim against another member. Any member seeking such records for such purpose shall be subject to disciplinary action for attempting to violate the confidentiality requirements of the organization. This policy is intended to promote pastoral and confessional communications without legal consequences and to protect potential privacy and confidentiality interests of third parties.

PRINCIPLE V—SUPERVISEE, STUDENT & EMPLOYEE RELATIONSHIPS

As members of AAPC we have an ethical concern for the integrity and welfare of our supervisees, students and employees. These relationships are maintained on a professional and confidential basis. We recognize our influential position with regard to both current and former supervisees, students and employees, and avoid exploiting their trust and dependency. We make every effort to avoid dual relationships with such persons that could impair our judgement or increase the risk of personal and/or financial exploitation.

A. We do not engage in ongoing counseling relationships with current supervisees, students and employees.

B. We do not engage in sexual or other harassment of supervisees, students, employees, research subjects or colleagues.

C. All forms of sexual behavior, as defined in Principle III,.G, with our supervisees, students, research subjects and employees (except in employee situations involving domestic partners) are unethical.

D. We advise our students, supervisees, and employees against offering or engaging in, or holding themselves out as competent to engage in, professional services beyond their training, level of experience and competence.

E. We do not harass or dismiss an employee who has acted in a reasonable, responsible and ethical manner to protect, or intervene on behalf of, a client or other member of the public or another employee.

PRINCIPLE VI—INTERPROFESSIONAL RELATIONSHIPS

As members of AAPC we relate to and cooperate with other professional persons in our community and beyond. We are part of a network of health care professionals and are expected to develop and maintain interdisciplinary and interprofessional relationships.

A. We do not offer ongoing clinical services to persons currently receiving treatment from another professional without prior knowledge of and in consultation with the other professional, with the clients' informed consent. Soliciting such clients is unethical.

B. We exercise care and interprofessional courtesy when approached for services by persons who claim or appear to have inappropriately terminated treatment with another professional.

PRINCIPLE VII—ADVERTISING

Any advertising by or for a member of AAPC, including announcements, public statements and promotional activities, is undertaken with the purpose of helping the public make informed judgements and choices.

A. We do not misrepresent our professional qualifications, affiliations and functions, or falsely imply sponsorship or certification by any organization.

B. We may use the following information to describe ourselves and the services we provide: name; highest relevant academic degree earned from an accredited institution; date, type and level of certification or licensure; AAPC membership level, clearly stated; address and telephone number; office hours; a brief review of services offered, e.g., individual, couple and group counseling; fee information; languages spoken; and policy regarding third party payments. Additional relevant information may be provided if it is legitimate, reasonable, free of deception and not otherwise prohibited by these principles. We may not use the initials "AAPC" after our names in the manner of an academic degree.

C. Announcements and brochures promoting our services describe them with accuracy and dignity, devoid of all claims or evaluation. We may send them to professional persons, religious institutions and other agencies, but to prospective individual clients only in response to inquires.

D. We do not make public statements which contain any of the following:
   1. A false, fraudulent, misleading, deceptive or unfair statement.
   2. A misrepresentation of fact or a statement likely to mislead or deceive because in context it makes only a partial disclosure of relevant facts.
   3. A testimonial from a client regarding the quality of services or products.
   4. A statement intended or likely to create false or unjustified expectations of favorable results.
   5. A statement implying unusual, unique, or one-of-a-kind abilities, including misrepresentation through sensationalism, exaggeration or superficiality.
   6. A statement intended or likely to exploit a client's fears, anxieties or emotions.
   7. A statement concerning the comparative desirability of offered services.
   8. A statement of direct solicitation of individual clients.

E. We do not compensate in any way a representative of the press, radio, television or other communication medium for the purpose of professional publicity and news items. A paid advertisement must be identified as such, unless it is contextually apparent that it is a paid advertisement. We are responsible for the content of such advertisement. Any advertisement to the public by radio or television is to be pre-recorded, approved by us and a recording of the actual transmission retained in our possession.

F. Advertisements or announcements by us of work-shops, clinics, seminars, growth groups or similar services or endeavors, are to give a clear statement of purpose and a clear description of the experiences to be provided. The education, training and experience of the provider(s) involved are to be appropriately specified.

G. Advertisements or announcements soliciting research participants, in which clinical or other professional services are offered as an inducement, make clear the nature of the services as well as the cost and other obligations or risks to be accepted by participants in the research.

© American Association of Pastoral Counselors. Reprinted with permission.

AMERICAN ASSOCIATION OF SCHOOL ADMINISTRATORS

Address: 1801 North Moore Street
             Arlington, VA 22209-9988
Telephone: 703/528-0700
WWW: www.aasa.org
Document: Professional Standards for
             Superintendency—Section Eight:
             Values and Ethics of Leadership
             (1993)

Standard 8: Values and Ethics of Leadership.
Understand and model appropriate value systems, ethics, and moral leadership; know the role of education in a democratic society; exhibit multicultural and ethnic understanding and related behavior; adapt educational programming to the needs of diverse constituencies; balance complex community demands in the best interest of the student; scan and monitor the environment for opportunities for staff and students; respond in an ethical and skillful way to the electronic and printed news media; and coordinate social agencies and human services to help each student grow and develop as a caring, informed citizen.

Indicators. A superintendent should know and be able to:
• Exhibit multicultural and ethnic understanding and sensitivity.
• Describe the role of schooling in a democratic society.
• Demonstrate ethical and personal integrity.
• Model accepted moral and ethical standards in all interactions.
• Describe a strategy to promote the value that moral and ethical practices are established and practiced in each classroom and school.
• Describe how education undergirds a free and democratic society.
• Describe a strategy to ensure that diversity of religion, ethnicity, and way of life in the district are not violated.
• Formulate a plan to coordinate social, health, and other community agencies to support each child in the district.

© American Association of School Administrators. Reprinted with permission.

AMERICAN ASSOCIATION OF UNIVERSITY PROFESSORS

Address: 1012 Fourteenth Street NW, Suite 500
             Washington, DC 20005-3465
Telephone: 202/737-5900 or 800/424-2973
WWW: www.aaup.org
Document: Statement on Professional Ethics
             (1987)

The statement which follows, a revision of a statement originally adopted in 1966, was approved by the Association's Committee B on Professional Ethics, adopted by the Association's Council in June 1987, and endorsed by the Seventy-third Annual Meeting.

INTRODUCTION

From its inception, the American Association of University Professors has recognized that membership in the academic profession carries with it special responsibilities. The Association has consistently affirmed these responsibilities in major policy statements, providing guidance to professors in such matters as their utterances as citizens, the exercise of their responsibilities to students and colleagues, and their conduct when resigning from an institution or when undertaking sponsored research. The *Statement on Professional Ethics* that follows sets forth those general standards that serve as a reminder of the variety of responsibilities assumed by all members of the profession.

In the enforcement of ethical standards, the academic profession differs from those of law and medicine, whose associations act to ensure the integrity of members engaged in private practice. In the academic profession the individual institution of higher learning provides this assurance and so should normally handle questions concerning propriety of conduct within its own framework by reference to a faculty group. The Association supports such local action and stands ready, through the general secretary and Committee B, to counsel with members of the academic community concerning questions of professional ethics and to inquire into complaints when local consideration is impossible or inappropriate. If the alleged offense is deemed sufficiently serious to raise the possibility of adverse action, the procedures should be in accordance with the 1940 *Statement of Principles on Academic Freedom and Tenure,* the 1958 *Statement on Procedural Standards in Faculty Dismissal Proceedings,* or the applicable provisions of the Association's *Recommended Institutional Regulations on Academic Freedom and Tenure.*

THE STATEMENT

I. Professors, guided by a deep conviction of the worth and dignity of the advancement of knowledge, recognize the special responsibilities placed upon them. Their primary responsibility to their subject is to seek and to state the truth as they see it. To this end professors devote their energies to developing and improving their scholarly competence. They accept the obligation to exercise critical self-discipline and judgment in using, extending, and transmitting knowledge. They practice intellectual honesty. Although professors may follow subsidiary interests, these interests must never seriously hamper or compromise their freedom of inquiry.

II. As teachers, professors encourage the free pursuit of learning in their students. They hold before them the best scholarly and ethical standards of their disciplines. Professors demonstrate respect for their students as individuals and adhere to their proper roles as intellectual guides and counselors. Professors make every reasonable effort to foster honest academic conduct and to ensure that their evaluations of students reflect each student's true merit. They respect the confidential nature of the relationship between professor and student. They avoid any exploitation, harassment, or discriminatory treatment of students. They acknowledge significant academic or scholarly assistance from them. They protect their academic freedom.

III. As colleagues, professors have obligations that derive from common membership in the community of scholars. Professors do not discriminate against or harass colleagues. They respect and defend the free inquiry of associates. In the exchange of criticism and ideas professors show due respect for the opinions of others. Professors acknowledge academic debt and strive to be objective in their professional judgment of colleagues. Professors accept their share of faculty responsibilities for the governance of their institution.

IV. As members of an academic institution, professors seek above all to be effective teachers and scholars. Although professors observe the stated regulations of the institution, provided the regulations do not contravene academic freedom, they maintain their right to criticize and seek revision. Professors give due regard to their paramount responsibilities within their institution in determining the amount and character of work done outside it. When considering the interruption or termination of their service, professors recognize the effect of their decision upon the program of the institution and give due notice of their intentions.

V. As members of their community, professors have the rights and obligations of other citizens. Professors measure the urgency of these obligations in the light of their responsibilities to their subject, to their students, to their profession, and to their institution. When they speak or act as private persons they avoid creating the impression of speaking or acting for their college or university. As citizens engaged in a profession that depends upon freedom for its health and integrity, professors have a particular obligation to promote conditions of free inquiry and to further public understanding of academic freedom.

© American Association of University Professors. Reprinted with permission.

AMERICAN BAR ASSOCIATION

Address: 750 North Lake Shore Drive
Chicago, IL 60611
Telephone: 312/988-5522
WWW: www.abanet.org
Document: Mission and Goals

(The ABA's Center for Professional Responsibility publishes two sets of model standards that apply to all lawyers and/or judges: The *ABA Model Rules of Professional Conduct* and the *ABA Model Code of Judicial Conduct*. These publications are not reprinted here but are available from the ABA Service Center. The ABA has a mission statement and set of goals; goal number five reflects the Association's commitment to ethics.—Eds.)

The mission of the American Bar Association is to be the national representative of the legal profession, serving the public and profession by promoting justice, professional excellence, and respect for the law.

The goals of the ABA reflect our commitment to these principles, as well as our determination to remain responsive to the challenges of a changing world. Each of the programs and activities of the ABA is intended to further one of the following goals:

I. To promote improvements in the American system of justice.
II. To promote meaningful access to legal representation and the American system of justice for all persons regardless of their economic or social condition.
III. To provide ongoing leadership in improving the law to serve the changing needs of society.
IV. To increase public understanding of, and respect for, the law, the legal process, and the role of the legal profession.
V. To achieve the highest standards of professionalism, competence, and ethical conduct.
VI. To serve as the national representative of the legal profession.
VII. To provide benefits, programs, and services which promote professional growth and enhance the quality of life of the members.
VIII. To advance the rule of law in the world.
IX. To promote full and equal participation in the legal profession by minorities and women.
X. To preserve and enhance the ideals of the legal profession as a common calling and its dedication to public service.
XI. To preserve the independence of the legal profession and the judiciary as fundamental to a free society.

© American Bar Association. Reprinted with permission.

AMERICAN BED AND BREAKFAST ASSOCIATION

Address: PO Box 1387
Midlothian, VA 23113-1387
Telephone: 804/379-2222
WWW: n/a
Document: Code of Ethics

• We acknowledge ethics and morality as inseparable elements of doing business and will test every decision against the highest standards of honesty, legality, fairness, impunity, and conscience.

- We will conduct ourselves personally and collectively at all times such as to bring credit to the service and tourism industry at large.
- We will concentrate our time, energy, and resources on the improvement of our own product and services and we will not denigrate our competition in the pursuit of our own success.
- We will treat all guests equally regardless of race, religion, nationality, creed, or sex.
- We will deliver standards of service and product with total consistency to every guest.
- We will provide a safe and sanitary environment at all times for every guest and employee.
- We will strive constantly, in words, actions, and deeds, to develop and maintain the highest level of trust, honesty, and understanding among guests, clients, employees, employers and the public at large.
- We will provide every employee at every level the knowledge, training, equipment, and motivation required to perform his or her own tasks according to our standards.
- We will guarantee that every employee at every level will have the same opportunity to perform, advance, and will be evaluated against the same standards as all employees engaged in the same or similar tasks.
- We will actively and consciously work to protect and preserve our natural environment and natural resources in all that we do.
- We will seek a fair and honest profit.

© American Bed and Breakfast Association. Reprinted with permission.

AMERICAN BOARD OF OPTICIANRY/NATIONAL CONTACT LENS EXAMINERS

Address: 10341 Democracy Lane
              Fairfax, VA 22030-2521
Telephone: 703/691-8355
WWW: www.opticians.org
Document: Disciplinary Guidelines (1993)

By applying for certification by ABO/NCLE, an applicant agrees to be subject to these Guidelines. These guidelines apply to any professionally related conduct of the person, or other conduct which materially and directly bears upon fitness to perform professional functions. These Guidelines apply to those matters over which the individual has control or responsibility. Proceedings concerning potential or actual violations of these Guidelines will be conducted pursuant to the Disciplinary Guidelines and Procedures.

The following acts relating to the practice of opticianry and contact lens technicianry shall be grounds for disciplinary action.

1. Procuring or attempting to procure ABO or NCLE certification or state licensure by misrepresentation, bribery, fraud or deception.
2. Theft or attempted theft of any ABO or NCLE exam.
3. Tampering with an ABO or NCLE exam.
4. Any false representation of ABO or NCLE certification.
5. Practicing with a revoked, suspended or inactive license in those states where a license is required.
6. In states where licensing is required, permitting any person under your supervision who is not licensed or participating in a state recognized student or apprenticeship program, to fit or dispense contact lenses, spectacles, eyeglasses or other optical devices which are part of the practice of opticianry or contact lens technicianry.
7. Failure to adequately supervise auxiliary staff, students or apprentice dispensing opticians within your supervision, to the extent that the patient's/customer's heal, welfare or safety is at risk.
8. Having been convicted in any state or federal court for any crime related to the practice of opticianry. A plea of guilty, non vult, nolo contendere or a similar disposition shall be deemed a conviction.
9. Having been disciplined for improper practice or misconduct as an optician by a duly authorized professional disciplinary agency of a state.
10. Failure to comply with an order or consent agreement relating to opticianry practice issued by or entered into with a state or federal court, licensing body, regulatory body, governmental agency, ABO, or NCLE.
11. Failure to report to ABO/NCLE, within 60 days, the revocation, suspension or surrender of a license to practice opticianry.
12. Failure to cooperate reasonably with an ABO/NCLE or state regulatory body's investigation of a disciplinary matter.

13. Advertising goods or services in a manner which is fraudulent, false, deceptive or misleading in form or content.

14. Attempting directly or indirectly, by way of intimidation, coercion or deception to obtain or retain a patient/customer, or to discourage a patient/customer from obtaining a second opinion.

15. Abandonment of a patient/customer or terminating imminently needed care of a patient/customer without adequate notice.

16. Paying or offering to pay a rebate, commission, compensation, or any other thing of value to a licensed physician, licensed optometrist, or any other person, in a manner which is unlawful, or which is for the mere act of referring a patient/customer to the dispensing optician, rather than as reasonable compensation for services rendered.

17. Engaging in substantial and/or repeated acts of negligent or incompetent professional conduct.

18. Engaging in fraud, deception, misrepresentation, false promise or false pretense in the practice of opticianry.

19. Failing to keep written prescription files as required by law.

20. The unauthorized material disclosure of confidential patient/customer information.

21. Deceptively altering patient/customer records.

22. Practicing opticianry or contact lens technicianry if the person is impaired by physical condition in such a manner that the services cannot be provided competently to patients/customers.

23. Exploitation or abuse of a patient/customer.

24. Assault and battery of a patient/customer.

25. Practicing in a manner involving contact with patients/customers while knowingly suffering from a contagious or infectious disease if such contact exposes a patient/customer to a serious and material health risk as defined by the Centers for Disease Control.

26. Engaging in discrimination in the provision of services based on a patient's/customer's age, sex, race, creed, color, national origin, disability, or other basis proscribed by law.

27. Fitting, dispensing, selling or otherwise providing prescription lenses including contact lenses to any individual without having a valid prescription for that individual.

28. Duplicating an eyeglass or contact lens, if prohibited by state law.

29. Failing to make fee or price information available upon presentation of a written prescription or sufficient information on which to base an estimation.

30. Engaging in other conduct which is determined by ABO/NCLE to be unethical or unprofessional as being inconsistent with generally recognized professional standards.

31. Professional conduct by an optician or contact lens technician that constitutes an extreme and unjustified deviation from the customary procedures or standards of care accepted in the ophthalmic community and that creates a serious risk of harm to or deception of patients/customers.

© American Board of Opticianry. Reprinted with permission.

AMERICAN CHEMICAL SOCIETY

Address: 1155 Sixteenth Street NW
            Washington, DC 20036
Telephone: 202/872-4600 or 800/227-5558
WWW: www.acs.org
Document: The Chemist's Code of Conduct
            (1994)

(A new edition of *The Chemist's Code of Conduct* is expected to be adopted in late 1998 or early 1999. This code remains in effect until then. ACS also publishes *Professional Employment Guidelines* and *Academic Professional Guidelines* which are not reprinted here.—Eds.)

The American Chemical Society expects its members to adhere to the highest ethical standards. Indeed, the federal Charter of the Society (1937) explicitly lists among its objectives "the improvement of the qualifications and usefulness of chemists through high standards of professional ethics, education, and attainments. . .".

Chemists have professional obligations to the public, to colleagues, and to science. One expression of these obligations is embodied in "The Chemist's Creed," approved by the ACS Council in 1965. The principles of conduct enumerated below are intended to replace "The Chemist's Creed." They were prepared by the Council Committee on Professional Relations, approved by the Council (March 16, 1994), and adopted by the Board of Directors (June 3, 1994) for the guidance of Society members in various professional dealings, especially those involving conflicts of interest.

Chemists Acknowledge Responsibilities To:

The Public

Chemists have a professional responsibility to serve the public interest and welfare and to further knowledge of science. Chemists should actively be concerned with the health and welfare of co-workers, consumer, and the community. Public comments on scientific matters should be made with care and precision, without unsubstantiated, exaggerated, or premature statements.

The Science of Chemistry

Chemists should seek to advance chemical science, understand the limitations of their knowledge, and respect the truth. Chemists should ensure that their scientific contributions, and those of the collaborators, are thorough, accurate, and unbiased in design, implementation, and presentation.

The Profession

Chemists should remain current with developments in their field, share ideas and information, keep accurate and complete laboratory records, maintain integrity in all conduct and publications, and give due credit to the contributions of others. Conflicts of interest and scientific misconduct, such as fabrication, falsification, and plagiarism, are incompatible with this Code.

The Employer

Chemists should promote and protect the legitimate interests of their employers, perform work honestly and competently, fulfill obligations, and safeguard proprietary information.

Employees

Chemists, as employers, should treat subordinates with respect for their professionalism and concern for their well-being, and provide them with a safe, congenial working environment, fair compensation,

and proper acknowledgment of their scientific contributions.

Students

Chemists should regard the tutelage of students as a trust conferred by society for the promotion of the student's learning and professional development. Each student should be treated respectfully and without exploitation.

Associates

Chemists should treat associates with respect, regardless of the level of their formal education, encourage them, learn with them, share ideas honestly, and give credit for their contributions.

Clients

Chemists should serve clients faithfully and incorruptibly, respect confidentiality, advise honestly, and charge fairly.

The Environment

Chemists should understand and anticipate the environmental consequences of their work. Chemists have responsibility to avoid pollution and to protect the environment.

AMERICAN COLLEGE OF HEALTH CARE ADMINISTRATORS

Address:	1800 Diagonal Road, Suite 355
	Alexandria, VA 22314-3571
Telephone:	703/739-7900 or 888/882-2422

WWW: www.achca.org
Document: Code of Ethics

Preamble: *The preservation of the highest standards of integrity and ethical principles is vital to the successful discharge of the professional responsibilities of all long-term health care administrators. This Code of Ethics has been promulgated by the American College of Health Care Administrators (ACHCA) in an effort to stress the fundamental rules considered essential to this basic purpose. It shall be the obligation of members to seek to avoid not only conduct specifically proscribed by the code, but also conduct that is inconsistent with its spirit and purpose. Failure to specify any particular responsibility or practice in this Code of Ethics should not be construed as denial of the existence of other responsibilities or practices. Recognizing that the ultimate responsibility for applying standards and ethics falls upon the individual, the ACHCA establishes the following Code of Ethics to make clear its expectation of the membership.*

EXPECTATION I

Individuals shall hold paramount the welfare of persons for whom care is provided.

PRESCRIPTIONS: The Health Care Administrator shall:

- Strive to provide to all those entrusted to his or her care the highest quality of appropriate services possible in light of resources or other constraints.
- Operate the facility consistent with laws, regulations, and standards of practice recognized in the field of health care administration.
- Consistent with law and professional standards, protect the confidentiality of information regarding individual recipients of care.
- Perform administrative duties with the personal integrity that will earn the confidence, trust, and respect of the general public.
- Take appropriate steps to avoid discrimination on basis of race, color, sex, religion, age, national origin, handicap, marital status, ancestry, or any other factor that is illegally discriminatory or not related to bona fide requirements of quality care.

PROSCRIPTION: The Health Care Administrator shall not:

- Disclose professional or personal information regarding recipients of service to unauthorized personnel unless required by law or to protect the public welfare.

EXPECTATION II

Individuals shall maintain high standards of professional competence.

PRESCRIPTIONS: The Health Care Administrator shall:

- Possess and maintain the competencies necessary to effectively perform his or her responsibilities.
- Practice administration in accordance with capabilities and proficiencies and, when appropriate, seek counsel from qualified others.
- Actively strive to enhance knowledge of and expertise in long-term care administration through continuing education and professional development.

PROSCRIPTIONS: The Health Care Administrator shall not:

- Misrepresent qualifications, education, experience, or affiliations.
- Provide services other than those for which he or she is prepared and qualified to perform.

EXPECTATION III

Individuals shall strive, in all matters relating to their professional functions, to maintain a professional posture that places paramount the interests of the facility and its residents.

PRESCRIPTIONS: The Health Care Administrator shall:

- Avoid partisanship and provide a forum for the fair resolution of any disputes which may arise in service delivery or facility management.
- Disclose to the governing body or other authority as may be appropriate, any actual or potential circumstance concerning him or her that might reasonably be thought to create a conflict of interest or have a substantial adverse impact on the facility or its residents.

PROSCRIPTION: The Health Care Administrator shall not:

- Participate in activities that reasonably may be thought to create a conflict of interest or have the potential to have a substantial adverse impact on the facility or its residents.

EXPECTATION IV

Individuals shall honor their responsibilities to the public, their profession, and their relationships with colleagues and members of related professions.

PRESCRIPTIONS: The Health Care Administrator shall:

• Foster increased knowledge within the profession of health care administration and support research efforts toward this end.

• Participate with others in the community to plan for and provide a full range of health care services.

• Share areas of expertise with colleagues, students, and the general public to increase awareness and promote understanding of health care in general and the profession in particular.

• Inform the ACHCA Standards and Ethics Committee of actual or potential violations of this Code of Ethics, and fully cooperate with ACHCA's sanctioned inquiries into matters of professional conduct related to this Code of Ethics.

PROSCRIPTION: The Health Care Administrator shall not:

• Defend, support, or ignore unethical conduct perpetrated by colleagues, peers or students.

© American College of Health Care Administrators. Reprinted with permission.

AmericanCollege *of* HealthcareExecutives

for leaders who care

AMERICAN COLLEGE OF HEALTHCARE EXECUTIVES

Address: One North Franklin Street, Suite 1700
              Chicago, IL 60606-3491
Telephone: 312/424-2800
WWW: www.ache.org
Document: American College of Healthcare
              Executives Code of Ethics (1995)

(Appendices I and II, entitled "American College of Healthcare Executives Grievance Procedure" and "Ethics Committee Action" are a material part of the *Code of Ethics* but are not reprinted here.—Eds.)

PREFACE

The *Code of Ethics* is administered by the Ethics Committee, which is appointed by the Board of Governors upon nomination by the Chairman. It is composed of at least nine Fellows of the College, each of whom serves a three-year term on a staggered basis, with three members retiring each year.

The Ethics Committee shall:

• Review and evaluate annually the *Code of Ethics*, and make any necessary recommendations for updating the *Code*.

• Review and recommend action to the Board of Governors on allegations brought forth regarding breaches of the *Code of Ethics*.

• Develop ethical policy statements to serve as guidelines of ethical conduct for healthcare executives and their professional relationships.

• Prepare an annual report of observations, accomplishments, and recommendations to the Board of Governors, and such other periodic reports as required.

The Ethics Committee invokes the *Code of Ethics* under authority of the ACHE *Bylaws*, Article II, Membership, Section 6, Resignation and Termination of Membership; Transfer to Inactive Status, subsection (b), as follows:

> Membership may be terminated or rendered inactive by action of the Board of Governors as a result of violation of the *Code of Ethics*; nonconformity with the *Bylaws* or *Regulations Governing Admission, Advancement, Recertification, and Reappointment*; conviction of a felony; or conviction of a crime of moral turpitude or a crime relating to the healthcare management profession. No such termination of membership or imposition of inactive status shall be effected without affording a reasonable opportunity for the member to consider the charges and to appear in his or her own defense before the Board of Governors or its designated hearing committee, as outlined in the "Grievance Procedure," Appendix I of the College's *Code of Ethics*.

PREAMBLE

The purpose of the *Code of Ethics* of the American College of Healthcare Executives is to serve as a guide to conduct for members. It contains standards of ethical behavior for healthcare executives in their professional relationships. These relationships include members of the healthcare executive's organization and other organizations. Also included are patients or others served, colleagues, the community and society as a whole. The *Code of Ethics* also incorporates standards of ethical behavior governing personal behavior, particularly when that conduct directly relates to the role and identity of the healthcare executive.

The fundamental objectives of the healthcare management professional are to enhance overall quality of life, dignity and well-being of every individual needing healthcare services; and to create a more equitable, accessible, effective and efficient healthcare system.

Healthcare executives have an obligation to act in ways that will merit the trust, confidence and respect of healthcare professionals and the general public. Therefore, healthcare executives should lead lives that embody an exemplary system of values and ethics.

In fulfilling their commitments and obligations to patients or others served, healthcare executives function as moral advocates. Since every management decision affects the health and well-being of both individuals and communities, healthcare executives must carefully evaluate the possible outcomes of their decisions. In organizations that deliver healthcare services, they must work to safeguard and foster the rights, interests and prerogatives of patients or others served. The role of moral advocate requires that healthcare executives speak out and take actions necessary to promote such rights, interests and prerogatives if they are threatened.

I. THE HEALTHCARE EXECUTIVE'S RESPONSIBILITIES TO THE PROFESSION OF HEALTHCARE MANAGEMENT

The healthcare executive shall:

A. Uphold the values, ethics and mission of the healthcare management profession;
B. Conduct all personal and professional activities with honesty, integrity, respect, fairness and good faith in a manner that will reflect well upon the profession;
C. Comply with all laws pertaining to healthcare management in the jurisdictions in which the healthcare executive is located, or conducts professional activities;
D. Maintain competence and proficiency in healthcare management by implementing a personal program of assessment and continuing professional education;

E. Avoid the exploitation of professional relationships for personal gain;
F. Use this *Code* to further the interests of the profession and not for selfish reasons;
G. Respect professional confidences;
H. Enhance the dignity and image of the healthcare management profession through positive public information programs; and
I. Refrain from participating in any activity that demeans the credibility and dignity of the healthcare management profession.

II. THE HEALTHCARE EXECUTIVE'S RESPONSIBILITIES TO PATIENTS OR OTHERS SERVED, TO THE ORGANIZATION AND TO EMPLOYEES

A. RESPONSIBILITIES TO PATIENTS OR OTHERS SERVED
The healthcare executive shall, within the scope of his or her authority:

1. Work to ensure the existence of a process to evaluate the quality of care or service to be rendered;
2. Avoid practicing or facilitating discrimination and institute safeguards to prevent discriminatory organizational practices;
3. Work to ensure the existence of a process that will advise patients or others served of the rights, opportunities, responsibilities and risks regarding available healthcare services;
4. Work to provide a process that ensures the autonomy and self-determination of patients or others served; and
5. Work to insure the existence of procedures that will safe-guard the confidentiality and privacy of patients or others served.

B. RESPONSIBILITIES TO THE ORGANIZATION
The healthcare executive shall, within the scope of his or her authority:

1. Provide healthcare services consistent with available resources and work to ensure the existence of a resource allocation process that considers ethical ramifications;
2. Conduct both competitive and cooperative activities in ways that improve community healthcare services;
3. Lead the organization in the use and improvement of standards of management and sound business practices;

4. Respect the customs and practices of patients or others served, consistent with the organization's philosophy; and

5. Be truthful in all forms of professional and organizational communication, and avoid disseminating information that is false, misleading, or deceptive.

C. RESPONSIBILITIES TO EMPLOYEES

Healthcare executives have an ethical and professional obligation to employees of the organizations they manage that encompass but are not limited to:

1. Working to create a working environment conducive for underscoring employee ethical conduct and behavior.

2. Working to ensure that individuals may freely express ethical concerns and providing mechanisms for discussing and addressing such concerns.

3. Working to ensure a working environment that is free from harassment, sexual and other; coercion of any kind, especially to perform illegal or unethical acts; and discrimination on the basis of race, creed, color, sex, ethnic origin, age or disability.

4. Working to ensure a working environment that is conducive to proper utilization of employees' skills and abilities.

5. Paying particular attention to the employee's work environment and job safety.

6. Working to establish appropriate grievance and appeals mechanisms.

III. CONFLICTS OF INTEREST

A conflict of interest may be only a matter of degree, but exists when the healthcare executive:

A. Acts to benefit directly or indirectly by using authority or inside information, or allows a friend, relative or associate to benefit from such authority or information.

B. Uses authority or information to make a decision to intentionally affect the organization in an adverse manner.

The healthcare executive shall:

A. Conduct all personal and professional relationships in such a way that all those affected are assured that management decisions are made in the best interests of the organization and the individual served by it;

B. Disclose to the appropriate authority any direct or indirect financial or personal interests that pose potential or actual conflicts of interest;

C. Accept no gifts or benefits offered with the express or implied expectation of influencing a management decision; and

D. Inform the appropriate authority and other involved parties of potential or actual conflicts of interest related to appointments or elections to boards or committees inside or outside the healthcare executive's organization.

IV. THE HEALTHCARE EXECUTIVE'S RESPONSIBILITIES TO COMMUNITY AND SOCIETY

The healthcare executive shall:

A. Work to identify and meet the needs of the community;

B. Work to insure that all people have reasonable access to healthcare services;

C. Participate in public dialogue on healthcare policy issues and advocate solutions that will improve health status and promote quality healthcare;

D. Consider the short-term and long-term impact of management decisions on both the community and on society; and

E. Provide prospective consumers with adequate and accurate information, enabling them to make enlightened judgments and decisions regarding services.

V. THE HEALTHCARE EXECUTIVE'S RESPONSIBILITY TO REPORT VIOLATIONS OF THE CODE

A member of the College who has reasonable grounds to believe that another member has violated this *Code* has a duty to communicate such facts to the Ethics Committee.

AMERICAN COLLEGE OF NURSE-MIDWIVES

Address:	818 Connecticut Avenue NW, Suite 900 Washington, DC 20006
Telephone:	202/728-9860
WWW:	www.midwife.org
Document:	Code of Ethics for Certified Nurse-Midwives (1990)

A Certified Nurse-Midwife has professional moral obligations. The purpose of this code is to identify obligations which guide the nurse-midwife in the practice of nurse-midwifery. This code further serves to clarify the expectations of the profession to consumers, the public, other professionals and to potential practitioners.

1. Nurse-midwifery exists for the good of women and their families. This good is safeguarded by practice in accordance with the ACNM Philosophy and ACNM Standards for the Practice of Nurse-Midwifery.

2. Nurse-midwives uphold the belief that childbearing and maturation are normal life processes. When intervention is indicated, it is integrated into care in a way that preserves the dignity of the woman and her family.

3. Decisions regarding nurse-midwifery care require client participation in an ongoing negotiation process in order to develop a safe plan of care. This process considers cultural diversity, individual autonomy, and legal responsibilities.

4. Nurse-midwives share professional information with their clients that leads to informed participation and consent. This sharing is done without coercion, or deception.

5. Nurse-midwives practice competently. They consult and refer when indicated by their professional scope of practice and/or personal limitations.

6. Nurse-midwives provide care without discrimination based on race, religion, life-style, sexual orientation, socio-economic status or nature of health problem.

7. Nurse-midwives maintain confidentiality except when there is a clear, serious and immediate danger or when mandated by law.

8. Nurse-midwives take appropriate action to protect clients from harm when endangered by incompetent or unethical practices.

9. Nurse-midwives interact respectfully with the people with whom they work and practice.

10. Nurse-midwives participate in developing and improving the care of women and families through supporting the profession of nurse-midwifery, research, and the education of nurse-midwifery students and nurse-midwives.

11. Nurse-midwives promote community, state, and national efforts, such as public education and legislation, to ensure access to quality care and to meet the health needs of women and their families.

THE AMERICAN COLLEGE OF OBSTETRICIANS AND GYNECOLOGISTS

Address:	409 Twelfth Street SW
	PO Box 96920
	Washington, DC 20090-6920
Telephone:	202/638-5577
WWW:	www.acog.org
Document:	Code of Professional Ethics of the American College of Obstetricians and Gynecologists

(The "Committee Opinions" mentioned below are not reprinted here.—Eds.)

Obstetrician-gynecologists, as members of the medical profession, have ethical responsibilities not only to patients, but also to society, to other health professionals, and to themselves. The following ethical foundations for professional activities in the field of obstetrics and gynecology are the supporting structures for the Code of Conduct. The Code implements many of these foundations in the form of rules of ethical conduct. Noncompliance with the Code may affect an individual's initial or continuing Fellowship in the American College of Obstetricians and Gynecologists. In addition to the Code, certain Committee Opinions of the American College of Obstetricians and Gynecologists provide ethical guidance. Fellows are urged to read and evaluate these Committee Opinions. Opinions relevant to specific points are referenced in the Code of Conduct.

Ethical Foundations

I. The patient-physician relationship: The welfare of the patient (*beneficence*) is central to all considerations in the patient-physician relationship. Included in this relationship is the obligation of physicians to respect the rights of patients, colleagues, and other health professionals. The respect for the right of individual patients to make their own choices about their health care (*autonomy*) is fundamental. The principle of justice requires strict avoidance of discrimination on the basis of race, color, religion, national origin, or any other basis that would constitute illegal discrimination (*justice*).

II. Physician conduct and practice: The obstetrician-gynecologist should deal honestly with patients and colleagues (*veracity*). This includes not misrepresenting himself or herself through any form of communication in an untruthful, misleading, or deceptive manner. Furthermore, maintenance of medical competence through study, application, and enhancement of medical knowledge and skills is an obligation of practicing physicians. Any behavior that diminishes a physician's capability to practice, such as substance abuse, must be immediately addressed and rehabilitative services instituted. The physician should modify his or her practice until the diminished capacity has been restored to an acceptable standard to avoid harm to patients (*nonmaleficence*). All physicians are obligated to respond to evidence of questionable conduct or unethical behavior by other physicians through appropriate procedures established by the relevant organization.

III. Avoiding conflicts of interest: Potential conflicts of interest are inherent in the practice of medicine. Physicians are expected to recognize such situations and deal with them through public disclosure. Conflicts of interest should be resolved in accordance with the best interest of the patient, respecting a woman's autonomy to make health care decisions. The physician should be an advocate for the patient through public disclosure of conflicts of interest raised by health payor policies (managed care or others or hospital policies).

IV. Professional relations: The obstetrician-gynecologist should respect and cooperate with other physicians, nurses, and other health-care professionals.

V. Societal responsibilities: The obstetrician-gynecologist has a continuing responsibility to society as a whole and should support and participate in activities that enhance the community. As a member of society, the obstetrician-gynecologist must respect the laws of that society. As professionals and members of medical societies, physicians are required to uphold the dignity and honor of the profession.

Code of Conduct

I. Patient-Physician Relationship

1. The patient-physician relationship is the central focus of all ethical concerns, and the welfare of the patient should form the basis of all medical judgments.

2. The obstetrician-gynecologist should serve as the patient's advocate and exercise all reasonable means to ensure that the most appropriate care is provided to the patient.

3. The patient-physician relationship has an ethical basis and is built on confidentiality, trust, and honesty. If no patient-physician relationship exists, a physician may refuse to provide care, except in emergencies. Both the patient and the obstetrician-gynecologist are free to establish or discontinue the patient-physician relationship. The obstetrician-gynecologist must adhere to all applicable legal or contractual constraints in dissolving the patient-physician relationship.

4. Sexual misconduct on the part of the obstetrician-gynecologist is an abuse of professional power and a violation of patient trust. Sexual contact or a romantic relationship between a physician and a current patient is always unethical (1).

5. The obstetrician-gynecologist has an obligation to obtain the informed consent of each patient (2,3). In obtaining informed consent for any course of medical or surgical treatment, the obstetrician-gynecologist should present to the patient, or to the person legally responsible for the patient, in understandable terms, pertinent medical facts and recommendations consistent with good medical practice. Such information should include alternate modes of treatment and the objectives, risks, benefits, possible complications, and anticipated results of such treatment.

6. It is unethical to prescribe, provide, or seek compensation for therapies that are of no benefit to the patient.

7. The obstetrician-gynecologist should respect the rights of patients, colleagues, and others and safeguard patient information and confidences within the limits of the law. If during the process of providing information for consent it is known that results of a particular test or other information must be given to governmental authorities or other third parties, that should be explained to the patient (4).

8. The obstetrician-gynecologist should not discriminate against patients based on race, color, national origin, religion, or on any other basis that would constitute illegal discrimination.

II. Physician Conduct and Practice

1. The obstetrician-gynecologist should recognize the boundaries of his or her particular competencies and expertise, and provide only those services and use only those techniques for which he or she is qualified by education, training, or experience.

2. The obstetrician-gynecologist should participate in continuing medical education activities to maintain current scientific and professional knowledge relevant to the medical services he or she renders. The obstetrician-gynecologist should provide medical care involving new therapies or techniques only after undertaking appropriate training and study.

3. In emerging areas of medical treatment where recognized medical guidelines do not exist, the obstetrician-gynecologist should exercise careful judgment and take appropriate precautions to protect patient welfare.

4. The obstetrician-gynecologist should not publicize or represent himself or herself in any untruthful, misleading, or deceptive manner to patients, colleagues, other health-care professionals, or the public (5).

5. The obstetrician-gynecologist who has reason to believe that he or she is infected with the human immunodeficiency virus or other serious infectious agents that might be communicated to patients should voluntarily be tested for the protection of his or her patients. In making decisions about patient-care activities, a physician infected with such an agent should adhere to the fundamental professional obligation to avoid harm to patients (6).

6. The obstetrician-gynecologist should not practice medicine while impaired by alcohol, drugs, or physical or mental disability. The obstetrician-gynecologist who experiences substance abuse problems or who is physically or emotionally impaired should seek appropriate assistance to address these problems and limit his or her practice until the impairment no longer affects the quality of patient care.

III. Conflicts of Interest

1. Potential conflicts of interest are inherent in the practice of medicine. Conflicts of interest should be resolved in accordance with the best interest of the patient, respecting a woman's autonomy to make health-care decisions. If there is concern about a possibly significant conflict of interest, the physician should disclose his or her concerns to the patient. If a conflict of interest cannot be resolved, the obstetrician-gynecologist should take steps to withdraw from the care of the patient. If conflicts of interest are unresolved, the physician should seek consultation with colleagues or an institutional ethics committee.

2. Commercial promotions of medical products and services may generate bias unrelated to product merit, creating, or appearing to create, inappropriate undue influence. The obstetrician-gynecologist should be aware of this potential conflict of interest and offer medical advice that is as accurate, balanced, complete, and devoid of bias as possible (7).

3. The obstetrician-gynecologist should prescribe drugs, devices, and other treatments based solely upon medical considerations and patient needs, regardless of any direct or indirect interests in or benefit from a pharmaceutical firm or other supplier.

4. When the obstetrician-gynecologist receives anything of substantial value, including royalties, from companies in the health-care industry, such as a manufacturer of pharmaceuticals and medical devices, this fact should be disclosed to patients and colleagues when material.

5. Financial and administrative constraints imposed by managed care may create disincentives to treatment otherwise recommended by the obstetrician-gynecologist as in the patient's best interest. Any pertinent constraints should be disclosed to the patient (8).

IV. Professional Relations

1. The obstetrician-gynecologist's relationships with other physicians, nurses, and health-care professionals should reflect fairness, honesty, and integrity, sharing a mutual respect and concern for the patient.

2. The obstetrician-gynecologist should consult, refer, or cooperate with other physicians, health-care professionals, and institutions to the extent necessary to serve the best interests of their patients.

3. The obstetrician-gynecologist should respect all laws, uphold the dignity and honor of the profession, and accept the profession's self-imposed discipline. The professional competence and conduct of obstetrician-gynecologists are best examined by professional associations, hospital peer-review committees, and state medical and/or licensing boards. These groups deserve the full participation and cooperation of the obstetrician-gynecologist.

4. The obstetrician-gynecologist should strive to address through the appropriate procedures the status of those physicians who demonstrate questionable competence, impairment, or unethical or illegal behavior. In addition, the obstetrician-gynecologist should cooperate with appropriate authorities to prevent the continuation of such behavior.

V. Societal Responsibilities

1. The obstetrician-gynecologist should support and participate in those health-care programs, practices, and activities that contribute positively, in a meaningful and cost-effective way, to the welfare of individual patients, the health-care system, or the public good.

2. Obstetrician-gynecologists who provide expert medical testimony in courts of law recognize their duty to testify truthfully. The obstetrician-gynecologist should not testify concerning matters about which he or she is not knowledgeable (9). The obstetrician-gynecologist should be prepared to have testimony, given in any judicial proceeding, subjected to peer review by an institution or professional organization to which he or she belongs. It is unethical for a physician to accept compensation that is contingent upon the outcome of litigation.

REFERENCES*

1. American College of Obstetricians and Gynecologists. Sexual misconduct in the practice of obstetrics and gynecology: ethical considerations. ACOG Committee Opinion 144. Washington, DC: ACOG, 1994.

2. American College of Obstetricians and Gynecologists. Ethical dimensions of informed consent. ACOG Committee Opinion 108. Washington, DC: ACOG, 1992.

3. American College of Obstetricians and Gynecologists. Informed refusal. ACOG Committee Opinion 166. Washington, DC: ACOG, 1995.

4. American College of Obstetricians and Gynecologists. Ethical guidance for patient testing. ACOG Committee Opinion 159. Washington, DC: ACOG, 1995.

5. American College of Obstetricians and Gynecologists. Deception. ACOG Committee Opinion 87. Washington, DC: ACOG, 1990.

6. American College of Obstetricians and Gynecologists. Human immunodeficiency virus infection: physicians' responsibilities. ACOG Committee Opinion 130. Washington, DC: ACOG, 1993.

7. American College of Obstetricians and Gynecologists. Guidelines for relationships with industry. ACOG Committee Opinion 182. Washington, DC: ACOG, 1997.

8. American College of Obstetricians and Gynecologists. Physician responsibility under managed care: patient advocacy in a changing health care environment. ACOG Committee Opinion 170. Washington, DC: ACOG, 1996.

9. American College of Obstetricians and Gynecologists. Ethical issues related to expert testimony by obstetricians and gynecologists. ACOG Committee Opinion 56. Washington, DC: ACOG, 1987.

American College of Obstetricians and Gynecologists. Code of Professional Ethics of the American College of Obstetricians and Gynecologists. Washington, DC, © ACOG 1997.

AMERICAN COLLEGE OF SURGEONS

Address: 633 North Saint Clair Street
             Chicago, IL 60611-3211
Telephone: 312/202-5000
WWW: www.facs.org
Document: Statements on Principles

Preamble

Founded to provide opportunities for the continuing education of surgeons, the American College of Surgeons has had a deep and effective concern for the improvement of patient care and for the ethical practice of medicine. The ethical practice of medicine establishes and ensures an environment in which all individuals are treated with respect and tolerance; discrimination or harassment on the basis of personal attributes, such as gender, race, or religion, are proscribed as being inconsistent with the ideals and principles of the American College of Surgeons. Applicants for Fellowship have always been evaluated from the standpoint of their professional competence and established reputation, and then judged as to their ethics. At the College's organizational meeting in 1913, the assemblage strongly endorsed a resolution that Fellows of the College must practice in strict honesty and must avoid any and all forms of fee splitting. Ever since, applicants have been refused Fellowship because of unacceptable financial practices or other unethical behavior. Further, Fellows have been disciplined or expelled for violation of the Fellowship Pledge and the Bylaws of the College.

Fellowship Pledge

Recognizing that the American College of Surgeons seeks to exemplify and develop the highest traditions of our ancient profession, I hereby pledge myself, as a condition of Fellowship in the College, to live in strict accordance with its principles and regulations.

I pledge myself to pursue the practice of surgery with honesty and to place the welfare and the rights of my patient above all else. I promise to deal with each patient as I would wish to be dealt with if I were in the patient's position, and I will set my fees commensurate with the services rendered. I will take no part in any arrangement, such as fee splitting or itinerant surgery, which induces referral or treatment for reason other than the patient's best welfare.

Upon my honor, I declare that I will advance my knowledge and skills, will respect my colleagues, and will seek their counsel when in doubt about my own abilities. In turn, I will willingly help my colleagues when requested.

Finally, I solemnly pledge myself to cooperate in advancing and extending the art and science of surgery by my Fellowship in the American College of Surgeons.

I. PRINCIPLES OF PATIENT CARE

Certain aspects of the ethical practice of medicine are of particular interest to surgeons. Related statements are presented in this section.

A. The responsibility of a surgeon includes preoperative diagnosis and care, the selection and performance of the operation, and postoperative surgical care.

A surgeon may delegate part of the care of patients to associates or residents under his or her personal direction, because modern surgery is often a team effort. However, the surgeon's personal responsibility must not be delegated or evaded. It is proper for the responsible surgeon to delegate the performance of part of a given operation to assistants, provided the surgeon is an active participant throughout the essential part of the operation. If a resident is to operate upon and take care of the patient, under the general supervision of an attending surgeon who will not participate actively in the operation, the patient should be so informed and consent thereto.

It is unethical to mislead a patient as to the identity of the doctor who performs the operation.

It is unethical to turn over the postoperative care of a patient completely to the referring physician.

Visits made by a referring physician during the postoperative period, for which charges are submitted but a needed service is not rendered, constitute a breach of ethics that comes under the category of unnecessary treatment.

When a patient is ready for discharge from the surgeon's care, it may be appropriate to transfer the day-to-day care to another physician.

B. Qualifications of a surgeon as a specialist carries the implication that practice will be conducted within specialty limits.

It is desirable that surgeons be highly educated, trained, and qualified to do the type of surgery they are to perform. A fine mark of such qualification, though not a rigid requirement, is certification either by a surgical board approved by the American Board of Medical Specialties or by the Royal College of Physicians and Surgeons of Canada.

Obviously, proper care of a patient on occasion may demand that a surgeon engage in practice outside usual specialty limits when no appropriately trained physician is available. This should not be a frequent or continuing occurrence.

C. Itinerant surgery is proscribed.

The elements of time and distance are not pertinent in determining whether an individual has performed "itinerant surgery." An ethical surgeon will not perform elective surgery at a distance from the usual location where he or she operates without personal determination of the diagnosis and of the adequacy of preoperative preparation. Postoperative care will be rendered by the operating surgeon unless it is delegated to another physician who is as well qualified to continue this essential aspect of total surgical care.

It is recognized that for many operations performed in an ambulatory setting, the pattern of the patient's postoperative visits to the surgeon may vary considerably; it is, however, the responsibility of the operating surgeon to establish communication to ensure that the patient receives proper continuity of care. Similar circumstances may pertain when patients travel great distances for elective surgery.

Emergency surgery that is performed in locations that are unusual for the surgeon may be necessary on occasion, but habitual or even frequent performance of operations under these circumstances cannot be condoned. If the condition of the patient permits and additional skills are required, the patient should be transported to a medical center where they are available. Not only does itinerant surgery violate ethical relations between surgeon and patient, it may also raise serious questions with regard to "ghost surgery."

D. Completion of an accredited residency program is the only valid way in which a physician can become a surgeon.

Some hospitals permit arrangements through which a staff member can achieve surgical privileges under the tutelage of a qualified surgeon in the operating room without serving in a formal, organized, accredited residency training program. This is an undesirable situation, because it frequently results in an inadequately trained physician who may aspire to be a surgeon. Opportunities for the type of surgical training that meets the approval of the College are numerous. Performance of surgical procedures under guidance is only one part of the training of a qualified surgeon.

E. Training of assistants.

Surgeons may participate in the training of allied health personnel to act as technical assistants. Such individuals must perform their duties under the direct supervision of the surgeon, who has the responsibility for all of their actions.

II. PRINCIPLES OF QUALIFICATIONS FOR SURGICAL PRIVILEGES

A. Qualifications of the responsible surgeon.

Eligibility to perform surgical procedures as the responsible surgeon must be based on an individual's adequate education and training, continued experience, and demonstrated proficiency.

Acceptable education will consist of graduation from a medical school approved by the Liaison Council on Medical Education or from a school that is acceptable to the medical licensing board of the state in which the surgeon is practicing (NOTE: Certain state and federal laws may require recognition of other types of health education), plus education leading to qualification as a surgical specialist.

A physician is considered to be a surgical specialist if the physician:

(1) Is certified by an American surgical specialty board approved by the American Board of Medical Specialties; or

(2) Has been judged eligible by such a board for its examination by reason of education, training, and experience; or

(3) Is a Fellow of the American College of Surgeons; or

(4) Has obtained, in a country outside the United States, graduate surgical education that satisfies the educational requirements for Fellowship in the American College of Surgeons.

It is recognized that surgical procedures may be performed by physicians who do not meet this definition, under the following conditions:

(1) A physician who has just completed formal training in an accredited surgical residency program as defined by the appropriate specialty, for whom the appropriate surgical board has not yet determined eligibility. (NOTE: Ordinarily, this situation would be within a time frame that would not exceed one year plus the board's practice requirement, if any).

(2) A physician who renders surgical care in (a) an emergency, or (b) an area of limited population where a surgical specialist is not available.

A resident in training in an approved surgical program may provide surgical care under supervision as determined by the surgical staff.

The granting and continuation of surgical privileges should be based upon the surgeon's record of demonstrated performance as evaluated by an established peer review mechanism and medical audit. Requests for privileges that are not generally associated with the field in which the applicant has been trained must be specifically requested and documented with evidence of appropriate training and experience.

In some geographically isolated and sparsely settled areas, fully trained surgeons in various fields may not be available. The performance of certain surgical procedures, especially of an emergency nature, by a physician without special surgical training may be in the best interest of the public in that area. The medical staff and the governing body of hospitals in such areas should periodically review the quality, the number, and the variety of surgical procedures being performed, as well as the surgical referral policies of the staff. Attention should be directed to any referral pattern in surgical care that may discourage the application of properly trained and qualified surgeons for staff membership.

B. Qualifications of the first assistant in the operation room.

The first assistant to the surgeon during a surgical operation should be a trained individual who is capable of participating in the operation and actively assisting the surgeon as part of a good working team. The first assistant provides aid in exposure, hemostasis, and other technical functions, thereby helping the surgeon carry out a safe operation with optimal results for the patient. This role will vary considerably with the surgical operation, specialty area, and type of hospital.

The American College of Surgeons supports the concept that, ideally, the first assistant to the surgeon at the operating table should be a qualified surgeon or resident in a surgical education program that is approved by the appropriate residency review committee and accredited by the Accreditation Council for Graduate Medical Education. It is a principle of surgical education and care that residents at appropriate levels of training should be provided with opportunities to assist at and participate in operations. Other physicians who are experienced in assisting the responsible surgeon may participate when a trained surgeon or a resident in an accredited program is not available.

Attainment of this ideal in all hospitals is recognized as being impracticable. In some circumstances it is necessary to utilize appropriately trained nonphysicians to serve as first assistants to qualified surgeons. Surgeon's assistants (SAs), or physician's assistants (PAs) with additional surgical training, may be employed if they meet national standards. These individuals are not authorized to operate independently.

Certified surgeon's or physician's assistants must make a formal application for appointment to the hospital, which should include:

(1) An outline of their qualifications and credentials.
(2) Stipulation of their requests to assist in a surgeon's practice including assisting at the operating table.
(3) Indication of the surgeon who will be responsible for the SA's or PA's performance.

The appropriate committee or board of the hospital should review such individuals' qualifications for hospital privileges.

Registered nurses with additional specialized training may also function as first assistants to the surgeon at the operating table in those situations or hospitals where more completely trained assistants are not available. If a nurse functions in this role, however, the size of the operating room team should not be reduced; the assigned nurse should function solely as the first assistant and not also as the scrub or instrument nurse. Similarly, surgical technologists may function as first assistants in the absence of more qualified individuals.

In some hospitals in this country, there may be no specifically trained and readily available surgical assistants in the operating room. Traditionally, the first assistant's role in such institutions has been filled by a variety of individuals from diverse backgrounds. It is the surgeon's responsibility to designate an individual who is most appropriate for this purpose in keeping with the bylaws of the medical staff of the hospital.

Practice privileges of individuals acting as first assistants should be based upon verified credentials, should be reviewed and approved by the hospital credentialing committee, and should be within the defined limits of state law.

C. Surgery in hospitals by persons not holding medical degrees.

Dentists

The policy of the American College of Surgeons has been well discussed and outlined in the *Bulletin of the American College of Surgeons* (May 1970, page 14). Important features of this policy are:

(1) The Division of Oral Surgery should be under the overall supervision of the surgeon-in-chief of the hospital or the chairman of the appropriate surgical department. In nondepartmentalized hospitals, the Division of Oral Surgery will be under the Chief of Staff or designated committee.

(2) The surgeon-in-chief, the departmental chairman, or the designated committee has the authority and responsibility for recommending to the hospital's governing board who shall, or shall not, perform surgical procedures.

(3) In the total care of patients with injuries in multiple regions or with complicated medical-surgical problems, the oral surgeon may be an essential member of the team and may act independently in an area of special competence. In instances requiring a team approach for the management of injuries in multiple regions or extensive and complicated medical-surgical problems, the surgeon who is captain of the team and who has final responsibility for the care of the patient must be a physician.

Podiatrists

(1) Licensed podiatrists may be hospital staff members and admit patients to the hospital in collaboration with a physician who shall be responsible for the overall aspects of the patient's care throughout the hospital stay.

(2) Surgical procedures that are performed by podiatrists must be under the overall supervision of the chief of the appropriate surgical service.

(3) The type and extent of operative procedures to be performed by podiatrists will be determined by the chief of surgery upon the advice of members of the surgical staff.

Chiropractors

Except as provided by law, there are no ethical or collective impediments to full professional association and cooperation between doctors of chiropractic and medical physicians.

III. PRINCIPLES OF QUALIFICATIONS FOR FELLOWSHIP

In this section are broad statements of the criteria that are used to determine the eligibility of applicants for Fellowship. These criteria are also used to evaluate the continuing eligibility of a Fellow. Precise, current requirements for applicants are published separately.

A. Licensure is a basic necessity.

The license must be valid in the state, province, or country in which the practice is conducted (unless the surgeon is a career officer in a federal medical service).

Some states issue a restricted license, or some form of certificate, to a resident or hospital employee for a limited time. An applicant for Fellowship must possess a full and unrestricted license.

B. Each Fellow must demonstrate professional and ethical fitness. Surgery is to be practiced with scientific honesty, placing the welfare of patients above all else.

For applicants, this fitness is determined based on reports from Fellows of the College who are used as references, and on reports from appropriate Credentials Committees, which are made to the Director and the Board of Regents.

Eligibility for Fellowship is gauged by the demonstrated surgical judgment and professional conscience of the applicant. The applicant's performance of surgery and its evaluation by peers are important considerations.

Each applicant must be approved by a three-fourths vote by the Regents. Any question as to the ethical practices of an applicant results in postponement to permit clarification. Reasonable documentation that an applicant fails to meet the standards results in his or her being "not approved."

Upon accepting Fellowship, the member must abide by the principles that are enunciated in the Fellowship Pledge, which appears on page 1 of these statements.

The same professional and ethical qualifications that are demanded of an applicant are requirements for Fellows. Deviations from these high principles during the Fellow's career can be cause for disciplinary action.

C. A surgeon must refuse to split fees.

Fee splitting as an inducement to refer a patient to another physician is unethical. The premise for referral must be quality of care. Violation of this tenet disqualifies an applicant. If a surgeon who is already a Fellow violates this principle, it is a cause for expulsion from Fellowship.

Many states have laws that forbid any form of fee splitting, and there is no state that sanctions it. Additionally, federal law makes illegal any form of rebate, kickback, or splitting of fees that includes any federal money. Thus, such illegal inducement cannot be considered an item of deductible business expense.

D. Physicians are to present their own statements for services.

A patient should have full knowledge of the services for which payment is made, the amount of the bill, and the recipient of the payment.

The patient's surgical experience may be divided into a period of diagnosis and preoperative care, the operation itself, postoperative care, and care during convalescence. When all of these services are performed by the surgeon, the patient should be billed accordingly. When the diagnosis and preoperative care have been accomplished by a referring physician, who may also render convalescent care, it is proper for the referring physician to charge for those services, and the surgeon should then charge for performance of the operation and for the postoperative care.

Since each attending physician has a contractual relationship with the patient, it is proper to bill the patient for the services that are performed. The surgeon should bill for personal services, and should not include charges for services performed by the referring physician.

When the surgeon employs an assistant who has no other professional relationship to the patient, the surgeon may pay this assistant and should disclose this expense in the patient's bill. If preferred, such an assistant may charge the patient directly.

A referring physician should send his or her own bill for services rendered, including assisting at an operation, but should not seek reimbursement for unnecessary duplication of postoperative hospital visits.

E. Partnerships, groups, clinics, or managed care organizations may bill as individuals.

Legally established associations of physicians in practice (partnerships, groups, clinics, or managed care organizations) are regarded as entities. When professional income is pooled and professional expenses are paid out of a common fund, the association may use a single bill to charge for the services of its members.

If a surgeon with an established practice at one location is also a consultant for an association at a different office, it is not ethical for the association to charge a patient for the surgeon's services. The surgeon should present a separate bill. If the association is paid for the use of space, services, and supplies, the payment should be justified by amounts for rent, salaries, and so on, that are common in the community; such payments should be totally unrelated to income that is generated from patients of the association.

F. Unnecessary surgery is condemned.

Whether due to repeated ineptness, lack of knowledge, or willful failure to apply acceptable indications for operations or other procedures, the performance of unnecessary surgery is an extremely serious violation of ethical principles for which disciplinary action is indicated. Committees in hospitals are organized to guard against such violations or repeated mistakes.

G. Fellows of the College are expected to make continuing efforts to improve their knowledge of surgery.

Every physician has the obligation to keep abreast of new knowledge and advances in the art and science of medicine. For the surgeon, attendance at meetings of the College and of other scientific societies is invaluable, as is continuing study of current journals and texts.

The Regents encourage periodic voluntary self-assessment by examination and professional improvement through continuing education programs.

H. Maintenance of Fellowship is jeopardized by infractions of College principles.

Upon receiving information indicating that a Fellow may be violating any principle of the College, the Director will follow the Bylaws of the College with regard to investigation and referral to the Central Judiciary Committee. If disciplinary action is imposed, it may take one of the following forms:

(1) Admonition—A written notification, warning, or serious rebuke.
(2) Censure—A written judgment, condemning the Fellow's action as wrong. This is a firm reprimand.
(3) Probation—A punitive action for a stated period of time, during which a Fellow
   a) loses the right to hold office or participate in a program
   b) retains other privileges or obligations of Fellowship
   c) will be reconsidered by the Central Judiciary Committee periodically, and at the end of the stated term.
(4) Suspension—A severe punitive action for a stated or indefinite time, during which the Fellow is subject to the following:
   a) the removal of the Fellow's name from the Yearbook and from the mailing list of the College
   b) a demand that the Fellowship certificate be returned to the College
   c) the obligation to pay visitor's registration fee when attending ACS meetings
   d) the waiving of annual dues.
   When suspension is lifted, the Fellow is returned to full privileges and obligations of Fellowship.

(5) Expulsion—The certificate of Fellowship and all other indicia of Fellowship previously issued by the College must be forthwith returned to the College. The surgeon shall not claim or pretend to be a Fellow of the American College of Surgeons thereafter.

I. Fellows are expected to report knowledge of violations of principles or bylaws.

When a Fellow is convinced that another fellow is violating the Fellowship Pledge, the Bylaws of the College, or its principles, a written confidential communication should be sent to the Director of the College. The information so submitted will then be further investigated and processed according to the provisions of the Bylaws.

IV. PRINCIPLES OF PUBLIC RELATIONS

Educational, sociological, and political developments make it essential that every doctor be concerned about public relations. Principles are unchanging, but they require interpretation and application in the light of current conditions. This section presents statements relevant to such principles.

A. Explanation of the nature and risk of an operation to the patient or to the patient's representative is essential.

Patients should understand the indications for the operation, the risk involved, and the result that it is hoped to attain. In the instance of a minor or a desperately ill or comatose patient, the responsible relative or guardian should be informed. Written consent should be obtained whenever the condition of the patient permits, before an operation is performed. A consent form should be signed by the patient. If the seriousness of the illness or other conditions do not make it feasible for the patient to do so, or if the patient is a minor, the form should be given to and signed by one or more persons who are authorized to do so by law.

B. Discussion of fees with patients prior to the submitting of a statement is recommended.

When a physician agrees to care for a patient, a contract is established (even if it is not written). This relationship implies agreement that the doctor will be compensated for services rendered to the patient. Whenever requested by the patient, a surgeon should fully discuss the fee with the patient. It is often desirable to discuss the fee prior to the operation.

C. Fees are to be commensurate with services rendered and with the patient's rights.

Surgeons have individual bases for their charges, and fees vary in different communities. The College has not attempted to establish fee schedules for its Fellows. Instead, applicants and Fellows are expected to make charges commensurate with what is considered to be reasonable by local mediation or peer review committees. Such charges may be related to the economic status of the patient.

D. Every patient's right to privacy must be respected.

The surgeon should maintain the confidentiality of information from and about the patient, except as such information must be communicated for the patient's proper care or as is required by law.

E. Surgeons should report new methods of or innovations in treatment to professional audiences to permit evaluation and authentication before release to public news media.

Both the patient's right to privacy and the medical profession's related rights must be observed, and any public release of scientific information should have the approval of the appropriate institutional committee, as well as the approval of the physician in charge of the patient. The best interests of patients and doctors are served when physicians observe the traditional practice of reporting innovations and discoveries to the profession before release to the news media. In issuing releases to audiovisual media or nonprofessional publications, the surgeon should be guided by patients' best interests. In addition, the release of such information should be designed for education and public information.

Communications to the public must not convey false, untrue, deceptive, or misleading information through statements, testimonials, photographs, graphics, or other means. Such communications must not create unjustified expectations of results and must include realistic assessments of safety, efficacy, and material risks, as well as the availability of alternatives. Communications must not misrepresent a surgeon's credentials, training, experience, or ability, and must not contain material claims of superiority that cannot be substantiated. If a surgeon pays for a communication, that fact must be disclosed unless the nature, format, or medium makes it apparent. The issuance of inaccurate communications to the public may result in disciplinary action by the Board of Regents.

F. Biomedical research must be conducted within ethical and legal guidelines.

Progress in medical care that is achieved through research depends on informed partnership between patients and physicians in the development of new drugs and treatment methods. Certain advances in the treatment of disease can be learned only through properly conducted clinical trials during which the results of varying treatments recommended by individual doctors are compared carefully.

When applicable, animal studies should precede the use of new and experimental techniques in humans. Research programs involving human beings should follow certain guidelines, including prior approval by an impartial committee on human experimentation, full description to the patient of procedures to be undertaken and explanation of the risk involved. There should be a justifiable expectation that the potential benefit of clinical trial outweighs the risk. The patient's personal rights must be respected, including an appropriate informed consent process and the right to withdraw consent at any time. There should be continuous observation and approval by the local committee that gave initial approval to the protocol.

G. Disclosure of commercial interest.

A Fellow's failure to disclose a financial interest in a commercial enterprise makes it unlikely that other professionals or the public can accurately evaluate statements made by the Fellow about the products or services. The statements may be misleading or deceptive. Failure to disclose remuneration or financial interest may constitute grounds for disciplinary action under Article VII, Section 1(I) of the College's Bylaws.

AMERICAN CONGRESS ON SURVEYING AND MAPPING

Address: 5410 Grosvenor Lane, Suite 100
             Bethesda, MD 20814-2144
Telephone: 301/493-0200

WWW: www.survmap.org
Document: Code of Ethics (1993)

CODE: As surveying and mapping professionals, we recognize that our ethical responsibilities extend to the public, to our clients, and to our peers. Accordingly, we acknowledge the following elements to identify our basic values: integrity, competence, and social awareness. Surveying and mapping professionals uphold and advance these values by

(I)   supporting and participating in the continuing development of the surveying and mapping professions;
(II) serving with honesty, with forthrightness, and within their areas of skill;
(III) using their expertise for the enhancement of human welfare and for the stewardship of resources.

CREED: As a professional surveyor, I dedicate my professional knowledge and skills to the advancement and betterment of human welfare. I pledge to give the utmost performance; to participate in none but honest enterprise; to live and work according to the laws of humankind and to the highest standards of professional conduct; to place service before profit, honor and standing of the profession before personal advantage, and the public welfare above all other considerations.

CANONS: In humility and with the need for divine guidance, I make this pledge: A professional surveyor should

(1) refrain from conduct that is detrimental to the public;
(2) abide by the rules and regulations pertaining to the practice of surveying within the licensing jurisdiction;
(3) accept assignments only in one's area of professional competence;
(4) develop and communicate a professional analysis and opinion without bias or personal interest;
(5) maintain the confidential nature of the surveyor-client relationship;
(6) use care to avoid advertising or solicitation that is misleading or otherwise contrary to the public interest;
(7) maintain professional integrity when dealing with members of other professions.

AMERICAN CONSULTING ENGINEERS COUNCIL

Address: 1015 Fifteenth Street NW, Suite 802
              Washington, DC 20005
Telephone: 202/347-7474
WWW: www.acec.org
Document: Professional and Ethical Conduct
              Guidelines (1980)

PREAMBLE
Consulting engineering is an important and learned profession. The members of the profession recognize that their work has a direct and vital impact on the quality of life for all people. Accordingly, the services provided by consulting engineers require honesty, impartiality, fairness and equity and must be dedicated to the protection of public health, safety and welfare. In the practice of their profession, consulting engineers must perform under a standard of professional behavior which requires adherence to the highest principles of ethical conduct on behalf of the public, clients, employees and the profession.

I. Fundamental Canons
Consulting engineers, in the fulfillment of their professional duties, shall:

1. Hold paramount the safety, health and welfare of the public in the performance of their professional duties.
2. Perform services only in areas of their competence.
3. Issue public statements only in an objective and truthful manner.
4. Act in professional matters for each client as faithful agents or trustees.
5. Avoid improper solicitation of professional assignments.

II. Rules of Practice
1. Consulting engineers shall hold paramount the safety, health and welfare of the public in the performance of their professional duties.
   a. Consulting engineers shall at all times recognize that their primary obligation is to protect the safety, health, property and welfare of the public. If their professional judgment is overruled under circumstances where the safety, health, property or welfare of the public are endangered, they shall notify their client and such other authority as may be appropriate.
   b. Consulting engineers shall approve only engineering work which, to the best of their knowledge and belief, is safe for public health, property and welfare and in conformity with accepted standards.
   c. Consulting engineers shall not reveal facts, data or information obtained in a professional capacity without the prior consent of the client except as authorized or required by law or these Guidelines.
   d. Consulting engineers shall not permit the use of their name or firm nor associate in business ventures with any person or firm which they have reason to believe is engaging in fraudulent or dishonest business or professional practices.
   e. Consulting engineers having knowledge of any alleged violation of these Guidelines shall cooperate with the proper authorities in furnishing such information or assistance as may be required.
2. Consulting engineers shall perform services only in the areas of their competence.
   a. Consulting engineers shall undertake assignments only when qualified by education or experience in the specific technical fields involved.
   b. Consulting engineers shall not affix their signatures to any plans or documents dealing with subject matter in which they lack competence nor to any plan or document not prepared under their direction and control.
   c. Consulting engineers may accept an assignment outside of their fields of competence to the extent that their services are restricted to those phases of the project in which they are qualified and to the extent that they are satisfied that all other phases of such project will be performed by registered or otherwise qualified

associates, consultants or employees, in which case they may then sign the documents for the total project.

3. Consulting engineers shall issue public statements only in an objective and truthful manner.

    a. Consulting engineers shall be objective and truthful in professional reports, statements or testimony. They shall include all relevant and pertinent information in such reports, statements or testimony.

    b. Consulting engineers may express publicly a professional opinion on technical subjects only when that opinion is founded upon adequate knowledge of the facts and competence in the subject matter.

    c. Consulting engineers shall issue no statements, criticisms, or arguments on technical matters which are inspired or paid for by interested parties, unless they have prefaced their comments by explicitly identifying the interested parties on whose behalf they are speaking and by revealing the existence of any interest they may have in the matters.

4. Consulting engineers shall act in professional matters for each client as faithful agents or trustees.

    a. Consulting engineers shall disclose all known or potential conflicts of interest to their clients by promptly informing them of any business association, interest or other circumstances which could influence or appear to influence their judgment of the quality of their services.

    b. Consulting engineers shall not accept compensation, financial or otherwise, from more than one party for services on the same project, or for services pertaining to the same project, unless the circumstances are fully disclosed to, and agreed to, by all interested parties.

    c. Consulting engineers in public service as members of a governmental body or department shall not participate in decisions with respect to professional services solicited or provided by them or their organizations in private engineering practices.

    d. Consulting engineers shall not solicit or accept a professional contract from a governmental body on which a principal officer of their organization serves as a member.

5. Consulting engineers shall avoid improper solicitation of professional assignments.

    a. Consulting engineers shall not falsify or permit misrepresentation of their, or their associates',

academic or professional qualifications. They shall not misrepresent or exaggerate their degree of responsibility in or for the subject matter of prior assignments. Brochures or other presentations incident to the solicitation of assignments shall not misrepresent pertinent facts concerning employees, associates, joint ventures or past accomplishments with the intent and purpose of enhancing their qualifications and their work.

    b. Consulting engineers shall not offer, give, solicit or receive, either directly or indirectly, any political contribution in an amount intended to influence the award of a contract by public authority, or which may be reasonably construed by the public of having the effect or intent to influence the award of the contract. They shall not offer any gift or other valuable consideration in order to secure work. They shall not pay a commission, percentage or brokerage fee in order to secure work except to a bona fide employee or bona fide established commercial or marketing agencies retained by them.

Special Note: These guidelines do not prohibit design competitions, free services, or contingent arrangements.

© American Consulting Engineers Council. Reprinted with permission.

AMERICAN CORRECTIONAL ASSOCIATION

Address:	4380 Forbes Boulevard Lanham, MD 20706-4322
Telephone:	301/918-1800 or 800/222-5646
WWW:	www.corrections.com/aca
Document:	Code of Ethics (1975. Most recently revised 1994.)

PREAMBLE

The American Correctional Association expects of its members unfailing honesty, respect for the dignity and individuality of human beings and a commitment to professional and compassionate service. To this end, we subscribe to the following principles.

Members shall respect and protect the civil and legal rights of all individuals.

Members shall treat every professional situation with concern for the welfare of the individuals involved and with no intent to personal gain.

Members shall maintain relationships with colleagues to promote mutual respect within the profession and improve the quality of service.

Members shall make public criticism of their colleagues or their agencies only when warranted, verifiable, and constructive.

Members shall respect the importance of all disciplines within the criminal justice system and work to improve cooperation with each segment.

Members shall honor the public's right to information and share information with the public to the extent permitted by law subject to individuals' right to privacy.

Members shall respect and protect the right of the public to be safeguarded from criminal activity.

Members shall refrain from using their positions to secure personal privileges or advantages.

Members shall refrain from allowing personal interest to impair objectivity in the performance of duty while acting in an official capacity.

Members shall refrain from entering into any formal or informal activity or agreement which presents a conflict of interest or is inconsistent with the conscientious performance of duties.

Members shall refrain from accepting any gifts, service, or favor that is or appears to be improper or implies an obligation inconsistent with the free and objective exercise of professional duties.

Members shall clearly differentiate between personal views/statements and views/statements/positions made on behalf of the agency or Association.

Members shall report to appropriate authorities any corrupt or unethical behaviors in which there is sufficient evidence to justify review.

Members shall refrain from discriminating against any individual because of race, gender, creed, national origin, religious affiliation, age, disability, or any other type of prohibited discrimination.

Members shall preserve the integrity of private information; they shall refrain from seeking information on individuals beyond that which is necessary to implement responsibilities and perform their duties; members shall refrain from revealing nonpublic information unless expressly authorized to do so.

Members shall make all appointments, promotions, and dismissals in accordance with established civil service rules, applicable contract agreements, and individual merit, rather than furtherance of personal interest.

Members shall respect, promote, and contribute to a work place that is safe, healthy, and free of harassment in any form.

© American Correctional Association. Reprinted with permission.

AMERICAN COUNSELING ASSOCIATION

Address: 5999 Stevenson Avenue
             Alexandria, VA 22304-3300
Telephone: 703/823-9800 or 800/347-6647
WWW: www.counseling.org
Document: Code of Ethics (1995)

Preamble

The American Counseling Association is an educational, scientific and professional organization whose members are dedicated to the enhancement of human development throughout the life span. Association members recognize diversity in our society and embrace a cross-cultural approach in support of the worth, dignity, potential, and uniqueness of each individual.

The specification of a code of ethics enables the association to clarify to current and future members, and to those served by members, the nature of the ethical responsibilities held in common by its members. As the code of ethics of the association, this document establishes principles that define the ethical behavior of association members. All members of the American Counseling Association are required to adhere to the Code of Ethics and the Standards of Practice. The Code of Ethics will serve as the basis for processing ethics complaints initiated against members of the association.

SECTION A:
THE COUNSELING RELATIONSHIP

A.1. Client Welfare

a. *Primary Responsibility.*
The primary responsibility of counselors is to respect the dignity and to promote the welfare of clients.

b. *Positive Growth and Development.*
Counselors encourage client growth and development in ways that foster the clients' interest and welfare; counselors avoid fostering dependent counseling relationships.

c. *Counseling Plans.*
Counselors and their clients work jointly in devising integrated, individual counseling plans that offer reasonable promise of success and are consistent with abilities and circumstances of clients. Counselors and clients regularly review counseling plans to ensure their continued viability and effectiveness, respecting clients' freedom of choice. (See A.3.b.)

d. *Family Involvement.*
Counselors recognize that families are usually important in clients' lives and strive to enlist family understanding and involvement as a positive resource, when appropriate.

e. *Career and Employment Needs.*
Counselors work with their clients in considering employment in jobs and circumstances that are consis-

tent with the clients' overall abilities, vocational limitations, physical restrictions, general temperament, interest and aptitude patterns, social skills, education, general qualifications, and other relevant characteristics and needs. Counselors neither place nor participate in placing clients in positions that will result in damaging the interest and the welfare of clients, employers, or the public.

A.2. Respecting Diversity

a. *Nondiscrimination.*
Counselors do not condone or engage in discrimination based on age, color, culture, disability, ethnic group, gender, race, religion, sexual orientation, marital status, or socioeconomic status. (See C.5.a., C.5.b., and D.1.i.)

b. *Respecting Differences.*
Counselors will actively attempt to understand the diverse cultural backgrounds of the clients with whom they work. This includes, but is not limited to, learning how the counselor's own cultural/ethnic/racial identity impacts her/his values and beliefs about the counseling process. (See E.8. and F.2.i.)

A.3. Client Rights

a. *Disclosure to Clients.*
When counseling is initiated, and throughout the counseling process as necessary, counselors inform clients of the purposes, goals, techniques, procedures, limitations, potential risks, and benefits of services to be performed, and other pertinent information. Counselors take steps to ensure that clients understand the implications of diagnosis, the intended use of tests and reports, fees, and billing arrangements. Clients have the right to expect confidentiality and to be provided with an explanation of its limitations, including supervision and/or treatment team professionals; to obtain clear information about their case records; to participate in the ongoing counseling plans; and to refuse any recommended services and be advised of the consequences of such refusal. (See E.5.a. and G.2.)

b. *Freedom of Choice.*
Counselors offer clients the freedom to choose whether to enter into a counseling relationship and to determine which professional(s) will provide counseling. Restrictions that limit choices of clients are fully explained. (See A.1.c.)

c. *Inability to Give Consent.*
When counseling minors or persons unable to give voluntary informed consent, counselors act in these clients' best interests. (See B.3.)

A.4. Clients Served by Others

If a client is receiving services from another mental health professional, counselors, with client consent, inform the professional persons already involved and develop clear agreements to avoid confusion and conflict for the client. (See C.6.c.)

A.5. Personal Needs and Values

a. *Personal Needs.*
In the counseling relationship, counselors are aware of the intimacy and responsibilities inherent in the counseling relationship, maintain respect for clients, and avoid actions that seek to meet their personal needs at the expense of clients.

b. *Personal Values.*
Counselors are aware of their own values, attitudes, beliefs, and behaviors and how these apply in a diverse society, and avoid imposing their values on clients. (See C.5.a.)

A.6. Dual Relationships

a. *Avoid When Possible.*
Counselors are aware of their influential positions with respect to clients, and they avoid exploiting the trust and dependency of clients. Counselors make every effort to avoid dual relationships with clients that could impair professional judgment or increase the risk of harm to clients. (Examples of such relationships include, but are not limited to, familial, social, financial, business, or close personal relationships with clients.) When a dual relationship cannot be avoided, counselors take appropriate professional precautions such as informed consent, consultation, supervision, and documentation to ensure that judgment is not impaired and no exploitation occurs. (See F.1.b.)

b. *Superior/Subordinate Relationships.*
Counselors do not accept as clients superiors or subordinates with whom they have administrative, supervisory, or evaluative relationships.

A.7. Sexual Intimacies With Clients

a. *Current Clients.*
Counselors do not have any type of sexual intimacies with clients and do not counsel persons with whom they have had a sexual relationship.

b. *Former Clients.*
Counselors do not engage in sexual intimacies with former clients within a minimum of 2 years after terminating the counseling relationship. Counselors who engage in such relationship after 2 years following termination have the responsibility to thoroughly examine and document that such relations did not have an exploitative nature, based on factors such as duration of counseling, amount of time since counseling, termination circumstances, client's personal history and mental status, adverse impact on the client, and actions by the counselor suggesting a plan to initiate a sexual relationship with the client after termination.

A.8. Multiple Clients

When counselors agree to provide counseling services to two or more persons who have a relationship (such as husband and wife, or parents and children), counselors clarify at the outset which person or persons are clients and the nature of the relationships they will have with each involved person. If it becomes apparent that counselors may be called upon to perform potentially conflicting roles, they clarify, adjust, or withdraw from roles appropriately. (See B.2. and B.4.d.)

A.9. Group Work

a. *Screening.*
Counselors screen prospective group counseling/therapy participants. To the extent possible, counselors select members whose needs and goals are compatible with goals of the group, who will not impede the group process, and whose well-being will not be jeopardized by the group experience.

b. *Protecting Clients.*
In a group setting, counselors take reasonable precautions to protect clients from physical or psychological trauma.

A.10. Fees and Bartering (See D.3.a. and D.3.b.)

a. *Advance Understanding.*
Counselors clearly explain to clients, prior to entering the counseling relationship, all financial arrangements related to professional services including the use of collection agencies or legal measures for nonpayment. (See A.11.c.)

b. *Establishing Fees.*
In establishing fees for professional counseling services, counselors consider the financial status of clients and locality. In the event that the established fee structure is inappropriate for a client, assistance is provided in attempting to find comparable services of acceptable cost. (See A.10.d., D.3.a., and D.3.b.)

c. *Bartering Discouraged.*

Counselors ordinarily refrain from accepting goods or services from clients in return for counseling services because such arrangements create inherent potential for conflicts, exploitation, and distortion of the professional relationship. Counselors may participate in bartering only if the relationship is not exploitative, if the client requests it, if a clear written contract is established, and if such arrangements are an accepted practice among professionals in the community. (See A.6.a.)

d. *Pro Bono Service.*

Counselors contribute to society by devoting a portion of their professional activity to services for which there is little or no financial return (pro bono).

A.11. Termination and Referral

a. *Abandonment Prohibited.*

Counselors do not abandon or neglect clients in counseling. Counselors assist in making appropriate arrangements for the continuation of treatment, when necessary, during interruptions such as vacations, and following termination.

b. *Inability to Assist Clients.*

If counselors determine an inability to be of professional assistance to clients, they avoid entering or immediately terminate a counseling relationship. Counselors are knowledgeable about referral resources and suggest appropriate alternatives. If clients decline the suggested referral, counselors should discontinue the relationship.

c. *Appropriate Termination.*

Counselors terminate a counseling relationship, securing client agreement when possible, when it is reasonably clear that the client is no longer benefiting, when services are no longer required, when counseling no longer serves the client's needs or interests, when clients do not pay fees charged, or when agency or institution limits do not allow provision of further counseling services. (See A.10.b. and C.2.g.)

A.12. Computer Technology

a. *Use of Computers.*

When computer applications are used in counseling services, counselors ensure that: (1) the client is intellectually, emotionally, and physically capable of using the computer application; (2) the computer application is appropriate for the needs of the client; (3) the client understands the purpose and operation of the computer applications; and (4) a follow-up of client use of a computer application is provided to correct possible misconceptions, discover inappropriate use, and assess subsequent needs.

b. *Explanation of Limitations.*

Counselors ensure that clients are provided information as a part of the counseling relationship that adequately explains the limitations of computer technology.

c. *Access to Computer Applications.*

Counselors provide for equal access to computer applications in counseling services. (See A.2.a.)

SECTION B: CONFIDENTIALITY

B.1. Right to Privacy

a. *Respect for Privacy.*

Counselors respect their clients' right to privacy and avoid illegal and unwarranted disclosures of confidential information. (See A.3.a. and B.6.a.)

b. *Client Waiver.*

The right to privacy may be waived by the client or their legally recognized representative.

c. *Exceptions.*

The general requirement that counselors keep information confidential does not apply when disclosure is required to prevent clear and imminent danger to the client or others or when legal requirements demand that confidential information be revealed. Counselors consult with other professionals when in doubt as to the validity of an exception.

d. *Contagious, Fatal Diseases.*

A counselor who receives information confirming that a client has a disease commonly known to be both communicable and fatal is justified in disclosing information to an identifiable third party, who by his or her relationship with the client is at a high risk of contracting the disease. Prior to making a disclosure the counselor should ascertain that the client has not already informed the third party about his or her disease and that the client is not intending to inform the third party in the immediate future. (See B.1.c and B.1.f.)

e. *Court-Ordered Disclosure.*

When court ordered to release confidential information without a client's permission, counselors request to the court that the disclosure not be required due to potential harm to the client or counseling relationship. (See B.1.c.)

f. *Minimal Disclosure.*

When circumstances require the disclosure of confidential information, only essential information is revealed. To the extent possible, clients are informed before confidential information is disclosed.

g. *Explanation of Limitations.*
When counseling is initiated and throughout the counseling process as necessary, counselors inform clients of the limitations of confidentiality and identify foreseeable situations in which confidentiality must be breached. (See G.2.a.)

h. *Subordinates.*
Counselors make every effort to ensure that privacy and confidentiality of clients are maintained by subordinates including employees, supervisees, clerical assistants, and volunteers. (See B.1.a.)

i. *Treatment Teams.*
If client treatment will involve a continued review by a treatment team, the client will be informed of the team's existence and composition.

B.2. Groups and Families

a. *Group Work.*
In group work, counselors clearly define confidentiality and the parameters for the specific group being entered, explain its importance, and discuss the difficulties related to confidentiality involved in group work. The fact that confidentiality cannot be guaranteed is clearly communicated to group members.

b. *Family Counseling.*
In family counseling, information about one family member cannot be disclosed to another member without permission. Counselors protect the privacy rights of each family member. (See A.8., B.3., and B.4.d.)

B.3. Minor or Incompetent Clients

When counseling clients who are minors or individuals who are unable to give voluntary, informed consent, parents or guardians may be included in the counseling process as appropriate. Counselors act in the best interests of clients and take measures to safeguard confidentiality. (See A.3.c.)

B.4. Records

a. *Requirement of Records.*
Counselors maintain records necessary for rendering professional services to their clients and as required by laws, regulations, or agency or institution procedures.

b. *Confidentiality of Records.*
Counselors are responsible for securing the safety and confidentiality of any counseling records they create, maintain, transfer, or destroy whether the records are written, taped, computerized, or stored in any other medium. (See B.1.a.)

c. *Permission to Record or Observe.*
Counselors obtain permission from clients prior to electronically recording or observing sessions. (See A.3.a.)

d. *Client Access.*
Counselors recognize that counseling records are kept for the benefit of clients, and therefore provide access to records and copies of records when requested by competent clients, unless the records contain information that may be misleading and detrimental to the client. In situations involving multiple clients, access to records is limited to those parts of records that do not include confidential information related to another client. (See A.8., B.1.a., and B.2.b.)

e. *Disclosure or Transfer.*
Counselors obtain written permission from clients to disclose or transfer records to legitimate third parties unless exceptions to confidentiality exist as listed in Section B.1. Steps are taken to ensure that receivers of counseling records are sensitive to their confidential nature.

B.5. Research and Training

a. *Data Disguise Required.*
Use of data derived from counseling relationships for purposes of training, research, or publication is confined to content that is disguised to ensure the anonymity of the individuals involved. (See B.1.g. and G.3.d.)

b. *Agreement for Identification.*
Identification of a client in a presentation or publication is permissible only when the client has reviewed the material and has agreed to its presentation or publication. (See G.3.d.)

B.6. Consultation

a. *Respect for Privacy.*
Information obtained in a consulting relationship is discussed for professional purposes only with persons clearly concerned with the case. Written and oral reports present data germane to the purposes of the consultation, and every effort is made to protect client identity and avoid undue invasion of privacy.

b. *Cooperating Agencies.*
Before sharing information, counselors make efforts to ensure that there are defined policies in other agen-

cies serving the counselor's clients that effectively protect the confidentiality of information.

SECTION C: PROFESSIONAL RESPONSIBILITY

C.1. Standards Knowledge

Counselors have a responsibility to read, understand, and follow the Code of Ethics and the Standards of Practice.

C.2. Professional Competence

a. *Boundaries of Competence.*

Counselors practice only within the boundaries of their competence, based on their education, training, supervised experience, state and national professional credentials, and appropriate professional experience. Counselors will demonstrate a commitment to gain knowledge, personal awareness, sensitivity, and skills pertinent to working with a diverse client population.

b. *New Specialty Areas of Practice.*

Counselors practice in specialty areas new to them only after appropriate education, training, and supervised experience. While developing skills in new specialty areas, counselors take steps to ensure the competence of their work and to protect others from possible harm.

c. *Qualified for Employment.*

Counselors accept employment only for positions for which they are qualified by education, training, supervised experience, state and national professional credentials, and appropriate professional experience. Counselors hire for professional counseling positions only individuals who are qualified and competent.

d. *Monitor Effectiveness.*

Counselors continually monitor their effectiveness as professionals and take steps to improve when necessary. Counselors in private practice take reasonable steps to seek out peer supervision to evaluate their efficacy as counselors.

e. *Ethical Issues Consultation.*

Counselors take reasonable steps to consult with other counselors or related professionals when they have questions regarding their ethical obligations or professional practice. (See H.1.)

f. *Continuing Education.*

Counselors recognize the need for continuing education to maintain a reasonable level of awareness of current scientific and professional information in their fields of activity. They take steps to maintain

competence in the skills they use, are open to new procedures, and keep current with the diverse and/or special populations with whom they work.

g. *Impairment.*

Counselors refrain from offering or accepting professional services when their physical, mental, or emotional problems are likely to harm a client or others. They are alert to the signs of impairment, seek assistance for problems, and, if necessary, limit, suspend, or terminate their professional responsibilities. (See A.11.c.)

C.3. Advertising and Soliciting Clients

a. *Accurate Advertising.*

There are no restrictions on advertising by counselors except those that can be specifically justified to protect the public from deceptive practices. Counselors advertise or represent their services to the public by identifying their credentials in an accurate manner that is not false, misleading, deceptive, or fraudulent. Counselors may only advertise the highest degree earned which is in counseling or a closely related field from a college or university that was accredited when the degree was awarded by one of the regional accrediting bodies recognized by the Council on Postsecondary Accreditation.

b. *Testimonials.*

Counselors who use testimonials do not solicit them from clients or other persons who, because of their particular circumstances, may be vulnerable to undue influence.

c. *Statements by Others.*

Counselors make reasonable efforts to ensure that statements made by others about them or the profession of counseling are accurate.

d. *Recruiting Through Employment.*

Counselors do not use their places of employment or institutional affiliation to recruit or gain clients, supervisees, or consultees for their private practices. (See C.5.e.)

e. *Products and Training Advertisements.*

Counselors who develop products related to their profession or conduct workshops or training events ensure that the advertisements concerning these products or events are accurate and disclose adequate information for consumers to make informed choices.

f. *Promoting to Those Served.*

Counselors do not use counseling, teaching, training, or supervisory relationships to promote their products or training events in a manner that is deceptive or would exert undue influence on individuals who may be vulnerable. Counselors may adopt textbooks they have authored for instruction purposes.

g. Professional Association Involvement.
Counselors actively participate in local, state, and national associations that foster the development and improvement of counseling.

C.4. Credentials

a. Credentials Claimed.
Counselors claim or imply only professional credentials possessed and are responsible for correcting any known misrepresentations of their credentials by others. Professional credentials include graduate degrees in counseling or closely related mental health fields, accreditation of graduate programs, national voluntary certifications, government-issued certifications or licenses, ACA professional membership, or any other credential that might indicate to the public specialized knowledge or expertise in counseling.

b. ACA Professional Membership.
ACA professional members may announce to the public their membership status. Regular members may not announce their ACA membership in a manner that might imply they are credentialed counselors.

c. Credential Guidelines.
Counselors follow the guidelines for use of credentials that have been established by the entities that issue the credentials.

d. Misrepresentation of Credentials.
Counselors do not attribute more to their credentials than the credentials represent, and do not imply that other counselors are not qualified because they do not possess certain credentials.

e. Doctoral Degrees from Other Fields.
Counselors who hold a master's degree in counseling or a closely related mental health field, but hold a doctoral degree from other than counseling or a closely related field, do not use the title, "Dr." in their practices and do not announce to the public in relation to their practice or status as a counselor that they hold a doctorate.

C.5. Public Responsibility

a. Nondiscrimination.
Counselors do not discriminate against clients, students, or supervisees in a manner that has a negative impact based on their age, color, culture, disability, ethnic group, gender, race, religion, sexual orientation, or socioeconomic status, or for any other reason. (See A.2.a.)

b. Sexual Harassment.
Counselors do not engage in sexual harassment. Sexual harassment is defined as sexual solicitation, physical advances, or verbal or nonverbal conduct that is sexual in nature, that occurs in connection with professional activities or roles, and that either: (1) is unwelcome, is offensive, or creates a hostile workplace environment, and counselors know or are told this; or (2) is sufficiently severe or intense to be perceived as harassment to a reasonable person in the context. Sexual harassment can consist of a single intense or severe act or multiple persistent or pervasive acts.

c. Reports to Third Parties.
Counselors are accurate, honest, and unbiased in reporting their professional activities and judgments to appropriate third parties including courts, health insurance companies, those who are the recipients of evaluation reports, and others. (See B.1.g.)

d. Media Presentations.
When counselors provide advice or comment by means of public lectures, demonstrations, radio or television programs, prerecorded tapes, printed articles, mailed material, or other media, they take reasonable precautions to ensure that (1) the statements are based on appropriate professional counseling literature and practice; (2) the statements are otherwise consistent with the Code of Ethics and the Standards of Practice; and (3) the recipients of the information are not encouraged to infer that a professional counseling relationship has been established. (See C.6.b.)

e. Unjustified Gains.
Counselors do not use their professional positions to seek or receive unjustified personal gains, sexual favors, unfair advantage, or unearned goods or services. (See C.3.d.)

C.6. Responsibility to Other Professionals

a. Different Approaches.
Counselors are respectful of approaches to professional counseling that differ from their own. Counselors know and take into account the traditions and practices of other professional groups with which they work.

b. Personal Public Statements.
When making personal statements in a public context, counselors clarify that they are speaking from their personal perspectives and that they are not

speaking on behalf of all counselors or the profession. (See C.5.d.)

c. *Clients Served by Others.*
When counselors learn that their clients are in a professional relationship with another mental health professional, they request release from clients to inform the other professionals and strive to establish positive and collaborative professional relationships. (See A.4.)

SECTION D: RELATIONSHIPS WITH OTHER PROFESSIONALS

D.1. Relationships With Employers and Employees

a. *Role Definition.*
Counselors define and describe for their employers and employees the parameters and levels of their professional roles.

b. *Agreements.*
Counselors establish working agreements with supervisors, colleagues, and subordinates regarding counseling or clinical relationships, confidentiality, adherence to professional standards, distinction between public and private material, maintenance and dissemination of recorded information, work load, and accountability. Working agreements in each instance are specified and made known to those concerned.

c. *Negative Conditions.*
Counselors alert their employers to conditions that may be potentially disruptive or damaging to the counselor's professional responsibilities or that may limit their effectiveness.

d. *Evaluation.*
Counselors submit regularly to professional review and evaluation by their supervisor or the appropriate representative of the employer.

e. *In-Service.*
Counselors are responsible for in-service development of self and staff.

f. *Goals.*
Counselors inform their staff of goals and programs.

g. *Practices.*
Counselors provide personnel and agency practices that respect and enhance the rights and welfare of each employee and recipient of agency services. Counselors strive to maintain the highest levels of professional services.

h. *Personnel Selection and Assignment.*
Counselors select competent staff and assign responsibilities compatible with their skills and experiences.

i. *Discrimination.*
Counselors, as either employers or employees, do not engage in or condone practices that are inhumane, illegal, or unjustifiable (such as considerations based on age, color, culture, disability, ethnic group, gender, race, religion, sexual orientation, or socioeconomic status) in hiring, promotion, or training. (See A.2.a. and C.5.b.)

j. *Professional Conduct.* Counselors have a responsibility both to clients and to the agency or institution within which services are performed to maintain high standards of professional conduct.

k. *Exploitative Relationships.* Counselors do not engage in exploitative relationships with individuals over whom they have supervisory, evaluative, or instructional control or authority.

l. *Employer Policies.* The acceptance of employment in an agency or institution implies that counselors are in agreement with its general policies and principles. Counselors strive to reach agreement with employers as to acceptable standards of conduct that allow for changes in institutional policy conducive to the growth and development of clients.

D.2. Consultation (See B.6.)

a. *Consultation as an Option.*
Counselors may choose to consult with any other professionally competent persons about their clients. In choosing consultants, counselors avoid placing the consultant in a conflict of interest situation that would preclude the consultant being a proper party to the counselor's efforts to help the client. Should counselors be engaged in a work setting that compromises this consultation standard, they consult with other professionals whenever possible to consider justifiable alternatives.

b. *Consultant Competency.*
Counselors are reasonably certain that they have or the organization represented has the necessary competencies and resources for giving the kind of consulting services needed and that appropriate referral resources are available.

c. *Understanding with Clients.*
When providing consultation, counselors attempt to develop with their clients a clear understanding of problem definition, goals for change, and predicted consequences of interventions selected.

d. *Consultant Goals.*

The consulting relationship is one in which client adaptability and growth toward self-direction are consistently encouraged and cultivated. (See A.1.b.)

D.3. Fees for Referral

a. *Accepting Fees from Agency Clients.*

Counselors refuse a private fee or other remuneration for rendering services to persons who are entitled to such services through the counselor's employing agency or institution. The policies of a particular agency may make explicit provisions for agency clients to receive counseling services from members of its staff in private practice. In such instances, the clients must be informed of other options open to them should they seek private counseling services. (See A.10.a., A.11.b., and C.3.d.)

b. *Referral Fees.*

Counselors do not accept a referral fee from other professionals.

D.4. Subcontractor Arrangements

When counselors work as subcontractors for counseling services for a third party, they have a duty to inform clients of the limitations of confidentiality that the organization may place on counselors in providing counseling services to clients. The limits of such confidentiality ordinarily are discussed as part of the intake session. (See B.1.e. and B.1.f.)

SECTION E: EVALUATION, ASSESSMENT, AND INTERPRETATION

E.1. General

a. *Appraisal Techniques.*

The primary purpose of educational and psychological assessment is to provide measures that are objective and interpretable in either comparative or absolute terms. Counselors recognize the need to interpret the statements in this section as applying to the whole range of appraisal techniques, including test and nontest data.

b. *Client Welfare.*

Counselors promote the welfare and best interests of the client in the development, publication, and utilization of educational and psychological assessment techniques. They do not misuse assessment results and interpretations and take reasonable steps to prevent others from misusing the information these techniques provide. They respect the client's right to know the results, the interpretations made, and the bases for their conclusions and recommendations.

E.2. Competence to Use and Interpret Tests

a. *Limits of Competence.*

Counselors recognize the limits of their competence and perform only those testing and assessment services for which they have been trained. They are familiar with reliability, validity, related standardization, error of measurement, and proper application of any technique utilized. Counselors using computer-based test interpretations are trained in the construct being measured and the specific instrument being used prior to using this type of computer application. Counselors take reasonable measures to ensure the proper use of psychological assessment techniques by persons under their supervision.

b. *Appropriate Use.*

Counselors are responsible for the appropriate application, scoring, interpretation, and use of assessment instruments, whether they score and interpret such tests themselves or use computerized or other services.

c. *Decisions Based on Results.*

Counselors responsible for decisions involving individuals or policies that are based on assessment results have a thorough understanding of educational and psychological measurement, including validation criteria, test research, and guidelines for test development and use.

d. *Accurate Information.*

Counselors provide accurate information and avoid false claims or misconceptions when making statements about assessment instruments or techniques. Special efforts are made to avoid unwarranted connotations of such terms as IQ and grade equivalent scores. (See C.5.c.)

E.3. Informed Consent

a. *Explanation to Clients.*

Prior to assessment, counselors explain the nature and purposes of assessment and the specific use of results in language the client (or other legally authorized person on behalf of the client) can understand, unless an explicit exception to this right has been agreed upon in advance. Regardless of whether scoring and interpretation are completed by counselors, by assistants, or by computer or other outside services, counselors take reasonable steps to ensure that appropriate explanations are given to the client.

b. *Recipients of Results.*

The examinee's welfare, explicit understanding, and prior agreement determine the recipients of test results. Counselors include accurate and appropriate interpretations with any release of individual or group test results. (See B.1.a. and C.5.c.)

E.4. Release of Information to Competent Professionals

a. Misuse of Results.
Counselors do not misuse assessment results, including test results, and interpretations, and take reasonable steps to prevent the misuse of such by others. (See C.5.c.)

b. Release of Raw Data.
Counselors ordinarily release data (e.g., protocols, counseling or interview notes, or questionnaires) in which the client is identified only with the consent of the client or the client's legal representative. Such data are usually released only to persons recognized by counselors as competent to interpret the data. (See B.1.a.)

E.5. Proper Diagnosis of Mental Disorders

a. Proper Diagnosis.
Counselors take special care to provide proper diagnosis of mental disorders. Assessment techniques (including personal interview) used to determine client care (e.g., locus of treatment, type of treatment, or recommended follow-up) are carefully selected and appropriately used. (See A.3.a. and C.5.c.)

b. Cultural Sensitivity.
Counselors recognize that culture affects the manner in which clients' problems are defined. Clients' socioeconomic and cultural experience is considered when diagnosing mental disorders.

E.6. Test Selection

a. Appropriateness of Instruments.
Counselors carefully consider the validity, reliability, psychometric limitations, and appropriateness of instruments when selecting tests for use in a given situation or with a particular client.

b. Culturally Diverse Populations.
Counselors are cautious when selecting tests for culturally diverse populations to avoid inappropriateness of testing that may be outside of socialized behavioral or cognitive patterns.

E.7. Conditions of Test Administration

a. Administration Conditions.
Counselors administer tests under the same conditions that were established in their standardization.

When tests are not administered under standard conditions or when unusual behavior or irregularities occur during the testing session, those conditions are noted in interpretation, and the results may be designated as invalid or of questionable validity.

b. Computer Administration.
Counselors are responsible for ensuring that administration programs function properly to provide clients with accurate results when a computer or other electronic methods are used for test administration. (See A.12.b.)

c. Unsupervised Test Taking.
Counselors do not permit unsupervised or inadequately supervised use of tests or assessments unless the tests or assessments are designed, intended, and validated for self-administration and/or scoring.

d. Disclosure of Favorable Conditions.
Prior to test administration, conditions that produce most favorable test results are made known to the examinee.

E.8. Diversity in Testing

Counselors are cautious in using assessment techniques, making evaluations, and interpreting the performance of populations not represented in the norm group on which an instrument was standardized. They recognize the effects of age, color, culture, disability, ethnic group, gender, race, religion, sexual orientation, and socioeconomic status on test administration and interpretation and place test results in proper perspective with other relevant factors. (See A.2.a.)

E.9. Test Scoring and Interpretation

a. Reporting Reservations.
In reporting assessment results, counselors indicate any reservations that exist regarding validity or reliability because of the circumstances of the assessment or the inappropriateness of the norms for the person tested.

b. Research Instruments.
Counselors exercise caution when interpreting the results of research instruments possessing insufficient technical data to support respondent results. The specific purposes for the use of such instruments are stated explicitly to the examinee.

c. Testing Services.
Counselors who provide test scoring and test interpretation services to support the assessment process

confirm the validity of such interpretations. They accurately describe the purpose, norms, validity, reliability, and applications of the procedures and any special qualifications applicable to their use. The public offering of an automated test interpretations service is considered a professional-to-professional consultation. The formal responsibility of the consultant is to the consultee, but the ultimate and overriding responsibility is to the client.

E.10. Test Security

Counselors maintain the integrity and security of tests and other assessment techniques consistent with legal and contractual obligations. Counselors do not appropriate, reproduce, or modify published tests or parts thereof without acknowledgment and permission from the publisher.

E.11. Obsolete Tests and Outdated Test Results

Counselors do not use data or test results that are obsolete or outdated for the current purpose. Counselors make every effort to prevent the misuse of obsolete measures and test data by others.

E.12. Test Construction

Counselors use established scientific procedures, relevant standards, and current professional knowledge for test design in the development, publication, and utilization of educational and psychological assessment techniques.

SECTION F: TEACHING, TRAINING, AND SUPERVISION

F.1. Counselor Educators and Trainers

a. *Educators as Teachers and Practitioners.*
Counselors who are responsible for developing, implementing, and supervising educational programs are skilled as teachers and practitioners. They are knowledgeable regarding the ethical, legal, and regulatory aspects of the profession, are skilled in applying that knowledge, and make students and supervisees aware of their responsibilities. Counselors conduct counselor education and training programs in an ethical manner and serve as role models for professional behavior. Counselor educators should make an effort to infuse material related to human diversity into all courses and/or workshops that are designed to promote the development of professional counselors.

b. *Relationship Boundaries with Students and Supervisees.*
Counselors clearly define and maintain ethical, professional, and social relationship boundaries with their students and supervisees. They are aware of the differential in power that exists and the student's or supervisee's possible incomprehension of that power differential. Counselors explain to students and supervisees the potential for the relationship to become exploitive.

c. *Sexual Relationships.*
Counselors do not engage in sexual relationships with students or supervisees and do not subject them to sexual harassment. (See A.6. and C.5.b)

d. *Contributions to Research.*
Counselors give credit to students or supervisees for their contributions to research and scholarly projects. Credit is given through coauthorship, acknowledgment, footnote statement, or other appropriate means, in accordance with such contributions. (See G.4.b. and G.4.c.)

e. *Close Relatives.*
Counselors do not accept close relatives as students or supervisees.

f. *Supervision Preparation.*
Counselors who offer clinical supervision services are adequately prepared in supervision methods and techniques. Counselors who are doctoral students serving as practicum or internship supervisors to master's level students are adequately prepared and supervised by the training program.

g. *Responsibility for Services to Clients.*
Counselors who supervise the counseling services of others take reasonable measures to ensure that counseling services provided to clients are professional.

h. *Endorsement.*
Counselors do not endorse students or supervisees for certification, licensure, employment, or completion of an academic or training program if they believe students or supervisees are not qualified for the endorsement. Counselors take reasonable steps to assist students or supervisees who are not qualified for endorsement to become qualified.

F.2. Counselor Education and Training Programs

a. *Orientation.*
Prior to admission, counselors orient prospective students to the counselor education or training program's expectations, including but not limited to the following: (1) the type and level of skill acquisition required for successful completion of the training, (2) subject matter to be covered, (3) basis for evaluation,

(4) training components that encourage self-growth or self-disclosure as part of the training process, (5) the type of supervision settings and requirements of the sites for required clinical field experiences, (6) student and supervisee evaluation and dismissal policies and procedures, and (7) up-to-date employment prospects for graduates.

b. *Integration of Study and Practice.*
Counselors establish counselor education and training programs that integrate academic study and supervised practice.

c. *Evaluation.*
Counselors clearly state to students and supervisees, in advance of training, the levels of competency expected, appraisal methods, and timing of evaluations for both didactic and experiential components. Counselors provide students and supervisees with periodic performance appraisal and evaluation feedback throughout the training program.

d. *Teaching Ethics.*
Counselors make students and supervisees aware of the ethical responsibilities and standards of the profession and the students' and supervisees' ethical responsibilities to the profession. (See C.1. and F.3.e.)

e. *Peer Relationships.*
When students or supervisees are assigned to lead counseling groups or provide clinical supervision for their peers, counselors take steps to ensure that students and supervisees placed in these roles do not have personal or adverse relationships with peers and that they understand they have the same ethical obligations as counselor educators, trainers, and supervisors. Counselors make every effort to ensure that the rights of peers are not compromised when students or supervisees are assigned to lead counseling groups or provide clinical supervision.

f. *Varied Theoretical Positions.*
Counselors present varied theoretical positions so that students and supervisees may make comparisons and have opportunities to develop their own positions. Counselors provide information concerning the scientific bases of professional practice. (See C.6.a.)

g. *Field Placements.*
Counselors develop clear policies within their training program regarding field placement and other clinical experiences. Counselors provide clearly stated roles and responsibilities for the student or supervisee, the site supervisor, and the program supervisor.

They confirm that site supervisors are qualified to provide supervision and are informed of their professional and ethical responsibilities in this role.

h. *Dual Relationships as Supervisors.*
Counselors avoid dual relationships such as performing the role of site supervisor and training program supervisor in the student's or supervisee's training program. Counselors do not accept any form of professional services, fees, commissions, reimbursement, or remuneration from a site for student or supervisee placement.

i. *Diversity in Programs.*
Counselors are responsive to their institution's and program's recruitment and retention needs for training program administrators, faculty, and students with diverse backgrounds and special needs. (See A.2.a.)

F.3. Students and Supervisees

a. *Limitations.*
Counselors, through ongoing evaluation and appraisal, are aware of the academic and personal limitations of students and supervisees that might impede performance. Counselors assist students and supervisees in securing remedial assistance when needed, and dismiss from the training program supervisees who are unable to provide competent service due to academic or personal limitations. Counselors seek professional consultation and document their decision to dismiss or refer students or supervisees for assistance. Counselors ensure that students and supervisees have recourse to address decisions made to require them to seek assistance or to dismiss them.

b. *Self-Growth Experiences.*
Counselors use professional judgment when designing training experiences conducted by the counselors themselves that require student and supervisee self-growth or self-disclosure. Safeguards are provided so that students and supervisees are aware of the ramifications their self-disclosure may have on counselors whose primary role as teacher, trainer, or supervisor requires acting on ethical obligations to the profession. Evaluative components of experiential training experiences explicitly delineate predetermined academic standards that are separate and not dependent on the student's level of self-disclosure. (See A.6.)

c. *Counseling for Students and Supervisees.*
If students or supervisees request counseling, supervisors or counselor educators provide them with ac-

ceptable referrals. Supervisors or counselor educators do not serve as counselor to students or supervisees over whom they hold administrative, teaching, or evaluative roles unless this is a brief role associated with a training experience. (See A.6.b.)

d. *Clients of Students and Supervisees.*
Counselors make every effort to ensure that the clients at field placements are aware of the services rendered and the qualifications of the students and supervisees rendering those services. Clients receive professional disclosure information and are informed of the limits of confidentiality. Client permission is obtained in order for the students and supervisees to use any information concerning the counseling relationship in the training process. (See B.1.e.)

e. *Standards for Students and Supervisees.*
Students and supervisees preparing to become counselors adhere to the Code of Ethics and the Standards of Practice. Students and supervisees have the same obligations to clients as those required of counselors. (See H.1.)

SECTION G: RESEARCH AND PUBLICATION

G.1. Research Responsibilities

a. *Use of Human Subjects.*
Counselors plan, design, conduct, and report research in a manner consistent with pertinent ethical principles, federal and state laws, host institutional regulations, and scientific standards governing research with human subjects. Counselors design and conduct research that reflects cultural sensitivity appropriateness.

b. *Deviation from Standard Practices.*
Counselors seek consultation and observe stringent safeguards to protect the rights of research participants when a research problem suggests a deviation from standard acceptable practices. (See B.6.)

c. *Precautions to Avoid Injury.*
Counselors who conduct research with human subjects are responsible for the subjects' welfare throughout the experiment and take reasonable precautions to avoid causing injurious psychological, physical, or social effects to their subjects.

d. *Principal Researcher Responsibility.*
The ultimate responsibility for ethical research practice lies with the principal researcher. All others involved in the research activities share ethical obligations and full responsibility for their own actions.

e. *Minimal Interference.*
Counselors take reasonable precautions to avoid causing disruptions in subjects' lives due to participation in research.

f. *Diversity.*
Counselors are sensitive to diversity and research issues with special populations. They seek consultation when appropriate. (See A.2.a. and B.6.)

G.2. Informed Consent

a. *Topics Disclosed.*
In obtaining informed consent for research, counselors use language that is understandable to research participants and that: (1) accurately explains the purpose and procedures to be followed; (2) identifies any procedures that are experimental or relatively untried; (3) describes the attendant discomforts and risks; (4) describes the benefits or changes in individuals or organizations that might be reasonably expected; (5) discloses appropriate alternative procedures that would be advantageous for subjects; (6) offers to answer any inquiries concerning the procedures; (7) describes any limitations on confidentiality; and (8) instructs that subjects are free to withdraw their consent and to discontinue participation in the project at any time. (See B.1.f.)

b. *Deception.*
Counselors do not conduct research involving deception unless alternative procedures are not feasible and the prospective value of the research justifies the deception. When the methodological requirements of a study necessitate concealment or deception, the investigator is required to explain clearly the reasons for this action as soon as possible.

c. *Voluntary Participation.*
Participation in research is typically voluntary and without any penalty for refusal to participate. Involuntary participation is appropriate only when it can be demonstrated that participation will have no harmful effects on subjects and is essential to the investigation.

d. *Confidentiality of Information.*
Information obtained about research participants during the course of an investigation is confidential. When the possibility exists that others may obtain access to such information, ethical research practice requires that the possibility, together with the plans for protecting confidentiality, be explained to participants as a part of the procedure for obtaining informed consent. (See B.1.e.)

e. *Persons Incapable of Giving Informed Consent.*
When a person is incapable of giving informed consent, counselors provide an appropriate explanation, obtain agreement for participation, and obtain appropriate consent from a legally authorized person.

f. *Commitments to Participants.*
Counselors take reasonable measures to honor all commitments to research participants.

g. *Explanations After Data Collection.*
After data are collected, counselors provide participants with full clarification of the nature of the study to remove any misconceptions. Where scientific or human values justify delaying or withholding information, counselors take reasonable measures to avoid causing harm.

h. *Agreements to Cooperate.*
Counselors who agree to cooperate with another individual in research or publication incur an obligation to cooperate as promised in terms of punctuality of performance and with regard to the completeness and accuracy of the information required.

i. *Informed Consent for Sponsors.*
In the pursuit of research, counselors give sponsors, institutions, and publication channels the same respect and opportunity for giving informed consent that they accord to individual research participants. Counselors are aware of their obligation to future research workers and ensure that host institutions are given feedback information and proper acknowledgment.

G.3. Reporting Results

a. *Information Affecting Outcome.*
When reporting research results, counselors explicitly mention all variables and conditions known to the investigator that may have affected the outcome of a study or the interpretation of data.

b. *Accurate Results.*
Counselors plan, conduct, and report research accurately and in a manner that minimizes the possibility that results will be misleading. They provide thorough discussions of the limitations of their data and alternative hypotheses. Counselors do not engage in fraudulent research, distort data, misrepresent data, or deliberately bias their results.

c. *Obligation to Report Unfavorable Results.*
Counselors communicate to other counselors the results of any research judged to be of professional value. Results that reflect unfavorably on institutions, programs, services, prevailing opinions, or vested interests are not withheld.

d. *Identity of Subjects.*
Counselors who supply data, aid in the research of another person, report research results, or make original data available take due care to disguise the identity of respective subjects in the absence of specific authorization from the subjects to do otherwise. (See B.1.g. and B.5.a.)

e. *Replication Studies.*
Counselors are obligated to make available sufficient original research data to qualified professionals who may wish to replicate the study.

G.4. Publication

a. *Recognition of Others.*
When conducting and reporting research, counselors are familiar with and give recognition to previous work on the topic, observe copyright laws, and give full credit to those to whom credit is due. (See F.1.d. and G.4.c.)

b. *Contributors.*
Counselors give credit through joint authorship, acknowledgment, footnote statements, or other appropriate means to those who have contributed significantly to research or concept development in accordance with such contributions. The principal contributor is listed first and minor technical or professional contributions are acknowledged in notes or introductory statements.

c. *Student Research.*
For an article that is substantially based on a student's dissertation or thesis, the student is listed as the principal author. (See F.1.d. and G.4.a.)

d. *Duplicate Submission.*
Counselors submit manuscripts for consideration to only one journal at a time. Manuscripts that are published in whole or in substantial part in another journal or published work are not submitted for publication without acknowledgment and permission from the previous publication.

e. *Professional Review.*
Counselors who review material submitted for publication, research, or other scholarly purposes respect the confidentiality and proprietary rights of those who submitted it.

SECTION H: RESOLVING ETHICAL ISSUES

H.1. Knowledge of Standards

Counselors are familiar with the Code of Ethics and the Standards of Practice and other applicable ethics codes from other professional organizations of which they are member, or from certification and licensure bodies. Lack of knowledge or misunderstanding of an ethical responsibility is not a defense against a charge of unethical conduct. (See F.3.e.)

H.2. Suspected Violations

a. *Ethical Behavior Expected.*

Counselors expect professional associates to adhere to the Code of Ethics. When counselors possess reasonable cause that raises doubts as to whether a counselor is acting in an ethical manner, they take appropriate action. (See H.2.d. and H.2.e.)

b. *Consultation.*

When uncertain as to whether a particular situation or course of action may be in violation of the Code of Ethics, counselors consult with other counselors who are knowledgeable about ethics, with colleagues, or with appropriate authorities.

c. *Organization Conflicts.*

If the demands of an organization with which counselors are affiliated pose a conflict with the Code of Ethics, counselors specify the nature of such conflicts and express to their supervisors or other responsible officials their commitment to the Code of Ethics. When possible, counselors work toward change within the organization to allow full adherence to the Code of Ethics.

d. *Informal Resolution.*

When counselors have reasonable cause to believe that another counselor is violating an ethical standard, they attempt to first resolve the issue informally with the other counselor if feasible, providing that such action does not violate confidentiality rights that may be involved.

e. *Reporting Suspected Violations.*

When an informal resolution is not appropriate or feasible, counselors, upon reasonable cause, take action such as reporting the suspected ethical violation to state or national ethics committees, unless this action conflicts with confidentiality rights that cannot be resolved.

f. *Unwarranted Complaints.*

Counselors do not initiate, participate in, or encourage the filing of ethics complaints that are unwarranted or intend to harm a counselor rather than to protect clients or the public.

H.3. Cooperation with Ethics Committees

Counselors assist in the process of enforcing the Code of Ethics. Counselors cooperate with investigations, proceedings, and requirements of the ACA Ethics Committee or ethics committees of other duly constituted associations or boards having jurisdiction over those charged with a violation. Counselors are familiar with the ACA Policies and Procedures and use it as a reference in assisting the enforcement of the Code of Ethics.

© American Counseling Association. Reprinted with permission.

AMERICAN DANCE THERAPY ASSOCIATION

Address:	2000 Century Plaza, Suite 108
	10632 Little Patuxent Parkway
	Columbia, MD 21044-3263
Telephone:	410/997-4040
WWW:	www.adta.org
Document:	Code of Ethical Practice of the
	American Dance Therapy
	Association (1969. Most recently
	revised 1997.)

(This code is designed to be used together with the *Ethical Standards of Practice of Dance Therapists Registered, Members of the Academy of Dance Therapists Registered, and Members of the American Dance Therapy Association*. Concomitant with the *Code of Ethical Practice*, the *Standards* are guidelines for personal conduct and serve as a model for practicing dance/movement therapists. The *Standards* are not reprinted here. — Eds.)

PREFACE TO CODE: The following Code of Ethical Practice sets forth ethical obligations of dance/movement therapists. The purpose of the Code is to define responsible professional behavior for dance/movement therapists and make this known to the community at large.

The ADTA defines dance/movement therapy as "the psychotherapeutic use of movement as a process which furthers the emotional, physical, cognitive and social integration of the individual."

The ethical obligations set forth in the principles below are rules of conduct governing the individual dance/movement therapist and the profession of dance/movement therapy for the purpose of protecting the public, safeguarding professional standards and fostering individual moral integrity.

At this time, no state has established license structures specifically for dance/movement therapists. However, in some states dance/movement therapists may qualify for licensure under other professional titles. Members of the American Dance Therapy Association, Dance Therapists Registered and members of the Academy of Dance Therapists Registered, are advised to carefully investigate their own state license structures as a means of staying informed of professional and legal rights and obligations of therapists, as well as legal rights and requirements for private practice.

CODE

A dance/movement therapist:

1. Practices upon completion of professional education and training and does not misrepresent the level of training completed.
2. Adheres to the treatment responsibilities of the therapeutic contract.
3. Knows and complies fully, with all laws and regulations pertaining to the protection of the public in the practice of dance/movement therapy.
4. Practices under supervision appropriate to professional status.
5. a. Engages in dance/movement therapy practice only when identified by the American Dance Therapy Association as a Dance Therapist Registered (DTR).
   b. Engages in private dance/movement therapy practice or training of dance/movement therapists only when identified by the American Dance Therapy Association as a member of the Academy of Dance Therapists Registered (ADTR).
6. Respects and protects the legal and personal rights of clients.

7. Affiliates professionally with individuals or organizations which practice according to approved ethical standards.
8. Represents the profession and the individual roles within the profession honestly; adheres to professional standards in announcing services and reporting unprofessional conduct.
9. Practices solely in the areas for which one has been trained and is professionally qualified to perform.
10. Plans and conducts dance/movement therapy consistent with overall treatment program of the setting.
11. A dance/movement therapist is qualified to engage in assessment of clients for the purposes of diagnosis, treatment planning, and/or research.

© American Dance Therapy Association. Reprinted with permission.

AMERICAN DENTAL ASSISTANTS ASSOCIATION

Address: 203 North LaSalle Street, Suite 1320
Chicago, IL 60601-1225
Telephone: 312/541-1550 or 800/733-2322
WWW: members.aol.com/adaa1/index.html
Document: Principles of Ethics and Code of Professional Conduct (1980)

FOREWORD

As an organization charged with representing a part of the professional individuals involved in the practice of dentistry, the American Dental Assistants Association has delineated the Principles of Ethics and the Code of Professional Conduct for members, officers and trustees. The Principles of Ethics are general goals to which each member should aspire and are not intended to be enforceable as rules of conduct for dental assistants. The Code of Professional Conduct is intended for use as a guide for the evaluation of elected officials and members.

AMERICAN DENTAL ASSISTANTS ASSOCIATION PRINCIPALS OF ETHICS

Each individual involved in the practice of dentistry assumes the obligation of maintaining and enriching the profession. Each member may choose to meet this obligation according to the dictates of personal conscience based on the needs of the human beings the profession of dentistry is committed to serve.

The spirit of the Golden Rule is the basic guiding principle of this concept. The member must strive to at all times maintain confidentiality, and exhibit respect for the dentist/employer. The member shall refrain from performing any professional service which is prohibited by state law and has the obligation to prove competence prior to providing services to any patient. The member shall constantly strive to upgrade and expand technical skills for the benefit of the employer and the consumer public. The member should additionally seek to sustain and improve the Local Organization, State Association, and the American Dental Assistants Association by active participation and personal commitment.

CODE OF PROFESSIONAL CONDUCT

As a member of the American Dental Assistants Association, I pledge to:

- Abide by the Bylaws of the Association;
- Maintain loyalty to the Association;
- Pursue the objectives of the Association;
- Hold in confidence the information entrusted to me by the Association;
- Serve all members of the Association in an impartial manner;
- Recognize and follow all laws and regulations relating to activities of the Association;
- Maintain respect for the members and the employees of the Association;
- Exercise and insist on sound business principles in the conduct of the affairs of the Association;
- Use legal and ethical means to influence legislation or regulation affecting members of the Association;
- Issue no false or misleading statements to fellow members or to the public;
- Refrain from disseminating malicious information concerning the Association or any member or employee of the American Dental Assistants Association;
- Maintain high standards of personal conduct and integrity;

- To not imply Association endorsement of personal opinions or positions;
- Cooperate in a reasonable and proper manner with staff and members;
- Accept no personal compensation from fellow members, except as approved by the Association;
- Promote and maintain the highest standards or performance in service to the Association;
- Assure public confidence in the integrity and service of the Association.

© American Dental Assistants Association. Reprinted with permission.

AMERICAN DENTAL ASSOCIATION

Address:	211 East Chicago Avenue
	Chicago, IL 60611-2678
Telephone:	312/440-2500
WWW:	www.ada.org
Document:	ADA Principles of Ethics and Code
	of Professional Conduct (Most
	recently revised 1997.)

I. INTRODUCTION

The dental profession holds a special position of trust within society. As a consequence, society affords the profession certain privileges that are not available to members of the public-at-large. In return, the profession makes a commitment to society that its members will adhere to high ethical standards of conduct. These standards are embodied in the *ADA Principles of Ethics and Code of Professional Conduct (ADA Code)*. The *ADA Code* is, in effect, a written expression of the obligations arising from the implied contract between the dental profession and society.

Members of the ADA voluntarily agree to abide by the *ADA Code* as a condition of membership in the Association. They recognize that continued public trust in the dental profession is based on the commitment of individual dentists to high ethical standards of conduct.

The *ADA Code* has three main components: The **Principles of Ethics**, the **Code of Professional Conduct** and the **Advisory Opinions**.

The **Principles of Ethics** are the aspirational goals of the profession. They provide guidance and offer justification for the *Code of Professional Conduct* and the *Advisory Opinions*. There are five fundamental principles that form the foundation of the *ADA Code*: patient autonomy, nonmaleficence, beneficence, justice and veracity. Principles can overlap each other as well as compete with each other for priority. More than one principle can justify a given element of the *Code of Professional Conduct*. Principles may at times need to be balanced against each other, but, otherwise, they are the profession's firm guideposts.

The **Code of Professional Conduct** is an expression of specific types of conduct that are either required or prohibited. The *Code of Professional Conduct* is a product of the ADA's legislative system. All elements of the *Code of Professional Conduct* result from resolutions that are adopted by the ADA's House of Delegates. The *Code of Professional Conduct* is binding on members of the ADA, and violations may result in disciplinary action.

The **Advisory Opinions** are interpretations that apply the *Code of Professional Conduct* to specific fact situations. They are adopted by the ADA's Council on Ethics, Bylaws and Judicial Affairs to provide guidance to the membership on how the Council might interpret the *Code of Professional Conduct* in a disciplinary proceeding.

The *ADA Code* is an evolving document and by its very nature cannot be a complete articulation of all ethical obligations. The *ADA Code* is the result of an on-going dialogue between the dental profession and society, and as such, is subject to continuous review.

Although ethics and the law are closely related, they are not the same. Ethical obligations may—and often do—exceed legal duties. In resolving any ethical problem not explicitly covered by the *ADA Code*, dentists should consider the ethical principles, the patient's needs and interests, and any applicable laws.

II. PREAMBLE

The American Dental Association calls upon dentists to follow high ethical standards which have the benefit of the patient as their primary goal. Recognition of this goal, and of the education and training of a dentist, has resulted in society affording to the profession the privilege and obligation of self-government.

The Association believes that dentists should possess not only knowledge, skill and technical competence but also those traits of character that foster adherence to ethical principles. Qualities of compassion, kindness, integrity, fairness and charity complement the ethical practice of dentistry and help to define the true professional.

The ethical dentist strives to do that which is right and good. The *ADA Code* is an instrument to help the dentist in this quest.

III. PRINCIPLES, CODE OF PROFESSIONAL CONDUCT AND ADVISORY OPINIONS

SECTION 1—PRINCIPLE: PATIENT AUTONOMY ("self-governance"). The dentist has a duty to respect the patient's rights to self-determination and confidentiality.

This principle expresses the concept that professionals have a duty to treat the patient according to the patient's desires, within the bounds of accepted treatment, and to protect the patient's confidentiality. Under this principle, the dentist's primary obligations include involving patients in treatment decisions in a meaningful way, with due consideration being given to the patient's needs, desires and abilities, and safeguarding the patient's privacy.

CODE OF PROFESSIONAL CONDUCT

1.A. PATIENT INVOLVEMENT.
The dentist should inform the patient of the proposed treatment, and any reasonable alternatives, in a manner that allows the patient to become involved in treatment decisions.

1.B. PATIENT RECORDS.
Dentists are obliged to safeguard the confidentiality of patient records. Dentists shall maintain patient records in a manner consistent with the protection of the welfare of the patient. Upon request of a patient or another dental practitioner, dentists shall provide any information that will be beneficial for the future treatment of that patient.

ADVISORY OPINIONS

1.B.1. FURNISHING COPIES OF RECORDS.
A dentist has the ethical obligation on request of either the patient or the patient's new dentist to furnish, either gratuitously or for nominal cost, such dental records or copies or summaries of them, including dental X-rays or copies of them, as will be beneficial for the future treatment of that patient. This obligation exists whether or not the patient's account is paid in full.

1.B.2. CONFIDENTIALITY OF PATIENT RECORDS.
The dominant theme in Code Section 1-B is the protection of the confidentiality of a patient's

records. The statement in this section that relevant information in the records should be released to another dental practitioner assumes that the dentist requesting the information is the patient's present dentist. The former dentist should be free to provide the present dentist with relevant information from the patient's records. This may often be required for the protection of both the patient and the present dentist. There may be circumstances where the former dentist has an ethical obligation to inform the present dentist of certain facts. Dentists should be aware, however, that the laws of the various jurisdictions in the United States are not uniform, and some confidentiality laws appear to prohibit the transfer of pertinent information, such as HIV seropositivity. Absent certain knowledge that the laws of the dentist's jurisdiction permit the forwarding of this information, a dentist should obtain the patient's written permission before forwarding health records which contain information of a sensitive nature, such as HIV seropositivity, chemical dependency or sexual preference. If it is necessary for a treating dentist to consult with another dentist or physician with respect to the patient, and the circumstances do not permit the patient to remain anonymous, the treating dentist should seek the permission of the patient prior to the release of data from the patient's records to the consulting practitioner. If the patient refuses, the treating dentist should then contemplate obtaining legal advice regarding the termination of the dentist/patient relationship.

SECTION 2—PRINCIPLE: NONMALEFICENCE ("do no harm"). The dentist has a duty to refrain from harming the patient.

This principle expresses the concept that professionals have a duty to protect the patient from harm. Under this principle, the dentist's primary obligations include keeping knowledge and skills current, knowing one's own limitations and when to refer to a specialist or other professional, and knowing when and under what circumstances delegation of patient care to auxiliaries is appropriate.

CODE OF PROFESSIONAL CONDUCT
2.A. EDUCATION.

The privilege of dentists to be accorded professional status rests primarily in the knowledge, skill and experience with which they serve their patients and society. All dentists, therefore, have the obligation of keeping their knowledge and skill current.

2.B. CONSULTATION AND REFERRAL.

Dentists shall be obliged to seek consultation, if possible, whenever the welfare of patients will be safeguarded or advanced by utilizing those who have special skills, knowledge, and experience. When patients visit or are referred to specialists or consulting dentists for consultation:

1. The specialists or consulting dentists upon completion of their care shall return the patient, unless the patient expressly reveals a different preference, to the referring dentist, or, if none, to the dentist of record for future care.
2. The specialists shall be obliged when there is no referring dentist and upon a completion of their treatment to inform patients when there is a need for further dental care.

ADVISORY OPINION
2.B.1. SECOND OPINIONS.

A dentist who has a patient referred by a third party for a "second opinion" regarding a diagnosis or treatment plan recommended by the patient's treating dentist should render the requested second opinion in accordance with this Code of Ethics. In the interest of the patient being afforded quality care, the dentist rendering the second opinion should not have a vested interest in the ensuing recommendation.

2.C. USE OF AUXILIARY PERSONNEL.

Dentists shall be obliged to protect the health of their patients by only assigning to qualified auxiliaries those duties which can be legally delegated. Dentists shall be further obliged to prescribe and supervise the patient care provided by all auxiliary personnel working under their direction.

2.D. PERSONAL IMPAIRMENT.

It is unethical for a dentist to practice while abusing controlled substances, alcohol or other chemical agents which impair the ability to practice. All dentists have an ethical obligation to urge chemically impaired colleagues to seek treatment. Dentists with first-hand knowledge that a colleague is practicing dentistry when so impaired have an ethical responsibility to report such evidence to the professional assistance committee of a dental society.

ADVISORY OPINION
2.D.1. ABILITY TO PRACTICE.

A dentist who becomes ill from any disease or impaired in any way shall, with consultation and advice from a qualified physician or other authority, limit the activities of practice to those areas that do not endanger the patients or members of the dental staff.

SECTION 3—PRINCIPLE: BENEFICENCE

("do good"). The dentist has a duty to promote the patient's welfare.

This principle expresses the concept that professionals have a duty to act for the benefit of others. Under this principle, the dentist's primary obligation is service to the patient and the public-at-large. The most important aspect of this obligation is the competent and timely delivery of dental care within the bounds of clinical circumstances presented by the patient, with due consideration being given to the needs, desires and values of the patient. The same ethical considerations apply whether the dentist engages in fee-for-service, managed care or some other practice arrangement. Dentists may choose to enter into contracts governing the provision of care to a group of patients; however, contract obligations do not excuse dentists from their ethical duty to put the patient's welfare first.

CODE OF PROFESSIONAL CONDUCT
3.A. COMMUNITY SERVICE.

Since dentists have an obligation to use their skills, knowledge and experience for the improvement of the dental health of the public and are encouraged to be leaders in their community, dentists in such service shall conduct themselves in such a manner as to maintain or elevate the esteem of the profession.

3.B. GOVERNMENT OF A PROFESSION.

Every profession owes society the responsibility to regulate itself. Such regulation is achieved largely through the influence of the professional societies. All dentists, therefore, have the dual obligation of making themselves a part of a professional society and of observing its rules of ethics.

3.C. RESEARCH AND DEVELOPMENT.

Dentists have the obligation of making the results and benefits of their investigative efforts available to all when they are useful in safeguarding or promoting the health of the public.

3.D. PATENTS AND COPYRIGHTS.

Patents and copyrights may be secured by dentists provided that such patents and copyrights shall not be used to restrict research or practice.

3.E. CHILD ABUSE.

Dentists shall be obliged to become familiar with the perioral signs of child abuse and to report suspected cases to the proper authorities consistent with state laws.

SECTION 4—PRINCIPLE: JUSTICE ("fairness"). The dentist has a duty to treat people fairly.

This principle expresses the concept that professionals have a duty to be fair in their dealings with patients, colleagues and society. Under this principle, the dentist's primary obligations include dealing with people justly and delivering dental care without prejudice. In its broadest sense, this principle expresses the concept that the dental profession should actively seek allies throughout society on specific activities that will help improve access to care for all.

CODE OF PROFESSIONAL CONDUCT
4.A. PATIENT SELECTION.

While dentists, in serving the public, may exercise reasonable discretion in selecting patients for their practices, dentists shall not refuse to accept patients into their practice or deny dental service to patients because of the patient's race, creed, color, sex or national origin.

ADVISORY OPINION
4.A.1. HIV POSITIVE PATIENTS.

A dentist has the general obligation to provide care to those in need. A decision not to provide treatment to an individual because the individual has AIDS or is HIV seropositive, based solely on that fact, is unethical. Decisions with regard to the type of dental treatment provided or referrals made or suggested, in such instances should be made on the same basis as they are made with other patients, that is, whether the individual dentist believes he or she has need of another's skills, knowledge, equipment or experience and whether the dentist believes, after consultation with the patient's physician if appropriate, the patient's health status would be significantly compromised by the provision of dental treatment.

4.B. EMERGENCY SERVICE.

Dentists shall be obliged to make reasonable arrangements for the emergency care of their patients of record. Dentists shall be obliged when consulted in an emergency by patients not of record to make reasonable arrangements for emergency care. If treatment is provided, the dentist, upon completion of treatment, is obliged to return the patient to his or her regular dentist unless the patient expressly reveals a different preference.

4.C. JUSTIFIABLE CRITICISM.

Dentists shall be obliged to report to the appropriate reviewing agency as determined by the local component or constituent society instances of gross or continual faulty treatment by other dentists. Patients should be informed of their present oral health status without disparaging comment about prior services. Dentists issuing a public statement with respect to the profession shall have a reasonable basis to believe that the comments made are true.

ADVISORY OPINION
4.C.1. MEANING OF "JUSTIFIABLE."

A dentist's duty to the public imposes a responsibility to report instances of gross or continual faulty treatment. However, the heading of this section is "Justifiable Criticism." Therefore, when informing a patient of the status of his or her oral health, the dentist should exercise care that the comments made are justifiable. For example, a difference of opinion as to preferred treatment should not be communicated to the patient in a manner which would imply mistreatment. There will necessarily be cases where it will be difficult to determine whether the comments made are justifiable. Therefore, this section is phrased to address the discretion of dentists and advises against disparaging statements against another dentist. However, it should be noted that, where comments are made which are obviously not supportable and therefore unjustified, such comments can be the basis for the institution of a disciplinary proceeding against the dentist making such statements.

4.D. EXPERT TESTIMONY.

Dentists may provide expert testimony when that testimony is essential to a just and fair disposition of a judicial or administrative action.

ADVISORY OPINION
4.D.1. CONTINGENT FEES.

It is unethical for a dentist to agree to a fee contingent upon the favorable outcome of the litigation in exchange for testifying as a dental expert.

4.E. REBATES AND SPLIT FEES.

Dentists shall not accept or tender "rebates" or "split fees."

SECTION 5—PRINCIPLE: VERACITY ("truthfulness"). The dentist has a duty to communicate truthfully.

This principle expresses the concept that professionals have a duty to be honest and trustworthy in their dealings with people. Under this principle, the dentist's primary obligations include respecting the position of trust inherent in the dentist-patient relationship, communicating truthfully and without deception, and maintaining intellectual integrity.

CODE OF PROFESSIONAL CONDUCT
5.A. REPRESENTATION OF CARE.

Dentists shall not represent the care being rendered to their patients in a false or misleading manner.

ADVISORY OPINIONS
5.A.1. DENTAL AMALGAM.

Based on available scientific data the ADA has determined through the adoption of Resolution 42H-1986 (*Trans*.1986:536) that the removal of amalgam restorations from the non-allergic patient for the alleged purpose of removing toxic substances from the body, when such treatment is performed solely at the recommendation or suggestion of the dentist, is improper and unethical.

5.A.2. UNSUBSTANTIATED REPRESENTATIONS.

A dentist who represents that dental treatment recommended or performed by the dentist has the capacity to cure or alleviate diseases, infections or other conditions, when such representations are not based upon accepted scientific knowledge or research, is acting unethically.

5.B. REPRESENTATION OF FEES.

Dentists shall not represent the fees being charged for providing care in a false or misleading manner.

ADVISORY OPINIONS
5.B.1. WAIVER OF COPAYMENT.

A dentist who accepts a third party* payment under a copayment plan as payment in full without disclosing to the third party* that the patient's payment portion will not be collected, is engaged in overbilling. The essence of this ethical impropriety is deception and misrepresentation; an overbilling dentist makes it appear to the third party* that the charge to the patient for services rendered is higher than it actually is.

5.B.2. OVERBILLING.

It is unethical for a dentist to increase a fee to a patient solely because the patient has insurance.

5.B.3. FEE DIFFERENTIAL.

Payments accepted by a dentist under a governmentally funded program, a component or constituent dental society sponsored access program, or a participating agreement entered into under a program of a third party* shall not be considered as evidence of overbilling in determining whether a charge to a patient, or to another third party* in behalf of a patient not covered under any of the aforecited programs constitutes overbilling under this section of the Code.

5.B.4. TREATMENT DATES.

A dentist who submits a claim form to a third party* reporting incorrect treatment dates for the purpose of assisting a patient in obtaining benefits under a dental plan, which benefits would otherwise be disallowed, is engaged in making an unethical, false or misleading representation to such third party.*

5.B.5. DENTAL PROCEDURES.

A dentist who incorrectly describes on a third party* claim form a dental procedure in order to receive a greater payment or reimbursement or incorrectly makes a non-covered procedure appear to be a covered procedure on such a claim form is engaged in making an unethical, false or misleading representation to such third party.*

5.B.6. UNNECESSARY SERVICES.

A dentist who recommends and performs unnecessary dental services or procedures is engaged in unethical conduct.

*A third party is any party to a dental prepayment contract that may collect premiums, assume financial risks, pay claims and/or provide administrative services.

5.C. DISCLOSURE OF CONFLICT OF INTEREST.

A dentist who presents educational or scientific information in an article, seminar or other program shall disclose to the readers or participants any monetary or other special interest the dentist may have with a company whose products are promoted or endorsed in the presentation. Disclosure shall be made in any promotional material and in the presentation itself.

5.D. DEVICES AND THERAPEUTIC METHODS.

Except for formal investigative studies, dentists shall be obliged to prescribe, dispense, or promote only those devices, drugs and other agents whose complete formulae are available to the dental profession. Dentists shall have the further obligation of not holding out as exclusive any device, agent, method or technique if that representation would be false or misleading in any material respect.

ADVISORY OPINIONS
5.D.1. REPORTING ADVERSE REACTIONS.

A dentist who suspects the occurrence of an adverse reaction to a drug or dental device has an obligation to communicate that information to the broader medical and dental community, including, in the case of a serious adverse event, the Food and Drug Administration (FDA).

5.D.2. MARKETING OR SALE OF PRODUCTS.

Dentists who, in the regular conduct of their practices, engage in the marketing or sale of products to their patients must take care not to exploit the trust inherent in the dentist-patient relationship for their own financial gain. Dentists should not induce their patients to buy a product by misrepresenting the product's therapeutic value or the dentist's professional expertise in recommending the product.

In the case of a health-related product, it is not enough for the dentist to rely on the manufacturer's or distributor's representations about the product's safety and efficacy. The dentist has an independent obligation to inquire into the truth and accuracy of such claims and verify that they are founded on accepted scientific knowledge or research.

Dentists should disclose to their patients all relevant information the patient needs to make an informed purchase decision, including whether the product is available elsewhere and whether there are any financial incentives for the dentist to recommend the product that would not be evident to the patient.

5.E. PROFESSIONAL ANNOUNCEMENT.

In order to properly serve the public, dentists should represent themselves in a manner that contributes to the esteem of the profession. Dentists should not misrepresent their training and competence in any way that would be false or misleading in any material respect.*

5.F. ADVERTISING.

Although any dentist may advertise, no dentist shall advertise or solicit patients in any form of communication in a manner that is false or misleading in any material respect.*

ADVISORY OPINIONS
5.F.1. ARTICLES AND NEWSLETTERS.

If a dental health article, message or newsletter is published under a dentist's byline to the public without making truthful disclosure of the source and authorship or is designed to give rise to questionable expectations for the purpose of inducing the public to utilize the services of the sponsoring dentist, the dentist is engaged in making a false or misleading representation to the public in a material respect.

5.F.2. EXAMPLES OF "FALSE OR MISLEADING."

The following examples are set forth to provide insight into the meaning of the term "false or misleading in a material respect." These examples are not meant to be all-inclusive. Rather, by restating the concept in alternative language and giving general examples, it is hoped that the membership will gain a better understanding of the term. With this in mind, statements shall be avoided which would: a) contain a material misrepresentation of fact, b) omit a fact necessary to make the statement considered as a whole not materially misleading, c) be intended or be likely to create an unjustified expectation about results the dentist can achieve, and d) contain a material, objective representation, whether express or implied, that the advertised services are superior in quality to those of other dentists, if that representation is not subject to reasonable substantiation.

Subjective statements about the quality of dental services can also raise ethical concerns. In particular, statements of opinion may be misleading if they are not honestly held, if they misrepresent the qualifications of the holder, or the basis of the opinion, or if the patient reasonably interprets them as implied statements of fact. Such statements will be evaluated on a case by case basis, considering how patients are likely to respond to the impression made by the advertisement as a whole. The fundamental issue is whether the advertisement, taken as a whole, is false or misleading in a material respect.

5.F.3. UNEARNED, NONHEALTH DEGREES.

The use of an unearned or nonhealth degree in any general announcements to the public by a dentist may be a representation to the public which is false or misleading in a material respect. A dentist may use the title Doctor, Dentist, DDS, or DMD, or any additional earned advanced degrees in health service areas. The use of unearned or nonhealth degrees could be misleading because of the likelihood that it will indicate to the public the attainment of a specialty or diplomate status.

For purposes of this advisory opinion, an unearned academic degree is one which is awarded by an educational institution not accredited by a generally recognized accrediting body or is an honorary degree. Generally, the use of honorary degrees or nonhealth degrees should be limited to scientific papers and curriculum vitae. In all instances state law should be consulted. In any review by the council of the use of nonhealth degrees or honorary degrees the council will apply the standard of whether the use of such is false or misleading in a material respect.

5.F.4. FELLOWSHIPS.

A dentist using the attainment of a fellowship in a direct advertisement to the general public may be making a representation to the public which is false or misleading in a material respect. Such use of a fellowship status may be misleading because of the likelihood that it will indicate to the dental consumer the attainment of a specialty status. However, when such use does not conflict with state law, the attainment of fellowship status may be indicated in scientific papers, curriculum vitae, third party payment forms and letterhead and stationery which is not used for the direct solicitation of patients. In any review by the council of the use of the attainment of fellowship status, the council will apply the standard of whether the use of such is false or misleading in a material respect.

5.F.5. REFERRAL SERVICES.

There are two basic types of referral services for dental care: not-for-profit and the commercial. The not-for-profit is commonly organized by dental societies or community services. It is open to all qualified practitioners in the area served. A fee is sometimes charged the practitioner to be listed with the service. A fee for such referral services is for the purpose of covering the expenses of the service and has no relation to the number of patients referred. In contrast, some commercial referral services restrict access to the referral service to a limited number of dentists in a particular geographic area. Prospective patients calling the service may be referred to a single subscribing dentist in the geographic area and the respective dentist billed for each patient referred. Commercial referral services often advertise to the public stressing that there is no charge for use of the service and the patient may not be informed of the referral fee paid by the dentist. There is a connotation to such advertisements that the referral that is being made is in the nature of a public service. A dentist is allowed to pay for any advertising permitted by the *Code*, but is generally not permitted to make payments to another person or entity for the referral of a patient for professional services. While the particular facts and circumstances relating to an individual commercial referral service will vary, the council believes that the aspects outlined above for commercial referral services violate the *Code* in that it constitutes advertising which is false or misleading in a material respect and violates the prohibitions in the *Code* against fee splitting.

5.F.6. HIV TEST RESULTS.

An advertisement or other communication intended to solicit patients which omits a material fact or facts necessary to put the information conveyed in the advertisement in a proper context can be misleading in a material respect. An advertisement to the public of HIV negative test results, without conveying additional information that will clarify the scientific significance of this fact, is an example of a misleading omission. A dental practice should not seek to attract patients on the basis of partial truths which create a false impression.

5.G. NAME OF PRACTICE.

Since the name under which a dentist conducts his or her practice may be a factor in the selection process of the patient, the use of a trade name or an assumed name that is false or misleading in any material respect is unethical. Use of the name of a dentist no longer actively associated with the practice may be continued for a period not to exceed one year.*

ADVISORY OPINION

5.G.1. DENTIST LEAVING PRACTICE.

Dentists leaving a practice who authorize continued use of their names should receive competent advice on the legal implications of this action. With permission of a departing dentist, his or her name may be used for more than one year, if, after the one year grace period has expired, prominent notice is provided to the public through such mediums as a sign at the office and a short statement on stationery and business cards that the departing dentist has retired from the practice.

5.H. ANNOUNCEMENT OF SPECIALIZATION AND LIMITATION OF PRACTICE.

This section and Section 5-I are designed to help the public make an informed selection between the practitioner who has completed an accredited program beyond the dental degree and a practitioner who has not completed such a program. The special areas of dental practice approved by the American Dental Association and the designation for ethical specialty announcement and limitation of practice are: dental public health, endodontics, oral and maxillofacial pathology, oral and maxillofacial surgery, orthodontics and dentofacial orthopedics, pediatric dentistry, periodontics and prosthodontics.

Dentists who choose to announce specialization should use "specialist in" or "practice limited to" and shall limit their practice exclusively to the announced special area(s) of dental practice, provided at the time of the announcement such dentists have met in each approved specialty for which they announce the existing educational requirements and standards set forth by the American Dental Association. Dentists who use their eligibility to announce as specialists to make the public believe that specialty services rendered in the dental office are being rendered by qualified specialists when such is not the case are engaged in unethical conduct. The burden of responsibility is on specialists to avoid any inference that general practitioners who are associated with specialists are qualified to announce themselves as specialists.

GENERAL STANDARDS.

The following are included within the standards of the American Dental Association for determining the education, experience and other appropriate requirements for announcing specialization and limitation of practice:

1. The special area(s) of dental practice and an appropriate certifying board must be approved by the American Dental Association.
2. Dentists who announce as specialists must have successfully completed an educational program accredited by the Commission on Dental Accreditation, two or more years in length, as specified by the Council on Dental Education, or be diplomates of an American Dental Association recognized certifying board. The scope of the individual specialist's practice shall be governed by the educational standards for the specialty in which the specialist is announcing.
3. The practice carried on by dentists who announce as specialists shall be limited exclusively to the special area(s) of dental practices announced by the dentist.

STANDARDS FOR MULTIPLE-SPECIALTY ANNOUNCEMENTS.

Educational criteria for announcement by dentists in additional recognized specialty areas are the successful completion of an educational program accredited by the Commission on Dental Accreditation in each area for which the dentist wishes to announce. Dentists who completed their advanced education in programs listed by the Council on Dental Education prior to the initiation of the accreditation process in 1967 and who are currently ethically announcing as specialists in a recognized area may announce in additional areas provided they are educationally qualified or are certified diplomates in each area for which they wish to announce. Documentation of successful completion of the educational program(s) must be submitted to the appropriate constituent society. The documentation must assure that the duration of the program(s) is a minimum of two years except for oral and maxillofacial surgery which must have been a minimum of three years in duration.*

ADVISORY OPINION
5.H.1. DIPLOMATE STATUS.
A dentist who announces in any means of communication with patients or the general public that he or she is certified or a diplomate in an area not recognized by the American Dental Association or the law of the jurisdiction where the dentist practices as a specialty area of dentistry is engaged in making a false representation to the public in a material respect.

5.H.2. DUAL DEGREED DENTISTS.
Nothing in Section 5-H shall be interpreted to prohibit a dual degreed dentist who practices medicine or osteopathy under a valid state license from announcing to the public as a dental specialist provided the dentist meets the educational, experience and other standards set forth in the *Code* for specialty announcement and further providing that the announcement is truthful and not materially misleading.

5-I. GENERAL PRACTITIONER ANNOUNCEMENT OF SERVICES.
General dentists who wish to announce the services available in their practices are permitted to announce the availability of those services so long as they avoid any communications that express or imply specialization. General dentists shall also state that the services are being provided by general dentists. No dentist shall announce available services in any way that would be false or misleading in any material respect.*

* Advertising, solicitation of patients or business or other promotional activities by dentists or dental care delivery organizations shall not be considered unethical or improper, except for those promotional activities which are false or misleading in any material respect. Notwithstanding any *ADA Principles of Ethics and Code of Professional Conduct* or other standards of dentist conduct which may be differently worded, this shall be the sole standard for determining the ethical propriety of such promotional activities. Any provision of an ADA constituent or component society's code of ethics or other standard of dentist conduct relating to dentists' or dental care delivery organizations' advertising, solicitation, or other promotional activities which is worded differently from the above standard shall be deemed to be in conflict with the *ADA Principles of Ethics and Code of Professional Conduct.*

IV. INTERPRETATION AND APPLICATION OF *PRINCIPLES OF ETHICS AND CODE OF PROFESSIONAL CONDUCT.*
The foregoing *ADA Principles of Ethics and Code of Professional Conduct* set forth the ethical duties that are binding on members of the American Dental Association. The component and constituent societies may adopt additional requirements or interpretations not in conflict with the *ADA Code.*

Anyone who believes that a member-dentist has acted unethically may bring the matter to the attention of the appropriate constituent (state) or component (local) dental society. Whenever possible, problems involving questions of ethics should be resolved at the state or local level. If a satisfactory resolution cannot be reached, the dental society may decide, after proper investigation, that the matter warrants issuing formal charges and conducting a disciplinary hearing pursuant to the procedures set forth in the ADA *Bylaws*, Chapter XII. PRINCIPLES OF ETHICS AND CODE OF PROFESSIONAL CONDUCT AND JUDICIAL PROCEDURE. The Council on Ethics, Bylaws and Judicial Affairs reminds constituent and component societies that before a dentist can be found to have breached any ethical obligation the dentist is entitled to a fair hearing.

A member who is found guilty of unethical conduct proscribed by the *ADA Code* or code of ethics of the constituent or component society, may be placed under a sentence of censure or suspension or may be expelled from membership in the Association. A member under a sentence of censure, suspension or expulsion has the right to appeal the decision to his or her constituent society and the ADA Council on Ethics, Bylaws and Judicial Affairs, as provided in Chapter XII of the ADA *Bylaws.*

© American Dental Association. Reprinted with permission.

AMERICAN DENTAL HYGIENISTS' ASSOCIATION

Address: 444 North Michigan Avenue,
              Suite 3400
              Chicago, IL 60611
Telephone: 312/440-8929
WWW: www.adha.org
Document: Code of Ethics for Dental Hygienists
              (1995)

(ADHA's *Code of Ethics for Dental Hygienists* is contained in the association's *Bylaws*. The entire *Bylaws* are not reprinted here.—Eds.)

1. Preamble

As dental hygienists, we are a community of professionals devoted to the prevention of disease and the promotion and improvement of the public's health. We are preventive oral health professionals who provide educational, clinical, and therapeutic services to the public. We strive to live meaningful, productive, satisfying lives that simultaneously serve us, our profession, our society, and the world. Our actions, behaviors, and attitudes are consistent with our commitment to public service. We endorse and incorporate the Code into our daily lives.

2. Purpose

The purpose of a professional code of ethics is to achieve high levels of ethical consciousness, decision making, and practice by the members of the profession. Specific objectives of the Dental Hygiene Code of Ethics are:

- to increase our professional and ethical consciousness and sense of ethical responsibility.

- to lead us to recognize ethical issues and choices and to guide us in making more informed ethical decisions.
- to establish a standard for professional judgment and conduct.
- to provide a statement of the ethical behavior the public can expect from us.

The Dental Hygiene Code of Ethics is meant to influence us throughout our careers. It stimulates our continuing study of ethical issues and challenges us to explore our ethical responsibilities. The Code establishes concise standards of behavior to guide the public's expectations of our profession and supports existing dental hygiene practice, laws and regulations. By holding ourselves accountable to meeting the standards stated in the Code, we enhance the public's trust on which our professional privilege and status are founded.

3. Key Concepts

Our beliefs, principles, values and ethics are concepts reflected in the Code. They are the essential elements of our comprehensive and definitive code of ethics, and are interrelated and mutually dependent.

4. Basic Beliefs

We recognize the importance of the following beliefs that guide our practice and provide context for our ethics:

- The services we provide contribute to the health and well being of society.
- Our education and licensure qualify us to serve the public by preventing and treating oral disease and helping individuals achieve and maintain optimal health.
- Individuals have intrinsic worth, are responsible for their own health, and are entitled to make choices regarding their health.
- Dental hygiene care is an essential component of overall health care and we function interdependently with other health care providers.
- All people should have access to health care, including oral health care.
- We are individually responsible for our actions and the quality of care we provide.

5. Fundamental Principles

These fundamental principles, universal concepts and general laws of conduct provide the foundation for our ethics.

Universality

The principle of universality assumes that, if one individual judges an action to be right or wrong in a given situation, other people considering the same action in the same situation would make the same judgement.

Complementarity

The principle of complementarity assumes the existence of an obligation to justice and basic human rights. It requires us to act toward others in the same way they would act toward us if roles were reversed. In all relationships, it means considering the values and perspective of others before making decisions or taking actions affecting them.

Ethics

Ethics are the general standards of right and wrong that guide behavior within society. As generally accepted actions, they can be judged by determining the extent to which they promote good and minimize harm. Ethics compel us to engage in health promotion/disease prevention activities.

Community

This principle expresses our concern for the bond between individuals, the community, and society in general. It leads us to preserve natural resources and inspires us to show concern for the global environment.

Responsibility

Responsibility is central to our ethics. We recognize that there are guidelines for making ethical choices and accept responsibility for knowing and applying them. We accept the consequences of our actions or the failure to act and are willing to make ethical choices and publicly affirm them.

6. Core Values

We acknowledge these values as general for our choices and actions.

Individual autonomy and respect for human beings

People have the right to be treated with respect. They have the right to informed consent prior to treatment, and they have the right to full disclosure of all relevant information so that they can make informed choices about their care.

Confidentiality

We respect the confidentiality of client information and relationships as a demonstration of the value we place on individual autonomy. We acknowledge our obligation to justify any violation of a confidence.

Societal Trust

We value client trust and understand that public trust in our profession is based on our actions and behavior.

Nonmaleficence

We accept our fundamental obligation to provide services in a manner that protects all clients and minimizes harm to them and others involved in their treatment.

Beneficence

We have a primary role in promoting the well being of individuals and the public by engaging in health promotion/disease prevention activities.

Justice and Fairness

We value justice and support the fair and equitable distribution of health care resources. We believe all people should have access to high-quality, affordable oral healthcare.

Veracity

We accept our obligation to tell the truth and assume that others will do the same. We value self-knowledge and seek truth and honesty in all relationships.

7. Standards of Professional Responsibility

We are obligated to practice our profession in a manner that supports our purpose, beliefs, and values in accordance with the fundamental principles that support our ethics. We acknowledge the following responsibilities:

To Ourselves as Individuals. . .

- Avoid self-deception, and continually strive for knowledge and personal growth.
- Establish and maintain a lifestyle that supports optimal health.
- Create a safe work environment.
- Assert our own interests in ways that are fair and equitable.
- Seek the advice and counsel of others when challenged with ethical dilemmas.
- Have realistic expectations ourselves and recognize our limitations.

To Ourselves as Professionals. . .

- Enhance professional competencies through continuous learning in order to practice according to high standards of care.
- Support dental hygiene peer-review systems and quality-assurance measures.
- Develop collaborative professional relationships and exchange knowledge to enhance our own life-long professional development.

To Family and Friends. . .

- Support the efforts of others to establish and maintain healthy lifestyles and respect the rights of friends and family.

To Clients. . .

- Provide oral health care utilizing high levels of professional knowledge, judgement, and skill.
- Maintain a work environment that minimizes the risk of harm.
- Serve all clients without discrimination and avoid action toward any individual or group that may be interpreted as discriminatory.
- Hold professional client relationships confidential.
- Communicate with clients in a respectful manner.
- Promote ethical behavior and high standards of care by all dental hygienists.
- Serve as an advocate for the welfare of clients.
- Provide clients with the information necessary to make informed decisions about their oral health and encourage their full participation in treatment decisions and goals.
- Refer clients to other healthcare providers when their needs are beyond our ability or scope of practice.
- Educate clients about high-quality oral heath care.

To Colleagues. . .

- Conduct professional activities and programs, and develop relationships in ways that are honest, responsible, and appropriately open and candid.
- Encourage a work environment that promotes individual professional growth and development.
- Collaborate with others to create a work environment that minimizes risk to the personal health and safety of our colleagues.
- Manage conflicts constructively.
- Support the efforts of other dental hygienists to communicate the dental hygiene philosophy and preventive oral care.
- Inform other health care professionals about the relationship between general and oral health.
- Promote human relationships that are mutually beneficial, including those with other health care professionals.

To Employees and Employers. . .

- Conduct professional activities and programs, and develop relationships in ways that are honest, responsible, open, and candid.
- Manage conflicts constructively.
- Support the right of our employees and employers to work in an environment that promotes wellness.
- Respect the employment rights of our employers and employees.

To the Dental Hygiene Profession. . .

- Participate in the development and advancement of our profession.
- Avoid conflicts of interest and declare them when they occur.
- Seek opportunities to increase public awareness and understanding of oral health practices.
- Act in ways that bring credit to our profession while demonstrating appropriate respect for colleagues in other professions.
- Contribute time, talent, and financial resources to support and promote our profession.
- Promote a positive image for our profession.
- Promote a framework for professional education that develops dental hygiene competencies to meet the oral and overall health needs of the public.

To the Community and Society. . .

- Recognize and uphold the laws and regulations governing our profession.
- Document and report inappropriate, inadequate, or substandard care and/or illegal activities by a health care provider, to the responsible authorities.
- Use peer review as a mechanism for identifying inappropriate, inadequate, or substandard care provided by dental hygienists.
- Comply with local, state, and federal statutes that promote public health and safety.
- Develop support systems and quality-assurance programs in the workplace to assist dental hygienists in providing the appropriate standard of care.
- Promote access to dental hygiene services for all, supporting justice and fairness in the distribution of healthcare resources.
- Act consistently with the ethics of the global scientific community of which our profession is a part.
- Create a healthful workplace ecosystem to support a healthy environment.
- Recognize and uphold our obligation to provide pro bono service.

To Scientific Investigation. . .

We accept responsibility for conducting research according to the fundamental principles underlying our ethical beliefs in compliance with universal codes, governmental standards, and professional guidelines for the care and management of experimental subjects. We acknowledge our ethical obligations to the scientific community:

- Conduct research that contributes knowledge that is valid and useful to our clients and society.
- Use research methods that meet accepted scientific standards.
- Use research resources appropriately.
- Systematically review and justify research in progress to insure the most favorable benefit-to-risk ratio to research subjects.
- Submit all proposals involving human subjects to an appropriate human subject review committee.
- Secure appropriate institutional committee approval for the conduct of research involving animals.
- Obtain informed consent from human subjects participating in research that is based on specifications published in Title 21 Code of Federal Regulations Part 46.
- Respect the confidentiality and privacy of data.
- Seek opportunities to advance dental hygiene knowledge through research by providing financial, human, and technical resources whenever possible.
- Report research results in a timely manner.
- Report research findings completely and honestly, drawing only those conclusions that are supported by the data presented.
- Report the names of investigators fairly and accurately.
- Interpret the research and the research of others accurately and objectively, drawing conclusions that are supported by the data presented and seeking clarity when uncertain.
- Critically evaluate research methods and results before applying new theory and technology in practice.
- Be knowledgeable concerning currently accepted preventive and therapeutic methods, products, and technology and their application to our practice.

AMERICAN DIETETIC ASSOCIATION

Address: 216 West Jackson Boulevard
                   Chicago, IL 60606-6995
Telephone: 312/899-0040

WWW: www.eatright.org
Document: Code of Ethics for the Profession of Dietetics (1942. Most recently revised 1962.)

(The American Dietetic Association was in the process of revising its code of ethics when this book went to press. A new code will be available in 1999. The current code's procedures for the review of alleged violations of the code are not reprinted here.—Eds.)

Preamble

The American Dietetic Association and its credentialing agency, the Commission on Dietetic Registration, believe it is in the best interests of the profession and the public it serves that a Code of Ethics provide guidance to dietetic practitioners in their professional practice and conduct. Dietetic practitioners have voluntarily developed a Code of Ethics to reflect the ethical principles guiding the dietetic profession and to outline commitments and obligations of the dietetic practitioner to self, client, society, and the profession.

The purpose of the Commission on Dietetic Registration is to assist in protecting the nutritional health, safety, and welfare of the public by establishing and enforcing qualifications for dietetic registration and for issuing voluntary credentials to individuals who have attained those qualifications. The Commission has adopted this Code to apply to individuals who hold these credentials.

The Ethics Code applies in its entirety to members of The American Dietetic Association who are Registered Dietitians (RDs) or Dietetic Technicians, Registered (DTRs). Except for sections solely dealing with the credential, the Code applies to all American Dietetic Association members who are not RDs or DTRs. Except for aspects solely dealing with membership, the Code applies to all RDs and DTRs who are not ADA members. All of the aforementioned are referred to in the Code as "dietetic practitioners."

Principles

1. The dietetic practitioner provides professional services with objectivity and with respect for the unique needs and values of individuals.
2. The dietetic practitioner avoids discrimination against other individuals on the basis of race, creed, religion, sex, age, and national origin.
3. The dietetic practitioner fulfills professional commitments in good faith.
4. The dietetic practitioner conducts him/herself with honesty, integrity, and fairness.

5. The dietetic practitioner remains free of conflict of interest while fulfilling the objectives and maintaining the integrity of the dietetic profession.

6. The dietetic practitioner maintains confidentiality of information.

7. The dietetic practitioner practices dietetics based on scientific principles and current information.

8. The dietetic practitioner assumes responsibility and accountability for personal competence in practice.

9. The dietetic practitioner recognizes and exercises professional judgment within the limits of his/her qualifications and seeks counsel or makes referrals as appropriate.

10. The dietetic practitioner provides sufficient information to enable clients to make their own informed decisions.

11. The dietetic practitioner who wishes to inform the public and colleagues of his/her services does so by using factual information. The dietetic practitioner does not advertise in a false or misleading manner.

12. The dietetic practitioner promotes or endorses products in a manner that is neither false nor misleading.

13. The dietetic practitioner permits use of his/her name for the purpose of certifying that dietetics services have been rendered only if he/she has provided or supervised the provision of those services.

14. The dietetic practitioner accurately presents professional qualifications and credentials.

    A. The dietetic practitioner uses "RD" or "registered dietitian" and "DTR" or "dietetic technician, registered" only when registration is current and authorized by the Commission on Dietetic Registration.

    B. The dietetic practitioner provides accurate information and complies with all requirements of the Commission on Dietetic Registration program in which he/she is seeking initial or continued credentials from the Commission on Dietetic Registration.

    C. The dietetic practitioner is subject to disciplinary action for aiding another person in violating any Commission on Dietetic Registration requirements or aiding another person in representing himself/herself as an RD or DTR when he/she is not.

15. The dietetic practitioner presents substantiated information and interprets controversial information without personal bias, recognizing that legitimate differences of opinion exist.

16. The dietetic practitioner makes all reasonable effort to avoid bias in any kind of professional evaluation. The dietetic practitioner provides objective evaluation of candidates for professional association memberships, awards, scholarships, or job advancements.

17. The dietetic practitioner voluntarily withdraws from professional practice under the following circumstances:

    A. The dietetic practitioner has engaged in any substance abuse that could affect his/her practice;

    B. The dietetic practitioner has been adjudged by a court to be mentally incompetent;

    C. The dietetic practitioner has an emotional or mental disability that affects his/her practice in a manner that could harm the client.

18. The dietetic practitioner complies with all applicable laws and regulations concerning the profession. The dietetic practitioner is subject to disciplinary action under the following circumstances:

    A. The dietetic practitioner has been convicted of a crime under the laws of the United States which is a felony or a misdemeanor, an essential element of which is dishonesty, and which is related to the practice of the profession.

    B. The dietetic practitioner has been disciplined by a state and at least one of the grounds for the discipline is the same or substantially equivalent to these principles.

    C. The dietetic practitioner has committed an act of misfeasance or malfeasance which is directly related to the practice of the profession as determined by a court of competent jurisdiction, a licensing board, or an agency of a governmental body.

19. The dietetic practitioner accepts the obligation to protect society and the profession by upholding the Code of Ethics for the Profession of Dietetics and by reporting alleged violations of the Code through the defined review process of The American Dietetic Association and its credentialing agency, the Commission on Dietetic Registration.

AMERICAN FEDERATION OF MUSICIANS OF THE UNITED STATES AND CANADA

Address: 1501 Broadway, Suite 600
              New York, NY 10036-5503
Telephone: 212/869-1330
WWW: www.afm.org
Document: The Music Code of Ethics (1998)

Music educators and professional musicians alike are committed to the importance of music as an essential component in the social and cultural fiber of our country. Many of the ways that they serve this commitment overlap—many professional musicians are music educators, and many music educators are, or have been, actively engaged in the field of professional performance. Based on training and expertise, however, educators and professional musicians serve fundamentally different functions:

- Music educators contribute to music in our society by promoting teaching music in schools, colleges and universities, and by promoting a greater interest in music and the study of music.
- Professional musicians contribute through their performance of music to the public in promoting the enjoyment and understanding of music.

When the line between these different functions is blurred, several problems may arise: Music educators may find that school programs they have built over the years are thrown into disarray. Musicians may suffer harm to their prestige and economic status. And those served by both educators and musicians—students and the public—may find that they are poorly educated and poorly entertained.

This Code of Ethics sets out guidelines that will help educators and performers avoid problems stemming from a lack of understanding of each others' role. It does not address the many other issues that shape ethical behavior in performance and in education.

Music Educators and the student groups they direct should be focused on the teaching and learning of music and on performances of music directly connected with the demonstration of performances at:

- School functions initiated by the schools as a part of a school program, whether in a school building or other site.
- Community functions organized in the interest of the schools strictly for educational purposes, such as those that might be originated by the parent and teachers association.
- School exhibits prepared as a courtesy on the part of a school district for educational organizations or educational conventional organizations or educational conventions being entertained in the district.
- Educational broadcasts that have the purpose of demonstrating or illustrating pupils' achievements in music study or that represent the culmination of a period of study and rehearsal. Included in this category are local, state, regional, and national school music festivals and competitions held under the auspices of schools, colleges, and/or educational organizations on a nonprofit basis and broadcast to acquaint the public with the results of music instruction in the schools.
- Student or amateur recordings for study purposes made in the classroom or in connection with contest, festival, or conference performances by students. These recordings are routinely licensed for distribution to students, but should not be offered for general sale to the public through commercial outlets.

In addition, it is appropriate for educators and the school groups they direct to take part in performances that go beyond typical school activities, but they should only do so where they have established that their participation will not interfere with the rights of professional musicians and where that participation occurs only after discussion with local musicians (through the local of the AF of M). Events in this category may include:

- Civic occasions of local, state, or national patriotic interest, of sufficient breadth to enlist the sympathies and cooperation of all persons, such as those held by the American Legion and Veterans of Foreign Wars in connection with Memorial Day services.

• Benefit performances for local charities, such as the Red Cross and hospitals (when and where local professional musicians would likewise donate their services.)

Professional Musicians provide entertainment. They should be the exclusive presenters of music for:

• Civic parades (where professional marching bands exist), ceremonies, expositions, community-center activities, regattas, nonscholastic contests, festivals, athletic games, activities, or celebrations, and the like, and national, state, and county fairs.

• Functions for the furtherance, directly or indirectly, of any public or private enterprise. This might include receptions or public events sponsored by chambers of commerce, boards of trade, and commercial clubs or associations.

• Any occasion that is partisan or sectarian in character or purpose. These occasions would include political rallies, private parties or weddings, and other similar functions.

• Functions of clubs, societies, and civic or fraternal organizations.

Interpreting the Code is simple. This is not to say that the principles set forth in this Code will never be subject to differing interpretations. But if educators and performers keep to the core ethical idea, *that education and entertainment have separate goals*, conflict should be kept to a minimum. Other things to keep in mind are:

• School groups should not be called on to provide entertainment at any time—they should be involved exclusively in education and the demonstration of education. Statements that funds are not available for employment to professional musicians; that if the talents of school musical organizations are not available, other musicians cannot or will not be employed; or that the student musicians are to play without remuneration of any kind, are immaterial.

• Enrichment of school programs by presentations from professional entertainers does not replace a balanced, sequential education in music provided by qualified teachers. Enrichment activities must always be planned in coordination with music educators and carried out in a way that helps, rather than hinders, the job of bringing students the skills and knowledge they need. The mere fact that it may be easier for school administration to bring in a unit from a local performing arts organization than to support a serious, ongoing curriculum in the

schools has no bearing on the ethics of a professional entertainer's involvement.

Should conflicts occur in issues touched by this Code, the American Federation of Musicians (AF of M) and Music Educators National Conference (MENC) suggest that those involved:

1. First, attempt to resolve the situation by contacting directly the other party involved.

2. Second, attempt resolution through the local representatives of the associations involved. The local of the AF of M should be accessible through directory assistance. The officers of MENC state affiliates can be found through the MENC site on the World Wide Web (www.menc.org) or by calling MENC headquarters at 1-800-336-3768.

3. Finally, especially difficult problems should be resolved through mediation. Help with this mediation is available by contacting the national offices of the AF of M and MENC.

This code is a continuing agreement that shall be reviewed regularly to make it responsive to changing conditions.

© American Federation of Musicians of the United States and Canada. Reprinted with permission.

AMERICAN FEDERATION OF POLICE

Address: 3801 Biscayne Boulevard
              Miami, FL 33137
Telephone: 305/573-9819
WWW: n/a
Document: Law Enforcement Profession's Code of Ethics

1. **As** a law enforcement officer, I regard myself as a member of an important and honorable profession.

2. **As** a law enforcement officer, I will keep myself in the best physical condition, so that I may at all times, perform my police duty with efficiency, and if necessary defend my uniform with honor. It is my duty to know the art of defense and be proficient in the use of my revolver.

3. **As** a law enforcement officer, it is my duty to know my work thoroughly and to inform myself on all other phases of law enforcement work. It is my further duty to avail myself of every opportunity to learn more about my professional work.

4. **As** a law enforcement officer, I should be exemplary in my conduct, edifying in my conversation, honest in my dealings, and obedient to all the laws of my city, state and nation, and I shall regard these as my sacred honor.

5. **As** a law enforcement officer, I should not, in the performance of duty, work for personal advantage or profit. I shall, at all times, recognize that I am a public servant obliged to give the most efficient and impartial service of which I am capable and I will be courteous in all my contacts.

6. **As** a law enforcement officer, I will regard my brother officer with the same standards as I hold for myself. It is my duty to guard his honor and life as I guard my own.

7. **As** a law enforcement officer, I should be loyal to my superiors, who determine my policies and accept responsibilities for my actions. It is my duty to do only those things which will reflect honor upon them, upon myself, and upon my profession.

AMERICAN FEDERATION OF TEACHERS

Address: 555 New Jersey Avenue NW
             Washington, DC 20001
Telephone: 202/879-4400
WWW: www.aft.org
Document: A Bill of Rights and Responsibilities
             for Learning: Standards of Conduct,
             Standards for Achievement

The traditional mission of our public schools has been to prepare our nation's young people for equal and responsible citizenship and productive adulthood. Today, we reaffirm that mission by remembering that democratic citizenship and productive adulthood begin with standards of conduct and standards for achievement in our schools. Other education reforms may work; high standards of conduct and achievement do work—and nothing else can work without them.

Recognizing that rights carry responsibilities, we declare that:

- All students and school staff have a right to schools that are safe, orderly and drug free.
- All students and school staff have a right to learn and work in school districts and schools that have clear discipline codes with fair and consistently enforced consequences for misbehavior.
- All students and school staff have a right to learn and work in school districts that have alternative educational placements for violent or chronically disruptive students.
- All students and school staff have a right to be treated with courtesy and respect.
- All students and school staff have a right to learn and work in school districts, schools and classrooms that have clearly stated and rigorous academic standards.
- All students and school staff have a right to learn and work in well-equipped schools that have the instructional materials needed to carry out a rigorous academic program.
- All students and school staff have a right to learn and work in schools where teachers know their subject matter and how to teach it.
- All students and school staff have a right to learn and work in school districts, schools and classrooms where high grades stand for high achievement and promotion is earned.
- All students and school staff have a right to learn and work in school districts and schools where getting a high school diploma means having the knowledge and skills essential for college or a good job.
- All students and school staff have a right to be supported by parents, the community, public officials and business in their efforts to uphold high standards of conduct and achievement.

AMERICAN HEALTH CARE ASSOCIATION

Address: 1201 L Street NW
             Washington, DC 20005
Telephone: 202/842-4444
WWW: www.ahca.org
Document: Code of Ethics

PREAMBLE

The American Health Care Association's (AHCA) Code of Ethics is concerned not only with what is right and what is good, but also with the association's obligation to others. The purpose of this Code is to contribute to a culture of ethical behavior in the long term care field. It is intended for AHCA as an organization. However, it is intended to serve as a model for AHCA's affiliates and their facility members.

This Code articulates a set of values and behaviors that AHCA believes is an appropriate standard of conduct for the organization and its leadership. AHCA believes it should be held accountable to its affiliates, their members, and the general public. This Code provides a guide for the way business should be conducted by AHCA and, by extension, its state affiliates and their member facilities.

This Code is not a tool of certification, nor does it contain sanctions to be imposed for not meeting the standards contained in the Code. Its primary sanction lies in the organizational and personal consciences of the Association, its state affiliates and their individual members.

In addition, this Code is an educational tool, designed to inspire individuals to act in a way that assures good care, sound community relationships and helps establish and reinforce public confidence in the entire long term care field.

AHCA believes that its affiliates and their members have a right to expect the Code's ideals to be embodied in the Association's positions and policies. Further, AHCA's affiliates and their members have the right to expect the Association's leaders to act in accordance with the values and standards of conduct articulated in this Code.

The following organizational values are the foundation of AHCA's Code of Ethics.

Concern for individuals in need

AHCA recognizes that a growing number of people in the United States need long term care. Many of those people have multiple needs: physical, emotional, spiritual, social and economic. AHCA exists not only to support its affiliates and their member facilities, but also to be an advocate for all people who need long term care services and supportive environments.

Quality service

People in need of long term care deserve quality services. AHCA is committed to providing its constituents with quality products and services, which in turn will assist providers in serving their patients well. AHCA advocates for quality care, including appropriate standards and their implementation. AHCA also advocates for appropriate funding through government and other entities to support the provision of quality long term care.

Service to the community

AHCA and its members perceive themselves to be good neighbors, contributing to the overall good of the community. AHCA supports this community service ideal and strives to mirror it in its values, ideals, and policies.

Integrity and honesty

Honesty is the glue of social relationships, both personal and corporate. AHCA is committed to honesty and integrity in all of its internal and external activities. To be honest is to be forthright and open. It requires individuals and organizations to actively provide complete and truthful information when making decisions or when influencing others to make responsible decisions.

Fairness

AHCA believes that in establishing policies, advocating for the long term care community, developing employment practices, pricing products and services, seeking grants or business opportunities, and in resolving disputes, the association and its members and staff must do what is fair and just. To be just is to do what is right and proper—free of prejudices—so as to achieve a balance of conflicting needs, rights and demands. Concepts of fairness must apply to dealing with/acknowledging conflicts of interest and, when appropriate, competing interests.

Accountability

AHCA, as a service organization, understands that it is accountable to its constituent members and, by extension, to those whom they serve. AHCA also understands that the association, its affiliates and their members are accountable to the public at large. AHCA recognizes that the association, its affiliates and their member facilities must comply with all laws and regulations that govern their operation.

Respect for employees

People are the heart of organizations. AHCA and its constituencies are committed to enhancing the individual well being and positive social interaction of all who are employed directly as well as those who are employed by its constituent organizations. AHCA, its affiliates and their members are committed to providing a safe and supportive work environment for their employees. AHCA and its members also recognize their responsibility to provide employees fair compensation and to deal with employees fairly.

Stewardship

AHCA recognizes that it occupies a privileged position as the voice of the long term care field in the United States. Many individuals and organizations support the association financially, at a significant cost to themselves and their organizations. Additionally, AHCA plays an important mediating role between people in need and governmental agencies with the capacity to relieve personal suffering. Such commitments and roles demand that AHCA use its resources—financial, social, and moral—prudently.

The Code of Ethics for AHCA is intended to direct people's actions toward a desired end. It is not intended as a set of policies or procedures for AHCA, but is an attempt to embody the Association's aspirations, values and beliefs.

Moral responsibility

As an organization with a moral responsibility, AHCA reflects on the ethical implications of its choices, but AHCA also recognizes that in many instances cherished values may be in conflict. Such conflicts do not excuse AHCA from recognizing differing perspectives or from making difficult decisions. AHCA holds itself accountable for its decisions and the way in which they are made.

Good business practice

As a trade organization, AHCA manifests a commitment to the values and behaviors which mark good business practice. Individuals in leadership have a re-

sponsibility to act responsibly and fairly to its state affiliates and to their member facilities. As an organization of state associations, AHCA is committed to the interests of those affiliates and is accountable to them and their member facilities.

Making difficult choices

Society often is faced with decisions that are divisive. Similarly, AHCA has and will continue to be faced with difficult choices. AHCA affirms that it is proper to forcefully present one's views but that it is also vital that we do so with civility and openness to other perspectives. In all of its decisionmaking, AHCA will adhere to the spirit and to the processes of its constitution and bylaws.

Acting responsibly

Individuals and organizations vested with powers to affect the life of AHCA have both the right and the responsibility to exercise their powers in the best interest of AHCA and the entire field of long term care. The staff, in turn, will exercise diligence both in providing truthful information for decisionmakers and in fulfilling responsibilities in accord with the will of the members.

Obligations to provide quality services

Because the field of long term care is in a state of flux, AHCA must constantly learn from the field and continually develop best practice models for use in the field. AHCA will forward standards and techniques to assist providers in meeting their obligations to provide high quality care and services.

Dealing with conflicting values

AHCA recognizes that its constituency involves families, volunteers, employees and suppliers, as well as individual facilities. While in many instances the interests of all constituencies are aligned, at times they are not. It is vital that any ambiguity and tension that arise from differing views and conflicting values be faced with forthrightness and sensitivity, recognizing that, at times, the interests of important, albeit secondary, constituencies must not only be heard, but they may be so compelling as to be controlling. In some instances, persons of good will differ about choices to be made. AHCA is committed to facing difficult issues and differing perspectives with honesty, forthrightness, and civility.

Use of information

AHCA recognizes that information can be used to confuse, obfuscate, and bolster a particular perspective. AHCA is committed to gathering and distributing relevant information to the best of its ability and to making it part of a fair and open decisionmaking process.

Responsible advocacy

AHCA has a special responsibility in the area of advocacy. AHCA must promote good practice within the field of long term care through promotion of education, training, research and the identification of best practice models. AHCA also must promote the development of ethically based practice by its behavior and through its various publications and other educational vehicles.

AHCA believes that the Association's policies and agenda must reflect a willingness to self regulate. While AHCA will support and help develop reasonable regulations that are fair and promote quality and cost efficiency, AHCA believes that quality must be internal to an organization and be motivated through strong leadership and clear vision. As an advocate for people in need of long term care, AHCA will promote reimbursement policies which make possible the provision of quality care to all individuals, including the economically disadvantaged. Similarly, AHCA will promote stewardship in the field so that both public and private resources will be used wisely and efficiently.

Potential conflicts of interest

All individuals within the AHCA leadership, both staff and volunteer, will be sensitive to potential conflicts and duality of interest. In areas that are questionable, leaders will declare such and subject themselves to the judgment of their peers as to the appropriateness of their participation in the decision at hand.

Respect for others

Respect for the dignity of others is a key element in all ethical behavior. AHCA recognizes the right to privacy and the importance of confidentiality. AHCA will be scrupulous in safeguarding these principles in the use of information—whether about individuals or about organizations.

Fairness in competition

Entrepreneurship and healthy competitiveness are part of American cultural values. However, fairness and decency are values of high moral order. Especially at a time when there are difficult societal decisions affecting the lives of all Americans, AHCA recognizes the importance of joining together with other

organizations with similar values and concern for people needing long term care.

© American Health Care Association. Reprinted with permission.

AMERICAN HEALTH INFORMATION MANAGEMENT ASSOCIATION

Address:	233 North Michigan Avenue, Suite 2150 Chicago, IL 60601-5519
Telephone:	312/233-1100
WWW:	www.ahima.org
Document:	AHIMA Code of Ethics (1993)

Preamble

The health information management professional abides by a set of ethical principles developed to safeguard the public and to contribute within the scope of the profession to quality and efficiency in health care. This Code of Ethics, adopted by the members of the American Health Information Management Association, defines the standards of behavior which promote ethical conduct.

  I. The Health Information Management Professional demonstrates behavior that reflects integrity, supports objectivity, and fosters trust in professional activities.
  II. The Health Information Management Professional respects the dignity of each human being.
  III. The Health Information Management Professional strives to improve personal competence and quality of services.
  IV. The Health Information Management Professional represents truthfully and accurately professional credentials, education, and experience.

V. The Health Information Management Professional refuses to participate in illegal or unethical acts and also refuses to conceal the illegal, incompetent, or unethical acts of others.

VI. The Health Information Management Professional protects the confidentiality of primary and secondary health records as mandated by law, professional standards, and the employer's policies.

VII. The Health Information Management Professional promotes to others the tenets of confidentiality.

VIII. The Health Information Management Professional adheres to pertinent laws and regulations while advocating changes which serve the best interest of the public.

IX. The Health Information Management Professional encourages appropriate use of health record information and advocates policies and systems that advance the management of health records and health information.

X. The Health Information Management Professional recognizes and supports the Association's mission.

© American Health Information Management Association. Reprinted with permission.

ORGANIZED 1884   INCORPORATED BY THE CONGRESS 1889

AMERICAN HISTORICAL ASSOCIATION

Address: 400 A Street SE
             Washington, DC 20003
Telephone: 202/544-2422
WWW: www.theaha.org
Document: Statement on Standards of
             Professional Conduct (1987. Most
             recently revised 1996.)

The historical profession is diverse, consisting of people who work in a variety of institutional settings and also as independent professionals. But all historians should be guided by the same principles of conduct.

1. Scholarship

Scholarship, the uncovering and exchange of new information and the shaping of interpretations, is basic to the activities of the historical profession. The profession communicates with students in textbooks and classrooms; to other scholars and the general public in books, articles, exhibits, films, and historic sites and structures; and to decision makers in memoranda and testimony.

Scholars must be not only competent in research and analysis but also cognizant of issues of professional conduct. **Integrity** is one of these issues. It requires an awareness of one's own bias and a readiness to follow sound method and analysis wherever they may lead. It demands disclosure of all significant qualifications of one's arguments. Historians should carefully document their findings and thereafter be prepared to make available to others their sources, evidence, and data, including the documentation they develop through interviews. Historians must not misrepresent evidence or the sources of evidence, must be free of the offense of plagiarism, and must not be indifferent to error or efforts to ignore or conceal it. They should acknowledge the receipt of any financial support, sponsorship, or unique privileges (including privileged access to research material) related to their research, and they should strive to bring the requests and demands of their employers and clients into harmony with the principles of the historical profession. They should also acknowledge assistance received from colleagues, students, and others.

Since historians must have **access to sources**—archival and other—in order to produce reliable history, they have a professional obligation to preserve sources and advocate free, open, equal, and nondiscriminatory access to them, and to avoid actions that might prejudice future access. Historians recognize the appropriateness of some national security and corporate and personal privacy claims but must challenge unnecessary restrictions. They must protect research collections and other historic resources and make those under their control available to other scholars as soon as possible.

Certain kinds of research and conditions attached to employment or to use of records impose obligations to maintain confidentiality, and oral historians often must make promises to interviewees as conditions for interviews. Scholars should honor any pledges made. At the same time, historians should seek definitions of conditions of confidentiality before work begins, press for redefinitions when experience demonstrates the unsatisfactory character of established regulations, and advise their readers of the conditions and rules that govern their work. They also have the obligation to decline to make their services available when policies are unnecessarily restrictive.

As **intellectual diversity** enhances the historical imagination and contributes to the development and vitality of the study of the past, historians should welcome rather than deplore it. When applied with integrity, the political, social, and religious beliefs of historians may inform their historical practice. When historians make interpretations and judgments, they should be careful not to present them in a way that forecloses discussion of alternative interpretations. Historians should be free from institutional and professional penalties for their beliefs and activities, provided they do not misrepresent themselves as speaking for their institutions or their professional organizations.

The bond that grows out of lives committed to the study of history should be evident in the **standards of civility** that govern the conduct of historians in their relations with one another. The preeminent value of all intellectual communities is reasoned discourse—the continuous colloquy among historians of diverse points of view. A commitment to such discourse makes possible the fruitful exchange of views, opinions, and knowledge.

2. Teaching

Communication skills are essential to historians' efforts to disseminate their scholarship beyond the profession. Those skills are not limited to writing books and articles but also involve teaching, which takes place in many locales—museums and historic sites as well as classrooms—and involves the use of visual materials and artifacts as well as words.

Quality in teaching involves **integrity** as well as competence. Integrity requires the presentation of differing interpretations with intellectual honesty; it also requires fairness and promptness in judging students' work on merit alone and a readiness to discuss their views with an open mind.

When so applied, the **political, social, and religious beliefs** of historians may inform their teaching. The right of the teacher to hold such convictions and to express them in teaching, however, does not justify the persistent intrusion of material unrelated to the subject of the course or the intentional use of falsification, misrepresentation, or concealment.

Freedom of expression is essential to the task of communicating historical thought and learning. To this end, historians should have substantial latitude in realizing their objectives, although they are obligated to see that their courses or other presentations reasonably correspond in coverage and emphasis to published descriptions.

3. Public Service

Historical knowledge provides a vital perspective in the analysis of contemporary social problems and political issues and at times may impose obligations on historians to enter policy arenas where difficulties abound. Oftentimes the work of historians may be used by others in ways that historians find objectionable. Some may seek to make partisans out of professionals or to discredit them by charging that they are not qualified to speak on an issue or are biased.

Historians entering public arenas as political advisers, expert witnesses, consultants, legislative witnesses, journalists, commentators, or staff may face a **choice of priorities** between professionalism and partisanship. They may want to prepare themselves by seeking advice from other experienced professionals. As historians, they must be sensitive to the complexities of history, the diversity among historians, and the limits as well as the strengths of their own points of view and experiences and of the discipline itself and its specialities. In such situations, historians must use sources, including the work of other scholars, with great care and should be prepared to explain the methods and assumptions in their research and the relations between evidence and interpretation and should be ready also to discuss alternative interpretations of the subjects being addressed.

4. Employment

Although some historians are self-employed, most work for academic institutions, corporations, government agencies, law firms, archives, historical societies, museums, parks, historic preservation programs, or in communications. In such institutions, they are usually in a position to influence employment policies, and thus they at least **share responsibility** for any unfair policies. To the extent that they can influence policies in their employing institutions, the AHA encourages historians to do all they possibly can to persuade their employers to accept and enforce such rules as will best insure **fairness in all decisions** about the appointment of historians and in all personnel decisions affecting the welfare of employed historians. If they are in an academic institution, they should urge the institution to accept the 1966 "Statement on Government of Colleges and Universities," jointly formulated by the American Association of University Professors (AAUP), the American Council on Education, and the Association of Governing Boards of Universities and Colleges. If in a nonacademic institution, they should urge the institution to adopt comparable standards.

Fairness begins with **recruitment**. Historians have an obligation to do all possible to insure that all employment opportunities in the field are widely publicized and that all professionally qualified persons have an equal opportunity to compete for any position. This means not only the placement of job notices in appropriate publications (for example, the *Chronicle of Higher Education*, AHA's *Perspectives*, or other more specialized professional placement newsletters) but also the inclusion in such notices of a completely accurate description of the position and of any contingencies, budgetary or otherwise, that might affect the continued availability of the position. An institution should not deceive possible candidates by omitting qualifications or characteristics that favor certain candidates over others (for example, a preference for unspecified minor fields). If an employer decides to alter a job description or selection criteria, the institution should readvertise.

Fairness also involves equal treatment of all qualified applicants and procedures which are considerate to all applicants. For example, an employing institution should promptly acknowledge all applications and, as soon as practicable, inform applicants who do not meet the selection criteria. Likewise, it should keep competitive applicants informed of the progress of the search and promptly notify those who are no longer under consideration. It should do all possible to accommodate finalists in arranging interviews, including the payment of expenses, where appropriate. Finally, it should insure that those who conduct interviews adhere to professional standards by respecting the dignity of candidates, focusing their questions on the qualifications needed for the position, and avoiding questions that violate federal antidiscrimination laws.

Employment decisions always involve judgments. But, except in those cases in which federal law allows a specific preference, institutions should base hiring decisions as well as all decisions relating to reappointment, promotion, tenure, apprenticeship, graduate student assistantships, awards, and fellowships solely on **professional qualifications** without regard to sex, race, color, national origin, sexual orientation, religion, political affiliation, veteran status, age, certain physical handicaps, or marital status.

Once employed, any person deserves the **professional respect and support** necessary for professional growth and advancement. Such respect precludes unequal treatment based on any nonprofessional criteria. In particular, it precludes any harassment or discrimination, which is unethical, unprofessional, and threatening to intellectual freedom. Harassment includes all behavior that prevents or impairs an individual's full enjoyment of educational or workplace rights, benefits, environment, or opportunities, such as generalized pejorative remarks or behavior or the use of professional authority to emphasize inappropriately the personal identity of a student or colleague. Sexual harassment, which includes inappropriate requests for sexual favors, unwanted sexual advances, and sexual assaults, is illegal and violates professional standards.

Historians should receive promotions and merit salary increases exclusively on the basis of professional qualifications and achievements. The best way to insure that such criteria are used is to establish **clear standards and procedures** known to all members of the institution. For example, academic historians need to know the relative weight given to scholarship, teaching, and service, and how they relate to decisions about tenure or promotion. An institution should have an established review process, should offer candidates for promotion or merit raises opportunities to substantiate their achievements, should provide early and specific notification of adverse tenure or promotion or salary decisions, and should provide an appeal mechanism.

Of particularly grave concern to historians are those institutional decisions that lead to disciplinary action, most important, questions of suspension and dismissal, since they may involve issues of academic freedom. All institutions employing historians should have clearly written policies governing both the grounds for disciplinary action and the procedures to be followed. Those procedures should embody the principles of due process, including adequate mechanisms for fact-finding and avenues for appeal. Academic institutions should adhere to the AAUP 1940 "Statement of Principles on Academic Freedom and Tenure." Other institutions that employ professional historians should provide a comparable standard of due process.

Historians who work **part-time or as adjunct or temporary faculty** should receive compensation in proportion to the share of a full-time work load they carry, including a proportionate share of fringe benefits available to their full-time colleagues; they also should have access to institutional facilities and support systems, including research support, and should be eligible to apply for relevant tenure opportunities. Employers should offer multiyear contracts to those likely to remain part-time for extended periods, and those individuals should have the attendant obligations of participation in governance and administrative tasks and access to the same procedural protections as full-time employees. Non-tenure-track employees also should be represented on the appropriate advisory and governing bodies, such as faculty senates.

5. Credentials
Historians are obligated to present their credentials **accurately and honestly** in all contexts. For example, care must be taken not to misrepresent one's qualifications in c.v.'s and in grant applications.

6. Implementation
Historians have a professional obligation to encourage the establishment of and to support guidelines and procedures concerning professionals in their employing institutions. Historians also have the responsibility to take appropriate action when confronted with violations of the profession's standards of conduct.

Initially, historians should utilize their employing institutions' grievance machinery. When this is not possible, feasible, or appropriate, alleged violations may be referred to the Professional Division of the AHA for consideration and possible resolution. The Division is not an investigatory body, although it may solicit and receive documents on cases.

The Division may refer cases to other organizations for formal arbitration or resolution; it may make statements on cases, or advise parties to the controversies to do so; and it may provide opportunities for persons to bring their views before the profession.

© American Historical Association. Reprinted with permission.

AMERICAN HOSPITAL ASSOCIATION

Address: One North Franklin
           Chicago, IL 60606

Telephone: 312/460-0034
WWW: www.aha.org
Document: Ethical Conduct for Health Care Institutions (1992)

Introduction
Health care institutions,* by virtue of their roles as health care providers, employers, and community health resources, have special responsibilities for ethical conduct and ethical practices that go beyond meeting minimum legal and regulatory standards. Their broad range of patient care, education, public health, social service, and business functions is essential to the health and well being of their communities. These roles and functions demand that health care organizations conduct themselves in an ethical manner that emphasizes a basic community service orientation and justifies the public trust. The health care institution's mission and values should be embodied in all its programs, services, and activities.

Because health care organizations must frequently seek a balance among the interests and values of individuals, the institution, and society, they often face ethical dilemmas in meeting the needs of their patients and their communities. This advisory is intended to assist members of the American Hospital Association to better identify and understand the ethical aspects and implications of institutional policies and practices. It is offered with the understanding that each institution's leadership in making policy and decisions must take into account the needs and values of the institution, its physicians, other care givers, and employees and those of individual patients, their families, and the community as a whole.

The governing board of the institution is responsible for establishing and periodically evaluating the ethical standards that guide institutional policies and practices. The governing board must also assure that its own policies, practices, and members comply with both legal and ethical standards of behavior. The chief executive officer is responsible for assuring that hospital medical staff, employees, and volunteers and auxilians understand and adhere to these standards and for promoting a hospital environment sensitive to differing values and conducive to ethical behavior.

This advisory examines the hospital's ethical responsibilities to its community and patients as well as those deriving from its organizational roles as employer and business entity. Although explicit responsibilities also are included in legal and accreditation requirements, it should be remembered that legal, accreditation, and ethical obligations often overlap and that ethical obligations often extend beyond legal and accreditation requirements.

Community Role

• Health care institutions should be concerned with the overall health status of their communities while continuing to provide direct patient services. They should take a leadership role in enhancing public health and continuity of care in the community by communicating and working with other health care and social agencies to improve the availability and provision of health promotion, education, and patient care services.

• Health care institutions are responsible for fair and effective use of available health care delivery resources to promote access to comprehensive and affordable health care services of high quality. This responsibility extends beyond the resources of the given institution to include efforts to coordinate with other health care organizations and professionals and to share in community solutions for providing care for the medically indigent and others in need of specific health services.

• All health care institutions are responsible for meeting community service obligations which may include special initiatives for care for the poor and uninsured, provision of needed medical or social services, education, and various programs designed to meet the specific needs of their communities.

• Health care institutions, being dependent upon community confidence and support, are accountable to the public, and therefore their communications and disclosure of information and data related to the institution should be clear, accurate, and sufficiently complete to assure that it is not misleading. Such disclosure should be aimed primarily at better public understanding of health issues, the services available to prevent and treat illness, and patient rights and responsibilities relating to health care decisions.

• Advertising may be used to advance the health care organization's goals and objectives and should, in all cases, support the mission of the health care organization. Advertising may be used to educate the public, to report to the community, to increase awareness of available services, to increase support for the organization, and to recruit employees. Health care advertising should be truthful, fair, accurate, complete, and sensitive to the health care

needs of the public. False or misleading statements, or statements that might lead the uninformed to draw false conclusions about the health care facility, its competitors, or other health care providers are unacceptable and unethical.**

• As health care institutions operate in an increasingly challenging environment, they should consider the overall welfare of their communities and their own missions in determining their activities, service mixes, and business. Health care organizations should be particularly sensitive to potential conflicts of interests involving individuals or groups associated with the medical staff, governing board, or executive management. Examples of such conflicts include ownership or other financial interests in competing provider organizations or groups contracting with the health care institution.

Patient's Care

• Health care institutions are responsible for providing each patient with care that is both appropriate and necessary for the patient's condition. Development and maintenance of organized programs for utilization review and quality improvement and of procedures to verify the credentials of physicians and other health professionals are basic to this obligation.

• Health care institutions in conjunction with attending physicians are responsible for assuring reasonable continuity of care and for informing patients of patient care alternatives when acute care is no longer needed.

• Health care institutions should ensure that the health care professionals and organizations with which they are formally or informally affiliated have appropriate credentials and/or accreditation and participate in organized programs to assess and assure continuous improvement in quality of care.

• Health care institutions should have policies and practices that assure the patient transfers are medically appropriate and legally permissible. Health care institutions should inform patients of the need for and alternatives to such transfers.

• Health care institutions should have policies and practices that support informed consent for diagnostic and therapeutic procedures and use of advance directives. Policies and practices must respect and promote the patient's responsibility for decision making.

• Health care institutions are responsible for assuring confidentially of patient-specific information. They are responsible for providing safeguards to prevent unauthorized release of information and establishing procedures for authorizing release of data.

- Health care institutions should assure that the psychological, social, spiritual, and physical needs and cultural beliefs and practices of patients and families are respected and should promote employee and medical staff sensitivity to the full range of such needs and practices. The religious and social beliefs and customs of patients should be accommodated whenever possible.

- Health care institutions should have specific mechanisms or procedures to resolve conflicting values and ethical dilemmas as well as complaints and disputes among patients/their families, medical staff, employees, the institution, and the community.

Organizational Conduct

The policies and practices of health care institutions should respect and support the professional ethical codes*** and responsibilities of their employees and medical staff members and be sensitive to institutional decisions that employees might interpret as compromising their ability to provide high-quality health care.

- Health care institutions should provide for fair and equitably-administered employee compensation, benefits, and other policies and practices.

- To the extent possible and consistent with the ethical commitments of the institution, health care institutions should accommodate the desires of employees and medical staff to embody religious and/or moral values in their professional activities.

- Health care institutions should have written policies on conflict of interest that apply to officers, governing board members, and medical staff, as well as others who may make or influence decisions for or on behalf of the institution, including contract employees. Particular attention should be given to potential conflicts related to referral sources, vendors, competing health care services, and investments. These policies should recognize that individuals in decision-making or administrative positions often have duality of interests that may not always present conflicts. But they should provide mechanisms for identifying and addressing dualities when they do exist.

- Health care institutions should communicate their mission, values, and priorities to their employees and volunteers, whose patient care and service activities are the most visible embodiment of the institution's ethical commitments and values.

AHA Resources

The American Hospital Association developed its first "code of ethics" for health care institutions called *Guidelines on Ethical Conduct and Relationships for Health Care Institutions* in 1973 as a complement to the *Code of Ethics for Hospital Executives* (available from the American College of Healthcare Executives). This management advisory is the most current version of this code. The AHA and its members are committed to regular review and updating of this advisory to assure that it is responsive to contemporary ethical issues facing health care institutions. This advisory identifies the major areas affecting the ethical conduct of health care institutions. It would be impossible for one advisory document to detail all of the factors and issues relating to each area. Additional information and guidance is available in the following AHA management advisories:

A *Patient's Bill of Rights, Advertising, Discharge Planning, Disclosure of Financial and Operating Information, Disclosure of Medical Record Information, Establishment of an Employee Grievance Procedure, Ethics Committees, Imperatives of Hospital Leadership, Physician Involvement in Governance, Quality Management, Resolution of Conflicts of Interest, The Patient's Choice of Treatment Options, Verifying Physician Credentials, Verifying Credentials of Medical Students and Residents.* The following AHA publications may also be useful: *Values in Conflict: Resolving Ethical Issues in Hospital Care* (AHA #025002), *Effective DNR Policies: Development, Revision, and Implementation* [out of print]. *Hospital Ethics Newsletter* [no longer published].

---

* The Term "health care institution" represents the mission, programs, and services as defined and implemented by the institution's leadership, including the governing board, executive management, and medical staff leadership. See also management advisories on *Imperatives of Hospital Leadership, Role and Functions of Hospital Executive Management, Role and Functions of the Hospital Governing Board,* and *Role and Functions of the Hospital Medical Staff.*

** Adapted from the AHA Management Advisory on Advertising, 1990.

*** For example, the American College of Healthcare Executives' *Code of Ethics* and professional codes of nursing, medicine, etc.

AMERICAN INSTITUTE OF AERONAUTICS AND ASTRONAUTICS

Address: 1801 Alexander Bell Drive, Suite 500
Reston, VA 20191-4344
Telephone: 703/264-7500 or 800/639-2422
WWW: www.aiaa.org
Document: AIAA Code of Ethics (1978)

PRECEPT

The AIAA member is to uphold and advance the honor and dignity of the aerospace profession, and in keeping with high standards of ethical conduct:

I. Will be honest and impartial, and will serve with devotion his employer and the public;

II. Will strive to increase the competence and prestige of the aerospace profession;

III. Will use his knowledge and skill for the advancement of human welfare.

RELATIONS WITH THE PUBLIC

1.1 The AIAA member will have proper regard for the safety, health, and welfare of the public in the performance of his professional duties.

1.2 The member will endeavor to extend public knowledge and appreciation of aerospace science and its achievements.

1.3 The member will be dignified and modest in explaining his work and merit and will ever uphold the honor and dignity of his profession.

1.4 The member will express an opinion on a professional subject only where it is founded on adequate knowledge and honest conviction.

1.5 The member will preface any ex parte statement, criticisms, or arguments that he may issue by clearly indicating on whose behalf they are made.

RELATIONS WITH EMPLOYERS AND CLIENTS

2.1 The AIAA member will act in professional matters as a faithful agent or trustee for each employer or client.

2.2 The member will act fairly and justly toward vendors and contractors, and will not accept from vendors or contractors any commissions or allowances that represent a conflict of interest.

2.3 The member will inform his employer or client if he is financially interested in any vendor or contractor, or in any invention, machines, or apparatus, that is involved in a project or work of his employer or client. The member will not allow such interest to affect his decision regarding services that he may be called upon to perform.

2.4 The member will indicate to his employer or client the adverse consequences to be expected if his judgment is overruled.

2.5 The member will undertake only those professional assignments for which he is qualified. The member will engage or advise his employer or client to engage specialists and will cooperate with them whenever his employer's or client's interests are served best by such an arrangement.

2.6 The member will not disclose information concerning the business affairs or technical processes of any present or former employer or client without his consent.

2.7 The member will not accept compensation—financial or otherwise—from more than one party for the same service, or for other services pertaining to the same work, without the consent of all interested parties.

2.8 The member will report to his employer or client any matters within his area of expertise that the member believes represent a contravention of public law, regulation, health, or safety.

RELATIONS WITH OTHER PROFESSIONALS

3.1 The AIAA member will take care that credit for professional work is given to those to whom credit is properly due.

3.2 The member will provide a prospective employee with complete information on working conditions and his proposed status of employment, and after employment will keep him informed of any changes in them.

3.3 The member will uphold the principle of appropriate and adequate compensation for those engaged in professional work, including those in subordinate capacities.

3.4 The member will endeavor to provide opportunity for the professional development and advancement of those in his employ or under his supervision.

3.5 The member will not injure maliciously the professional reputation, prospects, or practice of another professional.

3.6 The member will cooperate in advancing the aerospace profession by interchanging information and experience with other professionals and students, and by contributing to public communication media, and to the efforts of engineering and scientific societies and schools.

CODE ADMINISTRATION
Establish a three-member Ethical Conduct Panel (ECP) reporting to the Board of Directors to:

- Review all complaints, recommendations, criticism of, and questions concerning a code of ethics for all AIAA members and insure the privacy of all inquiries.
- By unanimous vote, recommend a course of action merited by the applicant.
- Where appropriate, present the ECP recommendations to the AIAA Board of Directors for approval and implementation.
- Report to each regular AIAA Board of Directors' meeting the disposition of all cases, including decisions not to act, received by the ECP in the period preceding each meeting.

The ECP will consist of three AIAA members selected by the Board of Directors. A member will serve for three years. One member will be appointed each year to provide two-thirds member continuity. If a member of the ECP disqualifies himself or herself, the Board shall appoint a replacement.

Note: As in AIAA's Constitution and Bylaws, the use of the masculine gender is intended to be interchangeable with the feminine gender wherever it occurs in this Code.

© American Institute of Aeronautics and Astronautics. Reprinted with permission.

THE AMERICAN INSTITUTE OF ARCHITECTS

Address: 1735 New York Avenue NW
Washington, DC 20006-5292

Telephone: 202/626-7300 or 800/242-3837
WWW: www.aiaonline.com
Document: Code of Ethics and Professional Conduct (1997)

Preamble
Members of The American Institute of Architects are dedicated to the highest standards of professionalism, integrity, and competence. This Code of Ethics and Professional Conduct states guidelines for the conduct of Members in fulfilling those obligations. The Code is arranged in three tiers of statements: Canons, Ethical Standards, and Rules of Conduct.

- Canons are broad principles of conduct.
- Ethical Standards (E.S.) are more specific goals toward which Members should aspire in professional performance and behavior.
- Rules of Conduct (**Rule**) are mandatory; violation of a rule is grounds for disciplinary action by the Institute. Rules of Conduct, in some instances, implement more than one Canon or Ethical Standard.

The Code applies to the professional activities of all classes of Members, wherever they occur. It addresses responsibilities to the public, which the profession serves and enriches; to the clients and users of architecture and in the building industries, who help to shape the built environment; and to the art and science of architecture, that continuum of knowledge and creation which is the heritage and legacy of the profession.

Commentary is provided for some of the Rules of Conduct. That commentary is meant to clarify or elaborate the intent of the Rule. The commentary is not part of the Code. Enforcement will be determined by application of the Rules of Conduct alone; the commentary will assist those seeking to conform their conduct to the Code and those charged with its enforcement.

Statement in Compliance With the 1990 Consent Decree: The following practices are not, in themselves, unethical, unprofessional, or contrary to any policy of The American Institute of Architects or any of its components:

(1) submitting, at any time, competitive bids or price quotations, including, in circumstances where price is the sole or principal consideration in the selection of an architect;
(2) providing discounts; or
(3) providing free services.

Individual architects or architecture firms, acting alone and not on behalf of the Institute or any of its components, are free to decide for themselves whether or not to engage in any of these practices. The Consent Decree permits the Institute, its components, or Members to advocate legislative or other government policies or actions relating to these practices. Finally, architects should continue to consult with state laws or regulations governing the practice of architecture.

CANON I
GENERAL OBLIGATIONS

MEMBERS SHOULD MAINTAIN AND ADVANCE THEIR KNOWLEDGE OF THE ART AND SCIENCE OF ARCHITECTURE, RESPECT THE BODY OF ARCHITECTURAL ACCOMPLISHMENT, CONTRIBUTE TO ITS GROWTH, THOUGHTFULLY CONSIDER THE SOCIAL AND ENVIRONMENTAL IMPACT OF THEIR PROFESSIONAL ACTIVITIES, AND EXERCISE LEARNED AND UNCOMPROMISED PROFESSIONAL JUDGMENT.

E.S. 1.1   Knowledge and Skill: Members should strive to improve their professional knowledge and skill.

Rule 1.101   In practicing architecture, Members shall demonstrate a consistent pattern of reasonable care and competence, and shall apply the technical knowledge and skill which is ordinarily applied by architects of good standing practicing in the same locality.

Commentary: By requiring a "consistent pattern" of adherence to the common law standard of competence, this allows for discipline of a Member who more than infrequently does not achieve that standard. Isolated instances of minor lapses would not provide the basis for discipline.

E.S. 1.2   Standards of Excellence: Members should continually seek to raise the standards of aesthetic excellence, architectural education, research, training, and practice.

E.S. 1.3   Natural and Cultural Heritage: Members should respect and help conserve their natural and cultural heritage while striving to improve the environment and the quality of life within it.

E.S. 1.4   Human Rights: Members should uphold human rights in all their professional endeavors.

Rule 1.401   Members shall not discriminate in their professional activities on the basis of race, religion, gender, national origin, age, disability, or sexual orientation.

E.S. 1.5   Allied Arts & Industries: Members should promote allied arts and contribute to the knowledge and capability of the building industries as a whole.

CANON II
OBLIGATIONS TO THE PUBLIC

MEMBERS SHOULD EMBRACE THE SPIRIT AND LETTER OF THE LAW GOVERNING THEIR PROFESSIONAL AFFAIRS AND SHOULD PROMOTE AND SERVE THE PUBLIC INTEREST IN THEIR PERSONAL AND PROFESSIONAL ACTIVITIES.

E.S. 2.1   Conduct: Members should uphold the law in the conduct of their professional activities.

Rule 2.101   Members shall not, in the conduct of their professional practice, knowingly violate the law.

Commentary: The violation of any law, local, state or federal, occurring in the conduct of a Member's professional practice, is made the basis for discipline by this rule. This includes the federal Copyright Act, which prohibits copying architectural works without the permission of the copyright owner. Allegations of violations of this rule must be based on an independent finding of a violation of the law by a court of competent jurisdiction or an administrative or regulatory body.

Rule 2.102   Members shall neither offer nor make any payment or gift to a public official with the intent of influencing the official's judgment in connection with an existing or prospective project in which the Members are interested.

Commentary: This does not prohibit campaign contributions made in conformity with applicable campaign financing laws.

Rule 2.103   Members serving in a public capacity shall not accept payments or gifts which are intended to influence their judgment.

Rule 2.104   Members shall not engage in conduct involving fraud or wanton disregard of the rights of others.

Commentary: This rule addresses serious misconduct whether or not related to a Member's professional practice. When an alleged violation of this rule is based on a violation of a law, then its proof must be based on an independent finding of a violation of the law by a court of competent jurisdiction or an administrative or regulatory body.

Rule 2.105 If, in the course of their work on a project, the Members become aware of a decision taken by their employer or client which violates any law or regulation and which will, in the Members' judgment, materially affect adversely the safety to the public of the finished project, the Members shall:

(a) advise their employer or client against the decision,

(b) refuse to consent to the decision, and

(c) report the decision to the local building inspector or other public official charged with the enforcement of the applicable laws and regulations, unless the Members are able to cause the matter to be satisfactorily resolved by other means.

Commentary: This rule extends only to violations of the building laws that threaten the public safety. The obligation under this rule applies only to the safety of the finished project, an obligation coextensive with the usual undertaking of an architect.

Rule 2.106 Members shall not counsel or assist a client in conduct that the architect knows, or reasonably should know, is fraudulent or illegal.

E.S. 2.2 Public Interest Services: Members should render public interest professional services and encourage their employees to render such services.

E.S. 2.3 Civic Responsibility: Members should be involved in civic activities as citizens and professionals, and should strive to improve public appreciation and understanding of architecture and the functions and responsibilities of architects.

Rule 2.301 Members making public statements on architectural issues shall disclose when they are being compensated for making such statements or when they have an economic interest in the issue.

CANON III
OBLIGATIONS TO THE CLIENT
MEMBERS SHOULD SERVE THEIR CLIENTS COMPETENTLY AND IN A PROFESSIONAL MANNER, AND SHOULD EXERCISE UNPREJUDICED AND UNBIASED JUDGMENT WHEN PERFORMING ALL PROFESSIONAL SERVICES.

E.S. 3.1 Competence: Members should serve their clients in a timely and competent manner.

Rule 3.101 In performing professional services, Members shall take into account applicable laws and regulations. Members may rely on the advice of other qualified persons as to the intent and meaning of such regulations.

Rule 3.102 Members shall undertake to perform professional services only when they, together with those whom they may engage as consultants, are qualified by education, training, or experience in the specific technical areas involved.

Commentary: This rule is meant to ensure that Members not undertake projects which are beyond their professional capacity. Members venturing into areas which require expertise they do not possess may obtain that expertise by additional education, training, or through the retention of consultants with the necessary expertise.

Rule 3.103 Members shall not materially alter the scope or objectives of a project without the client's consent.

E.S. 3.2 Conflict of Interest: Members should avoid conflicts of interest in their professional practices and fully disclose all unavoidable conflicts as they arise.

Rule 3.201 A Member shall not render professional services if the Member's professional judgment could be affected by responsibilities to another project or person, or by the Member's own interests, unless all those who rely on the Member's judgment consent after full disclosure.

Commentary: This rule is intended to embrace the full range of situations that may present a Member with a conflict between his interests or responsibilities and the interests of others. Those who are entitled to disclosure may include a client, owner, employee, contractor, or others who rely on or are affected by the Member's professional decisions. A Member who cannot appropriately communicate about a conflict directly with an affected person must take steps to ensure that disclosure is made by other means.

Rule 3.202   When acting by agreement of the parties as the independent interpreter of building contract documents and the judge of contract performance, Members shall render decisions impartially.

Commentary: This rule applies when the Member, though paid by the owner and owing the owner loyalty, is nonetheless required to act with impartiality in fulfilling the architect's professional responsibilities.

E.S. 3.3   Candor and Truthfulness: Members should be candid and truthful in their professional communications and keep their clients reasonably informed about the clients' projects.

Rule 3.301   Members shall not intentionally or recklessly mislead existing or prospective clients about the results that can be achieved through the use of the Members' services, nor shall the Members state that they can achieve results by means that violate applicable law or this **Code**.

Commentary: This rule is meant to preclude dishonest, reckless, or illegal representations by a Member either in the course of soliciting a client or during performance.

E.S. 3.4   Confidentiality: Members should safeguard the trust placed in them by their clients.

Rule 3.401   Members shall not knowingly disclose information that would adversely affect their client or that they have been asked to maintain in confidence, except as otherwise allowed or required by this **Code** or applicable law.

Commentary: To encourage the full and open exchange of information necessary for a successful professional relationship, Members must recognize and respect the sensitive nature of confidential client communications. Because the law does not recognize an architect-client privilege, however,

the rule permits a Member to reveal a confidence when a failure to do so would be unlawful or contrary to another ethical duty imposed by this **Code**.

CANON IV
OBLIGATIONS TO THE PROFESSION
MEMBERS SHOULD UPHOLD THE INTEGRITY AND DIGNITY OF THE PROFESSION.

E.S. 4.1   Honesty and Fairness: Members should pursue their professional activities with honesty and fairness.

Rule 4.101   Members having substantial information which leads to a reasonable belief that another Member has committed a violation of this **Code** which raises a serious question as to that Member's honesty, trustworthiness, or fitness as a Member, shall file a complaint with the National Ethics Council.

Commentary: Often, only an architect can recognize that the behavior of another architect poses a serious question as to that other's professional integrity. In those circumstances, the duty to the professional's calling requires that a complaint be filed. In most jurisdictions, a complaint that invokes professional standards is protected from a libel or slander action if the complaint was made in good faith. If in doubt, a Member should seek counsel before reporting on another under this rule.

Rule 4.102   Members shall not sign or seal drawings, specifications, reports, or other professional work for which they do not have responsible control.

Commentary: Responsible control means the degree of knowledge and supervision ordinarily required by the professional standard of care. With respect to the work of licensed consultants, Members may sign or seal such work if they have reviewed it, coordinated its preparation, or intend to be responsible for its adequacy.

Rule 4.103   Members speaking in their professional capacity shall not knowingly make false statements of material fact.

Commentary: This rule applies to statements in all professional contexts, including applications for licensure and AIA membership.

E.S. 4.2   Dignity and Integrity: Members should strive, through their actions, to promote the dignity and integrity of the profession, and to ensure that their representatives and employees conform their conduct to this **Code**.

Rule 4.201 Members shall not make misleading, deceptive, or false statements or claims about their professional qualifications, experience, or performance and shall accurately state the scope and nature of their responsibilities in connection with work for which they are claiming credit.

Commentary: This rule is meant to prevent Members from claiming or implying credit for work which they did not do, misleading others, and denying other participants in a project their proper share of credit.

Rule 4.202 Members shall make reasonable efforts to ensure that those over whom they have supervisory authority conform their conduct to this **Code**.

Commentary: What constitutes "reasonable efforts" under this rule is a common sense matter. As it makes sense to ensure that those over whom the architect exercises supervision be made generally aware of the **Code**, it can also make sense to bring a particular provision to the attention of a particular employee when a situation is present which might give rise to violation.

CANON V
OBLIGATIONS TO COLLEAGUES
MEMBERS SHOULD RESPECT THE RIGHTS AND ACKNOWLEDGE THE PROFESSIONAL ASPIRATIONS AND CONTRIBUTIONS OF THEIR COLLEAGUES.

E.S. 5.1 Professional Environment: Members should provide their associates and employees with a suitable working environment, compensate them fairly, and facilitate their professional development.

E.S. 5.2 Professional Recognition: Members should build their professional reputation on the merits of their own service and performance and should recognize and give credit to others for the professional work they have performed.

Rule 5.201 Members shall recognize and respect the professional contributions of their employees, employers, professional colleagues, and business associates.

Rule 5.202 Members leaving a firm shall not, without the permission of their employer or partner, take designs, drawings, data, reports, notes, or other materials relating to the firm's work, whether or not performed by the Member.

Rule 5.203 A Member shall not unreasonably withhold permission from a departing employee or partner to take copies of designs, drawings, data, reports, notes, or other materials relating to work performed by the employee or partner that are not confidential.

Commentary: A Member may impose reasonable conditions, such as the payment of copying costs, on the right of departing persons to take copies of their work.

© American Institute of Architects. Reprinted with permission.

AMERICAN INSTITUTE OF CERTIFIED PLANNERS

Address: 1776 Massachusetts Avenue NW, Suite 400 Washington, DC 20036-1904
Telephone: 202/872-0611
WWW: www.planning.org
Document: AICP Code of Ethics and Professional Conduct (1978. Most recently revised 1991.)

(In addition to the Code, the AICP publishes "Procedures Under the Code of Ethics and Professional Conduct" and "AICP Advisory Rulings," neither of which are reprinted here. The AICP, an institute of the American Planning Association, also subscribes to the "AICP/APA Ethical Principles in Planning." This document is reprinted under the APA entry. See p. 00.—Eds.)

This Code is a guide to the ethical conduct required of members of the American Institute of Certified Planners. The Code also aims at informing the public of the principles to which professional planners are committed. Systematic discussion of the application of these principles, among planners and with the public, is itself essential behavior to bring the Code into daily use.

The Code's standards of behavior provide a basis for adjudicating any charge that a member has acted unethically. However, the Code also provides more than the minimum threshold of enforceable acceptability. It sets aspirational standards that require conscious striving to attain.

The principles of the Code derive both from the general values of society and from the planning profession's special responsibility to serve the public interest. As the basic values of society are often in competition with each other, so also do the principles of this Code sometimes compete. For example, the need to provide full public information may compete with the need to respect confidences. Plans and programs often result from a balancing among divergent interests. An ethical judgment often also requires a conscientious balancing, based on the facts and context of a particular situation and on the precepts of the entire Code. Formal procedures for filing of complaints, investigation and resolution of alleged violations and the issuance of advisory rulings are part of the Code.

The Planner's Responsibility to the Public

A. A planner's primary obligation is to serve the public interest. While the definition of the public interest is formulated through continuous debate, a planner owes allegiance to a conscientiously attained concept of the public interest, which requires these special obligations:

1) A planner must have special concern for the long range consequences of present actions.
2) A planner must pay special attention to the interrelatedness of decisions.
3) A planner must strive to provide full, clear and accurate information on planning issues to citizens and governmental decision-makers.
4) A planner must strive to give citizens the opportunity to have a meaningful impact on the development of plans and programs. Participation should be broad enough to include people who lack formal organization or influence.
5) A planner must strive to expand choice and opportunity for all persons, recognizing a special responsibility to plan for the needs of disadvantaged groups and persons, and must urge the alteration of policies, institutions and decisions which oppose such needs.
6) A planner must strive to protect the integrity of the natural environment.
7) A planner must strive for excellence of environmental design and endeavor to conserve the heritage of the built environment.

The Planner's Responsibility to Clients and Employers

B. A planner owes diligent, creative, independent and competent performance of work in pursuit of the client's or employer's interest. Such performance should be consistent with the planner's faithful service to the public interest.

1) A planner must exercise independent professional judgment on behalf of clients and employers.
2) A planner must accept the decisions of a client or employer concerning the objectives and nature of the professional services to be performed unless the course of action to be pursued involves conduct which is illegal or inconsistent with the planner's primary obligation to the public interest.
3) A planner shall not perform work if there is an actual, apparent, or reasonably foreseeable conflict of interest, direct or indirect, or an appearance of impropriety, without full written disclosure concerning work for current or past clients and subsequent written consent by the current client or employer. A planner shall remove himself or herself from a project if there is any direct personal or financial gain including gains to family members. A planner shall not disclose information gained in the course of public activity for a private benefit unless the information would be offered impartially to any person.
4) A planner who has previously worked for a public planning body should not represent a private client, for one year after the planner's last date of employment with the planning body, in connection with any matter before that body that the planner may have influenced before leaving public employment.
5) A planner must not solicit prospective clients or employment through use of false or misleading claims, harassment or duress.
6) A planner must not sell or offer to sell services by stating or implying an ability to influence decisions by improper means.

7) A planner must not use the power of any office to seek or obtain a special advantage that is not in the public interest nor any special advantage that is not a matter of public knowledge.

8) A planner must not accept or continue to perform work beyond the planner's professional competence or accept work which cannot be performed with the promptness required by the prospective client or employer, or which is required by the circumstances of the assignment.

9) A planner must not reveal information gained in a professional relationship which the client or employer has requested to be held inviolate. Exceptions to this requirement of non-disclosure maybe made only when a) required by process of law, or b) required to prevent a clear violation of law, or c) required to prevent a substantial injury to the public. Disclosure pursuant to (b) and c) must not be made until after the planner has verified the facts and issues involved and, when practicable, has exhausted efforts to obtain reconsiderations of the matter and has sought separate opinions on the issue from other qualified professionals employed by the client or employer.

The Planner's Responsibility to the Profession and to Colleagues

C. A planner should contribute to the development of the profession by improving knowledge and techniques, making work relevant to solutions of community problems, and increasing public understanding of planning activities. A planner should treat fairly the professional views of qualified colleagues and members of other professions.

1) A planner must protect and enhance the integrity of the profession and must be responsible in criticism of the profession.

2) A planner must accurately represent the qualifications, views and findings of colleagues.

3) A planner who reviews the work of other professionals must do so in a fair, considerate, professional and equitable manner.

4) A planner must share the results of experience and research which contribute to the body of planning knowledge.

5) A planner must examine the applicability of planning theories, methods and standards to the facts and analysis of each particular situation and must not accept the applicability of a customary solution without first establishing its appropriateness to the situation.

6) A planner must contribute time and information to the professional development of students, interns, beginning professionals and other colleagues.

7) A planner must strive to increase the opportunities for women and members of recognized minorities to become professional planners.

8) A planner shall not commit an act of sexual harassment.

The Planner's Self-Responsibility

D. A planner should strive for high standards of professional integrity, proficiency and knowledge.

1) A planner must not commit a deliberately wrongful act which reflects adversely on the planner's professional fitness.

2) A planner must respect the rights of others and, in particular, must not improperly discriminate against persons.

3) A planner must strive to continue professional education.

4) A planner must accurately represent professional qualifications, education and affiliations.

5) A planner must systematically and critically analyze ethical issues in the practice of planning.

6) A planner must strive to contribute time and effort to groups lacking in adequate planning resources and to voluntary professional activities.

© American Institute of Certified Planners. Reprinted with permission.

AMERICAN INSTITUTE OF CERTIFIED PUBLIC ACCOUNTANTS

Address: 1211 Avenue of the Americas
             New York, NY 10036-8775
Telephone: 212/596-6200
WWW: www.aicpa.org
Document: Principles of Professional Conduct
             (1998)

(The AICPA *Code of Professional Conduct* has many parts. The part reprinted here is "Section 50: Principles of Professional Conduct." In addition to the *Principles of Professional Conduct*, the AICPA publishes a set of "Rules," which govern the performance of professional services by members. Rules are not reprinted here. The Council of the American Institute of Certified Public Accountants is authorized to designate bodies to promulgate technical standards under the Rules, and the bylaws require adherence to those Rules and standards.)

Section 51—Preamble

.01 Membership in the American Institute of Certified Public Accountants is voluntary. By accepting membership, a certified public accountant assumes an obligation of self-discipline above and beyond the requirements of laws and regulations.

.02 These Principles of the Code of Professional Conduct of the American Institute of Certified Public Accountants express the profession's recognition of its responsibilities to the public, to clients, and to colleagues. They guide members in the performance of their professional responsibilities and express the basic tenets of ethical and professional conduct. The Principles call for an unswerving commitment to honorable behavior, even at the sacrifice of personal advantage.

Section 52—Article I: Responsibilities

In carrying out their responsibilities as professionals, members should exercise sensitive professional and moral judgments in all their activities.

.01 As professionals, certified public accountants perform an essential role in society. Consistent with that role, members of the American Institute of Certified Public Accountants have responsibilities to all those who use their professional services. Members also have a continuing responsibility to cooperate with each other to improve the art of accounting, maintain the public's confidence, and carry out the profession's special responsibilities for self-governance. The collective efforts of all members are required to maintain and enhance the traditions of the profession.

Section 53—Article II: The Public Interest

Members should accept the obligation to act in a way that will serve the public interest, honor the public trust, and demonstrate commitment to professionalism.

.01 A distinguishing mark of a profession is acceptance of its responsibility to the public. The accounting profession's public consists of clients, credit grantors, governments, employers, investors, the business and financial community, and others who rely on the objectivity and integrity of certified public accountants to maintain the orderly functioning of commerce. This reliance imposes a public interest responsibility on certified public accountants. The public interest is defined as the collective well-being of the community of people and institutions the profession serves.

.02 In discharging their professional responsibilities, members may encounter conflicting pressures from among each of those groups. In resolving those conflicts, members should act with integrity, guided by the precept that when members fulfill their responsibility to the public, clients' and employers' interests are best served.

.03 Those who rely on certified public accountants expect them to discharge their responsibilities with integrity, objectivity, due professional care, and a genuine interest in serving the public. They are expected to provide quality services, enter into fee arrangements, and offer a range of services—all in a manner that demonstrates a level of professionalism consistent with these Principles of the Code of Professional Conduct.

.04 All who accept membership in the American Institute of Certified Public Accountants commit themselves to honor the public trust. In return for the faith that the public reposes in them, members should seek continually to demonstrate their dedication to professional excellence.

Section 54—Article III: Integrity

To maintain and broaden public confidence, members should perform all professional responsibilities with the highest sense of integrity.

.01 Integrity is an element of character fundamental to professional recognition. It is the quality from which the public trust derives and the benchmark against which a member must ultimately test all decisions.

.02 Integrity requires a member to be, among other things, honest and candid within the constraints of client confidentiality. Service and the public trust should not be subordinated to personal gain and advantage. Integrity can accommodate the inadvertent error and the honest difference of opinion; it cannot accommodate deceit or subordination of principle.

.03 Integrity is measured in terms of what is right and just. In the absence of specific rules, standards, or guidance, or in the face of conflicting opinions, a member should test decisions and deeds by asking: "Am I doing what a person of integrity would do? Have I retained my integrity?" Integrity requires a member to observe both the form and the spirit of technical and ethical standards; circumvention of those standards constitutes subordination of judgment.

.04 Integrity also requires a member to observe the principles of objectivity and independence and of due care.

Section 55—Article IV: Objectivity and Independence
A member should maintain objectivity and be free of conflicts of interest in discharging professional responsibilities. A member in public practice should be independent in fact and appearance when providing auditing and other attestation services.

.01 Objectivity is a state of mind, a quality that lends value to a member's services. It is a distinguishing feature of the profession. The principle of objectivity imposes the obligation to be impartial, intellectually honest, and free of conflicts of interest. Independence precludes relationships that may appear to impair a member's objectivity in rendering attestation services.

.02 Members often serve multiple interests in many different capacities and must demonstrate their objectivity in varying circumstances. Members in public practice render attest, tax, and management advisory services. Other members prepare financial statements in the employment of others, perform internal auditing services, and serve in financial and management capacities in industry, education, and government. They also educate and train those who aspire to admission into the profession. Regardless of service or capacity, members should protect the integrity of their work, maintain objectivity, and avoid any subordination of their judgment.

.03 For a member in public practice, the maintenance of objectivity and independence requires a continuing assessment of client relationships and public responsibility. Such a member who provides auditing and other attestation services should be independent in fact and appearance. In providing all other services, a member should maintain objectivity and avoid conflicts of interest.

.04 Although members not in public practice cannot maintain the appearance of independence, they nevertheless have the responsibility to maintain objectivity in rendering professional services. Members employed by others to prepare financial statements or to perform auditing, tax, or consulting services are charged with the same responsibility for objectivity as members in public practice and must be scrupulous in their application of generally accepted accounting principles and candid in all their dealings with members in public practice.

Section 56—Article V: Due Care
A member should observe the profession's technical and ethical standards, strive continually to improve competence and the quality of services, and discharge professional responsibility to the best of the member's ability.

.01 The quest for excellence is the essence of due care. Due care requires a member to discharge professional responsibilities with competence and diligence. It imposes the obligation to perform professional services to the best of a member's ability with concern for the best interest of those for whom the services are performed and consistent with the profession's responsibility to the public.

.02 Competence is derived from a synthesis of education and experience. It begins with a mastery of the common body of knowledge required for designation as a certified public accountant. The maintenance of competence requires a commitment to learning and professional improvement that must continue throughout a member's professional life. It is a member's individual responsibility. In all engagements and in all responsibilities, each member should undertake to achieve a level of competence that will assure that the quality of the member's services meets the high level of professionalism required by these Principles.

.03 Competence represents the attainment and maintenance of a level of understanding and knowledge that enables a member to render services with facility and acumen. It also establishes the limitations of a member's capabilities by dictating that consultation or referral may be required when a professional engagement exceeds the personal competence of a member or a member's firm. Each member is responsible for assessing his or her own competence—of evaluating whether education, experience, and judgment are adequate for the responsibility to be assumed.

.04 Members should be diligent in discharging responsibilities to clients, employers, and the public. Diligence imposes the responsibility to render services promptly and carefully, to be thorough, and to observe applicable technical and ethical standards.

.05 Due care requires a member to plan and supervise adequately any professional activity for which he or she is responsible.

Section 57—Article VI: Scope and Nature of Services

A member in public practice should observe the Principles of the Code of Professional Conduct in determining the scope and nature of services to be provided.

.01 The public interest aspect of certified public accountants' services requires that such services be consistent with acceptable professional behavior for certified public accountants. Integrity requires that service and the public trust not be subordinated to personal gain and advantage. Objectivity and independence require that members be free from conflicts of interest in discharging professional responsibilities. Due care requires that services be provided with competence and diligence.

.02 Each of these Principles should be considered by members in determining whether or not to provide specific services in individual circumstances. In some instances, they may represent an overall constraint on the nonaudit services that might be offered to a specific client. No hard-and-fast rules can be developed to help members reach these judgments, but they must be satisfied that they are meeting the spirit of the Principles in this regard.

.03 In order to accomplish this, members should :

• Practice in firms that have in place internal quality-control procedures to ensure that services are competently delivered and adequately supervised.
• Determine, in their individual judgments, whether the scope and nature of other services provided to an audit client would create a conflict of interest in the performance of the audit function for that client.
• Assess, in their individual judgments, whether an activity is consistent with their role as professionals (for example, Is such activity a reasonable extension or variation of existing services offered by the member or others in the profession?).

AICPA Professional Code of Professional Conduct, Copyright © 1992, 1994, 1996, 1998 by the American Institute of Certified Public Accountants, Inc., is reprinted with permission.

AMERICAN INSTITUTE OF CHEMICAL ENGINEERS

Address: 3 Park Avenue
                   New York, NY 10016-5991
Telephone: 212/591-8100 or 800/242-4363
WWW: www.aiche.org
Document: Code of Ethics (1992)

The Council of the American Institute of Chemical Engineers adopted this Code of Ethics to which it expects that the professional conduct of its members shall conform, and to which every applicant attests by signing his or her membership application.

Members of the American Institute of Chemical Engineers shall uphold and advance the integrity, honor, and dignity of the engineering profession by: being honest and impartial and serving with fidelity their employers, their clients, and the public; striving to increase the competence and prestige of the engineering profession; and using their knowledge and skill for the enhancement of human welfare. To achieve these goals, members shall:

1. Hold paramount the safety, health, and welfare of the public in performance of their professional duties.
2. Formally advise their employers or clients (and consider further disclosure, if warranted) if they perceive that a consequence of their duties will adversely affect the present or future health or safety of their colleagues or the public.
3. Accept responsibility for their actions and recognize the contributions of others; seek critical re-

view of their work and offer objective criticism of the work of others.

4. Issue statements or present information only in an objective and truthful manner.

5. Act in professional matters for each employer or client as faithful agents or trustees, and avoid conflicts of interest.

6. Treat fairly all colleagues and co-workers, recognizing their unique contributions and capabilities.

7. Perform professional services only in areas of their competence.

8. Build their professional reputations on the merits of their services.

9. Continue their professional development throughout their careers, and provide opportunities for the professional development of those under their supervision.

© American Institute of Chemical Engineers. Reprinted with permission.

THE AMERICAN INSTITUTE OF CHEMISTS

Address: 515 King Street, Suite 420
             Alexandria, VA 22314-1917
Telephone: 703/836-2090
WWW: www.theaic.org
Document: Code of Ethics (1983)

The profession of chemistry is increasingly important to the progress and the welfare of the community. The Chemist is frequently responsible for decisions affecting the lives and fortunes of others. To protect the public and maintain the honor of the profession, The American Institute of Chemists has established the following rules of conduct.

IT IS THE DUTY OF THE CHEMIST

1. To uphold the law; not to engage in illegal work nor cooperate with anyone so engaged;

2. To avoid associating or being identified with any enterprise of questionable character;

3. To be diligent in exposing and opposing such errors and frauds as the Chemist's special knowledge brings to light;

4. To sustain the institutions and burdens of the community as a responsible citizen;

5. To work and act in a strict spirit of fairness to employers, clients, contractors, and employees, and in a spirit of personal helpfulness and fraternity toward other members of the chemical profession.

6. To use only honorable means of competition for professional employment; to advertise only in a dignified and factual manner; to refrain from unfairly injuring, directly or indirectly, the professional reputation, prospects, or business of a fellow Chemist, or attempting to supplant a fellow Chemist already selected for employment; to perform services for a client only at rates that fairly reflect costs of equipment, supplies and overhead expenses as well as fair personal compensation;

7. To accept employment from more than one employer or client only when there is no conflict of interest; to accept commissions or compensation in any form from more than one interested party only with the full knowledge and consent of all parties concerned;

8. To perform all professional work in a manner that merits full confidence and trust; to be conservative in estimates, reports and testimony, especially if these are related to the promotion of a business enterprise or the protection of the public interest, and to state explicitly any known bias embodied therein; to advise client or employer of the probability of success before undertaking a project;

9. To review the professional work of other Chemists, when requested, fairly and in confidence, where they are: a) subordinates or employees, b) authors of proposals for grants or contracts, c) authors of technical papers, patents, or other publications, or d) involved in litigation;

10. To advance the profession by exchanging general information and experience with fellow Chemists and by contributing to the work of technical societies and to the technical press when such contribution does not conflict with the interests of a client or employer; to announce inventions and scientific advances first in this way rather than through the public press; to ensure that credit for technical work is given to its actual authors;

11. To work for any client or employer under a clear agreement, preferably in writing, as to the owner-

ship of data, plans, improvements, inventions, designs, or other intellectual property developed or discovered while so employed, understanding that in the absence of a written agreement: a) results based on information from the client or employer, not obtainable elsewhere, are the property of the client or employer, b) results based on knowledge or information belonging to the Chemist, or publicly available, are the property of the Chemist, the client or employer being entitled to their use only in the case or project for which the Chemist was retained, c) all work and results outside of the field for which the Chemist was retained or employed, and not using time or facilities belonging to a client or employer, are the property of the Chemist, and d) special data or information provided by a client or employer, or created by the Chemist and belonging to the client or employer, must be treated as confidential, used only in general as a part of the Chemist's professional experience, and published only after release by the client or employer.

12. To report any infractions of these principles of professional conduct to the authorities responsible for enforcement of applicable laws or regulations, or to the Ethics Committee of The American Institute of Chemists, as appropriate.

© The American Institute of Chemists. Reprinted with permission.

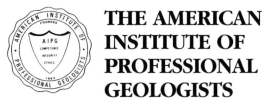

THE AMERICAN INSTITUTE OF PROFESSIONAL GEOLOGISTS

Address: 8703 Yates Drive, Suite 200
              Westminster, CO 80031-3681
Telephone: 303/412-6205
WWW: www.aipg.org
Document: AIPG Code of Ethics

Preamble

Members of The American Institute of Professional Geologists are dedicated to the highest standards of personal integrity and professional conduct. The Institute's Code of Ethics comprises three parts: the Canons, which are broad principles of conduct; the Ethical Standards, which are goals to which Members aspire; and the Rules of Conduct. Compliance with the Rules of Conduct is mandatory and violation of any Rule will be grounds for disciplinary action by the Institute. Under the Bylaws, the Institute may also impose discipline for legal violations and because of the suspension or revocation of registration or licensure, among other grounds. Disciplinary action may take the form of private admonition, public reprimand, suspension of membership, or termination. The Code of Ethics applies to all professional activities of Members and Affiliates, wherever and whenever they occur. The title "Member" where used in this Code of Ethics shall include Affiliates. A Member shall not be relieved of an ethical responsibility by virtue of his or her employment, because the Member has delegated an assignment to a subordinate, or because the Member was not involved in performing services for compensation.

Canon 1. General Obligations

Members should be guided by the highest standards of personal integrity and professional conduct.

Standard 1.1

Members should pursue honesty, integrity, loyalty, fairness, impartiality, candor, fidelity to trust, inviolability of confidence, and honorable conduct as a way of life.

> **Rule 1.1.1** By applying for or by continuing membership in the Institute, a Member agrees to comply with and uphold this Code of Ethics.

Canon 2. Obligations To The Public

Members should uphold the public health, safety, and welfare in the performance of professional services, and avoid even the appearance of impropriety.

Standard 2.1

Members should observe and comply with the requirements and intent of all applicable laws, codes, and regulations.

> **Rule 2.1.1** A Member shall not knowingly participate in any illegal activities, or knowingly permit the publication of his or her reports, maps, or other documents for illegal purpose.
>
> **Rule 2.1.2** A Member shall neither offer nor make any illegal payment, gift, or other valuable consideration to a public official for the purpose of influencing a decision by such official; nor shall a Member accept any payment, gift, or other valu-

able consideration which would appear to influence a decision made on behalf of the public by the Member acting in a position of public trust.

Rule 2.1.3 If a Member becomes aware of a decision or action by an employer, client, or colleague which violates any law or regulation, the Member shall advise against such action, and when such violation appears to materially affect the public health, safety, or welfare, shall advise the appropriate public officials responsible for the enforcement of such law or regulation.

Standard 2.2

Members should be accurate, truthful, and candid in all communications with the public.

Rule 2.2.1 A Member shall not knowingly engage in false or deceptive advertising, or make false, misleading, or deceptive representations or claims in regard to the profession of geology or which concern his or her own professional qualifications or abilities or those of other geologists.

Rule 2.2.2 A Member shall not issue a false statement or false information which the Member knows to be false or misleading, even though directed to do so by an employer or client.

Rule 2.2.3 A Member shall avoid making sensational, exaggerated, and or unwarranted statements that may mislead or deceive members of the public or any public body.

Standard 2.3

Members should participate as citizens and as professionals in public affairs.

Rule 2.3.1 A Member acting in a position of public trust shall exercise his or her authority impartially, and shall not seek to use his or her authority for personal profit or to secure any competitive advantage.

Standard 2.4

Members should promote public awareness of the effects of geology and geological processes on the quality of life.

Canon 3. Obligations to Employers and Clients

Members should serve their employers and clients faithfully and competently within their overall professional and ethical obligations.

Standard 3.1

Members should disclose any actual or potential conflicts of interest which may affect their ability to serve an employer or client faithfully.

Rule 3.1.1 A Member shall disclose to a prospective employer or client the existence of any owned or controlled mineral or other interest which may, either directly or indirectly, have a pertinent bearing on such employment.

Rule 3.1.2 A Member having or expecting to have beneficial interest in a property on which the Member reports shall state in the report the fact of the existence of such interest or expected interest.

Rule 3.1.3 A Member employed or retained by one employer or client shall not accept, without that employer's or client's written consent, an engagement by another if the interests of the two are in any manner conflicting.

Rule 3.1.4 A Member shall not accept referral fees from any person to whom an employer or client is referred; however, nothing herein shall prohibit a Member from being compensated by the employer or client for consultation, or for other services actually performed.

Rule 3.1.5 A Member shall not offer or pay referral fees to any person who refers an employer or client to the Member; however, nothing herein shall prohibit a Member from compensating the person giving the referral for consultation, or for other services actually performed.

Standard 3.2

Members should protect, to the fullest possible extent, the interest of an employer or client so far as is consistent with the public health, safety, and welfare and the Member's legal, professional, and ethical obligations.

Rule 3.2.1 A Member shall not use, directly or indirectly, any confidential information obtained from or in the course of performing services for an employer or client in any way which is adverse or detrimental to the interests of the employer or client, except with the prior consent of the employer or client or when disclosure is required by law.

Rule 3.2.2 A Member who has made an investigation for an employer or client shall not seek to profit economically from the information gained without written permission of the employer or client, unless it is clear that there can no longer be a conflict of interest with the original employer or client.

Rule 3.2.3 A Member shall not use his or her employer's or client's resources for private gain without the prior knowledge and consent of his or her employer or client.

Standard 3.3

Members should serve their employers and clients competently.

Rule 3.3.1 A Member shall perform professional services or issue professional advice which is only within the scope of the education and experience of the Member and the Member's professional associates, consultants, or employees, and shall advise the employer or client if any professional advice is outside of the Member's personal expertise.

Rule 3.3.2 A Member shall not give a professional opinion or submit a report without being as thoroughly informed as might be reasonably expected, considering the purpose for which the opinion or report is requested.

Rule 3.3.3 A Member shall engage, or advise an employer or client to engage, and cooperate with other experts and specialists whenever the employer's or client's interests would be best served by such service.

Standard 3.4
Members should serve their employers and clients diligently and perform their services in a timely manner.

Standard 3.5
Members who find that obligations to an employer or client conflict with professional or ethical standards should have such objectionable conditions corrected or resign.

Canon 4. Obligations to Professional Colleagues
Members should respect the rights, interests, and contributions of their professional colleagues.

Standard 4.1
Members should respect and acknowledge the professional status and contributions of their colleagues.

Rule 4.1.1 A Member shall give due credit for work done by others in the course of a professional assignment, and shall not knowingly accept credit due another.

Rule 4.1.2 A Member shall not plagiarize another in oral and written communications, or use materials prepared by others without appropriate attribution.

Canon 5. Obligations to the Institute and the Profession
Members should continually strive to improve the profession of geology so that it may be of ever increasing benefit to society.

Standard 5.1
Members should strive to improve their professional knowledge and skills.

Standard 5.2
Members should cooperate with others in the profession and encourage the dissemination of geological knowledge.

Standard 5.3
Members should work toward the improvement of standards of geological education, research, training, and practice.

Standard 5.4
Members should not only uphold these standards of ethics by precept and example but also encourage by counsel and advice to other Members, their adherence to such standards.

Standard 5.5
Members having knowledge of a violation of these Rules by another Member should bring substantiated evidence of such violation to the attention of the Institute.

© American Institute of Professional Geologists. Reprinted with permission.

AMERICAN JUDICATURE SOCIETY

Address: 180 North Michigan Avenue,
              Suite 600
              Chicago, IL 60601
Telephone: 312/558-6900
WWW: www.ajs.org
Document: Model Code of Conduct for
              Nonjudicial Court Employees (1989)

(In September 1987, AJS conducted a national survey of state court administrators about the existence and content of any rules in their states governing the behavior of nonjudicial court employees. The results appeared in the February 1988, *Judicature* article, "Ethical conduct of state court employees and administrators: the search for standards," by David T. Ozar, Cynthia Kelly and Yvette Begue. The authors continued their research and, working with AJS' executive committee, developed a model code which was approved for promulgation. The Model Code was published in the October-November 1989 issue of *Judicature* along with an article describing its background and development, "Ethical conduct of nonjudicial court employees: a proposed model code."—Eds.)

Introduction
The holding of public employment in the court system is a public trust justified by the confidence that

the citizenry reposes in the integrity of officers and employees of the judicial branch. A court employee, faithful to that trust, therefore shall observe high standards of conduct so that the integrity and independence of the courts may be preserved. Court employees shall carry out all duties assigned by law and shall put loyalty to the principles embodied in this Code above loyalty to persons or parties. A court employee shall uphold the Constitution, laws and legal regulations of the United States, the State of _____ and all governments therein, and never be a party to their evasion. A court employee shall abide by the standards set out in this Code and shall endeavor to expose violations of this Code wherever they may appear to exist.

Scope

1) Each jurisdiction must determine exactly which employees shall be covered by this Code. The Code should apply to all employees who directly or indirectly affect the court's operation. A suggested listing of such employees would include: court clerks, docket clerks, data processing personnel, bailiffs and judicial secretaries, as well as court managers and their staffs. This list is intended to be illustrative and does not imply that other employees should be omitted. For example, if janitors in the court building have authority to purchase supplies for the court, then the Code should apply to these employees as well.

2) This Code is not intended to apply to law clerks, who should be held to a higher standard of conduct, nor to court reporters who are bound by the *Code of Professional Conduct of the National Shorthand Reporters Association.*

3) The term, "court employee," includes within its scope those court employees who are also court managers.

4) The term, "court manager," includes within its scope all court employees who have important supervisory responsibilities. Each jurisdiction must identify the particular court employees who function as managers within that court system.

Section One: Abuse of Position

A) No employee shall use or attempt to use his or her official position to secure unwarranted privileges or exemptions for the employee or others.

B) No employee shall accept, solicit, or agree to accept any gift, favor or anything of value based upon any understanding, either explicit or implicit, that the official actions, decisions or judgment of any employee would be influenced thereby. Gifts that do not violate this prohibition against abuse of position are further regulated in Section Three, Subsection B6.

C) No employee shall discriminate by dispensing special favors to anyone, whether or not for remuneration, nor shall any employee so act that the employee is unduly affected or appears to be affected by kinship, rank, position or influence of any party or person.

D) No employee shall request or accept any fee or compensation, beyond that received by the employee in his or her official capacity, for advice or assistance given in the course of his or her public employment.

E) Each employee shall use the resources, property and funds under the employee's official control judiciously and solely in accordance with prescribed statutory and regulatory procedures.

F) Each employee shall immediately report to the appropriate authority any attempt to induce him or her to violate any of the standards set out above.

Section Two: Confidentiality

A) No court employee shall disclose to any unauthorized person for any purpose any confidential information acquired in the course of employment, or acquired through unauthorized disclosure by another.

B) Confidential information includes, but is not limited to, information on pending cases that is not already a matter of public record and information concerning the work product of any judge, law clerk, staff attorney or other employee including but not limited to, notes, papers, discussions and memoranda.

C) Confidential information that is available to specific individuals by reason of statute, court rule or administrative policy shall be provided only by persons authorized to do so.

D) Every court employee shall report confidential information to the appropriate authority when the employee reasonably believes this information is or may be evidence of a violation of law or of unethical conduct. No court employee shall be disciplined for disclosing such confidential information to an appropriate authority.

E) Court managers should educate court employees about what information is confidential and, where appropriate, should designate materials as confidential.

F) Court employees are not precluded from responding to inquiries concerning court procedures, but a court employee shall not give legal advice. Standard court procedures, such as the method for filing an appeal or starting a small claims action, should be summarized in writing and made available to litigants. All media requests for information should be referred to the court employee designated for that purpose.

G) No court employee shall either initiate or repeat ex parte communications from litigants, witnesses or attorneys to judges, jury members or any other person.

H) A former court employee should not disclose confidential information when disclosure by a current court employee would be a breach of confidentiality.

Section Three: Conflict of Interest

A) Every court employee shall avoid conflicts of interest, as defined below, in the performance of professional duties. Even though no misuse of office is involved, such a conflict of interest involving a court employee can seriously undermine the community's confidence and trust in the court system. Therefore, every court employee is required to exercise diligence in becoming aware of conflicts of interest, disclosing conflicts to the designated authority and ending them when they arise.

1) A conflict of interest exists when the court employee's objective ability or independence of judgment in the performance of his or her job is impaired or may reasonably appear to be impaired or when the court employee, or the employee's immediate family, as defined below, or business would derive financial gain as a result of the employee's position with the court system.

2) No conflict of interest exists if any benefit or detriment accrues to the employee as a member of a profession, business or group to the same extent as any other member of the profession, business or group who does not hold a position within the court system.

3) For the purpose of this Code, "immediate family" shall include the following, whether related by marriage, blood or adoption: spouse; dependent children; brother; sister; parent; grandparent; grandchildren; father-in-law, mother-in-law; sister-in-law, brother-in-law; son-in-law, daughter-in-law, stepfather, stepmother; stepson, stepdaughter; stepbrother, stepsister; half-brother, half-sister.

B) Prohibited Activities:

1) No court employee shall enter into any contract with the court system for services, supplies, equipment, leases or realty, apart from the employment contract relating to the employee's position, nor use that position to assist any member of his or her immediate family in securing a contract with the court system in a manner not available to any other interested party.

2) No court employee shall receive tips or other compensation for representing, assisting or consulting with parties engaged in transaction's or involved in proceedings with the court system.

3) No court employee shall participate in any business decision involving a party with whom either the court employee or any member of the employee's immediate family is negotiating for future employment.

4) No former court employee shall engage in transactions or represent others in transaction or proceedings with the court system for one year after termination of employment in any matter in which the former employee was substantially involved or in any dealings with offices or positions that the former employee once held.

5) No court employee shall knowingly employ, advocate or recommend for employment any member of his or her immediate family.

6) No court employee shall solicit, accept or agree to accept any gifts, loans, gratuities, discounts, favors, hospitality or services under circumstances from which it could reasonably be inferred that a major purpose of the donor is to influence the court employee in the performance of official duties.

   a) Nothing in this section shall prohibit an employee from accepting a public award presented in recognition of public service.

   b) Nothing in this section shall prohibit an employee from receiving a commercially reasonable loan made as part of the ordinary transaction of the lender's business.

   c) Nothing in this section shall prohibit any person from donating a gift to a group of employees, e.g., all the employees of an office or unit of the court system, provided that the value and circumstances of the gift are such that it could not be reasonably inferred that the gift would influence the employees in the performance of their official duties or that such influence was the purpose of the donor, and provided that any employee accepting such a gift promptly report the gift to the supervisor, who shall be responsible for its proper distribution. Gifts received with the understanding that they will influence employees' official actions, decisions or judgments are prohibited as abuse of office in Section One, Subsection B.

    d) Nothing in this section shall prohibit any person or group from donating a gift of historical or other significant value that is given for the benefit of the court system, provided that such a gift is received on behalf of the court system by the appropriate designated authority.

C) To secure conformity to the above standards, every court employee who has authority to enter into or to approve contracts in the name of the court system shall file a financial disclosure statement with the appropriate designated authority upon beginning employment in such position, at termination of employment, and annually while so employed. Such disclosure shall include all sources of and contractual arrangements for personal income, including investments and real property, business entity income and business position income held or received by themselves, their spouses or their dependent children, and shall follow the guidelines established by the appropriate designated authority.

D) Each full-time court employee's position with the court system must be the employee's primary employment. Outside employment is permissible only if it complies with all the following criteria:

1) The outside employment is not with an entity that regularly appears in court or conducts business with the court system, and it does not require the court employee to have frequent contact with attorneys who regularly appear in the court system; and

2) The outside employment is capable of being fulfilled outside of normal working hours and is not incompatible with the performance of the court employee's duties and responsibilities; and

3) The outside employment does not require the practice of law; and

4) The outside employment does not require or induce the court employee to disclose confidential information acquired in the course of and by reason of official duties; and

5) The outside employment shall not be within the judicial, executive or legislative branch of government without written consent of both employers; and

6) Where a conflict of interest exists or may reasonably appear to exist or where the outside employment reflects adversely on the integrity of the court, the employee shall inform the appropriate designated authority prior to accepting the other employment.

Section Four: Political Activity

A) Each employee retains the right to vote as the employee chooses and is free to participate actively in political campaigns during non-working hours. Such activity includes, but is not limited to, membership and holding office in a political party, campaigning for a candidate in a partisan election by making speeches and making contributions of time or money to individual candidates, political parties or other groups engaged in political activity. An employee who chooses to participate in political activity during off-duty hours shall not use his or her position or title within the court system in connection with such political activities.

B) With the exception of officers of the court who obtain their position by means of election, no employee shall be a candidate for or hold partisan elective office. With the same exception, an employee who declares an intention to run for partisan elective office shall take an unpaid leave of absence upon the filing of nomination papers. If elected, he or she shall resign. An employee may be a candidate for non-partisan office without separating from employment, provided that the employee complies with the requirements in this Code concerning performance of duties, conflicts of interest, etc.

C) No employee shall engage in any political activity during scheduled work hours, or when using government vehicles or equipment, or on court property. Political activity includes, but is not limited to:

1) Displaying campaign literature, badges, stickers, signs or other items of political advertising on behalf of any party, committee, agency or candidate for political office;

2) Using official authority or position, directly or indirectly, to influence or attempt to influence any other employee in the court system to become a member of any political organization or take part in any political activity;

3) Soliciting signatures for political candidacy;

4) Soliciting or receiving funds for political purposes.

D) No employee shall discriminate in favor of or against any employee or applicant for employment on account of political contributions or permitted political activities.

Section Five: Performance of Duties

A) Every court employee shall endeavor at all times to perform official duties properly and with diligence. Every court employee shall apply full-time energy to the business and responsibilities of the employee's office during working hours.

B) Every court employee shall carry out responsibilities as a servant of the public in as courteous a manner as possible.

C) Every court employee shall maintain or obtain current licenses or certificates as a condition of employment as required by law or court rule.

D) No court employee shall alter, falsify, destroy, mutilate backdate or fail to make required entries on any records within the employee's control. This provision does not prohibit alteration or expungement of records or documents pursuant to a court order.

E) No court employee shall discriminate on the basis of nor manifest, by words or conduct, bias or prejudice based on race, religion, national origin, gender, sexual orientation or political affiliation in the conduct of service to the court.

F) No court employee shall give legal advice or recommend the names of private attorneys.

G) No court employee shall refuse to enforce or otherwise carry out any properly issued rule or order of court, nor shall court employees exceed that authority. No court employee shall be required to perform any duties outside the scope of the assigned job description.

H) Every court employee shall immediately report violations of this Code to the appropriate designated authority.

I) Court employees who are law students, attorneys or members of other professional groups are also bound by the appropriate professional duties of those roles.

Section Six: Court Managers

A) Court managers regularly shall update their education.

B) Court managers shall require employees subject to their direction and control to observe the ethical standards set out in this Code.

C) Court managers shall diligently discharge their administrative responsibilities, maintain professional competence in judicial administration and facilitate the performance of other court employees.

D) Court managers shall take action regarding any unethical conduct of which they may become aware, initiating appropriate disciplinary measures against an employee for any such conduct and reporting to appropriate authorities evidence of any unethical conduct by judges or lawyers.

E) Court managers shall not act as leaders in or hold office in any political organization, make speeches for any political organization or publicly endorse a candidate for political office.

© American Judicature Society. Reprinted with permission.

AMERICAN LEAGUE OF LOBBYISTS

Address:	PO Box 30005
	Alexandria, VA 22310
Telephone:	703/960-3011
WWW:	www.alldc.org
Document:	Guidelines for Professional Conduct (1987)

The American League of Lobbyists believes that effective government depends on the greatest possible participation of those being governed. At the federal level, such participation focuses on the legislative and executive branches where professional and citizen lobbyists drawn from every major discipline represent literally every segment of society and every sector of the economy.

The League further believes that the heavy responsibility of the professional lobbyist, functioning in the eye of public opinion, requires standards of ethical behavior beyond those generally accepted by a free and moral society.

The League, therefore, offers the following guidelines which it urges be observed by its members and all those whose professional objectives are to influence national public policy decisions—

- The professional lobbyist accepts the fact that it is the system of representative government we enjoy that makes possible the practice of lobbying and, while keeping the interest of employer or client in a position of primacy, will temper the advocacy role with proper consideration for the general public interest.
- The professional lobbyist will protect confidences, not only those of the employer or client but also those of elected and appointed officials of government and professional colleagues.
- The professional lobbyist will always deal in accurate, current and factual information, whether it is being reported to the employer or client, government officials, the media or professional colleagues, and will not engage in misrepresentation of any nature.
- The professional lobbyist will acquire enough knowledge of public policy issues to be able to fairly present all points of view.
- The professional lobbyist will avoid conflicts of interest, not only conflict with the interests of the employer or client, but also those of colleagues pursuing the same or similar objectives, and where conflict is unavoidable will communicate the facts fully and freely to those affected.
- The professional lobbyist will comply with the laws and regulations governing lobbying as well as the standards of conduct applying to officials and staff of the Congress and the Executive Branch and will strive to go one step further and function in a manner that goes beyond these official enactments and promulgations.
- The personal conduct of the professional lobbyist should not bring discredit to the profession, government or individual colleagues.
- The professional lobbyist will refrain from any form of discrimination which is legally proscribed or simply generally recognized as such.
- A priority goal of the professional lobbyist should be to increase public understanding of the process and this objective should be pursued in every possible way—public appearances, media contacts, articles in company and other publications, and contacts in the normal course of everyday life.
- The professional lobbyist should constantly strive to upgrade the necessary skills by every means available, continuing formal education, attendance at meetings and seminars, and participation in ad hoc groups with like-minded colleagues.

© American League of Lobbyists. Reprinted with permission.

AMERICAN LIBRARY ASSOCIATION

Address:	50 East Huron Street. Chicago, IL 60611
Telephone:	800/545-2433
WWW:	www.ala.org
Document:	American Library Association Code of Ethics (1995)

As members of the American Library Association, we recognize the importance of codifying and making known to the profession and to the general public the ethical principles that guide the work of librarians, other professionals providing information services, library trustees and library staffs.

Ethical dilemmas occur when values are in conflict. The American Library Association Code of Ethics states the values to which we are committed, and embodies the ethical responsibilities of the profession in this changing information environment.

We significantly influence or control the selection, organization, preservation, and dissemination of information. In a political system grounded in an informed citizenry, we are members of a profession explicitly committed to intellectual freedom and the freedom of access to information. We have a special obligation to ensure the free flow of information and ideas to present and future generations.

The principles of this Code are expressed in broad statements to guide ethical decision making. These statements provide a framework; they cannot and do not dictate conduct to cover particular situations.

I. We provide the highest level of service to all library users through appropriate and usefully organized resources; equitable service policies; equitable access; and accurate, unbiased, and courteous responses to all requests.

II. We uphold the principles of intellectual freedom and resist all efforts to censor library resources.

III. We protect each library user's right to privacy and confidentiality with respect to information sought or received and resources consulted, borrowed, acquired or transmitted.

IV. We recognize and respect intellectual property rights.

V. We treat co-workers and other colleagues with respect, fairness and good faith, and advocate conditions of employment that safeguard the rights and welfare of all employees of our institutions.

VI. We do not advance private interests at the expense of library users, colleagues, or our employing institutions.

VII. We distinguish between our personal convictions and professional duties and do not allow our personal beliefs to interfere with fair representation of the aims of our institutions or the provision of access to their information resources.

VIII. We strive for excellence in the profession by maintaining and enhancing our own knowledge and skills, by encouraging the professional development of co-workers, and by fostering the aspirations of potential members of the profession.

© American Library Association. Reprinted with permission.

AMERICAN MARKETING ASSOCIATION

Address: 311 South Wacker Drive, Suite 5800
             Chicago, IL 60606
Telephone: 312/542-9000 or 800/262-1150
WWW: www.ama.org
Document: Code of Ethics

Members of the American Marketing Association are committed to ethical professional conduct. They have joined together in subscription to this Code of Ethics embracing the following topics:

Responsibilities of the marketer

Marketers must accept responsibility for the consequences of the activities and make every effort to ensure that their decisions, recommendations, and actions function to identify, serve, and satisfy all relevant publics: customers, organizations and society.

Marketers' professional conduct must be guided by:

1. The basic rule of professional ethics: not knowingly to do harm;
2. The adherence to all applicable laws and regulations;
3. The accurate representation of their education, training and experience; and
4. The active support, practice and promotion of this Code of Ethics.

Honesty and fairness

Marketers shall uphold and advance the integrity, honor and dignity of the marketing profession by:

1. Being honest in serving consumers, clients, employees, suppliers, distributors, and the public;
2. Not knowingly participating in conflict of interest without prior notice to all parties involved; and;
3. Establishing equitable fee schedules including the payment or receipt of usual, customary and/or legal compensation for marketing exchanges.

Rights and duties of parties in the marketing exchange process

Participants in the marketing exchange process should be able to expect that:

1. Products and services offered are safe and fit for their intended uses;
2. Communications about offered products and services are not deceptive;
3. All parties intend to discharge their obligations, financial and otherwise, in good faith; and
4. Appropriate internal methods exist for equitable adjustment and/or redress of grievances concerning purchases.

It is understood that the above would include, but is not limited to, the following responsibilities of the marketer:

In the area of product development and management,

• disclosure of all substantial risks associated with product or service usage;

- identification of any product component substitution that might materially change the product or impact on the buyer's purchase decision;
- identification of extra cost-added features.

In the area of promotions,
- avoidance of false and misleading advertising;
- rejection of high-pressure manipulations, or misleading sales tactics;
- avoidance of sales promotions that use deception or manipulation.

In the area of distribution,
- not manipulating the availability of a product for the purpose of exploitation;
- not using coercion in the marketing channel;
- not exerting undue influence over the reseller's choice to handle a product.

In the area of pricing,
- not engaging in price fixing;
- not practicing predatory pricing;
- disclosing the full price associated with any purchase.

In the area of marketing research,
- prohibiting selling or fundraising under the guise of conducting research;
- maintaining research integrity by avoiding misrepresentation and omission of pertinent research data;
- treating outside clients and suppliers fairly.

Organizational Relationships
Marketers should be aware of how their behavior may influence or impact the behavior of others in organizational relationships. They should not demand, encourage or apply coercion to obtain unethical behavior in their relationships with others, such as employees, suppliers, or customers.

1. Apply confidentiality and anonymity in professional relationships with regard to privileged information;
2. Meet their obligations and responsibilities in contracts and mutual agreements in a timely manner;
3. Avoid taking the work of others, in whole, or in part, and represent this work as their own or directly benefit from it without compensation or consent of the originator or owner;
4. Avoid manipulation to take advantage of situations to maximize personal welfare in a way that unfairly deprives or damages the organization of others.

Any AMA member found to be in violation of any provision of the Code of Ethics may have his or her Association membership suspended or revoked.

© American Marketing Association. Reprinted with permission.

AMERICAN MATHEMATICAL SOCIETY

Address: PO Box 6248
             Providence, RI 02904-6248
Telephone: 401/455-4000 or 800/321-4267
WWW: www.ams.org
Document: Ethical Guidelines of the American
             Mathematical Society (1995)

To assist in its chartered goal, ". . . the furtherance of the interests of mathematical scholarship and research . . .," and to help in the preservation of that atmosphere of mutual trust and ethical behavior required for science to prosper, the American Mathematical Society, through its Council, sets forth the following guidelines. While it speaks only for itself, these guidelines reflect its expectations of behavior both for its members and for all members of the wider mathematical community, including institutions engaged in the education or employment of mathematicians or in the publication of mathematics.

It is not intended that something not mentioned here is necessarily outside the scope of AMS interest. These guidelines are not a complete expression of the principles that underlie them but will, it is expected, be modified and amplified by events and experience. These are guidelines, not a collection of rigid rules.

The American Mathematical Society, through its Committee on Professional Ethics (COPE), may provide an avenue of redress for individual members injured in their capacity as mathematicians by violations of its ethical principles. COPE, in accordance with its procedures, will, in each case, determine the appropriate ways in which it can be helpful (including making recommendations to the Council of the Society). However, the AMS cannot enforce these guidelines and it cannot substitute for individual responsibility or for the responsibility of the mathematical community at large.

1. Mathematical Research and Its Presentation

The public reputation for honesty and integrity of the mathematical community and of the Society is its collective treasure and its publication record is its legacy. The correct attribution of mathematical results is essential, both as it encourages creativity, by benefiting the creator whose career may depend on the recognition of the work, and as it informs the community of when, where, and sometimes how original ideas have entered into the chain of mathematical thought. To that end, mathematicians have certain responsibilities which include the following:

- To endeavor to be knowledgeable in their field, especially as regards related work;
- To give proper credit (even to unpublished sources because the knowledge that something is true or false is valuable, however it is obtained);
- To use no language that suppresses or improperly detracts from the work of others;
- To correct in a timely way or withdraw work that is erroneous or previously published.

A claim of independence may not be based on ignorance of well disseminated results. Errors and oversights can occur, but it is the responsibility of the person making the error to set the record straight.

On appropriate occasions, it may be desirable to offer or accept joint authorship when independent researchers find that they have produced identical results. However, the authors listed for a paper must all have made a significant contribution to its content, and all who have made such a contribution must be offered the opportunity to be listed as an author. To claim a result in advance of its having been achieved with reasonable certainty injures the community by restraining those working toward the same goal. Publication of results that are announced must not be unreasonably delayed. Because the free exchange of ideas necessary to promote research is possible only when every individual's contribution is properly recognized, the Society will not knowingly publish anything that violates this principle, and it will seek to expose egregious violations anywhere in the mathematical community.

2. Social Responsibility of Mathematicians

The Society promotes mathematical research together with its unrestricted dissemination, and to that end encourages all and will strive to afford equal opportunity to all to engage in this endeavor. Mathematical ability must be respected wherever it is found, without regard to race, gender, ethnicity, age, sexual orientation, religious or political belief, or disability.

The growing importance of mathematics in society at large and of public funding of mathematics may increasingly place members of the mathematical community in conflicts of interest. The appearance of bias in reviewing, refereeing, or in funding decisions must be scrupulously avoided, particularly where decisions may affect one's own research, that of close colleagues, or of one's students; in extreme cases one must withdraw.

A reference or referee's report fully and accurately reflecting the writer's views is often given only on the understanding that it be confidential or that the name of the writer be withheld from certain interested parties; therefore, a request for a reference or report must be assumed, unless there is a statement to the contrary, to carry an implicit promise of confidentiality or anonymity which must be carefully kept unless negated by law. The writer of the reply must respond fairly, and keep confidential any privileged information, personal or mathematical, that the writer receives. If the requesting individual, institution, agency or company becomes aware that confidentiality or anonymity can not be maintained, that must immediately be communicated, and if known in advance, must be stated in the original request.

Where choices must be made and conflicts are unavoidable, as with editors or those who decide on appointments or promotions, it is essential to keep careful records which, even if held confidential at the time, would, when opened, demonstrate that the process was, indeed, fair. Freedom to publish must sometimes yield to security concerns, but mathematicians should resist excessive secrecy demands whether by government or private institutions.

When mathematical work may affect the public health, safety or general welfare, it is the responsibility of mathematicians to disclose the implications of their work to their employers and to the public, if necessary. Should this bring retaliation, the Society will examine the ways in which it may want to help the "whistle-blower," particularly when the disclosure has been made to the Society.

3. Education and Granting of Degrees

Holding a Ph.D. degree is virtually indispensable to an academic career in mathematics and is becoming increasingly important as a certificate of competence in the wider job market. An institution granting a degree in mathematics is certifying that competence and must take full responsibility for it by insuring the high level and originality of the thesis work, and sufficient knowledge by the recipient of important branches of mathematics outside the scope of the thesis. The original results in a thesis should be publishable in a recognized journal. When there is evidence of plagiarism it must be carefully investigated, even if it comes to light after granting the degree, and, if proven, the degree should be revoked.

Mathematicians and organizations involved in advising graduate students should honestly inform them about the employment prospects they may face upon completion of their degrees. No one should be exploited by the offer of a temporary position at a low salary and/or a heavy work load.

4. Publications

The Society will not take part in the publishing, printing or promoting of any research journal where there is some acceptance criterion, stated or unstated, that conflicts with the principles of these guidelines. It will promote the quick refereeing and timely publication of articles accepted to its journals.

Editors are responsible for the timely refereeing of articles and must judge articles by the state of knowledge at the time of submission. Editors and referees should accept a paper for publication only if they are reasonably certain the paper is correct.

The contents of an unpublished and uncirculated paper should be regarded by a journal as privileged information. If the contents of a paper become known in advance of publication solely as a result of its submission to or handling by a journal, and if a later paper based on knowledge of the privileged information is received anywhere (by the same or another journal), then any editor aware of the facts must refuse or delay publication of the later paper until after publication of the first—-unless the first author agrees to earlier publication of the later paper.

At the time a manuscript is submitted, editors should notify authors whenever a large backlog of accepted papers may produce inordinate delay in publication. A journal may not delay publication of a paper for reasons of an editor's self interest or of any interest other than the author's. The published article should bear the date on which the manuscript was originally submitted to the journal for publication, together with the dates of any revisions. Editors must be given and accept full scientific responsibility for their journals; when a demand is made by an outside agency for prior review or censorship of so-called "sensitive" articles, that demand must be resisted and, in any event, knowledge of the demand must be made public.

All mathematical publishers, particularly those who draw without charge on the resources of the mathematical community through the use of unpaid editors and referees, must recognize that they have made a compact with the community to disseminate information, and that compact must be weighed in their business decisions.

Both editors and referees must respect the confidentiality of materials submitted to them unless these have previously been made public, and above all may not appropriate to themselves ideas in work submitted to them or do anything that would impair the rights of authors to the fruits of their labors. Editors must preserve the anonymity of referees unless there is a credible allegation of misuse.

These are ethical obligations of all persons or organizations controlling mathematical publications, whatever their designation.

© American Mathematical Society. Reprinted with permission.

American Medical Association
Physicians dedicated to the health of America

AMERICAN MEDICAL ASSOCIATION

Address: 515 North State Street
             Chicago, IL 60610
Telephone: 312/464-5000

WWW: www.ama-assn.org
Document: Principles of Medical Ethics (1980)

Following is the text of the Principles of Medical Ethics; drafted by the special committee chaired by James S. Todd, MD, and adopted by the House of Delegates in July 1980.

Preamble:
The medical profession has long subscribed to a body of ethical statements developed primarily for the benefit of the patient. As a member of this profession, a physician must recognize responsibility not only to the patient, but also to society, or other health professionals, and to self. The following principles adopted by the American Medical Association are not laws, but standards of conduct which define the essentials of honorable behavior for the physician.

   I. A physician shall be dedicated to providing competent medical service with compassion and respect for human dignity.
   II. A physician shall deal honestly with patients and colleagues, and strive to expose those physicians deficient in character or competence, or who engage in fraud or deception.
   III. A physician shall respect the law and also recognize a responsibility to seek changes in those requirements which are contrary to the best interests of the patient.
   IV. A physician shall respect the rights of patients, of colleagues, and of other health professionals, and shall safeguard patient confidences within the constraints of the law.
   V. A physician shall continue to study, apply and advance scientific knowledge, make relevant information available to patients, colleagues, and the public, obtain consultation, and use the talents of other health professionals when indicated.
   VI. A physician shall, in the provision of appropriate patient care, except in emergencies, be free to choose whom to serve, with whom to associate, and the environment in which to provide medical services.
   VII. A physician shall recognize a responsibility to participate in activities contributing to an improved community.

AMERICAN MEDICAL TECHNOLOGISTS

Address: 710 Higgins Road
             Park Ridge, IL 60068-5765
Telephone: 847/823-5169
WWW: www.amt1.com
Document: Standards of Practice (1990)

The American Medical Technologists seeks to encourage, establish, and maintain the highest standards, traditions and principles of the practices which constitute the professions of the Registry.

Members of the Registry must recognize their responsibilities, not only to their patients, but also to society, to other health care professionals and to themselves.

The following Standards of Practice are principles adopted by the Board of Directors which define the essence of honorable and ethical behavior for a health care professional.

   I. While engaged in the Arts and Sciences which constitute the practice of their profession, AMT professionals shall be dedicated to the provision of competent service.
   II. The AMT professional shall place the welfare of the patient above all else.
   III. The AMT professional understands the importance of thoroughness in the performance of duty, compassion with patients, and the importance of the tasks which they may perform.

IV. The AMT professional shall always seek to respect the rights of patients and of fellow health care providers, and shall safeguard patient confidences.

V. AMT professionals will strive to increase their technical knowledge, shall continue to study, and shall continue to apply scientific advances in their specialty.

VI. The AMT professional shall respect the law and will pledge to avoid dishonest, unethical or illegal practices.

VII. AMT professionals understand that they are not to make or offer a diagnosis or interpretation unless they are duly licensed physicians/dentists or unless asked by the attending physician/dentist.

VIII. The AMT professional shall protect and value the judgment of the attending physician or dentist, providing this does not conflict with the behavior necessary to carry out Standard Number II above.

IX. AMT professionals recognize that any personal wrongdoing is their responsibility. It is also the professional health care provider's obligation to report to the proper authorities any knowledge of professional abuse.

X. The AMT professional pledges personal honor and integrity to cooperate in the advancement and expansion, by every lawful means, of the American Medical Technologists.

© American Medical Technologists. Reprinted with permission.

AMERICAN MENTAL HEALTH COUNSELORS ASSOCIATION

Address: 801 North Fairfax Street, Suite 304
              Alexandria, VA 22314
Telephone: 703/548-6002 or 800/326-2642
WWW: www.amhca.org
Document: AMHCA Code of Ethics (1987)

Preamble

Mental health counselors believe in the dignity and worth of the individual. They are committed to increasing knowledge of human behavior and understanding of themselves and others. While pursuing these endeavors, they make every reasonable effort to protect the welfare of those who seek their services or of any subject that may be the object of study. They use their skills only for purposes consistent with these values and do not knowingly permit their misuse by others. While demanding for themselves freedom of inquiry and community, mental health counselors accept the responsibility this freedom confers: competence, objectivity in the application of skills and concern for the best interests of clients, colleagues, and society in general. In the pursuit of these ideals, mental health counselors subscribe to the following principles:

Principle 1. Responsibility

In their commitment to the understanding of human behavior, mental health counselors value objectivity and integrity, and in providing services they maintain the highest standards. They accept responsibility for the consequences of their work and make every effort to insure that their services are used appropriately.

a. Mental health counselors accept ultimate responsibility for selecting appropriate areas for investigation and the methods relevant to minimize the possibility that their finding will be misleading. They provide thorough discussion of the limitations of their data and alternative hypotheses, especially where their work touches on social policy or might be misconstrued to the detriment of specific age, sex, ethnic, socio-economic, or other social categories. In publishing reports of their work, they never discard observations that may modify the interpretation of results. Mental health counselors take credit only for the work they have actually done. In pursuing research, mental health counselors ascertain that their efforts will not lead to changes in individuals or organizations unless such changes are part of the agreement at the time of obtaining informal consent. Mental health counselors clarify in advance the expectations for sharing and utilizing research data. They avoid dual relationships which may limit objectivity, whether theoretical, political, or monetary, so that interference with data, subjects, and milieu is kept to a minimum.

b. As employees of an institution or agency, mental health counselors have the responsibility of remaining alert to institutional pressures which may distort reports of counseling findings or use them in ways counter to the promotion of human welfare.

c. When serving as members of governmental or other organizational bodies, mental health counselors remain accountable as individuals to the Code of Ethics of the American Mental Health Counselors Association (AMHCA).

d. As teachers, mental health counselors recognize their primary obligation to help others acquire knowledge and skill. They maintain high standards of scholarship and objectivity by presenting counseling information fully and accurately, and by giving appropriate recognition to alternative viewpoints. As practitioners, mental health counselors know that they bear a heavy social responsibility because their recommendations and professional actions may alter the lives of others. They, therefore, remain fully cognizant of their impact and alert to personal, social, organizational, financial or political situations or pressures which might lead to misuse of their influence.

e. As practitioners, mental health counselors know that they bear a heavy social responsibility because their recommendations and professional actions may alter the lives of others. They, therefore, remain fully cognizant of their impact and alert to personal, social, organizational, financial or political situations or pressures which might lead to misuse of their influence.

f. Mental health counselors provide reasonable and timely feedback to employees, trainees, supervisors, students, clients, and others whose work they may evaluate.

Principle 2. Competence
The maintenance of high standards of professional competence is a responsibility shared by all mental health counselors in the interest of the public and the profession as a whole. Mental health counselors recognize the boundaries of their competence and the limitations of their techniques and only provide services, use techniques, or offer opinions as professionals that meet recognized standards. Throughout their careers, mental health counselors maintain knowledge of professional information related to the services they render.

a. Mental health counselors accurately represent their competence, education, training and experience.

b. As teachers, mental health counselors perform their duties based on careful preparation so that

their instruction is accurate, up-to-date and scholarly.

c. Mental health counselors recognize the need for continuing training to prepare themselves to serve persons of all ages and cultural backgrounds. They are open to new procedures and sensitive to differences between groups of people and changes in expectations and values over time.

d. Mental health counselors with the responsibility for decisions involving individuals or policies based on test results should know and understand literature relevant to the tests used and testing problems with which they deal.

e. Mental health counselors and practitioners recognize that their effectiveness depends in part upon their ability to maintain sound interpersonal relations, that temporary or more enduring aberrations on their part may interfere with their abilities or distort their appraisals of others. Therefore, they refrain from undertaking any activity in which their personal problems are likely to lead to inadequate professional services or harm to a client, or, if they are already engaged in such activity when they become aware of their personal problems, they would seek competent professional assistance to determine whether they should suspend or terminate services to one or all of their clients.

f. The mental health counselor has a responsibility both to the individual who is served and to the institution with which the service is performed to maintain high standards of professional conduct. The mental health counselor strives to maintain the highest levels of professional services offered to the individuals to be served. The mental health counselor also strives to assist the agency, organization or institution in providing the highest caliber of professional services. The acceptance of employment in an institution implies that the mental health counselor is in substantial agreement with the general policies and principles of the institution. If, despite concerted efforts, the member cannot reach agreement with the employer as to acceptable standards of conduct that allow for changes in institutional policy conducive to the positive growth and development of counselors, then terminating the affiliation should be seriously considered.

g. Ethical behavior among professional associates, mental health counselors and non-mental health counselors, is expected at all times. When information is possessed which raises serious doubt as to the ethical behavior of professional colleagues, whether association members or not, the mental health counselor is obligated to take action to attempt to rectify such a condition. Such action shall utilize the institution's channels first and then utilize procedures established by the state, division, or association.

h. The mental health counselor is aware of the intimacy of the counseling relationship and maintains a healthy respect for the personhood of the client and avoids engaging in activities that seek to meet the mental health counselor's personal needs at the expense of the client. Through awareness of the negative impact of both racial and sexual stereotyping and discrimination, the member strives to ensure the individual rights and personal dignity of the client in the counseling relationship.

Principle 3. Moral and Legal Standards

Mental health counselors' moral, ethical and legal standards of behavior are a personal matter to the same degree as they are for any other citizen, except as these may compromise the fulfillment of their professional responsibilities, or reduce the trust in counseling or counselors held by the general public.

Regarding their own behavior, mental health counselors should be aware of the prevailing community standards and of the possible impact upon the quality of professional services provided by their conformance to or deviation from these standards. Mental health counselors should also be aware of the possible impact of their public behavior upon the ability of colleagues to perform their professional duties.

a. To protect public confidence in the profession of counseling, mental health counselors will avoid public behavior that is clearly in violation of accepted moral and legal standards.

b. To protect students, mental health counselors/ teachers will be aware of the diverse backgrounds of students and, when dealing with topics that may give offense, will see that the material is treated objectively, that it is clearly relevant to the course, and that is treated in a manner for which the student is prepared.

c. Providers of counseling services conform to the statutes relating to such services as established by their state and its regulating professional board(s).

d. As employees, mental health counselors refuse to participate in employer's practices which are inconsistent with the moral and legal standards established by federal or state legislation regarding

the treatment of employees or of the public. In particular and for example, mental health counselors will not condone practices which result in illegal or otherwise unjustifiable discrimination on the basis of race, sex, religion or national origin in hiring, promotion or training.

e. In providing counseling services to clients mental health counselors avoid any action that will violate or diminish the legal and civil rights of clients or of others who may be affected by the action.

f. Sexual conduct, not limited to sexual intercourse, between mental health counselors and clients is specifically in violation of this code of ethics. This does not, however, prohibit the use of explicit instructional aids including films and video tapes. Such use is within accepted practices of trained and competent sex therapists.

Principle 4. Public Statements

Mental health counselors in their professional roles may be expected or required to make public statements providing counseling information, professional opinions, or supply information about the availability of counseling products and services. In making such statements, mental health counselors take full account of the limits and uncertainties of present counseling knowledge and techniques. They represent, as objectively as possible, their professional qualifications, affiliations, and functions, as well as those of the institutions or organizations with which the statements may be associated. All public statements, announcements of services, and promotional activities should serve the purpose of providing sufficient information to aid the consumer public in making informed judgments and choices on matters that concern it.

a. When announcing professional counseling services, mental health counselors limit the information to: name, highest relevant degree conferred, certification or licensure, address, telephone number, office hours, cost of services, and a brief explanation of the other types of services offered but not evaluative as to their quality or uniqueness. They will not contain testimonials by implication. They will not claim uniqueness of skill or methods beyond those acceptable and public scientific evidence.

b. In announcing the availability of counseling services or products, mental health counselors will not display their affiliations with organizations or agencies in a manner that implies the sponsorship or certification of the organization or agency. They will not name their employer or professional associations unless the services are in fact to be provided by or under the responsible, direct supervision and continuing control of such organizations or agencies.

c. Mental health counselors associated with the development of promotion of counseling devices, books, or other products offered for commercial sale will make every effort to insure that announcements and advertisements are presented in a professional and factually informative manner without unsupported claims of superiority and must be supported by scientifically acceptable evidence or by willingness to aid and encourage independent professional scrutiny or scientific test.

d. Mental health counselors engaged in radio, television or other public media activities will not participate in commercial announcements recommending to the general public the purchase or use of any proprietary or single-source product or service.

e. Mental health counselors who describe counseling or the services of professional counselors to the general public accept the obligation to present the material fairly and accurately, avoiding misrepresentation through sensationalism, exaggeration or superficiality. Mental health counselors will be guided by the primary obligation to aid the public in forming their own informed judgments, opinions and choices.

f. As teachers, mental health counselors ensure their statements in catalogs and course outlines are accurate, particularly in terms of subject matter to be covered, bases for grading, and nature of classroom experiences.

g. Mental health counselors accept the obligation to correct others who may represent their professional qualifications or associations with products or services in a manner incompatible with these guidelines.

h. Mental health counselors providing consultation, workshops, training, and other technical services may refer to previous satisfied clients in their advertising, provided there is no implication that such advertising refers to counseling services.

Principle 5. Confidentiality

Mental health counselors have a primary obligation to safeguard information about individuals obtained in the course of teaching, practice, or research. Personal information is communicated to others only with the person's written consent or in those circumstances where there is clear and imminent danger to the client, to others or to society. Disclosures of counseling information are restricted to what is necessary, relevant and verifiable.

a. All materials in the official record shall be shared with the client who shall have the right to decide what information may be shared with anyone beyond the immediate provider of service and to be informed of the implications of the materials to be shared.

b. The anonymity of clients served in public and other agencies is preserved, if at all possible, by withholding names and personal identifying data. If external conditions require reporting such information, the client shall be so informed.

c. Information received in confidence by one agency or person shall not be forwarded to another person or agency without the client's written permission.

d. Service providers have a responsibility to insure the accuracy and to indicate the validity of data shared with their parties.

e. Case reports presented in classes, professional meetings, or in publications shall be so disguised that no identification is possible unless the client or responsible authority has read the report and agreed in writing to its presentation or publication.

f. Counseling reports and records are maintained under conditions of security and provisions are made for their destruction when they have outlived their usefulness. Mental health counselors insure that privacy and confidentiality are maintained by all persons in the employ or volunteers, and community aides.

g. Mental health counselors who ask that an individual reveal personal information in the course of interviewing, testing or evaluation, or who allow such information to be divulged, do so only after making certain that the person or authorized representative is fully aware of the purposes of the interview, testing or evaluation and of the ways in which the information will be used.

h. Sessions with clients are taped or otherwise recorded only with their written permission or the written permission of a responsible guardian. Even with guardian written consent one should not record a session against the expressed wishes of a client.

i. Where a child or adolescent is the primary client, the interests of the minor shall be paramount.

j. In work with families, the rights of each family member should be safeguarded. The provider of service also has the responsibility to discuss the contents of the record with the parent and/or child, as appropriate, and to keep separate those parts which should remain the property of each family member.

Principle 6. Welfare of the Consumer

Mental health counselors respect the integrity and protect the welfare of the people and groups with whom they work. When there is a conflict of interest between the client and the mental health counselor employing institution, the mental health counselors clarify the nature and direction of their loyalties and responsibilities and keep all parties informed of their commitments. Mental health counselors fully inform consumers as to the purpose and nature of any evaluative treatment, educational or training procedure, and they freely acknowledge that clients, students, or subjects have freedom of choice with regard to participation.

a. Mental health counselors are continually cognizant both of their own needs and of their inherently powerful position *vis-a-vis* clients, in order to avoid exploiting the client's trust and dependency. Mental health counselors make every effort to avoid dual relationships with clients and/or relationships which might impair their professional judgment or increase the risk of client exploitation. Examples of such dual relationships include treating an employee or supervisor, treating a close friend or family relative and sexual relationships with clients.

b. Where mental health counselors work with members of an organization goes beyond reasonable conditions of employment, mental health counselors recognize possible conflicts of interest that may arise. When such conflicts occur, mental health counselors clarify the nature of the conflict and inform all parties of the nature and directions of the loyalties and responsibilities involved.

c. When acting as supervisors, trainers, or employers, mental health counselors accord recipients informed choice, confidentiality, and protection from physical and mental harm.

d. Financial arrangements in professional practice are in accord with professional standards that safeguard the best interests of the client and that are clearly understood by the client in advance of billing. This may best be done by the use of a contract. Mental health counselors are responsible for assisting clients in finding needed services in those instances where payment of the usual fee would be a hardship. No commission or rebate or other form of remuneration may be given or received for referral of clients for professional services, whether by an individual or by an agency.

e. Mental health counselors are responsible for making their services readily accessible to clients in a manner that facilitates the client's ability to make an informed choice when selecting a service provider. This responsibility includes a clear description of what the client may expect in the way of tests, reports, billing, therapeutic regime and schedules and the use of the mental health counselor's statement of professional disclosure.

f. Mental health counselors who find that their services are not beneficial to the client have the responsibility to make this known to the responsible persons.

g. Mental health counselors are accountable to the parties who refer and support counseling services and to the general public and are cognizant of the indirect or long-range effects of their intervention.

h. The mental health counselor attempts to terminate a private service or consulting relationship when it is reasonably clear to the mental health counselor that the consumer is not benefiting from it. If a consumer is receiving services from another mental health professional, mental health counselors do not offer their services directly to the consumer without informing the professional persons already involved in order to avoid confusion and conflict for the consumer.

i. The mental health counselor has the responsibility to screen prospective group participants, especially when the emphasis is on self-understanding and growth through self-disclosure. The member should maintain an awareness of the group participants' compatibility throughout the life of the group.

j. The mental health counselor may choose to consult with any other professionally competent person about a client. In choosing a consultant, the mental health counselor should avoid placing the consultant in a conflict of interest situation that would preclude the consultant's being a proper party to the mental health counselor's efforts to help the clients.

k. If the mental health counselor is unable to be of professional assistance to the client, the mental health counselor should avoid initiating the counseling relationship or the mental health counselor terminates the relationship. In either event, the member is obligated to suggest appropriate alternatives. (It is incumbent upon the mental health counselor to be knowledgeable about referral resources so that a satisfactory referral can be initiated.) In the event the client declines the suggested referral, the mental health counselor is not obligated to continue the relationship.

l. When the mental health counselor has other relationships, particularly of an administrative, supervisory, and/or evaluative nature, with an individual seeking counseling services, the mental health counselor should not serve as the counselor but should refer the individual to another professional. Only in instances where such an alternative is unavailable and where the individual's situation definitely warrants counseling intervention should the mental health counselor enter into and/or maintain a counseling relationship. Dual relationships with clients which might impair the member's objectivity and professional judgment (such as with close friends or relatives, sexual intimacies with any client, etc.) must be avoided and/or the counseling relationship terminated through referral to another competent professional.

m. All experimental methods of treatment must be clearly indicated to prospective recipients, and safety precautions are to be adhered to by the mental health counselor instituting treatment.

n. When the member is engaged in short-term group treatment/training programs e.g., marathons and other encounter-type or growth groups, the member ensures that there is professional assistance available during and following the group experience.

Principle 7. Professional Relationships
Mental health counselors act with due regard to the needs and feelings of their colleagues in counseling and other professions. Mental health counselors respect the prerogatives and obligations of the institutions or organizations with which they are associated.

a. Mental health counselors understand the areas of competence of related professions and make full use of other professional, technical, and administrative resources which best serve the interests of consumers. The absence of formal relationships with other professional workers does not relieve mental health counselors from the responsibility of securing for their clients the best possible professional service; indeed, this circumstance presents a challenge to the professional competence of mental health counselors, requiring special sensitivity to problems outside their areas of training, and foresight, diligence, and tact in obtaining the professional assistance needed by clients.

b. Mental health counselors know and take into account the traditions and practices of other professional groups with which they work and cooperate fully with members of such groups when research, services, and other functions are shared or in working for the benefit of public welfare.

c. Mental health counselors strive to provide positive conditions for those they employ and they spell out clearly the conditions of such employment. They encourage their employees to engage in activities that facilitate their further professional development.

d. Mental health counselors respect the viability, reputation, and the proprietary right of organizations which they serve. Mental health counselors show due regard for the interest of their present or prospective employers. In those instances where they are critical of policies, they attempt to effect change by constructive action within the organization.

e. In the pursuit of research, mental health counselors give sponsoring agencies, host institutions, and publication channels the same respect and opportunity for giving informed consent that they accord to individual research participants. They are aware of their obligation to future research workers and insure that host institutions are given feedback information and proper acknowledgment.

f. Credit is assigned to those who have contributed to a publication, in proportion to their contribution.

g. When a mental health counselor violates ethical standards, mental health counselors who know firsthand of such activities should, if possible, attempt to rectify the situation. Failing an informal solution, mental health counselors should bring such unethical activities to the attention of the appropriate state, and/or national committee on ethics and professional conduct. Only after all professional alternatives have been utilized will a mental health counselor begin legal action for resolution.

Principle 8. Utilization of Assessment Techniques

In the development, publication, and utilization of counseling assessment techniques, mental health counselors follow relevant standards. Individuals examined, or their legal guardians, have the right to know the results, the interpretations made, and where appropriate, the particulars on which final judgment was based. Test users should take precautions to protect test security but not at the expense of an individual's right to understand the basis for decisions that adversely affect that individual or that individual's dependents.

a. The client has the right to have and the provider has the responsibility to give explanations of test results in language the client can understand.

b. When a test is published or otherwise made available for operational use, it should be accompanied by a manual (or other published or readily available information) that makes every reasonable effort to describe fully the development of the test, the rationale, specifications followed in writing items analysis or other research. The test, the manual, the record forms and other accompanying material should help users make correct interpretations of the test results and should warn against common misuses. The test manual should state explicitly the purposes and applications for which the test is recommended and identify any special qualifications required to administer the test and to interpret it properly. Evidence of validity and reliability, along with other relevant research data, should be presented in support of any claims made.

c. Norms presented in test manuals should refer to defined and clearly described populations. These populations should be the groups with whom users of the test will ordinarily wish to compare the persons tested. Test users should consider the possibility of bias in tests or in test items. When indicated, there should be an investigation of possible differences in validity for ethnic, sex, or other subsamples that can be identified when the test is given.

d. Mental health counselors who have the responsibility for decisions about individuals or policies that are based on test results should have a thorough understanding of counseling or educational measurement and of validation and other test research.

e. Mental health counselors should develop procedures for systematically eliminating from data files test score information that has, because of the lapse of time, become obsolete.

f. Any individual or organization offering test scoring and interpretation services must be able to demonstrate that their programs are based on appropriate research to establish the validity of the programs and procedures used in arriving at interpretations. The public offering of an automated test interpretation service will be considered as a professional-to-professional consultation. In this the formal responsibility of the consultant is to the consultee but his/her ultimate and overriding responsibility is to the client.

g. Counseling services for the purpose of diagnosis, treatment, or personalized advice are provided only in the context of a professional relationship, and are not given by means of public lectures or demonstrations, newspapers or magazine articles, radio or television programs, mail, or similar media. The preparation of personnel reports and recommendations based on test data secured solely by mail is unethical unless such appraisals are an integral part of a continuing client relationship with a company, as a result of which the consulting clinical mental health counselor has intimate knowledge of the client's personal situation and can be assured thereby that his written appraisals will be adequate to the purpose and will be properly interpreted by the client. These reports must not be embellished with such detailed analyses of the subject's personality traits as would be appropriate only for intensive interviews with the subjects.

Principle 9. Pursuit of Research Activities

The decision to undertake research should rest upon a considered judgment by the individual mental health counselor about how best to contribute to counseling and to human welfare. Mental health counselors carry out their investigations with respect for the people who participate and with concern for their dignity and welfare.

a. In planning a study the investigator has the personal responsibility to make a careful evaluation of its ethical acceptability, taking into account the following principles for research with human beings. To the extent that this appraisal, weighing scientific and humane values, suggests a deviation from any principle, the investigator incurs an increasingly serious obligation to seek ethical advice and to observe more stringent safeguards to protect the rights of the human research participants.

b. Mental health counselors know and take into account the traditions and practices of other professional groups with members of such groups when research, services, and other functions are shared or in working for the benefit of public welfare.

c. Ethical practice requires the investigator to inform the participant of all features of the research that reasonably might be expected to influence willingness to participate, and to explain all other aspects of the research about which the participant inquires. Failure to make full disclosure gives added emphasis to the investigator's abiding responsibility to protect the welfare and dignity of the research participant.

d. Openness and honesty are essential characteristics of the relationship between investigator and research participant. When the methodological requirements of a study necessitate concealment or deception, the investigator is required to insure as soon as possible the participant's understanding of the reasons for this action and to restore the quality of the relationship with the investigator.

e. In the pursuit of research, mental health counselors give sponsoring agencies, host institutions, and publication channels the same respect and opportunity for giving informed consent that they accord to individual research participants. They are aware of their obligation to future research workers and insure that host institutions are given feedback information and proper acknowledgment.

f. Credit is assigned to those who have contributed to a publication, in proportion to their contribution.

g. The ethical investigator protects participants from physical and mental discomfort, harm and danger. If the risk of such consequences exists, the investigator is required to inform the participant of that fact, secure consent before proceeding, and take all possible measures to minimize distress. A research procedure may not be used if it is likely to cause serious and lasting harm to participants.

h. After the data are collected, ethical practice requires the investigator to provide the participant with a full clarification of the nature of the study and to remove any misconceptions that may have arisen. Where scientific or humane values justify delaying or withholding information the investigator acquires a special responsibility to assure that there are no damaging consequences for the participants.

i. Where research procedure may result in undesirable consequences for the participant, the investigator has the responsibility to detect and remove or correct these consequences, including, where relevant, long-term after effects.

j. Information obtained about the research participants during the course of an investigation is confidential. When the possibility exists that others may obtain access to such information, ethical research practice requires that the possibility, together with the plans for protecting confidentiality be explained to the participants as a part of the procedure for obtaining informed consent.

Principle 10. Private Practice

a. A mental health counselor should assist where permitted by legislation or judicial decision the profession in fulfilling its duty to make counseling services available in private settings.

b. In advertising services as a private practitioner the mental health counselor should advertise the services in such a manner so as to accurately inform the public as to services, expertise, profession and techniques of counseling in a professional manner. A mental health counselor who assumes an executive leadership role in the organization shall not permit his/her name to be used in professional notices during periods when not actively engaged in the private practice of counseling. The mental health counselor may list the following: highest relevant degree, type and level of certification or license, type and/or description of services and other relevant information. Such information should not contain false, inaccurate, misleading, partial, out-of-context or deceptive material or statements.

c. The mental health counselor may join in partnership/corporation with other mental health counselors and/or other professionals provided that each mental health counselor of the partnership or corporation makes clear the separate specialties by name in compliance with the regulations of the locality.

d. A mental health counselor has an obligation to withdraw from a counseling relationship if it is believed that employment will result in violation of the code of ethics, if their mental capacity or physical condition renders it difficult to carry out an effective professional relationship, or if the mental health counselor is discharged by the client because the counseling relationship is no longer productive for the client.

e. A mental health counselor should adhere to and support the regulations for private practice of the locality where the services are offered.

f. Mental health counselors are discouraged from deliberate attempts to utilize one's institutional affiliation to recruit clients for one's private practice. Mental health counselors are to refrain from offering their services in the private sector, when they are employed by an institution in which this is prohibited by stated policies reflecting conditions for employment.

Principle 11. Consulting

a. The mental health counselor acting as consultant must have a high degree of self-awareness of his/her own values, knowledge, skills and needs in entering a helping relationship which involves human and/or organizational change and that the focus of the relationship be on the issues to be resolved and not on the person(s) presenting the problem.

b. There should be understanding and agreement between the mental health counselor and client for the problem definition, changed goals and predicted consequences of interventions selected.

c. The mental health counselor must be reasonably certain that she/he or the organization represented have the necessary competencies and resources for giving the kind of help which is needed now or may develop later and that appropriate referral resources are available to the consultant, if needed later.

d. The mental health counselor relationship must be one in which client adaptability and growth toward self-direction are encouraged and cultivated. The mental health counselor must maintain this role consistently and not become a decision maker or substitute for the client.

e. When announcing consultant availability for services, the mental health counselor conscientiously adheres to professional standards.

f. The mental health counselor is expected to refuse a private fee or other remuneration for consultation with persons who are entitled to these services through the member's employing institution or agency. The policies of a particular agency may make explicit provisions for private practice with agency counselees by members of its staff. In such instances, the counselees must be apprised of other options open to them should they seek private counseling services.

Principle 12. Clients' Rights

The following apply to all consumers of mental health services, including both in- and out-patients in all state, county, local, and private care mental health facilities, as well as clients of mental health practitioners in private practice.

The client has the right:

a. to be treated with consideration and respect;

b. to expect quality service provided by concerned, competent staff;

c. to a clear statement of the purposes, goals, techniques, rules of procedure, and limitations as well as potential dangers of the services to be performed and all other information related to or likely to affect the on-going counseling relationship;

d. to obtain information about their case record and to have this information explained clearly and directly;

e. to full, knowledgeable, and responsible participation in the ongoing treatment plan, to the maximum feasible extent;

f. to expect complete confidentiality and that no information will be released without written consent;

g. to see and discuss their charges and payment records; and

h. to refuse any recommended services and be advised of the consequences of this action.

AMERICAN METEOROLOGICAL SOCIETY

Address: 45 Beacon Street
              Boston, MA 02108-3693
Telephone: 617/227-2425

WWW: www.ametsoc.org/AMS
Document: Guidelines for Professional Conduct (1989)

(The AMS "Guidelines for Professional Conduct" are part of its constitution and bylaws.—Eds.)

To enhance the benefits of the meteorological and related professions to humanity, to uphold the dignity and honor of the profession, and to provide guidance for individual members, institutional members, or for members in association with other professionals, the American Meteorological Society has adopted the following Guidelines for Professional Conduct. Only individuals and organizations who intend to abide by these Guidelines should seek admission or continuing membership in the Society; therefore, these Guidelines will appear on the membership application form and will be published at least annually in the official organ of the Society.

1. Relationship of members to the profession as a whole.
   A. Members should conduct themselves in such a manner as to reflect dignity and honor on their profession.
   B. Members who are professionally active should endeavor to keep abreast of relevant scientific and technical developments; they should continuously strive to improve their professional abilities.
   C. Members engaged in the development of new knowledge should make known to the scientific world their significant results through the media of technical or scientific publications or meetings.

2. Relationship of members to colleagues.
   Members should not take credit knowingly for work done by others; in publications or meetings, members should attempt to give credit where due.

3. Relationship of members to clients and the general public.
   A. Members should base their practice on sound scientific principles applied in a scientific manner.
   B. Members should not direct their professional activities into practices generally recognized as being detrimental to, or incompatible with, the general public welfare.
   C. Members undertaking work for a client should fully advise him or her as to the likelihood of success.

D. Members should refrain from making exaggerated or unwarranted claims and statements.
E. Members should refer requests for service that are beyond their professional capabilities or their scope of service to those properly qualified.
F. Members shall not use or display the official seal of the American Meteorological Society, the Radio Seal of Approval, the Television Seal of Approval or the designation Certified Consulting Meteorologist unless duly authorized by the Society.

© American Meteorological Society. Reprinted with permission.

AMERICAN NUCLEAR SOCIETY

Address: 555 North Kensington Avenue
La Grange Park, IL 60526
Telephone: 708/352-6611
WWW: www.ans.org
Document: The ANS Code of Ethics (1984)

(The *Canons of Ethics of Engineers* was formulated for the engineering profession in 1946 by the Committee on Engineering Ethics of the Engineers' Council for Professional Development, now the Accreditation Board for Engineering Technology (ABET). It is used as the basis of the codes for this and other engineering organizations.—Eds.)

Preamble: The ANS endorsed the Engineers' Council for Professional Development "Code of Ethics for Engineers" on March 29, 1973. ANS membership is 40 percent engineers, 40 percent scientists, and 20 percent others. Consequently, the word "engineer" in the original "Code of Ethics" was changed to "ANS member" on July 1, 1984, to more closely align the code to the ANS membership's vocations.

The Fundamental Principles
ANS members uphold and advance the integrity, honor and dignity of their professions by:
- using their knowledge and skill for the advancement of human welfare
- being honest and impartial and serving with fidelity the public, their employees, and clients

- striving to increase the competence and prestige of their professions
- supporting the professional and technical societies of their disciplines

The Fundamental Codes

1. ANS members shall hold paramount the safety, health and welfare of the public in the performance of their professional duties.
2. ANS members shall perform services only in the areas of their competence.
3. ANS members shall issue public statements only in an objective and truthful manner.
4. ANS members shall act in professional matters for each employer or client as faithful agents or trustees and shall avoid conflicts of interest.
5. ANS members shall build their professional reputation on the merit of their services and shall not compete unfairly with others.
6. ANS members shall act in such a manner as to uphold and enhance the honor, integrity, and dignity of the professions.
7. ANS members shall continue their professional development throughout their careers and shall provide opportunities for the professional development of those persons under their supervision.

© American Nuclear Society. Reprinted with permission.

AMERICAN NURSES ASSOCIATION

Address: 600 Maryland Avenue SW,
             Suite 100 West
             Washington, DC 20024-2571
Telephone: 202/651-7000
WWW: www.nursingworld.org
Document: Code for Nurses with Interpretive
             Statements (1950. Most recently
             revised 1985.)

PREAMBLE

A code of ethics makes explicit the primary goals and values of the profession. When individuals become nurses, they make a moral commitment to uphold the values and special moral obligations expressed in their code. The *Code for Nurses* is based on a belief about the nature of individuals, nursing, health, and

society. Nursing encompasses the protection, promotion, and restoration of health; the prevention of illness; and the alleviation of suffering in the care of clients, including individuals, families, groups, and communities. In the context of these functions, nursing is defined as the diagnosis and treatment of human responses to actual or potential health problems.

Since clients themselves are the primary decision makers in matters concerning their own health, treatment, and well-being, the goal of nursing actions is to support and enhance the client's responsibility and self-determination to the greatest extent possible. In this context, health is not necessarily an end in itself, but rather a means to a life that is meaningful from the client's perspective.

When making clinical judgments, nurses base their decisions on consideration of consequences and of universal moral principles, both of which prescribe and justify nursing actions. The most fundamental of these principles is respect for persons. Other principles stemming from this basic principle are autonomy (self-determination), beneficence (doing good), non-maleficence (avoiding harm), veracity (truth-telling), confidentiality (respecting privileged information), fidelity (keeping promises), and justice (treating people fairly).

In brief, then, the statements of the code and their interpretation provide guidance for conduct and relationships in carrying out nursing responsibilities consistent with the ethical obligations of the profession and with high quality in nursing care.

INTRODUCTION

A code of ethics indicates a profession's acceptance of the responsibility and trust with which it has been invested by society. Under the terms of the implicit contract between society and the nursing profession, society grants the profession considerable autonomy and authority to function in the conduct of its affairs. The development of a code of ethics is an essential activity of a profession and provides one means for the exercise of professional self-regulation.

Upon entering the profession, each nurse inherits a measure of both the responsibility and the trust that have accrued to nursing over the years, as well as the corresponding obligation to adhere to the profession's code of conduct and relationships for ethical practice. The *Code for Nurses with Interpretive Statements* is thus more a collective expression of nursing conscience and philosophy than a set of external rules imposed upon an individual practitioner of nursing. Personal and professional integrity can be assured only if an individual is committed to the profession's code of conduct.

A code of ethical conduct offers general principles to guide and evaluate nursing actions. It does not assure the virtues required for professional practice within the character of each nurse. In particular situations, the justification of behavior as ethical must satisfy not only the individual nurse acting as a moral agent but also the standards for professional peer review.

The *Code for Nurses* was adopted by the American Nurses Association in 1950 and has been revised periodically. It serves to inform both the nurse and society of the profession's expectations and requirements in ethical matters. The code and the interpretive statements together provide a framework within which nurses can make ethical decisions and discharge their responsibilities to the public, to other members of the health team, and to the profession.

Although a particular situation by its nature may determine the use of specific moral principles, the basic philosophical values, directives, and suggestions provided here are widely applicable to situations encountered in clinical practice. The *Code for Nurses* is not open to negotiation in employment settings, nor is it permissible for individuals or groups of nurses to adapt or change the language of this code.

The requirements of the code may often exceed those of the law. Violations of the law may subject the nurse to civil or criminal liability. The state nurses' associations, in fulfilling the profession's duty to society, may discipline their members for violations of the code. Loss of the respect and confidence of society and of one's colleagues is a serious sanction resulting from violation of the code. In addition, every nurse has a personal obligation to uphold and adhere to the code and to ensure that nursing colleagues do likewise.

Guidance and assistance in applying the code to local situations may be obtained from the American Nurses Association and the constituent state nurses' associations.

CODE FOR NURSES WITH INTERPRETIVE STATEMENTS

1. The nurse provides services with respect for human dignity and the uniqueness of the client, unrestricted by considerations of social or economic status, personal attributes, or the nature of health problems.

1.1 Respect for Human Dignity
The fundamental principle of nursing practice is respect for the inherent dignity and worth of every client. Nurses are morally obligated to respect human existence and the individuality of all persons who are the recipients of nursing actions. Nurses therefore must take all reasonable means to protect and preserve human life when there is hope of recovery or reasonable hope of benefit from life-prolonging treatment.

Truth telling and the process of reaching informed choice underlie the exercise of self-determination, which is basic to respect for persons. Clients should be as fully involved as possible in the planning and implementation of their own health care. Clients have the moral right to determine what will be done with their own person; to be given accurate information, and all the information necessary for making informed judgments; to be assisted with weighing the benefits and burdens of options in their treatment; to accept, refuse, or terminate treatment without coercion; and to be given necessary emotional support. Each nurse has an obligation to be knowledgeable about the moral and legal rights of all clients and to protect and support those rights. In situations in which the client lacks the capacity to make a decision, a surrogate decision maker should be designated.

Individuals are interdependent members of the community. Taking into account both individual rights and the interdependence of persons in decision making, the nurse recognizes those situations in which individual rights to autonomy in health care may temporarily be overridden to preserve the life of the human community; for example, when a disaster demands triage or when an individual presents a direct danger to others. The many variables involved make it imperative that each case be considered with full awareness of the need to preserve the rights and responsibilities of clients and the demands of justice. The suspension of individual rights must always be considered a deviation to be tolerated as briefly as possible.

1.2 Status and Attributes of Clients
The need for health care is universal, transcending all national, ethnic, racial, religious, cultural, political, educational, economic, developmental, personality, role, and sexual differences. Nursing care is delivered without prejudicial behavior. Individual value systems and life-styles should be considered in the planning of health care with and for each client. Attributes of clients influence nursing practice to the extent that they represent factors the nurse must understand, consider, and respect in tailoring care to personal

needs and in maintaining the individual's self-respect and dignity.

1.3 The Nature of Health Problems

The nurse's respect for the worth and dignity of the individual human being applies, irrespective of the nature of the health problem. It is reflected in care given the person who is disabled as well as one without disability, the person with long-term illness as well as one with acute illness, the recovering patient as well as one in the last phase of life. This respect extends to all who require the services of the nurse for the promotion of health, the prevention of illness, the restoration of health, the alleviation of suffering, and the provision of supportive care of the dying. The nurse does not act deliberately to terminate the life of any person.

The nurse's concern for human dignity and for the provision of high quality nursing care is not limited by personal attitudes or beliefs. If ethically opposed to interventions in a particular case because of the procedures to be used, the nurse is justified in refusing to participate. Such refusal should be made known in advance and in time for other appropriate arrangements to be made for the client's nursing care. If the nurse becomes involved in such a case and the client's life is in jeopardy, the nurse is obliged to provide for the client's safety, to avoid abandonment, and to withdraw only when assured that alternative sources of nursing care are available to the client.

The measures nurses take to care for the dying client and the client's family emphasize human contact. They enable the client to live with as much physical, emotional, and spiritual comfort as possible, and they maximize the values the client has treasured in life. Nursing care is directed toward the prevention and relief of the suffering commonly associated with the dying process. The nurse may provide interventions to relieve symptoms in the dying client even when the interventions entail substantial risks of hastening death.

1.4 The Setting for Health Care

The nurse adheres to the principle of nondiscriminatory, nonprejudicial care in every situation and endeavors to promote its acceptance by others. The setting shall not determine the nurse's readiness to respect clients and to render or obtain needed services.

2. The nurse safeguards the client's right to privacy by judiciously protecting information of a confidential nature.

2.1 The Client's Right to Privacy

The right to privacy is an inalienable human right. The client trusts the nurse to hold all information in confidence. This trust could be destroyed and the client's welfare jeopardized by injudicious disclosure of information provided in confidence. The duty of confidentiality, however, is not absolute when innocent parties are in direct jeopardy.

2.2 Protection of Information

The rights, well-being, and safety of the individual client should be the determining factors in arriving at any professional judgment concerning the disposition of confidential information received from the client relevant to his or her treatment. The standards of nursing practice and the nursing responsibility to provide high quality health services require that relevant data be shared with members of the health team. Only information pertinent to a client's treatment and welfare is disclosed, and it is disclosed only to those directly concerned with the client's care.

Information documenting the appropriateness, necessity, and quality of care required for the purposes of peer review, third-party payment, and other quality assurance mechanisms must be disclosed only under defined policies, mandates, or protocols. These written guidelines must assure that the rights, well-being, and safety of the client are maintained.

2.3 Access to Records

If in the course of providing care there is a need for the nurse to have access to the records of persons not under the nurse's care, the persons affected should be notified and, whenever possible, permission should be obtained first. Although records belong to the agency where the data are collected, the individual maintains the right of control over the information in the record. Similarly, professionals may exercise the right of control over information they have generated in the course of health care.

If the nurse wishes to use a client's treatment record for research or nonclinical purposes in which anonymity cannot be guaranteed, the client's consent must be obtained first. Ethically, this ensures the client's right to privacy; legally, it protects the client against unlawful invasion of privacy.

3. The nurse acts to safeguard the client and the public when health care and safety are affected by incompetent, unethical, or illegal practice by any person.

3.1 Safeguarding the Health and Safety of the Client

The nurse's primary commitment is to the health,

welfare, and safety of the client. As an advocate for the client, the nurse must be alert to and take appropriate action regarding any instances of incompetent, unethical, or illegal practice by any member of the health care team or the health care system, or any action on the part of others that places the rights or best interests of the client in jeopardy. To function effectively in this role, nurses must be aware of the employing institution's policies and procedures, nursing standards of practice, the *Code for Nurses* and laws governing nursing and health care practice with regard to incompetent, unethical, or illegal practice.

3.2 Acting on Questionable Practice
When the nurse is aware of inappropriate or questionable practice in the provision of health care, concern should be expressed to the person carrying out the questionable practice and attention called to the possible detrimental effect upon the client's welfare. When factors in the health care delivery system threaten the welfare of the client, similar action should be directed to the responsible administrative person. If indicated, the practice should then be reported to the appropriate authority within the institution, agency, or larger system.

There should be an established process for the reporting and handling of incompetent, unethical, or illegal practice within the employment setting so that such reporting can go through official channels without causing fear of reprisal. The nurse should be knowledgeable about the process and be prepared to use it if necessary. When questions are raised about the practices of individual practitioners or of health care systems, written documentation of the observed practices or behaviors must be available to the appropriate authorities. State nurses associations should be prepared to provide assistance and support in the development and evaluation of such processes and in reporting procedures.

When incompetent, unethical, or illegal practice on the part of anyone concerned with the client's care is not corrected within the employment setting and continues to jeopardize the client's welfare and safety, the problem should be reported to other appropriate authorities such as practice committees of the pertinent professional organizations or the legally constituted bodies concerned with licensing of specific categories of health workers or professional practitioners. Some situations may warrant the concern and involvement of all such groups. Accurate reporting and documentation undergird all actions.

3.3 Review Mechanisms
The nurse should participate in the planning, establishment, implementation, and evaluation of review mechanisms that serve to safeguard clients, such as duly constituted peer review processes or committees and ethics committees. Such ongoing review mechanisms are based on established criteria, have stated purposes, include a process for making recommendations, and facilitate improved delivery of nursing and other health services to clients wherever nursing services are provided.

4. The nurse assumes responsibility and accountability for individual nursing judgments and actions.

4.1 Acceptance of Responsibility and Accountability
The recipients of professional nursing services are entitled to high quality nursing care. Individual professional licensure is the protective mechanism legislated by the public to ensure the basic and minimum competencies of the professional nurse. Beyond that, society has accorded to the nursing profession the right to regulate its own practice. The regulation and control of nursing practice by nurses demand that individual practitioners of professional nursing must bear primary responsibility for the nursing care clients receive and must be individually accountable for their own practice.

4.2 Responsibility for Nursing Judgment and Action
Responsibility refers to the carrying out of duties associated with a particular role assumed by the nurse. Nursing obligations are reflected in the ANA publications *Nursing: A Social Policy Statement* and *Standards of Clinical Nursing Practice*. In recognizing the rights of clients, the standards describe a collaborative relationship between the nurse and the client through use of the nursing process. Nursing responsibilities include data collection and assessment of the health status of the client; formation of nursing diagnoses derived from client assessment; development of a nursing care plan that is directed toward designated goals, assists the client in maximizing his or her health capabilities, and provides for the client's participation in promoting, maintaining, and restoring his or her health; evaluation of the effectiveness of nursing care in achieving goals as determined by the client and the nurse; and subsequent reassessment and revision of the nursing care plan as warranted. In the process of assuming these responsibilities, the nurse is held accountable for them.

4.3 Accountability for Nursing Judgment and Action

Accountability refers to being answerable to someone for something one has done. It means providing an explanation or rationale to oneself, to clients, to peers, to the nursing profession, and to society. In order to be accountable, nurses act under a code of ethical conduct that is grounded in the moral principles of fidelity and respect for the dignity, worth, and self-determination of clients.

The nursing profession continues to develop ways to clarify nursing's accountability to society. The contract between the profession and society is made explicit through such mechanisms as (a) the *Code for Nurses,* (b) the standards of nursing practice, (c) the development of nursing theory derived from nursing research in order to guide nursing actions, (d) educational requirements for practice, (e) certification, and (f) mechanisms for evaluating the effectiveness of the nurse's performance of nursing responsibilities.

Nurses are accountable for judgments made and actions taken in the course of nursing practice. Neither physicians' orders nor the employing agency's policies relieve the nurse of accountability for actions taken and judgments made.

5. The nurse maintains competence in nursing.

5.1 Personal Responsibility for Competence

The profession of nursing is obligated to provide adequate and competent nursing care. Therefore it is the personal responsibility of each nurse to maintain competency in practice. For the client's optimum well-being and for the nurse's own professional development, the care of the client reflects and incorporates new techniques and knowledge in health care as these develop, especially as they relate to the nurse's particular field of practice. The nurse must be aware of the need for continued professional learning and must assume personal responsibility for currency of knowledge and skills.

5.2 Measurement of Competence in Nursing Practice

Evaluation of one's performance by peers is a hallmark of professionalism and a method by which the profession is held accountable to society. Nurses must be willing to have their practice reviewed and evaluated by their peers. Guidelines for evaluating the scope of practice and the appropriateness, effectiveness, and efficiency of nursing practice are found in nursing practice acts, ANA standards of practice, and other quality assurance mechanisms. Each nurse

is responsible for participating in the development of objective criteria for evaluation. In addition, the nurse engages in ongoing self-evaluation of clinical competency, decision-making abilities, and professional judgments.

5.3 Intraprofessional Responsibility for Competence in Nursing Care

Nurses share responsibility for high quality nursing care. Nurses are required to have knowledge relevant to the current scope of nursing practice, changing issues and concerns, and ethical concepts and principles. Since individual competencies vary, nurses refer clients to and consult with other nurses with expertise and recognized competencies in various fields of practice.

6. The nurse exercises informed judgment and uses individual competency and qualifications as criteria in seeking consultation, accepting responsibilities, and delegating nursing activities.

6.1 Changing Functions

Nurses are faced with decisions in the context of the increased complexity of health care, changing patterns in the delivery of health services, and the development of evolving nursing practice in response to the health needs of clients. As the scope of nursing practice changes, the nurse must exercise judgment in accepting responsibilities, seeking consultation, and assigning responsibilities to others who carry out nursing care.

6.2 Accepting Responsibilities

The nurse must not engage in practices prohibited by law or delegate to others activities prohibited by practice acts of other health care personnel or by other laws. Nurses determine the scope of their practice in light of their education, knowledge, competency and extent of experience. If the nurse concludes that he or she lacks competence or is inadequately prepared to carry out a specific function, the nurse has the responsibility to refuse that work and to seek alternative sources of care based on concern for the client's welfare. In that refusal, both the client and the nurse are protected. Inasmuch as the nurse is responsible for the continuous care of patients in health care settings, the nurse is frequently called upon to carry out components of care delegated by other health professionals as part of the client's treatment regimen. The nurse should not accept these interdependent functions if they are so extensive as to prevent the nurse from fulfilling the responsibility to provide appropriate nursing care to clients.

6.3 Consultation and Collaboration

The provision of health and illness care to clients is a complex process that requires a wide range of knowledge, skills, and collaborative efforts. Nurses must be aware of their own individual competencies. When the needs of the client are beyond the qualifications and competencies of the nurse, consultation and collaboration must be sought from qualified nurses, other health professionals or other appropriate sources. Participation on intradisciplinary or interdisciplinary teams is often an effective approach to the provision of high quality total health services.

6.4 Delegation of Nursing Activities

Inasmuch as the nurse is accountable for the quality of nursing care rendered to clients, nurses are accountable for the delegation of nursing care activities to other health workers. Therefore, the nurse must assess individual competency in assigning selected components of nursing care to other nursing service personnel. The nurse should not delegate to any member of the nursing team a function for which that person is not prepared or qualified. Employer policies or directives do not relieve the nurse of accountability for making judgments about the delegation of nursing care activities.

7. The nurse participates in activities that contribute to the ongoing development of the profession's body of knowledge.

7.1 The Nurse and Development of Knowledge

Every profession must engage in scholarly inquiry to identify, verify, and continually enlarge the body of knowledge that forms the foundation for its practice. A unique body of verified knowledge provides both framework and direction for the profession in all of its activities and for the practitioner in the provision of nursing care. The accrual of scientific and humanistic knowledge promotes the advancement of practice and the well-being of the profession's clients. Ongoing scholarly activity such as research and the development of theory is indispensable to the full discharge of a profession's obligations to society. Each nurse has a role in this area of professional activity, whether as an investigator in furthering knowledge, as a participant in research, or as a user of theoretical and empirical knowledge.

7.2 Protection of Rights of Human Participants in Research

Individual rights valued by society and by the nursing profession that have particular application in research include the right of adequately informed consent, the right to freedom from risk of injury, and the right of privacy and preservation of dignity. Inherent in these rights is respect for each individual's rights to exercise self-determination, to choose to participate or not, to have full information, and to terminate participation in research without penalty.

It is the duty of the nurse functioning in any research role to maintain vigilance in protecting the life, health, and privacy of human subjects from both anticipated and unanticipated risks and in assuring informed consent. Subjects' integrity, privacy, and rights must be especially safeguarded if the subjects are unable to protect themselves because of incapacity or because they are in a dependent relationship to the investigator. The investigation should be discontinued if its continuance might be harmful to the subject.

7.3 General Guidelines for Participating in Research

Before participating in research conducted by others, the nurse has an obligation to (a) obtain information about the intent and the nature of the research and (b) ascertain that the study proposal is approved by the appropriate bodies, such as institutional review boards.

Research should be conducted and directed by qualified persons. The nurse who participates in research in any capacity should be fully informed about both the nurse's and the client's rights and obligations.

8. The nurse participates in the profession's efforts to implement and improve standards of nursing.

8.1 Responsibility to the Public for Standards

Nursing is responsible and accountable for admitting to the profession only those individuals who have demonstrated the knowledge, skills, and commitment considered essential to professional practice. Nurse educators have a major responsibility for ensuring that these competencies and a demonstrated commitment to professional practice have been achieved before the entry of an individual into the practice of professional nursing.

Established standards and guidelines for nursing practice provide guidance for the delivery of professional nursing care and are a means for evaluating care received by the public. The nurse has a personal responsibility and commitment to clients for implementation and maintenance of optimal standards of nursing practice.

8.2 Responsibility to the Profession for Standards

Established standards reflect the practice of nursing grounded in ethical commitments and a body of knowledge. Professional standards or guidelines exist in nursing practice, nursing service, nursing education, and nursing research. The nurse has the responsibility to monitor these standards in daily practice and to participate actively in the profession's ongoing efforts to foster optimal standards of practice at the local, regional, state, and national levels of the health care system.

Nurse educators have the additional responsibility to maintain optimal standards of nursing practice and education in nursing education programs and in any other settings where planned learning activities for nursing students take place.

9. The nurse participates in the profession's efforts to establish and maintain conditions of employment conducive to high quality nursing care.

9.1 Responsibility for Conditions of Employment

The nurse must be concerned with conditions of employment that (a) enable the nurse to practice in accordance with the standards of nursing practice and (b) provide a care environment that meets the standards of nursing service. The provision of high quality nursing care is the responsibility of both the individual nurse and the nursing profession. Professional autonomy and self-regulation in the control of conditions of practice are necessary for implementing nursing standards.

9.2 Maintaining Conditions for High Quality Nursing Care

Articulation and control of nursing practice can be accomplished through individual agreement and collective action. A nurse may enter into an agreement with individuals or organizations to provide health care. Nurses may participate in collective action such as collective bargaining through their state nurses' association to determine the terms and conditions of employment conducive to high quality nursing care. Such agreements should be consistent with the profession's standards of practice, the state law regulating nursing practice, and the *Code for Nurses*.

10. The nurse participates in the profession's effort to protect the public from misinformation and misrepresentation and to maintain the integrity of nursing.

10.1 Protection from Misinformation and Misrepresentation

Nurses are responsible for advising clients against the use of products that endanger the clients' safety and welfare. The nurse shall not use any form of public or professional communication to make claims that are false, fraudulent, misleading, deceptive, or unfair.

The nurse does not give or imply endorsement to advertising, promotion, or sale of commercial products or services in a manner that may be interpreted as reflecting the opinion or judgment of the profession as a whole. The nurse may use knowledge of specific services or products in advising an individual client, since this may contribute to the client's health and well-being. In the course of providing information or education to clients or other practitioners about commercial products or services, however, a variety of similar products or services should be offered or described so the client or practitioner can make an informed choice.

10.2 Maintaining the Integrity of Nursing

The use of the title *registered nurse* is granted by state governments for the protection of the public. Use of that title carries with it the responsibility to act in the public interest. The nurse may use the title *R.N.* and symbols of academic degrees or other earned or honorary professional symbols of recognition in all ways that are legal and appropriate. The title and other symbols of the profession should not be used, however, for benefits unrelated to nursing practice or the profession, or used by those who may seek to exploit them for other purposes.

Nurses should refrain from casting a vote in any deliberations involving health care services or facilities where the nurse has business or other interests that could be construed as a conflict of interest.

11. The nurse collaborates with members of the health professions and other citizens in promoting community and national efforts to meet the health needs of the public.

11.1 Collaboration with Others to Meet Health Needs

The availability and accessibility of high quality health services to all people require collaborative planning at the local, state, national, and international levels that respects the interdependence of health professionals and clients in health care systems. Nursing care is an integral part of high quality health care, and nurses have an obligation to promote equitable access to nursing and health care for all people.

11.2 Responsibility to the Public

The nursing profession is committed to promoting the welfare and safety of all people. The goals and values of nursing are essential to effective delivery of health services. For the benefit of the individual client and the public at large, nursing's goals and commitments need adequate representation. Nurses should ensure this representation by active participation in decision making in institutional and political arenas to assure a just distribution of health care and nursing resources.

11.3 Relationships with Other Disciplines
The complexity of health care delivery systems requires a multidisciplinary approach to delivery of services that has the strong support and active participation of all the health professions. Nurses should actively promote the collaborative planning required to ensure the availability and accessibility of high quality health services to all persons whose health needs are unmet.

© American Nurses Association. Reprinted with permission.

The American
Occupational Therapy
Association, Inc.

AMERICAN OCCUPATIONAL THERAPY ASSOCIATION, INC.

Address: 4720 Montgomery Lane,
                PO Box 31220
                Bethesda, MD 20824-1220
Telephone: 301/652-2682
WWW: www.aota.org
Document: Occupational Therapy Code of Ethics
                (1994)

(This document replaces the 1988 *Occupational Therapy Code of Ethics (American Journal of Occupational Therapy,* 42, 795-796*)* which was rescinded by the 1994 Representative Assembly.—Eds.)

The American Occupational Therapy Association's Code of Ethics is a public statement of the values and principles used in promoting and maintaining high standards of behavior in occupational therapy. The American Occupational Therapy Association and its

members are committed to furthering people's ability to function within their total environment. To this end, occupational therapy personnel provide services for individuals in any stage of health and illness, to institutions, to other professionals and colleagues, to students, and to the general public.

The Occupational Therapy Code of Ethics is a set of principles that applies to occupational therapy personnel at all levels. The roles of practitioner (registered occupational therapist and certified occupational therapy assistant), educator, fieldwork educator, supervisor, administrator, consultant, fieldwork co-ordinator, faculty program director, researcher/scholar, entrepreneur, student, support staff, and occupational therapy aide are assumed.

Any action that is in violation of the spirit and purpose of this Code shall be considered unethical. To ensure compliance with the Code, enforcement procedures are established and maintained by the Commission on Standards and Ethics. Acceptance of membership in the American Occupational Therapy Association commits members to adherence to the *Code of Ethics* and its enforcement procedures.

Principle 1. Occupational therapy personnel shall demonstrate a concern for the well-being of the recipients of their services. (beneficence)
A. Occupational therapy personnel shall provide services in an equitable manner for all individuals.
B. Occupational therapy personnel shall maintain relationships that do not exploit the recipient of services sexually, physically, emotionally, financially, socially or in any other manner. Occupational therapy personnel shall avoid those relationships or activities that interfere with professional judgment and objectivity.
C. Occupational therapy personnel shall take all reasonable precautions to avoid harm to the recipient of services or to his or her property.
D. Occupational therapy personnel shall strive to ensure that fees are fair, reasonable, and commensurate with the service performed and are set with due regard for the service recipient's ability to pay.

Principle 2. Occupational therapy personnel shall respect the rights of the recipients of their services. (e.g., autonomy, privacy, confidentiality)
A. Occupational therapy personnel shall collaborate with service recipients or their surrogate(s) in determining goals and priorities throughout the intervention process.

B. Occupational therapy personnel shall fully inform the service recipients of the nature, risks, and potential outcomes of any interventions.

C. Occupational therapy personnel shall obtain informed consent from subjects involved in research activities indicating they have been fully advised of the potential risks and outcomes.

D. Occupational therapy personnel shall respect the individual's right to refuse professional services or involvement in research or educational activities.

E. Occupational therapy personnel shall protect the confidential nature of information gained from educational, practice, research, and investigational activities.

Principle 3. Occupational therapy personnel shall achieve and continually maintain high standards of competence. (duties)

A. Occupational therapy practitioners shall hold the appropriate national and state credentials for providing services.

B. Occupational therapy personnel shall use procedures that conform to the Standards of Practice of the American Occupational Therapy Association.

C. Occupational therapy personnel shall take responsibility for maintaining competence by participating in professional development and educational activities.

D. Occupational therapy personnel shall perform their duties on the basis of accurate and current information.

E. Occupational therapy practitioners shall protect service recipients by ensuring that duties assumed by or assigned to other occupational therapy personnel are commensurate with their qualifications and experience.

F. Occupational therapy practitioners shall provide appropriate supervision to individuals for whom the practitioners have supervisory responsibility.

G. Occupational therapists shall refer recipients to other service providers or consult with other service providers when additional knowledge and expertise are required.

Principle 4. Occupational therapy personnel shall comply with laws and Association policies guiding the profession of occupational therapy. (justice)

A. Occupational therapy personnel shall understand and abide by applicable Association policies; local, state, and federal laws; and institutional rules.

B. Occupational therapy personnel shall inform employers, employees, and colleagues about those laws and Association policies that apply to the profession of occupational therapy.

C. Occupational therapy practitioners shall require those they supervise in occupational therapy related activities to adhere to the *Code of Ethics*.

D. Occupational therapy personnel shall accurately record and report all information related to professional activities.

Principle 5. Occupational therapy personnel shall provide accurate information about occupational therapy services. (veracity)

A. Occupational therapy personnel shall accurately represent their qualifications, education, experience, training, and competence.

B. Occupational therapy personnel shall disclose any affiliations that may pose a conflict of interest.

C. Occupational therapy personnel shall refrain from using or participating in the use of any form of communication that contains false, fraudulent, deceptive, or unfair statements or claims.

Principle 6. Occupational therapy personnel shall treat colleagues and other professionals with fairness, discretion, and integrity. (fidelity, veracity)

A. Occupational therapy personnel shall safeguard confidential information about colleagues and staff.

B. Occupational therapy personnel shall accurately represent the qualifications, views, contributions, and findings of colleagues.

C. Occupational therapy personnel shall report any breaches of the *Code of Ethics* to the appropriate authority.

© American Occupational Therapy Association. Reprinted with permission.

AMERICAN OPTOMETRIC ASSOCIATION

Address: 243 North Lindbergh Boulevard
             St. Louis, MO 63141
Telephone: 314/991-4101

WWW: www.aoanet.org/
Document: Code of Ethics (1944)
              Standards of Conduct (1976)

Code of Ethics

It Shall Be the Ideal, the Resolve, and the Duty of the Members of The American Optometric Association:

- to keep the visual welfare of the patient uppermost at all times;
- to promote in every possible way, in collaboration with this Association, better care of the visual needs of mankind;
- to enhance continuously their educational and technical proficiency to the end that their patients shall receive the benefits of all acknowledged improvements in visual care;
- to see that no person shall lack for visual care, regardless of his financial status;
- to advise the patient whenever consultation with an optometric colleague or reference for other professional care seems advisable;
- to hold in professional confidence all information concerning a patient and to use such data only for the benefit of the patient;
- to conduct themselves as exemplary citizens;
- to maintain their offices and their practices in keeping with professional standards;
- to promote and maintain cordial and unselfish relationships with members of their own profession and of other professions for the exchange of information to the advantage of mankind.

Standards of Conduct

I. Basic Responsibilities of an Optometrist

Section A. The Welfare of Humanity

A health profession has as its prime objective the service it can render to humanity; monetary considerations should be a subordinate factor. In choosing the profession of optometry an individual assumes an obligation for personal conduct in accordance with professional ideals.

Section B. Continuing Competence

An optometrist should strive to keep current with every modern development in the profession, to enhance both knowledge and proficiency by the adoption of modern methods and scientific concepts of proven worth and to contribute personally to the general knowledge and advancement of the profession. All these things should be done with that freedom of action and thought that provides first for the welfare of the public.

II. Relationships With the Patient

Section A. Presence of a Pathological Condition

An optometrist should give to the patient or the patient's family a timely notice of manifestations of disease or abnormality.

Section B. Emergency Optometric Care

A request for optometric care in an emergency should receive immediate response. Once having undertaken an emergency case, an optometrist shall neither abandon nor neglect the patient.

Section C. Professional Fees

Professional fees charged the patient for examination, diagnosis and treatment shall be determined by the individual optometrist.

Section D. Charges for Materials

Charges for material should be clearly separated from professional fees.

III. Responsibilities to the Public

Section A. Informing the Public

An optometrist should honor the applicable provisions of valid State and Federal laws and rules regulating the advertising of ophthalmic materials and disseminating of information regarding professional services.

Section B. Patent

It is unprofessional for an optometrist to exploit a patent for lenses, appliances, or instruments used in the practice of optometry in such a way as to deprive the public of its benefits, either through refusal to grant licenses to competent manufacturers who can assure adequate production and unimpeachable quality, or through exorbitant demands in the form of royalty; or for similar forms of monopolistic control in which the interests of the public are exploited.

Section C. Rebates

It is unprofessional and unethical to accept rebates on prescriptions, lenses, or optical appliances used in the practice of optometry.

IV. Relationships With Other Optometrists

Section A. Intraprofessional Referral and Consultations

Intraprofessional referral and consultations are encouraged when the best interest of the patient indicates additional opinion. Protocol on the relationship and responsibilities between the referring and attending optometrist that customarily is followed by health professions shall prevail.

Section B. Official Position

An optometrist holding an official position in any optometric organization shall avoid any semblance of using this position for self-aggrandizement.

V. Relationship With Other Professionals

Section A. Interprofessional Referral and Consultations

Interprofessional referral and consultations are encouraged when the best interest of the patient indicates additional opinion. Protocol of the relationship and responsibilities between the referring and attending professional that customarily is followed by health professions shall prevail.

Section B. Public Health

Professional responsibility demands that the optometrist actively participate in public health activities with other health professionals to the end that every step be taken to safeguard the health and welfare of the public.

© American Optometric Association. Reprinted with permission.

AMERICAN OSTEOPATHIC ASSOCIATION

Address: 142 East Ontario Street
              Chicago, IL 60611
Telephone: 312/202-8000 or 800/621-1773
WWW: www.am-osteo-assn.org
Document: Code of Ethics (1996)

The American Osteopathic Association has formulated this Code to guide its member physicians in their professional lives. The standards presented are designed to address the osteopathic physician's ethical and professional responsibilities to patients, to society, to the AOA, to others involved in health care and to self.

Further, the American Osteopathic Association has adopted the position that actively practicing physicians should play the major role in the development and instruction of medical ethics.

Section 1. The physician shall keep in confidence whatever he may learn about a patient in the discharge of professional duties. Information shall be divulged by the physician when required by law or when authorized by the patient.

Section 2. The physician shall give a candid account of the patient's condition to the patient or to those responsible for the patient's care.

Section 3. A physician-patient relationship must be founded on mutual trust, cooperation, and respect. The patient, therefore, must have complete freedom to choose his physician. The physician must have complete freedom to choose patients whom he will serve. However, the physician should not refuse to accept patients because of the patient's race, creed, color, sex, national origin or handicap. In emergencies, a physician should make his services available.

Section 4. A physician is never justified in abandoning a patient. The physician shall give due notice to a patient or to those responsible for the patient's care when he withdraws from the case so that another physician may be engaged.

Section 5. A physician shall practice in accordance with the body of systematized and scientific knowledge related to the healing arts. A physician shall maintain competence in such systemized and scientific knowledge through study and clinical applications.

Section 6. The osteopathic profession has an obligation to society to maintain its high standards and, therefore, to continuously regulate itself. A substantial part of such regulation is due to the efforts and influence of the recognized local, state and national associations representing the osteopathic profession. A physician should maintain membership in and actively support such associations and abide by their rules and regulations.

Section 7. Under the law a physician may advertise, but no physician shall advertise or solicit patients directly or indirectly through the use of matters or activities which are false or misleading.

Section 8. A physician shall not hold forth or indicate possession of any degree recognized as the basis for licensure to practice the healing arts unless he is actually licensed on the basis of that degree in the state in which he practices. A physician shall designate his osteopathic school of practice in all professional uses of his name. Indications of specialty practice, membership in professional societies, and related matters shall be governed by rules promulgated by the American Osteopathic Association.

Section 9. A physician shall obtain consultation whenever requested to do so by the patient. A physician should not hesitate to seek consultation whenever he/she believes it advisable.

Section 10. In any dispute between or among physicians involving ethical or organizational matters, the matter in controversy should first be referred to the appropriate arbitrating bodies of the profession.

Section 11. In any dispute between or among physicians regarding the diagnosis and treatment of a patient, the attending physician has the responsibility for final decisions, consistent with any applicable osteopathic hospital rules or regulations.

Section 12. Any fee charged by a physician shall compensate the physician for services actually rendered. There shall be no division of professional fees for referrals of patients.

Section 13. A physician shall respect the law. When necessary a physician shall attempt to help to formulate the law by all proper means in order to improve patient care and public health.

Section 14. In addition to adhering to the foregoing ethical standards, a physician should whenever possible participate in community activities and services.

Section 15. It is considered sexual misconduct for a physician to have sexual contact with any current patient whom the physician has interviewed and/or upon whom a medical or surgical procedure has been performed.

Section 16. Sexual harassment by a physician is considered unethical. Sexual harassment is defined as physical or verbal intimidation of a sexual nature involving a colleague or subordinate in the workplace or academic setting, when such conduct creates an unreasonable, intimidating, hostile or offensive workplace or academic setting.

AMERICAN PHARMACEUTICAL ASSOCIATION— ACADEMY OF PHARMACY PRACTICE AND MANAGEMENT

Address: 2215 Constitution Avenue NW
             Washington, DC 20037-2985

Telephone: (202) 628-4410
WWW: www.aphanet.org
Document: Code of Ethics for Pharmacists (1994)

PREAMBLE

Pharmacists are health professionals who assist individuals in making the best use of medications. This Code, prepared and supported by pharmacists, is intended to state publicly the principles that form the fundamental basis of the roles and responsibilities of pharmacists. These principles, based on moral obligations and virtues, are established to guide pharmacists in relationships with patients, health professionals, and society.

I. A pharmacist respects the covenantal relationship between the patient and pharmacist.

Considering the patient-pharmacist relationship as a covenant means that pharmacist has moral obligations in response to the gift of trust received from society. In return for this gift, a pharmacist promises to help individuals achieve optimum benefit from their medications, to be committed to their welfare, and to maintain their trust.

II. A pharmacist promotes the good of every patient in a caring, compassionate, and confidential manner.

A pharmacist places concern for the well-being of the patient at the center of professional practice. In doing so, a pharmacist considers needs stated by the patient as well as those defined by health science. A pharmacist is dedicated to protecting the dignity of the patient. With a caring attitude and a compassionate spirit, a pharmacist focuses on serving the patient in a private and confidential manner.

III. A pharmacist respects the autonomy and dignity of each patient.

A pharmacist promotes the right of self-determination and recognizes individual self-worth by encouraging patients to participate in decisions about their health. A pharmacist communicates with patients in terms that are understandable. In all cases, a pharmacist respects personal and cultural differences among patients.

IV. A pharmacist acts with honesty and integrity in professional relationships.

A pharmacist has a duty to tell the truth and to act with conviction of conscience. A pharmacist avoids discriminatory practices, behavior or work conditions that impair professional judgment, and actions that compromise dedication to the best interests of patients.

V. A pharmacist maintains professional competence.

A pharmacist has a duty to maintain knowledge and abilities as new medications, devices, and technologies become available and as health information advances.

VI. A pharmacist respects the values and abilities of colleagues and other health professionals.

When appropriate, a pharmacist asks for the consultation of colleagues or other health professionals or refers the patient. A pharmacist acknowledges that colleagues and other health professionals may differ in the beliefs and values they apply to the care of the patient.

VII. A pharmacist serves individual, community, and societal needs.

The primary obligation of a pharmacist is to individual patients. However, the obligations of a pharmacist may at times extend beyond the individual to the community and society. In these situations, the pharmacist recognizes the responsibilities that accompany these obligations and acts accordingly.

VIII. A pharmacist seeks justice in the distribution of health resources.

When health resources are allocated, a pharmacist is fair and equitable, balancing the needs of patients and society.

AMERICAN PHYSICAL SOCIETY

Address: 1 Physics Ellipse
College Park, MD 20740-3844
Telephone: 301/209-3200
WWW: www.aps.org
Document: The American Physical Society Guidelines for Professional Conduct (1991)

The Constitution of *The American Physical Society* states that the objective of the Society shall be the advancement and diffusion of the knowledge of physics. It is the purpose of this statement to advance that objective by presenting ethical guidelines for Society members.

Each physicist is a citizen of the community of science. Each shares responsibility for the welfare of this community. Science is best advanced when there is mutual trust, based upon honest behavior, throughout the community. Acts of deception, or any other acts that deliberately compromise the advancement of science, are therefore unacceptable. Honesty must be regarded as the cornerstone of ethics in science.

The following are minimal standards of ethical behavior relating to several critical aspects of the physics profession.

Research Results

The results of research should be recorded and maintained in a form that allows analysis and review. Research data should be immediately available to scientific collaborators. Following publication, the data should be retained for a reasonable period in order to be available promptly and completely to responsible scientists. Exceptions may be appropriate in certain circumstances in order to preserve privacy, to assure patent protection, or for similar reasons.

Fabrication of data or selective reporting of data with the intent to mislead or deceive is an egregious departure from the expected norms of scientific conduct, as is the theft of data or research results from others.

Publication and Authorship Practices

Authorship should be limited to those who have made a significant contribution to the concept, design, execution and interpretation of the research study. All those who have made significant contributions should be offered the opportunity to be listed as authors. Other individuals who have contributed to the study should be acknowledged, but not be identified as authors. The sources of financial support for the project should be disclosed.

Plagiarism constitutes unethical scientific behavior and is never acceptable. Proper acknowledgment of the work of others used in a research project must always be given. Further, it is the obligation of each author to provide prompt retractions or corrections of errors in published works.

Peer Review

Peer review provides advice concerning research proposals, the publication of research results and career advancement of colleagues. It is an essential component of the scientific process.

Peer review can serve its intended function only if the members of the scientific community are prepared to provide thorough, fair and objective evaluations based on requisite expertise. Although peer review can be difficult and time-consuming, scientists have an obligation to participate in the process.

Privileged information or ideas that are obtained through peer review must be kept confidential and not be used for competitive gain.

Reviewers should disclose conflicts of interest resulting from direct competitive, collaborative, or other relationships with any of the authors, and avoid cases in which such conflicts preclude an objective evaluation.

Conflict of Interest

There are may professional activities of physicists that have the potential for a conflict of interest. Any professional relationship or action that may result in a conflict of interest must be fully disclosed. When objectivity and effectiveness cannot be maintained, the activity should be avoided or discontinued.

It should be recognized that honest error is an integral part of the scientific enterprise. It is not unethical to be wrong, provided that errors are promptly acknowledged and corrected when they are detected. Professional integrity in the formulation, conduct and reporting of physics activities reflects not only on the reputations of individual physicists and their organizations, but also on the image and credibility of the physics profession as perceived by scientific colleagues, government and the public. It is important that the traditions of ethical behavior be carefully maintained and transmitted with enthusiasm to future generations.

Physicists have an individual and a collective responsibility to ensure that there is no compromise with these guidelines.

© American Physical Society. Reprinted with permission.

AMERICAN PHYSICAL THERAPY ASSOCIATION

Address: 1111 North Fairfax Street
Alexandria, VA 22314-1488

Telephone: 703/684-2782 or 800/999-2782
WWW: www.apta.org
Documents: Code of Ethics for Physical
              Therapists (1981. Most recently
              revised 1991.) Standards of Ethical
              Conduct for the Physical Therapist
              Assistant (1982. Most recently
              revised 1991)

(The Judicial Committee of the American Physical Therapy Association has issued a companion *Guide for Professional Conduct* (not reprinted here), last amended January 1996 and available from the above address.—Eds.)

Code of Ethics for Physical Therapists
Preamble
This Code of Ethics sets forth ethical principles for the physical therapy profession. Members of this profession are responsible for maintaining and promoting ethical practice. This Code of Ethics, adopted by the American Physical Therapy Association, shall be binding on physical therapists who are members of the Association.

Principle 1
Physical therapists respect the rights and dignity of all individuals.

Principle 2
Physical therapists comply with the laws and regulations governing the practice of physical therapy.

Principle 3
Physical therapists accept responsibility for the exercise of sound judgment.

Principle 4
Physical therapists maintain and promote high standards for physical therapy practice, education, and research.

Principle 5
Physical therapists seek remuneration for their services that is deserved and reasonable.

Principle 6
Physical therapists provide accurate information to the consumer about the profession and about those services they provide.

Principle 7
Physical therapists accept the responsibility to protect the public and the profession from unethical, incompetent, or illegal acts.

Principle 8
Physical therapists participate in efforts to address the health needs of the public.

Standards of Ethical Conduct for the Physical Therapist Assistant

Preamble

Physical therapist assistants are responsible for maintaining and promoting high standards of conduct. These *Standards of Ethical Conduct for the Physical Therapist Assistant* shall be binding on physical therapist assistants who are affiliate members of the Association.

Standard 1

Physical therapist assistants provide services under the supervision of a physical therapist.

Standard 2

Physical therapist assistants respect the rights and dignity of all individuals.

Standard 3

Physical therapist assistants maintain and promote high standards in the provision of services, giving the welfare of patients their highest regard.

Standard 4

Physical therapist assistants provide services within the limits of the law.

Standard 5

Physical therapist assistants make those judgments that are commensurate with their qualifications as physical therapist assistants.

Standard 6

Physical therapist assistants accept the responsibility to protect the public and the profession from unethical, incompetent, or illegal acts.

© American Physical Therapy Association. Reprinted with permission.

THE AMERICAN PHYSIOLOGICAL SOCIETY

Address: 9650 Rockville Pike
Bethesda, MD 20814-3991

Telephone: 301/530-7164
WWW: www.faseb.org/aps
Document: The American Physiological Society
Policies on Research Ethics (1994)

(The polices reproduced here are selected from the *APS Operational Guide*, 1996.—Eds.)

Code of Ethics

Membership in the American Physiological Society includes the acceptance of and the responsibility to uphold the following Code of Ethics.

The role of the physiologist is to advance the field through teaching, research, and service. In the process, physiologists shall be honest in their reporting of research findings and ethical in their dealings with others. Moreover, physiologists shall be humane in the treatment of human and non-human subjects. Physiologists shall also have the professional responsibility to bring to the attention of appropriate authorities apparent violations of these principles.

Physiologists recognize the Society's responsibility to consider breaches of ethical behavior and to take any response deemed necessary in accordance with the Society's Bylaws, Article IX, Section 4 and as defined in the Operational Guide.

Appendix B
APS Operational Guide (1996), page 139
Adopted July 1993

Adherence to Ethical Guidelines

The American Physiological Society endorses the Recommendations from the Declaration of Helsinki and the Guiding Principles in the Care and Use of Animals and insists that all investigations involving humans and all animal experimentation reported in its publications be conducted in conformity with these principles. Editors/Associate Editors are expected to refuse papers in which evidence of the adherence to these principles is not apparent. They reserve the right to judge the appropriateness of the use of animals and humans in experiments published in the journals. Differences of opinion will be adjudicated by the Publications Committee.

Appendix C
APS Operational Guide (1996), page 142

Ethical Guidelines for Research

Recommendations from the Declaration of Helsinki

I. Basic Principles

1. Clinical research must conform to the moral and scientific principles that justify medical research

and should be based on laboratory and animal experiments or other scientifically established facts.

2. Clinical research should be conducted only by scientifically qualified persons and under the supervision of a qualified medical person.

3. Clinical research cannot legitimately be carried out unless the importance of the objective is in proportion to the inherent risk to the subject.

4. Every clinical research project should be preceded by careful assessment of inherent risks in comparison to foreseeable benefits to the subject or to others.

5. Special caution should be exercised by the doctor in performing clinical research in which the personality of the subject is liable to be altered by drugs or experimental procedure.

II. Clinical Research Combined with Professional Care

1. In the treatment of a sick person, the doctor must be free to use a new therapeutic measure, if in his judgment, it offers hope of saving life, re-establishing health, or alleviating suffering.

   If at all possible, consistent with patient psychology, the doctor should obtain the patient's freely given consent after the patient has been given a full explanation. In case of legal incapacity, consent should also be procured for the legal guardian; in case of physical incapacity, the permission of the legal guardian replaces that of the patient.

2. The doctor can combine clinical research with professional care, the objective being the acquisition of new medical knowledge, only to the extent that clinical research is justified by its therapeutic value for the patient.

III. Non-Therapeutic Clinical Research

1. In the purely scientific application of clinical research carried out on a human being, it is the duty of the doctor to remain the protector of the life and health of that person on whom clinical research is being carried out.

2. The nature, the purpose, and the risk of clinical research must be explained to the subject by the doctor.

3a. Clinical research on a human being cannot be undertaken without his free consent after he has been informed; if he is legally incompetent, the consent of the legal guardian should be procured.

3b. The subject of clinical research should be in such a mental, physical, and legal state as to be able to exercise fully his power of choice.

3c. Consent should, as rule, be obtained in writing. However, the responsibility for clinical research always remains with the research worker; it never falls on the subject even after consent is obtained.

4a. The investigator must respect the right of each individual to safeguard his personal integrity, especially if the subject is in a dependent relationship to the investigator.

4b. At any time during the course of clinical research the subject or his guardian should be free to withdraw permission for research to be continued.

   The investigator or the investigating team should discontinue the research if, in his or her judgment, it may, if continued, be harmful to the individual.

Appendix C
APS Operational Guide (1996), pages 140-141

Guiding Principles in the Care and Use of Animals

Animal experiments are to be undertaken only with the purpose of advancing knowledge. Consideration should be given to the appropriateness of experimental procedures, species of animals used, and number of animals required.

Only animals that are lawfully acquired shall be used in laboratory research, and their retention and use shall be in every case in compliance with federal, state, and local laws and regulations, and in accordance with the NIH Guide[1].

Animals used in research and education must receive every consideration for their comfort; they must be properly housed, fed, and their surroundings kept in sanitary conditions.

All experimental procedures must be carried out in accordance with the NIH Guide. Appropriate anesthetics must be used to eliminate sensibility to pain during all surgical procedures. Muscle relaxants or paralytics are not anesthetics, and they must not be used alone for surgical restraint, but may be used in conjunction with drugs known to produce adequate analgesia. The postoperative care of animals shall be such as to minimize discomfort and pain, and in any case shall be equivalent to accepted practices in veterinary medicine. All measures to minimize pain and

---

[1]*Guide for the Care and Use of Laboratory Animals* 7th edition, National Research Council, Institute of Laboratory Animal Resources Committee. Washington, DC: National Academy Press, 1996.

distress that would not compromise experimental results must be employed.

If the study requires the death of an animal, the most humane euthanasia method consistent with the study must be used.

When animals are used by students for their education or the advancements of science, such work shall be under the direct supervision of an experienced teacher or investigator.

Appendix C
APS Operational Guide (1996), page 142
Adopted 1953. Revised 1991

Conferees Statement of Principles for the Use of Animals in Research and Education

The Federation of American Societies for Experimental Biology (FASEB) affirms the essential contribution of animals in research and education aimed at improving the health of both humans and animals. The role of animals remains critical in understanding the fundamental processes of life, and in developing treatments for injury and disease. Members of the constituent Societies of FASEB believe that the use of animals in research and education is a privilege. This imposes a major responsibility to provide for their proper care and humane treatment. Good animal care and good science go hand-in-hand.

Therefore, the members of the constituent Societies of the Federation of American Societies for Experimental Biology support the following principles:

1. All work with animals shall be designed and performed in consideration of its relevance to the improvement of human or animal health and the advancement of knowledge for the good of society.
2. The acquisition, care and use of animals must be in accordance with applicable federal, state and local laws and regulations.
3. Each institution is responsible for providing a review procedure to assure that the use of animals in research and education conforms to the highest ethical, humane and scientific standards.
4. The minimum number of appropriate animals required to obtain valid results should be used. Good science demands judicious choices of appropriate methods, such as animals, computer simulations, or tissue and cell cultures.
5. Animals shall be housed and maintained under conditions appropriate to their species. Veterinary medical care shall be available.
6. Provision shall be made for the training and education of all personnel involved in the care and use of animals.
7. Sound scientific practice and humane considerations require that animals receive sedation, analgesia or anesthesia when appropriate. Animals should not be permitted to suffer severe or chronic pain or distress unnecessarily; such animals should be euthanized.

Developed by representatives of the constituent societies of FASEB at a consensus conference, June 1994. Adopted by the American Physiological Society Council, a founding member of FASEB, November 1994.

© American Physiological Society. Reprinted with permission.

AMERICAN PLANNING ASSOCIATION

Address: 122 South Michigan Avenue, Suite 1600 Chicago, IL 60603
Telephone: 312/431-9100
WWW: www.planning.org
Documents: AICP/APA Ethical Principles in Planning (1992)

This statement is a guide to ethical conduct for all who participate in the process of planning as advisors, advocates, and decision makers. It presents a set of principles to be held in common by certified planners, other practicing planners, appointed and elected officials, and others who participate in the process of planning.

The planning process exists to serve the public interest. While the public interest is a question of continuous debate, both in its general principles and in its case-by-case applications, it requires a conscientiously held view of the policies and actions that best serve the entire community. Section A presents what we hold to be necessary elements in such a view.

Planning issues commonly involve a conflict of values and, often, there are large private interests at stake. These accentuate the necessity for the highest standards of fairness and honesty among all participants. Section B presents specific standards.

Those who practice planning need to adhere to a special set of ethical requirements that must guide all who aspire to professionalism. These are presented in Section C.

Section D is the translation of the principles above into the AICP Code of Ethics and Professional Conduct. The Code is formally subscribed to by each certified planner. It includes an enforcement procedure that is administered by AICP. The Code, however, provides for more than the minimum threshold of enforceable acceptability. It also sets aspirational standards that require conscious striving to attain.

The ethical principles derive both from the general values of society and from the planner's special responsibility to serve the public interest. As the basic values of society are often in competition with each other, so do these principles sometimes compete. For example, the need to provide full public information may compete with the need to respect confidences. Plans and programs often result from a balancing among divergent interests. An ethical judgment often also requires a conscientious balancing, based on the facts and context of a particular situation and on the entire set of ethical principles.

This statement also aims to inform the public generally. It is also the basis for continuing systematic discussion of the application of its principles that is itself essential behavior to give them daily meaning.

A. The planning process must continuously pursue and faithfully serve the public interest.

Planning Process Participants should:

1. recognize the rights of citizens to participate in planning decisions;
2. strive to give citizens (including those who lack formal organization or influence) full, clear and accurate information on planning issues and the opportunity to have a meaningful role in the development of plans and programs;
3. strive to expand choice and opportunity for all persons, recognizing a special responsibility to plan for the needs of disadvantaged groups and persons;
4. assist in the clarification of community goals, objectives, and policies in plan making;
5. ensure that reports, records, and any other non-confidential information which is or will be, available to decision makers is made available to the public in a convenient format and sufficiently in advance of any decision;
6. strive to protect the integrity of the natural environment and the heritage of the built environment;
7. pay special attention to the interrelatedness of decisions and the long-range consequences of present actions.

B. Planning process participants continuously strive to achieve high standards of integrity and proficiency so that public respect for the planning process will be maintained.

Planning Process Participants should:

1. exercise fair, honest and independent judgment in their roles as decision makers and advisors;
2. make public disclosure of all "personal interests" they may have regarding any decision to be made in the planning process in which they serve, or are requested to serve, as advisor or decision maker (see also Advisory Ruling Number 2, "Conflicts of Interest When a Public Planner Has a Stake in Private Development" under Section D);
3. define "personal interest" broadly to include any actual or potential benefits or advantages that they, a spouse, family member or person living in their household might directly or indirectly obtain from a planning decision;
4. abstain completely from direct or indirect participation as an advisor or decision maker in any matter in which they have a personal interest, and leave any chamber in which such a matter is under deliberation, unless their personal interest has been made a matter of public record; their employer, if any, has given approval; and the public official, public agency or court with jurisdiction to rule on ethics matters has expressly authorized their participation;
5. seek no gifts or favors, nor offer any, under circumstances in which it might reasonably be inferred that the gifts or favors were intended or expected to influence a participant's objectivity as an advisor or decision maker in the planning process;
6. not participate as an advisor or decision maker on any plan or project in which they have previously participated as an advocate;
7. serve as advocates only when the client's objectives are legal and consistent with the public interest;
8. not participate as an advocate on any aspect of a plan or program on which they have previously served as advisor or decision maker unless their role as advocate is authorized by applicable law, agency regulation, or ruling of an ethics officer or agency; such participation as an advocate should be allowed only after prior disclosure to, and approval by, their affected client or employer; under no circumstance should such par-

ticipation commence earlier than one year following termination of the role as advisor or decision maker;

9. not use confidential information acquired in the course of their duties to further a personal interest;

10. not disclose confidential information acquired in the course of their duties except when required by law, to prevent a clear violation of law or to prevent substantial injury to third persons; provided that disclosure in the latter two situations may not be made until after verification of the facts and issues involved and consultation with other planning process participants to obtain their separate opinions;

11. not misrepresent facts or distort information for the purpose of achieving a desired outcome (see also Advisory Ruling Number 4: "Honesty in the Use of Information" under Section D);

12. not participate in any matter unless adequately prepared and sufficiently capacitated to render thorough and diligent service;

13. respect the rights of all persons and not improperly discriminate against or harass others based on characteristics which are protected under civil rights laws and regulations (see also Advisory Ruling Number 1: "Sexual Harassment").

C. APA members who are practicing planners continuously pursue improvement in their planning competence as well as in the development of peers and aspiring planners. They recognize that enhancement of planning as a profession leads to greater public respect for the planning process and thus serves the public interest.

APA Members who are practicing planners:

1. strive to achieve high standards of professionalism, including certification, integrity, knowledge, and professional development consistent with the AICP Code of Ethics;

2. do not commit a deliberately wrongful act which reflects adversely on planning as a profession or seek business by stating or implying that they are prepared, willing or able to influence decisions by improper means;

3. participate in continuing professional education;

4. contribute time and effort to groups lacking adequate planning resources and to voluntary professional activities;

5. accurately represent their qualifications to practice planning as well as their education and affiliations;

6. accurately represent the qualifications, views, and findings of colleagues;

7. treat fairly and comment responsibly on the professional views of colleagues and members of other professions;

8. share the results of experience and research which contribute to the body of planning knowledge;

9. examine the applicability of planning theories, methods and standards to the facts and analysis of each particular situation and do not accept the applicability of a customary solution without first establishing its appropriateness to the situation;

10. contribute time and information to the development of students, interns, beginning practitioners and other colleagues;

11. strive to increase the opportunities for women and members of recognized minorities to become professional planners;

12. systematically and critically analyze ethical issues in the practice of planning. (See also Advisory Ruling Number 3: "Outside Employment or Moonlighting").

Section D consists of the AICP Code of Ethics and Professional Conduct, Advisory Rulings, and Procedures. (The AICP Code of Ethics and Professional Conduct is reprinted under the entry for the American Institute of Certified Planners. See p. 00.—Eds.)

© American Planning Association. Reprinted with permission.

AMERICAN PODIATRIC MEDICAL ASSOCIATION

Address: 9312 Old Georgetown Road
            Bethesda, MD 20814-1698
Telephone: 301/571-9200
WWW: www.apma.org
Document: American Podiatric Code of Ethics
            (Most recently revised 1986.)

(The code appears to have originated about 1966; it has been printed in all issues of the *APMA Desk Reference* since that date. It was modestly revised in 1971, and then extensively revised in 1986 by the association's legal counsel.—Eds.)

SECTION I. PRINCIPLES OF ETHICS

This Code does not purport to include the entire field of podiatric medical ethics. The podiatrist is charged with many duties and obligations in addition to those set forth herein. Furthermore, every member of this Association shall be bound by the Code of Ethics of the American Podiatric Medical Association where not superseded herein.

The Principles of Ethics form the first part of this Code of Ethics. They are aspirational and inspirational model standards of exemplary professional conduct for all members of the Association. These Principles should not be regarded as limitations or restrictions, but as goals for which members should constantly strive.

A. **Ethics in Podiatric Medicine:** Ethics are moral values. An issue of ethics in podiatric medicine is resolved by the determination that the best interest of the patient is served.

B. **Providing Podiatric Medical Services:** Podiatric medical services must be provided with compassion, respect for human dignity, honesty, and integrity.

C. **Competence of the Podiatrist:** A podiatrist must maintain competence by continued study. That competence must be supplemented with the talents of other professionals and with consultation when indicated.

D. **Communication with the Patient:** Open communication with the patient is essential. Patient confidences must be safeguarded within the constraints of the law.

E. **Fees for Podiatric Medical Services:** Fees for podiatric medical services must not exploit patients or others who pay for the services.

F. **Identification of the Deficient Podiatrist:** Those podiatrists who engage in fraud or deception should be identified to appropriate authorities.

G. **Ethical Rules:** It is the duty of a podiatrist to place the patient's welfare and rights above all other considerations. To this end one must subscribe to ethical rules which are for the benefit of the patient.

SECTION 2. RULES OF ETHICS

The Rules of Ethics form the second part of this Code of Ethics. They are mandatory and direct specific standards of minimally-acceptable professional conduct for all members of the Association. The Rules of Ethics are enforceable for all members.

A. **Competence:** A podiatrist should perform only those procedures in which the podiatrist is competent by virtue of specific training or experience or is assisted by one who is. A podiatrist must not misrepresent credentials, training, experience, ability, or results.

B. **Patient Consent:** The performance of medical or surgical procedures shall be preceded by appropriate informed consent.

C. **Clinical Investigative Procedures:** Use of clinical investigative procedures shall be approved by adequate review mechanisms. Appropriate informed consent for these procedures must recognize their special nature and ramifications. A clinical investigative procedure is a method used to evaluate the authenticity or efficacy of a procedure or technique.

D. **Other Opinions and Referrals:** Additional opinion(s) shall be obtained if requested by the patient. Consultation(s) shall be obtained or referral(s) made whenever the welfare of the patient will be safeguarded or advanced by having recourse to practitioners who have special skills, knowledge, or experience.

E. **The Impaired Podiatrist:** A physically, mentally, or emotionally impaired podiatrist should withdraw from those aspects of practice affected by the impairment. If the podiatrist does not withdraw, it is the duty of other podiatrists who know of the impairment to take action to attempt to prevent him from harming himself or others.

F. **Preoperative Assessment:** Surgery shall be recommended only after a careful consideration of the patient's physical, social, emotional, and occupational needs. The preoperative workup must document the indications for surgery. Performance of unnecessary surgery is an extremely serious ethical violation.

G. **Postoperative Care:** Medical and surgical aspects of postoperative podiatric medical care, provided by a qualified podiatrist until the patient has recovered, are an integral part of patient management. If necessary postoperative care is not or will not be personally provided, the podiatrist must make arrangements with the mutual approval of the patient and of another qualified podiatrist or qualified practitioner of another branch of medicine who will provide postoperative care. Fees should reflect those arrangements with advance disclosure to the patient. In making those arrangements, the podiatrist must place the patient's welfare above all other considerations.

H. Delegation of Podiatric Medical Services: When a podiatrist delegates aspects of medical care to auxiliary health care personnel, the podiatrist must be assured that such personnel are qualified and adequately supervised. In delegating services, the podiatrist must place the patient's welfare above all other considerations. Delegation is defined as the assignment of specific services that need not be performed by the podiatrist, personally.

I. Medical and Surgical Procedures: A podiatrist must not misrepresent the services that are performed or the charges made for those services.

J. Procedures and Materials: A podiatrist should order only those procedures, devices, or pharmacological agents that are in the best interest of the patient. Ordering unnecessary procedures or materials for pecuniary gain is unethical.

K. Commercial Relationships: A podiatrist's clinical judgment and practice must not be affected by economic interest in, commitment to, or benefit from professionally-related commercial enterprises. The foregoing shall not limit membership or participation in health maintenance organizations, preferred provider organizations, or similar entities.

L. Communications to Colleagues: Communications to colleagues on research, including clinical investigations, must be accurate and truthful. Appropriate disclosure of commercial interest is required.

M. Communications to the Public: Communications to the public must be accurate. They must not convey false, untrue, deceptive, or misleading information through statements, testimonials, photographs, graphics, or other means. They must not omit material information, without which the communication would be deceptive. If communications (i.e., to the public) refer to benefits that involve significant risks, realistic assessments of their safety and efficacy must also be included, as well as the availability of alternatives and, where necessary to avoid deception, descriptions and/or assessments of the benefits or other attributes of those alternatives. Communications must not appeal primarily to an individual's anxiety or create unjustified expectations of results. Communications must not misrepresent a podiatrist's credentials, training, experience, or ability and must not contain material claims of superiority that cannot be substantiated. If a communication results from payment by a po-

diatrist, this must be disclosed unless the nature, format, or medium makes it apparent.

N. Professional Title: A podiatrist may use in connection with his name the titles, degrees, or designations authorized by law in his state. The title "doctor" or any abbreviation thereof cannot be used without the qualification "podiatrist" or "podiatric medicine — treatment of the foot and ankle," or other appropriate designations following the name.

A podiatrist who has been certified by a specialty board or group for one of the specialties approved by the American Podiatric Medical Association may use the appropriate term in connection with his specialty.

O. Split Fees, Commissions, and Rebates: It is unethical for podiatrists to pay or accept commissions in any form or manner on fees for professional services, references, consultations, pathology reports, radiograms, prescriptions, or on other services or articles supplied to patients.

Division of professional fees, or acceptance of rebates from fees paid by patients to x-ray, clinical or other laboratories, shoe stores, or other commercial establishments is unethical.

It is unethical for a podiatrist to pay for the recommendation of a patient.

The division of revenue in a partnership is outside the scope and application of this rule.

P. Patents and Copyrights: The podiatrist has the obligation of making the fruits of his discoveries and labors available to all when they are useful in safeguarding or promoting the health of the public. Patents and copyrights may be secured by a podiatrist provided that they and the remuneration derived from them are not used to restrict research, practice, or the benefits of the patented or copyrighted material.

Q. Waiver: Any member feeling aggrieved by reason of the enforcement of this code may submit a written request for waiver of specific provisions thereof and the reasons therefore to the Board of Directors and Ethics Committee which is authorized to grant said request upon good cause being shown therefore.

(Note: Throughout the Code of Ethics, the pronouns "he," "his," and "him" shall be intended to mean a member of either sex.)

AMERICAN POLITICAL SCIENCE ASSOCIATION

Address: 1527 New Hampshire Avenue NW
                Washington, DC 20036-1206
Telephone: 202/483-2512
WWW: www.apsanet.org
Document: Principles of Professional Conduct
                (1968. Most recently revised 1997.)

These principles, adopted by the Council of the American Political Science Association, embody in systematic form the principles established by the Association, the advisory opinions of the Committee on Professional Ethics, Rights and Freedoms, and other governing decisions adopted by the Association.

A. Freedom and Integrity of Research by Academic Political Scientists

Principles for Funding Agencies and Universities

1. Openness concerning material support of research is a basic principle of scholarship.

    1.1 In making grants for research, government and non-government sponsors should openly acknowledge research support and require that the grantee indicate in any published research financed by their grants the relevant sources of financial support.

    1.2 Where anonymity is requested by a non-governmental grantor and does not endanger the integrity of research, the character of the sponsorship rather than the identity of the grantor should be noted.

    1.3 Financial sponsors of research should avoid actions that would call into question the in-

tegrity of American academic institutions as centers of independent teaching and research. They should not sponsor research as a cover for intelligence activities.

    1.4 Political science research supported by government grants should be unclassified.

    1.5 After a research grant has been made, the grantor shall not impose any restriction on or require any clearance of research methods, procedures, or content.

    1.6 The grantor should assume no responsibility for the findings and conclusions of the researcher and should impose no restrictions or carry any responsibility for publication.

    1.7 Funding agencies should include in grants a stipulation that data gathered under the grants be made available to scholars at cost after a specified time, e.g., after a year has passed following the completion of the data-gathering process, or after the first substantial research report by the chief researcher has been completed.

2. The university or college should administer research funds according to principles of the funding agency, and in a manner which protects the integrity of the research.

    2.1 A university or college that administers research funds provided through contracts and grants from public and/or private sources must act to assure that research funds are used prudently and honorably.

    2.2 A university or college should not administer research funds derived from contracts or grants whose purpose and the character of whose sponsorship cannot be publicly disclosed.

    2.3 In administering research funds entrusted directly to its care, a university or college should do its best to ensure that no restrictions are placed on the availability of evidence to scholars or on their freedom to draw their own conclusions from the evidence and to share their findings with others.

Principles for Individual Researchers

3. In applying for research funds, the individual researcher should:

    3.1 clearly state the reasons for applying for support and not resort to stratagems of ambiguity to make the research more acceptable to a funding agency;

3.2 indicate clearly the actual amount of time the researcher personally plans to spend on the research;

3.3 indicate other sources of support of the research, if any; and

3.4 refuse to accept terms and conditions that the researcher believes will undermine his or her freedom and integrity as a scholar.

4. In conducting research so supported, the individual bears sole responsibility for the procedures, methods, and content of research. The researcher:

4.1 must avoid any deception or misrepresentation concerning his or her personal involvement or the involvement of respondents or subjects, and must avoid use of research as a cover for intelligence work or for partisan political purposes;

4.2 must refrain from using his or her professional status to obtain data and research materials for purposes other than scholarship;

4.3 with respect to research abroad, should not concurrently accept any additional support from agencies of the government for purposes that cannot be disclosed;

4.4 should carefully comply with the time, reporting, accounting, and other requirements set forth in the project instrument, and cooperate with institutional grant administrators in meeting these requirements; and

4.5 should avoid commingling project funds with personal funds, or funds of one project with those of another.

5. With respect to any public scholarly activity including publication of the results of research, the individual researcher:

5.1 bears sole responsibility for publication;

5.2 should disclose all relevant sources of financial support;

5.3 should indicate any condition imposed by financial sponsors or others on research publication, or other scholarly activities; and

5.4 should conscientiously acknowledge any assistance received in conducting research.

5.5 Authors are obliged to reveal the bases of any of their statements that are challenged specifically, except where confidentiality is involved.

5.6 When statements that are challenged are based on reproducible data, authors are obliged to facilitate replication. They may expect the challenger to pay the costs of reproducing the relevant data.

5.7 Challenges are to be sufficiently precise to indicate to the author what documentation or data are needed. Challengers are themselves in the status of authors in connection with the statements that they make.

6. Scholars have an ethical obligation to make a full and complete disclosure of all non-confidential sources involved in their research so that their work can be tested or replicated.

6.1 As citizens, they have an obligation to cooperate with grand juries, other law enforcement agencies, and institutional officials.

6.2 Conversely, scholars also have a professional duty not to divulge the identity of confidential sources of information or data developed in the course of research, whether to governmental or non-governmental officials or bodies, even though in the present state of American law they run the risk of suffering an applicable penalty.

6.3 Scholars must, however, exercise appropriate restraint in making claims as to the confidential nature of their sources, and resolve all reasonable doubts in favor of full disclosure.

7. Political scientists, like all scholars, are expected to practice intellectual honesty and to uphold the scholarly standards of their discipline.

7.1 Plagiarism, the deliberate appropriation of the work of others represented as one's own, not only may constitute a violation of the civil law but represents a serious breach of professional ethics.

7.2 Departments of political science should make it clear to both faculty and students that such misconduct will lead to disciplinary action and, in the case of serious offenses, may result in dismissal. Institutional rules and expected standards of conduct should be published in advance and distributed through such means as faculty and student handbooks.

7.3 Disciplinary proceedings should conform to norms of fairness and academic due process as formulated in relevant AAUP statements.

B. Responsibilities in the Classroom and to Students

8. Academic political scientists must be very careful not to impose their partisan views, conventional or otherwise, upon students or colleagues.

9. Teachers have an ethical obligation to choose materials for student use without respect to personal or collective gain.

9.1 Publishers are strongly discouraged from offering inducements for textbook choice apart from making examination copies available and lowering the suggested retail price of a book.

10. Faculty members must not expropriate the academic work of their students.

10.1 Teachers cannot represent themselves as authors of independent student research; and research assistance, paid or unpaid, requires full acknowledgment.

10.2 As advisers, faculty members are not entitled to claim joint authorship with a student of a thesis or dissertation.

11. Political science departments have an obligation to protect the procedural rights of graduate students.

11.1 Students should be advised at the time of their admittance as to the departmental and institutional requirements of the degree program they will be entering. If a department of political science changes the requirements of a program, students already enrolled and making normal progress toward their degrees should have the right to be governed by the requirements in force at the time of their entrance if they so desire.

11.2 Students should be advised at the time of their admittance under what conditions written or oral major examinations ("prelims," "comprehensives," etc.) are given and whether such examinations, if failed, may be retaken.

11.3 After submitting a proposal for a thesis or dissertation, a student should be informed by the chairperson of his or her committee of its action with regard to the acceptability of the proposal. Action on a proposal should be taken within a reasonable time and communicated to the student in writing.

11.4 If, in the opinion of the supervising faculty, a student's thesis or dissertation does not show satisfactory progress and should there arise questions of the acceptability of the final product, the student should be put on notice as soon as possible and in writing that his or her candidacy for the degree may be terminated.

11.5 Students should be advised of any changes in the composition of their thesis or dissertation committee. Faculty members should not participate in a thesis or dissertation examination unless they have had sufficient time to read the thesis or dissertation.

11.6 A student who fails a written or oral major examination ("prelims," "comprehensives," etc.) or has a thesis or dissertation required for the degree rejected should be informed by the examiners or readers as to the reasons for such failure or rejection. Upon request, this explanation should be rendered in writing.

11.7 Students should be informed upon entering a graduate program about any departmental or university grievance procedures for handling disputes that may arise between faculty and graduate students pertaining to the interpretation of degree requirements or the administration of the graduate program. Departments without an established grievance procedure are urged to develop such rules and to distribute them in writing to all their graduate students. Universities should provide an appeals process beyond the department level to insure adherence to proper procedural standards.

C. Political Activity of Academic Political Scientists

12. The college or university teacher is a citizen, and like other citizens, should be free to engage in political activities insofar as this can be done consistently with obligations as a teacher and scholar.

12.1 Effective service as a faculty member is often compatible with certain types of political activity, for example, holding a part time office in a political party or serving as a member of a governmental advisory board. Where a professor engages in full-time political activity, such as service in a state legislature, he or she should, as a rule, seek a leave of absence from the institution. Since political activity by academic political scientists is both legitimate and socially important, universities and colleges should have institutional arrangements to permit such activity, including reduction in the faculty member's work-load or a leave of absence subject to equitable adjustment of compensation.

12.2 A faculty member who seeks a leave to engage in political activity should recognize that he or she has a primary obligation to the institution and to grow as a teacher and scholar. The faculty member should consider the problems that a leave of absence may create for the administration, colleagues and students, and should not abuse the privilege by asking for leaves too frequently, or too late, or for too extended a period of time. A leave of absence incident to political activity should not affect unfavorably the tenure status of the faculty member.

12.3 Special problems arise if departments or schools endorse or sponsor political activities or public policies in the name of the entire faculty of the department or school. One of the purposes of tenure — to shelter unpopular or unorthodox teaching — is in some degree vitiated if the majority of a departmental faculty endorses or sponsors a particular political position in the name of the faculty of the department. Departments should adhere strictly to the rule that those faculty members who wish to endorse or sponsor a political position or activity do so in their own names without binding their colleagues. Departments as such should not endorse political positions.

D. Restrictions on the Use of the APSA Name or Office

13. When officers, members, or employees of the Association speak out on an issue of public policy, endorse a political candidate, or otherwise participate in political affairs, they should make it as clear as possible that they are not speaking on behalf of the Association unless they are so authorized by the Association, and they should not encourage any inference that they act for the Association unless so authorized by the Association. The use of the title of the office held in the APSA in political advertisements, even if labeled "for identification purposes only," may well be seen by others as an endorsement of a political position by the Association and should be avoided.

14. Officers and employees of the Association are free to engage in activities outside their obligations to the Association provided that such activities are consistent with their duties and responsibilities to the Association. When doubts arise

about the activities of subordinate staff members, they should be resolved by the Executive Director in consultation with the Administrative Committee of the Association. Similarly, when doubts arise about the activities of the Executive Director, they should be resolved by the Administrative Committee.

15. Officers or employees of the Association should not knowingly participate in transactions involving the Association, if they have a substantial economic interest in them. Under such circumstances, they should disqualify themselves from participating in transactions involving the Association.

E. Ethics in the Publication Process

16. Appraising manuscripts and reviewing books are serious scholarly responsibilities.

16.1 Those invited to make appraisals or to write reviews should disqualify themselves if they have a reasonable doubt about whether they can exercise the responsibility with scholarly detachment. Such doubt might be raised, for example, by an invitation to appraise the manuscript or review the book of a close personal friend or of a departmental colleague.

16.2 Insofar as possible, editors and book-review editors should themselves act in conformity with the above principles. Moreover, in connection with the appraisal of manuscripts, editors should take all reasonable precautions to avoid revealing the names of the author and the reader to each other.

17. When a piece of writing is jointly authored, it is presumed to be the intellectual product of the authors collectively, not individually, and this fact should govern its further use including its use by any of the original authors.

17.1 Passages of text and major themes and ideas used in subsequent work by any of the authors should be attributed to the original source following accepted standards for quotation and citation. Exceptions to this practice should occur only if a portion of the jointly authorized work has been clearly attributed in the original work to one of the authors.

18. Authors who submit manuscripts to more than one professional journal at the same time are obligated to inform each editor of the fact.

19. Political scientists seeking to reprint the previously published work of others have an ethical obligation to make sure that consent is obtained.

 19.1 The copyright holder should consent to the inclusion of previously published work only if the author consents. The copyright holder should either obtain the consent of the author or require that this be done by the party seeking permission to reprint.

 19.2 In cases where the copyright holder or the publisher of previously published work has not taken steps to obtain consent, the political scientist involved, as compiler and editor of the book, should secure the consent of the author of the material. Political scientists are encouraged to include in contracts with publishers a provision that the publisher must obtain the consent of the author or authors before allowing reprinting of the work.

 19.3 The copyright holder and the author are each entitled to a flat fee or a share of royalties in connection with permissions to reprint, specific terms depending on agreement with the party seeking permission. Either the copyright holder or the author may waive his or her right. Each may act on his or her own behalf, or by mutual consent one may act on behalf of both.

 19.4 Permission must be renewed, and financial arrangements are subject to renegotiation, whenever a book goes into a new edition.

 19.5 Any work reprinted may be changed only with the specific consent of the author. An author ordinarily is entitled to a complimentary copy of any publication in which his or her work is reprinted.

20. Responsibilities of Editors and Contributors to Edited Volumes

 20.1 Prospective editors shall not use the names of any individuals as contributors to an edited volume unless and until they have received permission of the contributors for use of their names.

 20.2 Once contracts are signed for an edited volume, and solicitations of manuscripts are made, editors have an obligation to include the solicited work in the publication if it conforms to the standards of scholarship previously established by the editors.

 20.3 Along with any other guidelines established by the editors, contracts and instructions to contributors should include clear specification of (1) manuscript length for the individual contributor; and (2) number of days for authors to respond to editors' alterations or suggestions for revision to the manuscript.

 20.4 Editors will normally have responsibility and authority for decisions on acceptability of manuscripts, and should clearly communicate this understanding, or any departure therefrom, to the contributors.

21. When a thesis or dissertation is published in whole or in part, the following rules apply:

 21.1 Authors are not ordinarily under an ethical obligation to acknowledge its origins.

 21.2 Authors are free to decide what acknowledgment, if any, to give to the professor under whose supervision they worked.

 21.3 Any financial support for the dissertation should be acknowledged in a manner consistent with principles for all published research.

F. Ethics in Recruitment, Hiring and Personnel Practices Process

22. Equal Employment Practices and Opportunities. It is Association policy that educational institutions not discriminate on the basis of gender, race, color, national origin, sexual orientation, marital status, physical handicap, disability, or religion in any condition of employment except in cases in which federal laws allow religious preference in hiring.

The guiding principle is that employment should be based on only those criteria which relate directly to professional competence.

In accordance with this policy, therefore, the Association will not indicate a preference, limitation, or specification based upon these classifications in job listings, except that religious preferences may be indicated when allowed by federal law.

However, it is Association policy to support the principles of affirmative action and to urge political science departments to pursue aggressively affirmative action programs and policies with regard to African Americans, Latinos, women, and other minorities.

23. Nepotism Rules.

Institutions employing political scientists should abolish nepotism rules, whether they apply departmentally or to an institution as a whole. Employment and advancement should be based solely on professional qualifications without regard for family relationships, subject only to appropriate rules governing conflict of interest.

24. Part-time Positions.

    Institutions employing political scientists should make more flexible use of part-time positions for fully qualified professional women and men, just as is now done for those professionals with joint appointments or part-time research positions. Part-time positions should carry full academic status, equivalent rank, promotion opportunities, equal rates of pay, commensurate departmental participation and commensurate fringe benefits, including access to research resources. The policy of flexible part-time positions is not intended to condone any practice such as moonlighting or any practice by employers used to circumvent normal career-ladder appointments.

25. Equal Employment Opportunities.

    It is Association policy that educational institutions not discriminate against job candidates on the basis of gender, race, color, national origin, sexual orientation, marital status, physical handicap, disability, or religion except in those cases in which federal laws allow religious preference in hiring.

    25.1 The guiding principle is that employment decisions should be based on only those criteria that relate directly to professional competence.

    25.2 It is Association policy that educational institutions not discriminate in any condition of employment (including the provision of domestic partner benefits) on the basis of gender, race, color, national origin, sexual orientation, age, marital status, physical handicap, disability, or religion except in those cases in which federal laws allow religious preferences in hiring.

    25.3 In pursuit of the objective of ending discrimination, it is Association policy to support the principles of affirmative action and urge political science departments to pursue aggressively affirmative action programs and policies with regard to African Americans, Latinos, women, minorities based on self-identified sexual orientation, and other minorities. (Appropriate strategies may differ for each group.)

    25.4 The Association will not indicate preference, limitation, or specification based upon the categories in paragraph 25.2 in job listings, except that religious preferences may be indicated when allowed by federal law.

26. Fraud in Claiming Advanced Degrees.

    26.1 If a person who seeks an academic position falsely claims to have an advanced degree, and if the falsity of the claim becomes known to the department or other appointing authorities of the institution in which the position is located, the chair or other appointing authorities ordinarily have an ethical obligation to report the fraud to the institution alleged to have granted the degree.

    26.2 If those who know of fraud are asked by a potential academic employer for an oral or written statement concerning the qualification of a person falsely claiming an advanced degree, the statement should ordinarily include an appropriate description of the fraud, especially if there is reason to believe that the person may persist in it.

27. Recommending a candidate for faculty appointment calls for honest and responsible judgment.

    27.1 The scholarly achievements and promise of the candidate should be assessed as fairly as possible.

    27.2 Also to be assessed are the characteristics of the candidate that relate to his or her probable effectiveness in the classroom and to the development of a stimulating rapport with professional colleagues.

    27.3 Should there be clear basis for question about the compatibility of the candidate's past behavior with legitimate expectations of the employing institution, the fact may be mentioned. It is permissible for the employing institution to expect that members of its faculty will abide by institutional rules that do not violate principles of academic freedom or political rights of citizenship. A candidate should be informed if references to such matters are in his or her record and should have an opportunity to place in the record a statement relating to such matters. Matters pertaining to the candidate that have no bearing on the legitimate expectations of the employing institution should not be mentioned.

27.4 When an academic department requests from a scholar outside the institution an evaluation regarding a political scientist, the normal expectation in the profession is that the letter of evaluation will be treated as confidential. If it is the department's policy to place such matters in an open file, or otherwise make these letters available to those who may desire to see them, then the department has an ethical obligation to inform the individual from whom a letter is requested that the letter will not be regarded as a confidential document. If one who is requested to write a letter of evaluation is informed in advance that the letter will be placed in an open file, then it is proper to exercise the option of not writing such a letter. Furthermore, the refusal to write a letter should not be a matter of record.

27.5 Letters of recommendation for political scientists who are still candidates for a degree, placed in files at their own or at other institutions, are by law open for inspection by them, unless they have waived this right of access. If they have not waived this right, the department has an obligation to inform the individuals from whom letters are requested that the confidentiality of their letters cannot be assured.

27.6 Letters of recommendation placed in files for post-secondary students are open for inspection by them, unless they have waived this right of access.

28. The Appointment Process.

28.1 Once an employing institution clearly indicates that it is giving serious consideration to an applicant for a faculty appointment, e.g., by interviewing him or her, it should inform the applicant of the status of his or her application, and of any change in status, within a reasonable time.

28.2 Once an employing institution offers a faculty appointment, the individual to whom the offer is made should respond within a reasonable time either with the decision or with a statement concerning his or her situation.

28.3 In connection with both points above, two weeks is to be considered a reasonable time unless the parties specifically agree otherwise.

28.4 An employing institution that offers a faculty appointment orally should immediately communicate the offer in writing.

28.5 The employing institution has an obligation to inform fully a candidate for employment concerning the terms and procedures used in making of offers of appointment.

29. Once an individual accepts an offer of employment from an institution, it is incumbent upon the individual not to seek or accept further employment for the same initial contract year unless a prior release is secured from the hiring institution.

G. Ethics in Tenure and Promotion

Among the most serious responsibilities in the academic community is the assessment of colleagues for tenure and promotion.

30. As a matter of principle, a department should use the same procedures and, insofar as possible, similar criteria for all candidates under review for tenure and promotion.

31. The candidate being reviewed has a professional right to know the motivating principles, customary standards, and principal procedures of the assessment process of his or her department.

31.1 The department is obligated to provide in writing to the candidate being assessed a statement that: (i) sets out the principal parts of the assessment process; (ii) explains the instructions under which external reviewers will operate; and (iii) provides an account of the process which the department and university will follow in coming to a decision on tenure or promotion.

31.2 The department is obligated (i) to inform the candidate, in writing, if procedures to be used depart in any way from the department's customary procedures; and (ii) to detail how and explain why procedures may differ in his or her case.

31.3 The department has a specific obligation to inform the candidate of the materials (e.g., manuscripts, proposals, publication) that are being sent out for review. The materials to be reviewed need not include all of the candidate's work, but should not exclude material the candidate judges indispensable to an assessment of his or her case.

32. External reviews are governed by a triad of rights and obligations: those of the department con-

ducting the review; those of the candidate under review; and those of the external reviewers. All three share values in common, for instance, a commitment to fairness and dispatch. But obligations and rights are not the same for all parties; each may give these values a differing weight, even a conflicting interpretation.

Guidelines, necessarily, must concern general principles. Guidelines for external review are not intended to be, and should not be read as, a uniform code, to be applied to all universities and colleges alike. Academic departments differ, for example, in educational mission, institutional resources, access to external reviewers and size. The proper procedure for one department or institution may not be the same for others.

32.1 Where external reviews are used in tenure and promotion decisions and if they are used in reappointment decisions, it is the right of faculty members to receive, and the obligation of academic departments to provide, external reviews that are expert, disinterested and timely.

32.2 Solicitations of outside letters of recommendation for promotion and tenure should always be phrased as an invitation which the recipient is free to reject. No presumption should be expressed that there is an obligation to perform this service, but rather that it is a professional courtesy of assistance to the department making the request. Refusal to perform this service should not be regarded as a negative statement about the candidate.

32.3 External reviewers perform a valuable professional service in assisting other departments and universities to assess candidates for tenure and promotion. It is not inappropriate for departments to offer an honorarium to external reviewers in the case of candidates for promotion and tenure who are not members of a reviewer's university. Institutions should inform the reviewer whether or not they will pay a fee and what that fee is when the initial contact is made with the reviewer.

32.4 Prior to selection of reviewers, the candidate being reviewed has a right to call to his or her department's attention possible reviewers he or she feels should be excluded on the grounds of personal bias. Depart-

ments and universities have an obligation to provide reviewers who will be objective and not harbor personal or professional biases against the candidate.

32.5 A department that solicits an external review on a confidential basis has an obligation to protect that confidentiality to the extent legally permissible.

32.6 The department conducting an external review, given its overall responsibility to assure an informed and timely evaluation, is ordinarily obliged: (i) to provide external reviewers a copy of the candidate's curriculum vitae and of the principal materials on which assessment is to be based; (ii) to ensure external reviewers sufficient time for a competent and conscientious assessment, as a rule not less than one month; (iii) to state if the assessment is a confidential one, and if not, the terms of departure from confidentiality; and (iv) to explain to external reviewers the relative importance of external reviews to the overall review process.

33. In 1947 APSA formally endorsed as Association policy the 1940 *Statement of Principles on Academic Freedom and Tenure* jointly developed by the American Association of University Professors (AAUP) and the Association of American Colleges (AAC).

AMERICAN PSYCHIATRIC ASSOCIATION

Address: 1400 K Street NW
             Washington, DC 20005
Telephone: 202/682-6000
WWW: www.psych.org

Document: The Principles of Medical Ethics with
             Annotations Especially Applicable to
             Psychiatry (1995)

(In 1973, the American Psychiatric Association published the first edition of *The Principles of Medical
Ethics with Annotations Especially Applicable to
Psychiatry*. Subsequently, revisions were published
as the Board of Trustees and the Assembly approved
additional annotations. In July of 1980, the American
Medical Association approved a new version of the
Principles of Medical Ethics (the first revision since
1957) and the APA Ethics Committee[1] incorporated
many of its annotations into the new Principles,
which resulted in the 1981 edition and subsequent revisions. The association also publishes a companion
volume, *Opinions of the Ethics Committee on the
Principles of Medical Ethics*, which is not reprinted
here. The Association's seal depicts Dr. Benjamin
Rush, regarded as "the Father of American Psychiatry;" he was also a signer of the Declaration of Independence. The stars under the name represent the 13
founding fathers of the Association who met in
Philadelphia in 1844.—Eds.)

FOREWORD
ALL PHYSICIANS should practice in accordance
with the medical code of ethics set forth in the Principles of Medical Ethics of the American Medical Association. An up-to-date expression and elaboration
of these statements is found in the Opinions and Reports of the Council on Ethical and Judicial Affairs of
the American Medical Association.[2] Psychiatrists are
strongly advised to be familiar with these documents.[3] (See p. 00.)

However, these general guidelines have sometimes been difficult to interpret for psychiatry, so
further annotations to the basic principles are offered in this document. While psychiatrists have the
same goals as all physicians, there are special ethical problems in psychiatric practice that differ in
coloring and degree from ethical problems in other
branches of medical practice, even though the basic
principles are the same. The annotations are not designed as absolutes and will be revised from time to
time so as to be applicable to current practices and
problems.

PRINCIPLES WITH ANNOTATIONS
Following are each of the AMA Principles of Medical
Ethics printed separately along with annotations es-
pecially applicable to psychiatry.

PREAMBLE
*The medical profession has long subscribed to a body
of ethical statements developed primarily for the benefit of the patient. As a member of this profession, a
physician must recognize responsibility not only to
patients but also to society, to other health professionals, and to self. The following Principles,
adopted by the American Medical Association, are
not laws but standards of conduct, which define the
essentials of honorable behavior for the physician.[4]*

SECTION 1
*A physician shall be dedicated to providing compe-
tent medical service with compassion and respect for
human dignity.*

1. The patient may place his/her trust in his/her psychiatrist knowing that the psychiatrist's ethics and
professional responsibilities preclude him/her
gratifying his/her own needs by exploiting the patient. The psychiatrist shall be ever vigilant about
the impact that his/her conduct has upon the
boundaries of the doctor/patient relationship, and
thus upon the well being of the patient. These requirements become particularly important because of the essentially private, highly personal,
and sometimes intensely emotional nature of the
relationship established with the psychiatrist.

2. A psychiatrist should not be a party to any type of
policy that excludes, segregates, or demeans the
dignity of any patient because of ethnic origin,
race, sex, creed, age, socioeconomic status, or
sexual orientation.

3. In accord with the requirements of law and accepted medical practice, it is ethical for a physician to submit his/her work to peer review and to
the ultimate authority of the medical staff executive body and the hospital administration and its
governing body. In case of dispute, the ethical
psychiatrist has the following steps available:

   a. Seek appeal from the medical staff decision
   to a joint conference committee, including
   members of the medical staff executive committee and the executive committee of the
   governing board. At this appeal, the ethical
   psychiatrist could request that outside opinions be considered.

   b. Appeal to the governing body itself.

   c. Appeal to state agencies regulating licensure of
   hospitals if, in the particular state, they concern
   themselves with matters of professional competency and quality of care.

d. Attempt to educate colleagues through development of research projects and data and presentations at professional meetings and in professional journals.

e. Seek redress in local courts, perhaps through an enjoining injunction against the governing body.

f. Public education as carried out by an ethical psychiatrist would not utilize appeals based solely upon emotion, but would be presented in a professional way and without any potential exploitation of patients through testimonials.

4. A psychiatrist should not be a participant in a legally authorized execution.

SECTION 2

A physician shall deal honestly with patients and colleagues, and strive to expose those physicians deficient in character or competence, or who engage in fraud or deception.

1. The requirement that the physician conduct himself/herself with propriety in his/her profession and in all the actions of his/her life is especially important in the case of the psychiatrist because the patient tends to model his/her behavior after that of his/her psychiatrist by identification. Further, the necessary intensity of the treatment relationship may tend to activate sexual and other needs and fantasies on the part of both patient and psychiatrist, while weakening the objectivity necessary for control. Additionally, the inherent inequality in the doctor-patient relationship may lead to exploitation of the patient. Sexual activity with a current or former patient is unethical.

2. The psychiatrist should diligently guard against exploiting information furnished by the patient and should not use the unique position of power afforded him/her by the psychotherapeutic situation to influence the patient in any way not directly relevant to the treatment goals.

3. A psychiatrist who regularly practices outside his/her area of professional competence should be considered unethical. Determination of professional competence should be made by peer review boards or other appropriate bodies.

4. Special consideration should be given to those psychiatrists who, due to illness, jeopardize the welfare of their patients and their own reputations and practices. It is ethical, even encouraged, for another psychiatrist to intercede in such situations.

5. Psychiatric services, like all medical services, are dispensed in the context of a contractual arrange-

ment between the patient and the treating physician. The provisions of the contractual arrangement, which are binding on the physician as well as on the patient, should be explicitly established.

6. It is ethical for the psychiatrist to make a charge for a missed appointment when this falls within the terms of the specific contractual agreement with the patient. Charging for a missed appointment or for one not cancelled 24 hours in advance need not, in itself, be considered unethical if a patient is fully advised that the physician will make such a charge. The practice, however, should be resorted to infrequently and always with the utmost consideration for the patient and his/her circumstances.

7. An arrangement in which a psychiatrist provides supervision or administration to other physicians or nonmedical persons for a percentage of their fees or gross income is not acceptable; this would constitute fee-splitting. In a team of practitioners, or a multidisciplinary team, it is ethical for the psychiatrist to receive income for administration, research, education, or consultation. This should be based upon a mutually agreed upon and set fee or salary, open to renegotiation when a change in the time demand occurs. (See also Section 5, Annotations 2, 3, and 4.)

SECTION 3

A physician shall respect the law and also recognize a responsibility to seek changes in those requirements which are contrary to the best interests of the patient.

1. It would seem self-evident that a psychiatrist who is a lawbreaker might be ethically unsuited to practice his/her profession. When such illegal activities bear directly upon his/her practice, this would obviously be the case. However, in other instances, illegal activities such as those concerning the right to protest social injustices might not bear on either the image of the psychiatrist or the ability of the specific psychiatrist to treat his/her patient ethically and well. While no committee or board could offer prior assurance that any illegal activity would not be considered unethical, it is conceivable that an individual could violate a law without being guilty of professionally unethical behavior. Physicians lose no right of citizenship on entry into the profession of medicine.

2. Where not specifically prohibited by local laws governing medical practice, the practice of acupuncture by a psychiatrist is not unethical per se. The psychi-

atrist should have professional competence in the use of acupuncture. Or, if he/she is supervising the use of acupuncture by nonmedical individuals, he/she should provide proper medical supervision. (See also Section 5, Annotations 3 and 4.)

SECTION 4

A physician shall respect the rights of patients, of colleagues, and of other health professionals, and shall safeguard patient confidences within the constraints of the law.

1. Psychiatric records, including even the identification of a person as a patient, must be protected with extreme care. Confidentiality is essential to psychiatric treatment. This is based in part on the special nature of psychiatric therapy as well as on the traditional ethical relationship between physician and patient. Growing concern regarding the civil rights of patients and the possible adverse effects of computerization, duplication equipment, and data banks makes the dissemination of confidential information an increasing hazard. Because of the sensitive and private nature of the information with which the psychiatrist deals, he/she must be circumspect in the information that he/she chooses to disclose to others about a patient. The welfare of the patient must be a continuing consideration.

2. A psychiatrist may release confidential information only with the authorization of the patient or under proper legal compulsion. The continuing duty of the psychiatrist to protect the patient includes fully apprising him/her of the connotations of waiving the privilege of privacy. This may become an issue when the patient is being investigated by a government agency, is applying for a position, or is involved in legal action. The same principles apply to the release of information concerning treatment to medical departments of government agencies, business organizations, labor unions, and insurance companies. Information gained in confidence about patients seen in student health services should not be released without the students' explicit permission.

3. Clinical and other materials used in teaching and writing must be adequately disguised in order to preserve the anonymity of the individuals involved.

4. The ethical responsibility of maintaining confidentiality holds equally for the consultations in which the patient may not have been present and in which the consultee was not a physician. In such instances, the physician consultant should alert the consultee to his/her duty of confidentiality.

5. Ethically the psychiatrist may disclose only that information which is relevant to a given situation. He/she should avoid offering speculation as fact. Sensitive information such as an individual's sexual orientation or fantasy material is usually unnecessary.

6. Psychiatrists are often asked to examine individuals for security purposes, to determine suitability for various jobs, and to determine legal competence. The psychiatrist must fully describe the nature and purpose and lack of confidentiality of the examination to the examinee at the beginning of the examination.

7. Careful judgment must be exercised by the psychiatrist in order to include, when appropriate, the parents or guardian in the treatment of a minor. At the same time, the psychiatrist must assure the minor proper confidentiality.

8. When in the clinical judgment of the treating psychiatrist the risk of danger is deemed to be significant, the psychiatrist may reveal confidential information disclosed by the patient.

9. When the psychiatrist is ordered by the court to reveal the confidences entrusted to him/her by patients, he/she may comply or he/she may ethically hold the right to dissent within the framework of the law. When the psychiatrist is in doubt, the right of the patient to confidentiality and, by extension, to unimpaired treatment, should be given priority. The psychiatrist should reserve the right to raise the question of adequate need for disclosure. In the event that the necessity for legal disclosure is demonstrated by the court, the psychiatrist may request the right to disclosure of only that information which is relevant to the legal question at hand.

10. With regard for the person's dignity and privacy and with truly informed consent, it is ethical to present a patient to a scientific gathering, if the confidentiality of the presentation is understood and accepted by the audience.

11. It is ethical to present a patient or former patient to a public gathering or to the news media only if the patient is fully informed of enduring loss of confidentiality, is competent, and consents in writing without coercion.

12. When involved in funded research, the ethical psychiatrist will advise human subjects of the funding source, retain his/her freedom to reveal data and results, and follow all appropriate and current guidelines relative to human subject protection.

13. Ethical considerations in medical practice preclude the psychiatric evaluation of any person charged with criminal acts prior to access to, or availability of, legal counsel. The only exception is the rendering of care to the person for the sole purpose of medical treatment.

14. Sexual involvement between a faculty member or supervisor and a trainee or student, in those situations in which an abuse of power can occur, often takes advantage of inequalities in the working relationship and may be unethical because: (a) any treatment of a patient being supervised may be deleteriously affected; (b) it may damage the trust relationship between teacher and student; and (c) teachers are important professional role models for their trainees and affect their trainees' future professional behavior.

SECTION 5

A physician shall continue to study, apply, and advance scientific knowledge, make relevant information available to patients, colleagues, and the public, obtain consultation, and use the talents of other health professionals when indicated.

1. Psychiatrists are responsible for their own continuing education and should be mindful of the fact that theirs must be a lifetime of learning.

2. In the practice of his/her specialty, the psychiatrist consults, associates, collaborates, or integrates his/her work with that of many professionals, including psychologists, psychometricians, social workers, alcoholism counselors, marriage counselors, public health nurses, etc. Furthermore, the nature of modern psychiatric practice extends his/her contacts to such people as teachers, juvenile and adult probation officers, attorneys, welfare workers, agency volunteers, and neighborhood aides. In referring patients for treatment, counseling, or rehabilitation to any of these practitioners, the psychiatrist should ensure that the allied professional or paraprofessional with whom he/she is dealing is a recognized member of his/her own discipline and is competent to carry out the therapeutic task required. The psychiatrist should have the same attitude toward members of the medical profession to whom he/she refers patients. Whenever he/she has reason to doubt the training, skill, or ethical qualifications of the allied professional, the psychiatrist should not refer cases to him/her.

3. When the psychiatrist assumes a collaborative or supervisory role with another mental health worker, he/she must expend sufficient time to assure that proper care is given. It is contrary to the interests of the patient and to patient care if he/she allows himself/herself to be used as a figurehead.

4. In relationships between psychiatrists and practicing licensed psychologists, the physician should not delegate to the psychologist or, in fact, to any nonmedical person any matter requiring the exercise of professional medical judgment.

5. The psychiatrist should agree to the request of a patient for consultation or to such a request from the family of an incompetent or minor patient. The psychiatrist may suggest possible consultants, but the patient or family should be given free choice of the consultant. If the psychiatrist disapproves of the professional qualifications of the consultant or if there is a difference of opinion that the primary therapist cannot resolve, he/she may, after suitable notice, withdraw from the case. If this disagreement occurs within an institution or agency framework, the differences should be resolved by the mediation or arbitration of higher professional authority within the institution or agency.

SECTION 6

A physician shall, in the provision of appropriate patient care, except in emergencies, be free to choose whom to serve, with whom to associate, and the environment in which to provide medical services.

1. Physicians generally agree that the doctor-patient relationship is such a vital factor in effective treatment of the patient that preservation of optimal conditions for development of a sound working relationship between a doctor and his/her patient should take precedence over all other considerations. Professional courtesy may lead to poor psychiatric care for physicians and their families because of embarrassment over the lack of a complete give-and-take contract.

2. An ethical psychiatrist may refuse to provide psychiatric treatment to a person who, in the psychiatrist's opinion, cannot be diagnosed as having a mental illness amenable to psychiatric treatment.

SECTION 7

A physician shall recognize a responsibility to participate in activities contributing to an improved community.

1. Psychiatrists should foster the cooperation of those legitimately concerned with the medical, psychological, social, and legal aspects of mental health and illness. Psychiatrists are encouraged to serve society by advising and consulting with the executive, legislative, and judiciary branches of the government. A psychiatrist should clarify whether he/she speaks as an individual or as a representative of an organization. Furthermore, psychiatrists should avoid cloaking their public statements with the authority of the profession (e.g., "Psychiatrists know that . . .").

2. Psychiatrists may interpret and share with the public their expertise in the various psychosocial issues that may affect mental health and illness. Psychiatrists should always be mindful of their separate roles as dedicated citizens and as experts in psychological medicine.

3. On occasion psychiatrists are asked for an opinion about an individual who is in the light of public attention, or who has disclosed information about himself/herself through public media. In such circumstances, a psychiatrist may share with the public his/her expertise about psychiatric issues in general. However, it is unethical for a psychiatrist to offer a professional opinion about that specific individual unless he/she has conducted an examination and has been granted proper authorization for such a statement.

4. The psychiatrist may permit his/her certification to be used for the involuntary treatment of any person only following his/her personal examination of that person. To do so, he/she must find that the person, because of mental illness, cannot form a judgment as to what is in his/her own best interests and that, without such treatment, substantial impairment is likely to occur to the person or others.

---

1. The committee included Herbert Klemmer, M.D., Chairperson, Miltiades Zaphiropoulos, M.D., Ewald Busse, M.D., John R. Saunders, M.D., and Robert McDevitt, M.D. J. Brand Brickman, M.D., William P. Camp, M.D., and Robert A. Moore, M.D. served as consultants to the APA Ethics Committee.

2. Current Opinions with Annotations of the Council on Ethical and Judicial Affairs, Chicago, American Medical Association, 1994.

3. Chapter 8, Section 1 of the Bylaws of the American Psychiatric Association states, "All members of the American Psychiatric Association shall be bound by the ethical code of the medical profession, specifically defined in The Principles of Medical Ethics of the American Medical Association." In interpreting the APA Constitution and Bylaws, it is the opinion of the Board of Trustees that inactive status in no way removes a physician member from responsibility to abide by the Principles of Medical Ethics.

4. Statements in italics are taken directly from the American Medical Association's Principles of Medical Ethics.

© American Psychiatric Association. Reprinted with permission.

AMERICAN PSYCHOANALYTIC ASSOCIATION

Address: 309 East 49th Street
                New York, NY 10017
Telephone: 212/752-0450
WWW: www.apsa.org
Document: Principles of Ethics for
                Psychoanalysts (1975. Most recently
                revised 1983.)

Preamble. These principles are intended to aid psychoanalysts individually and collectively in maintaining a high level of ethical conduct. They are not laws, but standards by which a psychoanalyst, or one in training to be a psychoanalyst, may determine the propriety of his/her conduct in his/her relationship with patients, with colleagues, with students, with members of allied professions, and with the public.

Objectives of the Profession and the Individual Psychoanalyst

Section 1. The principal objective of the profession of psychoanalysis is to offer a particular contribution to humanity, with full respect for enhancing the dignity of man. A psychoanalyst should strive continually to improve psychoanalytic knowledge and skill. He/she should make available to his/her patients and colleagues, as well as to other physicians, to other qualified professional persons, and to students, the benefits of his/her professional attainments.

Responsibilities to the Individual and to Society

Section 2. The honored ideals of the profession of psychoanalysis imply that the responsibilities of the psychoanalyst extend primarily to the individual, but also to society; these secondary responsibilities deserve his/her interest and participation in activities which have the purpose of preserving and improving both the health and the well-being of the individual and the community. When the interests of his/her patient conflict with the welfare of the community at large, the psychoanalyst must weigh the consequences of any action and arrive at a judgment based on all considerations.

Treatment to Have a Scientific Basis

Section 3. A psychoanalyst should practice a method of treatment founded on a scientific basis; he/she should not knowingly and voluntarily endorse anyone who violates this principle.

General Conduct of the Psychoanalyst

Section 4. A psychoanalyst should be courteous, considerate, professional and ethical in all his/her relationships. He/she should respect all laws, uphold the dignity and honor of the profession, and accept its self-imposed disciplines. He/she should accord members of allied professions the respect due their areas of competence.

Relationships with Patients and Colleagues

Section 5. A psychoanalyst should not solicit patients; he/she may choose whom he/she will treat. In an emergency, however, he/she should render service to the best of his/her ability unless he/she is of the opinion, based on his/her professional judgment, that it would be inappropriate or unwise to do so. In all situations, a psychoanalyst should merit the confidence of patients entrusted to his/her care, rendering to each a full measure of service. Having undertaken the care of a patient, he/she may not neglect him/her; and unless he/she has been discharged he/she may discontinue his/her services only after giving adequate notice. He/she should not render any professional service to the patient of a colleague, including therapists in allied professions, without the colleague's knowledge, unless, in his/her professional judgment, it would be in the best interests of the patient to do so. When he/she becomes aware that his/her patient is or has recently been in treatment with another therapist, he/she should ascertain that the patient has informed the other therapist of the consultation or desire for a change of therapist, or, if the patient has not done so, obtain consent, provided this will not interfere with the treatment, to inform the other therapist himself/herself as soon as may be practicable. He/she should, however, recognize and respect the patient's

right to terminate a relationship, including psychoanalytic treatment, and/or seek consultation or advice from others. In professional relationships, the first responsibility of the psychoanalyst is to the patient.

Protection of Confidentiality

Section 6. Except as required by law, a psychoanalyst may not reveal the confidences entrusted to him/her in the course of his/her professional work, or the particularities that he/she may observe in the characters of patients. Should he/she be required by a court of law to give testimony relating to the confidences of his/her patient, he/she should make use of all legal means to safeguard his/her patient's right to confidentiality.

When a psychoanalyst uses case material in exchanges with colleagues for scientific, educational or consultative purposes, he/she should exercise every precaution to assure that, unless specifically authorized by the patient, the identity of the patient is not revealed. When a psychoanalyst learns confidential information from a source other than the patient involved, he/she should, nonetheless, fully and appropriately respect its confidentiality.

Emoluments for Services

Section 7. A psychoanalyst is entitled to establish and to receive reasonable fees for his/her services. When undertaking the treatment of a patient, the psychoanalyst and the patient should agree on the fee and the conditions of payment. While it is expected that these terms will be fulfilled as a requirement for treatment, a psychoanalyst should implement them tactfully and humanely and with adequate regard for the realistic and therapeutic aspects of the fee and its payment. Fees may be charged for sessions missed by the patient when this policy has been prearranged. A psychoanalyst should neither pay nor receive a commission for referral of patients. He/she must not exploit the treatment of a patient for his/her own financial gain or to promote his/her personal advantage.

Dispensing of Drugs

Section 8. To the extent permitted by law, drugs or remedies may be dispensed, supplied, or prescribed by the psychoanalyst provided he/she is legally licensed to do so, and such action is appropriate to the treatment and done in the best interest of the patient.

Consultation

Section 9. A psychoanalyst should feel free to seek consultation on his/her own initiative or at the patient's request whenever he/she believes that this action may benefit the treatment. Consultation should be carefully considered in difficult cases.

Sexual Misconduct in Relation to Patients

Section 10. Sexual relationships between analyst and patient are antithetic to treatment and unacceptable under any circumstances. Any sexual activity with a patient constitutes a violation of this principle of ethics.

Remedial Measures for the Psychoanalyst

Section 11. When disorder within the psychoanalyst, however evidenced, is threatening or disturbing to the quality of his/her work, he/she should avail himself/herself promptly of remedial measures.

Safeguarding the Public and the Profession

Section 12. To safeguard the public and the profession:

(A) Each psychoanalyst should strive to protect against practice by psychoanalysts deficient in moral character or professional competence and should, consistent with the patient's right to confidentiality, report to the appropriate ethical body any unethical conduct by fellow members of the profession.

(B) Each psychoanalyst should strive to maintain and improve his/her psychoanalytic knowledge and to help his/her colleagues in this aim. When he/she is able, and when circumstances are appropriate, he/she should willingly promote knowledge of psychoanalysis and its derived applications.

(C) Training in the practice of psychoanalysis should reflect awareness of the special implications for the welfare of present and future patients and for the standards of psychoanalysis; the highest ethical and educational standards are required. While more than ethical standards are involved, the manner and spirit in which psychoanalytic education is offered clearly involves ethical issues. The psychoanalyst teacher has responsibilities to the public, his/her students, his/her profession, and himself/herself. These responsibilities must be given full attention both by the individual analyst, and, in the establishment of all training standards, by the Board on Professional Standards and its affiliated training programs. Accordingly, the educational standards and procedures of the Board on Professional Standards embody these ethical considerations and should be so accepted.

(D) Training in the practice of psychoanalysis, i.e., teaching courses, or conducting training analyses or providing supervision of psychoanalytic treatment, should be offered only when the highest ethical and educational standards are employed, and when there is careful selection of participants and thorough evaluation of the training and the progress of those enrolled in it. No psychoanalyst may claim or imply that training in psychoanalysis is directly or indirectly connected with or authorized by the American Psychoanalytic Association unless the educational standards and procedures of the Board on Professional Standards are fully observed and the training is conducted under the auspices of the Board on Professional Standards.

© American Psychoanalytic Association. Reprinted with permission.

AMERICAN
PSYCHOLOGICAL
ASSOCIATION

AMERICAN PSYCHOLOGICAL ASSOCIATION

Address: 750 First Street NE
                Washington, DC 20002-4242
Telephone: 202/336-5500 or 800/374-2721
WWW: www.apa.org
Document: Ethical Principles of Psychologists
                and Code of Conduct (1992)

(This Code originally appeared in *American Psychologist 47* (1992): 1597-1611.—Eds.)

INTRODUCTION

The American Psychological Association's (APA's) Ethical Principles of Psychologists and Code of Conduct (hereinafter referred to as the Ethics Code) consists of an Introduction, a Preamble, six General Principles (A—F), and specific Ethical Standards. The Introduction discusses the intent, organization, procedural considerations, and scope of application of the Ethics Code. The Preamble and General Principles are *aspirational* goals to guide psychologists toward the highest ideals of psychology. Although the Preamble and General Principles are not themselves enforceable rules, they should be considered by psychologists in arriving at an ethical course of action and may be considered by ethics bodies in interpreting the Ethical Standards. The Ethical Standards set forth *enforceable* rules for conduct as psychologists. Most of the Ethical Standards are written broadly, in order to apply to psychologists in varied roles, although the application of an Ethical Standard may vary depending on the context. The Ethical Standards are not exhaustive. The fact that a given conduct is not specifically addressed by the Ethics Code does not mean that it is necessarily either ethical or unethical.

Membership in the APA commits members to adhere to the APA Ethics Code and to the rules and procedures used to implement it. Psychologists and students, whether or not they are APA members, should be aware that the Ethics Code may be applied to them by state psychology boards, courts, or other public bodies.

This Ethics Code applies only to psychologists' work-related activities, that is, activities that are part of the psychologists' scientific and professional functions or that are psychological in nature. It includes the clinical or counseling practice of psychology, research, teaching, supervision of trainees, development of assessment instruments, conducting assessments, educational counseling, organizational consulting, social intervention, administration, and other activities as well. These work-related activities can be distinguished from the purely private conduct of a psychologist, which ordinarily is not within the purview of the Ethics Code.

The Ethics Code is intended to provide standards of professional conduct that can be applied by the APA and by other bodies that choose to adopt them. Whether or not a psychologist has violated the Ethics Code does not by itself determine whether he or she is legally liable in a court action, whether a contract is enforceable, or whether other legal consequences occur. These results are based on legal rather than ethical rules. However, compliance with or violation of the Ethics Code may be admissible as evidence in some legal proceedings, depending on the circumstances.

In the process of making decisions regarding their professional behavior, psychologists must consider this Ethics Code, in addition to applicable laws and psychology board regulations. If the Ethics Code establishes a higher standard of conduct than is required by law, psychologists must meet the higher ethical standard. If the Ethics Code standard appears to conflict with the requirements of law, then psychologists make known their commitment to the Ethics Code and take steps to resolve the conflict in a responsible manner. If neither law nor the Ethics Code resolves an issue, psychologists should consider other professional materials and the dictates of their own conscience, as well as seek consultation with others within the field when this is practical.

The procedures for filing, investigating, and resolving complaints of unethical conduct are described in the current Rules and Procedures of the APA Ethics Committee. The actions that APA may take for violations of the Ethics Code include actions such as reprimand, censure, termination of APA membership, and referral of the matter to other bodies. Complainants who seek remedies such as monetary damages in alleging ethical violations by a psychologist must resort to private negotiation, administrative bodies, or the courts. Actions that violate the Ethics Code may lead to the imposition of sanctions on a psychologist by bodies other than APA, including state psychological associations, other professional groups, psychology boards, other state or federal agencies, and payors for health services. In addition to actions for violation of the Ethics Code, the APA Bylaws provide that APA may take action against a member after his or her conviction of a felony, expulsion or suspension from an affiliated state psychological association, or suspension or loss of licensure.

PREAMBLE

Psychologists work to develop a valid and reliable body of scientific knowledge based on research. They may apply that knowledge to human behavior in a variety of contexts. In doing so, they perform many roles, such as researcher, educator, diagnostician, therapist, supervisor, consultant, administrator, social interventionist, and expert witness. Their goal is to broaden knowledge of behavior and, where appropriate, to apply it pragmatically to improve the condition of both the individual and society. Psychologists respect the central importance of freedom of inquiry and expression in research, teaching, and publication. They also strive to help the public in developing informed judgments and choices concerning human behavior. This Ethics Code provides a common set of values upon which psychologists build their professional and scientific work.

This Code is intended to provide both the general principles and the decision rules to cover most situations encountered by psychologists. It has as its primary goal the welfare and protection of the individuals and groups with whom psychologists work. It is the individual responsibility of each psychologist to aspire to the highest possible standards of conduct. Psychologists respect and protect human and civil rights, and do not knowingly participate in or condone unfair discriminatory practices.

The development of a dynamic set of ethical standards for a psychologist's work-related conduct requires a personal commitment to a lifelong effort to act ethically; to encourage ethical behavior by students, supervisees, employees, and colleagues, as appropriate; and to consult with others, as needed, concerning ethical problems. Each psychologist supplements, but does not violate, the Ethics Code's values and rules on the basis of guidance drawn from personal values, culture, and experience.

GENERAL PRINCIPLES

Principle A: Competence

Psychologists strive to maintain high standards of competence in their work. They recognize the boundaries of their particular competencies and the limitations of their expertise. They provide only those services and use only those techniques for which they are qualified by education, training, or experience. Psychologists are cognizant of the fact that the competencies required in serving, teaching, and/or studying groups of people vary with the distinctive characteristics of those groups. In those areas in which recognized professional standards do not yet exist, psychologists exercise careful judgment and take appropriate precautions to protect the welfare of those with whom they work. They maintain knowledge of relevant scientific and professional information related to the services they render, and they recognize the need for ongoing education. Psychologists make appropriate use of scientific, professional, technical, and administrative resources.

Principle B: Integrity

Psychologists seek to promote integrity in the science, teaching, and practice of psychology. In these activities psychologists are honest, fair, and respectful of others. In describing or reporting their qualifications, services, products, fees, research, or teaching, they do not make statements that are false, misleading, or deceptive. Psychologists strive to be aware of their own belief systems, values, needs, and limitations and the effect of these on their work. To the extent feasible, they attempt to clarify for relevant parties the roles they are performing and to function appropriately in accordance with those roles. Psychologists avoid improper and potentially harmful dual relationships.

Principle C: Professional and Scientific Responsibility

Psychologists uphold professional standards of conduct, clarify their professional roles and obligations, accept appropriate responsibility for their behavior, and adapt their methods to the needs of different populations. Psychologists consult with, refer to, or cooperate with other professionals and institutions to the extent needed to serve the best interests of their patients, clients, or other recipients of their services. Psychologists' moral standards and conduct are personal matters to the same degree as is true for any other person, except as psychologists' conduct may compromise their professional responsibilities or reduce the public's trust in psychology and psychologists. Psychologists are concerned about the ethical compliance of their colleagues' scientific and professional conduct. When appropriate, they consult with colleagues in order to prevent or avoid unethical conduct.

Principle D: Respect for People's Rights and Dignity

Psychologists accord appropriate respect to the fundamental rights, dignity, and worth of all people. They respect the rights of individuals to privacy, confidentiality, self-determination, and autonomy, mindful that legal and other obligations may lead to inconsistency and conflict with the exercise of these rights. Psychologists are aware of cultural, individual, and role differences, including those due to age, gender, race, ethnicity, national origin, religion, sexual orientation, disability, language, and socioeconomic status. Psychologists try to eliminate the effect on their work of biases based on those factors, and they do not knowingly participate in or condone unfair discriminatory practices.

Principle E: Concern for Others' Welfare

Psychologists seek to contribute to the welfare of those with whom they interact professionally. In their professional actions, psychologists weigh the welfare and rights of their patients or clients, students, supervisees, human research participants, and other affected persons, and the welfare of animal subjects of research. When conflicts occur among psychologists' obligations or concerns, they attempt to resolve these conflicts and to perform their roles in a responsible fashion that avoids or minimizes harm. Psychologists are sensitive to real and ascribed differences in power between themselves and others, and they do not exploit or mislead other people during or after professional relationships.

Principle F: Social Responsibility

Psychologists are aware of their professional and scientific responsibilities to the community and the society in which they work and live. They apply and make public their knowledge of psychology in order to contribute to human welfare. Psychologists are concerned about and work to mitigate the causes of human suffering. When undertaking research, they strive to advance human welfare and the science of psychology. Psychologists try to avoid misuse of their work. Psychologists comply with the law and encourage the development of law and social policy that serve the interests of their patients and clients and the public. They are encouraged to contribute a portion of their professional time for little or no personal advantage.

ETHICAL STANDARDS

1. General Standards

These General Standards are potentially applicable to the professional and scientific activities of all psychologists.

1.01 Applicability of the Ethics Code

The activity of a psychologist subject to the Ethics Code may be reviewed under these Ethical Standards only if the activity is part of his or her work-related functions or the activity is psychological in nature. Personal activities having no connection to or effect on psychological roles are not subject to the Ethics Code.

1.02 Relationship of Ethics and Law

If psychologists' ethical responsibilities conflict with law, psychologists make known their commitment to the Ethics Code and take steps to resolve the conflict in a responsible manner.

1.03 Professional and Scientific Relationship

Psychologists provide diagnostic, therapeutic, teaching, research, supervisory, consultative, or other psy-

chological services only in the context of a defined professional or scientific relationship or role. (See also Standards 2.01, Evaluation, Diagnosis, and Interventions in Professional Context, and 7.02, Forensic Assessments.)

1.04 Boundaries of Competence

(a) Psychologists provide services, teach, and conduct research only within the boundaries of their competence, based on their education, training, supervised experience, or appropriate professional experience.

(b) Psychologists provide services, teach, or conduct research in new areas or involving new techniques only after first undertaking appropriate study, training, supervision, and/or consultation from persons who are competent in those areas or techniques.

(c) In those emerging areas in which generally recognized standards for preparatory training do not yet exist, psychologists nevertheless take reasonable steps to ensure the competence of their work and to protect patients, clients, students, research participants, and others from harm.

1.05 Maintaining Expertise

Psychologists who engage in assessment, therapy, teaching, research, organizational consulting, or other professional activities maintain a reasonable level of awareness of current scientific and professional information in their fields of activity, and undertake ongoing efforts to maintain competence in the skills they use.

1.06 Basis for Scientific and Professional Judgments

Psychologists rely on scientifically and professionally derived knowledge when making scientific or professional judgments or when engaging in scholarly or professional endeavors.

1.07 Describing the Nature and Results of Psychological Services

(a) When psychologists provide assessment, evaluation, treatment, counseling, supervision, teaching, consultation, research, or other psychological services to an individual, a group, or an organization, they provide, using language that is reasonably understandable to the recipient of those services, appropriate information beforehand about the nature of such services and appropriate information later about results and conclusions. (See also Standard 2.09, Explaining Assessment Results.)

(b) If psychologists will be precluded by law or by organizational roles from providing such information to particular individuals or groups, they so inform those individuals or groups at the outset of the service.

1.08 Human Differences

Where differences of age, gender, race, ethnicity, national origin, religion, sexual orientation, disability, language, or socioeconomic status significantly affect psychologists' work concerning particular individuals or groups, psychologists obtain the training, experience, consultation, or supervision necessary to ensure the competence of their services, or they make appropriate referrals.

1.09 Respecting Others

In their work-related activities, psychologists respect the rights of others to hold values, attitudes, and opinions that differ from their own.

1.10 Nondiscrimination

In their work-related activities, psychologists do not engage in unfair discrimination based on age, gender, race, ethnicity, national origin, religion, sexual orientation, disability, socioeconomic status, or any basis proscribed by law.

1.11 Sexual Harassment

(a) Psychologists do not engage in sexual harassment. Sexual harassment is sexual solicitation, physical advances, or verbal or nonverbal conduct that is sexual in nature, that occurs in connection with the psychologist's activities or roles as a psychologist, and that either: (1) is unwelcome, is offensive, or creates a hostile workplace environment, and the psychologist knows or is told this; or (2) is sufficiently severe or intense to be abusive to a reasonable person in the context. Sexual harassment can consist of a single intense or severe act or of multiple persistent or pervasive acts.

(b) Psychologists accord sexual-harassment complainants and respondents dignity and respect. Psychologists do not participate in denying a person academic admittance or advancement, employment, tenure, or promotion, based solely upon their having made, or their being the subject of, sexual harassment charges. This does not preclude taking action based upon the outcome of such proceedings or consideration of other appropriate information.

1.12 Other Harassment

Psychologists do not knowingly engage in behavior that is harassing or demeaning to persons with whom

they interact in their work based on factors such as those persons' age, gender, race, ethnicity, national origin, religion, sexual orientation, disability, language, or socioeconomic status.

1.13 Personal Problems and Conflicts

(a) Psychologists recognize that their personal problems and conflicts may interfere with their effectiveness. Accordingly, they refrain from undertaking an activity when they know or should know that their personal problems are likely to lead to harm to a patient, client, colleague, student, research participant, or other person to whom they may owe a professional or scientific obligation.

(b) In addition, psychologists have an obligation to be alert to signs of, and to obtain assistance for, their personal problems at an early stage, in order to prevent significantly impaired performance.

(c) When psychologists become aware of personal problems that may interfere with their performing work-related duties adequately, they take appropriate measures, such as obtaining professional consultation or assistance, and determine whether they should limit, suspend, or terminate their work-related duties.

1.14 Avoiding Harm

Psychologists take reasonable steps to avoid harming their patients or clients, research participants, students, and others with whom they work, and to minimize harm where it is foreseeable and unavoidable.

1.15 Misuse of Psychologists' Influence

Because psychologists' scientific and professional judgments and actions may affect the lives of others, they are alert to and guard against personal, financial, social, organizational, or political factors that might lead to misuse of their influence.

1.16 Misuse of Psychologists' Work

(a) Psychologists do not participate in activities in which it appears likely that their skills or data will be misused by others, unless corrective mechanisms are available. (See also Standard 7.04, Truthfulness and Candor.)

(b) If psychologists learn of misuse or misrepresentation of their work, they take reasonable steps to correct or minimize the misuse or misrepresentation.

1.17 Multiple Relationships

(a) In many communities and situations, it may not be feasible or reasonable for psychologists to avoid social or other nonprofessional contacts with persons such as patients, clients, students, supervisees, or research participants. Psychologists must always be sensitive to the potential harmful effects of other contacts on their work and on those persons with whom they deal. A psychologist refrains from entering into or promising another personal, scientific, professional, financial, or other relationship with such persons if it appears likely that such a relationship reasonably might impair the psychologist's objectivity or otherwise interfere with the psychologist's effectively performing his or her functions as a psychologist, or might harm or exploit the other party.

(b) Likewise, whenever feasible, a psychologist refrains from taking on professional or scientific obligations when pre-existing relationships would create a risk of such harm.

(c) If a psychologist finds that, due to unforeseen factors, a potentially harmful multiple relationship has arisen, the psychologist attempts to resolve it with due regard for the best interests of the affected person and maximal compliance with the Ethics Code.

1.18 Barter (With Patients or Clients)

Psychologists ordinarily refrain from accepting goods, services, or other nonmonetary remuneration from patients or clients in return for psychological services because such arrangements create inherent potential for conflicts, exploitation, and distortion of the professional relationship. A psychologist may participate in bartering only if (1) it is not clinically contraindicated, and (2) the relationship is not exploitative. (See also Standards 1.17, Multiple Relationships, and 1.25, Fees and Financial Arrangements.)

1.19 Exploitative Relationships

(a) Psychologists do not exploit persons over whom they have supervisory, evaluative, or other authority such as students, supervisees, employees, research participants, and clients or patients. (See also Standards 4.05—4.07 regarding sexual involvement with clients or patients.)

(b) Psychologists do not engage in sexual relationships with students or supervisees in training over whom the psychologist has evaluative or direct authority, because such relationships are so likely to impair judgment or be exploitative.

1.20 Consultations and Referrals

(a) Psychologists arrange for appropriate consultations and referrals based principally on the best

interests of their patients or clients, with appropriate consent, and subject to other relevant considerations, including applicable law and contractual obligations. (See also Standards 5.01, Discussing the Limits of Confidentiality, and 5.06, Consultations.)

(b) When indicated and professionally appropriate, psychologists cooperate with other professionals in order to serve their patients or clients effectively and appropriately.

(c) Psychologists' referral practices are consistent with law.

1.21 Third-Party Requests for Services

(a) When a psychologist agrees to provide services to a person or entity at the request of a third party, the psychologist clarifies to the extent feasible, at the outset of the service, the nature of the relationship with each party. This clarification includes the role of the psychologist (such as therapist, organizational consultant, diagnostician, or expert witness), the probable uses of the services provided or the information obtained, and the fact that there may be limits to confidentiality.

(b) If there is a foreseeable risk of the psychologist's being called upon to perform conflicting roles because of the involvement of a third party, the psychologist clarifies the nature and direction of his or her responsibilities, keeps all parties appropriately informed as matters develop, and resolves the situation in accordance with this Ethics Code.

1.22 Delegation to and Supervision of Subordinates

(a) Psychologists delegate to their employees, supervisees, and research assistants only those responsibilities that such persons can reasonably be expected to perform competently, on the basis of their education, training, or experience, either independently or with the level of supervision being provided.

(b) Psychologists provide proper training and supervision to their employees or supervisees and take reasonable steps to see that such persons perform services responsibly, competently, and ethically.

(c) If institutional policies, procedures, or practices prevent fulfillment of this obligation, psychologists attempt to modify their role or to correct the situation to the extent feasible.

1.23 Documentation of Professional and Scientific Work

(a) Psychologists appropriately document their professional and scientific work in order to facilitate provision of services later by them or by other professionals, to ensure accountability, and to meet other requirements of institutions or the law.

(b) When psychologists have reason to believe that records of their professional services will be used in legal proceedings involving recipients of or participants in their work, they have a responsibility to create and maintain documentation in the kind of detail and quality that would be consistent with reasonable scrutiny in an adjudicative forum. (See also Standard 7.01, Professionalism, under Forensic Activities.)

1.24 Records and Data

Psychologists create, maintain, disseminate, store, retain, and dispose of records and data relating to their research, practice, and other work in accordance with law and in a manner that permits compliance with the requirements of this Ethics Code. (See also Standard 5.04, Maintenance of Records.)

1.25 Fees and Financial Arrangements

(a) As early as is feasible in a professional or scientific relationship, the psychologist and the patient, client, or other appropriate recipient of psychological services reach an agreement specifying the compensation and the billing arrangements.

(b) Psychologists do not exploit recipients of services or payors with respect to fees.

(c) Psychologists' fee practices are consistent with law.

(d) Psychologists do not misrepresent their fees.

(e) If limitations to services can be anticipated because of limitations in financing, this is discussed with the patient, client, or other appropriate recipient of services as early as is feasible. (See also Standard 4.08, Interruption of Services.)

(f) If the patient, client, or other recipient of services does not pay for services as agreed, and if the psychologist wishes to use collection agencies or legal measures to collect the fees, the psychologist first informs the person that such measures will be taken and provides that person an opportunity to make prompt payment. (See also Standard 5.11, Withholding Records for Nonpayment.)

1.26 Accuracy in Reports to Payors and Funding Sources

In their reports to payors for services or sources of research funding, psychologists accurately state the nature of the research or service provided, the fees or charges, and where applicable, the identity of the provider, the findings, and the diagnosis. (See also Standard 5.05, Disclosures.)

1.27 Referrals and Fees

When a psychologist pays, receives payment from, or divides fees with another professional other than in an employer—employee relationship, the payment to each is based on the services (clinical, consultative, administrative, or other) provided and is not based on the referral itself.

2. Evaluation, Assessment, or Intervention

2.01 Evaluation, Diagnosis, and Interventions in Professional Context

(a) Psychologists perform evaluations, diagnostic services, or interventions only within the context of a defined professional relationship. (See also Standards 1.03, Professional and Scientific Relationship.)

(b) Psychologists' assessments, recommendations, reports, and psychological diagnostic or evaluative statements are based on information and techniques (including personal interviews of the individual when appropriate) sufficient to provide appropriate substantiation for their findings. (See also Standard 7.02, Forensic Assessments.)

2.02 Competence and Appropriate Use of Assessments and Interventions

(a) Psychologists who develop, administer, score, interpret, or use psychological assessment techniques, interviews, tests, or instruments do so in a manner and for purposes that are appropriate in light of the research on or evidence of the usefulness and proper application of the techniques.

(b) Psychologists refrain from misuse of assessment techniques, interventions, results, and interpretations and take reasonable steps to prevent others from misusing the information these techniques provide. This includes refraining from releasing raw test results or raw data to persons, other than to patients or clients as appropriate, who are not qualified to use such information. (See also Standards 1.02, Relationship of Ethics and Law, and 1.04, Boundaries of Competence.)

2.03 Test Construction

Psychologists who develop and conduct research with tests and other assessment techniques use scientific procedures and current professional knowledge for test design, standardization, validation, reduction or elimination of bias, and recommendations for use.

2.04 Use of Assessment in General and With Special Populations

(a) Psychologists who perform interventions or administer, score, interpret, or use assessment techniques are familiar with the reliability, validation, and related standardization or outcome studies of, and proper applications and uses of, the techniques they use.

(b) Psychologists recognize limits to the certainty with which diagnoses, judgments, or predictions can be made about individuals.

(c) Psychologists attempt to identify situations in which particular interventions or assessment techniques or norms may not be applicable or may require adjustment in administration or interpretation because of factors such as individuals' gender, age, race, ethnicity, national origin, religion, sexual orientation, disability, language, or socioeconomic status.

2.05 Interpreting Assessment Results

When interpreting assessment results, including automated interpretations, psychologists take into account the various test factors and characteristics of the person being assessed that might affect psychologists' judgments or reduce the accuracy of their interpretations. They indicate any significant reservations they have about the accuracy or limitations of their interpretations.

2.06 Unqualified Persons

Psychologists do not promote the use of psychological assessment techniques by unqualified persons. (See also Standard 1.22, Delegation to and Supervision of Subordinates.)

2.07 Obsolete Tests and Outdated Test Results

(a) Psychologists do not base their assessment or intervention decisions or recommendations on data or test results that are outdated for the current purpose.

(b) Similarly, psychologists do not base such decisions or recommendations on tests and measures that are obsolete and not useful for the current purpose.

2.08 Test Scoring and Interpretation Services

(a) Psychologists who offer assessment or scoring procedures to other professionals accurately describe the purpose, norms, validity, reliability, and applications of the procedures and any special qualifications applicable to their use.

(b) Psychologists select scoring and interpretation services (including automated services) on the basis of evidence of the validity of the program and procedures as well as on other appropriate considerations.

(c) Psychologists retain appropriate responsibility for the appropriate application, interpretation, and use of assessment instruments, whether they score and interpret such tests themselves or use automated or other services.

2.09 Explaining Assessment Results

Unless the nature of the relationship is clearly explained to the person being assessed in advance and precludes provision of an explanation of results (such as in some organizational consulting, preemployment or security screenings, and forensic evaluations), psychologists ensure that an explanation of the results is provided using language that is reasonably understandable to the person assessed or to another legally authorized person on behalf of the client. Regardless of whether the scoring and interpretation are done by the psychologist, by assistants, or by automated or other outside services, psychologists take reasonable steps to ensure that appropriate explanations of results are given.

2.10 Maintaining Test Security

Psychologists make reasonable efforts to maintain the integrity and security of tests and other assessment techniques consistent with law, contractual obligations, and in a manner that permits compliance with the requirements of this Ethics Code. (See also Standard 1.02, Relationship of Ethics and Law.)

3. Advertising and Other Public Statements

3.01 Definition of Public Statements

Psychologists comply with this Ethics Code in public statements relating to their professional services, products, or publications or to the field of psychology. Public statements include but are not limited to paid or unpaid advertising, brochures, printed matter, directory listings, personal resumes or curriculum vitae, interviews or comments for use in media, statements in legal proceedings, lectures and public oral presentations, and published materials.

3.02 Statements by Others

(a) Psychologists who engage others to create or place public statements that promote their professional practice, products, or activities retain professional responsibility for such statements.

(b) In addition, psychologists make reasonable efforts to prevent others whom they do not control (such as employers, publishers, sponsors, organizational clients, and representatives of the print or broadcast media) from making deceptive statements concerning psychologists' practice or professional or scientific activities.

(c) If psychologists learn of deceptive statements about their work made by others, psychologists make reasonable efforts to correct such statements.

(d) Psychologists do not compensate employees of press, radio, television, or other communication media in return for publicity in a news item.

(e) A paid advertisement relating to the psychologist's activities must be identified as such, unless it is already apparent from the context.

3.03 Avoidance of False or Deceptive Statements

(a) Psychologists do not make public statements that are false, deceptive, misleading, or fraudulent, either because of what they state, convey, or suggest or because of what they omit, concerning their research, practice, or other work activities or those of persons or organizations with which they are affiliated. As examples (and not in limitation) of this standard, psychologists do not make false or deceptive statements concerning (1) their training, experience, or competence; (2) their academic degrees; (3) their credentials; (4) their institutional or association affiliations; (5) their services; (6) the scientific or clinical basis for, or results or degree of success of, their services; (7) their fees; or (8) their publications or research findings. (See also Standards 6.15, Deception in Research, and 6.18, Providing Participants With Information About the Study.)

(b) Psychologists claim as credentials for their psychological work, only degrees that (1) were earned from a regionally accredited educational institution or (2) were the basis for psychology licensure by the state in which they practice.

3.04 Media Presentations

When psychologists provide advice or comment by means of public lectures, demonstrations, radio or television programs, prerecorded tapes, printed articles, mailed material, or other media, they take reasonable precautions to ensure that (1) the statements are based on appropriate psychological literature and practice, (2) the statements are otherwise consistent with this Ethics Code, and (3) the recipients of the information are not encouraged to infer that a relationship has been established with them personally.

3.05 Testimonials

Psychologists do not solicit testimonials from current psychotherapy clients or patients or other persons who because of their particular circumstances are vulnerable to undue influence.

3.06 In-Person Solicitation

Psychologists do not engage, directly or through agents, in uninvited in-person solicitation of business from actual or potential psychotherapy patients or clients or other persons who because of their particular circumstances are vulnerable to undue influence. However, this does not preclude attempting to implement appropriate collateral contacts with significant others for the purpose of benefiting an already engaged therapy patient.

4. Therapy

4.01 Structuring the Relationship

(a) Psychologists discuss with clients or patients as early as is feasible in the therapeutic relationship appropriate issues, such as the nature and anticipated course of therapy, fees, and confidentiality. (See also Standards 1.25, Fees and Financial Arrangements, and 5.01, Discussing the Limits of Confidentiality.)

(b) When the psychologist's work with clients or patients will be supervised, the above discussion includes that fact, and the name of the supervisor, when the supervisor has legal responsibility for the case.

(c) When the therapist is a student intern, the client or patient is informed of that fact.

(d) Psychologists make reasonable efforts to answer patients' questions and to avoid apparent misunderstandings about therapy. Whenever possible, psychologists provide oral and/or written information, using language that is reasonably understandable to the patient or client.

4.02 Informed Consent to Therapy

(a) Psychologists obtain appropriate informed consent to therapy or related procedures, using language that is reasonably understandable to participants. The content of informed consent will vary depending on many circumstances; however, informed consent generally implies that the person (1) has the capacity to consent, (2) has been informed of significant information concerning the procedure, (3) has freely and without undue influence expressed consent, and (4) consent has been appropriately documented.

(b) When persons are legally incapable of giving informed consent, psychologists obtain informed permission from a legally authorized person, if such substitute consent is permitted by law.

(c) In addition, psychologists (1) inform those persons who are legally incapable of giving informed consent about the proposed interventions in a manner commensurate with the persons' psychological capacities, (2) seek their assent to those interventions, and (3) consider such persons' preferences and best interests.

4.03 Couple and Family Relationships

(a) When a psychologist agrees to provide services to several persons who have a relationship (such as husband and wife or parents and children), the psychologist attempts to clarify at the outset (1) which of the individuals are patients or clients and (2) the relationship the psychologist will have with each person. This clarification includes the role of the psychologist and the probable uses of the services provided or the information obtained. (See also Standard 5.01, Discussing the Limits of Confidentiality.)

(b) As soon as it becomes apparent that the psychologist may be called on to perform potentially conflicting roles (such as marital counselor to husband and wife, and then witness for one party in a divorce proceeding), the psychologist attempts to clarify and adjust, or withdraw from, roles appropriately. (See also Standard 7.03, Clarification of Role, under Forensic Activities.)

4.04 Providing Mental Health Services to Those Served by Others

In deciding whether to offer or provide services to those already receiving mental health services elsewhere, psychologists carefully consider the treatment issues and the potential patient's or client's welfare. The psychologist discusses these issues with the patient or client, or another legally authorized person on behalf of the client, in order to minimize the risk of confusion and conflict, consults with the other service providers when appropriate, and proceeds with caution and sensitivity to the therapeutic issues.

4.05 Sexual Intimacies With Current Patients or Clients

Psychologists do not engage in sexual intimacies with current patients or clients.

4.06 Therapy With Former Sexual Partners

Psychologists do not accept as therapy patients or clients persons with whom they have engaged in sexual intimacies.

4.07 Sexual Intimacies With Former Therapy Patients

(a) Psychologists do not engage in sexual intimacies with a former therapy patient or client for at least two years after cessation or termination of professional services.

(b) Because sexual intimacies with a former therapy patient or client are so frequently harmful to the patient or client, and because such intimacies undermine public confidence in the psychology profession and thereby deter the public's use of needed services, psychologists do not engage in sexual intimacies with former therapy patients and clients even after a two-year interval except in the most unusual circumstances. The psychologist who engages in such activity after the two years following cessation or termination of treatment bears the burden of demonstrating that there has been no exploitation, in light of all relevant factors, including (1) the amount of time that has passed since therapy terminated, (2) the nature and duration of the therapy, (3) the circumstances of termination, (4) the patient's or client's personal history, (5) the patient's or client's current mental status, (6) the likelihood of adverse impact on the patient or client and others, and (7) any statements or actions made by the therapist during the course of therapy suggesting or inviting the possibility of a posttermination sexual or romantic relationship with the patient or client. (See also Standard 1.17, Multiple Relationships.)

4.08 Interruption of Services

(a) Psychologists make reasonable efforts to plan for facilitating care in the event that psychological services are interrupted by factors such as the psychologist's illness, death, unavailability, or relocation or by the client's relocation or financial limitations. (See also Standard 5.09, Preserving Records and Data.)

(b) When entering into employment or contractual relationships, psychologists provide for orderly and appropriate resolution of responsibility for patient or client care in the event that the employment or contractual relationship ends, with paramount consideration given to the welfare of the patient or client.

4.09 Terminating the Professional Relationship

(a) Psychologists do not abandon patients or clients. (See also Standard 1.25e, under Fees and Financial Arrangements.)

(b) Psychologists terminate a professional relationship when it becomes reasonably clear that the patient or client no longer needs the service, is not benefiting, or is being harmed by continued service.

(c) Prior to termination for whatever reason, except where precluded by the patient's or client's conduct, the psychologist discusses the patient's or client's views and needs, provides appropriate pretermination counseling, suggests alternative service providers as appropriate, and takes other reasonable steps to facilitate transfer of responsibility to another provider if the patient or client needs one immediately.

5. Privacy and Confidentiality

These Standards are potentially applicable to the professional and scientific activities of all psychologists.

5.01 Discussing the Limits of Confidentiality

(a) Psychologists discuss with persons and organizations with whom they establish a scientific or professional relationship (including, to the extent feasible, minors and their legal representatives) (1) the relevant limitations on confidentiality, including limitations where applicable in group, marital, and family therapy or in organizational consulting, and (2) the foreseeable uses of the information generated through their services.

(b) Unless it is not feasible or is contraindicated, the discussion of confidentiality occurs at the outset of the relationship and thereafter as new circumstances may warrant.

(c) Permission for electronic recording of interviews is secured from clients and patients.

5.02 Maintaining Confidentiality

Psychologists have a primary obligation and take reasonable precautions to respect the confidentiality rights of those with whom they work or consult, recognizing that confidentiality may be established by law, institutional rules, or professional or scientific relationships. (See also Standard 6.26, Professional Reviewers.)

5.03 Minimizing Intrusions on Privacy

(a) In order to minimize intrusions on privacy, psychologists include in written and oral reports, consultations, and the like, only information germane to the purpose for which the communication is made.

(b) Psychologists discuss confidential information obtained in clinical or consulting relationships, or evaluative data concerning patients, individual or organizational clients, students, research participants, supervisees, and employees, only for appropriate scientific or professional purposes and only with persons clearly concerned with such matters.

5.04 Maintenance of Records

Psychologists maintain appropriate confidentiality in creating, storing, accessing, transferring, and disposing of records under their control, whether these are written, automated, or in any other medium. Psychologists maintain and dispose of records in accordance with law and in a manner that permits compliance with the requirements of this Ethics Code.

5.05 Disclosures

(a) Psychologists disclose confidential information without the consent of the individual only as mandated by law, or where permitted by law for a valid purpose, such as (1) to provide needed professional services to the patient or the individual or organizational client, (2) to obtain appropriate professional consultations, (3) to protect the patient or client or others from harm, or (4) to obtain payment for services, in which instance disclosure is limited to the minimum that is necessary to achieve the purpose.

(b) Psychologists also may disclose confidential information with the appropriate consent of the patient or the individual or organizational client (or of another legally authorized person on behalf of the patient or client), unless prohibited by law.

5.06 Consultations

When consulting with colleagues, (1) psychologists do not share confidential information that reasonably could lead to the identification of a patient, client, research participant, or other person or organization with whom they have a confidential relationship unless they have obtained the prior consent of the person or organization or the disclosure cannot be avoided, and (2) they share information only to the extent necessary to achieve the purposes of the consultation. (See also Standard 5.02, Maintaining Confidentiality.)

5.07 Confidential Information in Databases

(a) If confidential information concerning recipients of psychological services is to be entered into databases or systems of records available to persons whose access has not been consented to by the recipient, then psychologists use coding or other techniques to avoid the inclusion of personal identifiers.

(b) If a research protocol approved by an institutional review board or similar body requires the inclusion of personal identifiers, such identifiers are deleted before the information is made accessible to persons other than those of whom the subject was advised.

(c) If such deletion is not feasible, then before psychologists transfer such data to others or review such data collected by others, they take reasonable steps to determine that appropriate consent of personally identifiable individuals has been obtained.

5.08 Use of Confidential Information for Didactic or Other Purposes

(a) Psychologists do not disclose in their writings, lectures, or other public media, confidential, personally identifiable information concerning their patients, individual or organizational clients, students, research participants, or other recipients of their services that they obtained during the course of their work, unless the person or organization has consented in writing or unless there is other ethical or legal authorization for doing so.

(b) Ordinarily, in such scientific and professional presentations, psychologists disguise confidential information concerning such persons or organizations so that they are not individually identifiable to others and so that discussions do not cause harm to subjects who might identify themselves.

5.09 Preserving Records and Data

A psychologist makes plans in advance so that confidentiality of records and data is protected in the event of the psychologist's death, incapacity, or withdrawal from the position or practice.

5.10 Ownership of Records and Data

Recognizing that ownership of records and data is governed by legal principles, psychologists take reasonable and lawful steps so that records and data remain available to the extent needed to serve the best interests of patients, individual or organizational clients, research participants, or appropriate others.

5.11 Withholding Records for Nonpayment

Psychologists may not withhold records under their control that are requested and imminently needed for a patient's or client's treatment solely because payment has not been received, except as otherwise provided by law.

6. Teaching, Training Supervision, Research, and Publishing

6.01 Design of Education and Training Programs

Psychologists who are responsible for education and training programs seek to ensure that the programs are competently designed, provide the proper experiences, and meet the requirements for licensure, certification, or other goals for which claims are made by the program.

6.02 Descriptions of Education and Training Programs

(a) Psychologists responsible for education and training programs seek to ensure that there is a current and accurate description of the program content, training goals and objectives, and requirements that must be met for satisfactory completion of the program. This information must be made readily available to all interested parties.

(b) Psychologists seek to ensure that statements concerning their course outlines are accurate and not misleading, particularly regarding the subject matter to be covered, bases for evaluating progress, and the nature of course experiences. (See also Standard 3.03, Avoidance of False or Deceptive Statements.)

(c) To the degree to which they exercise control, psychologists responsible for announcements, catalogs, brochures, or advertisements describing workshops, seminars, or other non-degree-granting educational programs ensure that they accurately describe the audience for which the program is intended, the educational objectives, the presenters, and the fees involved.

6.03 Accuracy and Objectivity in Teaching

(a) When engaged in teaching or training, psychologists present psychological information accurately and with a reasonable degree of objectivity.

(b) When engaged in teaching or training, psychologists recognize the power they hold over students or supervisees and therefore make reasonable efforts to avoid engaging in conduct that is personally demeaning to students or supervisees. (See also Standards 1.09, Respecting Others, and 1.12, Other Harassment.)

6.04 Limitation on Teaching

Psychologists do not teach the use of techniques or procedures that require specialized training, licensure, or expertise, including but not limited to hypnosis, biofeedback, and projective techniques, to individuals who lack the prerequisite training, legal scope of practice, or expertise.

6.05 Assessing Student and Supervisee Performance

(a) In academic and supervisory relationships, psychologists establish an appropriate process for providing feedback to students and supervisees.

(b) Psychologists evaluate students and supervisees on the basis of their actual performance on relevant and established program requirements.

6.06 Planning Research

(a) Psychologists design, conduct, and report research in accordance with recognized standards of scientific competence and ethical research.

(b) Psychologists plan their research so as to minimize the possibility that results will be misleading.

(c) In planning research, psychologists consider its ethical acceptability under the Ethics Code. If an ethical issue is unclear, psychologists seek to resolve the issue through consultation with institutional review boards, animal care and use committees, peer consultations, or other proper mechanisms.

(d) Psychologists take reasonable steps to implement appropriate protections for the rights and welfare of human participants, other persons affected by the research, and the welfare of animal subjects.

6.07 Responsibility

(a) Psychologists conduct research competently and with due concern for the dignity and welfare of the participants.

(b) Psychologists are responsible for the ethical conduct of research conducted by them or by others under their supervision or control.

(c) Researchers and assistants are permitted to perform only those tasks for which they are appropriately trained and prepared.

(d) As part of the process of development and implementation of research projects, psychologists consult those with expertise concerning any special population under investigation or most likely to be affected.

6.08 Compliance With Law and Standards

Psychologists plan and conduct research in a manner consistent with federal and state law and regulations, as well as professional standards governing the conduct of research, and particularly those standards governing research with human participants and animal subjects.

6.09 Institutional Approval

Psychologists obtain from host institutions or organizations appropriate approval prior to conducting research, and they provide accurate information about their research proposals. They conduct the research in accordance with the approved research protocol.

6.10 Research Responsibilities

Prior to conducting research (except research involving only anonymous surveys, naturalistic observations, or similar research), psychologists enter into an agreement with participants that clarifies the nature of the research and the responsibilities of each party.

6.11 Informed Consent to Research

(a) Psychologists use language that is reasonably understandable to research participants in obtaining their appropriate informed consent (except as provided in Standard 6.12, Dispensing with Informed Consent). Such informed consent is appropriately documented.

(b) Using language that is reasonably understandable to participants, psychologists inform participants of the nature of the research; they inform participants that they are free to participate or to decline to participate or to withdraw from the research; they explain the foreseeable consequences of declining or withdrawing; they inform participants of significant factors that may be expected to influence their willingness to participate (such as risks, discomfort, adverse effects, or limitations on confidentiality, except as provided in Standard 6.15, Deception in Research); and they explain other aspects about which the prospective participants inquire.

(c) When psychologists conduct research with individuals such as students or subordinates, psychologists take special care to protect the prospective participants from adverse consequences of declining or withdrawing from participation.

(d) When research participation is a course requirement or opportunity for extra credit, the prospective participant is given the choice of equitable alternative activities.

(e) For persons who are legally incapable of giving informed consent, psychologists nevertheless (1) provide an appropriate explanation, (2) obtain the participant's assent, and (3) obtain appropriate permission from a legally authorized person, if such substitute consent is permitted by law.

6.12 Dispensing With Informed Consent

Before determining that planned research (such as research involving only anonymous questionnaires, naturalistic observations, or certain kinds of archival research) does not require the informed consent of research participants, psychologists consider applicable regulations and institutional review board requirements, and they consult with colleagues as appropriate.

6.13 Informed Consent in Research Filming or Recording

Psychologists obtain informed consent from research participants prior to filming or recording them in any form, unless the research involves simply naturalistic observations in public places and it is not anticipated that the recording will be used in a manner that could cause personal identification or harm.

6.14 Offering Inducements for Research Participants

(a) In offering professional services as an inducement to obtain research participants, psychologists make clear the nature of the services, as well as the risks, obligations, and limitations. (See also Standard 1.18, Barter [With Patients or Clients].)

(b) Psychologists do not offer excessive or inappropriate financial or other inducements to obtain research participants, particularly when it might tend to coerce participation.

6.15 Deception in Research

(a) Psychologists do not conduct a study involving deception unless they have determined that the use of deceptive techniques is justified by the study's prospective scientific, educational, or applied value and that equally effective alternative procedures that do not use deception are not feasible.

(b) Psychologists never deceive research participants about significant aspects that would affect their willingness to participate, such as physical risks, discomfort, or unpleasant emotional experiences.

(c) Any other deception that is an integral feature of the design and conduct of an experiment must be explained to participants as early as is feasible, preferably at the conclusion of their participation, but no later than at the conclusion of the research. (See also Standard 6.18, Providing Participants With Information About the Study.)

6.16 Sharing and Utilizing Data

Psychologists inform research participants of their anticipated sharing or further use of personally identifiable research data and of the possibility of unanticipated future uses.

6.17 Minimizing Invasiveness

In conducting research, psychologists interfere with the participants or milieu from which data are collected only in a manner that is warranted by an appropriate research design and that is consistent with psychologists' roles as scientific investigators.

6.18 Providing Participants With Information About the Study

(a) Psychologists provide a prompt opportunity for participants to obtain appropriate information about the nature, results, and conclusions of the research, and psychologists attempt to correct any misconceptions that participants may have.

(b) If scientific or humane values justify delaying or withholding this information, psychologists take reasonable measures to reduce the risk of harm.

6.19 Honoring Commitments

Psychologists take reasonable measures to honor all commitments they have made to research participants.

6.20 Care and Use of Animals in Research

(a) Psychologists who conduct research involving animals treat them humanely.

(b) Psychologists acquire, care for, use, and dispose of animals in compliance with current federal, state, and local laws and regulations, and with professional standards.

(c) Psychologists trained in research methods and experienced in the care of laboratory animals supervise all procedures involving animals and are responsible for ensuring appropriate consideration of their comfort, health, and humane treatment.

(d) Psychologists ensure that all individuals using animals under their supervision have received instruction in research methods and in the care, maintenance, and handling of the species being used, to the extent appropriate to their role.

(e) Responsibilities and activities of individuals assisting in a research project are consistent with their respective competencies.

(f) Psychologists make reasonable efforts to minimize the discomfort, infection, illness, and pain of animal subjects.

(g) A procedure subjecting animals to pain, stress, or privation is used only when an alternative procedure is unavailable and the goal is justified by its prospective scientific, educational, or applied value.

(h) Surgical procedures are performed under appropriate anesthesia; techniques to avoid infection and minimize pain are followed during and after surgery.

(i) When it is appropriate that the animal's life be terminated, it is done rapidly, with an effort to minimize pain, and in accordance with accepted procedures.

6.21 Reporting of Results

(a) Psychologists do not fabricate data or falsify results in their publications.

(b) If psychologists discover significant errors in their published data, they take reasonable steps to correct such errors in a correction, retraction, erratum, or other appropriate publication means.

6.22 Plagiarism

Psychologists do not present substantial portions or elements of another's work or data as their own, even if the other work or data source is cited occasionally.

6.23 Publication Credit

(a) Psychologists take responsibility and credit, including authorship credit, only for work they have actually performed or to which they have contributed.

(b) Principal authorship and other publication credits accurately reflect the relative scientific or professional contributions of the individuals involved, regardless of their relative status. Mere possession of an institutional position, such as Department Chair, does not justify authorship credit. Minor contributions to the research or to the writing for publications are appropriately acknowledged, such as in footnotes or in an introductory statement.

(c) A student is usually listed as principal author on any multiple-authored article that is substantially based on the student's dissertation or thesis.

6.24 Duplicate Publication of Data

Psychologists do not publish, as original data, data that have been previously published. This does not preclude republishing data when they are accompanied by proper acknowledgment.

6.25 Sharing Data

After research results are published, psychologists do not withhold the data on which their conclusions are based from other competent professionals who seek to verify the substantive claims through reanalysis and who intend to use such data only for that purpose, provided that the confidentiality of the participants can be protected and unless legal rights concerning proprietary data preclude their release.

6.26 Professional Reviewers

Psychologists who review material submitted for publication, grant, or other research proposal review respect the confidentiality of and the proprietary rights in such information of those who submitted it.

7. Forensic Activities

7.01 Professionalism

Psychologists who perform forensic functions, such as assessments, interviews, consultations, reports, or expert testimony, must comply with all other provisions of this Ethics Code to the extent that they apply to such activities. In addition, psychologists base their forensic work on appropriate knowledge of and competence in the areas underlying such work, including specialized knowledge concerning special populations. (See also Standards 1.06, Basis for Scientific and Professional Judgments; 1.08, Human Differences; 1.15, Misuse of Psychologists' Influence; and 1.23, Documentation of Professional and Scientific Work.)

7.02 Forensic Assessments

(a) Psychologists' forensic assessments, recommendations, and reports are based on information and techniques (including personal interviews of the individual, when appropriate) sufficient to provide appropriate substantiation for their findings. (See also Standards 1.03, Professional and Scientific Relationship; 1.23, Documentation of Professional and Scientific Work; 2.01, Evaluation, Diagnosis, and Interventions in Professional Context; and 2.05, Interpreting Assessment Results.)

(b) Except as noted in (c), below, psychologists provide written or oral forensic reports or testimony of the psychological characteristics of an individual only after they have conducted an examination of the individual adequate to support their statements or conclusions.

(c) When, despite reasonable efforts, such an examination is not feasible, psychologists clarify the impact of their limited information on the reliability and validity of their reports and testimony, and they appropriately limit the nature and extent of their conclusions or recommendations.

7.03 Clarification of Role

In most circumstances, psychologists avoid performing multiple and potentially conflicting roles in forensic matters. When psychologists may be called on to serve in more than one role in a legal proceeding—for example, as consultant or expert for one party or for the court and as a fact witness—they clarify role expectations and the extent of confidentiality in advance to the extent feasible, and thereafter as changes occur, in order to avoid compromising their professional judgment and objectivity and in order to avoid misleading others regarding their role.

7.04 Truthfulness and Candor

(a) In forensic testimony and reports, psychologists testify truthfully, honestly, and candidly and, consistent with applicable legal procedures, describe fairly the bases for their testimony and conclusions.

(b) Whenever necessary to avoid misleading, psychologists acknowledge the limits of their data or conclusions.

7.05 Prior Relationships

A prior professional relationship with a party does not preclude psychologists from testifying as fact witnesses or from testifying to their services to the extent permitted by applicable law. Psychologists appropriately take into account ways in which the prior relationship might affect their professional objectivity or opinions and disclose the potential conflict to the relevant parties.

7.06 Compliance With Law and Rules

In performing forensic roles, psychologists are reasonably familiar with the rules governing their roles. Psychologists are aware of the occasionally competing demands placed upon them by these principles and the requirements of the court system, and attempt to resolve these conflicts by making known their commitment to this Ethics Code and taking steps to resolve the conflict in a responsible manner. (See also Standard 1.02, Relationship of Ethics and Law.)

8. Resolving Ethical Issues

8.01 Familiarity With Ethics Code

Psychologists have an obligation to be familiar with this Ethics Code, other applicable ethics codes, and their application to psychologists' work. Lack of awareness or misunderstanding of an ethical standard is not itself a defense to a charge of unethical conduct.

8.02 Confronting Ethical Issues

When a psychologist is uncertain whether a particular situation or course of action would violate this Ethics Code, the psychologist ordinarily consults with other psychologists knowledgeable about ethical issues, with state or national psychology ethics committees, or with other appropriate authorities in order to choose a proper response.

8.03 Conflicts Between Ethics and Organizational Demands

If the demands of an organization with which psychologists are affiliated conflict with this Ethics Code, psy-

chologists clarify the nature of the conflict, make known their commitment to the Ethics Code, and to the extent feasible, seek to resolve the conflict in a way that permits the fullest adherence to the Ethics Code.

8.04 Informal Resolution of Ethical Violations

When psychologists believe that there may have been an ethical violation by another psychologist, they attempt to resolve the issue by bringing it to the attention of that individual if an informal resolution appears appropriate and the intervention does not violate any confidentiality rights that may be involved.

8.05 Reporting Ethical Violations

If an apparent ethical violation is not appropriate for informal resolution under Standard 8.04 or is not resolved properly in that fashion, psychologists take further action appropriate to the situation, unless such action conflicts with confidentiality rights in ways that cannot be resolved. Such action might include referral to state or national committees on professional ethics or to state licensing boards.

8.06 Cooperating With Ethics Committees

Psychologists cooperate in ethics investigations, proceedings, and resulting requirements of the APA or any affiliated state psychological association to which they belong. In doing so, they make reasonable efforts to resolve any issues as to confidentiality. Failure to cooperate is itself an ethics violation.

8.07 Improper Complaints

Psychologists do not file or encourage the filing of ethics complaints that are frivolous and are intended to harm the respondent rather than to protect the public.

© American Psychological Association. Reprinted with permission.

AMERICAN PSYCHOLOGICAL SOCIETY

Address: 1010 Vermont Avenue NW, Suite 1100 Washington, DC 20005-4907
Telephone: 202/783-2077
WWW: www.psychologicalscience.org

The American Psychological Society uses the code of the American Psychological Association. See p. 00.

198   *American Purchasing Society, Inc.*

AMERICAN PURCHASING SOCIETY, INC.

Address: 430 West Downer Place
             Aurora, IL 60506
Telephone: 630/859-0250
WWW: www.american-purchasing.com
Document: Code of Ethics

1. Maintain loyalty to your employer. Pursue your organization's objectives consistent with this code as long as no federal, state or local laws are violated.
2. Buy without personal prejudice from suppliers who offer the optimum value when all factors are considered.
3. Exercise and insist on honesty. Denounce all forms of unscrupulous business practices.
4. Avoid all conflicts of interest which would jeopardize impartiality in your business transactions.
5. Be truthful with your suppliers, potential suppliers, and all others with whom you do business.
6. Maintain high standards of personal conduct.
7. Refuse to accept gratuities offered by suppliers or potential suppliers.

Code of Conduct
1. Strive constantly to improve one's knowledge of methods, materials, and processes that affect purchasing performance.
2. Exercise and insist on sound business principles in the conduct of all transactions.
3. Be receptive to competent counsel from colleagues and demonstrate a willingness to share in support of the purchasing profession.

AMERICAN SOCIETY FOR MICROBIOLOGY

Address: 1752 N Street NW
             Washington, DC 20036-2804
Telephone: 202/737-3600
WWW: www.asmusa.org
Document: ASM Code of Ethics (1988)

Fundamental Principles
Members of ASM accept that the following fundamental principles advance their profession and uphold its integrity and dignity.

1. They will use their knowledge and skills for the advancement of human welfare.
2. They will be honest and impartial in their interactions with the public, their employers, their clients, patients in whose diagnosis and treatment they are involved, their colleagues, their students, and their employees.
3. They will strive to increase the competence and prestige of the profession of microbiology by responsible action and by sharing the results of their research through academic, commercial, or public service.
4. They will endeavor to continue to expand their professional knowledge and skills, and they will support the aims of the societies of their discipline.

Canons
To these fundamental principles are subtended the following Canons of Ethics:

1. Microbiologists recognize a duty to the public to propagate a true understanding of science. They will avoid making statements known to be premature, false, misleading, or exaggerated and will discourage any use of microbiology contrary to the welfare of human kind. They will work for proper and beneficent application of scientific

discoveries and will call to the attention of the public or the appropriate authorities misuses of microbiology or of information derived from microbiology.

2. Microbiologists are encouraged to communicate knowledge obtained in their research through discussions with their peers and through publications in the scientific literature.

3. In their scientific publications, microbiologists will strive for accuracy not only in the reporting and interpretation of their observations, but also in the proper citation of pertinent previous contributions by others.

4. Microbiologists will endeavor to recognize conflicts of interest and to avoid the abuse of privileged positions. Such privileged positions include, but are not limited to, (i) the review and evaluation of manuscripts and grant applications, (ii) evaluation of candidates for employment or promotion, (iii) ASM committee or staff positions, (iv) service in consulting activities, (v) access to specimen materials and information regarding their sources, (vi) student guidance, and (vii) simultaneous service in profit-making and not-for-profit organizations.

5. Microbiologists recognize their responsibility to make available to other members of the profession the unique materials that were the source of published data, so far as this does not infringe upon proprietary rights.

6. Microbiologists recognize responsibilities to students, technicians, and other associates working under their supervision to consider them colleagues, to provide training where required, and to assign appropriate recognition for their contributions. By direction and example, these colleagues should be taught adherence to the ethical standards herein described.

7. Members shall not represent any position as being that of ASM unless that position has been approved by the appropriate unit of ASM.

8. Members of ASM recognize ASM's responsibility to consider breaches of this Code of Ethics and to recommend appropriate responses. These responses are defined under ethical Review Process.

9. Microbiologists accepting membership in ASM by that action agree to abide by this Code of Ethics.

Advancing excellence in public service. . .

AMERICAN SOCIETY FOR PUBLIC ADMINISTRATION

Address: 1120 G Street NW, Suite 700
                  Washington, DC 20005-3885
Telephone: 202/393-7878
WWW: www.aspanet.org
Document: Code of Ethics (1984. Most recently revised 1994.)

The American Society for Public Administration (ASPA) exists to advance the science, processes, and art of public administration. The Society affirms its responsibility to develop the spirit of professionalism within its membership, and to increase public awareness of ethical principles in public service by its example. To this end, we, the members of the Society, commit ourselves to the following principles:

I. Serve the Public Interest
Serve the public, beyond serving oneself.
   ASPA members are committed to:

1. Exercise discretionary authority to promote the public interest.
2. Oppose all forms of discrimination and harassment, and promote affirmative action.
3. Recognize and support the public's right to know the public's business.
4. Involve citizens in policy decision-making.
5. Exercise compassion, benevolence, fairness and optimism.
6. Respond to the public in ways that are complete, clear, and easy to understand.
7. Assist citizens in their dealings with government.
8. Be prepared to make decisions that may not be popular.

II. Respect the Constitution and the Law

Respect, support, and study government constitutions and laws that define responsibilities of public agencies, employees, and all citizens.

ASPA members are committed to:

1. Understand and apply legislation and regulations relevant to their professional role.
2. Work to improve and change laws and policies that are counter-productive or obsolete.
3. Eliminate unlawful discrimination.
4. Prevent all forms of mismanagement of public funds by establishing and maintaining strong fiscal and management controls, and by supporting audits and investigative activities.
5. Respect and protect privileged information.
6. Encourage and facilitate legitimate dissent activities in government and protect the whistleblowing rights of public employees.
7. Promote constitutional principles of equality, fairness, representativeness, responsiveness and due process in protecting citizen's rights.

III. Demonstrate Personal Integrity

Demonstrate the highest standards in all activities to inspire public confidence and trust in public service.

ASPA members are committed to:

1. Maintain truthfulness and honesty and to not compromise them for advancement, honor, or personal gain.
2. Ensure that others receive credit for their work and contributions.
3. Zealously guard against conflict of interest or its appearance: *e.g.*, nepotism, improper outside employment, misuse of public resources or the acceptance of gifts.
4. Respect superiors, subordinates, colleagues and the public.
5. Take responsibility for their own errors.
6. Conduct official acts without partisanship.

IV. Promote Ethical Organizations

Strengthen organizational capabilities to apply ethics, efficiency and effectiveness in serving the public.

ASPA members are committed to:

1. Enhance organizational capacity for open communication, creativity, and dedication.
2. Subordinate institutional loyalties to the public good.
3. Establish procedures that promote ethical behavior and hold individuals and organizations accountable for their conduct.
4. Provide organization members with an administrative means for dissent, assurance of due process and safeguards against reprisal.
5. Promote merit principles that protect against arbitrary and capricious actions.
6. Promote organizational accountability through appropriate controls and procedures.
7. Encourage organizations to adopt, distribute, and periodically review a code of ethics as a living document.

V. Strive for Professional Excellence

Strengthen individual capabilities and encourage the professional development of others.

ASPA members are committed to:

1. Provide support and encouragement to upgrade competence.
2. Accept as a personal duty the responsibility to keep up to date on emerging issues and potential problems.
3. Encourage others, throughout their careers, to participate in professional activities and associations.
4. Allocate time to meet with students and provide a bridge between classroom studies and the realities of public service.

© American Society for Public Administration. Reprinted with permission.

AMERICAN SOCIETY FOR QUALITY

Address:	611 East Wisconsin Avenue, PO BOX 3005 Milwaukee, WI 53201-3005
Telephone:	414/272-8575
WWW:	www.asq.org
Document:	Code of Ethics

To uphold and advance the honor and dignity of the profession, and in keeping with high standards of ethical conduct, I acknowledge that I:

FUNDAMENTAL PRINCIPLES

1. Will be honest and impartial, and will serve with devotion my employer, my clients, and the public.

2. Will strive to increase the competence and prestige of the profession.
3. Will use my knowledge and skill for the advancement of human welfare, and in promoting the safety and reliability of products for public use.
4. Will earnestly endeavor to aid the work of the Society.

RELATIONS WITH THE PUBLIC

1. Will do whatever I can to promote the reliability and safety of all products that come within my jurisdiction.
2. Will endeavor to extend public knowledge of the work of the Society and its members that relates to the public welfare.
3. Will be dignified and modest in explaining my work and merit.
4. Will preface any public statements that I may issue by clearly indicating on whose behalf they are made.

RELATIONS WITH EMPLOYERS
AND CLIENTS

1. Will act in professional matters as a faithful agent or trustee for each employer or client.
2. Will inform each client or employer of any business connections, interests or affiliations which might influence my judgment or impair the equitable character of my services.
3. Will indicate to my employer or client the adverse consequences to be expected if my professional judgment is overruled.
4. Will not disclose information concerning the business affairs or technical processes of any present or former employer or client without his consent.
5. Will not accept compensation from more than one party for the same service without the consent of all parties. If employed, I will engage in supplementary employment of consulting practice only with the consent of my employer.

RELATIONS WITH PEERS

1. Will take care that credit for the work of others is given to those to whom it is due.
2. Will endeavor to aid the professional development and advancement of those in my employ or under my supervision.
3. Will not compete unfairly with others; will extend my friendship and confidence to all associates and those with whom I have business relations.

AMERICAN SOCIETY OF AGRONOMY

Address:	677 South Segoe Road
	Madison, WI 53711
Telephone:	608/273-8080
WWW:	www.agronomy.org
Document:	Statement of Ethics (1992)

Members of the American Society of Agronomy acknowledge that they are scientifically and professionally involved with the interdependence of natural, social, and technological systems. They are dedicated to the acquisition and dissemination of knowledge that advances the sciences and professions involving plants, soils, and their environment.

In an effort to promote the highest quality of scientific and professional conduct among its members, the American Society of Agronomy endorses the following guiding principles, which represent basic scientific and professional values of our profession.

Members shall:

1. Uphold the highest standards of scientific investigation and professional comportment, and an uncompromising commitment to the advancement of knowledge.
2. Honor the rights and accomplishments of others and properly credit the work and ideas of others.
3. Strive to avoid conflicts of interest.
4. Demonstrate social responsibility in scientific and professional practice, by considering whom their scientific and professional activities benefit, and whom they neglect.

5. Provide honest and impartial advice on subjects about which they are informed and qualified.
6. As mentors of the next generation of scientific and professional leaders, strive to instill these ethical standards in students at all educational levels.

© American Society of Agronomy. Reprinted with permission.

AMERICAN SOCIETY OF ANESTHESIOLOGISTS

Address: 520 North Northwest Highway.
                Park Ridge, IL 60068-2573
Telephone: 847/825-5586
WWW: www.ASAhq.org
Document: Guidelines for the Ethical Practice of
                Anesthesiology (1967. Most recently
                revised 1995.)

Preamble
Membership in the American Society of Anesthesiologists is a privilege of physicians who are dedicated to the ethical provision of health care. The Society recognizes the Principles of Medical Ethics of the American Medical Association (AMA) as the basic guide to the ethical conduct of its members. (See p. 00)

The practice of anesthesiology involves special problems relating to the quality and standards of patient care. Therefore, the Society requires its members to adhere to the AMA Principles of Medical Ethics and any other specific ethical guidelines adopted by this Society.

Definitions
Medical Direction: Anesthesia direction, management or instruction provided by an anesthesiologist whose responsibilities include:

1. Preanesthetic evaluation of the patient.
2. Prescription of the anesthesia plan.
3. Personal participation in the most demanding procedures in this plan, especially those of induction and emergence.
4. Following the course of anesthesia administration at frequent intervals.
5. Remaining physically available for the immediate diagnosis and treatment of emergencies.

6. Providing indicated postanesthesia care.

An anesthesiologist engaged in medical direction should not personally be administering another anesthetic and should use sound judgment in initiating other concurrent anesthetic and emergency procedures.

There may be specific circumstances when elements of the following guidelines may not apply and wherein individualized decisions may be appropriate.

I. Anesthesiologists have ethical responsibilities to their patients.
1. The patient-physician relationship involves special obligations for the physician that include placing the patient's interests foremost, faithfully caring for the patient and being truthful.
2. Anesthesiologists respect the right of every patient to self-determination. Anesthesiologists should include patients, including minors, in medical decision-making that is appropriate to their developmental capacity and the medical issues involved.
3. Anesthetized patients are particularly vulnerable, and anesthesiologists should strive to care for each patient's physical and psychological safety, comfort and dignity. Anesthesiologists should monitor themselves and their colleagues to protect the anesthetized patient from any disrespectful or abusive behavior.
4. Anesthesiologists should keep confidential patients' medical and personal information.
5. Anesthesiologists should provide preoperative evaluation and care and should facilitate the process of informed decision-making, especially regarding the choice of anesthetic technique.
6. If responsibility for a patient's care is to be shared with other physicians or nonphysician anesthesia providers, this arrangement should be explained to the patient. When directing nonphysician anesthesia providers, anesthesiologists should provide or ensure the same level of preoperative evaluation, care and counseling as when personally providing these same aspects of anesthesia care.
7. When directing nonphysician anesthesia providers or physicians in training in the actual delivery of anesthetics, anesthesiologists should remain personally and continuously available for direction and supervision during the anesthetic; they should directly participate in the most demanding aspects of the anesthetic care.

8. Anesthesiologists should provide for appropriate postanesthetic care for their patients.

9. Anesthesiologists should not participate in exploitive financial relationships.

10. Anesthesiologists share with all physicians the responsibility to provide care for patients irrespective of their ability to pay for their care. Anesthesiologists should provide such care with the same diligence and skill as for patients who do pay for their care.

II. Anesthesiologists have ethical responsibilities to medical colleagues.

1. Anesthesiologists should promote a cooperative and respectful relationship with their professional colleagues that facilitates quality medical care for patients. This responsibility respects the efforts and duties of other care providers including physicians, medical students, nurses, technicians and assistants.

2. Anesthesiologists should provide timely medical consultation when requested and should seek consultation when appropriate.

3. Anesthesiologists should cooperate with colleagues to improve the quality, effectiveness and efficiency of medical care.

4. Anesthesiologists should advise colleagues whose ability to practice medicine becomes temporarily or permanently impaired to appropriately modify or discontinue their practice. They should assist, to the extent of their own abilities, with the re-education or rehabilitation of a colleague who is returning to practice.

5. Anesthesiologists should not take financial advantage of other physicians, nonphysician anesthesia providers or staff members. Verbal and written contracts should be honest and understandable, and should be respected.

III. Anesthesiologists have ethical responsibilities to the health care facilities in which they practice.

1. Anesthesiologists should serve on health care facility or specialty committees. This responsibility includes making good faith efforts to review the practice of colleagues and to help develop departmental or health care facility procedural guidelines for the benefit of the health care facility and all of its patients.

2. Anesthesiologists share with all medical staff members the responsibility to observe and report to appropriate authorities any potentially negligent practices or conditions which may present a hazard to patients or health care facility personnel.

3. Anesthesiologists personally handle many controlled and potentially dangerous substances and, therefore, have a special responsibility to keep these substances secure from illicit use. Anesthesiologists should work within their health care facility to develop and maintain an adequate monitoring system for controlled substances.

IV. Anesthesiologists have ethical responsibilities to themselves.

1. The achievement and maintenance of competence and skill in the specialty is the primary professional duty of all anesthesiologists. This responsibility does not end with completion of residency training or certification by the American Board of Anesthesiology.

2. The practice of quality anesthesia care requires that anesthesiologists maintain their physical and mental health and special sensory capabilities. If in doubt about their health, then anesthesiologists should seek medical evaluation and care. During this period of evaluation or treatment, anesthesiologists should modify or cease their practice.

V. Anesthesiologists have ethical responsibilities to their community and to society.

1. A physician shall recognize a responsibility to participate in activities contributing to an improved community.

Guidelines for the Ethical Practice of Anesthesiology (1995) is reprinted with permission of the American Society of Anesthesiologists, 520 N. Northwest Highway, Park Ridge, Illinois 60068-2573. © Copyright 1998.

AMERICAN SOCIETY OF APPRAISERS

Address: 555 Herndon Parkway, Suite 125
             Herndon, VA 20170
Telephone: 703/478-2228
WWW: www.appraisers.org

Document: Principles of Appraisal Practice and
             Code of Ethics (1952. Most recently
             revised 1996.)

(The original code, adopted in June, 1952, was developed by a Joint Consolidation Committee which
helped merge the Technical Valuation Society and the
American Society of Technical Appraisers to form
the American Society of Appraisers.—Eds.)

FOREWORD

In a Society which not only permits but encourages
the private ownership of productive property and one
which also engages in large and multitudinous public
works, there appears, on every hand, a necessity for
the appraisal of property. In fact, property appraisals
are used throughout the economic, governmental,
legal, and social activities of such a society.

As the vocation of property appraisal has developed during past decades from a business occupation
into a profession, certain concepts have emerged and
become clear. The word "property" is now given to
physical things and also to the legal rights of ownership of tangible or intangible entities. Appraising is
now considered to encompass three classes of operations, namely,

(1) The estimation of the cost of producing or re-
    placing physical property,
(2) The forecasting of the monetary earning power
    of certain classes of property,
(3) The valuation or determination of the worth of
    property.

Because of the specialized knowledge and abilities
required of the appraiser which are not possessed by
the layman, there has now come to be established a
fiduciary relationship between him and those who
rely upon his findings.

The American Society of Appraisers occupies a
unique position among professional appraisal societies in that it recognizes and is concerned with all
classes of property: **real, personal, tangible,** and **intangible,** including real estate, machinery and equipment, buildings and other structures, furnishings,
works of art, natural resources, public utilities, gems
and jewelry, investment securities, and so forth. It is
also unique in that it recognizes the threefold character of the appraisal function.

In recognizing the need for the highest professional competence among appraisers, the American
Society of Appraisers actively supports recognized
institutions of higher learning in their scholastic pro-

grams which are designed to provide the necessary
academic background to both appraiser aspirants and
to the qualified professionals who desire to update
and broaden their professional skills.

The Society has established an Educational Foundation to assist those institutions of higher learning
which actively provide scholastic training and research in the various appraisal disciplines.

The necessity for a set of authoritative principles
and a code of professional ethics, broad enough to
cover all classes of property as well as the complexities of the various appraisal procedures, is a pressing
one. Previous statements of principles have dealt almost exclusively with real estate. Existing codes of
ethics are, in large measure, couched in such general
moralistic terms that they are impractical for specific
application.

Violation of any provision or rule of the Code
should not give rise to a civil cause of action and
should not create any presumption or evidence that a
legal duty has been breached nor should it create any
special relationship between the appraiser or any
other person. This Code is designed to provide guidance to appraisers and to provide a structure for regulating conduct of members of the ASA through disciplinary actions. Violations of the Code are not
designed or intended to be the basis of any civil liability. (January 1990)

To meet the need for a comprehensive set of guideposts and for a specific code of ethics, the Society has
prepared and presents herewith *The Principles of Appraisal Practice and Code of Ethics* of the American
Society of Appraisers.

INTRODUCTION

1.1 Membership Composition of the American So-
ciety of Appraisers

The American Society of Appraisers is a professional
organization of individuals. Each of its members who
has demonstrated, to the satisfaction of the Society,
that he is qualified to appraise one or more of the existing kinds of property, has been granted the right to
use the identification, Member of the American Society of Appraisers. Members and Senior Members
may use the appropriate designations authorized by
the Board of Governors.

1.2 Definition of "Appraisal Practice" and
"Property"

1.21 The term appraisal practice, as defined by the
      Society, applies to any of the four following op-
      erations, singly or in combination, these opera-

tions being executed within a framework of general principles of technical procedure and personal conduct:

(1) Determination of the value of property (the transitive verb *determine* having the meaning: "to come to a decision concerning, as the result of investigation, reasoning, etc.");

(2) Forecasting of the earning power of property;

(3) Estimation of the cost of

    (a) Production of a new property *(production* having the meaning: "brought into being by assembly of elements, fabrication, construction, manufacture, or natural growth of living things");

    (b) Replacement of an existing property by purchase or production of an equivalent property;

    (c) Reproduction of an existing property by purchase or production of an identical property.

(4) Determining non-monetary benefits or characteristics that contribute to value. The rendering of judgments as to age, remaining life, condition, quality, or authenticity of physical property, amenities; an estimate of the amount of a natural resource, population increase, nature of market, rate of absorption, etc.

1.22 In a valuation and in a forecast of earning power, the word property is used to describe the *rights* to the future *benefits of something owned* or *possessed to the exclusion of other persons.* The "something owned" may be tangible, intangible or both. In a cost estimation, the word *property* is used to describe the "something owned" without regard to its ownership.

1.3 Purpose of Promulgating the Principles of Appraisal Practice and Code of Ethics

The Principles of Appraisal Practice and Code of Ethics of the American Society of Appraisers are promulgated to:

1.31 Inform those who use the services of appraisers what, in the opinion of the Society, constitutes competent and ethical appraisal practice;

1.32 Serve as a guide to its own members in achieving competency in appraisal practice and in adhering to ethical standards;

1.33 Aid in the accomplishment of the purposes of the Society, which include:

    (a) Fosterage of appraisal education,

    (b) Improvement and development of appraisal techniques,

    (c) Encouragement of sound professional practices,

    (d) Establishment of criteria of sound performance for use of employers of staff appraisers,

    (e) Enforcement of ethical conduct and practice by its members;

1.34 Provide means, auxiliary to those used in examining applicants for admission to the grades of Members and Senior Member of the Society, for judging their skill, competence, and understanding of ethical principles;

1.35 Epitomize those appraisal practices that experience has found to be effective in protecting the public against exploitation.

OBJECTIVES OF APPRAISAL WORK

2.1 Various Kinds of Objectives of Appraisal Work

An appraisal is undertaken for one or more of several objectives, namely: to determine the value of a property; to estimate the cost of producing, acquiring, altering, or completing a property; to estimate the monetary amount of damages to a property; and to forecast the monetary earning power of a property. In specific instances, the work may have additional objectives, such as: the formulation of conclusions and recommendations or the presentations of alternatives (and their consequences) for the client's actions.

2.2 Objective Character of the Results of an Appraisal Undertaking

The primary objective of a monetary appraisal, is determination of a numerical result, either as a range or most probable point magnitude—the dollar amount of a value, the dollar amount of an estimated cost, the dollar amount of an estimated earning power. This numerical result is objective and unrelated to the desires, wishes, or needs of the client who engages the appraiser to perform the work. The amount of this figure is as independent of what someone desires it to be as a physicist's measurement of the melting point of lead or an accountant's statement of the amount of net profits of a corporation. All the principles of appraisal ethics stem from this central fact.

APPRAISER'S PRIMARY DUTY AND RESPONSIBILITY

The appraiser's duty and responsibility, in each subject case, is twofold.

3.1 Appraiser's Obligation to Determine and Describe the Apposite Kind of Value or Estimated Cost

First, because there are several kinds of value and several kinds of cost estimates, each of which has a legitimate place as the end point of some class of appraisal engagement, it is the appraiser's obligation to ascertain which one of these is pertinent to the particular undertaking. In meeting this obligation, the appraiser may consider his client's instructions and/or may obtain legal or other professional advice, but the selection of the apposite kind of value or estimated cost is the appraiser's sole responsibility. Also, it is his obligation, in this connection, fully to explain and describe what is meant by the particular value or cost estimate which he has determined, in order to obviate misunderstanding and to prevent unwitting or deliberate misapplication. For example, an appraisal engagement which calls for the determination of the replacement cost of a merchant's inventory of goods, for insurance purposes, would not be properly discharged by an appraisal of its retail market value; and an engagement which calls for the determination of the current market value of a multi-tenant office building leasehold estate, would not be properly discharged by a determination of the depreciated new cost of replacement of the improvements.

3.2 Appraiser's Obligation to Determine Numerical Results with Whatever Degree of Accuracy the Particular Objectives of the Appraisal Necessitate

Second, it is the appraiser's obligation to determine the appropriate and applicable numerical results with as high a degree of accuracy as the particular objectives of the appraisal necessitate.

3.3 Appraiser's Obligation to Avoid Giving a False Numerical Result

Obviously, the appraiser has every obligation to avoid giving a false figure. The numerical result of an appraisal could be false for one of two reasons: it could be false because it is a grossly inaccurate estimate of the apposite kind of value or cost estimate, or it could be false, even though numerically accurate, because it is an estimate of an inapposite kind of value of cost estimate.

3.4 Appraiser's Obligation to Attain Competency and to Practice Ethically

In order to meet his obligations, the appraiser must be competent in his field. This competency he attains by education, training, study, practice, and experience.

He must also recognize, understand, and bide by those ethical principles that are interwoven with and are an essential part of truly professional practice.

3.5 Professional Character of Appraisal Practice

The members of the Society are engaged in a professional activity. A profession is based on an organized body of specific knowledge—knowledge not possessed by laymen. It is of such a character that it requires a high degree of intelligence and considerable expenditure of time and effort to acquire it and to become adept in its application. An appraiser's client relies on the appraiser's professional knowledge and abilities to whatever extent may be necessary to accomplish the objectives of the work. Members of the Society recognize this relationship.

3.6 Appraiser's Responsibility to Third Parties

Under certain specific circumstances an appraisal report may be given by a client to a third party for their use. If the purpose of the appraisal includes a specific use by a third party, the third party has a right to rely on the validity and objectivity of the appraiser's findings as regards the specific stated purpose and intended use for which the appraisal was originally made. Members of the Society recognize their responsibility to those parties, other than the client, who may be specifically entitled to make use of their reports.

APPRAISER'S OBLIGATION TO HIS CLIENT

The appraiser's primary obligation to his client is to reach complete, accurate, and pertinent conclusions and numerical results regardless of the client's wishes or instructions in this regard. The relationship between client and appraiser is not one of principal and agent. However, the appraiser's obligation to his client goes somewhat beyond this primary obligation. These secondary obligations are set forth in the following sections.

4.1 Confidential Character of an Appraisal Engagement

The fact that an appraiser has been employed to make an appraisal is a confidential matter. In some instances, the very fact of employment may be information that a client, whether private or a public agency, prefers for valid reasons to keep confidential. Knowledge by outsiders of the fact of employment of an appraiser may jeopardize a client's proposed enterprise or transaction. Consequently, it is improper for the appraiser to disclose the fact of his engagement, unless the client approves of the disclosure or clearly has no interest in keeping the fact of the engagement confidential, or unless the appraiser is required by due process of law to disclose the fact of his engagement.

In the absence of an express agreement to the contrary, the identifiable contents of an appraisal report are the property of the appraiser's client or employer and, ethically, cannot be submitted to any professional Society as evidence of professional qualifications, and cannot be published in any identifiable form without the client's or employer's consent.

4.2 Appraiser's Obligation to Give Competent Service

It is not proper for an appraiser to accept an engagement to make an appraisal of property of a type he is not qualified to appraise or in a field outside his Society membership classification, unless (a) he fully acquaints the client with the limitations of his qualifications or (b) he associates himself with another appraiser or appraisers who possess the required qualifications.

As a corollary to the above principle, the Society declares that it is unethical for an appraiser to claim or imply that he has professional qualifications which he does not possess or to state his qualifications in a form which may be subject to erroneous interpretation. (See Sec. 7.8)

4.3 Appraiser's Obligation Relative to Giving Testimony

When an appraiser is engaged by one of the parties in a controversy, it is unethical for the appraiser to suppress any facts, data, or opinions which are adverse to the case his client is trying to establish; or to overemphasize any facts, data, or opinions which are favorable to his client's case; or in any other particulars to become an advocate. It is the appraiser's obligation to present the data, analysis, and value without bias, regardless of the effect of such unbiased presentation on his client's case. (Also, see Sec. 7.5)

4.4 Appraiser's Obligation to Document Appraisal Testimony

When a member accepts employment to make an appraisal, or to testify as to value of property before a court of law or other judicial or quasi-judicial forums, the appraiser shall, before testifying, complete an adequate written appraisal report, or have complete documentation and substantiation available in his files.

4.5 Appraiser's Obligation Relative to Serving More Than One Client in the Same Matter

When two or more potential clients seek an appraiser's services with respect to the same property or

with respect to the same legal action, the appraiser may not properly serve more than one, except with the consent of all parties.

4.6 Agreements and Contracts for Appraisal Services

It is good practice to have a written contract, or at least a clear oral agreement, between appraiser and client, covering objectives and scope of work, time of delivery of report, and amount of fees. In certain circumstances, it may be desirable to include in the appraisal-service contract a statement covering the objective character of appraisal findings and a statement that the appraiser cannot act as an advocate or negotiator.

APPRAISER'S OBLIGATION TO OTHER APPRAISERS AND TO THE SOCIETY

5.1 Protection of Professional Reputation of Other Appraiser's

The appraiser has an obligation to protect the professional reputation of all appraisers (whether members of the Society or not) who subscribe to and practice in accord with the Principles of Appraisal Practice of the Society. The Society declares that it is unethical for an appraiser to injure, or attempt to injure, by false or malicious statements or by innuendo the professional reputation or prospects of any appraiser.

5.2 Appraiser's Obligation Relative to Society's Disciplinary Actions

A member of the society, having knowledge of an act by another member which, in his opinion, is in violation of the ethical principles incorporated in the *Principles of Appraisal Practice and Code of Ethics* of the Society, has the obligation to report the matter in accordance with the procedure specified in the Constitution and Bylaws.

It is the appraiser's obligation to cooperate with the Society and its officers in all matters, including investigation, censure, discipline, or dismissal of members who are charged with violation of the *Principles of Appraisal Practice and Code of Ethics* of the Society.

APPRAISAL METHODS AND PRACTICES

6.1 Various Kinds of Value

The Society recognizes that different kinds of property may have different kinds of value depending on the particular attendant circumstances and, further, that there are both basic and subordinate kinds of value.

Good professional practice requires that the appraiser describe in sufficient detail, in each case, the nature and meaning of the specific value that he is determining.

6.2 Selection of Appraisal Method

The procedure and method for determining the particular value in question is a matter for the appraiser himself to determine—he cannot be held responsible for the result unless he has a free hand in selecting the process by which that result is to be obtained. However, good appraisal practice requires that the method selected be adequate for the purpose, embrace consideration of all the factors that have a bearing on the value, and be presented in a clear and logical manner.

6.3 Fractional Appraisals

Certain classes of properties (real estate, business enterprise, collections of chattels, for example) can be considered as made up of components (for example, in the case of real estate: land and buildings; in the case of a business enterprise: land, buildings, machinery and equipment, contracts, and goodwill). If an element is considered as an integrated part of the whole property, its value, in general, is different from the value the same element has if considered as a fraction separated from the whole property.

An appraisal of an element of a whole property, considered by itself and ignoring its relation to the rest of the whole property, is called a "fractional appraisal." There are legitimate uses for fractional appraisals (appraisal of buildings for fire insurance purposes; appraisal to determine the value of land as if cleared of existing improvements; appraisal in connection with public utility rate-making, etc.) but good practice requires that a fractional appraisal be labeled as such and that the limitations on its use by the client and/or third parties be clearly stated.

6.4 Contingent and Limiting Conditions Affecting an Appraisal

In many instances the validity of the appraiser's conclusions as to the value of a subject property is contingent upon the validity of statements, information, and/or data upon which he has relied, supplied to him by members of other professions or secured by him from official sources. Such material may be obtained, for example, from architects, engineers, lawyers, accountants, government officials, government agencies, etc. It is proper for the appraiser to rely upon and use such material provided (1) he states in his report that he has done so, (2) he stands ready to make his

sources and/or the material itself available for any required verification, and (3) he does not pass to others the responsibility for matters that are, or should be, within the scope of his own professional knowledge. Good appraisal practice requires that the appraiser state any other contingent or limiting conditions which affect the appraisal, such as, for example, that the value is contingent upon the completion of projected public or private improvements, etc.

6.5 Hypothetical Appraisals

A hypothetical appraisal is an appraisal based on assumed conditions which are contrary to fact or which are improbable of realization or consummation. The Society takes the position that there are legitimate uses for some hypothetical appraisals, but that it is improper and unethical to issue a hypothetical appraisal report unless (1) the value is clearly labeled as hypothetical (2) the legitimate purpose for which the appraisal was made is stated, and (3) the conditions which were assumed contrary to fact are set forth.

A hypothetical appraisal showing the value of a company which it is proposed to form by merging two existing companies would be deemed to serve a legitimate purpose. On the other hand, a hypothetical appraisal of a projected apartment house, based on an assumed rent schedule which is so much above the market that it is practically impossible for it to be realized, would not serve any legitimate purpose and its issuance might well lead to the defrauding of some unwary investor.

6.6 Appraisals In Which Access to Pertinent Data is Denied

Situations sometimes occur in which data that the appraiser considers pertinent to the making of a valid appraisal are in existence but access to them is denied to the appraiser, either by the client or some other party (for example: the past production records of an oil field; the records of prior revenue and expense of a motel property; etc.). In such a case, the appraiser, at his option, may properly decline to carry out the assignment. In the event he considers such data *essential* to the making of a valid appraisal, he may not properly proceed with the assignment.

6.7 Ranges of Value or Estimated Cost and Reliability Estimates

Some appraisal engagements call for the determination of a probable range of value or estimated cost, either with or without a collateral statement of the most probable figure within that range. It is entirely within the scope of good appraisal practice to give a range of value or estimated cost.

Inasmuch as the appraiser's determination of the amount of a value or an estimated cost cannot, by its very nature, be exact, it is good appraisal practice to append to such numerical results a statement as to the degree of reliability to be accorded thereto. Such reliability estimates are usually expressed as plus and minus percentages.

6.8 Values or Estimated Costs Under Different Hypotheses

The objective of an appraisal undertaking may be the determination of different values or different cost estimates based on different hypotheses. It is entirely within the scope of good appraisal practice to give such differing numerical results, provided the appraiser adheres to the principles set forth in Sec. 3.1 and Sec. 6.5.

6.9 Inspection, Investigation, Analysis, and Description of Subject Property

The valuation of a property is a procedure based on an analysis of all the characteristics of the property which contribute to or detract from its value; good appraisal practice requires that the appraiser's inspection, investigation, and study be thorough enough to uncover all of the pertinent characteristics.

Good appraisal practice requires that the description of the property, tangible or intangible, which is the subject of a valuation, cover adequately (a) identification of the property (b) statement of the legal rights and restrictions comprised in the ownership, and (c) the characteristics of the property which contribute to or detract from its value.

In the case of chattels and prospective real estate improvements, identification is particularly important in order to prevent unscrupulous persons from representing the appraisal as applying to substituted inferior property.

In general, the legal rights of the ownership of chattels are obvious and need not be stated; but, in the case of real property, statements of zoning restrictions, building codes, easements, leases, etc., are essential elements of the description. It is understood, however, that the legal rights of the ownership of an interest in real property are matters of legal, not appraisal, opinion, and that the appraiser discharges his obligations in this regard by stating the sources of these data. (See Sec. 6.4) In the case of intangible properties (patents, contracts, franchises, etc.) the documentary provisions not only define what the

property is, they also set forth the legal rights and descriptions.

The physical condition of chattels or real property is an element contributing to or detracting from their value; good appraisal practice requires adequate inspection and investigation to determine it.

6.10 Collaboration Between Appraisers and Utilization of the Services of Members of Other Professions

Collaboration between appraisers is desirable, in some situations, to expedite the completion of work and, in other situations, to obtain the benefits of combined judgment or combined data. Such collaboration is entirely proper providing all the collaborators sign a joint report or, if there be dissenting opinions, providing these dissenting opinions are made a part of the report.

In some cases, the nature of the appraisal undertaking calls for special professional knowledge and abilities in addition to those possessed by the appraiser. In such an instance, it is both necessary and proper for the appraiser to employ other appraisers and/or members of other professions to obtain data and derive conclusions relative to specific parts of the work. The principal appraiser builds his final conclusions in part, on these contributions, taking responsibility for the final result but subject to the validity of the underlying or constituent contributions. (See Sec. 6.4)

UNETHICAL AND UNPROFESSIONAL APPRAISAL PRACTICES

The principles of appraisal practice given in Sec. 6 relate to the primary objective of an appraisal undertaking, namely the determination of the apposite numerical result with that degree of accuracy required by the attendant circumstances, where as the principles given in this section (Sec. 7) relate to the establishment and maintenance of the confidence of clients and other interested parties in the validity of the results of appraisal undertakings. To this end, certain practices are declared by the Society to be unethical and unprofessional.

7.1 Contingent Fees

If an appraiser were to accept an engagement for which the amount of his compensation is contingent upon the amount of an award in a property settlement or a court action where his services are employed; or is contingent upon the amount of a tax reduction obtained by a client where his services are used; or is contingent upon the consummation of the sale or financing of a property in connection with which his services are utilized or is contingent upon his reaching any finding or conclusion specified by his client; then, anyone considering using the results of the appraiser's undertaking might well suspect that these results were biased and self-serving and therefore, invalid. Such suspicion would militate against the establishment and maintenance of trust and confidence in the results of appraisal work, generally; therefore the Society declares that the contracting for or acceptance of any such contingent fee is unethical and unprofessional.

As a corollary to the above principle relative to contingent fees, the Society declares that it is unethical and unprofessional for an appraiser (a) to contract for or accept compensation for appraisal services in the form of a commission, rebate, division of brokerage commissions, or any similar forms and (b) to receive or pay finder's or referral fees.

7.2 Percentage Fees
The Society takes the position that it is unprofessional and unethical for the appraiser to contract to do work for a fixed percentage of the amount of value, or of the estimated cost (as the case may be) which he determines at the conclusion of his work.

7.3 Disinterested Appraisals
Anyone using an appraiser who has an interest or a contemplated future interest in the property appraised, might well suspect that the report was biased and self-serving and, therefore, that the findings were invalid. Such suspicion tends to break down trust and confidence in the results of appraisal work, generally.

Interests which an appraiser may have in a property which is to be appraised, include ownership of the subject property; acting, or having some expectation of acting, as agent in the purchase, sale, or financing of the subject property; and managing, or have some expectation of managing, the subject property. Such interests are particularly apt to exist if the appraiser, while engaged in professional appraisal practice, is also engaged in a related retail business (real estate, jewelry, furs, antiques, fine arts, etc.).

The Society declares that, subject to the provision for disclosure given in the following paragraph, it is unethical and unprofessional for an appraiser to accept an assignment to appraise a property in which he has an interest or a contemplated future interest. However, if a prospective client, after full disclosure by the appraiser of his present or contemplated future

interest in the subject property, still desires to have the appraiser do the work, the latter may properly accept the engagement provided he discloses the nature and extent of his interest in his appraisal report.

7.4 Responsibility Connected with Signatures to Appraisal Reports
The user of an appraisal report, before placing reliance on its conclusions, is entitled to assume that the party signing the report is responsible for the findings, either because he did the work himself or because the work was done under his supervision.

In cases where two or more appraisers are employed to prepare a joint report, the user thereof is entitled to assume that, if all of them sign it, they are jointly and severally responsible for the validity of all of the findings therein; and, if all do not sign, he has a right to know what the dissenting opinions are.

In cases where two or more appraisers have been engaged by a single client to make independent appraisals of the same property, the client has the right to expect that he will receive opinions which have been reached independently and that he may use them as checks against each other and/or have evidence of the range within which the numerical results lie.

To implement these principles, the Society declares that it is unethical (a) to misrepresent who made an appraisal by appending the signature of any person who neither did the work himself nor had the work done under his supervision, (b) in the case of a joint report to omit any signatures or any dissenting opinions, (c) in case two or more appraisers have collaborated in an appraisal undertaking, for them, or any of them, to issue separate appraisal reports, and (d) in case two or more appraisers have been engaged by a single client to make independent appraisals of the same property, for them to collaborate or consult with one another or make use of each other's findings or figures.

An appraisal firm or corporation may properly use a corporate signature with the signature of a responsible officer thereof. But the person who actually did the appraisal for the corporation must sign the corporate appraisal report or the report must acknowledge the person who actually made the appraisal.

7.5 Advocacy
If an appraiser, in the writing of a report or in giving an exposition of it before third parties or in giving testimony in a court action suppresses or minimizes any facts, data, or opinions which, if fully stated,

might militate against the accomplishment of his client's objective or, if he adds any irrelevant data or unwarranted favorable opinions or places an improper emphasis on any relevant facts for the purpose of aiding his client in accomplishing his objective, he is, in the opinion of the Society, an advocate. Advocacy, as here described, affects adversely the establishment and maintenance of trust and confidence in the results of professional appraisal practice and the Society declares that it is unethical and unprofessional. (Also, see Sec. 4.3)

7.6 Unconsidered Opinions and Preliminary Reports

If an appraiser gives an opinion as to the value, earning power, or estimated cost of a property without having ascertained and weighed all of the pertinent facts, such opinion, except by an extraordinary coincidence, will be inaccurate. The giving of such offhand opinions tends to belittle the importance of inspection, investigation, and analysis in appraisal procedure and lessens the confidence with which the results of good appraisal practice are received, and therefore the Society declares the giving of hasty and unconsidered opinions to be unprofessional.

If an appraiser makes a preliminary report without including a statement to the effect that it is preliminary and that the figures given are subject to refinement or change when the final report is completed, there is the possibility that some user of the report, being under the impression that it is a final and completed report, will accord the figures a degree of accuracy and reliability they do not possess. The results of such misplaced confidence could be damaging to the reputation of professional appraisers, generally, as well as of the appraiser concerned. To obviate this possibility, the Society declares it to be unprofessional appraisal practice to omit a proper limiting and qualifying statement in a preliminary report.

7.7 Advertising and Solicitation

It is not unethical to advertise the availability of appraisal services. It is unethical to use any inaccurate, misleading, false or deceptive claim, promise or representation in connection with any advertisement. These unethical practices are considered by the Society to be detrimental to the establishment and maintenance of public confidence in the results of appraisal work. The Society declares that such practices on the part of an appraiser constitute unethical and

unprofessional conduct. It would be unethical to do the following:

(a) Misrepresent in any way one's connection or affiliation with the ASA or any other organization;

(b) Misrepresent one's background, education, training or expertise;

(c) Misrepresent services available or an appraiser's prior or current service to any client, or identify any client without the express written permission of such client to be identified in advertising;

(d) Represent, guarantee or imply that a particular valuation or estimate of value or result of an engagement will be tailored or adjusted to any particular use or conclusion other than that an appraisal will be based upon an honest and accurate adherence to the Principles of Appraisal Practice.

7.8 Misuse of Membership Designations

The Constitution and Bylaws of the Society establish three professional grades of membership, namely, Member, Senior Member, and Fellow. (An Affiliate or Candidate does not hold a professional grade of membership in the Society.) The designation "A.M.," meaning Accredited Member, may be used in the grade of a Member. The designation "A.S.A.," meaning Accredited Senior Appraiser, may be used only in the grade of Senior Member, except those Senior Members certified in the classification of Real Property Residential (1-4 Units) who use the designation "A.S.A Residential." The designation "F.A.S.A." may be used only by Fellows. The Society declares that it is unethical for a member to claim or imply that he holds a higher degree of membership than he has attained. (Also, see Bylaws Art. B-27.)

7.9 Causes for Disciplinary Action by the Society

Disciplinary action against the members of the Society is taken in the event of violations of specific provisions of the Society's Constitution and Bylaws or of its *Principles of Appraisal Practice and the Code of Ethics* incorporated therein. Such actions are under of jurisdiction of the International President, the International Ethics Committee, and the Board of Governors. Violations may fall under six categories:

(1) Deviations from good appraisal practice
(2) Failure to fulfill obligations and responsibilities
(3) Unprofessional conduct
(4) Unethical conduct
(5) Conviction in any judicial tribunal of (a) any felony or (b) any misdemeanor for which the maximum penalty is three (3) years in jail or

more regardless of the actual sentence imposed or (c) any misdemeanor involving honesty or veracity, i.e., involving theft or false statement regardless of the actual sentence imposed.

(6) Any unlawful, illegal or immoral conduct (even if not convicted in a judicial tribunal) which would bring disrepute to the appraisal profession or to the American Society of Appraisers.

After due investigation, the Society may take action in the form of suggestion, censure, suspension, or expulsion, in which last event the member will be required to surrender his Certificate, membership pin, and other evidences of his membership after its termination.

APPRAISAL REPORTS

In preceding sections it was stated that good appraisal practice, as defined by the Society, requires the inclusion of certain specific explanations, descriptions, and statements in an appraisal report. These are summarized herewith. (These requirements do not apply to reports prepared by a staff appraiser for the exclusive and non-public use of his employer; but do apply to reports prepared by a public appraiser, i.e., one who offers his services for a fee to the general public.)

8.1 Description of the Property Which Is the Subject of an Appraisal Report

It is required that the property with which an appraisal report is concerned, whether tangible, intangible, real, or personal, be fully described therein, the elements of such description being: (a) identification, (b) legal rights and restrictions encompassed in the ownership, where these are not obvious, (c) value characteristics, and (d) physical condition, where applicable. (See Sec. 6.8)

8.2 Statement of the Objectives of the Appraisal Work

It is required that an appraisal report include a statement of the objectives for which the work was performed: to determine a value, to estimate a cost, to forecast an earning power, to ascertain certain facts, to reach conclusions and make recommendations for action in specified matters, etc. (See Sec. 2.1)

It is required that the meaning attached by the appraiser to any specific kind of value or estimated cost which is the objective of the appraisal undertaking be described and explained in the appraisal report. (See Sec. 6.1)

It is required that an appraisal report include a statement as to the date which the value estimate, cost estimate or forecast of income applies.

When appropriate, an analysis of the highest and the best use of the property should be included in the investigation and study.

8.3 Statement of the Contingent and Limiting Conditions to Which the Appraisal Findings Are Subject

It is required that statements, information, and/or data, which were obtained by the appraiser from members of other professions, or official or other presumably reliable sources, and the validity of which affects the appraisal findings, be summarized or stated in full in the appraisal report and the sources given, so that verification desired by any user of the report may be accomplished. (See Sec. 6.4)

If an appraisal is a hypothetical one, it is required that it be labeled as hypothetical, that the reason a hypothetical appraisal was made be stated, and that the assumed hypothetical conditions be set forth. (See Sec. 6.5)

If an appraisal is a fractional appraisal, it is required that it be labeled as fractional and that the limitations on the use of the reported figure be stated. (See Sec. 6.3)

If a preliminary appraisal report is issued, namely, one in which the figures are subject to refinement or change, it is required that the report be labeled as preliminary and that the limitation on its use be stated. (See Sec. 7.6)

8.4 Description and Explanation in the Appraisal Report of the Appraisal Method Used

It is required that the method selected by the appraiser as applicable to the subject appraisal undertaking be described and explained in the appraisal report. (See Sec. 6.2)

8.5 Statement of the Appraiser's Disinterestedness

It is required that the appraiser include a statement in his appraisal report that he has no present or contemplated future interest in the subject property or any other interest which might tend to prevent his making a fair and unbiased appraisal or, if he does have such an interest, to set forth fully the nature and extent of that interest. (See Sec. 7.3)

8.6 Appraisers Responsibility to Communicate Each Analysis, Opinion and Conclusion in a Manner that is not Misleading

The appraiser should state in each report, "I hereby certify that, to the best of my knowledge and belief, the statements of fact contained in this report are true and correct, and this report has been prepared in conformity with the Uniform Standards of Professional Appraisal Practice of The Appraisal Foundation and the Principles of Appraisal Practice and Code of Ethics of the American Society of Appraisers."

8.7 Mandatory Recertification Statement

All Senior Member appraisers should state in each report "The American Society of Appraisers has a mandatory recertification program for all of its Senior members. 'I am' or 'I am not' in compliance with that program."

8.8 Signatures to Appraisal Reports and the Inclusion of Dissenting Opinions

It is required that the party who makes the appraisal or who has the appraisal made under his supervision sign the appraisal report. (See Sec. 7.4)

It is required that all collaborating appraisers, issuing a joint report, who agree with the findings, sign the report; and that any collaborating appraiser who disagrees with any or all of the findings of the others, prepare, sign, and include in the appraisal report his dissenting opinion. (See Sec. 7.4)

© American Society of Appraisers. Reprinted with permission.

**CERTIFIED
ASSOCIATION
EXECUTIVE**

AMERICAN SOCIETY OF ASSOCIATION EXECUTIVES

Address: 1575 I Street NW
Washington, DC 20005-1168
Telephone: 202/626-2723
WWW: www.asaenet.org
Document: Standards of Conduct (1997)

(The ASAE publishes extensively in the field of professional ethics. Interested students are referred in particular to "Codes of Ethics and Professional Standards," in *The Value of Associations to American Society* (Washington, DC, 1990), 63-77; Samuel B. Shapiro, "ASAE Ethical Codes," in *A Coming of Age: A History of the Profession of Association Management* (Washington, DC, 1987), 151-61; and Lawrence J. Lad, *Current Principles and Practices in Association Self-Regulation* (Washington, DC, 1992).—Eds.)

As a member of the American Society of Association Executives, I pledge myself to:

• Maintain the highest standard of personal conduct.

• Actively promote and encourage the highest level of ethics within the industry or profession my association represents.

• Maintain loyalty to the association that employs me, and pursue its objectives in ways that are consistent with the public interest.

• Recognize and discharge my responsibility and that of my association to uphold all laws and regulations relating to my association's policies and activities.

• Strive for excellence in all aspects of management of my association.

• Use only legal and ethical means in all association activities.

• Serve all members of my association impartially, provide no special privilege to any individual member, and accept no personal compensation from a member except with full disclosure and with the knowledge and consent of my association's governing board.

• Maintain the confidentiality of privileged information entrusted or known to me by virtue of my office.

• Refuse to engage in, or countenance, activities for personal gain at the expense of my association or its industry or profession.

• Refuse to engage in, or countenance, discrimination on the basis of race, sex, age, religion, national origin, sexual orientation, or disability.

• Always communicate association internal and external statements in a truthful and accurate manner by assuring that there is integrity in the data and information used by my association.

• Cooperate in every reasonable and proper way with other association executives, and work with them in the advancement of the profession of association management.

• Use every opportunity to improve public understanding of the role of associations.

This Code of Standards of Conduct for members of the American Society of Association Executives has been adopted to promote and maintain the highest standards of association service and personal conduct among its members. Adherence to these standards is expected from members of the society, and serves to assure public confidence in the integrity and service of association executives.

©1997 American Society of Association Executives. Reprinted with permission.

AMERICAN SOCIETY OF CIVIL ENGINEERS

Address: 1801 Alexander Bell Drive
Reston, VA 20191-4400
Telephone: 703/295-6300 or 800/548-2723
WWW: www.asce.org
Document: Code of Ethics (1976. Most recently revised 1996.)

(The *Canons of Ethics of Engineers* was formulated for the engineering profession in 1946 by the Committee on Engineering Ethics of the Engineers' Council for Professional Development, now the Accreditation Board for Engineering Technology (ABET). It is used as the basis of the codes for this and other engineering organizations.—Eds.)

Fundamental Principles

Engineers uphold and advance the integrity, honor and dignity of the engineering profession by:

1. using their knowledge and skill for the enhancement of human welfare and the environment;
2. being honest and impartial and serving with fidelity the public, their employers and clients;
3. striving to increase the competence and prestige of the engineering profession; and
4. supporting the professional and technical societies of their disciplines.

Fundamental Canons

1. Engineers shall hold paramount the safety, health and welfare of the public and shall strive to comply with the principles of sustainable development in the performance of their professional duties.
2. Engineers shall perform services only in areas of their competence.
3. Engineers shall issue public statements only in an objective and truthful manner.
4. Engineers shall act in professional matters for each employer or client as faithful agents or trustees, and shall avoid conflicts of interest.
5. Engineers shall build their professional reputation on the merit of their services and shall not compete unfairly with others.
6. Engineers shall act in such a manner as to uphold and enhance the honor, integrity, and dignity of the engineering profession.
7. Engineers shall continue their professional development throughout their careers, and shall provide opportunities for the professional development of those engineers under their supervision.

Guidelines to Practice Under the Fundamental Canons of Ethics

CANON 1.

Engineers shall hold paramount the safety, health and welfare of the public and shall strive to comply with the principles of sustainable development in the performance of their professional duties.

a. Engineers shall recognize that the lives, safety, health and welfare of the general public are dependent upon engineering judgments, decisions and practices incorporated into structures, machines, products, processes and devices.

b. Engineers shall approve or seal only those design documents, reviewed or prepared by them, which are determined to be safe for public health and welfare in conformity with accepted engineering standards.

c. Engineers whose professional judgment is overruled under circumstances where the safety, health and welfare of the public are endangered, or the principles of sustainable development ignored, shall inform their clients or employers of the possible consequences.

d. Engineers who have knowledge or reason to believe that another person or firm may be in violation of any of the provisions of Canon 1 shall present such information to the proper authority in writing and shall cooperate with the proper authority in furnishing such further information or assistance as may be required.

e. Engineers should seek opportunities to be of constructive service in civic affairs and work for the advancement of the safety, health and well-being of their communities, and the protection of the environment through the practice of sustainable development.

f. Engineers should be committed to improving the environment by adherence to the principles of sustainable development so as to enhance the quality of life of the general public.

CANON 2.

Engineers shall perform services only in areas of their competence.

a. Engineers shall undertake to perform engineering assignments only when qualified by education or experience in the technical field of engineering involved.

b. Engineers may accept an assignment requiring education or experience outside of their own fields of competence, provided their services are restricted to those phases of the project in which they are qualified. All other phases of such project shall be performed by qualified associates, consultants, or employees.

c. Engineers shall not affix their signatures or seals to any engineering plan or document dealing with subject matter in which they lack competence by virtue of education or experience or to any such plan or document not reviewed or prepared under their supervisory control.

CANON 3.

Engineers shall issue public statements only in an objective and truthful manner.

a. Engineers should endeavor to extend the public knowledge of engineering and sustainable development, and shall not participate in the dissemination of untrue, unfair or exaggerated statements regarding engineering.

b. Engineers shall be objective and truthful in professional reports, statements, or testimony. They shall include all relevant and pertinent information in such reports, statements, or testimony.

c. Engineers, when serving as expert witnesses, shall express an engineering opinion only when it is founded upon adequate knowledge of the facts, upon a background of technical competence, and upon honest conviction.

d. Engineers shall issue no statements, criticisms, or arguments on engineering matters which are inspired or paid for by interested parties, unless they indicate on whose behalf the statements are made.

e. Engineers shall be dignified and modest in explaining their work and merit, and will avoid any act tending to promote their own interests at the expense of the integrity, honor and dignity of the profession.

CANON 4.

Engineers shall act in professional matters for each employer or client as faithful agents or trustees, and shall avoid conflicts of interest.

a. Engineers shall avoid all known or potential conflicts of interest with their employers or clients and shall promptly inform their employers or clients of any business association, interests, or circumstances which could influence their judgment or the quality of their services.

b. Engineers shall not accept compensation from more than one party for services on the same project, or for services pertaining to the same project, unless the circumstances are fully disclosed to and agreed to, by all interested parties.

c. Engineers shall not solicit or accept gratuities, directly or indirectly, from contractors, their agents, or other parties dealing with their clients or employers in connection with work for which they are responsible.

d. Engineers in public service as members, advisors, or employees of a governmental body or department shall not participate in considerations or actions with respect to services solicited or provided by them or their organization in private or public engineering practice.

e. Engineers shall advise their employers or clients when, as a result of their studies, they believe a project will not be successful.

f. Engineers shall not use confidential information coming to them in the course of their assignments as a means of making personal profit if such action is adverse to the interests of their clients, employers or the public.

g. Engineers shall not accept professional employment outside of their regular work or interest without the knowledge of their employers.

CANON 5.

Engineers shall build their professional reputation on the merit of their services and shall not compete unfairly with others.

a. Engineers shall not give, solicit or receive either directly or indirectly, any political contribution, gratuity, or unlawful consideration in order to secure work, exclusive of securing salaried positions through employment agencies.

b. Engineers should negotiate contracts for professional services fairly and on the basis of demonstrated competence and qualifications for the type of professional service required.

c. Engineers may request, propose or accept professional commissions on a contingent basis only under circumstances in which their professional judgments would not be compromised.

d. Engineers shall not falsify or permit misrepresentation of their academic or professional qualifications or experience.

e. Engineers shall give proper credit for engineering work to those to whom credit is due, and shall recognize the proprietary interests of others. Whenever possible, they shall name the person or persons who may be responsible for designs, inventions, writings or other accomplishments.

f. Engineers may advertise professional services in a way that does not contain misleading language or is in any other manner derogatory to the dignity of the profession. Examples of permissible advertising are as follows:

Professional cards in recognized, dignified publications, and listings in rosters or directories published by responsible organizations, provided that the cards or listings are consistent in size and content and are in a section of the publication regularly devoted to such professional cards.

Brochures which factually describe experience, facilities, personnel and capacity to render service, providing they are not misleading with respect to the engineer's participation in projects described.

Display advertising in recognized dignified business and professional publications, providing it is factual and is not misleading with respect to the engineer's extent of participation in projects described.

A statement of the engineers' names or the name of the firm and statement of the type of service posted on projects for which they render services.

Preparation or authorization of descriptive articles for the lay or technical press, which are factual and dignified. Such articles shall not imply anything more than direct participation in the project described.

Permission by engineers for their names to be used in commercial advertisements, such as may be published by contractors, material suppliers, etc., only by means of a modest, dignified notation acknowledging the engineers' participation in the project described. Such permission shall not include public endorsement of proprietary products.

g Engineers shall not maliciously or falsely, directly or indirectly, injure the professional reputation, prospects, practice or employment of another engineer or indiscriminately criticize another's work.

h. Engineers shall not use equipment, supplies, laboratory or office facilities of their employers to carry on outside private practice without the consent of their employers.

CANON 6.

Engineers shall act in such a manner as to uphold and enhance the honor, integrity, and dignity of the engineering profession.

a. Engineers shall not knowingly act in a manner which will be derogatory to the honor, integrity, or dignity of the engineering profession or knowingly engage in business or professional practices of a fraudulent, dishonest or unethical nature.

CANON 7.

Engineers shall continue their professional development throughout their careers, and shall provide opportunities for the professional development of those engineers under their supervision.

a. Engineers should keep current in their specialty fields by engaging in professional practice, participating in continuing education courses, reading in the technical literature, and attending professional meetings and seminars.

b. Engineers should encourage their engineering employees to become registered at the earliest possible date.

c. Engineers should encourage engineering employees to attend and present papers at professional and technical society meetings.

d. Engineers shall uphold the principle of mutually satisfying relationships between employers and employees with respect to terms of employment including professional grade descriptions, salary ranges, and fringe benefits.

AMERICAN SOCIETY OF HEALTH-SYSTEM PHARMACISTS

Address: 7272 Wisconsin Avenue
    Bethesda, MD 20814
Telephone: 301/657-3000
WWW: www.ashp.org

The American Society of Health-System Pharmacists uses the same code of ethics as the American Pharmaceutical Association. See p. 158.

AMERICAN SOCIETY OF HEATING, REFRIGERATING, AND AIR CONDITIONING ENGINEERS

Address: 1791 Tullie Circle NE
    Atlanta, GA 30329
Telephone: 404/636-8400
WWW: www.ashrae.org
Document: Code of Ethics (1986)

As members of a Society "organized and operated for the exclusive purpose of advancing the arts and sciences of heating, refrigeration, air conditioning and ventilation, the allied arts and sciences and related human factors for the benefit of the general public," we recognize that honesty, fairness, courtesy, competence and integrity must characterize our conduct.

With the foregoing in mind

- Our efforts shall be directed at all times to the enhancement of the public health, safety and welfare.
- Our services shall be offered only in areas of our competence.
- Our products shall be offered only in areas of their suitability.
- Our public statements shall be issued only in an objective and truthful manner.
- Our endeavors shall carefully avoid conflicts of interest and the appearance of conflicts of interest.
- The confidentiality of clients' and employers' business affairs, proprietary information, and procedures shall be respected.

© American Society of Heating, Refrigerating and Air-Conditioning Engineers. Reprinted with permission.

ASID
American Society
of Interior Designers

AMERICAN SOCIETY OF INTERIOR DESIGNERS

Address: 608 Massachusetts Avenue NE
    Washington, DC 20002
Telephone: 202/546-3480
WWW: www.asid.org
Document: ASID Code of Ethics and Professional Conduct

1.0 PREAMBLE
Members of the American Society of Interior Designers are required to conduct their professional practice in a manner that will inspire the respect of clients, suppliers of goods and services to the profession, and fellow professional designers, as well as the general public. It is the individual responsibility of every member of the Society to uphold this Code and the Bylaws of the Society.

2.0 RESPONSIBILITY TO THE PUBLIC
2.1 Members shall comply with all existing laws, regulations and codes governing business procedures and the practice of interior design as established by the state or other jurisdiction in which they practice.

2.2 Members shall not seal or sign drawings, specifications, or other interior design documents except where the member or the member's firm has prepared, supervised or professionally reviewed and approved such documents, as allowed by relevant state law.

2.3 Members shall at all times consider the health, safety and welfare of the public in spaces they design. Members agree, whenever possible, to notify property managers, landlords, and/or public officials of conditions within a built environment that endanger the health, safety and/or welfare of occupants.

2.4 Members shall not engage in any form of false or misleading advertising or promotional activities and shall not imply through advertising or other means that staff members or employees of their firm are qualified interior designers unless such be the fact.

2.5 Members shall neither offer, nor make any payments or gifts to any public official, nor take any other action, with the intent of unduly influencing the official's judgement in connection with an existing or prospective project in which the members are interested.

2.6 Members shall not assist or abet improper or illegal conduct of anyone in connection with a project.

3.0 RESPONSIBILITY TO THE CLIENT

3.1 Members' contracts with a client shall clearly set forth the scope and nature of the project involved, the services to be performed and the method of compensation for those services.

3.2 Members may offer professional services to a client for any form of legal compensation.

3.3 Members shall not undertake any professional responsibility unless they are, by training and experience, competent to adequately perform the work required.

3.4 Members shall fully disclose to a client all compensation which the Member shall receive in connection with the project and shall not accept any form of undisclosed compensation from any person or firm with whom the member deals in connection with the project.

3.5 Members shall not divulge any confidential information about the client or the client's project, or utilize photographs or specifications of the project, without the express permission of the client, with an exception for those specifications or drawings over which the designer retains proprietary rights.

3.6 Members shall be candid and truthful in all their professional communications.

3.7 Members shall act with fiscal responsibility in the best interest of their clients and shall maintain sound business relationships with suppliers, industry and trades to insure the best service possible to the public.

4.0 RESPONSIBILITY TO OTHER INTERIOR DESIGNERS AND COLLEAGUES

4.1 Members shall not interfere with the performance of another interior designer's contractual or professional relationship with a client.

4.2 Members shall not initiate, or participate in, any discussion or activity which might result in an unjust injury to another interior designer's reputation or business relationships.

4.3 Members may, when requested and it does not present a conflict of interest, render a second opinion to a client, or serve as an expert witness in a judicial or arbitration proceeding.

4.4 Members shall not endorse the application for ASID membership and/or certification, registration or licensing of an individual known to be unqualified with respect to education, training, experience or character, nor shall a Member knowingly misrepresent the experience, professional expertise or moral character of that individual.

4.5 Members shall only take credit for work that has actually been created by that Member or the Member's firm, and under the Member's supervision.

4.6 Members should respect the confidentiality of sensitive information obtained in the course of their professional activities.

5.0 RESPONSIBILITY TO THE PROFESSION

5.1 Members agree to maintain standards of professional and personal conduct that will reflect in a responsible manner on the Society and the profession.

5.2 Members shall seek to continually upgrade their professional knowledge and competency with respect to the interior design profession.

5.3 Members agree, whenever possible, to encourage and contribute to the sharing of knowledge and information between interior designers and other allied professional disciplines, industry and the public.

6.0 RESPONSIBILITY TO THE EMPLOYER

6.1 Members leaving an employer's service shall not take drawings, designs, data, reports, notes, client lists, or other materials relating to work performed in the employer's service except with permission of the employer.

6.2 A member shall not unreasonably withhold permission from departing employees to take copies of material relating to their work while an employee of the member's firm, which are not proprietary and confidential in nature.

6.3 Members shall not divulge any confidential information obtained during the course of their employment about the client or the client's project or utilize photographs or specifications of the project, without the express permission of both client and employer.

7.0 ENFORCEMENT

7.1 The Society shall follow standard procedures for the enforcement of this Code as approved by the Society's Board of Directors.

7.2 Members having a reasonable belief, based upon substantial information, that another member has acted in violation of this Code, shall report such information in accordance with accepted procedures.

7.3 Any deviation from this Code, or any action taken by a Member which is detrimental to the Society and the profession as a whole shall be deemed unprofessional conduct subject to discipline by the Society's Board of Directors.

AMERICAN SOCIETY OF INTERNAL MEDICINE

Address: 2011 Pennsylvania Avenue NW,
Suite 800
Washington, DC 20066-1837
Telephone: 215/351-2600 or 800/523-1546
WWW: www.asim.org
Document: Ethics (1996)

Patient/Physician Covenant:

ASIM supports the Patient/Physician Covenant as published in the *Journal of the American Medical Association* (JAMA), May 17, 1995, volume 273, number 19, page 1553. Medicine is, at its center, a moral enterprise grounded in a covenant of trust. This covenant obliges physicians to be competent and to use their competence in the patient's best interests. Physicians, therefore, are both intellectually and morally obliged to act as advocates for the patient wherever their welfare is threatened and for their health at all times.

Patient Directives and Utilization Review:

The prior existence of advance directives (expressions of intent to forgo resuscitative, extraordinary, unwanted or other care highly unlikely to improve or stabilize health status) should not jeopardize the provision of medically appropriate care, if the care is consistent with agreed upon limits.

• Individual physicians should not in any way be reprimanded by reviewing bodies for abiding by the wishes of patients when providing appropriate care to individuals who have exercised advance directives.

ASIM urges the AMA and other organizations representing hospice physicians to study the problem of utilization reviewers *a priori* limiting access to or questioning the appropriateness of care for individuals who have agreed to "no code" status and publicize the implications tor utilization management (UM) determinations to hospital medical staff UM committees and to payers and health plans.

Terminal Illness:

The following AMA policy statement is endorsed by ASIM:

• The intentional termination of the life of one human being by another—mercy killing or euthanasia—is contrary to public policy, medical tradition, and the most fundamental measures of human value and worth.

• The cessation of the employment of extraordinary means to prolong the life of the body when there is irrefutable evidence that biological death is imminent is the decision of the patient and/or the lawful representative, acting in the patient's best interest.

• The advice and judgment of the physician or physicians involved should be readily available to the patient and/or the immediate family and/or the lawful representative in all such situations.

- No physician, other licensed health care provider, or hospital should be civilly or criminally liable under these guidelines, nor should there be any criminal or civil penalties of any sort imposed for conduct pursuant to these guidelines.
- Except as stated above, all matters not in the public domain relating to a patient's terminal illness are the private right of the patient and are protected from public scrutiny by the privacy and confidentiality of the physician-patient relationship.

Right to Forego Life Sustaining Treatment:
ASIM reaffirms the principle of patient autonomy and the patient's right to self-determination.

- ASIM reaffirms that the right to self-determination includes the right to refuse medical treatment including artificially administered nutrition and hydration.
- ASIM reaffirms that a patient lacking decision-making capacity such as patient in an irreversible coma or a patient in a persistent vegetative state, is entitled to have appropriate decisions with respect to continuing or foregoing life-sustaining treatment, made by a surrogate decision maker such as an agent designated in a Durable Power of Attorney for Health Care, a family member, or a significant other.
- ASIM reaffirms that a patient's right to self-determination with respect to foregoing life-sustaining treatment supersedes the interests of health care providers and of the state in preserving life.

Dissemination of Information Regarding Power of Attorney For Health Care and Living Wills:
ASIM actively supports federal legislation that assures the rights of a person to self-determine their medical treatment, particularly in regards to withdrawal or refusal of life-sustaining treatment, while preserving the pivotal role of the doctor/patient relationship.

- ASIM believes that physicians should be educated about issues related to patient self-determination and the importance of communicating with patients about this matter including: Informing patients of their rights and responsibilities in regards to refusing various types of treatment during a terminal or life-threatening illness; encouraging patients to discuss these and related issues with their physicians; and encouraging patients to exercise their option of executing Durable Power of Attorney for Health Care and/or a Living Will.

Ethical Considerations in Health Care:
When making treatment decisions that involve ethical choices, health care professionals and patients (or their authorized representatives) should strive for a high level of mutual understanding and shared decision-making.

- The establishment of ethics committees at health care facilities to provide ethical guidance to protect patients' rights and responsibilities should be encouraged.
- The inclusion of ethics in the curricula of health professions education programs and emphasis on ethical concerns in the traditional peer review process should be encouraged.

Moral and Ethical Issues in the Use of Health Care Technologies:
The criteria on which to base professional recommendations for the application or withdrawal of health care technology should be developed by the individual health care facility in which the technology is to be used, and should be consistent with professional and ethical considerations. Each health care facility should establish a permanent ethics committee, composed of health professionals and lay representatives from the general community, to develop the criteria. Each facility should, on an ad hoc basis, convene ethics committees to advise health professionals and patients regarding the application of criteria to individual cases. In those cases in which a technology is used outside a health care facility, local consortia of health professionals and lay people should be created to develop criteria governing the application or withdrawal of health care technology.

- Recommendations by a health professional to apply or withdraw a health care technology in the diagnosis or treatment of an individual patient must be based on clinically valid criteria consistent with professional and ethical standards. In particular, such decisions should not be based on the patient's chronological (as opposed to biological) age, sex, race, ethnic origin, current wealth or probable future income, but should take into consideration the quality of life resulting from application or withdrawal of the technology.
- The health care professional responsible for managing and coordinating an individual's health care should have the responsibility for determining whether application of a technology is clinically appropriate and consistent with the criteria established by the health care facility. That health care

professional is also responsible for communicating recommendations, including the rationale for such recommendations, to the patient. The decision to use or not to use the technology should be made jointly by the health professional and the patient or his or her representative. When the decision to withdraw or deny a technology cannot be made by the patient or his or her representative and the health professional, either party should have the right to seek the counsel of an ethics committee.

• Competent terminally ill individuals should have the freedom to make their own decisions regarding the withholding or withdrawal of treatment. Appropriate individuals should be encouraged to develop guidelines for the withholding or withdrawal of treatment and state legislatures should be encouraged to pass "right to die" legislation.

• In making decisions as to whether to commit resources to the development of capital-intensive technology in a given area, the appropriate balance between individual and societal rights should be considered. Such decisions should take into consideration the recommendations and findings of local and regional planning entities as to the need for such technology in relation to the need for alternative services that might be offered and the appropriate distribution of the technology itself.

© American Society of Internal Medicine. Reprinted with permission.

AMERICAN SOCIETY OF JOURNALISTS AND AUTHORS

Address: 1501 Broadway, Suite 302
New York, NY 10036
Telephone: 212/997-0947
WWW: www.asja.org
Document: ASJA Code of Ethics and Fair Practices (Most recently revised 1997.)

Preamble
Over the years, an unwritten code governing editor-writer relationships has arisen. The American Society of Journalists and Authors has compiled the major principles and practices of that code that are generally recognized as fair and equitable.

The ASJA has also established a Committee on Editor-Writer Relations to investigate and mediate disagreements brought before it, either by members or by editors. In its activity this committee shall rely on the following guidelines.

1. Truthfulness, Accuracy, Editing
The writer shall at all times perform professionally and to the best of his or her ability, assuming primary responsibility for truth and accuracy. No writer shall deliberately write into an article a dishonest, distorted, or inaccurate statement.

Editors may correct or delete copy for purposes of style, grammar, conciseness or arrangement, but may not change the intent or sense without the writer's permission.

2. Sources
A writer shall be prepared to support all statements made in his or her manuscripts, if requested. It is understood, however, that the publisher shall respect any and all promises of confidentiality made by the writer in obtaining information.

3. Ideas and Proposals
An idea shall be defined not as a subject alone but as a subject combined with an approach.

A proposal of an idea ("query") by a professional writer shall receive a personal response within three weeks. If such a communication is in writing, it is properly viewed and treated as business correspondence, with no return postage or other materials required for reply,

A writer shall be considered to have a proprietary right to an idea suggested to an editor.

4. Acceptance of an Assignment
A request from an editor that the writer proceed with an idea, however worded and whether oral or written, shall be considered an assignment. (The word "assignment" here is understood to mean a definite order for an article.) It shall be the obligation of the writer to proceed as rapidly as possible toward the completion of an assignment, to meet a deadline mutually agreed upon, and not to agree to unreasonable deadlines.

5. Conflict of Interest
The writer shall reveal to the editor, before acceptance of an assignment, any actual or potential conflict of interest, including but not limited to any financial interest in any product, firm, or commercial venture relating to the subject of the article.

6. Report on Assignment

If in the course of research or during the writing of the article, the writer concludes that the assignment will not result in a satisfactory article, he or she shall be obliged to so inform the editor.

7. Withdrawal

Should a disagreement arise between the editor and writer as to the merit or handling of an assignment, the editor may remove the writer on payment of mutually satisfactory compensation for the effort already expended, or the writer may withdraw without compensation and, if the idea for the assignment originated with the writer, may take the idea elsewhere without penalty.

8. Agreements

The practice of written confirmation of all agreements between editors and writers is strongly recommended, and such confirmation may originate with the editor, the writer, or an agent. Such a memorandum of confirmation should list all aspects of the assignment including subject, approach, length, special instructions, payments, deadline, and guarantee (if any). Failing prompt contradictory response to such a memorandum, both parties are entitled to assume that the terms set forth therein are binding.

All terms and conditions should be agreed upon at the time of assignment, with no changes permitted except by written agreement signed by both parties.

9. Rewriting

No writer's work shall be rewritten without his or her advance consent. If an editor requests a writer to rewrite a manuscript, the writer shall be obliged to do so but shall alternatively be entitled to withdraw the manuscript and offer it elsewhere.

10. Bylines

Lacking any stipulation to the contrary, a byline is the author's unquestioned right. All advertisements of the article should also carry the author's name. If an author's byline is omitted from the published article, no matter what the cause or reason, the publisher shall be liable to compensate the author financially for the omission.

11. Updating

If delay in publication necessitates extensive updating of an article, such updating shall be done by the author, to whom additional compensation shall be paid.

12. Reversion of Rights

Reasonable and good-faith efforts should be made to schedule an article within six months and publish it within twelve months. In the event that circumstances prevent such timely publication, the writer should be informed within twelve months as to the publication's continued interest in the article and plans to publish it. If publication is unlikely, the manuscript and all rights therein should revert to the author without penalty or cost to the author.

13. Payment for Assignments

An assignment presumes an obligation upon the publisher to pay for the writer's work upon satisfactory completion of the assignment, according to the agreed terms. Should a manuscript that has been accepted, orally or in writing, by a publisher or any representative or employee of the publisher, later be deemed unacceptable, the publisher shall nevertheless be obliged to pay the writer in full according to the agreed terms.

If an editor withdraws or terminates an assignment, due to no fault of the writer, after work has begun but prior to completion of a manuscript, the writer is entitled to compensation for work already put in; such compensation shall be negotiated between editor and author and shall be commensurate with the amount of work already completed. If a complete assignment is not accepted, due to no fault of the writer, the writer is still entitled to full payment.

14. Time of Payments

The writer is entitled to full payment for an accepted article within 30 days of delivery. No article payment, or any portion thereof, should ever be subject to publication or to scheduling for publication.

15. Expenses

Unless otherwise stipulated by the editor at the time of an assignment, a writer shall assume that normal, out-of-pocket expenses will be reimbursed by the publisher. Any extraordinary expenses anticipated by the writer shall be discussed with the editor prior to incurring them.

16. Insurance

A magazine that gives a writer an assignment involving any extraordinary hazard shall insure the writer against death or disability during the course of travel or the hazard, or, failing that, shall honor the cost of such temporary insurance as an expense account item.

17. Loss of Personal Belongings

If, as a result of circumstances or events directly connected with a perilous assignment and due to no fault of the writer, a writer suffers loss of personal belongings or professional equipment or incurs bodily injury, the publisher shall compensate the writer in full.

18. Copyright, Additional Rights

It shall be understood, unless otherwise stipulated in writing, that sale of an article manuscript entitles the purchaser to first North American publication rights only, and that all other rights are retained by the author. Under no circumstances shall an independent writer be required to sign a so-called "all rights transferred" or "work made for hire" agreement as a condition of assignment, of payment or of publication.

19. Reprints

All revenues from reprints shall revert to the author exclusively, and it is incumbent upon a publication to refer all requests for reprints to the author. The author has a right to charge for such reprints and must request that the original publication be credited.

20. Agents

In the absence of any agreement to the contrary, a writer shall not be obliged to pay an agent a fee on work negotiated, accomplished and paid for without the assistance of the agent. An agent should not charge a client a separate fee covering "legal" review of a contract for a book or other project.

21. TV and Radio Promotion

The writer is entitled to be paid for personal participation in TV or radio programs promoting periodicals in which the writer's work appears.

22. Indemnity

No writer should be obliged to indemnify any magazine or book publisher against any claim, actions, or proceedings arising from an article or book, except where there are valid claims of plagiarism or copyright violation.

23. Proofs

The editor shall submit edited proofs of the author's work to the author for approval, sufficiently in advance of publication that any errors may be brought to the editors' attention. If for any reason a publication is unable to so deliver or transmit proofs to the author, the author is entitled to review the proofs in the publication's office.

AMERICAN SOCIETY OF LANDSCAPE ARCHITECTS

A S L A

Address:	636 Eye Street NW
	Washington, DC 20001-3736
Telephone:	202/898-2444
WWW:	www.asla.org
Document:	Code of Professional Conduct (1995)

PREAMBLE:

The profession of landscape architecture, so named in 1867, was built on the foundation of several principles: dedication to the public health, safety, and welfare and recognition and protection of the land and its resources. These principles form the foundations, as well, of this Code. The Code also contains important principles relating to duties to clients and to members of the Society.

The Code is arranged so that each canon contains ethical standards—essentially goals members should strive to meet. Some of the ethical standards contain objective rules. Violation of rules (R) might subject an ASLA member to a complaint while violation of ethical standards (ES) will not. Therefore the word "should" is used in the ethical standards and "shall" is used in the rules. Enacted by the Board of Trustees, April 2, 1995.

CANON I. PROFESSIONAL RESPONSIBILITY

ES1.1 Members should understand and obey laws governing their professional practice and business matters and conduct their professional duties with honesty.

> **R1.101** Members, in the conduct of their professional practice, shall not violate the law, including any federal, state or local laws, and particularly laws and regulations in the areas of antitrust, employment, environment and land-use planning, and those governing professional practice.

> **R1.102** A member shall not give, lend or promise anything of value to any public official, or representative of a prospective client, in order to influence the judgment or actions in the

letting of contracts, of that official or representative of a prospective client.

Comment: However, the provision of pro bono services will not violate this rule.

R1.103 Members in government service shall not accept private practice work with anyone doing business with their agency, or with whom the member has any government contact on matters involving applications for grants, contracts or planning and zoning actions.

R1.104 Members shall recognize the contributions of others engaged in the planning, design and construction of the physical environment and shall give them appropriate recognition and due credit for professional work, and shall not maliciously injure or attempt to injure the reputation, prospects, practice or employment position of those persons so engaged.

R1.105 Members shall not mislead, through advertising or other means, existing or prospective clients about the results that can be achieved through the use of the members' services, nor shall the members state that they can achieve results by means that violate this code or the law.

Comment: So long as they are not misleading, advertisements in any medium are not prohibited by this Code .

R1.106 Members shall not accept compensation for their services from more than one party on a project, unless the circumstances are agreed to in writing by all parties.

R1.107 A member shall truthfully, without exaggeration, misleading, deceptive or false statements or claims, inform the client, employer, or public about personal qualifications, capabilities and experience.

Comment: Members shall not take credit for work performed under the direction of a former employer beyond the limits of their personal involvement and shall give credit to the performing firm. Employers should give departing employees access to work that they performed, reproduced at cost, and a description of the employee's involvement in the work should be noted on each product, and signed by the employer.

R1.108 Members shall not reveal information obtained in the course of their professional activities which they have been asked to maintain in confidence, or which could affect the interests of another adversely. Unique exceptions: to stop an act which creates harm, a significant risk to the public health, safety and welfare, which cannot otherwise be prevented, to establish claims or defense on behalf of members, or in order to comply with applicable law, regulations or with this code.

R1.109 Members shall neither copy nor reproduce the copyrighted works of other landscape architects or design professionals, without prior written approval of the author.

ES1.2 Members should seek to make full disclosure of relevant information to the clients, public and other interested parties who rely on their advice and professional work product.

R1.201 Members making public statements on landscape architectural issues shall disclose compensation other than fee and their role and any economic interest in a project.

R1.202 Members shall make full disclosure during the solicitation and conduction of a project of the roles and professional status of all project team members and consultants, including their state licenses and professional degrees held, if any; availability of coverage of liability and errors and omissions insurance coverage; and any other material potential limitations.

R1.203 Members shall make full disclosure to the client or employer of any financial or other interest which bears upon the service or project. If a client or employer objects to such association, financial interest, or other interest, the member shall either terminate such association or interest, or give up the commission or employment.

ES1.3 Members should endeavor to protect the interests of their clients and the public through competent performance of their work; participate in continuing education, educational research, and development and dissemination of technical information relating to planning, design, construction and management of the physical environment.

> **R1.301** Members shall undertake to perform professional services only when they, together with those persons whom they may engage as consultants, are qualified by education, training, or experience in the specific technical areas involved.

> **R1.302** Members shall not sign or seal drawings, specifications, reports, or other professional work for which they do not have direct professional knowledge or direct supervisory control.

> **R1.303** Members shall continually seek to raise the standards of aesthetic, ecological and cultural excellence through compliance with applicable state requirements for continuing professional education.

ES1.4 Members should strive to promote diversity throughout the profession of landscape architecture.

> **R1.401** Members shall not conduct or participate in any employment practices or professional activities which discriminate on the basis of race, religion, gender national origin, age, disability, or sexual orientation.

CANON II. ENVIRONMENTAL ETHICS

ES2.1 Members should accept responsibility for the consequences of their design, planning, management and policy decisions on the health of natural systems and cultural communities and their harmony, equity and balance with one another.

Comment: The concept of accepting responsibility does not imply acceptance of legal liability.

ES2.2 Members should generate design, planning, management strategies and policy from the basis of the cultural context and the ecosystem to which each landscape belongs at the local, regional and global scale.

ES2.3 Members should develop, use and specify products, materials, technologies and techniques which exemplify the principles of sustainable development and landscape regeneration.

ES2.4 Members should seek constant improvement in knowledge, abilities, and skills, in educational institutions, and professional practices and organizations to more effectively achieve sustainable development.

ES2.5 Members should actively engage in shaping decisions, attitudes and values that support human health, environmental protection and sustainable development.

CANON III. MEMBER DUTIES

ES3.1 Members should work to insure that they, their employees or supervisees, and other members adhere to this code of conduct and the bylaws of the ASLA.

> **R3.101** Members having information which leads to a reasonable belief that another member has committed a violation of this code, shall report such information.

> **Comment:** Often a landscape architect can recognize that the behavior of another poses a serious question as to the other's professional integrity. It is the duty of the professional to bring the matter to the attention of the committee [to be named], which action, if done in good faith, is in some jurisdictions protected from libel or slander action. If in doubt, the member reporting under this rule should seek counsel prior to making such a report.

> **R3.102** The official seal or logo of the ASLA may not be used other than as specified in the bylaws.

> **R3.103** Members, associates, and affiliates shall adhere to the specific applicable terms of the bylaws regarding use of references to ASLA membership.

ES3.2 Members should endeavor to participate in pro bono works in the service of the public good and to serve in elected and appointed capacities which improve public appreciation and understanding of landscape architecture, environmental systems, and the functions and responsibilities of landscape architects.

© American Society of Landscape Architects. Reprinted with permission.

 **ASME International**

AMERICAN SOCIETY OF MECHANICAL ENGINEERS

Address: Three Park Avenue
             New York, NY 10016-5990
Telephone: 212/705-7722 or 800/843-2763
WWW: www.asme.org
Document: Code of Ethics of Engineers

The *Canons of Ethics of Engineers* was formulated for the engineering profession in 1946 by the Committee on Engineering Ethics of the Engineers' Council for Professional Development, now the Accreditation Board for Engineering Technology (ABET). It is used as the basis of the codes for this and other engineering organizations.—Eds.)

THE FUNDAMENTAL PRINCIPLES
Engineers uphold and advance the integrity, honor, and dignity of the engineering profession by:

   I. *using their knowledge and skill for the enhancement of human welfare;*
  II. *being honest and impartial, and serving with fidelity the public, their employers and clients, and*
 III. *striving to increase the competence and prestige of the engineering profession.*

THE FUNDAMENTAL CANONS
1. Engineers shall hold paramount the safety, health and welfare of the public in the performance of their professional duties.
2. Engineers shall perform services only in the areas of their competence.
3. Engineers shall continue their professional development throughout their careers and shall provide

opportunities for the professional and ethical development of those engineers under their supervision.
4. Engineers shall act in professional matters for each employer or client as faithful agents or trustees, and shall avoid conflicts of interest or the appearance of conflicts of interest.
5. Engineers shall build their professional reputation on the merit of their services and shall not compete unfairly with others.
6. Engineers shall associate only with reputable persons or organizations.
7. Engineers shall issue public statements only in an objective and truthful manner.

© The American Society of Mechanical Engineers. Reprinted with permission.

AMERICAN SOCIETY OF NEWSPAPER EDITORS

Address: 11690B Sunrise Valley Drive
             Reston, VA 20191-1409
Telephone: 703/453-1122
WWW: www.asne.org
Document: ASNE Statement of Principles
             (1975)

(ASNE's Statement of Principles was originally adopted in 1922 as the *Canons of Journalism*. The document was revised and renamed *Statement of Principles* in 1975. Discussion of the background to this code may be found in the chapter "Ethics, an Eternal Problem" in Alice Fox Pitts's book, *Read All About It! 50 years of ASNE* (Easton, PA, 1974).—Eds.)

PREAMBLE.
The First Amendment, protecting freedom of expression from abridgment by any law, guarantees to

the people through their press a constitutional right, and thereby places on newspaper people a particular responsibility. Thus journalism demands of its practitioners not only industry and knowledge but also the pursuit of a standard of integrity proportionate to the journalist's singular obligation. To this end the American Society of Newspaper Editors sets forth this Statement of Principles as a standard encouraging the highest ethical and professional performance.

ARTICLE I—Responsibility.

The primary purpose of gathering and distributing news and opinion is to serve the general welfare by informing the people and enabling them to make judgments on the issues of the time. Newspapermen and women who abuse the power of their professional role for selfish motives or unworthy purposes are faithless to that public trust. The American press was made free not just to inform or just to serve as a forum for debate but also to bring an independent scrutiny to bear on the forces of power in the society, including the conduct of official power at all levels of government.

ARTICLE II—Freedom of the Press.

Freedom of the press belongs to the people. It must be defended against encroachment or assault from any quarter, public or private. Journalists must be constantly alert to see that the public's business is conducted in public. They must be vigilant against all who would exploit the press for selfish purposes.

ARTICLE III—Independence.

Journalists must avoid impropriety and the appearance of impropriety as well as any conflict of interest or the appearance of conflict. They should neither accept anything nor pursue any activity that might compromise or seem to compromise their integrity.

ARTICLE IV—Truth and Accuracy.

Good faith with the reader is the foundation of good journalism. Every effort must be made to assure that the news content is accurate, free from bias and in context, and that all sides are presented fairly. Editorials, analytical articles and commentary should be held to the same standards of accuracy with respect to facts as news reports. Significant errors of fact, as well as errors of omission, should be corrected promptly and prominently.

ARTICLE V—Impartiality.

To be impartial does not require the press to be unquestioning or to refrain from editorial expression.

Sound practice, however, demands a clear distinction for the reader between news reports and opinion. Articles that contain opinion or personal interpretation should be clearly identified.

ARTICLE VI—Fair Play.

Journalists should respect the rights of people involved in the news, observe the common standards of decency and stand accountable to the public for the fairness and accuracy of their news reports. Persons publicly accused should be given the earliest opportunity to respond. Pledges of confidentiality to news sources must be honored at all costs, and therefore should not be given lightly. Unless there is clear and pressing need to maintain confidences, sources of information should be identified.

These principles are intended to preserve, protect and strengthen the bond of trust and respect between American journalists and the American people, a bond that is essential to sustain the grant of freedom entrusted to both by the nation's founders.

© American Society of Newspaper Editors. Reprinted with permission.

AMERICAN SOCIETY OF
PLASTIC AND RECONSTRUCTIVE
SURGEONS

AMERICAN SOCIETY OF PLASTIC AND RECONSTRUCTIVE SURGEONS

Address:	444 East Algonquin Road
	Arlington Heights, IL 60005
Telephone:	847/228-9900
WWW:	www.plasticsurgery.org
Document:	Code of Ethics for the American
	Society of Plastic and Reconstructive
	Surgeons (1992. Most recently
	revised 1996.)

Preamble

As stated in its *Bylaws*, the American Society of Plastic and Reconstructive Surgeons, (ASPRS) is organized:

To benefit humanity by advancing the art and science of plastic and reconstructive surgery; to promote the highest standard of professional skill and competence among plastic surgeons; to promote the exchange of information among plastic surgeons; to promote the highest standard of personal conduct among plastic surgeons and physicians; to provide the public with information about the scientific progress in plastic and reconstructive surgery; to promote the purpose and effectiveness of plastic surgeons as is consistent with the public interest.

Membership in ASPRS is granted by the voting membership of ASPRS to those surgeons who are competent practitioners of the art and science of plastic surgery. Competence in plastic surgery involves attainment and maintenance of high standards of medical and ethical conduct. Medical competence is fostered by successful completion of the examinations of the American Board of Plastic Surgery. Ethical competence is fostered by the adoption and enforcement of a *Code of Ethics*, adherence to which is prerequisite for admission to and maintenance of membership in ASPRS. Members are expected to act in accord with the *General and Specific Principles of the Code of Ethics* of ASPRS in all contacts with patients, peers and the general public. Further, members are individually responsible and accountable for their actions and words, as well as the use of their names. Members shall be subject to disciplinary action, including expulsion, for violation of any of the *General or Specific Principles* of this Code.

Section 1.—General Principles

I. The principal objective of the medical profession is to render services to humanity with full respect for human dignity. Physicians should merit the confidence of patients entrusted to their care, rendering to each a full measure of service and devotion.

II. Physicians should strive continually to improve medical knowledge and skill, and must make available to their patients and colleagues the benefits of their professional attainments. Physicians have an affirmative duty to disclose new medical advances to patients and colleagues.

III. Physicians should practice a method of healing founded on a scientific basis, and should not voluntarily associate professionally with anyone who violates this principle.

IV. The medical profession should safeguard the public and itself against physicians deficient in moral character or professional competence. Physicians should observe all laws, uphold the dignity and honor of the profession, and accept its self-imposed disciplines. They should expose, without hesitation, illegal or unethical conduct of fellow members of the profession.

V. Physicians may choose whom to serve. In emergency situations, however, physicians should render service to the best of their ability. Having undertaken the care of a patient, a physician may not neglect the patient; and until the patient has been discharged, a physician may discontinue services only after giving adequate notice.

VI. Physicians should provide services under the terms and conditions which permit the free and complete exercise of sound medical judgement and skill. Nothing contained in this provision shall be constructed to limit price competition among physicians.

VII. In the practice of medicine, a physician should receive professional income only for medical services actually rendered or supervised by the physician, where the physician is personally and identifiably responsible. No physician shall pay nor receive a commission for referral of patients.

VIII. A physician should seek consultation upon request, in doubtful or difficult cases or whenever it appears that the quality of medical service any be enhanced thereby.

IX. A physician may not reveal a patient's confidence, or the deficiencies observed in the character of patients, unless required to do so by law or unless it becomes necessary in order to protect the welfare of the individual or of the community.

X. The honored ideals of the medical profession imply that the responsibilities of the physician extend not only to the individual, but also to society. Activities which have the purpose of improving both the health and well-being of the individual and the community deserve the interest and participation of the physician.

XI. To assist the public in obtaining medical services, physicians are permitted to make known their services through advertising. Advertising, however, entails the risk that the physician may employ practices that are false, fraudulent, deceptive, or misleading. Regulation is, therefore, necessary and in the public interest. Subsection II of the *Specific Principles* governing advertising permits public dissemination of truthful information about medical services, while prohibiting false, fraudulent, deceptive or misleading communications, and restricting direct solicitation.

Section 2.—Specific Principles

I. Each member may be subject to disciplinary action, including expulsion, if:

A. The member's right to practice medicine is limited, suspended, or terminated in any state, province, or country for violation of a medical practice act or other statute or governmental regulation or the member is disciplined by any medical licensing authority.

B. The member exhibits medical incompetence.

C. The member is convicted of (or pleads guilty to) a felony or any crime relating to or arising out of the practice of medicine or involving moral turpitude.

D. The member engages in sexual misconduct in the practice of medicine.

E. The member is involved in improper financial dealings such as:

1. Payment and/or acceptance of rebates or referral fees to any person, including agents and employees of the member.

2. Charging exorbitant fees, particularly of non-contractual nature (e.g., emergency care). Fees are exorbitant when they are wholly disproportionate to the services rendered. The reasonableness of fees depends upon the novelty and difficulty of the procedures involved; the skill required to provide proper care; the time and labor required; the fee charged for similar services by similarly situated peers; and whether or not the patient had agreed in advance to the fee.

3. Except in instances of emergencies or urgent and life threatening disease or injury, nothing in the Principle shall be construed to prohibit a member from requiring prepayment of professional fees for an elective surgical operation.

F. The member, either on the member's behalf or, on behalf of a partner or associate or any physician or other affiliated health care provider, uses or participates in the use of any form of communication (including computer imaging and electronic communications) containing a false, fraudulent, deceptive, or misleading statement or claim, including a statement or claim which: (*11/96*)

1. Contains a misrepresentation of fact, or omits to state any material fact necessary to make the statements, considered as a whole, not deceptive or misleading.

2. Contains images of persons or facsimiles thereof which falsely or deceptively portray a physical or medical condition, injury, disease, including obesity, or recovery of relief therefrom.

3. Contains a testimonial pertaining to the quality and efficacy of medical care if the experience of the endorser does not represent the typical experience of other patients or if, due to the infrequency and/or complexity of such care, results in other cases cannot be predicted with any degree of accuracy.

4. Is intended or is likely to create false or unjustified expectations of favorable results.

5. Contains a representation or statement of opinion as to the superior quality of professional services which is not susceptible to verification by the public or contains a statement representing that the member possesses the skills or provides services superior to those of other physicians with similar training unless such representation can be factually substantiated.

6. Appeals primarily to layperson's fears, anxieties, or emotional vulnerabilities.

7. Contains, in reference to any matter material to a patient's decision to utilize a member's services, a representation of fact or implication that is likely to cause an ordinary prudent person to misunderstand or be deceived, or fails to contain reasonable warnings or disclosures necessary to make a representation or implication not deceptive.

8. Contains a prediction of future success or guarantees that satisfaction or a cure will result from the performance of the member's services.

9. States or implies that a member is a board certified specialist unless the member is

certified by a board recognized by the American Board of Medical Specialties.

10. Concerns illegal transactions.

11. Is not identified as a paid advertisement or solicitation unless it is apparent from the context that it is a paid announcement or advertisement.

12. Relates to professional fees other than:

    (a) A statement of the fixed fee charged for a specific professional service, provided that the description of such service would not be misunderstood or be deceptive and that the statement indicates whether additional fees may be incurred for related professional services which may be required in individual cases, and

    (b) A statement of the range of fees for specifically described professional services, provided that there is reasonable disclosure of relevant variables and considerations affecting fees so that the statement would not be misunderstood or be deceptive, including, without limitation, an indication whether additional fees may be incurred for related professional services which may be required in individual cases.

13. Is intended or is likely to attract patients by use of puffery or exaggerated claims.

G. The member performs an unjustified surgical operation or a surgical operation that is not calculated to improve or benefit the patient.

H. The member practices or advertises under a trade name which is false, fraudulent, deceptive or misleading.

 I. The member performs a surgical operation or operations (except on patients whose chances of recovery would be prejudiced by removal to another hospital) under circumstances in which the responsibility for diagnosis or care of the patient is delegated to another who is not qualified to undertake it.

J. The member participates in a charity raffle, fund raising event, contest or other promotion in which the prize is any procedure and the member agrees to perform such procedure. (*1/83, 9/94*)

K. The member seeks or obtains a patent for any invention or discovery of a method or process for performing a surgical procedure, except if the method or process is performed by or as a necessary component of a machine or composition of matter or improvement thereof which is itself patentable subject matter. (*10/95*)

L. The member exhibits unprofessional conduct as defined in the General or Specific Principles of this Code.

II. Advertising

A. Subject to the limitations of Article I, Section F, a member may advertise through public communications media such as professional announcements, telephone and medical directories, computer bulletin boards, Internet web pages and broadcast and electronic media. The following are examples or the types of useful information that could be included in ethical advertising. The list is illustrative and should not be interpreted as excluding other relevant information consistent with the ethical guidelines established herein. (*11/96*)

1. A statement of regular, e-mail, or website addresses, and telephone numbers of the member's offices.

2. A statement of office hours regularly maintained by the member.

3. A statement of language, other than English, fluently spoken by the physician or a person in the physician's office.

4. A statement as to specialty board certification or a statement that the physician's practice is limited to specific fields.

5. A statement that the member provides services under specified private or public insurance plans or health care plans.

6. A statement of names of schools and postgraduate clinical training programs from which the member has graduated together with the degrees received.

7. A listing of the member's publications in educational journals.

8. A statement of teaching positions currently or formerly held by the member together with pertinent dates.

9. A statement of the member's affiliations with hospitals or clinics.

10. A statement that the member regularly accepts installment payments of fees and/or credit cards.

B. A member shall not compensate or give anything of value directly or indirectly to a representative of the press, radio, or television or other communication medium in anticipation or return of recommending the member's services or for professional publicity. If a communication to the public results from a payment by a member, such as a payment to a public relations agent, this must be disclosed unless the nature, format or medium of communication makes that fact apparent. A member may pay the reasonable cost of advertising permitted by this code. A copy or record of an advertisement in its entirety shall be kept for one year after its dissemination. If the paid advertisement is communicated by television or radio, it shall be pre-recorded and approved for broadcast by the member and a recording of the actual transmission shall be retained by the member for one year after its dissemination. A member shall be held personally responsible for any violation of the Code of Ethics by a public relations, advertising or similar firm which he or she retains. (*9/93*)

III. Solicitation

   A. Solicitation means in-person communication to specific individuals to attract them as patients.
   B. A member shall refrain from engaging in systematic verbal solicitation of patients in person, by telephone, or through agents.
   C. A member shall not initiate contact with a prospective patient knowing that the physical, emotional, or mental state or degree of education of the person solicited is such that the person could not exercise reasonable judgement in employing a plastic surgeon.
   D. A member who has given unsolicited, in-person advice to a layperson that the individual should have medical or health care shall not accept employment resulting from that advice if:
      1. The advice embodies or implies a statement or claim that is false, fraudulent, deceptive or misleading within the meaning of Article I, Section F.
      2. The advice involves the use by the member of undue influence, coercion, duress, harassment, intimidation, unwarranted promises of benefits, over persuasion, overreaching, or pressure for immediate response.

      3. The member has been given notice that the individual non-patient does not want to receive communication from the member.

IV. Expert Testimony (*11/96*)

   It is in the public interest that medical expert testimony be readily available, objective and unbiased. Members have an obligation to testify as expert witnesses when appropriate. However, members whose testimony, including testimony as to credentials or qualifications, is false, deceptive, or misleading may be subject to disciplinary action, including expulsion. Further to help limit possibly misleading testimony, members serving as expert witnesses should:
   1. Have recent and substantive experience in the area in which they testify,
   2. Thoroughly review the medical facts and testify to their content fairly, honestly and impartially,
   3. Be familiar with the standards of practice prevailing at the time of the occurrence,
   4. Neither condemn performance that clearly falls within generally accepted practice standards nor endorse or condone performance that clearly falls outside of such standards.

V. Conflicts of Interest

   A physician's clinical judgement and practice must not be affected by economic interest in, commitment to, or benefit from professionally-related commercial enterprises or other actual or potential conflicts of interest. Disclosure of professionally-related commercial interests and any other interests that may influence clinical decision-making is required in communications to patients, the public, and colleagues. When a physician's interest conflicts so greatly with the patient's interest as to be incompatible, the physician should make alternative arrangements for the care of the patient.

   In the context of physician ownership interest in a commercial venture, the physician has an obligation to disclose the ownership interest to the patient or referring colleagues prior to utilization; the physician's activities must be in strict conformance with the law; and the patient should have free choice to use the physician's facility or therapy or to seek the needed services elsewhere.

VI. Enforcement

   Any member charged with a violation of any ethical standard set forth herein may be subject to disciplinary measures, including censure, suspension or expulsion, as described in Article XVIII of the Society's Bylaws.

© American Society of Plastic and Reconstructive Surgeons. Reprinted with permission.

AMERICAN SOCIETY OF SAFETY ENGINEERS

Address: 1800 East Oakton Street
                Des Plaines, IL 60018-2187
Telephone: 847/699-2929
WWW: www.asse.org
Document: Code of Professional Conduct (1974.
                Most recently revised 1993.)

(Prior to 1974, the American Society of Safety Engineers used the code of ethics of the National Society of Professional Engineers. Their code was adapted from the original code formulated by the Committee on Engineering Ethics of the Engineers' Council for Professional Development, now the Accreditation Board for Engineering Technology (ABET). The following version of the code, specifically addressed to safety engineers, acknowledges the fact that substantive changes in bylaws and membership has established safety engineering as a profession with unique responsibilities.—Eds.)

FUNDAMENTAL PRINCIPLES

As a member of the American Society of Safety Engineers, I recognize that my work has an impact on the protection of people, property and the environment.

In order to assume professional responsibility, I shall uphold and advance the integrity, honor and dignity of the safety, health and environmental professional by:

1. Enhancing protection of people, property and the environment through knowledge and skill;

2. Being honest, impartial, and serving the public, employers and clients with fidelity;

3. Striving to increase my competence in and the prestige of the safety profession; and

4. Avoiding circumstances where compromise of the professional conduct or conflict of interest may arise.

FUNDAMENTAL CANONS

In fulfillment of my duties as a safety professional, I shall:

1. Hold paramount the protection of people, property and the environment;

2. Advise employers, clients, employees or appropriate authorities when my professional judgement indicates that the protection of people, property and the environment is unacceptably at risk;

3. Strive for continuous self-development while participating in the safety profession;

4. Perform professional services only in the areas of my competence;

5. Issue public statements only in an objective and truthful manner and in accordance with the authority bestowed upon me;

6. Act in professional matters as faithful agent or trustee and avoid conflict of interest;

7. Build my professional reputation on merit of service; and

8. Assure equal opportunities for individuals under my supervision.

As a member of ASSE, I shall comply with these provisions of the "Code of Professional Conduct."

© American Society of Safety Engineers. Reprinted with permission.

AMERICAN SOCIETY OF TRANSPORTATION AND LOGISTICS, INC.

Address: 229 Peachtree Street, Suite 401
                Atlanta, GA 30303
Telephone: 404/524-3555
WWW: www.astl.org

Document: Code of Ethics of the American
             Society of Transportation and
             Logistics, Inc.

ONE—A person holding membership in the Society, by virtue of having successfully met all of its examination requirements, may use the designation of either "Certified in Transportation and Logistics" (CTL), or "Certified Member—American Society of Transportation and Logistics" (CM-AST&L). A person holding membership in the Society by virtue of having qualified under the Founder requirements, may use the designation "Founder Member—American Society of Transportation and Logistics" (FM-AST&L). A person holding membership in the Society, by virtue of having qualified under the Sustaining requirements, may use the designation "Sustaining Member—American Society of Transportation and Logistics" (SM-AST&L). A person holding membership in the Society, by virtue of having qualified under the Educator requirements, may use the designation "Educator Member—American Society of Transportation and Logistics" (EM-AST&L). A person holding membership in the Society, by virtue of having qualified under the Associate or Affiliate requirements, may use the designation "Associate or Affiliate Member—American Society of Transportation and Logistics" (AM-AST&L or AF-AST&L). A person who has qualified in any of the above categories and who has retired from active pursuit of the profession shall be entitled to use the designation "Member Emeritus—American Society of Transportation and Logistics" (ME-AST&L).

TWO—A person holding membership in the Society shall strictly observe any law or laws regarding the use and application of the title "Transportation and Logistics Manager," or other similar designations, which may be in effect in the particular state or states in which such member resides, is employed, or engages in practice.

THREE—The conduct of those holding membership in this Society with each other and before the public generally should be characterized by candor and fairness, and should be such as to uphold at all times the honor of their calling and to maintain the dignity of their profession.

FOUR—A person holding membership in the Society shall consider and hold confidential all information received in the course of employment, and shall not disclose same except upon authority of the client or

clients to which such information properly belongs, or when required to do so by a mandate of law.

FIVE—No one holding membership in the Society shall undertake to render professional services under any circumstances or upon any terms that would jeopardize the good name of the profession or impair the standing of any other person.

SIX—Those holding membership in the Society are hereby deemed responsible for the professional conduct of persons in their employ. Consequently, they should, through exemplary conduct on their own part, strive at all times to secure observance by their employees of this code of ethics.

© American Society of Transportation and Logistics, Inc. Reprinted with permission.

MEMBER
ASTA
**American Society
of Travel Agents**
*Integrity in Travel®
Worldwide*

AMERICAN SOCIETY OF TRAVEL AGENTS

Address: 1101 King Street
               Alexandria, VA 22314
Telephone: 703/739-2782
WWW: www.astanet.com
Document: Code of Ethics (1997)

Preamble
We live in a world in which travel has become both increasingly important and complex in its variety of modes and choices. Travelers are faced with a myriad of alternatives as to transportation, accommodations and other travel services. Travelers must depend on travel agencies and others in the industry to guide them honestly and competently. Similarly, carriers, hotels and other suppliers must provide to the traveler the product as it was advertised. All ASTA members pledge themselves to conduct their business activities in a manner that promotes the ideal of integrity in travel and agree to act in accordance with the following Principles of the ASTA Code of Ethics. Complaints arising under this Code should be filed in writing with the ASTA Consumer Affairs Department.

Responsibilities of All Members

1. Accuracy.
ASTA members will be factual and accurate when providing information about their services and the services of any firm they represent. They will not use deceptive practices.

2. Disclosure.
ASTA members will provide complete details about terms and conditions of any travel service, including cancellation and service fee policies, before accepting non-refundable payment for the booking.

3. Notice.
ASTA members operating tours will promptly advise the agent or client who reserved the space of any change in itinerary, services, features or price. If substantial changes are made that are within the control of the operator, the client will be allowed to cancel without penalty.

4. Delivery.
ASTA members operating tours will provide all components as stated in their brochure or written confirmation, or provide alternate services of equal or greater value, or provide appropriate compensation.

5. Responsiveness.
ASTA members will promptly respond to their clients' complaints.

6. Refunds.
ASTA members will remit any undisputed funds under their control within the specified time limit. Reasons for delay in providing funds will be given to the claimant promptly.

7. Cooperation.
ASTA members will cooperate with any inquiry conducted by ASTA to resolve any dispute involving consumers or another member.

8. Confidences.
ASTA members will not use improperly obtained client lists or other confidential information obtained from an employee's former employer.

9. Confidentiality.
ASTA members will treat every client transaction confidentially and not disclose any information without permission of the client, unless required by law.

10. Affiliation.
ASTA members will not falsely represent a person's affiliation with their firm.

11. Credentials.
An ASTA member shall not, in exchange for money or otherwise, provide travel agent credentials to any person as to whom there is no reasonable expectation that the person will engage in a bona fide effort to sell or manage the sale of travel services to the general public on behalf of the member through the period of validity of such credentials. This principle applies to the ASTA member and all affiliated or commonly controlled enterprises.

12. Conflict of Interest.
ASTA members will not allow any preferred relationship with a supplier to interfere with the interests of their clients.

13. Compliance.
ASTA members shall abide by all federal, state and local laws and regulations.

Conclusion
Adherence to the Principles of the ASTA Code of Ethics signifies competence, fair dealing and high integrity. Failure to adhere to these Principles may subject a member to disciplinary action, as set forth in ASTA's Bylaws.

© American Society of Travel Agents, Inc. Reprinted with permission.

AMERICAN SOCIOLOGICAL ASSOCIATION

**AMERICAN
SOCIOLOGICAL
ASSOCIATION**

Address: 1307 New York Avenue NW, Suite 700
             Washington, DC 20005

Telephone: 202/383-9005
WWW: www.asanet.org
Document: Code of Ethics (1997)

INTRODUCTION

The American Sociological Association's (ASA's) Code of Ethics sets forth the principles and ethical standards that underlie sociologists' professional responsibilities and conduct. These principles and standards should be used as guidelines when examining everyday professional activities. They constitute normative statements for sociologists and provide guidance on issues that sociologists may encounter in their professional work.

ASA's Code of Ethics consists of an Introduction, a Preamble, five General Principles, and specific Ethical Standards. This Code is also accompanied by the Rules and Procedures of the ASA Committee on Professional Ethics which describe the procedures for filing, investigating, and resolving complaints of unethical conduct.

The Preamble and General Principles of the Code are aspirational goals to guide sociologists toward the highest ideals of sociology. Although the Preamble and General Principles are not enforceable rules, they should be considered by sociologists in arriving at an ethical course of action and may be considered by ethics bodies in interpreting the Ethical Standards.

The Ethical Standards set forth enforceable rules for conduct by sociologists. Most of the Ethical Standards are written broadly in order to apply to sociologists in varied roles, and the application of an Ethical Standard may vary depending on the context. The Ethical Standards are not exhaustive. Any conduct that is not specifically addressed by this Code of Ethics is not necessarily ethical or unethical.

Membership in the ASA commits members to adhere to the ASA Code of Ethics and to the Policies and Procedures of the ASA Committee on Professional Ethics. Members are advised of this obligation upon joining the Association and that violations of the Code may lead to the imposition of sanctions, including termination of membership. ASA members subject to the Code of Ethics may be reviewed under these Ethical Standards only if the activity is part of or affects their work-related functions, or if the activity is sociological in nature. Personal activities having no connection to or effect on sociologists' performance of their professional roles are not subject to the Code of Ethics.

PREAMBLE

This Code of Ethics articulates a common set of values upon which sociologists build their professional and scientific work. The Code is intended to provide both the general principles and the rules to cover professional situations encountered by sociologists. It has as its primary goal the welfare and protection of the individuals and groups with whom sociologists work. It is the individual responsibility of each sociologist to aspire to the highest possible standards of conduct in research, teaching, practice, and service.

The development of a dynamic set of ethical standards for a sociologist's work-related conduct requires a personal commitment to a lifelong effort to act ethically; to encourage ethical behavior by students, supervisors, supervisees, employers, employees, and colleagues; and to consult with others as needed concerning ethical problems. Each sociologist supplements, but does not violate, the values and rules specified in the Code of Ethics based on guidance drawn from personal values, culture, and experience.

GENERAL PRINCIPLES

The following General Principles are aspirational and serve as a guide for sociologists in determining ethical courses of action in various contexts. They exemplify the highest ideals of professional conduct.

Principle A: Professional Competence

Sociologists strive to maintain the highest levels of competence in their work; they recognize the limitations of their expertise; and they undertake only those tasks for which they are qualified by education, training, or experience. They recognize the need for ongoing education in order to remain professionally competent; and they utilize the appropriate scientific, professional, technical, and administrative resources needed to ensure competence in their professional activities. They consult with other professionals when necessary for the benefit of their students, research participants, and clients.

Principle B: Integrity

Sociologists are honest, fair, and respectful of others in their professional activities—in research, teaching, practice, and service. Sociologists do not knowingly act in ways that jeopardize either their own or others' professional welfare. Sociologists conduct their affairs in ways that inspire trust and confidence; they do not knowingly make statements that are false, misleading, or deceptive.

Principle C: Professional and Scientific Responsibility

Sociologists adhere to the highest scientific and professional standards and accept responsibility for their work. Sociologists understand that they form a community and show respect for other sociologists even when they disagree on theoretical, methodological, or personal approaches to professional activities. Sociologists value the public trust in sociology and are concerned about their ethical behavior and that of other sociologists that might compromise that trust. While endeavoring always to be collegial, sociologists must never let the desire to be collegial outweigh their shared responsibility for ethical behavior. When appropriate, they consult with colleagues in order to prevent or avoid unethical conduct.

Principle D: Respect for People's Rights, Dignity, and Diversity

Sociologists respect the rights, dignity, and worth of all people. They strive to eliminate bias in their professional activities, and they do not tolerate any forms of discrimination based on age; gender; race; ethnicity; national origin; religion; sexual orientation; disability; health conditions; or marital, domestic, or parental status. They are sensitive to cultural, individual, and role differences in serving, teaching, and studying groups of people with distinctive characteristics. In all of their work-related activities, sociologists acknowledge the rights of others to hold values, attitudes, and opinions that differ from their own.

Principle E: Social Responsibility

Sociologists are aware of their professional and scientific responsibility to the communities and societies in which they live and work. They apply and make public their knowledge in order to contribute to the public good. When undertaking research, they strive to advance the science of sociology and to serve the public good.

ETHICAL STANDARDS

1. Professional and Scientific Standards

Sociologists adhere to the highest possible technical standards that are reasonable and responsible in their research, teaching, practice, and service activities. They rely on scientifically and professionally derived knowledge; act with honesty and integrity; and avoid untrue, deceptive, or undocumented statements in undertaking work-related functions or activities.

2. Competence

(a) Sociologists conduct research, teach, practice, and provide service only within the boundaries of their competence, based on their education, training, supervised experience, or appropriate professional experience.

(b) Sociologists conduct research, teach, practice, and provide service in new areas or involving new techniques only after they have taken reasonable steps to ensure the competence of their work in these areas.

(c) Sociologists who engage in research, teaching, practice, or service maintain awareness of current scientific and professional information in their fields of activity, and undertake continuing efforts to maintain competence in the skills they use.

(d) Sociologists refrain from undertaking an activity when their personal circumstances may interfere with their professional work or lead to harm for a student, supervisee, human subject, client, colleague, or other person to whom they have a scientific, teaching, consulting, or other professional obligation.

3. Representation and Misuse of Expertise

(a) In research, teaching, practice, service, or other situations where sociologists render professional judgments or present their expertise, they accurately and fairly represent their areas and degrees of expertise.

(b) Sociologists do not accept grants, contracts, consultation, or work assignments from individual or organizational clients or sponsors that appear likely to require violation of the standards in this Code of Ethics. Sociologists dissociate themselves from such activities when they discover a violation and are unable to achieve its correction.

(c) Because sociologists' scientific and professional judgments and actions may affect the lives of others, they are alert to and guard against personal, financial, social, organizational, or political factors that might lead to misuse of their knowledge, expertise, or influence.

(d) If sociologists learn of misuse or misrepresentation of their work, they take reasonable steps to correct or minimize the misuse or misrepresentation.

4. Delegation and Supervision

(a) Sociologists provide proper training and supervision to their students, supervisees, or employees and take reasonable steps to see that such persons perform services responsibly, competently, and ethically.

(b) Sociologists delegate to their students, supervisees, or employees only those responsibilities that such persons, based on their education, training, or experience, can reasonably be expected to perform either independently or with the level of supervision provided.

5. Nondiscrimination

Sociologists do not engage in discrimination in their work based on age; gender; race; ethnicity; national origin; religion; sexual orientation; disability; health conditions; marital, domestic, or parental status; or any other applicable basis proscribed by law.

6. Non-exploitation

(a) Whether for personal, economic, or professional advantage, sociologists do not exploit persons over whom they have direct or indirect supervisory, evaluative, or other authority such as students, supervisees, employees, or research participants.

(b) Sociologists do not directly supervise or exercise evaluative authority over any person with whom they have a sexual relationship, including students, supervisees, employees, or research participants.

7. Harassment

Sociologists do not engage in harassment of any person, including students, supervisees, employees, or research participants. Harassment consists of a single intense and severe act or of multiple persistent or pervasive acts which are demeaning, abusive, offensive, or create a hostile professional or workplace environment. Sexual harassment may include sexual solicitation, physical advance, or verbal or non-verbal conduct that is sexual in nature. Racial harassment may include unnecessary, exaggerated, or unwarranted attention or attack, whether verbal or non-verbal, because of a person's race or ethnicity.

8. Employment Decisions

Sociologists have an obligation to adhere to the highest ethical standards when participating in employment related decisions, when seeking employment, or when planning to resign from a position.

8.01 Fair Employment Practices

(a) When participating in employment-related decisions, sociologists make every effort to ensure equal opportunity and fair treatment to all full- and part-time employees. They do not discrimi-

nate in hiring, promotion, salary, treatment, or any other conditions of employment or career development on the basis of age; gender; race; ethnicity; national origin; religion; sexual orientation; disability; health conditions; marital, domestic, or parental status; or any other applicable basis proscribed by law.

(b) When participating in employment-related decisions, sociologists specify the requirements for hiring, promotion, tenure, and termination and communicate these requirements thoroughly to full- and part-time employees and prospective employees.

(c) When participating in employment-related decisions, sociologists have the responsibility to be informed of fair employment codes, to communicate this information to employees, and to help create an atmosphere upholding fair employment practices for full- and part-time employees.

(d) When participating in employment-related decisions, sociologists inform prospective full- and part-time employees of any constraints on research and publication and negotiate clear understandings about any conditions that may limit research and scholarly activity.

8.02 Responsibilities of Employees

(a) When seeking employment, sociologists provide prospective employers with accurate and complete information on their professional qualifications and experiences.

(b) When leaving a position, permanently or temporarily, sociologists provide their employers with adequate notice and take reasonable steps to reduce negative effects of leaving.

9. Conflicts of Interest

Sociologists maintain the highest degree of integrity in their professional work and avoid conflicts of interest and the appearance of conflict. Conflicts of interest arise when sociologists' personal or financial interests prevent them from performing their professional work in an unbiased manner. In research, teaching, practice, and service, sociologists are alert to situations that might cause a conflict of interest and take appropriate action to prevent conflict or disclose it to appropriate parties.

9.01 Adherence to Professional Standards

Irrespective of their personal or financial interests or those of their employers or clients, sociologists adhere to professional and scientific standards in (1) the collection, analysis, or interpretation of data; (2) the reporting of research; (3) the teaching, professional presentation, or public dissemination of sociological knowledge; and (4) the identification or implementation of appropriate contractual, consulting, or service activities.

9.02 Disclosure
Sociologists disclose relevant sources of financial support and relevant personal or professional relationships that may have the appearance of or potential for a conflict of interest to an employer or client, to the sponsors of their professional work, or in public speeches and writing.

9.03 Avoidance of Personal Gain
(a) Under all circumstances, sociologists do not use or otherwise seek to gain from information or material received in a confidential context (e.g., knowledge obtained from reviewing a manuscript or serving on a proposal review panel), unless they have authorization to do so or until that information is otherwise made publicly available.
(b) Under all circumstances, sociologists do not seek to gain from information or material in an employment or client relationship without permission of the employer or client.

9.04 Decisionmaking in the Workplace
In their workplace, sociologists take appropriate steps to avoid conflicts of interest or the appearance of conflicts, and carefully scrutinize *potentially biasing* affiliations or relationships. In research, teaching, practice, or service, such potentially biasing affiliations or relationships include, but are not limited to, situations involving family, business, or close personal friendships or those with whom sociologists have had strong conflict or disagreement.

9.05 Decisionmaking Outside of the Workplace
In professional activities outside of their workplace, sociologists in *all* circumstances abstain from engaging in deliberations and decisions that allocate or withhold benefits or rewards from individuals or institutions if they have *biasing* affiliations or relationships. These biasing affiliations or relationships are: 1) current employment or being considered for employment at an organization or institution that could be construed as benefiting from the decision; 2) current officer or board member of an organization or institution that could be construed as benefiting from the decision; 3) current employment or being considered for employment at the same organization or institution where an individual could benefit from the

decision; 4) a spouse, domestic partner, or known relative who as an individual could benefit from the decision; or 5) a current business or professional partner, research collaborator, employee, supervisee, or student who as an individual could benefit from the decision.

10. Public Communication
Sociologists adhere to the highest professional standards in public communications about their professional services, credentials and expertise, work products, or publications, whether these communications are from themselves or from others.

10.01 Public Communications
(a) Sociologists take steps to ensure the accuracy of all public communications. Such public communications include, but are not limited to, directory listings; personal resumes or curriculum vitae; advertising; brochures or printed matter; interviews or comments to the media; statements in legal proceedings; lectures and public oral presentations; or other published materials.
(b) Sociologists do not make public statements that are false, deceptive, misleading, or fraudulent, either because of what they state, convey, or suggest or because of what they omit, concerning their research, practice, or other work activities or those of persons or organizations with which they are affiliated. Such activities include, but are not limited to, false or deceptive statements concerning sociologists' (1) training, experience, or competence; (2) academic degrees; (3) credentials; (4) institutional or association affiliations; (5) services; (6) fees; or (7) publications or research findings. Sociologists do not make false or deceptive statements concerning the scientific basis for, results of, or degree of success from their professional services.
(c) When sociologists provide professional advice or comment by means of public lectures, demonstrations, radio or television programs, prerecorded tapes, printed articles, mailed material, or other media, they take reasonable precautions to ensure that (1) the statements are based on appropriate research, literature, and practice; and (2) the statements are otherwise consistent with this Code of Ethics.

10.02 Statements by Others
(a) Sociologists who engage or employ others to create or place public statements that promote their

work products, professional services, or other activities retain responsibility for such statements.

(b) Sociologists make reasonable efforts to prevent others whom they do not directly engage, employ, or supervise (such as employers, publishers, sponsors, organizational clients, members of the media) from making deceptive statements concerning their professional research, teaching, or practice activities.

(c) In working with the press, radio, television, or other communications media or in advertising in the media, sociologists are cognizant of potential conflicts of interest or appearances of such conflicts (e.g., they do not provide compensation to employees of the media), and they adhere to the highest standards of professional honesty (e.g., they acknowledge paid advertising).

11. Confidentiality

Sociologists have an obligation to ensure that confidential information is protected. They do so to ensure the integrity of research and the open communication with research participants and to protect sensitive information obtained in research, teaching, practice, and service. When gathering confidential information, sociologists should take into account the long-term uses of the information, including its potential placement in public archives or the examination of the information by other researchers or practitioners.

11.01 Maintaining Confidentiality

(a) Sociologists take reasonable precautions to protect the confidentiality rights of research participants, students, employees, clients, or others.

(b) Confidential information provided by research participants, students, employees, clients, or others is treated as such by sociologists even if there is no legal protection or privilege to do so. Sociologists have an obligation to protect confidential information, and not allow information gained in confidence from being used in ways that would unfairly compromise research participants, students, employees, clients, or others.

(c) Information provided under an understanding of confidentiality is treated as such even after the death of those providing that information.

(d) Sociologists maintain the integrity of confidential deliberations, activities, or roles, including, where applicable, that of professional committees, review panels, or advisory groups (e.g., the ASA Committee on Professional Ethics).

(e) Sociologists, to the extent possible, protect the confidentiality of student records, performance data, and personal information, whether verbal or written, given in the context of academic consultation, supervision, or advising.

(f) The obligation to maintain confidentiality extends to members of research or training teams and collaborating organizations who have access to the information. To ensure that access to confidential information is restricted, it is the responsibility of researchers, administrators, and principal investigators to instruct staff to take the steps necessary to protect confidentiality.

(g) When using private information about individuals collected by other persons or institutions, sociologists protect the confidentiality of individually identifiable information. Information is private when an individual can reasonably expect that the information will not be made public with personal identifiers (e.g., medical or employment records).

11.02 Limits of Confidentiality

(a) Sociologists inform themselves fully about all laws and rules which may limit or alter guarantees of confidentiality. They determine their ability to guarantee absolute confidentiality and, as appropriate, inform research participants, students, employees, clients, or others of any limitations to this guarantee at the outset consistent with ethical standards set forth in 11.02(b).

(b) Sociologists may confront unanticipated circumstances where they become aware of information that is clearly health- or life-threatening to research participants, students, employees, clients, or others. In these cases, sociologists balance the importance of guarantees of confidentiality with other principles in this Code of Ethics, standards of conduct, and applicable law.

(c) Confidentiality is not required with respect to observations in public places, activities conducted in public, or other settings where no rules of privacy are provided by law or custom. Similarly, confidentiality is not required in the case of information available from public records.

11.03 Discussing Confidentiality and Its Limits

(a) When sociologists establish a scientific or professional relationship with persons, they discuss (1) the relevant limitations on confidentiality, and (2) the foreseeable uses of the information generated through their professional work.

(b) Unless it is not feasible or is counter-productive, the discussion of confidentiality occurs at the outset of the relationship and thereafter as new circumstances may warrant.

11.04 Anticipation of Possible Uses of Information

(a) When research requires maintaining personal identifiers in databases or systems of records, sociologists delete such identifiers before the information is made publicly available.

(b) When confidential information concerning research participants, clients, or other recipients of service is entered into databases or systems of records available to persons without the prior consent of the relevant parties, sociologists protect anonymity by not including personal identifiers or by employing other techniques that mask or control disclosure of individual identities.

(c) When deletion of personal identifiers is not feasible, sociologists take reasonable steps to determine that appropriate consent of personally-identifiable individuals has been obtained before they transfer such data to others or review such data collected by others.

11.05 Electronic Transmission of Confidential Information

Sociologists use extreme care in delivering or transferring any confidential data, information, or communication over public computer networks. Sociologists are attentive to the problems of maintaining confidentiality and control over sensitive material and data when use of technological innovations, such as public computer networks, may open their professional and scientific communication to unauthorized persons.

11.06 Anonymity of Sources

(a) Sociologists do not disclose in their writings, lectures, or other public media confidential, personally identifiable information concerning their research participants, students, individual or organizational clients, or other recipients of their service which is obtained during the course of their work, unless consent from individuals or their legal representatives has been obtained.

(b) When confidential information is used in scientific and professional presentations, sociologists disguise the identity of research participants, students, individual or organizational clients, or other recipients of their service.

11.07 Minimizing Intrusions on Privacy

(a) To minimize intrusions on privacy, sociologists include in written and oral reports, consultations, and public communications only information germane to the purpose for which the communication is made.

(b) Sociologists discuss confidential information or evaluative data concerning research participants, students, supervisees, employees, and individual or organizational clients only for appropriate scientific or professional purposes and only with persons clearly concerned with such matters.

11.08 Preservation of Confidential Information

(a) Sociologists take reasonable steps to ensure that records, data, or information are preserved in a confidential manner consistent with the requirements of this Code of Ethics, recognizing that ownership of records, data, or information may also be governed by law or institutional principles.

(b) Sociologists plan so that confidentiality of records, data, or information is protected in the event of the sociologist's death, incapacity, or withdrawal from the position or practice.

(c) When sociologists transfer confidential records, data, or information to other persons or organizations, they obtain assurances that the recipients of the records, data, or information will employ measures to protect confidentiality at least equal to those originally pledged.

12. Informed Consent

Informed consent is a basic ethical tenet of scientific research on human populations. Sociologists do not involve a human being as a subject in research without the informed consent of the subject or the subject's legally authorized representative, except as otherwise specified in this Code. Sociologists recognize the possibility of undue influence or subtle pressures on subjects that may derive from researchers' expertise or authority, and they take this into account in designing informed consent procedures.

12.01 Scope of Informed Consent

(a) Sociologists conducting research obtain consent from research participants or their legally authorized representatives (1) when data are collected from research participants through any form of communication, interaction, or intervention; or (2) when behavior of research participants occurs in a private context where an individual can reasonably expect that no observation or reporting is taking place.

(b) Despite the paramount importance of consent, sociologists may seek waivers of this standard when (1) the research involves no more than minimal risk for research participants, and (2) the research could not practicably be carried out were informed consent to be required. Sociologists recognize that waivers of consent require approval from institutional review boards or, in the absence of such boards, from another authoritative body with expertise on the ethics of research. Under such circumstances, the confidentiality of any personally identifiable information must be maintained unless otherwise set forth in 11.02(b).

(c) Sociologists may conduct research in public places or use publicly available information about individuals (e.g., naturalistic observations in public places, analysis of public records, or archival research) without obtaining consent. If, under such circumstances, sociologists have any doubt whatsoever about the need for informed consent, they consult with institutional review boards or, in the absence of such boards, with another authoritative body with expertise on the ethics of research before proceeding with such research.

(d) In undertaking research with vulnerable populations (e.g., youth, recent immigrant populations, the mentally ill), sociologists take special care to ensure that the voluntary nature of the research is understood and that consent is not coerced. In all other respects, sociologists adhere to the principles set forth in 12.01(a)-(c).

(e) Sociologists are familiar with and conform to applicable state and federal regulations and, where applicable, institutional review board requirements for obtaining informed consent for research.

12.02 Informed Consent Process

(a) When informed consent is required, sociologists enter into an agreement with research participants or their legal representatives that clarifies the nature of the research and the responsibilities of the investigator prior to conducting the research.

(b) When informed consent is required, sociologists use language that is understandable to and respectful of research participants or their legal representatives.

(c) When informed consent is required, sociologists provide research participants or their legal representatives with the opportunity to ask questions about any aspect of the research, at any time during or after their participation in the research.

(d) When informed consent is required, sociologists inform research participants or their legal representatives of the nature of the research; they indicate to participants that their participation or continued participation is voluntary; they inform participants of significant factors that may be expected to influence their willingness to participate (e.g., possible risks and benefits of their participation); and they explain other aspects of the research and respond to questions from prospective participants. Also, if relevant, sociologists explain that refusal to participate or withdrawal from participation in the research involves no penalty, and they explain any foreseeable consequences of declining or withdrawing. Sociologists explicitly discuss confidentiality and, if applicable, the extent to which confidentiality may be limited as set forth in 11.02(b).

(e) When informed consent is required, sociologists keep records regarding said consent. They recognize that consent is a process that involves oral and/or written consent.

(f) Sociologists honor all commitments they have made to research participants as part of the informed consent process except where unanticipated circumstances demand otherwise as set forth in 11.02(b).

12.03 Informed Consent of Students and Subordinates

When undertaking research at their own institutions or organizations with research participants who are students or subordinates, sociologists take special care to protect the prospective subjects from adverse consequences of declining or withdrawing from participation.

12.04 Informed Consent with Children

(a) In undertaking research with children, sociologists obtain the consent of children to participate, to the extent that they are capable of providing such consent, except under circumstances where consent may not be required as set forth in 12.01(b).

(b) In undertaking research with children, sociologists obtain the consent of a parent or a legally authorized guardian. Sociologists may seek waivers of parental or guardian consent when (1) the research involves no more than minimal risk for the research participants, and (2) the research could not practically be carried out were consent to be required, or (3) the consent of a parent or guardian is not a reasonable requirement to protect the child (e.g., neglected or abused children).

(c) Sociologists recognize that waivers of consent from a child and a parent or guardian require approval from institutional review boards or, in the absence of such boards, from another authoritative body with expertise on the ethics of research. Under such circumstances, the confidentiality of any personally identifiable information must be maintained unless otherwise set forth in 11.02(b).

12.05 Use of Deception in Research

(a) Sociologists do not use deceptive techniques (1) unless they have determined that their use will not be harmful to research participants; is justified by the study's prospective scientific, educational, or applied value; and that equally effective alternative procedures that do not use deception are not feasible, and (2) unless they have obtained the approval of institutional review boards or, in the absence of such boards, with another authoritative body with expertise on the ethics of research.

(b) Sociologists never deceive research participants about significant aspects of the research that would affect their willingness to participate, such as physical risks, discomfort, or unpleasant emotional experiences.

(c) When deception is an integral feature of the design and conduct of research, sociologists attempt to correct any misconception that research participants may have no later than at the conclusion of the research.

(d) On rare occasions, sociologists may need to conceal their identity in order to undertake research that could not practically be carried out were they to be known as researchers. Under such circumstances, sociologists undertake the research if it involves no more than minimal risk for the research participants and if they have obtained approval to proceed in this manner from an institutional review board or, in the absence of such boards, from another authoritative body with expertise on the ethics of research. Under such circumstances, confidentiality must be maintained unless otherwise set forth in 11.02(b).

12.06 Use of Recording Technology

Sociologists obtain informed consent from research participants, students, employees, clients, or others prior to videotaping, filming, or recording them in any form, unless these activities involve simply naturalistic observations in public places and it is not anticipated that the recording will be used in a manner that could cause personal identification or harm.

13. Research Planning, Implementation, and Dissemination

Sociologists have an obligation to promote the integrity of research and to ensure that they comply with the ethical tenets of science in the planning, implementation, and dissemination of research. They do so in order to advance knowledge, to minimize the possibility that results will be misleading, and to protect the rights of research participants.

13.01 Planning and Implementation

(a) In planning and implementing research, sociologists minimize the possibility that results will be misleading.

(b) Sociologists take steps to implement protections for the rights and welfare of research participants and other persons affected by the research.

(c) In their research, sociologists do not encourage activities or themselves behave in ways that are health- or life-threatening to research participants or others.

(d) In planning and implementing research, sociologists consult those with expertise concerning any special population under investigation or likely to be affected.

(e) In planning and implementing research, sociologists consider its ethical acceptability as set forth in the Code of Ethics. If the best ethical practice is unclear, sociologists consult with institutional review boards or, in the absence of such review processes, with another authoritative body with expertise on the ethics of research.

(f) Sociologists are responsible for the ethical conduct of research conducted by them or by others under their supervision or authority.

13.02 Unanticipated Research Opportunities

If during the course of teaching, practice, service, or non-professional activities, sociologists determine that they wish to undertake research that was not previously anticipated, they make known their intentions and take steps to ensure that the research can be undertaken consonant with ethical principles, especially those relating to confidentiality and informed consent. Under such circumstances, sociologists seek the approval of institutional review boards or, in the absence of such review processes, another authoritative body with expertise on the ethics of research.

13.03 Offering Inducements for Research Participants
Sociologists do not offer excessive or inappropriate financial or other inducements to obtain the participation of research participants, particularly when it might coerce participation. Sociologists may provide incentives to the extent that resources are available and appropriate.

13.04 Reporting on Research
(a) Sociologists disseminate their research findings except where unanticipated circumstances (e.g., the health of the researcher) or proprietary agreements with employers, contractors, or clients preclude such dissemination.
(b) Sociologists do not fabricate data or falsify results in their publications or presentations.
(c) In presenting their work, sociologists report their findings fully and do not omit relevant data. They report results whether they support or contradict the expected outcomes.
(d) Sociologists take particular care to state all relevant qualifications on the findings and interpretation of their research. Sociologists also disclose underlying assumptions, theories, methods, measures, and research designs that might bear upon findings and interpretations of their work.
(e) Consistent with the spirit of full disclosure of methods and analyses, once findings are publicly disseminated, sociologists permit their open assessment and verification by other responsible researchers with appropriate safeguards, where applicable, to protect the anonymity of research participants.
(f) If sociologists discover significant errors in their publication or presentation of data, they take reasonable steps to correct such errors in a correction, a retraction, published errata, or other public fora as appropriate.
(g) Sociologists report sources of financial support in their written papers and note any special relations to any sponsor. In special circumstances, sociologists may withhold the names of specific sponsors if they provide an adequate and full description of the nature and interest of the sponsor.

(h) Sociologists take special care to report accurately the results of others' scholarship by using correct information and citations when presenting the work of others in publications, teaching, practice, and service settings.

13.05 Data Sharing
(a) Sociologists share data and pertinent documentation as a regular practice. Sociologists make their data available after completion of the project or its major publications, except where proprietary agreements with employers, contractors, or clients preclude such accessibility or when it is impossible to share data and protect the confidentiality of the data or the anonymity of research participants (e.g., raw field notes or detailed information from ethnographic interviews).
(b) Sociologists anticipate data sharing as an integral part of a research plan whenever data sharing is feasible.
(c) Sociologists share data in a form that is consonant with research participants' interests and protect the confidentiality of the information they have been given. They maintain the confidentiality of data, whether legally required or not; remove personal identifiers before data are shared; and if necessary use other disclosure avoidance techniques.
(d) Sociologists who do not otherwise place data in public archives keep data available and retain documentation relating to the research for a reasonable period of time after publication or dissemination of results.
(e) Sociologists may ask persons who request their data for further analysis to bear the associated incremental costs, if necessary.
(f) Sociologists who use data from others for further analyses explicitly acknowledge the contribution of the initial researchers.

14. Plagiarism
(a) In publications, presentations, teaching, practice, and service, sociologists explicitly identify, credit, and reference the author when they take data or material verbatim from another person's written work, whether it is published, unpublished, or electronically available.
(b) In their publications, presentations, teaching, practice, and service, sociologists provide acknowledgment of and reference to the use of others' work, even if the work is not quoted verbatim or paraphrased, and they do not present

others' work as their own whether it is published, unpublished, or electronically available.

15. Authorship Credit

(a) Sociologists take responsibility and credit, including authorship credit, only for work they have actually performed or to which they have contributed.

(b) Sociologists ensure that principal authorship and other publication credits are based on the relative scientific or professional contributions of the individuals involved, regardless of their status. In claiming or determining the ordering of authorship, sociologists seek to reflect accurately the contributions of main participants in the research and writing process.

(c) A student is usually listed as principal author on any multiple authored publication that substantially derives from the student's dissertation or thesis.

16. Publication Process

Sociologists adhere to the highest ethical standards when participating in publication and review processes when they are authors or editors.

16.01 Submission of Manuscripts for Publication

(a) In cases of multiple authorship, sociologists confer with all other authors prior to submitting work for publication and establish mutually acceptable agreements regarding submission.

(b) In submitting a manuscript to a professional journal, book series, or edited book, sociologists grant that publication first claim to publication except where explicit policies allow multiple submissions. Sociologists do not submit a manuscript to a second publication until after an official decision has been received from the first publication or until the manuscript is withdrawn. Sociologists submitting a manuscript for publication in a journal, book series, or edited book can withdraw a manuscript from consideration up until an official acceptance is made.

(c) Sociologists may submit a book manuscript to multiple publishers. However, once sociologists have signed a contract, they cannot withdraw a manuscript from publication unless there is reasonable cause to do so.

16.02 Duplicate Publication of Data

When sociologists publish data or findings that they have previously published elsewhere, they accompany these publications by proper acknowledgment.

16.03 Responsibilities of Editors

(a) When serving as editors of journals or book series, sociologists are fair in the application of standards and operate without personal or ideological favoritism or malice. As editors, sociologists are cognizant of any potential conflicts of interest.

(b) When serving as editors of journals or book series, sociologists ensure the confidential nature of the review process and supervise editorial office staff, including students, in accordance with practices that maintain confidentiality.

(c) When serving as editors of journals or book series, sociologists are bound to publish all manuscripts accepted for publication unless major errors or ethical violations are discovered after acceptance (e.g., plagiarism or scientific misconduct).

(d) When serving as editors of journals or book series, sociologists ensure the anonymity of reviewers unless they otherwise receive permission from reviewers to reveal their identity. Editors ensure that their staff conform to this practice.

(e) When serving as journal editors, sociologists ensure the anonymity of authors unless and until a manuscript is accepted for publication or unless the established practices of the journal are known to be otherwise.

(f) When serving as journal editors, sociologists take steps to provide for the timely review of all manuscripts and respond promptly to inquiries about the status of the review.

17. Responsibilities of Reviewers

(a) In reviewing material submitted for publication, grant support, or other evaluation purposes, sociologists respect the confidentiality of the process and the proprietary rights in such information of those who submitted it.

(b) Sociologists disclose conflicts of interest or decline requests for reviews of the work of others where conflicts of interest are involved.

(c) Sociologists decline requests for reviews of the work of others when they believe that the review process may be biased or when they have questions about the integrity of the process.

(d) If asked to review a manuscript, book, or proposal they have previously reviewed, sociologists make it known to the person making the request (e.g., editor, program officer) unless it is clear that they are being asked to provide a reappraisal.

18. Education, Teaching, and Training

As teachers, supervisors, and trainers, sociologists follow the highest ethical standards in order to ensure the quality of sociological education and the integrity of the teacher-student relationship.

18.01 Administration of Education Programs

(a) Sociologists who are responsible for education and training programs seek to ensure that the programs are competently designed, provide the proper experiences, and meet all goals for which claims are made by the program.

(b) Sociologists responsible for education and training programs seek to ensure that there is an accurate description of the program content, training goals and objectives, and requirements that must be met for satisfactory completion of the program.

(c) Sociologists responsible for education and training programs take steps to ensure that graduate assistants and temporary instructors have the substantive knowledge required to teach courses and the teaching skills needed to facilitate student learning.

(d) Sociologists responsible for education and training programs have an obligation to ensure that ethics are taught to their graduate students as part of their professional preparation.

18.02 Teaching and Training

(a) Sociologists conscientiously perform their teaching responsibilities. They have appropriate skills and knowledge or are receiving appropriate training.

(b) Sociologists provide accurate information at the outset about their courses, particularly regarding the subject matter to be covered, bases for evaluation, and the nature of course experiences.

(c) Sociologists make decisions concerning textbooks, course content, course requirements, and grading solely on the basis of educational criteria without regard for financial or other incentives.

(d) Sociologists provide proper training and supervision to their teaching assistants and other teaching trainees and take reasonable steps to ensure that such persons perform these teaching responsibilities responsibly, competently, and ethically.

(e) Sociologists do not permit personal animosities or intellectual differences with colleagues to foreclose students' or supervisors' access to these colleagues or to interfere with student or supervisee learning, academic progress, or professional development.

19. Contractual and Consulting Services

(a) Sociologists undertake grants, contracts, or consultation only when they are knowledgeable about the substance, methods, and techniques they plan to use or have a plan for incorporating appropriate expertise.

(b) In undertaking grants, contracts, or consultation, sociologists base the results of their professional work on appropriate information and techniques.

(c) When financial support for a project has been accepted under a grant, contract, or consultation, sociologists make reasonable efforts to complete the proposed work on schedule.

(d) In undertaking grants, contracts, or consultation, sociologists accurately document and appropriately retain their professional and scientific work.

(e) In establishing a contractual arrangement for research, consultation, or other services, sociologists clarify, to the extent feasible at the outset, the nature of the relationship with the individual, organizational, or institutional client. This clarification includes, as appropriate, the nature of the services to be performed, the probable uses of the services provided, possibilities for the sociologist's future use of the work for scholarly or publication purposes, the timetable for delivery of those services, and compensation and billing arrangements.

20. Adherence to the Code of Ethics

Sociologists have an obligation to confront, address, and attempt to resolve ethical issues according to this Code of Ethics.

20.01 Familiarity with the Code of Ethics

Sociologists have an obligation to be familiar with this Code of Ethics, other applicable ethics codes, and their application to sociologists' work. Lack of awareness or misunderstanding of an ethical standard is not, in itself, a defense to a charge of unethical conduct.

20.02 Confronting Ethical Issues

(a) When sociologists are uncertain whether a particular situation or course of action would violate the Code of Ethics, they consult with other sociologists knowledgeable about ethical issues, with ASA's Committee on Professional Ethics, or with other organizational entities such as institutional review boards.

(b) When sociologists take actions or are confronted with choices where there is a conflict between ethical standards enunciated in the Code of Ethics and laws or legal requirements, they make known their commitment to the Code and take steps to resolve the conflict in a responsible manner by consulting with colleagues, professional organizations, or the ASA's Committee on Professional Ethics.

20.03 Fair Treatment of Parties in Ethical Disputes

(a) Sociologists do not discriminate against a person on the basis of his or her having made an ethical complaint.

(b) Sociologists do not discriminate against a person based on his or her having been the subject of an ethical complaint. This does not preclude taking action based upon the outcome of an ethical complaint.

20.04 Reporting Ethical Violations of Others

When sociologists have substantial reason to believe that there may have been an ethical violation by another sociologist, they attempt to resolve the issue by bringing it to the attention of that individual if an informal resolution appears appropriate or possible, or they seek advice about whether or how to proceed based on this belief, assuming that such activity does not violate any confidentiality rights. Such action might include referral to ASA's Committee on Professional Ethics.

20.05 Cooperating with Ethics Committees

Sociologists cooperate in ethics investigations, proceedings, and resulting requirements of the American Sociological Association. In doing so, they make reasonable efforts to resolve any issues of confidentiality. Failure to cooperate may be an ethics violation.

20.06 Improper Complaints

Sociologists do not file or encourage the filing of ethics complaints that are frivolous and are intended to harm the alleged violator rather than to protect the integrity of the discipline and the public.

Note: This revised edition of the ASA Code of Ethics builds on the 1989 edition of the Code and the 1992 version of the American Psychological Association's Ethical Principles of Psychologists and Code of Conduct.

AMERICAN
SPEECH-LANGUAGE-
HEARING
ASSOCIATION

AMERICAN SPEECH-LANGUAGE-HEARING ASSOCIATION

Address:	10801 Rockville Pike
	Rockville, MD 20852
Telephone:	800/498-2071
WWW:	www.asha.org
Document:	Code of Ethics (1994)

Preamble

The preservation of the highest standards of integrity and ethical principles is vital to the responsible discharge of obligations in the professions of speech-language pathology and audiology. This Code of Ethics sets forth the fundamental principles and rules considered essential to this purpose.

Every individual who is (a) a member of the American Speech-Language-Hearing Association, whether certified or not, (b) a nonmember holding the Certificate of Clinical Competence from the Association, (c) an applicant for membership or certification, or (d) a Clinical Fellow seeking to fulfill standards for certification shall abide by this Code of Ethics.

Any action that violates the spirit and purpose of this Code shall be considered unethical. Failure to specify any particular responsibility or practice in this Code of Ethics shall not be construed as denial of the existence of such responsibilities or practices.

The fundamentals of ethical conduct are described by Principles of Ethics and by Rules of Ethics as they relate to responsibility to persons served, to the public, and to the professions of speech-language pathology and audiology.

Principles of Ethics, aspirational and inspirational in nature, form the underlying moral basis for the Code of Ethics. Individuals shall observe these principles as affirmative obligations under all conditions of professional activity.

Rules of Ethics are specific statements of minimally acceptable professional conduct or of prohibitions and are applicable to all individuals.

Principle of Ethics I

Individuals shall honor their responsibility to hold paramount the welfare of persons they serve professionally.

Rules of Ethics

A. Individuals shall provide all services competently.

B. Individuals shall use every resource, including referral when appropriate, to ensure that high-quality service is provided.

C. Individuals shall not discriminate in the delivery of professional services on the basis of race or ethnicity, gender, age, religion, national origin, sexual orientation, or disability.

D. Individuals shall fully inform the persons they serve of the nature and possible effects of services rendered and products dispensed.

E. Individuals shall evaluate the effectiveness of services rendered and of products dispensed and shall provide services or dispense products only when benefit can reasonably be expected.

F. Individuals shall not guarantee the results of any treatment or procedure, directly or by implication; however, they may make a reasonable statement of prognosis.

G. Individuals shall not evaluate or treat speech, language, or hearing disorders solely by correspondence.

H. Individuals shall maintain adequate records of professional services rendered and products dispensed and shall allow access to these records when appropriately authorized.

I. Individuals shall not reveal, without authorization, any professional or personal information about the person served professionally, unless required by law to do so, or unless doing so is necessary to protect the welfare of the person or of the community.

J. Individuals shall not charge for services not rendered, nor shall they misrepresent,[1] in any fashion, services rendered or products dispensed.

K. Individuals shall use persons in research or as subjects of teaching demonstrations only with their informed consent.

L. Individuals whose professional services are adversely affected by substance abuse or other health-related conditions shall seek professional assistance and, where appropriate, withdraw from the affected areas of practice.

Principle of Ethics II

Individuals shall honor their responsibility to achieve and maintain the highest level of professional competence.

Rules of Ethics

A. Individuals shall engage in the provision of clinical services only when they hold the appropriate Certificate of Clinical Competence or when they are in the certification process and are supervised by an individual who holds the appropriate Certificate of Clinical Competence.

B. Individuals shall engage in only those aspects of the professions that are within the scope of their competence, considering their level of education, training, and experience.

C. Individuals shall continue their professional development throughout their careers.

D. Individuals shall delegate the provision of clinical services only to persons who are certified or to persons in the education or certification process who are appropriately supervised. The provision of support services may be delegated to persons who are neither certified nor in the certification process only when a certificate holder provides appropriate supervision.

E. Individuals shall prohibit any of their professional staff from providing services that exceed the staff member's competence, considering the staff member's level of education, training, and experience.

F. Individuals shall ensure that all equipment used in the provision of services is in proper working order and is properly calibrated.

Principle of Ethics III

Individuals shall honor their responsibility to the public by promoting public understanding of the professions, by supporting the development of services designed to fulfill the unmet needs of the public, and by providing accurate information in all communications involving any aspect of the professions.

Rules of Ethics

A. Individuals shall not misrepresent their credentials, competence, education, training, or experience.

B. Individuals shall not participate in professional activities that constitute a conflict of interest.

C. Individuals shall not misrepresent diagnostic information, services rendered, or products dispensed or engage in any scheme or artifice to defraud in connection with obtaining payment or reimbursement for such services or products.

D. Individuals' statements to the public shall provide accurate information about the nature and management of communication disorders, about the professions, and about professional services.

E. Individuals' statements to the public—advertising, announcing, and marketing their professional services, reporting research results, and promoting product—shall adhere to prevailing professional standards and shall not contain misrepresentations.

Principle of Ethics IV

Individuals shall honor their responsibilities to the professions and their relationships with colleagues, students, and members of allied professions. Individuals shall uphold the dignity and autonomy of the professions, maintain harmonious interprofessional and intraprofessional relationships, and accept the professions' self-imposed standards.

Rules of Ethics

A. Individuals shall prohibit anyone under their supervision from engaging in any practice that violates the Code of Ethics.

B. Individuals shall not engage in dishonesty, fraud, deceit, misrepresentation, or any form of conduct that adversely reflects on the professions or on the individual's fitness to serve persons professionally.

C. Individuals shall assign credit only to those who have contributed to a publication, presentation, or product. Credit shall be assigned in proportion to the contribution and only with the contributor's consent.

D. Individuals' statements to colleagues about professional services, research results, and products shall adhere to prevailing professional standards and shall contain no misrepresentations.

E. Individuals shall not provide professional services without exercising independent professional judgment, regardless of referral source or prescription.

F. Individuals shall not discriminate in their relationships with colleagues, students, and members of allied professions on the basis of race or ethnicity, gender, age, religion, national origin, sexual orientation, or disability.

G. Individuals who have reason to believe that the Code of Ethics has been violated shall inform the Ethical Practice Board.

H. Individuals shall cooperate fully with the Ethical Practice Board in its investigation and adjudication of matters related to this Code of Ethics.

---

1. For purposes of this Code of Ethics, misrepresentation includes any untrue statements or statements that are likely to mislead. Misrepresentation also includes the failure to state any information that is material and that ought, in fairness, to be considered.

© American Speech-Language-Hearing Association. Reprinted with permission.

AMERICAN STATISTICAL ASSOCIATION

Address: 1429 Duke Street
Alexandria, VA 22314-3402
Telephone: 703/684-1221
WWW: www.amstat.org
Document: Ethical Guidelines for Statistical Practice (1995)

Statisticians have a public duty to maintain integrity in their professional work, particularly in the application of statistical skills to problems where private interests may inappropriately affect the development or application of statistical knowledge. For these reasons, statisticians should

- present their findings and interpretations honestly and objectively
- avoid untrue, deceptive, or undocumented statements
- disclose any financial or other interests that may affect, or appear to affect, their professional statements

Recognizing that collecting data for a statistical inquiry may impose a burden on respondents, that it may be viewed by some as an invasion of privacy, and that it often involves legitimate confidentiality considerations, statisticians should

- collect only the data needed for the purpose of their inquiry
- inform each potential respondent about the general nature and sponsorship of the inquiry and the intended uses of the data
- establish their intentions, where pertinent, to protect the confidentiality of information collected from respondents, strive to ensure that these intentions realistically reflect their ability to do so, and clearly state pledges of confidentiality and their limitations to the respondents
- ensure that the means are adequate to protect confidentiality to the extent pledged or intended, that processing and use of data conform with the pledges made, that appropriate care is taken with

directly identifying information (using such steps as destroying this type of information or removing it from the file when it is no longer needed for the inquiry), that appropriate techniques are applied to control statistical disclosure

- ensure that, whenever data are transferred to other persons or organizations, this transfer conforms with the established confidentiality pledges, and require written assurance from the recipients of the data that the measures employed to protect confidentiality will be at least equal to those originally pledged

Recognizing that statistical work must be visible and open to assessment with respect to quality and appropriateness in order to advance knowledge, and that such assessment may involve an explanation of the assumptions, methodology, and data processing used, statisticians should

- delineate the boundaries of the inquiry as well as the boundaries of the statistical inferences which can be derived from it
- emphasize that statistical analysis may be an essential component of an inquiry and should be acknowledged in the same manner as other essential components
- be prepared to document data sources used in an inquiry; known inaccuracies in the data; and steps taken to correct or to refine the data, statistical procedures applied to the data, and the assumptions required for their application
- make the data available for analysis by other responsible parties with appropriate safeguards for privacy concerns
- recognize that the selection of a statistical procedure may to some extent be a matter of judgment and that other statisticians may select alternative procedures
- direct any criticism of a statistical inquiry to the inquiry itself and not to the individuals conducting it

Recognizing that a client or employer may be unfamiliar with statistical practice and be dependent upon the statistician for expert advice, statisticians should

- make clear their qualifications to undertake the statistical inquiry at hand
- inform a client or employer of all factors that may affect or conflict with their impartiality
- accept no contingency fee arrangements
- fulfill all commitments in any inquiry undertaken
- apply statistical procedures without concern for a favorable outcome
- state clearly, accurately, and completely to a client the characteristics of alternate statistical procedures

along with the recommended methodology and the usefulness and implications of all possible approaches

- disclose no private information about or belonging to any present or former client without the client's approval

Background

These Ethical Guidelines for Statistical Practice identify ethical relationships with the public, government, clients or employers, and other professionals. This document is open-ended; it establishes procedures for amending its contents and for broadening its scope. The main vehicle for such changes is the ASA Committee on Professional Ethics.

Additional requirements may be incorporated into the body of this document for any of the following purposes:

- to extend the general guidelines
- to identify further points of ethical contact between statisticians and the public, government, their clients or employers, and other professionals
- to establish ethical principles for the use of statistics in a specialized area such as medicine, law, or survey research
- to set ethical principles for publishing statistical reports
- to document procedures for resolving disputes on questions of professional ethics

Reprinted with permission from the American Statistical Association. Copyright 1995 by the American Statistical Association. All rights reserved.

AMERICAN UROLOGICAL ASSOCIATION

Address: 1120 North Charles Street
            Baltimore, MD 21201
Telephone: 410/727-1100
WWW: www.auanet.org

The American Urological Association uses the code of the American Medical Association. See p. 00.

APPRAISAL INSTITUTE

Address: 875 North Michigan Avenue,
                 Suite 2400
                 Chicago, IL 60611-1980
Telephone: 312/335-4100
WWW: www.appraisalinstitute.org
Document: Code of Professional Ethics of the
                 Appraisal Institute (1997)

(The Appraisal Institute has also adopted and published *Explanatory Comments Relating to the Code of Professional Ethics*, which provides additional information concerning the background, interpretation, and application of Canons and Ethical Rules. It is not reprinted here.—Eds.)

Preamble

The importance of the role of the real property appraiser, consultant, and review appraiser in our economy places ethical obligations upon the men and women who serve in these capacities. In recognition of these obligations, the Appraisal Institute has adopted this Code of Professional Ethics. Each Member of the Appraisal Institute is required to conduct his or her activities in accordance with the requirements of the Code of Professional Ethics, adopted periodically by the Board of Directors, and with the Standards of Professional Appraisal Practice as adopted periodically by the Board of Directors. Each Member of the Appraisal Institute is urged to bring to the attention of the national Ethics and Counseling Committee any significant factual information that such Member may possess which reasonably tends to indicate that another Member may have failed to observe the requirements of the Code of Professional Ethics or the Standards of Professional Appraisal Practice.

Definitions

As used in the Code, the following definitions apply. The definitions of appraisal, consulting, real estate, real property, report, and review are quoted from the Uniform Standards of Professional Appraisal Practice and are included for ease of reference.

APPRAISAL: (noun) The act or process of estimating value; an estimate of value.

(adjective) Of or pertaining to appraising and related functions.

ASSIGNMENT: Assignments include appraisal, consulting, and review.

CONSULTING: The act or process of providing information, analysis of real estate data and recommendations or conclusions on diversified problems in real estate, other than estimating value.

FILE MEMORANDA: Sufficient information to demonstrate substantial compliance with the Standards of Professional Appraisal Practice including in statement, outline, or reference form: work sheets, data sheets and related material.

KNOW OR KNOWINGLY: Means that the Member realizes what he or she is doing, is aware of the nature of his or her conduct and is not acting through mistake or accident.

Knowledge can be inferred from the Member's conduct and from all the facts and circumstances surrounding the case. The determination of "knowingly" should be made in the context of the Member's training, appraisal background and other relevant experience. A Member will be deemed to have acted (or failed to act) "knowingly" if he or she acted in disregard of the requirements of the Code of Professional Ethics or Standards of Professional Appraisal Practice or the recognized appraisal methods and techniques as set forth in the Appraisal Institute's courses, seminars, textbooks and other publications. The term "knowingly" includes not only what the Member knew, but also what the Member reasonably should have known given all the facts and circumstances of the case and the Member's training, appraisal background and experience.

MEMBER: Shall mean a Designated Member, Associate Member, or Affiliate Member of the Appraisal Institute.

REAL ESTATE: An identified parcel or tract of land, including improvements, if any.

REAL PROPERTY: The interest, benefits, and rights inherent in the ownership of real estate.

REPORT: Any communication, written or oral, of an appraisal, review, or consultation service that is transmitted to the client upon completion of an assignment.

Appraisal reports, real estate counseling reports, real estate tax counseling reports, real estate offering memorandum, mortgage banking offers, highest and best use studies, market demand and economic feasibility studies and all other reports resulting from an assignment are reports regardless of their title.

REVIEW: The act or process of critically studying a report prepared by another.

Since a clear understanding of defined terms is essential to a proper understanding of the Code of Professional Ethics, it is the responsibility of each Member to be familiar with and understand each defined term in the Code when following and applying the Canons and Ethical Rules set forth in the Code and discussed in the Explanatory Comments.

Exceptions to Ethical Rules

If any Ethical Rule set forth in the Code of Professional Ethics is contrary to the law or public policy of any jurisdiction, such Ethical Rule shall be void and of no force or effect in such jurisdiction.

In stating each individual Ethical Rule, no attempt has been made to enumerate all of the various circumstances and conditions that will excuse a Member from the strict observance of such Rule; however, the Appraisal Institute recognizes that illness, acts of God, and various other events beyond the control of a Member may make it inequitable to insist upon a strict observance of a Rule in a particular case. When a Member in the exercise of reasonable care, violates an Ethical Rule due to illness, acts of God or other circumstances beyond his or her control, it is expected that the agency of the Appraisal Institute charged with responsibility for enforcing the Code of Professional Ethics will act in a manner that will avoid an inequitable result.

CANON 1

A MEMBER MUST REFRAIN FROM CONDUCT THAT IS DETRIMENTAL TO THE APPRAISAL INSTITUTE, THE APPRAISAL PROFESSION AND THE PUBLIC

Ethical Rules

E.R. 1-1   It is unethical to knowingly:
- a)   act in a manner that is misleading or fraudulent;
- b)   use, or permit an employee or third party to use, a misleading report;
- c)   communicate, or permit an employee or third party to communicate, any report in a manner that is misleading;
- d)   contribute to or participate in an appraisal, review, or consulting opinion that reasonable appraisers would not believe to be justified; or
- e)   contribute to or participate in the preparation or delivery of a report containing an appraisal, review or consulting opinion that reasonable appraisers would not believe to be justified, whether or not such report is signed or delivered by the Member.

E.R. 1-2   It is unethical to engage in misconduct of any kind that leads to a conviction of a crime involving fraud, dishonesty, or false statements or a crime involving moral turpitude.

CANON 2

A MEMBER MUST ASSIST THE APPRAISAL INSTITUTE IN CARRYING OUT ITS RESPONSIBILITIES TO THE USERS OF APPRAISAL SERVICES AND THE PUBLIC

Ethical Rules

E.R. 2-1   It is unethical:
- a)   to knowingly violate the rules set forth in the Regulations of the Appraisal Institute that govern the confidentiality of the admissions process or the confidentiality of the peer review process.
- b)   for a Member who has made a referral of a peer review matter, or who has any knowledge of the existence of such referral or any subsequent screening or review of the matter, to fail to treat such knowledge confidentially.

E.R. 2-2   It is unethical to accept an appointment to, or to fail to immediately resign from, an Appraisal Institute committee dealing with admissions or peer review activity if the Member is unable or unwilling to fulfill the responsibilities of a member of said committee.

E.R. 2-3   It is unethical for a Member:
- a)   To knowingly make false statements or submit misleading information to a duly qualified Admissions Committee or on an application, or to refrain from promptly submitting any relevant information in the possession of such Member when re-

quested to do so by a duly qualified Admissions Committee or on an application.

b) To knowingly submit misleading information to a duly authorized peer review committee (or member or agent thereof); or, when requested to do so by a duly authorized peer review committee (or member or agent thereof), to refrain from promptly submitting any relevant information in the possession or control of the Member; to refuse to appear for a personal interview or participate in an interview conducted by telephone; or to refuse to promptly answer all relevant questions concerning the matter being investigated.

c) To fail or refuse to promptly submit a written report or file memoranda containing data, reasoning and conclusions, or to fail or refuse to submit a Permission to Review relating to a report or file memoranda when requested to do so by the Director of Screening or any duly authorized member of the Screening Staff.

d) To fail or refuse to promptly submit any relevant information in the possession of the Member concerning the status of litigation related to a peer review matter when requested to do so by the Ethics and Counseling Department; or, to knowingly submit misleading information to the Ethics and Counseling Department concerning the status of litigation related to an Ethics and Counseling matter or to the Ethics Administration Division Chair concerning a possible violation of Ethical Rule 5-2 (or its predecessors) or correction of such a violation.

e) To fail to notify the Ethics and Counseling Department prior to resumption of any activity governed by the Code of Professional Ethics or the Standards of Professional Appraisal Practice if the Member previously gave notice that such activity had ceased and, as a result, one or more pending peer review files were closed.

E.R. 2-4   It is unethical to fail to comply with the terms of a summons issued by a duly authorized peer review committee.

E.R. 2-5   It is unethical to fail to prepare either a written report or file memoranda containing the data, reasoning and conclusions

for each assignment within a reasonable time after completing the assignment.

E.R. 2-6   It is unethical to give testimony as to an appraisal, review, or consulting opinion in a deposition or affidavit, or before any board, commission, tribunal or court, unless a written report or file memoranda is prepared prior to giving such testimony.

E.R. 2-7   It is unethical to fail to preserve each written report, file memoranda, and any related file for;

a) a period of five years from the date of preparation of such report or file memoranda;

b) a period of two years following final disposition of a proceeding in which testimony was given;

c) a period commencing upon notification that an assignment is the subject of a peer review matter until notification by the Appraisal Institute of final disposition of the peer review matter;

d) a period commencing upon a request from Admissions relating to an assignment until notification by the Appraisal Institute of the completion of review by Admissions; or

e) a period of two years following the final disposition of a review of an assignment by a state licensing and/or certification board, whichever period shall be the last to expire.

E.R. 2-8   It is unethical to enter into a contract for an assignment that precludes compliance with the Standards of Professional Appraisal Practice, the Code of Professional Ethics, the Bylaws, or any Regulation of the Appraisal Institute.

E.R. 2-9   It is unethical to enter into a contract for the performance of an assignment that does not provide that all assignments will be developed and all reports will be prepared in conformity with and subject to the requirements of this Code of Professional Ethics and the Standards of Professional Appraisal Practice.

E.R. 2-10 It is unethical for a Member who is employed by a business entity engaged in assignments to fail to sincerely and demonstrably seek other employment if

a) such business entity fails to comply with the Appraisal Institute's rules relating to

b) such business entity fails to comply with the Appraisal Institute's rules relating to advertising or the solicitation of business.

E.R. 2-11 It is unethical, in the performance of an assignment, to sign a report without accepting responsibility for the contents of the entire report unless the Member clearly and precisely indicates in the report the portion or portions of the report for which responsibility is or is not accepted.

CANON 3
IN THE PERFORMANCE OF AN ASSIGNMENT, A MEMBER MUST DEVELOP AND COMMUNICATE EACH ANALYSIS AND OPINION WITHOUT BEING MISLEADING, WITHOUT BIAS FOR THE CLIENT'S INTEREST AND WITHOUT ACCOMMODATION OF HIS OR HER OWN INTERESTS

Ethical Rules

E.R. 3-1 It is unethical, in the performance of an assignment, to develop an analysis or opinion that is biased or misleading or to prepare, orally present, sign, or deliver a report that fails to accurately communicate his or her analyses or opinions or that the Member knows to contain any biased analysis or opinion. Further, it is unethical for a Member to knowingly permit a business entity that is wholly or majority owned or wholly or partially controlled by such Member to develop an analysis or opinion that is misleading or biased or to prepare, orally present, sign, or deliver a report that contains any biased analysis or opinion or a report that fails to accurately communicate the Member's analyses or opinions.

E.R. 3-2 Reserved.

(NOTE: OLD E.R. 3-1 AND E.R. 3-2 HAVE BEEN COMBINED INTO NEW E.R. 3-1.)

E.R. 3-3 It is unethical to accept or perform an assignment that is contingent upon reporting a predetermined analysis or opinion.

E.R. 3-4 It is unethical to accept or perform an assignment if the compensation to be paid for the performance of such assignment is contingent upon the opinion or conclusion reached, the attainment of a stipulated result, or the occurrence of a subsequent event.

The above restriction on contingent compensation does not apply to those consulting assignments where the appraiser is not acting in a disinterested manner and would not reasonably be perceived as performing a service that requires impartiality. It is unethical to perform such an assignment without disclosing in the report that the compensation is contingent. The Member must explain the basis for the contingency in the report and in any transmittal letter in which conclusions are stated.

E.R. 3-5 It is unethical to accept or perform an assignment that is based upon a hypothetical condition, unless

a) the use of the hypothesis is clearly disclosed; and

b) the assumption of the hypothetical condition is clearly required for legal purposes, for purposes of reasonable analysis, or for purposes of comparison and would not be misleading; and

c) the report clearly describes the rationale for this assumption, the nature of the hypothetical condition, and its effect on the result of the assignment.

E.R. 3-6 It is unethical to accept an assignment if a Member has any direct or indirect, current, or prospective personal interest in the subject of the assignment or outcome of the assignment or any personal bias toward the parties involved in the assignment, unless

a) prior to accepting the assignment, the Member carefully considers the facts and concludes that his or her professional judgment will not be affected and reasonable persons, under the same circumstances, would reach the same conclusion; and

b) such personal interest or bias is disclosed to the client prior to acceptance of the assignment; and

c) such personal interest or bias is fully and accurately disclosed in each written and oral report resulting from such assignment.

E.R. 3-7   It is unethical for a Member, during the period that commences at the time that he or she is contacted concerning an assignment and expires a reasonable length of time after the completion of such assignment, to deliberately acquire property or assume a position that could possibly affect his or her judgment or violate his or her fiduciary duty to the client unless, prior to such acquisition or change of position,

a)   the Member carefully considers the facts and reasonably concludes that the proposed acquisition or change of position will not affect his or her judgment or violate his or her fiduciary duty to the client; and

b)   the Member makes full disclosure to the client and obtains from the client a written statement consenting to or approving such acquisition or change of position; and

c)   at the time of such disclosure, the Member gives the client the right to terminate the assignment without payment of any fee or other charge; and

d)   the facts concerning such acquisition or change of position are completely and accurately described in each written and oral report resulting from the assignment.

E.R. 3-8   It is unethical, in the performance of an assignment, to fail to acknowledge by name in any written report each individual who rendered significant professional assistance.

CANON 4
A MEMBER MUST NOT VIOLATE THE CONFIDENTIAL NATURE OF THE APPRAISER-CLIENT RELATIONSHIP

Ethical Rules

E.R. 4-1   It is unethical to disclose the analyses, opinions, or conclusions of an assignment to anyone other than

a)   the client and those persons specifically authorized by the client to receive such information;

b)   third parties, when and to the extent that the Member is legally required to do so by statute, ordinance, or order of court; and

c)   the duly authorized committees of the Appraisal Institute.

E.R. 4-2   If the client furnishes confidential factual data to a Member in the course of an assignment, it is unethical to disclose such confidential factual data to anyone other than

a)   those persons specifically authorized by the client to receive such information;

b)   third parties, when and to the extent that the Member is legally required to do so by statute, ordinance, or order of court; and

c)   the duly authorized committees of the Appraisal Institute,
unless such confidential factual data has subsequently been made public.

E.R. 4-3   If a Member is furnished confidential factual data by a client and a third party subsequently requests an assignment that will be materially affected by the use of, or the failure to use, such confidential factual data, it is unethical to accept such subsequent assignment, unless

a)   the source that provided such confidential factual data permits such data to be used in the subsequent assignment;

b)   such confidential factual data has subsequently been made public; or

c)   the Member is able to obtain data from other sources that is sufficient to support a properly developed analysis or opinion.

E.R. 4-4   It is unethical for a Member serving on an Appraisal Institute committee to discuss or disclose confidential information or factual data derived through committee activities with anyone other than

a)   the appraiser whose report, file memoranda, or file contains the confidential information or factual data;

b)   the appraiser's client and those persons specifically authorized by such client to receive such information;

c)   third parties, when and to the extent that the Member is legally required to do so by statute, ordinance, or order of court; and

d)   committee members within the scope of the Bylaws and Regulations of the Appraisal Institute.

CANON 5
A MEMBER MUST USE CARE TO AVOID ADVERTISING OR SOLICITATIONS THAT ARE MISLEADING OR OTHERWISE CONTRARY TO THE PUBLIC INTEREST

Ethical Rules

E.R. 5-1 It is unethical to utilize misleading advertising. Further, it is unethical to knowingly permit a business entity that is wholly or partially owned or controlled by a Member to utilize misleading advertising.

E.R. 5-2 It is unethical to use or refer to the Appraisal Institute or its membership designations in a manner that is misleading, or to use or display the registered designations or emblems of the Appraisal Institute in a manner contrary to Regulation No. 5.

E.R. 5-3 It is unethical for a Member to solicit assignments in a misleading manner. Further, it is unethical to knowingly permit a business entity wholly or partially owned or controlled by a Member to solicit assignments in a misleading manner.

E.R. 5-4 It is unethical for a Member to pay an undisclosed fee, commission, or thing of value for the procurement of an assignment, or for a Member to knowingly permit a business entity owned or controlled by such Member, to pay an undisclosed fee, commission, or thing of value for procuring an assignment. The disclosure of fees, commissions and things of value paid in connection with the procurement of an assignment must appear in the certification of any resulting written report and in any transmittal letter in which conclusions are stated.

Intra-company payments to employees or partners for business development are not deemed to be a "fee, commission, or thing of value" for the purpose of this Rule.

E.R. 5-5 *Reserved.*

E.R. 5-6 It is unethical to prepare or use in any manner a resume or statement of qualifications that is misleading.

ARCHAEOLOGICAL INSTITUTE OF AMERICA

Address: 656 Beacon Street
              Boston, MA 02215-2006
Telephone: 617/353-9361
WWW: www.archaeological.org
Document: Code of Ethics (1990)
Code of Professional Standards (1994)

(The Archaeological Institute of America wholeheartedly endorses the *UNESCO Draft Convention on the Means of Prohibiting and Preventing the Illicit Import, Export, and Transfer of Ownership of Cultural Property.* In addition, the AIA endorses the following *Code of Ethics*, developed by James Russell and Clemency Chase Coggins in conjunction with the Professional Responsibilities Committee (PRC) of the Institute. *The Code of Professional Standards* was developed by K. D. Vitelli in conjunction with the PRC and was passed by the Council on December 29, 1994. *Grievance Procedures*, developed by Claire L. Lyons in conjunction with the PRC and approved on December 29, 1996, is not reprinted here.—Eds.)

Code of Ethics
The Archaeological Institute of America is dedicated to the greater understanding of archaeology, to the protection and preservation of the world's archaeological resources and the information they contain, and to the encouragement and support of archaeological research and publication.

In accordance with these principles, members of the AIA should:

1. Seek to ensure that the exploration of archaeological sites be conducted according to the highest standards under the direct supervision of qualified personnel, and that the results of such research be made public;
2. Refuse to participate in the illegal trade in antiquities derived from excavation in any country after December 30, 1970, when the AIA Council endorsed the UNESCO Convention on Cultural Property, and refrain from activities that enhance the commercial value of such objects;
3. Inform appropriate authorities of threats to, or plunder of archaeological sites, and illegal import or export of archaeological material.

Code of Professional Standards

PREAMBLE

This Code applies to those members of the AIA who play an active, professional role in the recovery, care, study, or publication of archaeological material, including cultural resources located under water. Within the Institute they enjoy the privileges of organizing sessions and submitting papers for the Annual Meetings, of lecturing to local societies, participating in the AIA committees that shape and direct the discipline, participating in the placement service, and of being listed in the *Directory of Professionals in Archaeology*.

Along with those privileges come special responsibilities. Our members should inform themselves about and abide by the laws of the countries in which they live and work. They should treat others at home and in the field with respect and sensitivity. As primary stewards of the archaeological record, they should work actively to preserve that record in all its dimensions and for the long term; and they should give due consideration to the interests of others, both colleagues and the lay public, who are affected by the research.

The AIA recognizes that archaeology is a discipline dealing, in all its aspects, with the human condition, and that archaeological research must often balance competing ethical principles. This Code of Professional Standards does not seek to legislate all aspects of professional behavior and it realizes the conflicts embedded in many of the issues addressed. The Code sets forth three broad areas of responsibility and provides examples of the kinds of considerations called for by each. It aims to encourage all professional archaeologists to keep ethical considerations in mind as they plan and conduct research.

I. RESPONSIBILITIES TO THE ARCHAEOLOGICAL RECORD

Professional archaeologists incur responsibilities to the archaeological record, the physical remains and all the associated information about those remains, including those located under water.

1. Professional archaeologists should adhere to the Guidelines of the AIA general Code of Ethics concerning illegal antiquities in their research and publications.
2. The purposes and consequences of all archaeological research should be carefully considered before the beginning of work. Approaches and methods should be chosen that require a minimum of damage to the archaeological record. Although excavation is sometimes the appropriate means of research, archaeological survey, study of previously excavated material, and other means should be considered before resort is made to excavation.
3. The recovery and study of archaeological material from all periods should be carried out only under the supervision of qualified personnel.
4. Archaeologists should anticipate and provide for adequate and accessible long-term storage and curatorial facilities for all archaeological materials, records and archives.
5. Archaeologists should make public the results of their research in a timely fashion, making evidence available to others if publication is not accomplished within a reasonable time.
6. All research projects should contain specific plans for conservation, preservation, and publication from the very outset, and funds should be secured for such purposes.

II. RESPONSIBILITIES TO THE PUBLIC

Because the archaeological record represents the heritage of all people, it is the responsibility of professional archaeologists to communicate with the general public about the nature of archaeological research and the importance of archaeological resources. Archaeologists also have specific responsibilities to the local communities where they carry out research and field work, as well as to their home institutions and communities.

Archaeologists should be sensitive to cultural mores and attitudes, and be aware of the impact research and field work may have on a local population, both during and after the work. Such considerations should be taken into account in designing the project's strategy.

1. Professional archaeologists should be actively engaged in public outreach through lecturing, popular writing, school programs, and other educational initiatives.
2. Plans for field work should consider the ecological impact of the project and its overall impact on the local communities.
3. Professional archaeologists should not participate in projects whose primary goal is private gain.
4. For field projects, archaeologists should consult with appropriate representatives of the local community during the planning stage, invite local participation in the project, and regularly inform the local community about the results of the research.
5. Archaeologists should respect the cultural norms and dignity of local inhabitants in areas where archaeological research is carried out.
6. The legitimate concerns of people who claim descent from, or some other connection with, cultures of the past must be balanced against the scholarly integrity of the discipline. A mutually acceptable accommodation should be sought.

III. RESPONSIBILITIES TO COLLEAGUES

Professional archaeologists owe consideration to colleagues, striving at all times to be fair, never plagiarize, and give credit where due.

1. Archaeologists involved in cooperative projects should strive for harmony and fairness; those in positions of authority should behave with consideration toward those under their authority, while all team members should strive to promote the success of the broader undertaking.
2. The Principal Investigator(s) of archaeological projects should maintain acceptable standards of safety and ascertain that staff members are adequately insured.
3. Professional archaeologists should maintain confidentiality of information gleaned in reviewing grant proposals and other such privileged sources.
4. Professional archaeologists should not practice discrimination or harassment based on sex, religion, age, race, national origin, disability, or sexual orientation; project sponsors should establish the means to eliminate and/or investigate complaints of discrimination or harassment.
5. Archaeologists should honor reasonable requests from colleagues for access to materials and records, preserving existing rights to publication,

but sharing information useful for the research of others. Scholars seeking access to unpublished information should not expect to receive interpretive information if that is also unpublished and in progress.
6. Before studying and/or publishing any unpublished material archaeologists should secure proper permission, normally in writing, from the appropriate project director or the appointed representative of the sponsoring institution and/or the antiquities authorities in the country of origin.
7. Scholars studying material from a particular site should keep the project director informed of their progress and intentions; project directors should return the courtesy.
8. Members of cooperative projects should prepare and evaluate reports in a timely and collegial fashion.

© Archaeological Institute of America. Reprinted with permission.

ASSOCIATED BUILDERS AND CONTRACTORS

Address:	1300 North 17th Street
	Rosslyn, VA 22209
Telephone:	703/812-2000
WWW:	www.abc.org
Document:	Code of Ethics (1971)

As a member of the Associated Builders and Contractors, Inc., I will strive to observe the following principles in the conduct of my business:

1. Maintain a standard of performance with the Owner's best interest and my obligations.
2. Quote only realistic prices and completion dates and perform accordingly.
3. Cooperate to the fullest extent with the Architect and other agents of the owner toward fulfillment of a common goal.
4. Solicit quotations only from firms with whom I am willing to do business.
5. Make all payments promptly within the terms of the contract.

6. Observe and foster the highest standards of safety and working conditions for my employees.

7. Establish realistic wage schedules for my employees commensurate with their ability and their industry so that they may enjoy the dignity to which they are entitled.

8. Actively participate in the training of skilled tradesmen for the future welfare of the Merit Shop industry.

© Associated Builders and Contractors. Reprinted with permission.

ASSOCIATION FOR CAREER AND TECHNICAL EDUCATION

Address: 1410 King Street
             Alexandria, VA 22314
Telephone: 703/683-3111
WWW: www.avaonline.org
Document: Code of Ethics (1979)

The vocational educator believes in the worth and dignity of each individual and in the value of vocational education in enhancing individual development. Consequently, vocational educators strive for the highest ethical standards to merit the respect and confidence of students, colleagues, and the community. They use their skills and knowledge to develop each of their students or colleagues to maximize human potential. This code of ethics provides a framework by which to guide vocational educators and the institutions through which they work in attaining the highest degree of professionalism.

With respect to self, the vocational educator:

• Represents personal and professional qualifications in a true and accurate manner.

• Maintains confidentiality of students and colleagues except where disclosure is compelled by law or to serve a compelling professional need.

• Bases professional action and decisions upon sound, objective rationale without influence of favors, gifts, or personal or political advantage.

• Recognizes and accepts responsibility for individual actions, judgments, and decisions.

• Strives throughout one's career to master, maintain, and improve professional competence through study, work, travel, and exploration.

• Contributes to the growing body of specialized knowledge, concepts, and skills which characterize vocational education.

• Strives for the advancement of vocational education, upholds its honor and dignity, and works to strengthen it in the community, state, and nation.

• Participates actively in the work of professional organizations to define and improve standards of vocational education preparation and service.

• Establishes and maintains conditions on employment conducive to providing high quality vocational education.

• Performs one's duty as a teacher on the basis of careful preparation so instruction is accurate, current, objective, and scholarly, designed to enhance the student's individual capabilities.

• Exercises professional judgment in presenting, interpreting, and critiquing ideas, including controversial issues.

• Joins with other professionals whose mission is to improve the delivery of vocational education to the nation's citizens.

With respect to others, the vocational educator:

• Uses individual competence as a principal criterion in accepting delegated responsibilities and assigning duties to others.

• Provides statements about a colleague or student in a fair, objective manner without embarrassment or ridicule.

• Provides educational and/or career options to all students or colleagues.

• Evaluates students and colleagues without regard to race, color, creed, sex, status, or any other factor unrelated to the need for vocational education, allowing any student or colleague to participate in a program who can benefit from it, and providing the same benefits or advantages to all students or colleagues in the program.

• Respects the rights and reputation of the student, colleague with whom one works, and the institution or organization with which one is affiliated.

• Acts to safeguard the health and safety of students and colleagues against incompetent, unethical, or illegal behavior of any person, whether student or colleague.

- Protects vocational education by promoting admission to the profession of persons who are fully qualified because of character, education, and experience, according to legally established criteria and standards.
- Promotes improvement of legalities affecting vocational education.
- Exercises professional judgment in the choice of teaching methods and materials appropriate to the needs and interests of each student.
- Influences effectively the formation of policies and procedures which affect one's professional work.

© Association for Career and Technical Education. Reprinted with permission.

ASSOCIATION FOR COMPUTING MACHINERY

Address: 1515 Broadway, 17th Floor
New York, NY 10036-5701
Telephone: 212/626-0500 or 800/342-6626
WWW: www.acm.org
Document: ACM Code of Ethics and
Professional Conduct (1997)

(The ACM also publishes a companion "Using the New ACM Code of Ethics in Decision Making," reprinted from *Communications of the ACM, Vol. 36, No.2 (February 1993)*. It is not reprinted here but is available at the above address.—Eds.)

Preamble.

Commitment to ethical professional conduct is expected of every member (voting members, associate members, and student members) of the Association for Computing Machinery (ACM).

This Code, consisting of 24 imperatives formulated as statements of personal responsibility, identifies the elements of such a commitment. It contains many, but not all, issues professionals are likely to face. Section 1 outlines fundamental ethical considerations, while Section 2 addresses additional, more specific considerations of professional conduct. Statements in Section 3 pertain more specifically to individuals who have a leadership role, whether in the workplace or in a volunteer capacity such as with organizations like ACM. Principles involving compliance with this Code are given in Section 4.

The Code shall be supplemented by a set of Guidelines, which provide explanation to assist members in dealing with the various issues contained in the Code. It is expected that the Guidelines will be changed more frequently than the Code.

The Code and its supplementary Guidelines are intended to serve as a basis for ethical decision making in the conduct of professional work. Secondarily, they may serve as a basis for judging the merit of a formal complaint pertaining to the violation of professional ethical standards.

It should be noted that although computing is not mentioned in the imperatives of Section 1.0, the Code is concerned with how these fundamental imperatives apply to one's conduct as a computing professional. These imperatives are expressed in a general form to emphasize that ethical principles which apply to computer ethics are derived from more general ethical principles.

It is understood that some words and phrases in a code of ethics are subject to varying interpretations, and that any ethical principle may conflict with other ethical principles in specific situations. Questions related to ethical conflicts can best be answered by thoughtful consideration of fundamental principles, rather than reliance on detailed regulations.

1. General Moral Imperatives. As an ACM member I will . . ..

1.1 Contribute to society and human well-being
This principle concerning the quality of life of all people affirms an obligation to protect fundamental human rights and to respect the diversity of all cultures. An essential aim of computing professionals is to minimize negative consequences of computing systems, including threats to health and safety. When designing or implementing systems, computing professionals must attempt to ensure that the products of their efforts will be used in socially responsible ways, will meet social needs, and will avoid harmful effects to health and welfare.

In addition to a safe social environment, human well-being includes a safe natural environment. Therefore, computing professionals who design and develop systems must be alert to, and make others aware of, any potential damage to the local or global environment.

1.2 Avoid harm to others

"Harm" means injury or negative consequences, such as undesirable loss of information, loss of property, property damage, or unwanted environmental impacts. This principle prohibits use of computing technology in ways that result in harm to any of the following: users, the general public, employees, employers. Harmful actions include intentional destruction or modification of files and programs leading to serious loss of resources or unnecessary expenditure of human resources such as the time and effort required to purge systems of "computer viruses."

Well-intended actions, including those that accomplish assigned duties, may lead to harm unexpectedly. In such an event the responsible person or persons are obligated to undo or mitigate the negative consequences as much as possible. One way to avoid unintentional harm is to carefully consider potential impacts on all those affected by decisions made during design and implementation.

To minimize the possibility of indirectly harming others, computing professionals must minimize malfunctions by following generally accepted standards for system design and testing. Furthermore, it is often necessary to assess the social consequences of systems to project the likelihood of any serious harm to others. If system features are misrepresented to users, coworkers, or supervisors, the individual computing professional is responsible for any resulting injury. In the work environment the computing professional has the additional obligation to report any signs of system dangers that might result in serious personal or social damage. If one's superiors do not act to curtail or mitigate such dangers, it may be necessary to "blow the whistle" to help correct the problem or reduce the risk. However, capricious or misguided reporting of violations can, itself, be harmful. Before reporting violations, all relevant aspects of the incident must be thoroughly assessed. In particular, the assessment of risk and responsibility must be credible. It is suggested that advice be sought from other computing professionals. (See principle 2.5 regarding thorough evaluations.)

1.3 Be honest and trustworthy

Honesty is an essential component of trust. Without trust an organization cannot function effectively. The honest computing professional will not make deliberately false or deceptive claims about a system or system design, but will instead provide full disclosure of all pertinent system limitations and problems. A computer professional has a duty to be honest about his or her own qualifications, and about any circumstances that might lead to conflicts of interest.

Membership in volunteer organizations such as ACM may at times place individuals in situations where their statements or actions could be interpreted as carrying the "weight" of a larger group of professionals. An ACM member will exercise care to not misrepresent ACM or positions and policies of ACM or any ACM units.

1.4 Be fair and take action not to discriminate

The values of equality, tolerance, respect for others, and the principles of equal justice govern this imperative. Discrimination on the basis of race, sex, religion, age, disability, national origin, or other such factors is an explicit violation of ACM policy and will not be tolerated.

Inequities between different groups of people may result from the use or misuse of information and technology. In a fair society, all individuals would have equal opportunity to participate in, or benefit from, the use of computer resources regardless of race, sex, religion, age, disability, national origin or other such similar factors. However, these ideals do not justify unauthorized use of computer resources nor do they provide an adequate basis for violation of any other ethical imperatives of this code.

1.5 Honor property rights including copyrights and patents

Violation of copyrights, patents, trade secrets and the terms of license agreements is prohibited by law in most circumstances. Even when software is not so protected, such violations are contrary to professional behavior. Copies of software should be made only with proper authorization. Unauthorized duplication of materials must not be condoned.

1.6 Give proper credit for intellectual property

Computing professionals are obligated to protect the integrity of intellectual property. Specifically, one must not take credit for others' ideas or work, even in cases where the work has not been explicitly protected, for example, by copyright or patent.

1.7 Respect the privacy of others

Computing and communication technology enables the collection and exchange of personal information on a scale unprecedented in the history of civilization. Thus there is increased potential for violating the privacy of individuals and groups. It is the responsibility of professionals to maintain the privacy and integrity of data describing individuals. This includes taking precautions to ensure the accuracy of data, as well as protecting it from unauthorized access or accidental disclosure to inappropriate individuals. Furthermore, procedures must be established to allow individuals to review their records and correct inaccuracies.

This imperative implies that only the necessary amount of personal information be collected in a system, that retention and disposal periods for that information be clearly defined and enforced, and that personal information gathered for a specific purpose not be used for other purposes without consent of the individual(s). These principles apply to electronic communications, including electronic mail, and prohibit procedures that capture or monitor electronic user data, including messages, without the permission of users or *bona fide* authorization related to system operation and maintenance. User data observed during the normal duties of system operation and maintenance must be treated with strictest confidentiality, except in cases where it is evidence for the violation of law, organizational regulations, or this Code. In these cases, the nature or contents of that information must be disclosed only to proper authorities (see 1.9).

1.8 Honor confidentiality
The principle of honesty extends to issues of confidentiality of information whenever one has made an explicit promise to honor confidentiality or, implicitly, when private information not directly related to the performance of one's duties becomes available. The ethical concern is to respect all obligations of confidentiality to employers, clients, and users unless discharged from such obligations by requirements of the law or other principles of this Code.

2. More Specific Professional Responsibilities. As an ACM computing professional I will . . .

2.1 Strive to achieve the highest quality, effectiveness and dignity in both the process and products of professional work
Excellence is perhaps the most important obligation of a professional. The computing professional must strive to achieve quality and to be cognizant of the serious negative consequences that may result from poor quality in a system.

2.2 Acquire and maintain professional competence
Excellence depends on individuals who take respon-

sibility for acquiring and maintaining professional competence. A professional must participate in setting standards for appropriate levels of competence, and strive to achieve those standards. Upgrading technical knowledge and competence can be achieved in several ways: doing independent study; attending seminars, conferences, or courses; and being involved in professional organizations.

2.3 Know and respect existing laws pertaining to professional work
ACM members must obey existing local, state, province, national, and international laws unless there is a compelling ethical basis not to do so. Policies and procedures of the organizations in which one participates must also be obeyed. But compliance must be balanced with the recognition that sometimes existing laws and rules may be immoral or inappropriate and, therefore, must be challenged.

Violation of a law or regulation may be ethical when that law or rule has inadequate moral basis or when it conflicts with another law judged to be more important. If one decides to violate a law or rule because it is viewed as unethical, or for any other reason, one must fully accept responsibility for one's actions and for the consequences.

2.4 Accept and provide appropriate professional review
Quality professional work, especially in the computing profession, depends on professional reviewing and critiquing. Whenever appropriate, individual members should seek and utilize peer review as well as provide critical review of the work of others.

2.5 Give comprehensive and thorough evaluations of computer systems and their impacts, including analysis of possible risks
Computer professionals must strive to be perceptive, thorough, and objective when evaluating, recommending, and presenting system descriptions and alternatives. Computer professionals are in a position of special trust, and therefore have a special responsibility to provide objective, credible evaluations to employers, clients, users, and the public. When providing evaluations the professional must also identify any relevant conflicts of interest, as stated in imperative 1.3.

As noted in the discussion of principle 1.2 on avoiding harm, any signs of danger from systems must be reported to those who have opportunity and/or responsibility to resolve them. See the guidelines for imperative 1.2 for more details concerning harm, including the reporting of professional violations.

2.6 Honor contracts, agreements, and assigned responsibilities

Honoring one's commitments is a matter of integrity and honesty. For the computer professional this includes ensuring that system elements perform as intended. Also, when one contracts for work with another party, one has an obligation to keep that party properly informed about progress toward completing that work.

A computing professional has a responsibility to request a change in any assignment that he or she feels cannot be completed as defined. Only after serious consideration and with full disclosure of risks and concerns to the employer or client, should one accept the assignment. The major underlying principle here is the obligation to accept personal accountability for professional work. On some occasions other ethical principles may take greater priority.

A judgment that a specific assignment should not be performed may not be accepted. Having clearly identified one's concerns and reasons for that judgment, but failing to procure a change in that assignment, one may yet be obligated, by contract or by law, to proceed as directed. The computing professional's ethical judgment should be the final guide in deciding whether or not to proceed. Regardless of the decision, one must accept the responsibility for the consequences. However, performing assignments "against one's own judgment" does not relieve the professional of responsibility for any negative consequences.

2.7 Improve public understanding of computing and its consequences

Computing professionals have a responsibility to share technical knowledge with the public by encouraging understanding of computing, including the impacts of computer systems and their limitations. This imperative implies an obligation to counter any false views related to computing.

2.8 Access computing and communication resources only when authorized to do so

Theft or destruction of tangible and electronic property is prohibited by imperative 1.2—"Avoid harm to others." Trespassing and unauthorized use of a computer or communication system is addressed by this imperative. Trespassing includes accessing communication networks and computer systems, or accounts and/or files associated with those systems, without explicit authorization to do so. Individuals and organizations have the right to restrict access to their systems so long as they do not violate the discrimination principle (see 1.4).

No one should enter or use another's computer system, software, or data files without permission. One must always have appropriate approval before using system resources, including .rm57 communication ports, file space, other system peripherals, and computer time.

3. Organizational Leadership Imperatives. As an ACM member and an organizational leader, I will . . . [Background Note: This section draws extensively from the draft IFIP Code of Ethics, especially its sections on organizational ethics and international concerns. The ethical obligations of organizations tend to be neglected in most codes of professional conduct, perhaps because these codes are written from the perspective of the individual member. This dilemma is addressed by stating these imperatives from the perspective of the organizational leader. In this context "leader" is viewed as any organizational member who has leadership or educational responsibilities. These imperatives generally may apply to organizations as well as their leaders. In this context "organizations" are corporations, government agencies, and other "employers," as well as volunteer professional organizations.]

3.1 Articulate social responsibilities of members of an organizational unit and encourage full acceptance of those responsibilities

Because organizations of all kinds have impacts on the public, they must accept responsibilities to society. Organizational procedures and attitudes oriented toward quality and the welfare of society will reduce harm to members of the public, thereby serving public interest and fulfilling social responsibility. Therefore, organizational leaders must encourage full participation in meeting social responsibilities as well as quality performance.

3.2 Manage personnel and resources to design and build information systems that enhance the quality of working life

Organizational leaders are responsible for ensuring that computer systems enhance, not degrade, the quality of working life. When implementing a computer system, organizations must consider the personal and professional development, physical safety, and human dignity of all workers. Appropriate human-computer ergonomic standards should be considered in system design and in the workplace.

3.3 Acknowledge and support proper and authorized uses of an organization's computing and communication resources

Because computer systems can become tools to harm as well as to benefit an organization, the leadership has the responsibility to clearly define appropriate and inappropriate uses of organizational computing resources. While the number and scope of such rules should be minimal, they should be fully enforced when established.

3.4 Ensure that users and those who will be affected by a system have their needs clearly articulated during the assessment and design of requirements. Later the system must be validated to meet requirements

Current system users, potential users and other persons whose lives may be affected by a system must have their needs assessed and incorporated in the statement of requirements. System validation should ensure compliance with those requirements.

3.5 Articulate and support policies that protect the dignity of users and others affected by a computing system

Designing or implementing systems that deliberately or inadvertently demean individuals or groups is ethically unacceptable. Computer professionals who are in decision making positions should verify that systems are designed and implemented to protect personal privacy and enhance personal dignity.

3.6 Create opportunities for members of the organization to learn the principles and limitations of computer systems

This complements the imperative on public understanding (2.7). Educational opportunities are essential to facilitate optimal participation of all organizational members. Opportunities must be available to all members to help them improve their knowledge and skills in computing, including courses that familiarize them with the consequences and limitations of particular types of systems. In particular, professionals must be made aware of the dangers of building systems around oversimplified models, the improbability of anticipating and designing for every possible operating condition, and other issues related to the complexity of this profession.

4. Compliance with the Code. As an ACM member I will . . .

4.1 Uphold and promote the principles of this Code

The future of the computing profession depends on both technical and ethical excellence. Not only is it important for ACM computing professionals to adhere to the principles expressed in this Code, each member should encourage and support adherence by other members.

4.2 Treat violations of this code as inconsistent with membership in the ACM

Adherence of professionals to a code of ethics is largely a voluntary matter. However, if a member does not follow this code by engaging in gross misconduct, membership in ACM may be terminated.

Copyright waived. Reprinted with permission.

ASSOCIATION FOR INVESTMENT MANAGEMENT AND RESEARCH

Address:	560 Ray C. Hunt Drive PO Box 3668 Charlottesville, VA 22903-0668
Telephone:	804/951-5499 or 800/247-8132
WWW:	www.aimr.org
Document:	Code of Ethics and Standards of Professional Conduct (1996)

The Code of Ethics

Members of the Association for Investment Management and Research shall:

- Act with integrity, competence, dignity, and in an ethical manner when dealing with the public, clients, prospects, employers, employees, and fellow members.
- Practice and encourage others to practice in a professional and ethical manner that will reflect credit on members and their profession.
- Strive to maintain and improve their competence and the competence of others in the profession.

• Use reasonable care and exercise independent professional judgment.

The Standards of Professional Conduct

STANDARD I: FUNDAMENTAL RESPONSIBILITIES

Members shall:

A. Maintain knowledge of and comply with all applicable laws, rules, and regulations (including AIMR's Code of Ethics and Standards of Professional Conduct) of any government, regulatory organization, licensing agency, or professional association governing the members' professional activities.

B. Not knowingly participate or assist in any violation of such laws, rules, or regulations.

STANDARD II: RELATIONSHIPS WITH AND RESPONSIBILITIES TO THE PROFESSION

A. Use of Professional Designation.

1. Membership in AIMR, the Financial Analysts Federation (FAF), or the Institute of Chartered Financial Analysts (ICFA) may be referenced by members of these organizations only in a dignified and judicious manner. The use of the reference may be accompanied by an accurate explanation of the requirements that have been met to obtain membership in these organizations.

2. Holders of the Chartered Financial Analyst designation may use the professional designation "Chartered Financial Analyst," or the mark "CFA," and are encouraged to do so, but only in a dignified and judicious manner. The use of the designation may be accompanied by an accurate explanation of the requirements that have been met to obtain the designation.

3. Candidates may reference their participation in the CFA Program, but the reference must clearly state that an individual is a candidate for the CFA designation and may not imply that the candidate has achieved any type of partial designation.

B. Professional Misconduct.

Members shall not engage in any professional conduct involving dishonesty, fraud, deceit, or misrepresentation or commit any act that reflects adversely on their honesty, trustworthiness, or professional competence.

C. Prohibition against Plagiarism.

Members shall not copy or use, in substantially the same form as the original, material prepared by another without acknowledging and identifying the name of the author, publisher, or source of such material. Members may use, without acknowledgment, factual information published by recognized financial and statistical reporting services or similar sources.

STANDARD III: RELATIONSHIPS WITH AND RESPONSIBILITIES TO THE EMPLOYER

A. Obligation to Inform Employer of Code and Standards.

Members shall:

1. Inform their employer, through their direct supervisor, that they are obligated to comply with the Code and Standards and are subject to disciplinary sanctions for violations thereof.

2. Deliver a copy of the Code and Standards to their employer if the employer does not have a copy.

B. Duty to Employer.

Members shall not undertake any independent practice that could result in compensation or other benefit in competition with their employer unless they obtain written consent from both their employer and the persons or entities for whom they undertake independent practice.

C. Disclosure of Conflicts to Employer.

Members shall:

1. Disclose to their employer all matters, including beneficial ownership of securities or other investments, that reasonably could be expected to interfere with their duty to their employer or ability to make unbiased and objective recommendations.

2. Comply with any prohibitions on activities imposed by their employer if a conflict of interest exists.

D. Disclosure of Additional Compensation Arrangements.

Members shall disclose to their employer in writing all monetary compensation or other benefits that they receive for their services that are in addition to compensation or benefits conferred by a member's employer.

E. Responsibilities of Supervisors.

Members with supervisory responsibility, authority, or the ability to influence the conduct of others shall exercise reasonable supervision over those subject to their supervision or authority to prevent any violation of applicable statutes, regulations, or provisions of the Code and Standards. In so doing, members are entitled to rely on reasonable procedures designed to detect and prevent such violations.

STANDARD IV: RELATIONSHIPS WITH AND RESPONSIBILITIES TO CLIENTS AND PROSPECTS

A. Investment Process.

A.1 Reasonable Basis and Representations.
Members shall:

a. Exercise diligence and thoroughness in making investment recommendations or in taking investment actions.

b. Have a reasonable and adequate basis, supported by appropriate research and investigation, for such recommendations or actions.

c. Make reasonable and diligent efforts to avoid any material misrepresentation in any research report or investment recommendation.

d. Maintain appropriate records to support the reasonableness of such recommendations or actions.

A.2 Research Reports.
Members shall:

a. Use reasonable judgment regarding the inclusion or exclusion of relevant factors in research reports.

b. Distinguish between facts and opinions in research reports.

c. Indicate the basic characteristics of the investment involved when preparing for public distribution a research report that is not directly related to a specific portfolio or client.

A.3 Independence and Objectivity.
Members shall use reasonable care and judgment to achieve and maintain independence and objectivity in making investment recommendations or taking investment action.

B. Interactions with Clients and Prospects.

B.1 Fiduciary Duties.
In relationships with clients, members shall use particular care in determining applicable fiduciary duty and shall comply with such duty as to those persons and interests to whom the duty is owed. Members must act for the benefit of their clients and place their clients' interests before their own.

B.2 Portfolio Investment Recommendations and Actions.
Members shall:

a. Make a reasonable inquiry into a client's financial situation, investment experience, and investment objectives prior to making any investment recommendations and shall update this information as necessary, but no less frequently than annually, to allow the members to adjust their investment rec-

ommendations to reflect changed circumstances.

b. Consider the appropriateness and suitability of investment recommendations or actions for each portfolio or client. In determining appropriateness and suitability, members shall consider applicable relevant factors, including the needs and circumstances of the portfolio or client, the basic characteristics of the investment involved, and the basic characteristics of the total portfolio. Members shall not make a recommendation unless they reasonably determine that the recommendation is suitable to the client's financial situation, investment experience, and investment objectives.

c. Distinguish between facts and opinions in the presentation of investment recommendations.

d. Disclose to clients and prospects the basic format and general principles of the investment processes by which securities are selected and portfolios are constructed and shall promptly disclose to clients and prospects any changes that might significantly affect those processes.

B.3 Fair Dealing.
Members shall deal fairly and objectively with all clients and prospects when disseminating investment recommendations, disseminating material changes in prior investment recommendations, and taking investment action.

B.4 Priority of Transactions.
Transactions for clients and employers shall have priority over transactions in securities or other investments of which a member is the beneficial owner so that such personal transactions do not operate adversely to their clients' or employer's interests. If members make a recommendation regarding the purchase or sale of a security or other investment, they shall give their clients and employers adequate opportunity to act on the recommendation before acting on their own behalf. For purposes of the Code and Standards, a member is a "beneficial owner" if the member has:

a. a direct or indirect pecuniary interest in the securities;

b. the power to vote or direct the voting of the shares of the securities or investments;

c. the power to dispose or direct the disposition of the security or investment.

B.5 Preservation of Confidentiality.
Members shall preserve the confidentiality of information communicated by clients, prospects, or employers concerning matters within the scope of the

client-member, prospect-member, or employer-member relationship unless the member receives information concerning illegal activities on the part of the client, prospect, or employer.

B.6 Prohibition against Misrepresentation.

Members shall not make any statements, orally or in writing, that misrepresent:

a. the services that they or their firms are capable of performing;
b. their qualifications or the qualifications of their firm;
c. the member's academic or professional credentials.

Members shall not make or imply, orally or in writing, any assurances or guarantees regarding any investment except to communicate accurate information regarding the terms of the investment instrument and the issuer's obligations under the instrument.

B.7 Disclosure of Conflicts to Clients and Prospects.

Members shall disclose to their clients and prospects all matters, including beneficial ownership of securities or other investments, that reasonably could be expected to impair the member's ability to make unbiased and objective recommendations.

B.8 Disclosure of Referral Fees.

Members shall disclose to clients and prospects any consideration or benefit received by the member or delivered to others for the recommendation of any services to the client or prospect.

STANDARD V: RELATIONSHIPS WITH AND RESPONSIBILITIES TO THE INVESTING PUBLIC

A. Prohibition against Use of Material Nonpublic Information.

Members who possess material nonpublic information related to the value of a security shall not trade or cause others to trade in that security if such trading would breach a duty or if the information was misappropriated or relates to a tender offer. If members receive material nonpublic information in confidence, they shall not breach that confidence by trading or causing others to trade in securities to which such information relates. Members shall make reasonable efforts to achieve public dissemination of material nonpublic information disclosed in breach of a duty.

B. Performance Presentation.

1. Members shall not make any statements, orally or in writing, that misrepresent the investment performance that they or their firm have accomplished or can reasonably be expected to achieve.

2. If members communicate individual or firm performance information directly or indirectly to clients or prospective clients, or in a manner intended to be received by clients or prospective clients, members shall make every reasonable effort to assure that such performance information is a fair, accurate, and complete presentation of such performance.

© Association for Investment Management and Research. Reprinted with permission.

Association of Clinical Research Professionals

ASSOCIATION OF CLINICAL RESEARCH PROFESSIONALS

Address:	1012 14th Street NW, Suite 807
	Washington, DC 20005
Telephone:	202/737-8100
WWW:	www.acrpnet.org
Document:	Code of Ethics for the Association of
	Clinical Research Professionals

I, as a Member of the Association of Clinical Research Professionals, shall:

• Strive to conduct myself and my work with objectivity and integrity.

• Hold as inviolate that credible science is fundamental to all clinical research.

• Seek to communicate information concerning subject health and safety in a timely and responsible manner, with due regard for the significance and credibility of the available data.

• Present my scientific statements or endorsements with full disclosure of whether or not factual supportive data are available.

• Abstain from professional judgments influenced by conflict of interest and, insofar as possible, make full and complete disclosure in situations that may imply a conflict of interest.

- Observe the spirit as well as the law, regulations, and ethical standards with regard to the rights and welfare of human participants involved in research procedures.
- Practice high standards of occupational health and safety for the benefit of human participants involved in research procedures, my co-workers and other personnel.

© Association of Clinical Research Professionals. Reprinted with permission.

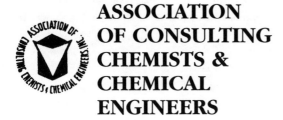

ASSOCIATION OF CONSULTING CHEMISTS & CHEMICAL ENGINEERS

Address: PO Box 297
               Sparta, NJ 07871
Telephone: 973/729-6671
WWW: www.chemconsult.org
Document: Standards of Consulting (1997)

(The original *Code of Ethics* of the ACC&CE was drafted in 1931 and updated in 1961. The Association currently uses the *Standards of Consulting* form reprinted here, rather than the *Code of Ethics*.—Eds.)

Members of the ASSOCIATION OF CONSULTING CHEMISTS AND CHEMICAL ENGINEERS share a serious commitment to high standards of consulting. Every member has signed that he or she subscribes to the Association's Code of Ethics. In essence, this code may be summarized as follows:

In his or her relationships with clients a member should:

- Serve the client's interests in a professional manner.
- Render accurate and conscientious services, under the terms of any verbal or written agreement with the client.
- Disclose no proprietary or secret information gained from association with the client without the client's consent.
- Avoid conflicts of interest with and among clients.
- Request compensation for services rendered commensurate with the amount, quality and special nature of the work.

In his or her relationships with other consultants a member should:

- Treat other professional consultants with fairness and courtesy.
- Be helpful and supportive to other consultants.
- Support and contribute to high standards in the practice of consulting as a profession.

In his or her relationship with the public a member should:

- Refuse to be connected with any illegal work.
- Demonstrate by example that consulting is a valuable and useful part of society.
- Aid and support efforts to advance knowledge of chemistry, chemical engineering, bioengineering and related fields and the application of this knowledge to practical purposes.
- Support projects and causes that are in the general public interest where the expertise of the consultant is relevant.
- Expose and oppose all errors and frauds within the range of his or her special knowledge and skills.

Anyone concerned with the professional conduct of a member should bring the matter to the attention of the Association where it will be referred to the Professional Welfare and Ethics Committee for resolution.

© Association of Consulting Chemists & Chemical Engineers. Reprinted with permission.

ASSOCIATION OF INFORMATION TECHNOLOGY PROFESSIONALS

Address: 315 South Northwest Highway, Suite 200
               Park Ridge, IL 60068-4278

Telephone: 847/825-8124 or 800/224-9371
WWW: www.aitp.org
Document: Code of Ethics (1997)

(The current *Code of Ethics* was originally adopted January 1, 1983. It was updated to reflect the Association's name change from "Data Processing Management Association" to "Association of Information Technology Professionals" in 1997.—Eds.)

I acknowledge:

That I have an obligation to management, therefore, I shall promote the understanding of information processing methods and procedures to management using every resource at my command.

That I have an obligation to my fellow members, therefore, I shall uphold the high ideals of AITP as outlined in its Association Bylaws. Further, I shall cooperate with my fellow members and shall treat them with honesty and respect at all times.

That I have an obligation to society and will participate to the best of my ability in the dissemination of knowledge pertaining to the general development and understanding of information processing. Further, I shall not use knowledge of a confidential nature to further my personal interest, nor shall I violate the privacy and confidentially of information entrusted to me or to which I may gain access.

That I have an obligation to my employer whose trust I hold, therefore, I shall endeavor to discharge this obligation to the best of my ability, to guard my employer's interests, and to advise him or her wisely and honestly.

That I have an obligation to my college or university, therefore, I shall uphold its ethical and moral principles.

That I have an obligation to my country, therefore, in my personal, business, and social contacts, I shall uphold my nation and shall honor the chosen way of life of my fellow citizens.

I accept these obligations as a personal responsibility and as a member of this Association, I shall actively discharge these obligations and I dedicate myself to that end.

Standards of Conduct

These standards expand on the Code of Ethics by providing specific statements of behavior in support of each element of the code. They are not objectives to be strived for, they are rules that no true professional will violate. It is first of all expected that an information processing professional will abide by the appropriate laws of their country and community. The following standards address tenets that apply to the profession.

In recognition of my obligation to management I shall:

- Keep my personal knowledge up-to-date and insure that proper expertise is available when needed.
- Share my knowledge with others and present factual and objective information to management to the best of my ability.
- Accept full responsibility for work that I perform.
- Not misuse the authority entrusted to me.
- Not misrepresent or withhold information concerning the capabilities of equipment, software or systems.
- Not take advantage of the lack of knowledge or inexperience on the part of others.

In recognition of my obligation to my fellow members and the profession I shall:

- Be honest in all my professional relationships.
- Take appropriate action in regard to any illegal or unethical practices that come to my attention. However, I will bring charges against any person only when I have reasonable basis for believing in the truth of the allegations and without regard to personal interest.
- Endeavor to share my special knowledge.
- Cooperate with others in achieving understanding and in identifying problems.
- Not use or take credit for the work of others without specific acknowledgment and authorization.
- Not take advantage of the lack of knowledge or inexperience on the part of others for personal gain.

In recognition of my obligation to society I shall:

- Protect the privacy and confidentiality of all information entrusted to me.
- Use my skill and knowledge to inform the public in all areas of my expertise.
- To the best of my ability, insure that the products of my work are used in a socially responsible way.
- Support, respect, and abide by the appropriate local, state, provincial, and federal laws.
- Never misrepresent or withhold information that is germane to a problem or situation of public concern nor will I allow any such known information to remain unchallenged.
- Not use knowledge of a confidential or personal nature in any unauthorized manner or to achieve personal gain.

In recognition of my obligation to my employer I shall:

- Make every effort to ensure that I have the most current knowledge and that the proper expertise is available when needed.
- Avoid conflict of interest and insure that my employer is aware of any potential conflicts.
- Present a fair, honest, and objective viewpoint.
- Protect the proper interests of my employer at all times.
- Protect the privacy and confidentiality of all information entrusted to me.
- Not misrepresent or withhold information that is germane to the situation.
- Not attempt to use the resources of my employer for personal gain or for any purpose without proper approval.
- Not exploit the weakness of a computer system for personal gain or personal satisfaction.

© Association of Information Technology Professionals. Reprinted with permission.

ASSOCIATION OF MANAGEMENT CONSULTING FIRMS

Address: 380 Lexinton Avenue, Suite 1700
             New York, NY 10168
Telephone: 212/551-7887
WWW: www.amcf.org

The Association of Management Consulting Firms abides by the same *Code of Ethics* as the Institute of Management Consultants, a sister member of the Council of Consulting Organizations. See p. 00.

ASSOCIATION OF PROFESSIONAL GENEALOGISTS

Address: PO Box 40393
             Denver, CO 80204-0393
Telephone: 408/737-7149
WWW: www.apgen.org
Document: APG Code of Ethics (1982)

As a member of the **Association of Professional Genealogists** I agree that professionalism in genealogy requires ethical conduct in all relationships with the present or potential genealogical community. I therefore agree to abide by the following standards:

The professional genealogist promotes a coherent, truthful approach to genealogy, family history, and local history.

The professional presents research results and opinions in a clear, well-organized manner; fully and accurately cites sources; and does not withhold, suppress, or knowingly misquote or misinterpret sources or data.

The professional genealogist promotes the trust and security of genealogical consumers.

The professional honestly advertises services and credentials, avoiding the use of misleading or exaggerated representations; explains without concealment or misrepresentation all fees, charges, and payment structures; abides by agreements regarding project scope, number of hours, and deadlines or reporting schedules; keeps adequate, accessible records of financial and project-specific contacts with the consumer; and does not knowingly violate or encourage others to violate laws and regulations

concerning copyright, right to privacy, business finances, or other
pertinent subjects.

The professional genealogist supports records access and preservation.

The professional is courteous to research facility personnel and treats records with care and respect; supports efforts to locate, collect, and preserve the records by compiling, cataloging, reproducing, and indexing documents; and does not mutilate, rearrange, or remove from its proper custodian any printed, original microfilm, or electronic record.

The professional genealogist promotes the welfare of the genealogical community.

The professional gives proper credit to those who supply information and provide assistance; does not knowingly supplant another researcher; encourages applicable education, accreditation, and certification; and refrains from public behavior, oral remarks, or written communications that defame the profession, individual genealogists, or the Association of Professional Genealogists.

© Association of Professional Genealogists. Reprinted with permission.

ASSOCIATION OF TRIAL LAWYERS OF AMERICA

Address: 1050 31st Street NW
             Washington, DC 20007
Telephone: 202/965-3500

WWW: www.atlanet.com
Document: Code of Conduct (1988)

1. No ATLA member shall personally, or through a representative, contact any party, or an aggrieved survivor in an attempt to solicit a potential client when there has been no request for such contact from the injured party, an aggrieved survivor, or a relative of either, or the injured parties' union representative.

2. No ATLA member shall go to the scene of an event which caused injury unless requested to do so by an interested party, an aggrieved survivor, a relative of either or by an attorney representing an injured party or survivor.

3. No ATLA member shall initiate a television appearance or initiate any comment to any news media concerning an event causing injury within 10 days of the event unless the member forgoes any financial return from the compensation of those injured or killed, provided, however, that an individual designated by a bar association to state the official position of such bar association may initiate such media contact to communicate such position.

4. No ATLA member shall personally, or through an associate attorney, file a complaint with a specific *ad damnum* amount unless required by local rules of court. If such amount is stated, it shall be based upon good faith evaluation of facts which the member can demonstrate.

5. No ATLA member shall personally, or through a representative, make representations of trial experience or past results of litigation either of which is in any way false or misleading.

6. No ATLA member shall personally, or through a representative, initiate personal contact with a potential client (who is not a client, former client, relative or close personal friend of the attorney) for the purpose of advising that individual of the possibility of an unrecognized legal claim for damages unless the member forgoes any financial interest in the compensation of the injured party.

7. No ATLA member shall file or maintain a frivolous suit, issue, or position. However, no ATLA member should refrain from urging or arguing any suit, issue, or position that he believes in good faith to have merit.

8. The ATLA Board of Governors has condemned attorneys or legal clinics who advertise for clients in personal injury cases and who have no intention of handling the cases themselves, but do so for the sole purpose of brokering the case to other attorneys. Any ATLA member who enters a contract of representation on behalf of a claimant shall, at the time of retention, fully advise the client, in writing, of all relationships with other attorneys who will be involved in the presentation, the role each attorney shall play, and the proposed division of fees among them. The client shall also be promptly advised of all changes affecting the representation.

9. No ATLA member shall knowingly accept a referral from a person, whether an ATLA member or not, who obtained the representation by conduct which this code prohibits.

© Association of Trial Lawyers of America. Reprinted with permission.

BOARD FOR CERTIFICATION OF GENEALOGISTS

Address: PO Box 14291
            Washington, DC 20044
Telephone: n/a
WWW: www.genealogy.org/~bcg
Document: Standards of Conduct (1964. Updated
            regularly.)

To protect the public

- I will not publish or publicize as fact anything I know to be false, doubtful, or unproven; nor will I be a party, directly or indirectly, to such action by others.
- I will identify my sources for all information and cite only those documents I have personally used.
- I will quote documents precisely, avoiding any alterations that I do not clearly identify as editorial interpretations.
- I will present the purpose, practice, scope, and possibilities of genealogical research within a realistic framework.
- I will delineate my abilities, publications, and/or fees in a true and realistic fashion.

To protect the consumer (client or colleague)

- I will keep confidential any personal or genealogical information given to me, unless I receive written consent to the contrary.
- I will reveal to the consumer any personal or financial interests that might compromise my professional obligations.
- I will undertake paid research commissions only after a clear agreement as to scope and fee.
- I will, to the best of my abilities, address my research to the issue raised by the consumer and report to that question.
- I will seek from the consumer all prior information and documentation related to the research and will not knowingly repeat the work, as billable hours, without explanation as to good cause.
- I will furnish only facts I can substantiate with adequate documentation; and I will not withhold any data necessary for the consumer's purpose.
- If the research question involves analysis of data in order to establish a genealogical relationship or identity, I will report that the conclusions are based on the weight of the available evidence and that absolute proof of genealogical relationships is usually not possible.
- If I cannot resolve a research problem within the limitations of time or budget established by contract, I will explain the reasons why.
- If other feasible avenues are available, I will suggest them; but I will not misrepresent the possibilities of additional research.
- I will return any advance payment that exceeds the hours and expenses incurred.

- I will not publish or circulate research or reports to which the consumer has a proprietary right, without prior written consent of the consumer; I will observe these rights, whether my report was made directly to the consumer or to an employer or agent.

To protect the profession

- I will act, speak, and write in a manner I believe to be in the best interests of the profession and scholarship of genealogy.
- I will participate in exposing genealogical fraud; but I will not otherwise knowingly injure or attempt to injure, the reputation, prospects, or practice of another genealogist.
- I will not attempt to supplant another genealogist already employed by a client or agency. I will substitute for another researcher only with specific written consent of and instructions provided by the client or agency.
- I will not represent as my work the work of another. This includes works that are copyrighted, in the public domain, or unpublished. This pledge includes reports, lecture materials, audio/visual tapes, compiled records, and authored essays.
- I will not reproduce for public dissemination, in an oral or written fashion, the work of another genealogist, writer, or lecturer, without that person's written consent. In citing another's work, I will give proper credit.

© Board for Certification of Genealogists. Reprinted with permission.

BOARD OF CERTIFIED SAFETY PROFESSIONALS

Address:	208 Burwash Avenue
	Savoy, IL 61874-9571
Telephone:	217/359-9263
WWW:	www.bcsp.com
Document:	Code of Professional Conduct (1989)

Purpose

This Code sets forth the principles and standards of professional conduct to be observed by holders of documents of certification conferred by The Board of Certified Safety Professionals.

Principles

Certificants shall, in their professional activities, sustain and advance the integrity, honor and prestige of the Safety Profession by:

1. Using their knowledge and skill for the enhancement of the safety and health of people and the protection of property and the environment.
2. Being honest and impartial, and serving the public, employees, employers and clients with fidelity.
3. Striving to increase their own competence and the prestige of the safety profession.
4. Avoiding circumstances where compromise of professional conduct or conflict of interest may arise.

Standards

Certificants shall:

1. Hold paramount the safety and health of people and the protection of property and the environment in performance of professional duties and exercise their obligation to advise employers, clients or appropriate authorities of danger to people, property or the environment.
2. Perform professional services and assignments only in areas of their competence.
3. Issue public statements only in an objective and truthful manner.
4. Act in professional matters for employers or clients as faithful agents or trustees.
5. Build their professional reputation on merit of service.
6. Strive for continuous self-development while participation in their chosen professional safety discipline.

© Board of Certified Safety Professionals. Reprinted with permission.

BOTANICAL SOCIETY OF AMERICA

Address:	c/o Kimberly E. Hiser
	Business Manager, Botanical Society
	of America
	1735 Neil Avenue
	Columbus, Ohio 43210-1293

Telephone: 614/292-3519
WWW: www.botany.org
Document: Guidelines for Professional Ethics
(Draft, 1997)

In conducting their research, teaching, and service, botanists often must confront difficult ethical issues related both to their field of specialty, data collection needs and methods, and to the dissemination and use of their findings both in research and teaching. Because botanists are a diverse group with varying scientific backgrounds and professional affiliations, their ethical problems are both diverse and complex. This document presents guidelines for professional behavior for members of the Botanical Society of America.

1. MEMBERS OF THE BOTANICAL SOCIETY OF AMERICA HAVE RESPONSIBILITIES TO THE PUBLIC:

A. They will strive to use and disseminate their knowledge, skills, and training to enhance the well-being of humans through teaching, research, and service. They will specifically refuse to work professionally on any research or teach concepts that in their judgment will result in misinformation or harm;

B. They will strive to maintain professional competence and will not offer advice on subjects about which they are uninformed;

C. They will not engage in nor will they allow the dissemination of information about botany that is false, misleading, or will lead to the destruction of rare and/or endangered/threatened plant species;

D. They will not be a party to any misconduct or unethical behavior, and when perceived in others, they will take appropriate corrective steps.

2. MEMBERS OF THE BOTANICAL SOCIETY OF AMERICA HAVE RESPONSIBILITIES TO THE RESEARCH COMMUNITY:

A. They will communicate clearly and honestly to all with whom they work the objectives and possible consequences of their research by oral and/or printed means. They will support the peer review process. If the research has a commercial objective, researchers will make that explicit, and will disclose within reason the expectations for results;

B. They will comply with all rules and limitations that local people, their communities, or their institutions place on the research, provided that such rules and limitations do not violate other guidelines listed here. They will not attempt to gain information through deception, nor will they "trick" people into revealing "secret" information. They will offer to supply any reports or materials resulting from their research;

C. They will respect any request for confidence made by those providing data or materials, provided that maintaining such confidence does not compromise other ethical considerations;

D. They will respect individuals' rights to anonymity and the rights of privacy of those with whom they work;

E. When materials or information obtained from colleagues can be reasonably expected to have commercial value, members will arrange with employers for equitable compensation for those who have provided the information and/or plants, and will do all in their power to ensure that fair compensation is made;

F. They will refrain from any activity which appears to represent a conflict of interest;

G. They will ensure humane treatment of animals used for plant experimentation;

H. They will adhere to the authorship and publication practices in the field of science and the *American Journal of Botany.*

3. MEMBERS OF THE BOTANICAL SOCIETY OF AMERICA HAVE RESPONSIBILITIES TO HOST GOVERNMENTS AND OTHER HOST INSTITUTIONS:

A. They will comply honestly and completely with all regulations requesting disclosure of project objectives, sponsorship and methods, as well as supply reports and specimens to perform specified services (e.g., seminars and training);

B. They will, when the situation requires, make clear that they will not compromise their professional ethics as a condition of their receiving clearance to do research. Specifically, they will take no actions that might jeopardize the safety or well being of either those with whom they are working or any other individuals;

C. They will assist their colleagues in enhancing the physical and human resources of their institutions and nations.

4. MEMBERS OF THE BOTANICAL SOCIETY OF AMERICA HAVE RESPONSIBILITIES TO THE PROFESSION:

A. They will maintain a level of integrity and professional behavior in the field so as not to jeopardize future research by others;

B. They will not present as their own the work of others, and will credit earlier published studies and individuals whose results they are confirming;

C. They will not allow, to the limits of their abilities, their materials to be used for fraudulent or harmful purposes;

D. They will not allow nor practice discrimination or harassment in any form, and when they perceive it in the actions of others, they will take the appropriate corrective steps;

E. They will serve as mentors, where appropriate, and maintain a professional image both within and outside the discipline of botany.

5. MEMBERS OF THE BOTANICAL SOCIETY OF AMERICA HAVE RESPONSIBILITIES TO THOSE WHO SUPPORT THEIR RESEARCH, TEACHING, AND SERVICE THAT ARE CONSISTENT WITH THE ETHICAL GUIDELINES OF THE BOTANICAL SOCIETY OF AMERICA.

© Botanical Society of America. Reprinted with permission.

CERTIFIED FINANCIAL PLANNER BOARD OF STANDARDS

Address: 1700 Broadway, Suite 2100
               Denver, Colorado 80290-2101
Telephone: 303/830-7500
WWW: www.CFP-Board.org
Document: Code of Ethics and Professional
Responsibility (1998)

Preamble and Applicability
The Code of Ethics and Professional Responsibility (Code) has been adopted by the Certified Financial Planner Board of Standards, Inc. (CFP Board) to provide principles and rules to all persons whom it has recognized and certified to use the CFP certification mark and the marks CFP and Certified Financial Planner (collectively "the marks"). The CFP Board determines who is recognized and certified to use the marks. Implicit in the acceptance of this authorization is an obligation not only to comply with the mandates and requirements of all applicable laws and regulations but also to take responsibility to act in an ethical and professionally responsible manner in all professional services and activities.

For purposes of this Code, a person recognized and certified by the CFP Board to use the marks is called a CFP designee or Certified Financial Planner designee. This Code applies to CFP designees actively involved in the practice of personal financial planning, in other areas of financial services, in industry, in related professions, in government, in education or in any other professional activity in which the marks are used in the performance of their professional responsibilities. This Code also applies to candidates for the CFP designation who are registered as such with the CFP Board. For purposes of this Code, the term CFP designee shall be deemed to include candidates.

Composition and Scope
The Code consists of two parts: Part I—Principles and Part II—Rules. The Principles are statements expressing in general terms the ethical and professional ideals expected of CFP designees and which they should strive to display in their professional activities. As such the Principles are aspirational in character but are intended to provide a source of guidance for a CFP designee. The comments following each Principle further explain the meaning of the Principle. The Rules provide practical guidelines derived from the tenets embodied in the Principles. As such, the Rules set forth the standards of ethical and professionally responsible conduct expected to be followed in particular situations. This Code does not undertake to define standards of professional conduct of CFP designees for purposes of civil liability.

Due to the nature of a CFP designee's particular field of endeavor, certain Rules may not be applicable to that CFP designee's activities. For example, a CFP designee who is engaged solely in the sale of securities as a registered representative is not subject to the written disclosure requirements of Rule 402 (applicable to CFP designees engaged in personal financial planning) although he or she may have disclosure responsibilities under Rule 401. A CFP designee is obligated to determine what responsibilities the CFP designee has in each professional relationship including, for example, duties that arise in particular circumstances from a position of trust or confidence that a CFP designee may have. The CFP designee is obligated to meet those responsibilities.

The Code is structured so that the presentation of the Rules parallels the presentation of the Principles. For example, the Rules which relate to Principle 1—

Integrity, are numbered in the 100 to 199 series while those Rules relating to Principle 2—Objectivity, are numbered in the 200 to 299 series.

Compliance

The CFP Board of Governors requires adherence to this Code by all those it recognizes and certifies to use the marks. Compliance with the Code, individually and by the profession as a whole, depends on each CFP designee's knowledge of and voluntary compliance with the Principles and applicable Rules, on the influence of fellow professional and public opinion, and on disciplinary proceedings, when necessary, involving CFP designees who fail to comply with the applicable provisions of the Code.

Terminology In This Code

"**Client**" denotes a person, persons, or entity for whom professional services are rendered. Where the service of the practitioner are provided to an entity (corporation, trust, partnership, estate, etc.), the client is the entity, acting through its legally authorized representative.

"**Commission**" denotes the compensation received by an agent or broker when the same is calculated as a percentage on the amount of his or her sales or purchase transactions.

"**Conflict(s) of interest(s)**" denotes circumstances, relationships or other facts about the CFP designee's own financial, business, property and/or personal interests which will or reasonably may impair the CFP designee's rendering of disinterested advice, recommendations or services.

"**Fee-only**" denotes a method of compensation in which compensation is received solely from a client with neither the personal financial planning practitioner nor any related party receiving compensation which is contingent upon the purchase or sale of any financial product. A "related party" for this purpose shall mean an individual or entity from whom any direct or indirect economic benefit is derived by the personal financial planning practitioner as a result of implementing a recommendation made by the personal financial planning practitioner.

"**Personal financial planning**" or "**financial planning**" denotes the process of determining whether and how an individual can meet life goals through the proper management of financial resources.

"**Personal financial planning process**" or "**financial planning process**" denotes the process which typically includes, but is not limited to, the six ele-

ments of establishing and defining the client-planner relationship, gathering client data including goals, analyzing and evaluating the client's financial status, developing and presenting financial planning recommendations and/or alternatives, implementing the financial planning recommendations and monitoring the financial planning recommendations.

"**Personal financial planning subject areas**" or "**financial planning subject areas**" denotes the basic subject fields covered in the financial planning process which typically include, but are not limited to, financial statement preparation and analysis (including cash flow analysis/planning and budgeting), investment planning (including portfolio design, i.e., asset allocation, and portfolio management), income tax planning, education planning, risk management, retirement planning, and estate planning.

"**Personal financial planning professional**" or "**financial planning professional**" denotes a person who is capable and qualified to offer objective, integrated, and comprehensive financial advice to or for the benefit of individuals to help them achieve their financial objectives. A financial planning professional must have the ability to provide financial planning services to clients, using the financial planning process covering the basic financial planning subjects.

"**Personal financial planning practitioner**" or "**financial planning practitioner**" denotes a person who is capable and qualified to offer objective, integrated, and comprehensive financial advice to or for the benefit of clients to help them achieve their financial objectives and who engages in financial planning using the financial planning process in working with clients.

Part I—Principles

Introduction

These Principles of the Code express the professions recognition of its responsibilities to the public, to clients, to colleagues, and to employers. They apply to all CFP designees and provide guidance to them in the performance of their professional services.

Principle 1—Integrity

A CFP designee shall offer and provide professional services with integrity.

As discussed in Composition and Scope, CFP designees may be placed by clients in positions of trust and confidence. The ultimate source of such public trust is the CFP designee's personal integrity. In deciding what is right and just, a CFP designee should rely on his or her integrity as the appropriate touchstone. Integrity demands honesty and candor which must not be subordinated to personal gain and advantage. Within the characteristic of integrity, allowance can be made for innocent error and legitimate difference of opinion; but integrity cannot co-exist with deceit or subordination of one's principles. Integrity requires a CFP designee to observe not only the letter but also the spirit of this Code.

Principle 2—Objectivity

A CFP designee shall be objective in providing professional services to clients.

Objectivity requires intellectual honesty and impartiality. It is an essential quality for any professional. Regardless of the particular service rendered or the capacity in which a CFP designee functions, a CFP designee should protect the integrity of his or her work, maintain objectivity, and avoid subordination of his or her judgment that would be in violation of this Code.

Principle 3—Competence

A CFP designee shall provide services to clients competently and maintain the necessary knowledge and skill to continue to do so in those areas in which the designee is engaged.

One is competent only when he or she has attained and maintained an adequate level of knowledge and skill, and applies that knowledge effectively in providing services to clients. Competence also includes the wisdom to recognize the limitations of that knowledge and when consultation or client referral is appropriate. A CFP designee, by virtue of having earned the CFP designation, is deemed to be qualified to practice financial planning. However, in addition to assimilating the common body of knowledge required and acquiring the necessary experience for designation, a CFP designee shall make a continuing commitment to learning and professional improvement.

Principle 4—Fairness

A CFP designee shall perform professional services in a manner that is fair and reasonable to clients, principals, partners, and employers and shall disclose conflict(s) of interest(s) in providing such services.

Fairness requires impartiality, intellectual honesty, and disclosure of conflict(s) of interest(s). It involves a subordination of one's own feelings, prejudices, and desires so as to achieve a proper balance of conflicting interests. Fairness is treating others in the same fashion that you would want to be treated and is an essential trait of any professional.

Principle 5—Confidentiality

A CFP designee shall not disclose any confidential client information without the specific consent of the client unless in response to proper legal process, to defend against charges of wrongdoing by the CFP designee or in connection with a civil dispute between the CFP designee and client.

A client, by seeking the services of a CFP designee, may be interested in creating a relationship of personal trust and confidence with the CFP designee. This type of relationship can only be built upon the understanding that information supplied to the CFP designee or other information will be confidential. In order to provide the contemplated services effectively and to protect the client's privacy, the CFP designee shall safeguard the confidentiality of such information.

Principle 6—Professionalism

A CFP designee's conduct in all matters shall reflect credit upon the profession.

Because of the importance of the professional services rendered by CFP designees, there are attendant responsibilities to behave with dignity and courtesy to all those who use those services, fellow professionals, and those in related professions. A CFP designee also has an obligation to cooperate with fellow CFP designees to enhance and maintain the profession's public image and to work jointly with other CFP designees to improve the quality of services. It is only through the combined efforts of all CFP designees in cooperation with other professionals, that this vision can be realized.

Principle 7—Diligence

A CFP designee shall act diligently in providing professional services.

Diligence is the provision of services in a reasonably prompt and thorough manner. Diligence also includes proper planning for and supervision of the rendering of professional services.

Part II—Rules

Introduction

As stated in Part I—Principles, the Principles apply to all CFP designees. However, due to the nature of a CFP designee's particular field of endeavor, certain

Rules may not be applicable to that CFP designee's activities. The universe of activities by CFP designees is indeed diverse and a particular CFP designee may be performing all, some or none of the typical services provided by financial planning professionals. As a result, in considering the Rules in Part II, a CFP designee must first recognize what specific services he or she is rendering and then determine whether or not a specific Rule is applicable to those services. To assist the CFP designee in making these determinations, this Code includes a series of definitions of terminology used throughout the Code. Based upon these definitions, a CFP designee should be able to determine which services he or she provides and, therefore, which Rules are applicable to those services.

Rules that Relate to the Principle of Integrity

Rule 101

A CFP designee shall not solicit clients through false or misleading communications or advertisements:

(a) **Misleading Advertising:** A CFP designee shall not make a false or misleading communication about the size, scope or areas of competence of the CFP designee's practice or of any organization with which the CFP designee is associated; and

(b) **Promotional Activities:** In promotional activities, a CFP designee shall not make materially false or misleading communications to the public or create unjustified expectations regarding matters relating to financial planning or the professional activities and competence of the CFP designee. The term "promotional activities" includes, but is not limited to, speeches, interviews, books and/or printed publications, seminars, radio and television shows, and video cassettes; and

(c) **Representation of Authority:** A CFP designee shall not give the impression that a CFP designee is representing the views of the CFP Board or any other group unless the CFP designee has been authorized to do so. Personal opinions shall be clearly identified as such.

Rule 102

In the course of professional activities, a CFP designee shall not engage in conduct involving dishonesty, fraud, deceit or misrepresentation, or knowingly make a false or misleading statement to a client, employer, employee, professional colleague, governmental or other regulatory body or official, or any other person or entity.

Rule 103

A CFP designee has the following responsibilities regarding funds and/or other property of clients:

(a) In exercising custody of or discretionary authority over client funds or other property, a CFP designee shall act only in accordance with the authority set forth in the governing legal instrument (e.g., special power of attorney, trust, letters testamentary, etc.); and

(b) A CFP designee shall identify and keep complete records of all funds or other property of a client in the custody of or under the discretionary authority of the CFP designee; and

(c) Upon receiving funds or other property of a client, a CFP designee shall promptly or as otherwise permitted by law or provided by agreement with the client, deliver to the client or third party any funds or other property which the client or third party is entitled to receive and, upon request by the client, render a full accounting regarding such funds or other property; and

(d) A CFP designee shall not commingle client funds or other property with a CFP designee's personal funds and/or other property or the funds and/or other property of a CFP designee's firm. Commingling one or more clients' funds or other property together is permitted, subject to compliance with applicable legal requirements and provided accurate records are maintained for each client's funds or other property; and

(e) A CFP designee who takes custody of all or any part of a client's assets for investment purposes, shall do so with the care required of a fiduciary.

Rules that Relate to the Principle of Objectivity

Rule 201

A CFP designee shall exercise reasonable and prudent professional judgment in providing professional services.

Rule 202

A financial planning practitioner shall act in the interest of the client.

Rules that Relate to the Principle of Competence

Rule 301

A CFP designee shall keep informed of developments in the field of financial planning and participate in continuing education throughout the CFP designee's professional career in order to improve professional competence in all areas in which the CFP designee is engaged. As a distinct part of this requirement, a CFP designee shall satisfy all minimum continuing education requirements established for CFP designees by the CFP Board.

Rule 302

A CFP designee shall offer advice only in those areas in which the CFP designee has competence. In areas where the CFP designee is not professionally competent, the CFP designee shall seek the counsel of qualified individuals and/or refer clients to such parties.

Rules that Relate to the Principle of Fairness

Rule 401

In rendering professional services, a CFP designee shall disclose to the client:

(a) Material information relevant to the professional relationship, including but not limited to conflict(s) of interest(s), changes in the CFP designee's business affiliation, address, telephone number, credentials, qualifications, licenses, compensation structure and any agency relationships, and the scope of the CFP designee's authority in that capacity.

(b) The information required by all laws applicable to the relationship in a manner complying with such laws.

Rule 402

A financial planning practitioner shall make timely written disclosure of all material information relative to the professional relationship. In all circumstances such disclosure shall include conflict(s) of interest(s) and sources of compensation. Written disclosures that include the following information are considered to be in compliance with this Rule:

(a) A statement of the basic philosophy of the CFP designee (or firm) in working with clients. The disclosure shall include the philosophy, theory and/or principles of financial planning which will be utilized by the CFP designee; and

(b) Resumes of principals and employees of a firm who are expected to provide financial planning services to the client and a description of those services. Such disclosures shall include educational background, professional/employment history, professional designations and licenses held, and areas of competence and specialization; and

(c) A statement of compensation, which in reasonable detail discloses the source(s) and any contingencies or other aspects material to the fee and/or commission arrangement. Any estimates made shall be clearly identified as such and shall be based on reasonable assumptions. Referral fees, if any, shall be fully disclosed; and

(d) A statement indicating whether the CFP designee's compensation arrangements involve fee-only, commission-only, or fee and commission. A CFP designee shall not hold out as a fee-only financial planning practitioner if the CFP designee receives commissions or other forms of economic benefit from related parties; and

(e) A statement describing material agency or employment relationships a CFP designee (or firm) has with third parties and the fees or commissions resulting from such relationships; and

(f) A statement identifying conflict(s) of interest(s).

Rule 403

A CFP designee providing financial planning shall disclose in writing, prior to establishing a client relationship, relationships which reasonably may compromise the CFP designee's objectivity or independence.

Rule 404

Should conflict(s) of interest(s) develop after a professional relationship has been commenced, but before the services contemplated by that relationship have been completed, a CFP designee shall promptly disclose the conflict(s) of interest(s) to the client or other necessary persons.

Rule 405

In addition to the disclosure by financial planning practitioners regarding sources of compensation required under Rule 402, such disclosure shall be made annually thereafter for ongoing clients. The annual disclosure requirement may be satisfied by offering to provide clients with the current copy of SEC form ADV, Part II or the disclosure called for by Rule 402.

Rule 406

A CFP designee's compensation shall be fair and reasonable.

Rule 407

Prior to establishing a client relationship, and consistent with the confidentiality requirements of Rule 501, a CFP designee may provide references which may include recommendations from present and/or former clients.

Rule 408

When acting as an agent for a principal, a CFP designee shall assure that the scope of his or her authority is clearly defined and properly documented.

Rule 409

Whether a CFP designee is employed by a financial planning firm, an investment institution, or serves as an agent for such an organization, or is self-employed, all CFP designees shall adhere to the same standards of disclosure and service.

Rule 410

A CFP designee who is an employee shall perform professional services with dedication to the lawful objectives of the employer and in accordance with this Code.

Rule 411

A CFP designee shall:

(a) Advise the CFP designee's employer of outside affiliations which reasonably may compromise service to an employer; and
(b) Provide timely notice to the employer and clients, unless precluded by contractual obligation, in the event of change of employment or CFP Board licensing status.

Rule 412

A CFP designee doing business as a partner or principal of a financial services firm owes to the CFP designee's partners or co-owners a responsibility to act in good faith. This includes, but is not limited to, disclosure of relevant and material financial information while in business together.

Rule 413

A CFP designee shall join a financial planning firm as a partner or principal only on the basis of mutual disclosure of relevant and material information regarding credentials, competence, experience, licensing and/or legal status, and financial stability of the parties involved.

Rule 414

A CFP designee who is a partner or co-owner of a financial services firm who elects to withdraw from the firm shall do so in compliance with any applicable agreement, and shall deal with his or her business interest in a fair and equitable manner.

Rule 415

A CFP designee shall inform his or her employer, partners or co-owners of compensation or other benefit arrangements in connection with his or her services to clients which are in addition to compensation from the employer, partners or co-owners for such services.

Rule 416

If a CFP designee enters into a business transaction with a client, the transaction shall be on terms which are fair and reasonable to the client and the CFP designee shall disclose the risks of the transaction, conflict(s) of interest(s) of the CFP designee, and other relevant information, if any, necessary to make the transaction fair to the client.

Rules that Relate to the Principle of Confidentiality

Rule 501

A CFP designee shall not reveal—or use for his or her own benefit—without the client's consent, any personally identifiable information relating to the client relationship or the affairs of the client, except and to the extent disclosure or use is reasonably necessary:

(a) To establish an advisory or brokerage account, to effect a transaction for the client, or as otherwise impliedly authorized in order to carry out the client engagement; or
(b) To comply with legal requirements or legal process; or
(c) To defend the CFP designee against charges of wrongdoing; or
(d) In connection with a civil dispute between the CFP designee and the client.

For purposes of this rule, the proscribed use of client information is improper whether or not it actually causes harm to the client.

Rule 502

A CFP designee shall maintain the same standards of confidentiality to employers as to clients.

Rule 503

A CFP designee doing business as a partner or principal of a financial services firm owes to the CFP designee's partners or co-owners a responsibility to act in good faith. This includes, but is not limited to, adherence to reasonable expectations of confidentiality both while in business together and thereafter.

Rules that Relate to the Principle of Professionalism

Rule 601

A CFP designee shall use the marks in compliance with the rules and regulations of the CFP Board, as established and amended from time to time.

Rule 602

A CFP designee shall show respect for other financial planning professionals, and related occupational groups, by engaging in fair and honorable competitive practices. Collegiality among CFP designees shall not, however, impede enforcement of this Code.

Rule 603

A CFP designee who has knowledge, which is not required to be kept confidential under this Code, that another CFP designee has committed a violation of this Code which raises substantial questions as to the designee's honesty, trustworthiness or fitness as a CFP designee in other respects, shall promptly inform the CFP Board. This rule does not require disclosure of information or reporting based on knowledge gained as a consultant or expert witness in anticipation of or related to litigation or other dispute resolution mechanisms. For purposes of this rule, knowledge means no substantial doubt.

Rule 604

A CFP designee who has knowledge, which is not required under this Code to be kept confidential, and which raises a substantial question of unprofessional, fraudulent or illegal conduct by a CFP designee or other financial professional, shall promptly inform the appropriate regulatory and/or professional disciplinary body. This rule does not require disclosure or reporting of information gained as a consultant or expert witness in anticipation of or related to litigation or other dispute resolution mechanisms. For purposes of this Rule, knowledge means no substantial doubt.

Rule 605

A CFP designee who has reason to suspect illegal conduct within the CFP designee's organization shall make timely disclosure of the available evidence to the CFP designee's immediate supervisor and/or partners or co-owners. If the CFP designee is convinced that illegal conduct exists within the CFP designee's organization, and that appropriate measures are not taken to remedy the situation, the CFP designee shall, where appropriate, alert the appropriate regulatory authorities including the CFP Board in a timely manner.

Rule 606

In all professional activities a CFP designee shall perform services in accordance with:

(a) Applicable laws, rules, and regulations of governmental agencies and other applicable authorities; and

(b) Applicable rules, regulations, and other established policies of the CFP Board.

Rule 607

A CFP designee shall not engage in any conduct which reflects adversely on his or her integrity or fitness as a CFP designee, upon the marks, or upon the profession.

Rule 608

The Investment Advisers Act of 1940 requires registration of investment advisers with the U.S. Securities and Exchange Commission and similar state statutes may require registration with state securities agencies. CFP designees shall disclose to clients their firm's status as registered investment advisers. Under present standards of acceptable business conduct, it is proper to use registered investment adviser if the CFP designee is registered individually. If the CFP designee is registered through his or her firm, then the CFP designee is not a registered investment adviser but a person associated with an investment adviser. The firm is the registered investment adviser. Moreover, RIA or R.I.A. following a CFP designee's name in advertising, letterhead stationery, and business cards may be misleading and is not permitted either by this Code or by SEC regulations.

Rule 609

A CFP designee shall not practice any other profession or offer to provide such services unless the CFP designee is qualified to practice in those fields and is licensed as required by state law.

Rule 610

A CFP designee shall return the client's original records in a timely manner after their return has been requested by a client.

Rule 611

A CFP designee shall not bring or threaten to bring a disciplinary proceeding under this Code, or report or threaten to report information to the CFP Board pursuant to Rules 603 and/or 604, or make or threaten to make use of this Code for no substantial purpose other than to harass, maliciously injure, embarrass and/or unfairly burden another CFP designee.

Rule 612

A CFP designee shall comply with all applicable post-certification requirements established by the CFP Board including, but not limited to, payment of the annual CFP designee fee as well as signing and returning the Licensee's Statement annually in connection with the license renewal process.

Rules that Relate to the Principle of Diligence

Rule 701

A CFP designee shall provide services diligently.

Rule 702

A financial planning practitioner shall enter into an engagement only after securing sufficient information to satisfy the CFP designee that:

(a The relationship is warranted by the individual's needs and objectives; and

(b) The CFP designee has the ability to either provide requisite competent services or to involve other professionals who can provide such services.

Rule 703

A financial planning practitioner shall make and/or implement only recommendations which are suitable for the client.

Rule 704

Consistent with the nature and scope of the engagement, a CFP designee shall make a reasonable investigation regarding the financial products recommended to clients. Such an investigation may be made by the CFP designee or by others provided the CFP designee acts reasonably in relying upon such investigation.

Rule 705

A CFP designee shall properly supervise subordinates with regard to their delivery of financial planning services, and shall not accept or condone conduct in violation of this Code.

CHARTERED PROPERTY CASUALTY UNDERWRITER SOCIETY

Address: PO Box 3009
             Malvern, PA 19355-0709
Telephone: 610/251-2728
WWW: www.cpcusociety.org
Document: Code of Ethics

(The following ethics statements are taken from the Bylaws of the CPCUS.—Eds.)

SECTION 3.

The Board of Directors, by affirmative vote of two-thirds of its voting members, shall have the authority to expel, suspend, censure, or reprimand any member for conduct in violation of the standards of the Society as set forth in Section 4 of this article, or for conduct in violation of the CPCU professional commitment as adopted and promulgated from time to time by the American Institute for Chartered Property Casualty Underwriters, Inc. The Board of Directors, by affirmative vote of two-thirds of its voting members, shall have the authority to remove any of the board members listed in Article III, Section 2 upon recommendation by the Executive Committee.

SECTION 4.

It may be a basis for disciplinary action to commit any of the following acts:

a. Specified Unethical Practices.

(1) To violate any law or regulation duly enacted by any governmental body whose authority has been established by law.

(2) To willfully misrepresent or conceal a material fact in insurance and risk management business dealings in violation of a duty or obligation.

(3) To breach the confidential relationship that a member has with his client or with his principal.

(4) To willfully misrepresent the nature or significance of the CPCU designation.

(5) To write, speak, or act in such a way as to lead another to reasonably believe that the member is officially representing the Society or a chapter of the Society unless the member has been duly authorized to do so.

(6) To aid and abet in the performance of any unethical practice proscribed under this Section.

(7) To engage in conduct which has been the subject of a presidential or Board of Directors directive to cease and desist.

b. Unspecified Unethical Practices.

(1) A member shall not engage in practices which tend to discredit the Society or the business of insurance and risk management.

(2) A member shall not fail to use due diligence to ascertain the needs of his or her client or principal and shall not undertake any assignment if

it is apparent that it cannot be performed by him or her in a proper and professional manner.

(3) A member shall not fail to use his or her full knowledge and ability to perform his or her duties to his or her client or principal.

Reprinted with permission of the CPCU Society, Malvern, Pennsylvania.

CHILD WELFARE LEAGUE OF AMERICA

Address: 440 First Street NW, Suite 310
                    Washington, DC 20001
Telephone: 202/638-2952
WWW: www.cwla.org

The Child Welfare League of America subscribes to the code of the National Association of Social Workers. See p. 00.

Clinical Social
Work Federation

CLINICAL SOCIAL WORK FEDERATION

Address: PO Box 3740
                    Arlington, VA 22203
Telephone: 703/522-3866
WWW: www.cswf.org
Document: Code of Ethics (1997)

PREAMBLE

The principal objective of the profession of clinical social work is the enhancement of the mental health and the well-being of the individuals and families who seek services from its practitioners. The professional practice of clinical social workers is shaped by ethical principles which are rooted in the basic values of the social work profession. These core values include a commitment to the dignity, well-being, and self-determination of the individual; a commitment to professional practice characterized by competence and integrity, and a commitment to a society which offers opportunities to all its members in a just and non-discriminatory manner. Clinical social workers examine practice situations in terms of the ethical dilemmas that they present, with a critical analysis of how the formulation of a solution fulfills the core requirements of ethical practice; non-malfeasance, (doing no harm to clients); beneficence, (helping clients), and autonomy (enhancing the self-determination of clients).

The following represents a specific codification of those ethical principles. It is intended to serve as a standard for clinical social workers in all of their professional functions, and to inspire their will to act in a manner consistent with those tenets. The clinical social worker is expected to take into consideration all principles in this code that have a bearing upon any situation in which ethical judgment is to be exercised, and to select a course of action consistent with the spirit, as well as the letter of the code.

Individual members of the Clinical Social Work Federation and of the various State Societies for Clinical Social Work agree to adhere to the precepts expressed in this Code, and to practice in a manner which is consistent with them. When the practice of a member is alleged to deviate from the Code of Ethics, the Code is to be used as a standard for the evaluation of the nature and seriousness of the deviation.

I. GENERAL RESPONSIBILITIES OF CLINICAL SOCIAL WORKERS

Clinical social workers maintain high standards in all of their professional roles, and value professional competence, objectivity, and integrity. They accept responsibility for the consequences of their work, and ensure that their services are used in an appropriate manner.

a) Clinical social workers bear a heavy professional responsibility because their actions and recommendations may significantly affect the lives of others. They practice only within their sphere of competence, and maintain and enhance that competence through participation in continuing professional development throughout their careers. They refrain from undertaking or continuing any professional activity in which their personal difficulties, or any other limitations, might lead to the inadequate provision of service.

b) Clinical social workers do not exploit professional relationships sexually, financially, or for any other professional and/or personal advantage. They maintain this standard of conduct toward all those who may be professionally associated with them.

c) Clinical social workers often function as employees in clinics, hospitals, and agencies, or, as providers on managed care panels. In these positions, they are responsible for identifying and actively working to modify policies or procedures which may come into conflict with the standards of their profession. If such a conflict arises, the primary responsibility of the clinical social worker is to uphold the ethical standards of the profession. These standards require that commitment to the welfare of the client(s) is the primary obligation.

d) Clinical social workers have an additional responsibility, both to the profession which provides the basis of their practice, and to those who are entering that profession. As teachers, supervisors, and mentors, they are responsible for maintaining high standards of objectivity and scholarship. In all of their professional activities they consistently examine, and attempt to expand, the knowledge base on which practice in the profession is centered.

II. RESPONSIBILITY TO CLIENTS

The primary responsibility of the clinical social worker is to the individual client, the family or the group with whom he or she has a professional relationship. Clinical social workers respect the dignity, protect the welfare, and maximize the self-determination of the clients with whom they work.

1. INFORMED CONSENT TO TREATMENT

a) Clinical social work treatment takes place within a context of informed consent. This requires that the client(s) be informed of the extent and nature of the services being offered as well as the mutual limits, rights, opportunities, and obligations associated with the provision of and payment for those services. In order for the consent to be valid, the client(s) must be informed in a manner which is clear to them, must choose freely and without undue influence, and must have the capacity to make an informed choice. In instances where

clients are not of legal age or competent to give a meaningful consent, they will be informed in a manner which is consistent with their level of understanding. In such situations, authorization for treatment will be obtained from an appropriate third party, such as a parent or other legal guardian.

b) Clinical social workers have a duty to understand the potential impact on all aspects of treatment resulting from participation in various third party payment mechanisms, and to disclose fully their knowledge of these features to the client. Such features might include, but are not limited to; limitations of confidentiality; payment limitations related to provider choice; a summary of the treatment review process required by the plan; the comparative treatment orientations of the plan and of the clinical social worker; the possibility that benefits may be limited under the plan; the clinical social worker's relationship to the plan and any incentives to limit or deny care; and, the availability of alternative treatment options.

2. PRACTICE MANAGEMENT AND TERMINATION

a) Clinical social workers enter into and/or continue professional relationships based on their ability to meet the needs of clients appropriately. The clinical social worker terminates services and relationships with clients when such services and relationships are no longer in the client's best interest. Clinical social workers do not abandon clients by withdrawing services precipitously, except under extraordinary circumstances.

Clinical social workers give careful consideration to all factors involved in termination and take care to minimize the possible adverse effects it might have on the client(s). When interruption or termination of service is anticipated, the clinical social worker gives reasonable notification and provides for transfer, referral, or continuation of service in a manner as consistent as possible with the client's needs and preferences.

b) Clinical social workers providing services which are reimbursed by third party payers continue to have primary responsibility for the welfare of the client(s). The failure of the third party to authorize continued benefits does not remove the obligation of the clinical social worker to assure necessary treatment, if this is in the client's best interests. When benefits are ended, the clinical social worker has a number of options including; acceptance of private payment for continued services, at either regular or reduced rates; provision of services on an unpaid basis; and, referral to appropriate alternative treatment sources.

c) A clinical social worker who disagrees with the denial of continued benefits by a third party payer is responsible for discussing this action with the client(s), and for devising a clinically appropriate plan, which may or may not include appeal of the decision. Further pursuit of the appeals process will be based on such factors as; the degree to which the clinical social worker believes that further treatment is necessary for the client's well-being; the degree to which the client(s) wishes to pursue the appeals process, and; the degree to which there are alternative means available for the client(s) to continue treatment.

d) Clinical social workers keep records for each individual and family they treat which reflect relevant administrative rules, contractual obligations, and local and federal statutes. They are required to be knowledgeable about statutes relating to client access to records, and to fulfill their responsibility as required by law. When access to records is permitted, the clinical social worker will take appropriate, legally permitted steps to protect the privacy of all third parties who may be named in the records.

e) All requirements regarding the establishment, maintenance, and disposal of records relate equally to written and to electronic records.

Clinical social workers establish a policy on record retention and disposal, or are aware of agency policies regarding these issues, and communicate it to the client. In the event of the death or incapacity of a client, they safeguard the record, within existing statutes, and the information contained therein. Clinical social workers have a plan or procedure for the proper handling of client records in the event of their own death or disability which both protects privacy, and ensures that legitimate access functions can be properly carried out.

3. RELATIONSHIPS WITH CLIENTS

a) Clinical social workers are responsible for setting clear and appropriate professional boundaries, especially in those instances in which dual or multiple relationships are unavoidable. They do not engage in dual or multiple relationships in which there is any risk of their professional judgment being compromised, or of the client being harmed or exploited. When clinical social workers provide services to two or more persons who have a relationship with each other, they clarify with all parties the nature of the professional responsibilities to each of them, and the ways in which appropriate boundaries will be maintained.

b) Clinical social workers do not, under any circumstances, engage in romantic or sexual contact with either current or former clients. Clinical social workers are also mindful of how their relationship with the family and/or friends of their clients might affect their work with the client. Consequently, they also avoid romantic or sexual involvements with members of the client's family, or with others with whom the client has a close, personal relationship.

c) Clinical social workers are aware of the authority which is inherent in their professional role. They do not engage in any activity that will abuse their professional relationships or exploit others for personal, political, or business interests. As practitioners, supervisors, teachers, administrators, and researchers their primary professional responsibility is always the welfare of the client(s) with whom they work.

d) When the clinical social worker must act on behalf of a client, that action should always safeguard the interests and concerns of that client. When another person has been authorized to act on behalf of a client, the clinical social worker should deal with that person in a manner which will safeguard the interests and concerns of the client.

e) Clinical social workers recognize and support the right to self determination of clients who may choose not to relinquish their privacy by pursuing third party reimbursement for treatment, even when they are eligible for such reimbursement. In such instances, the clinical social worker makes every effort to assist the client in making alternative financial arrangements so that treatment can proceed.

f) When a clinical social worker determines that a conflict potentially detrimental to the treatment process has arisen, he or she should inform the individual(s) to whom he or she has a professional responsibility of the nature of the conflict and the way in which it might affect the provision of service.

4. COMPETENCE

a) Clinical social workers are aware of the scope in which they are entitled to practice. This scope is defined by their areas of personal competence; by their license or other legal recognition; and by their training and/or experience. They are responsible for confining their practice to those areas in which they are legally authorized and in which they are qualified to practice. When necessary, they utilize the knowledge and experience of members of other professions. In using such consultants or supervisors, the clinical social worker is responsible for ensuring that they are recognized members of their own profession, and are qualified and competent to carry out the service required.

b) Clinical social workers recognize that the privacy and intimacy of the therapeutic relationship may unrealistically intensify the client's feelings for them. The maintenance of professional boundaries and objectivity is crucial to effective and responsible treatment. Clinical social workers maintain self awareness and take care to prevent the possible harmful intrusion of their own unresolved personal issues into the therapeutic relationship. They take appropriate steps to resolve the situation when there is a danger of this occurring. Such steps could include, but are not limited to; seeking additional supervision or consultation; seeking additional personal treatment; and, if necessary, making alternative arrangements for the treatment of the client(s).

c) Clinical social workers recognize the responsibility to remain abreast of knowledge and developments in the field which may benefit their client(s). Ongoing involvement in supervision, consultation, and continuing education are some of the ways in which this responsibility can be fulfilled. It is particularly important for the clinical social worker to secure appropriate training, supervision, or consultation when attempting to use a treatment technique with which he or she is unfamiliar.

III. CONFIDENTIALITY

Clinical social workers have a primary obligation to maintain the privacy of both current and former clients, whether living or deceased, and to maintain the confidentiality of material that has been transmitted to them in any of their professional roles. Exceptions to this responsibility will occur only when there are overriding legal or professional reasons and, whenever possible, with the written informed consent of the client(s).

a) Clinical social workers discuss fully with clients both the nature of confidentiality, and potential limits to confidentiality which may arise during the course of their work. Confidential information should only be released, whenever possible, with the written permission of the client(s). As part of the process of obtaining such a release, the clinical social worker should inform the client(s) about the nature of the information being sought, the purpose(s) for which it is being sought, to whom the information will be released, how the client(s) may withdraw permission for its release, and, the length of time that the release will be in effect.

b) Clinical social workers know and observe both legal and professional standards for maintaining the privacy of records, and mandatory reporting obligations. Mandatory reporting obligations may include, but are not limited to; the reporting of the abuse or neglect of children or of vulnerable adults; the duty to take steps to protect or warn a third party who may be endangered by the client(s); and, any duty to report the misconduct or impairment of another professional. Additional limits to confidentiality may occur because of parental access to the records of a minor, the access of legal guardians to the records of some adults, access by the courts to mandated reports, and access by third party payers to information for the purpose of treatment authorization or audit. When confidential information is released to a third party, the clinical social worker will ensure that the information divulged is limited to the minimum amount required to accomplish the purpose for which the release is being made.

c) Clinical social workers treating couples, families, and groups seek agreement among the parties involved regarding each individual's right to confidentiality, and the mutual obligation to protect the confidentiality of information shared by other parties to the treatment. Clients involved in this type of treatment should, however, be informed that the clinical social worker cannot guarantee that all participants will honor their agreement to maintain confidentiality.

d) When confidential information is used for purposes of professional education, research, or publication, the primary responsibility of the clinical social worker is the protection of the client(s) from possible harm, embarrassment, or exploitation. When extensive material is used for any of these purposes the clinical social worker makes every effort to obtain the informed consent of the client(s) for such use, and will not proceed if the client(s) denies this consent. Whether or not a consent is obtained, every effort will be made to protect the true identity of the client. Any such presentation will be limited to the amount necessary for the professional purpose, and will be shared only with other responsible individuals.

e) The development of new technologies for the storage and transmission of data poses a great danger to the privacy of individuals. Clinical social workers take special precautions to protect the confidentiality of material stored or transmitted through computers, electronic mail, facsimile machines, telephones, telephone answering machines, and all other electronic or computer technology. When using these technologies, disclosure of identifying information regarding the client(s) should be avoided whenever possible.

IV. RELATIONSHIPS WITH COLLEAGUES
Clinical social workers act with integrity in their relationships with colleagues and members of other professions. They know and take into account the traditions, practices, and areas of competence of other professionals and cooperate with them fully for the welfare of clients.

a) Clinical social workers represent accurately the views, qualifications, and findings of colleagues. When expressing judgment on these matters they do so in a manner that is sensitive to the best interests of both colleagues and clients.

b) If a clinical social worker's services are sought by an individual who is already receiving similar services from another professional, consideration for the client's welfare is the primary concern. This concern requires that the clinical social worker proceed with great caution, carefully considering the existing professional relationship, the therapeutic issues involved, and whether it is therapeutically and ethically appropriate to be involved in the situation.

c) As supervisors, consultants, or employers, clinical social workers are responsible for providing competent professional guidance and a role model to colleagues, employees, and students. They foster working conditions that assure consistency, respect, privacy, and protection from physical or mental harm. Clinical social workers do not abuse the authority of their position by harassing or pressuring colleagues, employees, or students for

sexual reasons, financial gain, or any other purpose. They refrain from actions that are unwanted by the recipient, and can reasonably be interpreted as pressuring or intimidating the recipient.

d) Clinical social workers carry out their responsibility to both clients and the profession by maintaining high standards of practice within the professional community. They take appropriate measures to discourage, prevent, expose, and correct unethical or incompetent behavior by colleagues, and also assist and defend colleagues believed to be unjustly charged with such conduct. They discourage the practice of clinical social work by those who fail to meet accepted standards of training and experience, or who are practicing outside of their area of competence.

e) Clinical social workers who have knowledge of a colleague's impairment, misconduct, or incompetence attempt to bring about remediation through whatever means is appropriate. Such actions may include, but are not limited to; direct discussion with the colleague, with permission from the client(s) if this is needed; a report, if mandatory, to a regulatory body, professional organization, or employer; a report to a supervisor, or other agency administrator.

V. FEE ARRANGEMENTS
When setting fees, clinical social workers should give consideration to the client's ability to pay and make every effort to establish fees that are fair, reasonable, and commensurate with the value of the service performed.

a) In the initial contact with the client(s) fees for services and policies regarding fee collection should be clarified. This clarification should also take into account any financial constraint which may affect the treatment process.

b) It is unethical for a clinical social worker to offer, give, solicit, or receive any fee or other consideration to or from a third party for the referral of a client. They accept reimbursement from clients and from third party payers only for services directly rendered to the client(s). Clinical social workers may, however, participate in contractual arrangements in which they agree to discount their fees.

c) A clinical social worker who contracts with a third party payer agrees to abide by the conditions of the contract. If, however, the clinical social worker believes the contract contains elements which violate the ethics of the profession, the clinical social worker seeks to redress this situation through appropriate courses of action which may include; obtaining the other party's agreement to delete the clause; or, refusing to sign the contract.

d) Barter arrangements, in which goods or services are accepted from clients as payment for professional services, should be avoided as much as possible. Such plans, especially when they involve provision of services by the client(s), have the potential to constitute dual relationships which will damage the treatment. Barter arrangements may be entered into only in rare situations, and may only involve provision of goods, as opposed to services, in exchange for treatment. Such arrangements can only be entered into upon the specific request of the client, and when the following additional criteria are met; traditional payment methods are not possible; the client(s) is not coerced or exploited in any way, and; the arrangement is not detrimental to the client(s) or to the professional relationship.

e) Clinical social workers employed by an agency or clinic, and also engaged in private practice, conform to contractual agreements with the employing facility. They do not solicit or accept a private fee or consideration of any kind for providing a service to which the client is entitled through the employing facility.

VI. CLINICAL SOCIAL WORKERS' RESPONSIBILITIES TO THE COMMUNITY

Clinical social workers are aware of the social codes and ethical expectations in their communities, and recognize that violation of accepted societal, ethical, legal, and moral standards on their part may compromise the fulfillment of their professional responsibilities and/or reduce public trust in the profession.

a) Clinical social workers do not, in any of their capacities, practice, condone, facilitate, or collaborate with any form of discrimination on the basis of race, religion, color, national origin, gender, sexual orientation, age, socioeconomic status, or physical or emotional disability.

b) Clinical social workers practice their profession in compliance with legal standards, and do not participate in arrangements or activities which undermine or violate the law. When they believe, however, that laws or community standards are in conflict with the principles and ethics of the pro-

fession, they make known the conflict and work responsibly toward change that is in the public interest.

c) Clinical social workers recognize a responsibility to participate in activities leading toward improved social conditions. They should advocate and work for conditions and resources that give all persons equal access to the services and opportunities required to meet basic needs and to develop to the fullest potential.

VII. RESEARCH AND SCHOLARLY ACTIVITIES

In planning, conducting, and reporting a study, the investigator has the responsibility to make a careful evaluation of its ethical acceptability, taking into account the following additional principles for research with human subjects. To the extent that this appraisal, weighing scientific and humane values, suggests a compromise of any principle, the investigator incurs an increasingly serious obligation to observe stringent safeguards to protect the rights and well-being of research participants.

a) In conducting research in institutions or organizations, clinical social workers obtain appropriate authority to carry out their work. Host organizations are given proper credit for their contributions to the project.

b) Ethically acceptable research begins with the establishment of a clear and fair agreement between the investigator and the research participant that clarifies the responsibilities of each. The investigator has the obligation to honor all commitments included in that agreement.

c) Responsibility for the establishment and maintenance of acceptable ethical practice in research always remains with the investigator. The investigator is also responsible for the ethical treatment of research participants by collaborators, assistants, students, and employees, all of whom incur parallel obligations.

d) Ethical practice requires the investigator to inform the participant of all features of the research that might reasonably be expected to influence willingness to participate, and to explain all other aspects of the research about which the participant inquires. After the data are collected, the investigator provides the participant with information about the nature of the study in order to remove any misconceptions that may have arisen.

e) The ethical investigator protects participants from physical and mental discomfort, harm, and danger. If a risk of such consequences exists, the investigator is required to inform the participant of that fact, secure consent before proceeding, and take all possible measures to minimize distress. A research procedure must not be used if it is likely to cause serious or lasting harm to a participant.

f) The methodological requirements of the study may necessitate concealment, deception, or minimal risk to participants. In such cases, the investigator must be able to justify the use of these techniques and to ensure, as soon as possible, the participant's understanding of the reasons and sufficient justification for the procedure in question.

g) Ethical practice requires the investigator to respect the individual's freedom to decline to participate in, or withdraw from, research and to so inform prospective participants. The obligation to protect this freedom requires special vigilance when the investigator is, in any manner, in a position of authority over the participant. It is unethical to penalize a participant in any way for withdrawing from or refusing to participate in a research project.

h) Information obtained about the individual research participants during the course of an investigation is confidential unless otherwise agreed to in advance.

i) Investigation of human subjects in studies which use drugs, are conducted only in conjunction with licensed physicians.

j) Clinical social workers take credit only for work actually done in scholarly and research projects, and give appropriate credit to the contributions of others in a manner which is proportional to the degree to which those contributions are represented in the final product.

k) Research findings must be presented accurately and completely, with full discussion of both their usefulness and their limitations. Clinical social workers are responsible for attempting to prevent any distortion or misuse of their findings.

VIII. PUBLIC STATEMENTS

Public statements, announcements of services, and promotional activities of clinical social workers serve the purpose of providing sufficient information to aid consumers in making informed judgments and choices. Clinical social workers state accurately, objectively, and without misrepresentation their professional qualifications, affilia-tions, and functions as well as those of the institutions or organizations with which they or their statements may be associated. In addition, they should correct the misrepresentations of others with respect to these matters.

a) In announcing availability for professional services, protection of the public is the primary concern. A clinical social worker may use any information so long as it describes his or her credentials and the services provided accurately and without misrepresentation. Information usually found helpful by the public includes the name of the professional; highest relevant academic degree from an accredited institution; specialized post-graduate training; type and level of state certification or license; any advanced certifications held; address and telephone number; office hours; type of service provided; languages spoken; and, policy with regard to third party payments.

b) In announcements of available professional services, information regarding fees and fee policies may also be found helpful by prospective clients. Appropriate announcements of this type could include such general terms as "moderate fees." It is unethical to make statements regarding fees or fee policies which are deceptive, or misrepresent the actual fee arrangements.

c) The clinical social worker is responsible for assuring that all advertising is in conformity with the ethical standards of the profession. Publications announcing any type of clinical social work service describe those services accurately. They do not falsely or deceptively claim or imply superior personal or professional competence.

d) Clinical social workers are free to make public appearances and engage in public discussion regarding issues such as, for example, the relative value of alternative treatment approaches. Diagnostic and therapeutic services for clients, however, are rendered only in the context of a professional relationship. Such services are not given by means of public lectures, newspaper or magazine articles, radio or television programs, or anything of a similar nature. Professional use of the media or of other public forums is appropriate when the purpose is to educate the public about professional matters regarding which the clinical social worker has special knowledge or expertise.

e) Clinical social workers respect the rights and reputation of any professional organization with which they are affiliated, and do not falsely imply sponsorship or certification by any organization. When making public statements, the clinical social worker will make clear which are personal opinions, and which are authorized statements on behalf of the organization.

© Clinical Social Work Federation. Reprinted with permission.

COLLEGE OF AMERICAN PATHOLOGISTS

Address: 325 Waukegan Road
Northfield, IL 60093-2750
Telephone: 847/832-7000
WWW: www.cap.org

The College of American Pathologists subscribes to the code of ethics of the American Medical Association. See p. 00.

COMMUNITY ASSOCIATIONS INSTITUTE

COMMUNITY ASSOCIATIONS INSTITUTE

Address: 1630 Duke Street
Alexandria, VA 22314
Telephone: 703/548-8600
WWW: www.caionline.com
Document: Professional Manager Code of Ethics (Most recently revised 1993.)

(The Professional Manager Code of Ethics is further amplified in the *Code Clarification Document* provided by the Community Associations Institute. It is not reprinted here.—Eds.)

The Manager Shall:

1. Comply with current standards or practices as may be established from time to time by CAI and each state in which the Manager practices;
2. Participate in continuing professional education through CAI and other organizations and maintain a CAI membership;
3. Not make any inaccurate or misleading representations or statements to a prospective client;
4. Undertake only those engagements the Manager can reasonably expect to perform with professional competence;
5. Exercise due care and exhibit adequate planning and supervision;
6. Disclose in writing to the client any actual, potential or perceived conflict of interest if the client may have dealings with another party in some way related to the Manager;
7. Not knowingly misrepresent facts to benefit the Manager;
8. Refuse any compensation, gratuity or other form of remuneration from individuals or companies who act on behalf of the client;
9. Insure that homeowners receive timely notice as required by state statutes or legal documents and protect their right of appeal;
10. Disclose to the client the extent of fidelity insurance carried on behalf of the Manager and/or client and any subsequent changes in coverage which may occur during the Manager's engagement;
11. See that the funds held for the client by the Manager are in separate accounts, are not misappropriated, and are returned to the client at the end of the Manager's engagement;
12. Recognize that the original records, files, and books held by the Manger are the property of the client to be returned to the client at the end of the Manager's engagement.

© Community Associations Institute. Reprinted with permission.

THE DIRECT MARKETING ASSOCIATION

Address: 1120 Avenue of the Americas
New York, NY 10036-6700

Telephone: 212/768-7277
WWW: www.the-dma.org
Document: Guidelines for Ethical Business
              Practice (1998)

The Direct Marketing Association's Guidelines for Ethical Business Practice are intended to provide individuals and organizations involved in direct marketing in all media with generally accepted principles of conduct. These guidelines reflect The DMA's long-standing policy of high levels of ethics and the responsibility of the Association, its members, and all marketers to maintain consumer and community relationships that are based on fair and ethical principles. In addition to providing general guidance to the industry, the Guidelines for Ethical Business Practice are used by The DMA's Committee on Ethical Business Practice, an industry peer review committee, as the standard to which direct marketing promotions that are the subject of complaint to The DMA are compared.

These self-regulatory guidelines are intended to be honored in light of their aims and principles. All marketers should support the guidelines in spirit and not treat their provisions as obstacles to be circumvented by legal ingenuity.

These guidelines also represent The DMA's general philosophy that self-regulatory measures are preferable to governmental mandates. Self-regulatory actions are more readily adaptable to changing techniques and economic and social conditions. They encourage widespread use of sound business practices.

Because dishonest, misleading or offensive communications discredit all means of advertising and marketing, including direct marketing, observance of these guidelines by all concerned is expected. All persons involved in direct marketing should take reasonable steps to encourage other industry members to follow these guidelines as well.

The Terms of the Offer

HONESTY AND CLARITY OF OFFER

Article #1

All offers should be clear, honest and complete so that the consumer may know the exact nature of what is being offered, the price, the terms of payment (including all extra charges) and the commitment involved in the placing of an order. Before publication of an offer, marketers should be prepared to substantiate any claims or offers made. Advertisements or specific claims which are untrue, misleading, deceptive or fraudulent should not be used.

ACCURACY AND CONSISTENCY

Article #2

Simple and consistent statements or representations of all the essential points of the offer should appear in the promotional material. The overall impression of an offer should not be contradicted by individual statements, representations or disclaimers.

CLARITY OF REPRESENTATIONS

Article #3

Representations which, by their size, placement, duration or other characteristics, are unlikely to be noticed or are difficult to understand should not be used if they are material to the offer.

ACTUAL CONDITIONS

Article #4

All descriptions, promises and claims of limitation should be in accordance with actual conditions, situations and circumstances existing at the time of the promotion.

DISPARAGEMENT

Article #5

Disparagement of any person or group on grounds addressed by federal or state laws that prohibit discrimination is unacceptable.

DECENCY

Article #6

Solicitations should not be sent to consumers who have indicated to the marketer that they consider those solicitations to be vulgar, immoral, profane, pornographic or offensive in any way and who do not want to receive them.

PHOTOGRAPHS AND ART WORK

Article #7

Photographs, illustrations, artwork and the situations they describe should be accurate portrayals and current reproductions of the products, services or other subjects they represent.

DISCLOSURE OF SPONSOR AND INTENT

Article #8

All marketing contacts should disclose the name of the sponsor and each purpose of the contact. No one should make offers or solicitations in the guise of one purpose when the intent is a different purpose.

ACCESSIBILITY

Article #9

Every offer and shipment should clearly identify the marketer's name and postal address or telephone number, or both, at which the consumer may obtain service. If an offer is made online, an e-mail address should also be identified.

SOLICITATION IN THE GUISE OF AN INVOICE OR GOVERNMENTAL NOTIFICATION

Article #10

Offers that are likely to be mistaken for bills, invoices or notices from public utilities or governmental agencies should not be used.

POSTAGE, SHIPPING OR HANDLING CHARGES

Article #11

Postage, shipping or handling charges, if any, should bear a reasonable relationship to actual costs incurred.

Marketing to Children

MARKETING TO CHILDREN

Article #12

Offers and the manner in which they are presented that are suitable for adults only should not be made to children. In determining the suitability of a communication with children online or in any other media, marketers should address the age range, knowledge, sophistication and maturity of their intended audience.

PARENTAL RESPONSIBILITY AND CHOICE

Article #13

Marketers should provide notice and an opportunity to opt out of the marketing process so that parents have the ability to limit the collection, use and disclosure of their children's names, addresses or other personally identifiable information.

INFORMATION FROM OR ABOUT CHILDREN

Article #14

Marketers should take into account the age range, knowledge, sophistication and maturity of children when collecting information from them. Marketers should limit the collection, use and dissemination of information collected from or about children to information required for the promotion, sale and delivery of goods and services, provision of customer services, conducting market research and engaging in other appropriate marketing activities.

Marketers should effectively explain that the information is being requested for marketing purposes. Information not appropriate for marketing purposes should not be collected.

Upon request from a parent, marketers should promptly provide the source and general nature of information maintained about a child. Marketers should implement strict security measures to ensure against unauthorized access, alteration or dissemination of the data collected from or about children.

Special Offers and Claims

USE OF THE WORD "FREE" AND OTHER SIMILAR REPRESENTATIONS

Article #15

A product or service which is offered without cost or obligation to the recipient may be unqualifiedly described as "free."

If a product or service is offered as "free," all qualifications and conditions should be clearly and conspicuously disclosed, in close conjunction with the use of the term "free" or other similar phrase.

When the term "free" or other similar representations are made (for example, 2-for-1, half-price or 1-cent offers), the product or service required to be purchased should not have been increased in price or decreased in quality or quantity.

PRICE COMPARISONS

Article #16

Price comparisons including those between a marketer's current price and a former, future or suggested price, or between a marketer's price and the price of a competitor's comparable product should be fair and accurate.

In each case of comparison to a former, manufacturer's suggested or competitor's comparable product price, recent substantial sales should have been made at that price in the same trade area.

For comparisons with a future price, there should be a reasonable expectation that the new price will be charged in the foreseeable future.

GUARANTEES

Article #17

If a product or service is offered with a guarantee or a warranty, either the terms and conditions should be set forth in full in the promotion, or the promotion should state how the consumer may obtain a copy.

The guarantee should clearly state the name and address of guarantor and the duration of the guarantee.

Any requests for repair, replacement or refund under the terms of a guarantee or warranty should be honored promptly. In an unqualified offer of refund, repair or replacement, the customer's preference shall prevail.

USE OF TEST OR SURVEY DATA

Article #18

All test or survey data referred to in advertising should be valid and reliable as to source and methodology, and should support the specific claim for which it is cited. Advertising claims should not distort test or survey results or take them out of context.

TESTIMONIALS AND ENDORSEMENTS

Article #19

Testimonials and endorsements should be used only if they are:

a. Authorized by the person quoted;
b. Genuine and related to the experience of the person giving them both at the time made and at the time of the promotion; and
c. Not taken out of context so as to distort the endorser's opinion or experience with the product.

Sweepstakes

USE OF THE TERM "SWEEPSTAKES"

Article #20

Sweepstakes are promotional devices by which items of value (prizes) are awarded to participants by chance without the promoter's requiring the participants to render something of value (consideration) to be eligible to participate. The co-existence of all three elements—prize, chance and consideration—in the same promotion constitutes a lottery. It is illegal for any private enterprise to run a lottery without specific governmental authorization.

When skill replaces chance, the promotion becomes a skill contest. When gifts (premiums or other items of value) are given to all participants independent of the element of chance, the promotion is not a sweepstakes. Promotions that are not sweepstakes should not be held out as such.

Only those promotional devices which satisfy the definition stated above should be called or held out to be a sweepstakes.

NO-PURCHASE OPTION

Article #21

Promotions should clearly state that no purchase is required to win sweepstakes prizes. They should not represent that those who make a purchase or otherwise render consideration with their entry will have a better chance of winning or will be eligible to win more or larger prizes than those who do not make a purchase or otherwise render consideration. The method for entering without ordering should be easy to find, read and understand. When response devices used only for entering the sweepstakes are provided, they should be as easy to find as those utilized for ordering the product or service.

CHANCES OF WINNING

Article #22

No sweepstakes promotion, or any of its parts, should represent that a recipient or entrant has won a prize or that any entry stands a greater chance of winning a prize than any other entry when this is not the case. Winners should be selected in a manner that ensures fair application of the laws of chance.

PRIZES

Article #23

Sweepstakes prizes should be advertised in a manner that is clear, honest and complete so that the consumer may know the exact nature of what is being offered. For prizes paid over time, the annual payment schedule and number of years should be clearly disclosed. Photographs, illustrations, artwork and the situations they represent should be accurate portrayals of the prizes listed in the promotion.

No award or prize should be held forth directly or by implication as having substantial monetary value if it is of nominal worth. The value of a non-cash prize should be stated at regular retail value, whether actual cost to the sponsor is greater or less.

All prizes should be awarded and delivered without cost to the participant. If there are certain conditions under which a prize or prizes will not be awarded, that fact should be disclosed in a manner that is easy to find, read and understand.

PREMIUMS

Article #24

Premiums should be advertised in a manner that is clear, honest and complete so that the consumer may know the exact nature of what is being offered.

A premium, gift or item should not be called or held out to be a "prize" if it is offered to every recipient of or participant in a promotion. If all participants will receive a premium, gift or item, that fact should be clearly disclosed.

DISCLOSURE OF RULES

Article #25

All terms and conditions of the sweepstakes, including entry procedures and rules, should be easy to find, read and understand. Disclosures set out in the rules section concerning no-purchase option, prizes and chances of winning should not contradict the overall impression created by the promotion.

The following should be set forth clearly in the rules:

- No purchase of the advertised product or service is required in order to win a prize.
- Procedures for entry.
- If applicable, disclosure that a facsimile of the entry blank or other alternate means (such as a 3 × 5 card) may be used to enter the sweepstakes.
- The termination date for eligibility in the sweepstakes. The termination date should specify whether it is a date of mailing or receipt of entry deadline.
- The number, retail value (of non-cash prizes) and complete description of all prizes offered, and whether cash may be awarded instead of merchandise. If a cash prize is to be awarded by installment payments, that fact should be clearly disclosed, along with the nature and timing of the payments.
- The approximate odds of winning each prize or a statement that such odds depend on number of entrants.
- The method by which winners will be selected.
- The geographic area covered by the sweepstakes and those areas in which the offer is void.
- All eligibility requirements, if any.
- Approximate dates when winners will be selected and notified.
- Publicity rights regarding the use of winner's name.
- Taxes are the responsibility of the winner.
- Provision of a mailing address to allow consumers to receive a list of winners of prizes over $25.00 in value.

Fulfillment

UNORDERED MERCHANDISE

Article #26

Merchandise should not be shipped without having first received the customer's permission. The exceptions are samples or gifts clearly marked as such, and merchandise mailed by a charitable organization soliciting contributions, as long as all items are sent with a clear and conspicuous statement informing the recipient of an unqualified right to treat the product as a gift and to do with it as the recipient sees fit, at no cost or obligation to the recipient.

PRODUCT AVAILABILITY AND SHIPMENT

Article #27

Direct marketers should offer merchandise only when it is on hand or when there is a reasonable expectation of its timely receipt.

Direct marketers should ship all orders according to the terms of the offer or within 30 days where there is no promised shipping date, unless otherwise directed by the consumer, and should promptly notify consumers of any delays.

DRY TESTING

Article #28

Direct marketers should engage in dry testing only when the special nature of the offer is made clear in the promotion.

Collection, Use and Maintenance of Marketing Data

COLLECTION, USE AND TRANSFER OF PERSONALLY IDENTIFIABLE DATA

Article #29

Consumers who provide data that may be rented, sold or exchanged for marketing purposes should be informed periodically by marketers of their policy concerning the rental, sale or exchange of such data and of the opportunity to opt out of the marketing process. Should that policy substantially change, marketers have an obligation to inform consumers of that change prior to the rental, sale or exchange of such data, and to offer consumers an opportunity to opt out of the marketing process at that time. All individual opt out requests should be honored. Marketers should maintain and use their own systems, policies and procedures, and, at no cost to consumers, refrain from using or transferring such data, as the case may be, as requested by consumers.

List compilers should maintain and use their own systems, policies and procedures, and at no cost to consumers refrain from using or transferring data, as the case may be, as requested by consumers. For each list that is rented, sold or exchanged, the applicable DMA Preference Service name removal list (e.g., Mail Preference Service, Telephone Preference Service) should be employed prior to use.

Data about consumers who have opted out of use or transfer should not, per their requests, be used, rented, sold or exchanged.

Upon request by a consumer, marketers should disclose the source from which they obtained personally identifiable data about that consumer.

PERSONAL DATA
Article #30
Marketers should be sensitive to the issue of consumer privacy and should only collect, combine, rent, sell, exchange or use marketing data. Marketing data should be used only for marketing purposes.

Data and selection criteria that by reasonable standards may be considered sensitive and/or intimate should not be disclosed, displayed or provide the basis for lists made available for rental, sale or exchange when there is a reasonable expectation by the consumer that the information will be kept confidential.

PROMOTION OF MARKETING LISTS
Article #31
Any advertising or promotion for marketing lists being offered for rental, sale or exchange should reflect the fact that a marketing list is an aggregate collection of marketing data. Such promotions should also reflect a sensitivity for the consumers on those lists.

MARKETING LIST USAGE
Article #32
List owners, brokers, managers, compilers and users of marketing lists should ascertain the nature of the list's intended usage for each different marketing use prior to rental, sale, exchange, transfer or use of the list. List owners, brokers, managers and compilers should not permit the rental, sale, exchange or transfer of their marketing lists, nor should users use any marketing lists for an offer that is in violation of these guidelines.

Telephone Marketing
REASONABLE HOURS
Article #33
Telephone contacts should be made during reasonable hours as specified by federal and state laws and regulations.

TAPING OF CONVERSATIONS
Article #34
Taping of telephone conversations by telemarketers should only be conducted with notice to or consent of all parties, or the use of a beeping device, as required by applicable federal and state laws and regulations.

RESTRICTED CONTACTS
Article #35
A telephone marketer should not knowingly call a consumer who has an unlisted or unpublished telephone number, or a telephone number for which the called party must pay the charges, except in instances where the number was provided by the consumer to that marketer.

Random dialing techniques, whether manual or automated, in which those parties to be called are left to chance should not be used in sales and marketing solicitations.

Sequential dialing techniques, whether a manual or automated process, in which selection of those parties to be called is based on the location of their telephone numbers in a sequence of telephone numbers should not be used.

USE OF AUTOMATED DIALING EQUIPMENT
Article #36
When using automated dialing equipment for any reason, telephone marketers should only use equipment which allows the telephone to immediately release the line when the called party terminates the connection.

ADRMPS (Automatic Dialers and Recorded Message Players) and prerecorded messages should be used only in accordance with tariffs, federal, state, and local laws, FCC regulations and these guidelines. Telephone marketers should use a live operator to obtain a consumer's permission before delivering a recorded message.

When using any automated dialing equipment to reach a multi-line location, the equipment should release each line used before connecting to another.

USE OF TELEPHONE FACSIMILE MACHINES
Article #37
Unless there is a prior business relationship with the recipient, or unless the recipient has given prior permission, unsolicited advertisements should not be transmitted by facsimile. Each permitted transmission to a fax machine must clearly contain on each page or on the first page, the date and time the transmission is sent, the identity of the sender and the telephone number of the sender or the sending machine.

PROMOTIONS FOR RESPONSE BY TOLL-FREE AND PAY-PER-CALL NUMBERS

Article #38

Promotions for response by 800 or other toll-free numbers should be used only when there is no charge to the consumer for the call itself and when there is no transfer from a toll-free number to a pay call.

Promotions for response by using 900 numbers or any other type of pay-per-call programs should clearly and conspicuously disclose all charges for the call. A preamble at the beginning of the 900 or other pay-per-call should include the nature of the service or program, charge per minute and the total estimated charge for the call, as well as the name, address and telephone number of the sponsor. The caller should be given the option to disconnect the call at any time during the preamble without incurring any charge.

The 900 number or other pay-per-call should only use equipment that ceases accumulating time and charges immediately upon disconnection by the caller.

DISCLOSURE AND TACTICS

Article #39

Prior to asking consumers for payment authorization, telephone marketers should disclose the cost of the merchandise or service and all terms and conditions, including payment plans, whether or not there is a no refund or a no cancellation policy in place, limitations, and the amount or existence of any extra charges such as shipping and handling and insurance. At no time should high pressure tactics be utilized.

Fund-Raising

Article #40

In addition to compliance with these guidelines, fund-raisers and other charitable solicitors should, whenever requested by donors or potential donors, provide financial information regarding use of funds.

Laws, Codes, and Regulations

Article #41

Direct marketers should operate in accordance with laws and regulations of the United States Postal Service, the Federal Trade Commission, the Federal Communications Commission, the Federal Reserve Board, and other applicable federal, state and local laws governing advertising, marketing practices and the transaction of business.

ECOLOGICAL SOCIETY OF AMERICA

Address: 1707 H Street NW,
             Suite 400
             Washington, DC 20006
Telephone: 202/833-8773
WWW: www.sdsc.edu/esa/esa.htm
Document: Code of Ethics

PREAMBLE

This code provides guiding principles of conduct for all members of the Ecological Society of America. Ecologists are faced with the vital and often conflicting tasks of resolving the needs of society and the needs of naturally functioning and managed ecosystems. The solution of complex ecological problems will require the help of persons from all walks of life. If ecology is to progress it must include the pure scientists seeking new information and the practitioners who apply that knowledge to solving practical problems. Of prime importance is the training of new ecologists, obtaining new information, applying the knowledge that we already have, and communicating with all segments of society. A Code of Ethics is essential to the continuation of an honorable and respected position for the Profession.

GENERAL: ALL MEMBERS OF THE ECOLOGICAL SOCIETY OF AMERICA

1. Will use their knowledge, skills, and training when appropriate to find ways to harmonize society's needs, demands, and actions with the maintenance and enhancement of natural and managed ecosystems.
2. Will offer professional advice only on those subjects in which they are informed and qualified through professional training and experience.
3. Will not represent themselves as spokespersons for the Society without Council authority.

4. Will avoid and discourage the dissemination of false, erroneous, biased, unwarranted, or exaggerated statements concerning ecology.

5. Will conduct their professional affairs in an ethical manner as prescribed in this Code, will endeavor to protect the ecological profession from misunderstanding and misrepresentation, and will cooperate with one another to assure the rapid interchange and dissemination of ecological knowledge.

6. In any communication, will not plagiarize; will give full and proper credit to, and will avoid misinterpretation of, the work and ideas of others.

7. Will report accurately, truthfully, fully, and clearly, to the limit of their abilities, the ecological and other information pertinent to a given project and will convey their findings objectively. Therefore, will not fabricate or falsify results or commit scientific fraud.

8. Will exercise utmost care in laboratory and field research to avoid or minimize adverse environmental effects resulting from their presence, activities, or equipment. They will sacrifice only those organisms needed to obtain data essential to their work.

9. Will comply with Federal requirements for protection of researchers, human subjects, or the public or for ensuring the welfare of laboratory animals, and will comply with relevant legal requirements governing research.

10. Within reasonable limits of time and finance, will volunteer their special knowledge, skill, and training to the public for the benefit of society and the environment.

11. Will not discriminate against others on the basis of sex, sexual orientation, creed, religion, race, color, national origin, age, economic status, cultural mores, physical handicaps, or organizational affiliation.

12. Will clearly differentiate facts, opinions, theories, hypotheses, and ideas; will provide ethical leadership in accord with this Code, and will not mislead students concerning their limitations, training or abilities.

13. Should, when they have substantial evidence of a breach of this Code by another member, bring such conduct to the attention of the offender and to the Council.

14. Will neither seek employment, grants, or gain nor attempt to injure the reputation or opportunities for employment of another ecologist or scientist in a related profession by false, biased, or undocumented claims or accusations, by any other malicious action, or by offers of gifts or favors.

15. Will not practice or condone sexual harassment, nor any form of sexual intimidation or exploitation.

CERTIFIED: ALL ECOLOGISTS CERTIFIED BY ESA

All ecologists certified by ESA must adhere particularly to the following section in addition to the other sections of this code:

1. Will present, upon request, evidence of their qualifications, including professional training, publications, and experience, to any rightful petitioner.

2. Will keep informed of advances in ecological knowledge and techniques, as well as in related aspects of science and society, and will integrate such knowledge and techniques into their professional activities including teaching.

3. Will inform a prospective or current employer or client of any professional or personal interests which may impair the objectivity of their work, and provide their clients with access to the provisions of this Code.

4. Will respect any request for confidentiality expressed by their employers or clients, provided that such confidentiality will not contribute to unnecessary or significant degradation of the environment and does not jeopardize the health, safety, or welfare of the public. Should a conflict develop between such confidentiality and the safety of life or property of the public, members of the Society shall notify their employers or clients of the conflict in writing, and will be guided by their conscience in taking further action.

5. Will not seek employment by unethical bidding, but shall expect the prospective employer or client to select Certified Ecologists on the basis of ability and experience. All salaries or fees and the extent and kinds of service to be rendered shall be described fully prior to employment.

6. Will not use the security or resources of salaried academic, institutional, or governmental positions to compete unethically or unfairly with consulting ecologists in private practice.

7. Will accept compensation for a particular service or report from one source only, except with the full knowledge and consent of all concerned parties.

8. Will utilize, or will recommend that an employer, client, or grantor utilize the best available experts whenever such action is essential to solving a problem.

9. Will not associate with, or allow the use of their names, reports, maps, or other technical materials by any enterprise known to be illegal, fraudulent, or of questionable character, or contrary to the welfare of the public or the environment.

10. May advertise their services in a dignified and factual manner, but must avoid exaggeration, self-praise, or undue conspicuousness.

PUBLICATION: PERSONS WHO REVIEW, EDIT, OR PUBLISH PAPERS

1. Will not claim authorship of a paper unless they have made a substantial contribution, such as:
   a. conceived the ideas and the design of the experiments
   b. participated in the active execution of the study
   c. analyzed and interpreted the data
   d. wrote the manuscript

2. Will not submit for publication any manuscript containing data they are not authorized to use. Where not otherwise specified by contract or explicit agreement, the principal investigator(s) of a research project should be assumed to retain the right to control authorization or use of the data.

3. Will not submit a manuscript, representing as new research results that have been published or submitted elsewhere.

4. Will not submit a manuscript for publication in a book or journal while it is under review for possible publication in another book or journal.

5a. When serving as an editor or reviewer of a manuscript, will treat that manuscript as confidential, recognizing that it is the intellectual property of the author(s).

5b. Will not use the ideas or results of others in manuscripts submitted for publication without full attribution of the source. If the ideas or data have not been published, will not use them without permission of the author.

6. Will not include in a manuscript any illustrations or tables from another manuscript without permission of the owner of the copyright.

7. Will not serve as editor or reviewer of a manuscript if present or past connections with the author or the author's institution may prevent an objective evaluation of the work.

8. Will not purposefully delay publication of another person's manuscript to gain advantage over that person.

9. Will promptly report to the editor any errors in research results or interpretations they have discovered after a manuscript is submitted for publication or is published.

COMMITTEE ON PROFESSIONAL ETHICS: PURPOSE

The Committee will review as needed ethical issues of concern to members of ESA and will keep the members informed about these issues. It will propose to the Council modifications of the Code of Ethics as needed, and will serve as a liaison to the Professional Society Ethics Group of the AAAS (*American Association for the Advancement of Science*). It will help the President and Council of ESA any time that someone informs them of ethical misconduct by a member of ESA.

© Ecological Society of America. Reprinted with permission.

ENTOMOLOGICAL SOCIETY OF AMERICA

Address:	9301 Annapolis Road
	Lanham, MD 20706-3115
Telephone:	301/731-4535
WWW:	www.entsoc.org
Document:	Statement of Ethics of the
	Entomological Society of America
	(1996)

Preamble:

The purpose of The Society is to promote the science of entomology in all of its subdisciplines for the advancement of science and the benefit of society, to publish and encourage publications pertaining to entomology, and to assure cooperation in all measures leading to these ends.

In accordance with this purpose, The Society encourages its members to:

1. treat all people with civility, avoiding harassment and discrimination,

2. uphold the highest standards of truthfulness and honesty in all scientific and professional endeavors,

3. evaluate the work of colleagues fairly and with open-mindedness,
4. recognize past and present contributors to science and not claim credit for accomplishments of others,
5. disclose potential conflicts of interest,
6. offer professional advice only on those subjects in which they are qualified,
7. expose scientific and professional misconduct promptly,
8. comply with all laws and regulations that apply to our science and profession.

Code of Ethics for Board Certified Entomologists
PREAMBLE

The profession of Entomology is increasingly important to the welfare and progress of human society. Professional entomologists have the position and authority to render effective service to humanity, in keeping with high standards of ethical conduct. In order that the honor and dignity of the profession be advanced and maintained, the Entomological Society of America has established the following code to define the professional conduct and ethics, binding on Board Certified Entomologists.

OBLIGATIONS TO SOCIETY

1.1 The Board Certified Entomologist's knowledge and skills will be used for the betterment of human welfare.
1.2 The Board Certified Entomologist will share in sustaining the laws, institutions, and burdens of the community.

OBLIGATIONS TO THE PUBLIC

2.1 The Board Certified Entomologist will have proper regard for the safety, health, and welfare of the public in the performance of professional duties.
2.2 The Board Certified Entomologist will be honest and impartial, and will preface any one-sided statements, criticisms, or arguments by clearly indicating on whose behalf they are made.
2.3 The Board Certified Entomologist will express an opinion on an entomological subject only when it is founded on adequate knowledge and honest conviction; and will be factual in all estimates, reports, and testimony.

OBLIGATIONS TO THE PROFESSION

3.1 The Board Certified Entomologist will strive to advance the science and art of entomology, to guard and uphold its high standard of honor, and conform with the principles of professional conduct.

3.2 The Board Certified Entomologist will cooperate in upbuilding the profession by exchanging information with fellow entomologists, and by contributing to the work of technical societies and the technical press, where disclosure of such information does not conflict with the interests of clients and employers.
3.3 The Board Certified Entomologist will defend the prestige of the profession, and will report to the Entomological Society of America any persons or organizations using the words entomologist, entomology, or derivatives thereof in a manner implying performance or supervision by a Board Certified Entomologist when such is not true.

OBLIGATIONS TO EMPLOYERS AND CLIENTS

4.1 The Board Certified Entomologist will act as a faithful agent or trustee for each employer or client, and will not knowingly engage in illegal work or cooperate with any person so engaged.
4.2 The Board Certified Entomologist will undertake only those entomological assignments for which the Entomologist is qualified. The Board Certified Entomologist will obtain or advise the employer or client to obtain the assistance of specialists whenever the employer's or client's interests are so served best, and will cooperate with the specialists.
4.3 The Board Certified Entomologist will indicate to the employer or client alternatives to recommended courses of action and the expected consequences of each recommended action and alternative.
4.4 The Board Certified Entomologist will inform the employer or client as to any financial interest the Entomologist has in any person, material, device, or concept which is or might become involved in a project or work for the employer or client. Decisions regarding entomological services to be performed shall not be influenced by such financial interests.
4.5 The Board Certified Entomologist will act fairly and justly toward vendors and contractors, selecting their products and services on the basis of merit and value.
4.6 The Board Certified Entomologist will not disclose information concerning the business affairs or technical processes of present or former employers or clients without their consent.
4.7 The Board Certified Entomologist will not accept compensation, financial or otherwise, from

more than one party for the same service, or for other services pertaining to the same work, without the consent of all interested parties.

OBLIGATIONS TO FELLOW ENTOMOLOGISTS

5.1 The Board Certified Entomologist will give credit for entomological work to whom it is due.

5.2 The Board Certified Entomologist will promote solidarity and harmony with fellow entomologists, respect their judgement, and support them collectively and individually whenever possible against unjust claims and accusations.

5.3 The Board Certified Entomologist will not accept any engagement to review the professional work of a fellow entomologist (except in editing scientific papers and in litigation) without the knowledge of such entomologist, unless the entomologist's connection with the work has been terminated.

5.4 The Board Certified Entomologist will not injure intentionally the professional reputation, prospects, or practice of another entomologist. However, proof that another entomologist has been unethical, illegal, or unfair should be communicated to the Entomological Society of America.

5.5 The Board Certified Entomologist will provide a prospective entomology employee with complete information on working conditions and the proposed status of employment, and during employment will keep the employee informed of any changes therein.

5.6 The Board Certified Entomologist who employs or supervises other entomologists will endeavor to provide opportunity for their professional development and advancement.

FEDERAL BAR ASSOCIATION

Address: 2215 M Street NW
Washington, DC 20037
Telephone: 202/785-1614
WWW: www.fedbar.org

Document: Model Rules of Professional Conduct for Federal Lawyers (1990)

(*Model Rules of Professional Conduct for Federal Lawyers*, Washington, DC: Federal Bar Association, 1990, is a 48-page document of rules interspersed with extensive comment and cross references. Only the Rules are reprinted here, but readers interested in further amplification are recommended to consult a copy of the complete document.—Eds.)

Preamble: A Federal Lawyer's Responsibilities (1990)

A Federal lawyer is a representative of clients, an officer of the legal system, and a public citizen having special responsibility for the quality of justice. The Federal lawyer should demonstrate the highest standards of ethical conduct, personal dignity, truthfulness, honesty, fortitude, and professional integrity. The Federal lawyer should also promote public service.

As a representative of clients, a Federal lawyer performs various functions. As an advisor, a Federal lawyer provides a client with informed understanding of the client's rights and obligations and explains their practical implications. As an advocate, a Federal lawyer zealously asserts the client's position under the law and the ethical rules of the adversary system. As negotiator, a Federal lawyer seeks results advantageous to the client, but consistent with the requirement of honest dealing with others. As a mediator between clients, a Federal lawyer seeks to reconcile their divergent interests as an advisor and, to a limited extent, as a spokesperson for each client. A Federal lawyer acts as evaluator by examining client's legal affairs and reporting about them to the client or to others.

In all professional functions a Federal lawyer should be competent, prompt, diligent, and honest. A Federal lawyer should maintain communication with a client concerning the representation. A Federal lawyer should keep in confidence information relating to representation of a client, except insofar as disclosure is required or permitted by these Rules or other law.

A Federal lawyer's conduct should conform to the requirements of the law, both in professional service to clients and in the Federal lawyer's personal affairs. A Federal lawyer should use legal procedures only for their lawfully intended purposes and not to harass or intimidate others. A Federal lawyer should demonstrate respect for the legal system and for those who serve it, including judges, other Federal lawyers, and public officials. To the Federal Agency, the Federal lawyer owes the duties of professional dignity and integrity. While it is a Federal lawyer's duty, when necessary, to challenge the rectitude of official action, it is also a Federal lawyer's duty to uphold legal process.

As a public citizen, a Federal lawyer should seek improvement of the law, the administration of justice, and the quality of service rendered by the legal profession. Federal lawyers should strive at all times to uphold the honor and dignity of the Federal legal profession and to improve the administration of justice. As a member of a learned profession, a Federal lawyer should cultivate knowledge of the law beyond its use for clients, employ that knowledge in reform of the law where needed, and work to strengthen legal education.

Many of a Federal lawyer's professional responsibilities are prescribed in these Rules, as well as in substantive and procedural law. However, a Federal lawyer is also guided by personal conscience and the approbation of professional peers. A Federal lawyer should strive to attain the highest level of skill, to improve the law and the legal profession, to exemplify the legal profession's ideals of public service, and to respect the truth finding role of the courts.

A Federal lawyer's responsibilities as a representative of clients, an officer of the legal system, and a public citizen are usually harmonious. Thus, when an opposing party is well represented, a Federal lawyer can be zealous in advocating the interests of a client and justice will be served. A Federal lawyer also can be sure that preserving client confidence ordinarily serves the public interest because people are more likely to ask legal advice, and thereby heed their legal obligations, when they know their communications will be private.

A Federal lawyer should always uphold and promote the highest standards for the practice of law within the Federal sector. A Federal lawyer should seek to advance the development of sound Federal laws and the establishment and maintenance of an efficient Federal legal and judicial system. A Federal lawyer should promote the public's confidence in the Federal legal system. A Federal lawyer also should promote the highest professional standards for and the professional well being of all Federal lawyers. A Federal lawyer should seek to encourage outstanding lawyers to enter the Federal service.

In addition to the high standards of conduct expected of all Federal lawyers, the Government lawyer has a specific responsibility to strive to promote the public interest. The Government lawyer should not realize personal gain from the performance of official duties and should avoid any interest or activity that is in conflict with the Government lawyer's official duties. The Government lawyer should strive for personal professional excellence and encourage the professional development of other staff members and those seeking to enter the field of Government law practice.

Due to the nature of legal practice, however, Federal lawyers encounter conflicting responsibilities. Virtually all difficult ethical problems arise from conflicts between a Federal lawyer's responsibilities to clients, to the legal system, and to the Federal lawyer's own interest in remaining an upright person. These Rules prescribe terms for resolving such conflicts. Within the framework of these Rules many difficult issues of professional discretion can arise. Such issues must be resolved through the exercise of sensitive professional and moral judgment guided by the basic principles underlying these Rules.

SCOPE

These Rules, in conjunction with laws and regulations that control the practice of Federal lawyers, are intended to govern the ethical conduct of Federal lawyers.

They have been adopted by the National Council of the Federal Bar Association. The Federal Bar Association is not empowered to discipline members or enforce these Rules. As such, these Rules regulate professional conduct of Federal lawyers and impose certain duties only to the extent to which they are adopted by a Federal Agency. The Federal Bar Association encourages Federal agencies to adopt rules of professional responsibility based, in whole or in part, on these Rules. If so adopted, failure to comply with an obligation or prohibition imposed by a Rule may be the basis for invoking administrative or disciplinary action. The Rules presuppose that disciplinary assessment of a Federal lawyer's conduct will be made on the basis of the facts and circumstances as they existed at the time of the conduct in question and in recognition of the fact that a Federal lawyer often has to act upon uncertain or incomplete evidence of the situation. Moreover, these Rules presuppose that whether or not discipline should be imposed for a violation, and severity of a sanction, depend on all of the circumstances, such as the willfulness and seriousness of the violation, extenuating factors, and whether there have been previous violations. Violations of a Rule should not give rise to a cause of action nor should they create a presumption that a legal duty has been breached. These Rules are designed to provide guidance to Federal lawyers and to provide a structure for regulating conduct. They are not designed to be a basis for civil liability.

Furthermore, the purpose of these Rules can be subverted when they are invoked by opposing parties as procedural weapons. The fact that a Rule is a just basis for a Federal lawyer's self-assessment, or for sanctioning a Federal lawyer under the administration of a disciplinary authority, does not imply that an antagonist in a collateral proceeding or transaction has standing to seek enforcement of the Rule. Accordingly, nothing in these Rules should be deemed to augment any substantive legal duty of Federal lawyers or the extra-disciplinary consequences of violating such duty.

They are to be used in conjunction with laws and regulation that control the practice of Federal lawyers. Although not punitive in nature, the Rules establish the minimum standards of ethical conduct demanded of Federal lawyers.

The ethical conduct of lawyers specially retained by the Government is also intended to be governed by these Rules of Professional Conduct.

These Rules presuppose a larger legal context shaping the Federal lawyer's role. That context includes statutes and court rules relating to matters of licensing, laws defining specific obligations of Federal lawyers, and substantive and procedural law in general. Compliance with these Rules, as with all laws in an open society, depends primarily upon understanding and voluntary compliance, secondarily upon reinforcement by peer and public opinion, and finally, when applicable and necessary, upon enforcement through disciplinary proceedings. These Rules do not, however, exhaust the moral and ethical considerations that should inform a Federal lawyer, for no worthwhile human activity can be completely defined by legal rules. These Rules simply provide a framework for the ethical practice of law.

Furthermore, for purposes of determining the Federal lawyer's authority and responsibility, principles of substantive law external to these Rules determine whether a client-lawyer relationship exists. Whether a client-lawyer relationship exists for any specific purpose can depend on the circumstances and may be a question of fact.

Moreover, these Rules are not intended to govern or affect judicial application of either the attorney-

client or work product privilege. Those privileges were developed to promote compliance with law and fairness in litigation. In reliance on the attorney-client privilege, clients are entitled to expect that communications within the scope of the privilege will be protected against compelled disclosure. The attorney-client privilege is that of the client and not of the Federal lawyer. The fact that in exceptional situations the Federal lawyer under these Rules is required or permitted to disclose client confidence does not vitiate the proposition that, as a general matter, the client has a reasonable expectation that information relating to the client will not be voluntarily disclosed and that disclosure of such information may be compelled only in accordance with recognized exceptions to the attorney-client and work product privileges.

The Federal lawyer's exercise of discretion not to disclose information under Rule 1.6(c) should not be subject to reexamination. Permitting such reexamination would be incompatible with the general policy of promoting compliance with law through assurances that communications will be protected against disclosure.

These Rules of Professional Conduct are rules of reason. They should be interpreted with reference to the purposes of legal representation and of the law itself. Some of these Rules are imperative, cast in the terms "shall" or "shall not." These define proper conduct for purposes of professional discipline. Others, generally cast in the term "may" are permissive and define areas under these Rules in which the Federal lawyer has professional discretion. No disciplinary action should be taken when the Federal lawyer chooses not to act or acts within the bounds of such discretion. Other Rules define the nature of relationships between the Federal lawyer and others. These Rules are thus partly obligatory and partly descriptive in that they define a Federal lawyer's professional role. Many of the comments use the term "should". Comments do not add obligations to these Rules, but provide guidance for practicing in compliance with these Rules. The comments are interpretative, while the text of each Rule is authoritative.

The Preamble and this note on Scope provide general orientation.

DEFINITIONS

Within the scope of these Rules:

"Attorney-client" is the term used to describe the evidentiary privilege against disclosure of communications between a Federal lawyer's client and the Federal lawyer. It is not used to describe the relationship between a Federal lawyer and the lawyer's client.

"Belief" or "believes" mean that the individual involved actually concludes the fact in question to be true. A(n) individual's belief may be inferred from circumstances.

"Client-lawyer" is used to express the professional relationship between a Federal lawyer and the lawyer's client. The term is not used to reference any evidentiary privileges, such as the "attorney-client" privilege.

"Consult" or "consultation" means communication of information reasonably sufficient to permit the client to appreciate the significance of the matter in question.

"Federal Agency" means: (1) An Executive agency, including an Executive department, military department, Government corporation, Government controlled corporation, and an independent establishment; (2) The Congress, committees of Congress, members of Congress who employ lawyers, and Congressional agencies; (3) The courts of the United States and agencies of the Judiciary; (4) The Governments of the territories and possessions of the United States; or (5) The Government of the District of Columbia.

"Federal lawyer" means a Government lawyer or a Non-Government lawyer, as hereinafter defined.

"Firm" means the organizational entity through which Non-Government lawyers transact business. The term includes private law firms, the legal departments of corporations and other business entities that hire lawyers as employees, and legal service organizations. The term does not include a Federal Agency.

"Government employee" means an officer or employee of a Federal Agency. The term includes members of the Armed Forces.

"Government lawyer" means a Government employee who holds a position as an attorney with a Federal Agency or serves as a judge advocate in one of the Armed Forces, but only while performing official duties. The term includes a lawyer in private practice who has contracted with or been specially retained by a Federal Agency to represent the Agency or another person while engaged in the performance of the contractual obligation.

"Fraud" or "fraudulent" means conduct having deceit as its purpose and does not encompass merely negligent misrepresentation or failure to apprise another of relevant information.

"Individual" is used to describe a single human being.

"Knowingly," "known," or "knows" means actual knowledge of the fact in question. A person's knowledge may be inferred from circumstances.

"Law" as used in these Rules includes statutes, treaties and international agreements, legal precedents, Federal Agency regulations, directives, and orders.

"Non-Government lawyer" means an individual who is a member of the bar of a Federal court or the highest court of a State or Territory, who represents persons before a Federal Agency. When a Government lawyer is engaged in the private practice of law or pro bono representation not related to the Government lawyer's official duties, the lawyer is considered a Non-Government lawyer.

"Person" means an individual, a corporation, a company, an association, a firm, a partnership, a society, a joint stock company, or any other legal entity.

"Reasonable" or "reasonably" when used in relation to conduct by Federal lawyer means the conduct of a reasonably prudent and competent lawyer.

"Reasonable belief" or "reasonably believes" when used in reference to a Federal lawyer means that the lawyer believes the matter in question and that the circumstances are such that the belief is reasonable.

"Reasonably should know" when used in reference to a Federal lawyer means that a lawyer of reasonable prudence and competence would ascertain the matter in question.

"Substantial" when used in reference to degree or extent means a material matter of clear and weighty importance.

"Supervisory lawyer" means a Federal lawyer within an office or organization with authority over or responsibility for the direction, coordination, evaluation, or assignment of responsibilities and work of subordinate lawyers, contract legal representation, nonlawyer assistants (e.g., paralegals), and clerical personnel.

"Tribunal" means a court, board, hearing officer, investigating officer, judge, jury, panel, or other body or official that receives evidence and makes a ruling or determination.

CLIENT-LAWYER RELATIONSHIP

RULE 1.1 Competence

A Federal lawyer shall provide competent representation to a client. Competent representation requires the legal knowledge, skill, thoroughness, and preparation reasonably necessary for the representation.

RULE 1.2 Scope of Representation

(a) A Federal lawyer shall abide by a client's decisions concerning the objectives of representation, subject to paragraphs (c), (d), (e), and (f), and shall consult with the client as to the means by which these decisions are to be pursued. A Federal lawyer shall abide by a client's decision whether to accept an offer of settlement of a matter. In a criminal case, and to the extent applicable in civil cases and administrative hearings, the Federal lawyer shall abide by the client's decision, after consultation with the Federal lawyer, as to choice of counsel (as provided by law), a plea to be entered, selection of trial forum, whether to enter into a pretrial agreement, and whether the client will testify.

(b) A Federal lawyer's representation of a client, including representation by appointment, does not constitute an endorsement of the client's political, economic, social, or moral views or activities.

(c) A Federal lawyer may limit the objectives of the representation if the client consents after consultation or as required by law and communicated to the client.

(d) A Federal lawyer shall not counsel a client to engage, or assist a client, in conduct that the lawyer knows is criminal or fraudulent, but a Federal lawyer may discuss the legal and moral consequences of any proposed course of conduct with a client and may counsel or assist a client to make a good faith effort to determine the validity, scope, meaning, or application of the law.

(e) When a Federal lawyer knows that a client expects assistance not permitted by these Rules of Professional Conduct or other law, the lawyer shall advise the client of the relevant limitations on the lawyer's conduct.

(f) A Government lawyer's authority and control over decisions concerning the representation may, by law, be expanded beyond the limits imposed by paragraphs (a) and (c).

RULE 1.3 Diligence

A Federal lawyer shall act with reasonable diligence and promptness in representing a client.

RULE 1.4 Communication

(a) A Federal lawyer shall keep a client reasonably informed about the status of a matter and promptly comply with reasonable requests for information.

(b) A Federal lawyer shall explain a matter to the extent reasonably necessary to permit the client to make informed decisions regarding the representation.

RULE 1.5 Fees

(a) A Federal lawyer shall be regulated by the Rules of Professional Conduct or other applicable rules of the jurisdictions in which the Federal lawyer is licensed or is practicing law, and otherwise by law in regard to matters concerning fees.

(b) A Government lawyer, in connection with the Government lawyer's official duties, may not request or accept any compensation from a client other than that provided by the United States for the performance of duties.

RULE 1.6 Confidentiality of Information

(a) A Federal lawyer shall not reveal information relating to the representation of a client unless the client consents after consultation, except for disclosures that are impliedly authorized in order to carry out the representation, and except as stated in paragraphs (b), (c), and (d).

(b) A Federal lawyer shall reveal such information to the extent the Federal lawyer reasonably believes necessary to prevent the client from committing a criminal act that the Federal lawyer believes is likely to result in imminent death or substantial bodily harm, or imminent and significant impairment of national security or defense.

(c) A Federal lawyer may reveal such information to the extent the Federal lawyer reasonably believes necessary to establish a claim or defense on behalf of the Federal lawyer in a controversy between the Federal lawyer and the client, to establish a defense to a criminal charge or civil claim against the Federal lawyer based upon conduct in which the client was involved, or to respond to allegations in any proceeding concerning the Federal lawyer's representation of the client.

(d) A Government lawyer may reveal such information when required or authorized by law.

RULE 1.7 Conflict of Interest: General Rule

(a) A Federal lawyer shall not represent a client if the representation of that client will be directly adverse to another client, unless:
  (1) The Federal lawyer reasonably believes the representation will not adversely affect the relationship with the other client; and
  (2) Each client consents after consultation.

(b) A Federal lawyer shall not represent a client if the representation of that client may be materially limited by the lawyer's responsibilities to another client or to a third person, or by the Federal lawyer's own interests, unless:

(1) The Federal lawyer reasonably believes the representation will not be adversely affected; and

(2) The client consents after consultation. When representation of multiple clients in a single matter is undertaken, the consultation shall include explanation of the implications of the common representation and the advantages and risks involved.

RULE 1.8 Conflict of Interest: Prohibited Transactions

(a) A Federal lawyer shall not enter into a business transaction with a client or knowingly acquire an ownership, possessory, security, or other pecuniary interest adverse to a client unless:

(1) The transaction and terms on which the Federal lawyer requires the interest are fair and reasonable to the client and are fully disclosed and transmitted in writing to the client in a manner which can be reasonably understood by the client;

(2) The client is given a reasonable opportunity to seek the advice of independent counsel in the transaction; and

(3) The client consents in writing thereto.

(b) A Federal lawyer shall not use information relating to representation of a client to the disadvantage of the client unless the client consents after consultation.

(c) A Federal lawyer shall not prepare an instrument giving the lawyer or an individual related to the lawyer as parent, child, sibling, or spouse any substantial gift from a client, including a testamentary gift, except where the client is related to the donee.

(d) While representing a client, a Federal lawyer shall not make or negotiate an agreement giving the lawyer literary or edit rights to a portrayal or account based in substantial part on information relating to the representation.

(e) A Federal lawyer shall not provide financial assistance to a client in connection with pending or contemplated litigation, except that:

(1) A Non-Government lawyer practicing before a Federal Agency may advance court costs and expenses of litigation, the repayment of which may be contingent on the outcome of the matter; and

(2) A Non-Government lawyer practicing before a Federal Agency representing an indigent client may pay court costs and expenses of litigation on behalf of the client.

(f) A Federal lawyer shall not accept compensation for representing a client from one other than the client unless:

(1) The client consents after consultation;

(2) There is no interference with the Federal lawyer's independence of professional judgment or with the Federal lawyer-client relationship; and

(3) Information relative to representation of a client is protected as required by Rule 1.6.

(g) A Federal lawyer who represents two or more clients shall not participate in making an aggregate settlement of the claims of or against the clients, or in a criminal case an aggregate agreement as to guilty pleas or nolo contendere pleas, unless each client consents after consultation, including disclosure of the existence and nature of all the claims or pleas involved and of the participation of each person in the settlement.

(h) A Federal lawyer shall not:

(1) Make an agreement prospectively limiting the lawyer's liability to a client for malpractice unless permitted by law and the client is independently represented in making the agreement.

(2) Settle a claim for liability due to allegations of malpractice with an unrepresented client or former client without first advising that person in writing that independent representation is appropriate in connection therewith.

(i) A Federal lawyer related to another lawyer as parent, child, sibling, or spouse shall not represent a client if the client's interest is directly adverse to a person who the Federal lawyer knows is represented by the other lawyer, except with the consent of the client after consultation regarding the relationship.

(j) A Non-Government lawyer shall not acquire a proprietary interest in the cause of action or subject matter of litigation the lawyer is conducting for a client, except that the lawyer may:

(1) Acquire a lien granted by law to secure the Non-Government lawyer's fee or expenses; and

(2) Contract with a client for a reasonable contingent fee in a civil case.

Rule 1.9 Conflict of Interest: Former Client

(a) A Federal lawyer who has formerly represented a client in a matter shall not thereafter represent another person in the same or a substantially related matter in which the person's interests are materially adverse to the interests of the client unless the former client consents after consultation.

(b) A Federal lawyer shall not knowingly represent a person in the same or a substantially related matter in which a firm with which the lawyer formerly was associated had previously represented a client:

    (1) Whose interests are materially adverse to that person; and

    (2) About whom the lawyer had acquired information protected by Rules 1.6 and 1.9(c) that is material to the matter; unless the former client consents after consultation.

(c) A Federal lawyer who has formerly represented a client in a matter or whose present or former firm has formerly represented a client in a matter shall not thereafter:

    (1) Use information relating to the representation to the disadvantage of the former client except as Rule 1.6 would permit with respect to a client or when the information has become generally known.

    (2) Reveal information relating to the representation except as Rule 1.6 or Rule 3.3. would permit or require with respect to a client.

Rule 1.10 Imputed Disqualification: General Rule

(a) Government lawyers working in the same Federal Agency are not automatically disqualified from representing a client because any of them practicing alone would be prohibited from doing so by Rules 1.7, 1.8(c), 1.9, or 2.2.

(b) When a Federal lawyer has terminated an association with a firm, the firm is not prohibited from thereafter representing a person with interests materially adverse to those of a client represented by the formerly associated lawyer and not currently represented by the firm, unless:

    (1) The matter is the same or substantially related to that in which the formerly associated lawyer represented the client; and

    (2) Any Federal lawyer remaining in the firm has information protected by Rules 1.6 and 1.9(c) that is material to the matter.

(c) A disqualification under this Rule may be waived by the affected client under the conditions stated in Rule 1.7.

RULE 1.11 Successive Government and Private Employment

(a) Except as law may otherwise expressly permit, a Federal lawyer shall not represent a private client in connection with a matter in which the Federal lawyer participated personally and substantially as a Government employee unless the appropriate Government Agency consents after consultation. No lawyer in a firm with which that lawyer is associated may knowingly undertake or continue representation in such matter unless:

    (1) The disqualified Federal lawyer is screened from any participation in the matter and is apportioned no part of the fee therefrom; and

    (2) Written notice is promptly given to the appropriate government Agency to enable it to ascertain compliance with the provisions of this Rule.

(b) Except as law may otherwise expressly permit, a Federal lawyer having information that the lawyer knows is confidential Government information about a person acquired when the lawyer was a Government employee shall not represent a private client whose interests are adverse to that person in a matter in which the information could be used to the material disadvantage of that person. A firm with which that lawyer is associated may undertake or continue representation in the matter only if the disqualified lawyer is screened from any participation in the matter and is apportioned no part of the fee therefrom.

(c) Except as law may otherwise expressly permit, a Federal lawyer serving as a Government employee shall not:

    (1) Participate in a matter in which the Federal lawyer participated personally and substantially while in private practice or nongovernmental employment, unless under applicable law no one is, or by lawful delegation may be, authorized to act in the lawyer's stead in the matter.

    (2) Negotiate for private employment with any person who is involved as a party or as attorney for a party in a matter in which the Federal lawyer is participating personally and substantially.

(d) As used in this Rule, the term "matter" includes:
  (1) Any judicial or other proceeding, application, request for a ruling or other determination, contract, claim, controversy, investigation, charge, accusation, arrest, or other particular matter involving a specific party or parties.
  (2) Any other matter covered by the conflict of interest rules of the appropriate Federal Agency.
(e) As used in this Rule, the term "confidential Governmental information" means information which has been obtained under Governmental authority and that, at the time this Rule is applied, the Government is prohibited by law from disclosing to the public or has a legal privilege not to disclose, and which is not otherwise available to the public.

RULE 1.12 Former Judge or Arbitrator

(a) Except as stated in paragraph (d), a Federal lawyer shall not represent anyone in connection with a matter in which the lawyer participated personally and substantially as a judge or other adjudicative officer, arbitrator, or law clerk to such a person, unless all parties to the proceeding consent after disclosure.
(b) A Federal lawyer shall not negotiate for employment with any person who is involved as a party or as attorney for a party in a matter in which the lawyer is participating personally and substantially as a judge or other adjudicative officer, or arbitrator.
(c) If a Federal lawyer is disqualified by paragraph (a), no Federal lawyer in a firm with which the lawyer is associated may knowingly undertake or continue representation in the matter unless:
  (1) The disqualified Federal lawyer is screened from any participation in the matter and is apportioned no part of the fee therefrom.
  (2) Written notice is promptly given to the appropriate tribunal to enable it to ascertain compliance with the provisions of this Rule.
(d) An arbitrator selected as a partisan of a party in a multi-member arbitration panel is not prohibited from subsequently representing that party.

RULE 1.13 The Federal Agency as the Client

(a) Except when representing another client pursuant to paragraphs (e), (f) and (g), a Government lawyer represents the Federal Agency that employs the Government lawyer. Government lawyers are often formally employed by a Federal Agency but assigned to an organizational element within the Federal Agency. Unless otherwise specifically provided, the Federal Agency, not the organizational element, is ordinarily considered the client. The Federal Agency acts through its authorized officials. These officials include the heads of organizational elements within the Federal Agency. When a Government lawyer is assigned to an organizational element and designated to provide legal services and advice to the head of that organization, the client-lawyer relationship exists between the Government lawyer and the Federal agency, as represented by the head of the organization, as to matters within the scope of the official business of the organization. The head of the organization may only invoke the attorney-client privilege or the rule of confidentiality for the benefit of the Federal Agency. In so invoking, either the attorney-client privilege or attorney-client confidentiality on behalf of the Federal Agency, the head of the organization is subject to being overruled by higher agency authority.

(b) If a Government lawyer knows that a Government employee is acting, intending to act, or refusing to act in a matter related to the representation in a manner such that either a violation of a legal obligation to the Federal Agency or a violation of law reasonably might be imputed to the Federal Agency, the Government lawyer shall proceed as is reasonably necessary in the best interest of the Federal Agency. In determining how to proceed, the Government lawyer shall give due consideration to the seriousness of the violation and its consequences, the scope and nature of the Government lawyer's representation, the responsibility in the Federal Agency, the apparent motivation of the person involved, the policies of the Federal Agency concerning such matters, and any other relevant considerations. Any measures taken shall be designed to minimize disruption of the Federal Agency and the risk of revealing information relating to the representation to persons outside the Federal Agency. Such measures may include, among others:
  (1) Advising the person that, in the Government lawyer's opinion, the action, planned action, or refusal to act is contrary to law; advising the person of the Federal Agency's policy on the matter concerned; advising the person that

his or her personal legal interests are at risk and that he or she should consult independent counsel, because their may be a conflict of interest with the Government lawyer's responsibility to the organization; and asking the person to reconsider the matter.

(2) Advising the person that a separate legal opinion on the matter be sought for presentation to appropriate authority in Federal Agency.

(3) Advising the person that the lawyer is ethically obligated to preserve the interests of the Federal Agency and, as a result, must consider discussing the matter with supervisory lawyers within the Government lawyer's office or at a higher level within the Federal Agency.

(4) Referring the matter to or seeking guidance from higher authority in the Federal Agency, including, if warranted by the seriousness of the matter, referral to the highest authority that can act on behalf of the Federal Agency.

(c) If, despite the Government lawyer's efforts in accordance with paragraph (b), the highest authority that can act concerning the matter insists upon action, or refusal to act, that is clearly a violation of law, the Government lawyer shall terminate representation with respect to the matter in question. In no event may the Government lawyer participate or assist in the illegal activity.

(d) In dealing with the Government employee, a Government lawyer shall explain the identity of the client when it is apparent that the Federal Agency's interests are adverse to those of the Government employee.

(e) A Government lawyer shall not form a client-lawyer relationship or represent a client other than the Federal Agency unless specifically assigned or authorized by competent authority.

(f) A Government lawyer representing the Federal Agency may also represent any of its Government employees subject to the provisions of paragraph (f), Rule 1.7, and other applicable authority. If the Federal Agency's consent to dual representation is required by Rule 1.7, the consent shall be given by an appropriate official of the Federal Agency, other than the individual to be represented.

(g) A Government lawyer who has been duly assigned or authorized to represent an individual who is subject to disciplinary action or adminis-

trative proceedings, or to provide civil legal assistance to an individual has, for those purposes, a lawyer-client relationship with that individual.

RULE 1.14 Client Under a Disability

(a) When a client's ability to make adequately considered decisions in connection with the representation is impaired, whether because of minority, mental disability, or for some other reason, the Federal lawyer shall, as far as reasonably possible, maintain a normal client-lawyer relationship with the client.

(b) A Federal lawyer may seek the appointment of a guardian or take other protective action with respect to a client, only when the Federal lawyer reasonably believes the client cannot adequately act in the client's own interest.

RULE 1.15 Safekeeping Property

(a) A Federal lawyer shall hold property of clients or third persons that is in the lawyer's possession in connection with a representation separate from the lawyer's own property. Funds shall be kept in a separate account maintained in the state in which the Federal lawyer's office is situated, or elsewhere with the consent of the client or third person. Other property shall be identified as belonging to the client and safeguarded appropriately. Complete records of such account funds and other property shall be kept by the lawyer and shall be preserved for a period of five years after termination of the representation.

(b) Upon receiving funds or other property in which a client or third person has an interest, a Federal lawyer shall promptly notify the client or the third person. Except as stated in this Rule or as otherwise permitted by law or by agreement with the client, the lawyer shall promptly deliver to the client or third person any funds or other property that the client or third person is entitled to receive and, upon request by the client or third person, shall promptly render full accounting regarding such property.

(c) When in the course of representation a Federal lawyer is in possession of property in which both the lawyer and another person claim interests, the property shall be kept separate by the lawyer until an accounting is made and their respective interests are severed. If a dispute arises concerning their respective interests, the portion in dispute shall be kept separate by the lawyer until the dispute is resolved.

(d) When property of a client or third party is admitted into evidence or otherwise included in the record of a proceeding, the Federal lawyer should take reasonable action to ensure its prompt return.

RULE 1.16 Declining or Terminating Representation

(a) Except as stated in paragraph (c), a Federal lawyer shall not represent a client, or, once representation has commenced, shall seek to withdraw from the representation of a client, if:

   (1) The representation will result in violation of these Rules of Professional Conduct or law.

   (2) The Federal lawyer's physical or mental condition materially impairs the lawyer's ability to represent the client.

   (3) The Federal lawyer is dismissed by the client.

(b) Except as stated in paragraph (c), a Federal lawyer may seek to withdraw from representing a client if withdrawal can be accomplished without material adverse effect on the interests of the client, or if:

   (1) The client persists in a course of action involving the Federal lawyer's services that the lawyer reasonably believes is criminal or fraudulent.

   (2) The client has used the Federal lawyer's services to perpetrate a crime or fraud.

   (3) A client insists upon pursuing an objective that the Federal lawyer considers repugnant or imprudent.

   (4) The client fails substantially to fulfill an obligation to the Federal lawyer regarding the lawyer's services and has been given reasonable warning that the Federal lawyer will seek to withdraw unless the obligation is fulfilled.

   (5) The representation will result in an unreasonable financial burden on the Federal lawyer or has been rendered unreasonable by the client.

   (6) Other good cause for withdrawal exists.

(c) When properly ordered to do so by a tribunal or other competent authority, a Federal lawyer shall continue representation notwithstanding good cause for terminating the representation.

(d) Upon termination of representation, a Federal lawyer shall take steps to the extent reasonably practicable to protect a client's interests, such as giving reasonable notice to the client, allowing time for employment of other counsel, surrendering papers and property to which the client is entitled, and refunding any advance payment of fees that has not been earned. The Federal lawyer may retain papers relating to the client to the extent permitted by law.

COUNSELOR

RULE 2.1 Advisor

In representing a client, a Federal lawyer shall exercise independent professional judgment and render candid advise. In rendering advice, a Federal lawyer may refer not only to law but to other considerations, such as moral, social, and political factors, that may be relevant to the client's situation, but not in conflict with the law.

RULE 2.2 Intermediary

(a) A Federal lawyer may act as an intermediary between individuals if:

   (1) The Federal lawyer consults with each client concerning the implications of common representation, including the advantages and risks involved and the effect on the attorney-client confidentiality, and obtains each client's consent to the common representation;

   (2) The Federal lawyer reasonably believes that the matter can be resolved on terms compatible with each client's best interest, that each client will be able to make adequately informed decisions in the matter, and that there is little risk of material prejudice to the interests of any of the clients if the contemplated resolution is unsuccessful; and

   (3) The Federal lawyer reasonably believes that the common representation can be undertaken impartially and without improper effect on other responsibilities the lawyer has to any of the clients.

(b) While acting as an intermediary, the Federal lawyer shall consult with each client concerning the decisions to be made and the considerations relevant in making them, so each client can make adequately informed decisions.

(c) A Federal lawyer shall withdraw as an intermediary if any of the clients so requests or if any of the conditions stated in paragraph (a) is no longer satisfied. Upon withdrawal, the lawyer shall not represent any of the clients in the matter that was the subject of the common representation unless each client consents.

RULE 2.3 Evaluation for Use by Third Persons

(a) A Federal lawyer may undertake an evaluation of a matter affecting a client for the use of someone other than the client if:

  (1) The Federal lawyer reasonably believes that making the evaluation is compatible with other aspects of the lawyer's relationship with the client, and

  (2) The client consents after sufficient consultation.

(b) Except a disclosure is required in connection with a report of an evaluation, information relating to the evaluation is otherwise protected by Rule 1.6.

ADVOCATE

RULE 3. 1 Meritorious Claims and Contentions

A Federal lawyer shall not bring or defend a proceeding, or assert or controvert an issue therein, unless there is a basis for doing so that is not frivolous. This basis may include a good faith argument for an extending, modifying, or reversing existing law. A Federal lawyer for the defendant in a criminal proceeding, of the respondent in a proceeding that could result in incarceration or other adverse action, may nevertheless so defend the proceeding as to require that every element of the case be established.

RULE 3.2 Expediting Litigation

A Federal lawyer shall make reasonable efforts to expedite litigation and other proceedings consistent with the interests of the client and the lawyer's responsibilities to the tribunal to avoid unwarranted delay.

RULE 3.3 Candor Toward the Tribunal

(a) A Federal lawyer shall not knowingly:

  (1) Make a false statement of material fact or law to a tribunal.

  (2) Fail to disclose a material fact to a tribunal when disclosure is necessary to avoid assisting a criminal or fraudulent act by the client.

  (3) Fail to disclose to the tribunal legal authority in the controlling jurisdiction known to the Federal lawyer to be directly adverse to the position of the client and not disclosed by opposing counsel.

  (4) Offer evidence that the lawyer knows to be false. If a Federal lawyer has offered material evidence and comes to know of its falsity, the lawyer shall take reasonable remedial measures.

  (5) Disobey an obligation or order imposed by a tribunal, unless done openly before the tribunal in a good faith assertion that no valid obligation or order should exist.

(b) The duties stated in paragraph (a) continue to the conclusion of the proceeding, and apply even if compliance requires disclosure of information otherwise protected by Rule 1.6.

(c) A Federal lawyer may refuse to offer evidence that the lawyer reasonably believes to be false.

(d) In an ex parte proceeding, a Federal lawyer shall disclose to the tribunal all material facts known to the lawyer that are reasonably necessary to enable the tribunal to make an informed decision, whether or not the facts are adverse.

RULE 3.4 Fairness to Opposing Party and Counsel

A Federal lawyer shall not:

(a) Unlawfully obstruct another party's access to evidence or unlawfully alter, destroy, or conceal a document or other material having potential evidentiary value. A Federal lawyer shall not counsel or assist another person to do any such act.

(b) Falsify evidence, counsel, or assist a witness to testify falsely, or offer an inducement to a witness that is prohibited by law.

(c) Knowingly disobey an obligation to an opposing party and counsel under the rules of a tribunal, except for an open refusal based on an assertion that no valid obligation exists.

(d) In pretrial procedure, make a frivolous discovery request or fail to make reasonably diligent efforts to comply with a legally proper discovery request by an opposing party.

(e) In pretrial, allude to any matter that the lawyer does not reasonably believe is relevant or that will not be supported by admissible evidence, assert personal knowledge of facts in issue except when testifying as a witness, or state a personal opinion as to the justness of a cause, the credibility of a witness, the culpability of a civil litigant, or the guilt or innocence of a defendant.

(f) Request a person other than a client to refrain from voluntarily giving relevant information to another party unless:

  (1) The person is a relative or an employee or other agent of a client; and

  (2) The Federal lawyer reasonably believes the person's interests will not be adversely affected by refraining from giving such information.

RULE 3.5 Impartiality and Decorum of the Tribunal

A Federal lawyer shall not:

(a) Seek to influence a tribunal, a member of a tribunal, a prospective member of a tribunal, or other official by means prohibited by law.

(b) Communicate ex parte with such a person about the matter except as permitted by law.

(c) Engage in conduct intended to disrupt a tribunal.

RULE 3.6 Tribunal Publicity

(a) A Federal lawyer shall not make an extrajudicial statement that a reasonable person would expect to be disseminated by means of public communication if the lawyer knows or reasonably should know that it will have a substantial likelihood of materially prejudicing an adjudicative proceeding or an official review process thereof.

(b) A statement referred to in paragraph (a) ordinarily is likely to have such an effect when it refers to a civil matter triable to a jury, a criminal matter, any other proceeding that could result in incarceration, or other adverse action and that statement relates to:

(1) The character, credibility, reputation, or criminal record of a party, suspect in a criminal investigation, or witness, the identity of a witness, or the expected testimony of a party or witness.

(2) The possibility of a plea of guilty to the offense or the existence or contents of any confession, admission, or statement given by a defendant or suspect, or that person's refusal or failure to make a statement.

(3) The performance or results of any examination or test, the refusal or failure of a person to submit to an examination or test, or the identity or nature of physical evidence expected to be presented.

(4) Any opinion as to the guilt or innocence of a defendant or suspect in an original case or proceeding that could result in incarceration or other adverse action.

(5) Information the Federal lawyer knows or reasonably should know is likely to be inadmissible as evidence in a trial and that would, if disclosed, create a substantial risk of prejudicing an impartial trial.

(6) A defendant's having been charged with a crime, unless included therein is a statement explaining that the charge is merely an accusation and the defendant is presumed innocent until and unless proven guilty.

(c) Notwithstanding paragraphs (a) and (b)(1-5), a Federal lawyer involved in the investigation or litigation of a matter may state without elaboration:

(1) The general nature of the claim or defense.

(2) Information contained in a public record.

(3) That an investigation of the matter is in progress, including the general scope of the investigation, the offense or claim or defense involved and, except when prohibited by law, the identity of the persons involved.

(4) The scheduling or result of any step in litigation.

(5) A request for assistance in obtaining evidence and information necessary in litigation.

(6) A warning of danger concerning the behavior of the person involved, when there is reason to believe the likelihood of substantial harm to an individual or to the public interest exists.

(7) In a criminal case:

  (i) The identity, place of business, occupation, and family status of the defendant.

  (ii) If the defendant has not been apprehended, information necessary to aid in apprehension of that person.

  (iii) The fact, time, and place of apprehension.

  (iv) The identity of investigating and apprehending officers or agencies and the length of the investigation.

(d) The protection and release of information in matters pertaining to the Government shall be consistent with law.

RULE 3.7 Federal Lawyer as Witness

(a) A Federal lawyer shall not act as advocate at a trial in which the lawyer is likely to be a necessary witness except when:

(1) The testimony relates to an uncontested issue.

(2) The testimony relates to the nature, value, and quality of legal services rendered in the case.

(3) Disqualification of the Federal lawyer would work substantial hardship on the client.

(b) A Federal lawyer may act as advocate in a matter in which another lawyer in the Federal lawyer's agency or firm is likely to be called as a witness unless precluded from doing so by Rule 1.7 or Rule 1.9.

RULE 3.8 Special Responsibilities of a Prosecutor

A prosecutor shall:

(a) Refrain from prosecuting a charge that the prosecutor knows is not supported by probable cause, or if not authorized to decline the prosecution of a charge to recommend to the appropriate authority that any charge not warranted by the evidence be withdrawn;

(b) Make reasonable efforts to ensure that the defendant has been advised of the right to and the procedure for obtaining counsel and has been given reasonable opportunity to obtain counsel;

(c) Not seek to obtain from an unrepresented defendant a waiver of important pretrial rights;

(d) Make timely disclosure to the defense of all evidence or information known to the Federal lawyer that tends to negate the guilt of the defendant or mitigates the offense, and, in connection with sentencing, disclose to the defense all unprivileged mitigating information known to the Federal lawyer, except when the Federal lawyer is relieved of this responsibility by a protective order or regulation; and

(e) Exercise reasonable care to prevent investigators, law enforcement personnel, employees, or other persons assisting or associated with the Federal lawyer in a criminal case from making extrajudicial statements that the prosecutor would be prohibited from making under Rule 3.6.

(f) Respect the attorney-client privilege of defendants and not diminish the privilege through investigative or judicial processes.

RULE 3.9 Advocate in Nonadjudicative Proceedings

A Federal lawyer representing a client before a legislative or administrative tribunal in a nonadjudicative proceeding shall disclose that the appearance is in a representative capacity and shall conform to the provisions of rules 3.3(a)–(c), 3.4(a)–(c), and 3.5.

TRANSACTIONS WITH PERSONS OTHER THAN CLIENTS

RULE 4.1 Truthfulness in Statements to Others

In the course of representing a client a Federal lawyer shall not knowingly:

(a) Make a false statement of material fact or law to a third person.

(b) Fail to disclose a material fact to a third person when disclosure is necessary to avoid assisting a criminal or fraudulent act by a client, unless disclosure is prohibited by Rule 1.6.

RULE 4.2 Communication with Persons Represented by Counsel

(a) In representing a client, a Federal lawyer shall not communicate about the subject of the representation with a party the lawyer knows to be represented by another lawyer in the matter, unless the Federal lawyer has the consent of the other lawyer; in a criminal matter, the individual initiates the communication with the Government lawyer and voluntarily and knowingly waives the right to counsel for the purposes of that communication; or the Federal lawyer otherwise is authorized by law to do so.

(b) This Rule does not prohibit communications by a Non-Government lawyer with Federal Agency officials who have the authority to resolve a matter affecting the lawyer's client, whether or not the lawyer's communications relate to matters that are the subject of the representation, provided that the lawyer discloses the lawyer's identity; the fact that the lawyer represents a client in a matter involving the official's Federal Agency; and that the matter is being handled for the Federal Agency by a Government lawyer.

RULE 4.3 Dealing with Unrepresented Persons

In dealing on behalf of a client with a person who is not represented by counsel, a Federal lawyer shall not state or imply that the lawyer is disinterested. When the Federal lawyer knows or reasonably should know that the unrepresented person misunderstands the lawyer's role in the matter, the lawyer shall make reasonable efforts to correct the misunderstanding.

RULE 4.4 Respect for Rights of Third Persons

In representing a client, a Federal lawyer shall not use means that have no substantial purpose other than to embarrass, delay, or burden a third person, or use methods of obtaining evidence that violate the legal rights of such a person.

LEGAL OFFICES
RULE 5.1 Responsibilities of a Supervisory Lawyer

(a) A supervisory lawyer shall make reasonable efforts to ensure that all Federal lawyers conform to these Rules of Professional Conduct.

(b) A Federal lawyer shall be responsible for another Federal lawyer's violation of these Rules of Professional Conduct if:

(1) The Federal lawyer orders or, with knowledge of the specific conduct, ratifies the conduct involved; or

(2) The Federal lawyer has direct Supervisory authority over the other Federal lawyer and knows of the conduct at a time when its consequences can be avoided or mitigated, but fails to take reasonable remedial action.

(c) A Federal lawyer, who is a supervisory lawyer, is responsible for ensuring that the subordinate lawyer is properly trained and is competent to perform the duties to which the subordinate lawyer is assigned.

(d) A Government lawyer, who is a supervisory lawyer, should encourage subordinate lawyers to participate in pro bono publico service activities and the activities of bar associations and law reform organizations.

RULE 5.2 Responsibilities of a Subordinate Federal Lawyer

(a) A Federal lawyer is bound by these Rules of Professional Conduct notwithstanding the Federal lawyer's acting at the direction of another person.

(b) A Subordinate Federal lawyer does not violate these Rules of Professional Conduct if that lawyer acts in accordance with a supervisory lawyer's reasonable resolution of an arguable question of professional duty.

RULE 5.3 Responsibilities Regarding Nonlawyer Assistants

With respect to a nonlawyer under the authority, supervision, or direction of a Federal lawyer:

(a) A supervisory lawyer shall make reasonable efforts to ensure that the office has in effect measures giving reasonable assurance that the person's conduct is compatible with the professional obligations of the Federal lawyer.

(b) A Federal lawyer having direct supervisory authority over the nonlawyer shall make reasonable efforts to ensure that the nonlawyer's conduct is compatible with the professional obligations of the Federal lawyer.

(c) A Federal lawyer shall be responsible for conduct of the nonlawyer that would be a violation (of) these Rules if engaged in by the Federal lawyer if:

(1) The Federal lawyer orders or, with the knowledge of the specific conduct, ratifies the conduct involved; or

(2) The Federal lawyer has direct supervisory authority over the nonlawyer, and knows of the conduct at a time when its consequences can be avoided or mitigated but fails to take reasonable remedial action.

RULE 5.4 Professional Independence of a Federal Lawyer

(a) A Federal lawyer is expected to exercise professional independence of judgment during the representation of a client, consistent with these Rules.

(b) Notwithstanding a Government lawyer's status as a Government employee, a Government lawyer detailed or assigned to represent an individual Government employee or another person as the client is expected to exercise loyalty and professional independence during the representation, consistent with these Rules and to the same extent as required by a Non-Government lawyer in private practice.

(c) A Supervisory Government lawyer may not base an adverse evaluation or other prejudicial action against a Subordinate Government lawyer on the Subordinate Government lawyer's exercise of professional independence under (b) above.

(d) A Government lawyer shall obey the lawful orders of superiors when representing the United States and individual clients, but a Government lawyer shall not permit a nonlawyer to direct or regulate the Government lawyer's professional judgment in rendering legal services.

(e) A Non-Government lawyer shall not permit a nonlawyer who recommends, employs, or pays the Non-Government lawyer to render legal services for another to direct or regulate the Non-Government lawyer's professional judgment in rendering legal services.

(f) A Non-Government lawyer shall comply with the Rules of Professional Conduct or other applicable laws of the jurisdiction in which the Non-Government lawyer is licensed or is practicing law concerning the limitations on sharing fees and the organizational form of their practice.

RULE 5.5 Unauthorized Practice of Law

A Federal lawyer shall not:

(a) Except as authorized by law, practice law in a jurisdiction where doing so violates the regulation of the legal profession in that jurisdiction; or

(b) Assist a person who is not a member of the bar in the performance of activity that constitutes the unauthorized practice of law.

PUBLIC SERVICE

RULE 6.1 Pro Bono Publico Service

(a) A Federal lawyer should render public interest legal service. A Federal lawyer may discharge this responsibility by providing professional services at no fee or a reduced fee to persons of limited means or to public service or charitable groups or organizations, by service in activities for improving the law, the legal system or the legal profession, and by financial support for organizations that provide legal service to persons of limited means.

(b) A Government lawyer should provide pro bono legal services consistent with applicable law.

RULE 6.2 Accepting Appointments

A Federal lawyer shall not seek to avoid appointment by a tribunal to represent a person except for good cause, such as:

(a) Representing the client is contrary to law or in violation of these Rules.

(b) Representing the client is likely to result in an unreasonable financial burden on the Federal lawyer.

(c) The client or the cause is so repugnant to the lawyer as to be likely to impair the client-lawyer relationship or the lawyer's ability to represent the client.

RULE 6.3 Membership in Legal Services Organization

A Federal lawyer may serve as a director, officer, or member of a legal services organization, apart from the law firm or Federal Agency in which the lawyer practices, notwithstanding that the organization serves persons having interests adverse to a client of the Federal lawyer. The Federal lawyer shall not knowingly participate in a decision or action of the organization:

(a) If participating in the decision or action would be incompatible with the Federal lawyer's obligations to a client under Rule 1.7; or

(b) Where the decision or action could have a material adverse effect on the representation of a client of the organization whose interests are adverse to a client of the Federal lawyer.

RULE 6.4 Membership in Bar Associations and Law Reform Activities Affecting Client Interests

A Federal lawyer may serve as a member, director, or officer of a bar association or an organization involved in reform of the law or its administration, notwithstanding that the reform may affect the inter-

ests of a client. The Federal lawyer shall not knowingly participate in a decision or action of the organization if participating in the decision would be incompatible with the Federal lawyer's obligations to the client under Rule 1.7. When the Federal lawyer knows the interests of the client may be materially benefitted by a decision in which the Federal lawyer participates, the Federal lawyer shall disclose that fact, but need not identify the client.

INFORMATION ABOUT LEGAL SERVICES

RULE 7.1 Communications Concerning a Federal Agency's Legal Services

A Government lawyer may advertise the Federal Agency's legal services through the public media, such as a telephone directory, newspaper, or other periodicals, outdoor sign, radio, television, or through written communications.

MAINTAINING THE INTEGRITY OF THE PROFESSION

RULE 8.1 Bar Admission and Disciplinary Matters

An applicant for admission to a bar or employment as a lawyer with a Federal Agency, a Federal lawyer seeking the right to practice before a Federal Agency, or a Federal lawyer in connection with a disciplinary matter, shall not:

(a) Knowingly make a false statement of material fact.

(b) Fail to disclose a fact necessary to correct a misapprehension known by the person to have arisen in the matter, or knowingly fail to respond to a lawful demand for information from an admission or disciplinary authority, except that the Rule does not require disclosure of information otherwise protected by Rule 1.6.

RULE 8.2 Judicial and Legal Officials

A Federal lawyer shall not make a statement the lawyer knows to be false or with reckless disregard as to its truth or falsity concerning the qualifications or integrity of a tribunal or of a candidate for election or appointment to judicial or legal office.

RULE 8.3 Reporting Professional Misconduct

(a) A Federal lawyer having knowledge that another Federal lawyer has committed a violation of these Rules of Professional Conduct that raises a substantial question as to that lawyer's honesty, trustworthiness, or fitness as a Federal lawyer in other respects, shall report such a violation to the appropriate official as provided by law.

(b) A Federal lawyer having knowledge that a judge has committed a violation of applicable rules of judicial conduct that raises a substantial question as to the judge's fitness for office shall report such a violation to the appropriate official as provided by law.

(c) This Rule does not require disclosure of information otherwise protected by Rule 1.6.

RULE 8.4 Misconduct

It is professional misconduct for a Federal lawyer to:

(a) Violate or attempt to violate these Rules of Professional Conduct, knowingly assist or induce another to do so, or do so through the acts of another.

(b) Commit a criminal act that reflects adversely on the Federal lawyer's honesty, trustworthiness, or fitness as a Federal lawyer in other respects.

(c) Engage in conduct involving dishonesty, fraud, deceit, or misrepresentation.

(d) Engage in conduct prejudicial to the administration of justice.

(e) State or imply an ability to influence improperly a government Federal Agency or official.

(f) Knowingly assist a judge or judicial officer in conduct that violates applicable rules of judicial conduct or other law.

RULE 8.5 Jurisdiction

(a) A Federal lawyer shall comply with the rules of professional conduct applicable to the Federal Agency that employs the Government lawyer or the Federal Agency before which the Federal lawyer practices.

(b) If the Federal Agency has not adopted or promulgated rules of professional conduct, the Federal lawyer shall comply with the rules of professional conduct of the state bars in which the Federal lawyer is admitted to practice.

© Federal Bar Association. Reprinted with permission.

FINANCIAL EXECUTIVES INSTITUTE

Telephone: 973/898-4600
WWW: www.fei.org
Document: Code of Ethics (1985)

As a member of Financial Executives Institute, I will:

- Conduct my business and personal affairs at all times with honesty and integrity. Provide complete, appropriate and relevant information in an objective manner when reporting to management, stockholders, employees, government agencies, other institutions and the public.

- Comply with rules and regulations of federal, state, provincial and local governments and other appropriate private and public regulatory agencies.

- Discharge duties and responsibilities to my employer to the best of my ability, including complete communication on all matters within my jurisdiction.

- Maintain the confidentiality of information acquired in the course of my work except when authorized or otherwise legally obligated to disclose. Confidential information acquired in the course of my work will not be used for my personal advantage.

- Maintain an appropriate level of professional competence through continuing development of my knowledge and skills.

- Refrain from committing acts discreditable to myself, my employer, FEI or fellow members of the Institute.

© Financial Executives Institute. Reprinted with permission.

GAMA INTERNATIONAL *Growth through sharing*

GENERAL AGENTS AND MANAGERS ASSOCIATION

Address: 10 Madison Avenue, Box 1938
Morristown, NJ 07962-1938

Address: 1922 F Street NW
Washington, DC 20006-4389

Telephone: 202/331-6088
WWW: www.gamaweb.com
Document: Statement of Principles

Because the institution of life insurance renders an economic and social service that is unique and of great benefit to society, because it is a trusteeship that requires constant service, and because matters that affect its progress are of vital concern to all, and because the representatives of life insurance constitute its most important liaison with the public which it serves; and because it is of the utmost importance to maintain the high ethical standards of the institution of life insurance;

Therefore, I believe it to be my responsibility:

To select my agents and managers carefully, using the best available techniques, so that only the qualified shall be placed under contract.

To build a sales organization by recruiting people new to the business who intend to make life insurance, in one or more of its branches, their full-time career.

To provide adequate training and supervision, using the best available methods and materials, so that the agents placed under contract give sound advice, render quality service to policyholders, and achieve financial success at the earliest possible moment.

To encourage my associates to continue their development with sound self-improvement programs from year to year, such as LUTC*, CLU**, and other similar courses, to the end that they may reach the highest level of proficiency, and achieve prestige and maximum satisfaction in their work.

To encourage membership in and support the local Association of Life Underwriters by attendance and participation in meetings and activities and to follow their rules of conduct.

To present fairly and honestly, and without exaggeration, all facts which a prospective agent or manager should have in determining whether to accept a contract with my agency.

To urge any agent or manager with whom I am discussing potential employment to review the agent's or manager's current employment situation with the agent's present general agent or manager before reaching a decision.

To take a leadership role in advocacy of the agency distribution system and in the fundamental belief that

life and disability insurance are upon death, disability, old age and during emergencies the best products to provide cash and income when most needed by my fellow citizens who seek self-determination and personal freedom.

In general, I shall endeavor and encourage others to practice the "Golden Rule" in all aspects of our professional lives and, in so doing, strive to gain the respect of our contemporaries and lift our profession to the highest level of public esteem.

(*Life Underwriter Training Course. **Certified Life Underwriter.—Eds.)

© General Agents and Managers Association. Reprinted with permission.

GENETICS SOCIETY OF AMERICA

Address: 9650 Rockville Pike.
Bethesda, MD 20814-3998
Telephone: 301/571-1825
WWW: www.faseb.org/genetics/gsa/
gsamenu.htm
Document: Code of Ethical Principles for
Genetics Professionals (1995)

(The following code, the fruit of work undertaken by the Council of Regional Networks (CORN) Ethics Committee, "is not a Code of Ethics in the proper sense, but a collection of statements on which consensus could be reached." These "rather terse" statements were published in the *American Journal of Medical Genetics 65* (1996), together with "An Explication" which is not reprinted here.—Eds.)

PREAMBLE

Genetics impacts the health of all individuals, their offspring and future generations. The practice of medical genetics has generated principles of ethics to guide those who strive to serve humanity within this profession. The principal tenets are presented here for the guidance of each professional and the information of the public. The evolution of these principles should be only in the direction of higher levels of service to both the individual and the community, and enhancement of the freedom and rights of those who come under the care of anyone belonging to the profession.

RESPONSIBILITIES TO PATIENTS AND FAMILIES

The relationships among genetics professionals, patients, and their families are founded on the principles of autonomy and privacy. The genetics professional should:

1. Serve patients and their families with equity and with respect for each person's feelings, beliefs, ethno-cultural traditions, and social circumstances;
2. Provide counseling that is nondirective, supportive, and responsive to the individual's requests, and should respect the choices of patients and families;
3. Convey information sensitively to patients, and in language they understand, so that they may make independent decisions and give informed consent;
4. Refer, when indicated or requested, to other experts for specialized services or to confirm diagnosis;
5. Honor the confidentiality of information shared in the relationship with patients and their families;
6. Urge patients and families to share genetic information with relatives at risk, pointing out the possible need for this early in the relationship;
7. Inform persons who participate as subjects of research that they may refuse testing, or refuse to receive information, and that they may withdraw from research programs without change in care;
8. Inform patients of possible conflicts of interest and of possible commercial and other uses of their biological specimens, of duration of storage, and of confidentiality of personal identifiers.

RESPONSIBILITIES TO SOCIETY

Individuals within the professional genetics community have a responsibility to provide assistance to society as a whole in the understanding of genetics. Genetics professionals should:

1. Participate actively in the development and support of appropriate regulation of genetics services to ensure that the highest quality is maintained;
2. Achieve appropriate balance between the rights of individuals and the needs of public health in the use of genetic information;
3. Promote educational activities designed to inform the community of developments in genetics, and assist the community in formulating reasonable expectations and in understanding implications;

4. Stimulate public discussion of issues arising from advances in genetics, ensure that public debates include objective and well-documented science, and participate in formulation of public policy and attitudes toward genetics to promote socially responsible change;
5. Distinguish, in public statements, that which one perceives as fact, professional consensus, competing schools of thought, or personal opinion;
6. Guard against discrimination on the basis of genetic status, race, gender, sexual orientation, religion, or socioeconomic status in the provision of genetics services;
7. Support equitable access to genetics services as part of any health care system;
8. Support regulation of genetic research that provides ethical standards, including informed consent and confidentiality;
9. Use genetic knowledge and techniques to support and broaden the choice of patients, and not to promote eugenic programs.

RESPONSIBILITIES TO THE PROFESSION

Genetics encompasses many disciplines in which professionals are trained. Mutual respect and assistance among professionals are essential for proper patient care. Genetics professionals should:

1. Maintain professional competency through continual learning;
2. Share expertise attained through training, experience, and research by teaching, publishing, collegial interchange, and nurturing those who seek competency in the disciplines;
3. Support and encourage one another in ethical conduct, and in resolving professional differences with mutual respect and for the benefit of the patient;
4. Share appropriate information with the referring source, toward the collaborative development of a plan of care for the patient;
5. Guard against the profession's limiting, or cooperating in the limiting, of any individual's or group's human rights on the basis of genetic characteristics.

"Code of Ethical Principles for Genetics Professionals." Baumiller, Robert C.; Comley, Sarah; Cunningham, George; Fisher, Nancy; Fox, Lynda; Henderson, Merrill; Lebel, Robert; McGrath, Geraldine; Pelias, Mary Z.; Porter, Ian; Willson, Nancy Roper. *American Journal of Medical Genetics.* Copyright © 1996 Wiley-Liss, Inc. Reprinted by permission of Wiley-Liss, Inc, a division of John Wiley & Sons, Inc.

GUILD OF PRESCRIPTION OPTICIANS OF AMERICA

Address: 10341 Democracy Lane
Fairfax, VA 22030-2521
Telephone: 703/691-8355 or 800/443-8997
WWW: www.opticians.org
Document: Code of Ethics (1926. Most recently revised 1983.)

(The Guild of Prescription Opticians of America was founded in 1926 to represent opticians who dispensed eyewear directly to the consumer. In 1972, this organization reorganized into the Opticians Association of America, representing a larger constituency including retail optical firm owners, optical corporations, and state societies of opticians among others. The Guild of Prescription Opticians of America originally produced the following code of ethics, which is still in effect today.—Eds.)

I. To maintain the highest level of professional opticianry, thereby protecting the consumers' interests.

II. To meet the high standards of the Guild to ensure that efficiency and service are always provided.

III. To furnish a source for eye care products and services, independent of those prescribing for eye care needs.

IV. To promote the conservation of human eyesight.

V. To supply only the finest quality optical products and services, representing the state of the art in opticianry.

VI. To participate in and encourage continuing education for eye care professionals.

HUMAN FACTORS AND ERGONOMICS SOCIETY

Address: PO Box 1369
Santa Monica, CA 90406-1369
Telephone: 310/394-1811
WWW: www.hfes.org
Document: Human Factors and Ergonomics Society Code of Ethics (1989)

Preamble

The Human Factors and Ergonomics Society is dedicated to the betterment of humankind through the scientific inquiry into and application of those principles that relate to the interface of humans with their natural, residential, recreational, and vocational environments and the procedures, practices, and design considerations that increase a human's performance and safety at those interfaces. To promote and sustain the highest levels of professional and scientific performance by its members, the Human Factors and Ergonomics Society has adopted this Code of Ethics. No special oath to these Articles is necessary; its provisions are incumbent on all classes of membership of the Society.

No such code can be expected to completely anticipate all of the various and complex arrangements that professionals create, nor can it fully explore the many ramifications of these arrangements. The following Articles, then, are a guide and serve to set the tenor of professional behavior. The details must be left to the conscience and goodwill of the elected and appointed officers of the Society who must administer adherence to this code.

Article I-Professional Qualifications

Human factors scientists and engineers have the responsibility of factually representing their professional qualifications as well as those of the institution they represent.

Principle 1

Members limit their practice to those areas of human factors wherein they maintain a competence by virtue of training and/or experience and not extend their endeavors beyond their realm of competence. They enter into additional areas of human factors practice and teaching only after sufficient professional preparation or with proper professional oversight.

Principle 2

Where a brief or summary statement of qualifications would be deceptive or misleading, members present their educational background in the detail and with the additional explanation necessary for an accurate interpretation of their area of study and the level of attainment achieved. Members do likewise with their representations of their work experience so that there is little chance for a misunderstanding of the extensiveness or intensiveness of their work achievements.

Principle 3

Members represent their employers' capabilities and interests accurately so as not to mislead their clients or potential clients or damage the business interests or reputation of their employers.

Principle 4

Members, when representing their professional affiliations, factually represent their current or past affiliations with any institution or organization as well as factually represent the aims and purposes of those institutions or organizations.

Principle 5

Members do not use their affiliation with the Human Factors and Ergonomics Society or its Chapters for purposes not consonant with the stated purposes of the Society, nor do they announce their affiliation with the Human Factors and Ergonomics Society in such a way as to falsely imply sponsorship or approval by that organization.

Article II-General Conduct

Human factors scientists and engineers have the responsibility of comporting themselves in a manner consistent with that generally expected of the professional community.

Principle 1

In the conduct of their professional activities, members do everything necessary to reflect personal integrity as well as to convey the integrity of their profession.

Principle 2

Members avoid sensationalism, exaggeration, and superficiality that constitutes deception, and must similarly avoid any misrepresentation in all public statements, presentations, and submissions to mass media.

Principle 3

Members avoid all situations that contain elements of conflict of interest or must provide full disclosure of those conflicts to all potentially affected parties.

Principle 4

Members do not use a position as a teacher, a granting or contracting official, an employer or employee, or any other position of influence to coerce or harass others.

Principle 5

Members do not use race, handicap, sex, sexual preference, age, religion, or national origin as a consideration in hiring, promotion, or training or in any research or application where such consideration is irrelevant to the situational demands for performance.

Principle 6

Members factually represent all aspects of an employment offer, fully disclosing the terms and conditions of work, the length of employment, research projects and facilities available, work assignments, and opportunities for advancement.

Principle 7

Where responsible for design, members include considerations for the safety of person and property, and, through the appropriate source, notify those concerned when a hazardous condition exists.

Principle 8

Members clearly present the adverse safety and health consequences to be expected from deviations proposed if their technical judgment is overruled by technical or administrative authority.

Article III-Publications

Human factors scientists and engineers generally have the obligation to report their work to the general scientific community and to give credit to those who have contributed on a professional level to that publication.

Principle 1

Members give credit, proportional to their contribution, to all those responsible for the formulation, experimental design, analysis, or other treatment of the material if their contribution was on a professional level. Such credit should be extended by a listing of all contributors' names in the publication. That listing can be in the form of joint authorship with the name of the most substantial contributor listed as senior author, or by a footnote or introductory statement when the contribution is minor. This Principle deals with credit for professional contributions only and in no way affects copyright ownership.

Principle 2

Members ensure that their work is reported factually, bearing professional responsibility for all elements of their reportage, including the accuracy of analysis, quotation from other works, and conclusions drawn. Members maintain the highest standards of scientific experimentation and analysis.

Principle 3
Members maintain a position of objectivity when editing publications and reviewing papers that reflect views other than their own, as well as papers that present data in conflict with those they themselves may have previously published.

Article IV-Subject Precautions
Human factors scientists and engineers have the responsibility of treating both human and animal subjects humanely and in accordance with federal, state, and local laws or regulations, as well as the generally accepted procedures within the scientific community.

Principle 1
Members determine, through consultation with colleagues or institutional review committees, that the exposure of human or animal research subjects to hazards, stress, divulgence of history or preferences, or tedium is commensurate with the significance of the problem being researched.

Principle 2
Members determine the degree of hazard present in the exposure of human or animal research subjects, avoiding any exposures to human subjects that may result in death, dismemberment, permanent dysfunction or extreme pain, and utilize the lowest levels of exposure to both human and animal subjects consistent with the phenomenon under consideration.

Principle 3
Members ensure the ethical treatment of human and animal research subjects by collaborators, assistants, students, and employees.

Principle 4
Members establish an informed consent with human research subjects when required by institutional, state, or federal codes or regulations, making explicit in plain language the terms of participation, particularly with respect to any elements of risk or stress involved, and adhere to those terms throughout the experiment. One of these terms must be that the subject has the right to terminate participation at any time without prejudice.

Principle 5
Members do not coerce potential human research subjects to participate as subjects, nor do they use

undue monetary rewards to induce subjects to take risks they would not otherwise take.

Principle 6
Members preserve the confidentiality of any information obtained from human research subjects that, if divulged, may have harmful effects on those subjects.

© Human Factors and Ergonomists Society. Reprinted with permission.

iDSA

INDUSTRIAL DESIGNERS SOCIETY OF AMERICA

Address: 1142 East Walker Road
Great Falls, VA 22066
Telephone: 703/759-0100
WWW: www.idsa.org
Document: Code of Ethics and Articles of Ethical Practice

(The Code of Ethics sets forth the fundamental ethical principles of IDSA. Since there is always room for interpretation when applying principles to a specific set of circumstances, the Ethics Advisory Council was formed to give guidance on ethics issues and to interpret the Code. Although they are not reprinted here, a number of summary opinions have been issued by the EAC to supplement the Code.—Eds.)

Recognizing that industrial designers affect the quality of life in our increasingly independent and complex society; that responsible ethical decision making often requires conviction, courage and ingenuity in today's competitive business context: We, the members of the Industrial Designers Society of America, will endeavor to meet the standards set forth in this code, and strive to support and defend one another in doing so.

Fundamental Ethical Principles

We will uphold and advance the integrity of our profession by:

1. supporting one another in achieving our goals of maintaining high professional standards and levels of competence, and honoring commitments we make to others;
2. being honest and fair in serving the public, our clients, employers, peers, employees and students regardless of gender, race, creed, ethnic origin, age, disability or sexual orientation;
3. striving to maintain sufficient knowledge of relevant current events and trends so as to be able to assess the economic and environmental effects of our decisions;
4. using our knowledge and skill for the enrichment of human well-being, present and future; and
5. supporting equality of rights under the law and opposing any denial or abridgement of equal rights by the United States or by any individual state on account of gender, race, creed, ethnic origin, age, disability or sexual orientation.

Articles of Ethical Practice

The following articles provide an outline of ethical guidelines designed to advance the quality of our profession. They provide general principles in which the "Ethics Advisory Council" can resolve more specific questions that may arise.

Article I:

We are responsible to the public for their safety, and their economic and general well-being is our foremost professional concern. We will participate only in projects we judge to be ethically sound and in conformance with pertinent legal regulations; we will advise our clients and employers when we have serious reservations concerning projects we have been assigned.

Article II:

We will provide our employers and clients with original and innovative design service of high quality; by serving their interests as faithful agents; by treating privileged information with discretion; by communicating effectively with their appropriate staff members; by avoiding conflicts of interest; and by establishing clear contractual understandings regarding obligations of both parties. Only with agreement of all concerned will we work on competing product lines simultaneously.

Article III:

We will compete fairly with our colleagues by building our professional reputation primarily on the quality of our work; by issuing only truthful, objective and non-misleading public statements and promotional materials; by respecting competitors' contractual relationships with their clients; and by commenting only with candor and fairness regarding the character of work of other industrial designers.

Article IV:

We will be responsible to our employees by facilitating their professional development insofar as possible; by establishing clear contractual understandings; by maintaining safe and appropriate work environments; by properly crediting work accomplished; and by providing fair and adequate compensation for salary and overtime hours.

Article V:

We will be responsible to design education by holding as one of our fundamental concerns the education of design students; by advocating implementation of sufficiently inclusive curricula and requiring satisfactory proficiency to enable students to enter the profession with adequate knowledge and skills; by providing opportunities for internships (and collaboratives) with and observation of practicing designers; by respecting students' rights to ownership of their designs; and by fairly crediting them for work accomplished.

Article VI:

We will advance the interests of our profession by abiding by this Code; by providing a forum within the Society for the ongoing review of ethical concerns; and by publishing, as appropriate, interpretations of this Code.

**INSTITUTE FOR
CERTIFICATION
OF COMPUTING
PROFESSIONALS**

| Address: | 2200 East Devon Avenue, Suite 247 Des Plaines, IL 60018-4503 |

Telephone: 847/299-4227
WWW: www.iccp.org
Document: ICCP Code of Ethics

Certified computing professionals, consistent with their obligation to the public at large, should promote the understanding of information processing methods and procedures using every resource at their command.

Certified computing professionals have an obligation to their profession to uphold the high ideals and level of personal knowledge as evidenced by the Certificate held. They should also encourage the dissemination of knowledge pertaining to the development of the computing profession.

Certified computing professionals have an obligation to serve the interests of their employers and clients loyally, diligently and honestly.

Certified computing professionals must not engage in any conduct or commit any act which is a discredit to the reputation or integrity of the information processing profession.

Certified computing professionals must not imply that the Certificates which they hold are their sole claim to professional competence.

Codes of Conduct and Good Practice for Certified Computing Professionals

The essential elements relating to conduct that identify a professional activity are:

A high standard of skill and knowledge.
A confidential relationship with people served.
Public reliance upon the standards of conduct and established practice.
The observance of an ethical code.

Therefore, these Codes have been formulated to strengthen the professional status of certified computing professionals.

1. Preamble

1.1: The basic issue, which may arise in connection with any ethical proceedings before a Certification Council, is whether a holder of a Certificate administered by that Council has acted in a manner which violates the Code of Ethics for certified computing professionals.

1.2: Therefore, the ICCP has elaborated the existing Code of Conduct, which defines more specifically an individual's professional responsibility. This step was taken in recognition of questions and concerns as to what constitutes professional and ethical conduct in the computing profession.

1.3: The ICCP has reserved for and delegated to each Certification Council the right to revoke any Certificate which has been issued under its administration in the event that the recipient violates the Code of Ethics, as amplified by the Code of Conduct. The revocation proceedings are specified by rules governing the business of the Certification Council and provide protection of the rights of any individual who may be subject to revocation of a certificate held. The ICCP may bypass revocation proceedings and automatically revoke any Certificate for non-compliance with mandatory recertification processes, providing the certificate was awarded subject to mandatory recertification requirements.

1.4: Insofar as violation of the Code of Conduct may be difficult to adjudicate, the ICCP has also promulgated a Code of Good Practice, the violation of which does not in itself constitute a reason to revoke a Certificate. However, any evidence concerning a serious and consistent breach of the Code of Good Practice may be considered as additional circumstantial evidence in any ethical proceedings before a Certification Council.

1.5: Whereas the Code of Conduct is of a fundamental nature, the Code of Good Practice is expected to be amended from time to time to accommodate changes in the social environment and to keep up with the development of the information processing profession.

1.6: A Certification Council will not consider a complaint where the holder's conduct is already subject to legal proceedings. Any complaint will only be considered when the legal action is completed, or it is established that no legal proceedings will take place.

1.7: Recognizing that the language contained in all sections of either the Code of Conduct or Code of Good Practice is subject to interpretations beyond those intended, the ICCP intends to confine all Codes to the matters pertaining to personal actions of individual certified computing professionals in situations for which they can be held directly accountable without reasonable doubt.

1.8: Certified computing professionals have a responsibility to respect intellectual property rights, including copyrights, patents and trademarks. Violation of copyrights, patents and terms of license agreements is prohibited by law in most circumstances. Even when not so protected, such violations are contrary to professional behavior. Software should be copied only with proper authorization. Unauthorized duplication of both printed and electronic materials must be discouraged including those cases where the work has not been explicitly protected by any means. Credit should not be taken for the work of others. The work of others should not be used without specific acknowledgment and authorization.

2. Code of Conduct

2.1: Disclosure: Subject to the confidential relationships between oneself and one's employer or client, one is expected not to transmit information which one acquires during the practice of one's profession in any situation which may seriously affect a third party.

2.2: Social Responsibility: One is expected to accept a responsibility to the public to diminish, through a continuing educational process, confusion and misconceptions surrounding the information processing industry. One is expected to be cognizant of and act in accordance with all procedures and regulations to improve public safety through the protection of information vital to the security of the nation and its people, both collectively and individually.

2.3: Conclusions and Opinions: One is expected to state a conclusion on a subject in one's field only when it can be demonstrated that it has been founded on adequate knowledge. One will state a qualified opinion when expressing a view in an area within one's professional competence but not supported by relevant facts.

2.4: Identification: One shall properly qualify oneself when expressing an opinion outside one's professional competence in the event that such an opinion could be identified by a third party as expert testimony, or if by inference the opinion can be expected to be used improperly.

2.5: Integrity: One will not knowingly lay claims to competence one does not demonstrably possess. One shall not take advantage of the lack of knowledge or inexperience of others.

2.6: Conflict of Interest: One shall act with strict impartiality when purporting to give independent advice. In the event that the advice given is currently or potentially influential to one's personal benefit, full and detailed disclosure to all relevant interested parties will be made at the time the advice is provided. One's employer especially should be made aware of any potential conflicts of interest. One will not denigrate the honesty or competence of a fellow professional or a competitor, with the intent to gain an unfair advantage.

2.7: Accountability: The degree of professional accountability for results will be dependent on the position held and type of work performed. For instance: a senior executive is accountable for the quality of work performed by all individuals the person supervises and for ensuring that recipients of information are fully aware of known limitations in the results provided. The personal accountability of consultants and technical experts is especially important because of the positions of unique trust inherent in their advisory roles. Consequently, they are accountable for seeing to it that known limitations of their work are fully disclosed, documented and explained. Furthermore information processing professionals have a responsibility to take appropriate action regarding any illegal or unethical practices that come to their attention. Charges should be brought against a person only when a reasonable basis for the allegations has been established, without regard to personal interest.

2.8: Protection of Privacy: One shall protect the privacy and confidentiality of all entrusted information. One shall have special regard for the potential effects of computing-based systems on the right of privacy of individuals whether this is within one's own organization, among customers or suppliers, or in relation to the general public. Because of the privileged capability of computing professionals to gain access to computerized files, especially strong strictures will be applied to those who have used their position of trust to obtain information from computerized files for their personal gain.

Where it is possible that decisions can be made within a computing-based system could adversely affect the personal security, work or career of an individual, the system design shall specifically provide for decision review by a responsible executive who will thus remain accountable and identifiable for that decision.

3. Code of Good Practice

3.1: Education: One has a special responsibility to keep oneself fully aware of developments in information processing technology relevant to one's current professional occupation. One will contribute to the interchange of technical and professional information by encouraging and participating in educational activities directed to both fellow professionals and to the public at large. One will do all in one's power to further public understanding of computing systems. One will contribute to the growth of knowledge in the field to the extent that one's expertise, and ability allow.

3.2: Personal Conduct: Insofar as one's personal and professional activities interact visibly to the same public, one is expected to support, respect and abide by the appropriate laws and in general to apply the same high standards of behavior in one's personal life as are demanded in one's professional activities.

3.3: Competence: One shall at all times exercise technical and professional competence at least to the level one claims. One shall not deliberately withhold information in one's possession unless disclosure of that information could harm or seriously affect another party, or unless one is bound by a proper, clearly defined confidential relationship. One shall not deliberately destroy or diminish the value or effectiveness of a computing-based system through acts of commission or omission.

3.4: Statements: One shall not make false or exaggerated statements as to the state of affairs existing or expected regarding any aspect of information technology or the use of computers. In communicating with lay persons, one shall use general language wherever possible and shall not use technical terms or expressions unless there exist no adequate equivalents in the general language.

3.5: Discretion: One shall exercise maximum discretion in disclosing, or permitting to be disclosed, or using to one's own advantage, any information relating the affairs of one's present or previous employers or clients.

3.6: Conflict of Interest: One shall not knowingly hold, assume, or accept a position or a client with which one's interests conflict or are likely to conflict with one's current duties or clients unless that interest has been disclosed in advance to all parties involved.

3.7: Public Safety: One has a responsibility to protect fundamental human rights and dignity and to respect cultural diversity. Those who design, develop and maintain computing systems shall be alert to and make others aware of any potential damage to the local and global environment. When developing information systems, computing professionals must ensure that their efforts are used to benefit humanity. Harmful effects to general health and welfare of the public shall be avoided.

3.8: Violations: One is expected to report violations of the Code, testify in ethical proceedings where one has expert or firsthand knowledge, and serve on panels to judge complaints of violations of ethical conduct.

4. Procedural Requirements for Revocation of Certificate Awarded

4.1: The ICCP may automatically revoke Certificates for non-compliance with mandatory recertification processes, providing the certificate was awarded subject to mandatory recertification requirements.

4.2: A Certification Council, on behalf of the Institute for Certification of Computing Professionals, has the right to revoke any Certificate which has been awarded by it in the event that the recipient violates the Codes, or engages in conduct which is a discredit or disgrace to the computing profession.

4.3: The grounds for revocation, except for failure to comply with mandatory recertification requirements, will be based upon the opinion of at least two-thirds of the members of the Council.

4.4: Procedure for handling revocation:

1. A formal written statement of charges alleging facts which constitute the grounds for revocation will be prepared.
2. A copy of said charges will be forwarded to the person accused, fixing a time within which such person may file with the Council answers to the charges.
3. If the charges are denied in the answer, the Council will fix a time for the hearing and give notice of the time and place of the hearing to the person accused.
4. Presentation of evidence in support of the charges will be made by the secretary (a nonvoting member) of the Certification Council.
5. Presentation of the evidence in defense of the charges will be made by the accused or the designated representative of the accused.
6. Ample opportunity for both sides to present facts and arguments will be allowed at the hearing.
7. At the conclusion of the hearing, the Council will determine whether or not the charges have been sufficiently established by the evidence and whether the Certificate should be revoked or should not be revoked.
8. The accused will be notified of the decision by registered mail.
9. The accused has the right to request review of the decision by the Executive Committee of ICCP, provided an appeal in writing is submitted to the President of ICCP within 30 days of the accused's receipt of the Council's decision.

INSTITUTE OF CERTIFIED MANAGEMENT ACCOUNTANTS

Address: 10 Paragon Drive
              Montvale, NJ 07645-1759
Telephone: 201/573-9000 or 800/638-4427
WWW: raw.rutgers.edu/raw/ima/icma.htm

The Institute of Certified Management Accountants subscribes to the same code of ethics as the Institute of Management Accountants. See p. 00.

INSTITUTE OF ELECTRICAL AND ELECTRONICS ENGINEERS

Address: Three Park Avenue, 17th Floor
              New York, NY 10016-5997
Telephone: 212/419-7900
WWW: www.ieee.org
Document: IEEE Code of Ethics (1990)

(The original IEEE code was adopted in 1974, generated by a subcommittee of the IEEE United States Activity Committee, which subsequently became the US Activities Board (USAB). In 1987 the IEEE Board of Directors amended the code without consulting any other body. In 1990 a complete revision (leading to the present version) was approved by the Board of Directors after an extensive process in which the work of an ad hoc committee of USAB was reviewed by a number of IEEE entities.—Eds.)

We, the members of the IEEE, in recognition of the importance of our technologies in affecting the quality of life throughout the world, and in accepting a personal obligation to our profession, its members and the communities we serve, do hereby commit ourselves to conduct of the highest ethical and professional manner and agree:

1. to accept responsibility in making engineering decisions consistent with the safety, health, and welfare of the public, and to disclose promptly factors that might endanger the public or the environment;
2. to avoid real or perceived conflicts of interest whenever possible, and to disclose them to affected parties when they do exist;
3. to be honest and realistic in stating claims or estimates based on available data;
4. to reject bribery in all of its forms;
5. to improve understanding of technology; its appropriate application, and potential consequences;
6. to maintain and improve our technical competence and to undertake technological tasks for others only if qualified by training or experience, or after full disclosure of pertinent limitations;
7. to seek, accept, and offer honest criticism of technical work, to acknowledge and correct errors, and to credit properly the contributions of others;
8. to treat fairly all persons regardless of such factors as race, religion, gender, disability, age, or national origin;
9. to avoid injuring others, their property, reputation, or employment by false or malicious action;
10. to assist colleagues and co-workers in their professional development and to support them in following this code of ethics.

INSTITUTE OF INDUSTRIAL ENGINEERS

Address: 25 Technology Park/Atlanta
              Norcross, GA 30092
Telephone: 770/449-0460
WWW: www.iienet.org
Document: Engineering Code of Ethics

(The *Canons of Ethics of Engineers* was formulated for the engineering profession in 1946 by the Committee on Engineering Ethics of the Engineers' Council for Professional Development, now the Accreditation Board for Engineering Technology (ABET). It is used as the basis of the codes for this and other engineering organizations.—Eds.)

IIE endorses the Canon of Ethics provided by the Accreditation Board for Engineering and Technology.

The Fundamental Principles

Engineers uphold and advance the integrity, honor and dignity of the engineering profession by:

1. Using their knowledge and skill for the enhancement of human welfare;
2. Being honest and impartial, and serving with fidelity the public, their employers and clients;
3. Striving to increase the competence and prestige of the engineering profession; and
4. Supporting the professional and technical societies of their disciplines.

The Fundamental Canons

1. Engineers shall hold paramount the safety, health and welfare of the public in the performance of their professional duties.

2. Engineers shall perform services only in the areas of their competence.
3. Engineers shall issue public statements only in an objective and truthful manner.
4. Engineers shall act in professional matters for each employer or client as faithful agents or trustees, and shall avoid conflicts of interest.
5. Engineers shall build their professional reputation on the merit of their services and shall not compete unfairly with others.
6. Engineers shall associate only with reputable persons or organizations.
7. Engineers shall continue their professional development throughout their careers and shall provide opportunities for the professional development of those engineers under their supervision.

© Institute of Industrial Engineers. Reprinted with permission.

INSTITUTE OF INTERNAL AUDITORS

Address: 249 Maitland Avenue
              Altamonte Springs, FL 32701-4201
Telephone: 407/830-7600
WWW: www.theiia.org
Document: The Institute of Internal Auditors
              Code of Ethics (1988)

(The following *Code of Ethics* specifies the professional responsibilities and behavior for IIA members and Certified Internal Auditors (CIAs). In 1988, two codes of ethics—one for members and one for CIAs—were consolidated into one code. Additionally, several new articles were added to address the expanded responsibilities and expectations placed upon the profession.—Eds.)

PURPOSE: A distinguishing mark of a profession is acceptance by its members of responsibility to the interests of those it serves. Members of The Institute of Internal Auditors (Members) and Certified Internal

Auditors (CIAs) must maintain high standards of conduct in order to effectively discharge this responsibility. The Institute of Internal Auditors (Institute) adopts this *Code of Ethics* for Members and CIAs.

APPLICABILITY: This *Code of Ethics* is applicable to all Members and CIAs. Membership in The Institute and acceptance of the "Certified Internal Auditor" designation are voluntary actions. By acceptance, Members and CIAs assume an obligation of self-discipline above and beyond the requirements of laws and regulations.

The standards of conduct set forth in this *Code of Ethics* provide basic principles in the practice of internal auditing. Members and CIAs should realize that their individual judgment is required in the application of these principles.

CIA shall use the "Certified Internal Auditor" designation with discretion and in a dignified manner, fully aware of what the designation denotes. The designation shall also be used in a manner consistent with all statutory requirements.

Members who are judged by the Board of Directors of The Institute to be in violation of the standards of conduct of the *Code of Ethics* shall be subject to forfeiture of their membership in The Institute. CIAs who are similarly judged also shall be subject to forfeiture of the "Certified Internal Auditor" designation.

STANDARDS OF CONDUCT

  I. Members and CIAs shall exercise honesty, objectivity, and diligence in the performance of their duties and responsibilities.
 II. Members and CIAs shall exhibit loyalty in all matters pertaining to the affairs of their organization or to whomever they may be rendering a service. However, Members and CIAs shall not knowingly be a party to any illegal or improper activity.
III. Members and CIAs shall not knowingly engage in acts or activities which are discreditable to the profession of internal auditing or to their organization.
 IV. Members and CIAs shall refrain from entering into any activity which may be in conflict with the interest of their organization or which would prejudice their ability to carry out objectively their duties and responsibilities.
  V. Members and CIAs shall not accept anything of value from an employee, client, customer, supplier, or business associate of their organization which would impair or be presumed to impair their professional judgment.

 VI. Members and CIAs shall undertake only those services which they can reasonably expect to complete with professional competence.
VII. Members and CIAs shall adopt suitable means to comply with the *Standards for the Professional Practice of Internal Auditing.*
VIII. Members and CIAs shall be prudent in the use of information acquired in the course of their duties. They shall not use confidential information for any personal gain nor in any manner which would be contrary to law or detrimental to the welfare of their organization.
 IX. Members and CIAs, when reporting on the results of their work, shall reveal all material facts known to them which, if not revealed, could either distort reports of operations under review or conceal unlawful practices.
  X. Members and CIAs shall continually strive for improvement in their proficiency, and in the effectiveness and quality of their service.
 XI. Members and CIAs, in the practice of their profession, shall be ever mindful of their obligation to maintain the high standards of competence, morality, and dignity promulgated by The Institute. Members shall abide by the *By-laws* and uphold the objectives of The Institute.

INSTITUTE of MANAGEMENT ACCOUNTANTS

CERTIFIED MANAGEMENT ACCOUNTANT PROGRAM
CERTIFIED IN FINANCIAL MANAGEMENT PROGRAM

INSTITUTE OF MANAGEMENT ACCOUNTANTS

Address: 10 Paragon Drive
             Montvale, NJ 07645-1759
Telephone: 201/573-9000 or 800/638-4427

WWW: www.imanet.org

Document: Standards of Ethical Conduct for Practitioners of Management Accounting and Financial Management (1983. Most recently revised 1997.)

(This statement was originally issued by the IMA, then known as the National Association of Accountants, as a *Statement on Management Accounting* on June 1, 1983. It was drafted by the Ad Hoc Committee on Professional Ethics.—Eds.)

Practitioners of management accounting and financial management have an obligation to the public, their profession, the organization they serve, and themselves, to maintain the highest standards of ethical conduct. In recognition of this obligation, the Institute of Management Accountants has promulgated the following standards of ethical conduct for practitioners of management accounting and financial management. Adherence to these standards, both domestically and internationally, is integral to achieving the *Objectives of Management Accounting*. Practitioners of management accounting and financial management shall not commit acts contrary to these standards nor shall they condone the commission of such acts by others within their organizations.

COMPETENCE

Practitioners of management accounting and financial management have a responsibility to:

- Maintain an appropriate level of professional competence by ongoing development of their knowledge and skills.
- Perform their professional duties in accordance with relevant laws, regulations, and technical standards.
- Prepare complete and clear reports and recommendations after appropriate analyses of relevant and reliable information.

CONFIDENTIALITY

Practitioners of management accounting and financial management have a responsibility to:

- Refrain from disclosing confidential information acquired in the course of their work except when authorized, unless legally obligated to do so.
- Inform subordinates as appropriate regarding the confidentiality of information acquired in the course of their work and monitor their activities to assure the maintenance of that confidentiality.
- Refrain from using or appearing to use confidential information acquired in the course of their work for

unethical or illegal advantage either personally or through third parties.

INTEGRITY

Practitioners of management accounting and financial management have a responsibility to:

- Avoid actual or apparent conflicts of interest and advise all appropriate parties of any potential conflict.
- Refrain from engaging in any activity that would prejudice their ability to carry out their duties ethically.
- Refuse any gift, favor, or hospitality that would influence or would appear to influence their actions.
- Refrain from either actively or passively subverting the attainment of the organization's legitimate and ethical objectives.
- Recognize and communicate professional limitations or other constraints that would preclude responsible judgement or successful performance of an activity.
- Communicate unfavorable as well as favorable information and professional judgements or opinions.
- Refrain from engaging in or supporting any activity that would discredit the profession.

OBJECTIVITY

Practitioners of management accounting and financial management have a responsibility to:

- Communicate information fairly and objectively.
- Disclose fully all relevant information that could reasonably be expected to influence an intended user's understanding of the reports, comments, and recommendations presented.

RESOLUTION OF ETHICAL CONFLICT

In applying the standards of ethical conduct, practitioners of management accounting and financial management may encounter problems in identifying unethical behavior or in resolving an ethical conflict. When faced with significant ethical issues, practitioners of management accounting and financial management should follow the established policies of the organization bearing on the resolution of such conflict. If these policies do not resolve the ethical conflict, such practitioners should consider the following courses of action.

- Discuss such problems with the immediate superior except when it appears that the superior is involved, in which case the problem should be presented initially to the next higher managerial level. If a satisfactory resolution cannot be achieved when the problem is initially presented, submit the issues to the next higher managerial level. If the immediate superior is the chief executive officer, or equivalent, the acceptable reviewing authority may be a group such as the audit committee, executive committee, board of directors, board of trustees, or owners. Contact with levels above the immediate superior should be initiated only with the superior's knowledge, assuming the superior is not involved. Except where legally prescribed, communication of such problems to authorities or individuals not employed or engaged by the organization is not considered appropriate.

- Clarify relevant ethical issues by confidential discussion with an objective advisor (e.g., IMA Ethics Counseling service) to obtain a better understanding of possible courses of action.
- Consult your own attorney as to legal obligations and rights concerning the ethical conflict.
- If the ethical conflict still exits after exhausting all levels of internal review, there may be no other recourse on significant matters than to resign from the organization and to submit an informative memorandum to an appropriate representative of the organization. After resignation, depending on the nature of the ethical conflict, it may also be appropriate to notify other parties.

INSTITUTE OF MANAGEMENT CONSULTANTS

Address: 1200 Nineteenth Street NW, Suite 300
               Washington, DC 20036-2422
Telephone: 202/857-5334 or 800/221-2557
WWW: www.imcusa.org
Document: Code of Ethics (1991)

(In addition to the *Code of Ethics* below, the IMC uses *Code of Ethics—Enforcement Procedures* and *Implementation of the Code of Ethics*, not reprinted here. The IMC is a division of the Council of Consulting Organizations, Inc.—Eds.)

Clients

1. We will serve our clients with integrity, competence, and objectivity.
2. We will keep client information and records of client engagements confidential and will use proprietary client information only with the client's permission.
3. We will not take advantage of confidential client information for ourselves or our firms.
4. We will not allow conflicts of interest which provide a competitive advantage to one client through our use of confidential information from another client who is a direct competitor without that competitor's permission.

Engagements

5. We will accept only engagements for which we are qualified by our experience and competence.
6. We will assign staff to client engagements in accord with their experience, knowledge, and expertise.
7. We will immediately acknowledge any influences on our objectivity to our clients and will offer to withdraw from a consulting engagement when our objectivity or integrity may be impaired.

Fees

8. We will agree independently and in advance on the basis for our fees and expenses and will charge fees and expenses that are reasonable, legitimate, and commensurate with the services we deliver and the responsibility we accept.
9. We will disclose to our clients in advance any fees or commissions that we will receive for equipment, supplies or services we recommend to our clients.

Profession

10. We will respect the intellectual property rights of our clients, other consulting firms, and sole practitioners and will not use proprietary information or methodologies without permission.
11. We will not advertise our services in a deceptive manner and will not misrepresent the consulting profession, consulting firms, or sole practitioners.
12. We will report violations of this Code of Ethics.

INSTITUTE OF REAL ESTATE MANAGEMENT

Address: 430 North Michigan Avenue
Chicago, IL 60611-4090
Telephone: 312/329-6000
WWW: www.irem.org
Document: Code of Professional Ethics of the
CERTIFIED PROPERTY
MANAGER® (CPM®) (1994)

(The Institute of Real Estate Management (IREM) established a code of ethical standards at the time the association was founded in 1933. The *Individual Member's Pledge* from the original bylaws was followed by the more formal *Rules of Professional Conduct* in 1939. These rules were subsequently refined and substantially modified on numerous occasions, most recently in November, 1994. All IREM members have earned IREM's CERTIFIED PROPERTY MANAGER® (CPM®) designation.—Eds.)

Introduction
To establish and maintain public confidence in the honesty, integrity, professionalism, and ability of the professional property manager is fundamental to the future success of the Institute of Real Estate Management and its members. This Code and performance pursuant to its provisions will be beneficial to the general public and contribute to the continued development of a mutually beneficial relationship among CERTIFIED PROPERTY MANAGER® members, candidates for membership, REALTORS®, clients, employers, and the public.

The Institute of Real Estate Management, as the professional society of property management, seeks to work closely with all other segments of the real estate industry to protect and enhance the interests of the public. To this end, members of the Institute have adopted and, as a condition of membership, subscribe to this Code of Professional Ethics. By doing so, they give notice that they clearly recognize the vital need to preserve and encourage fair and equitable practices and competition among all who are engaged in the profession of property management.

Those who are members of the Institute are dedicated individuals who are sincerely concerned with the protection and interests of those who come in contact with the industry. To this end, members of the Institute have subscribed to this professional pledge:

Pledge
I pledge myself to the advancement of professional property management through the mutual efforts of members of the Institute of Real Estate Management and by any other proper means available to me.

I pledge myself to seek and maintain an equitable, honorable, and cooperative association with fellow members of the Institute and with all others who may become a part of my business and professional life.

I pledge myself to place honesty, integrity, and industriousness above all else; to pursue my gainful efforts with diligent study and education to the end that service to my clients shall always be maintained at the highest possible level.

I pledge myself to comply with the principles and declarations of the Institute of Real Estate Management as set forth in its Bylaws, Regulations, and this Code of Professional Ethics.

Article 1. Fiduciary Obligation to Clients
A CERTIFIED PROPERTY MANAGER® shall at all times exercise loyalty to the interests of the client and shall not engage in any activity which could be reasonably construed as contrary to the best interests of the client. A CERTIFIED PROPERTY MANAGER® shall not represent personal or business interests divergent or conflicting with those of the client, unless the client is first notified in writing of the activity or potential conflict of interest, and consents in writing to such representation. A CERTIFIED PROPERTY

MANAGER®, as a fiduciary for the client, shall not accept, directly or indirectly, any rebate, fee, commission, discount, or other benefit, monetary or otherwise, which has not been fully disclosed to and approved by the client.

Article 2. Disclosure
A CERTIFIED PROPERTY MANAGER® shall not disclose to a third party any confidential or proprietary information which would be injurious or damaging to a client concerning the client's business or personal affairs without the client's prior written consent, unless such disclosure is required or compelled by law or regulations.

Article 3. Accounting and Reporting
A CERTIFIED PROPERTY MANAGER® shall at all times keep and maintain accurate financial and business records concerning each property managed for the client, which records shall be available for inspection at all reasonable times by the client. A CERTIFIED PROPERTY MANAGER® shall furnish to the client, at mutually agreed upon intervals, regular reports concerning the client's properties.

Article 4. Protection of Funds
A CERTIFIED PROPERTY MANAGER® shall not commingle personal or company funds with the funds of a client or use one client's funds for the benefit of another client, but shall keep the client's funds in a fiduciary account in an insured financial institution or as otherwise directed in writing by the client. A CERTIFIED PROPERTY MANAGER® shall at all times exert due diligence for the maintenance and protection of the client's funds against all reasonably foreseeable contingencies and losses.

Article 5. Relations with Other Members of the Profession
A CERTIFIED PROPERTY MANAGER® shall not make, authorize or otherwise encourage any unfounded derogatory or disparaging comments concerning the practices of another CERTIFIED PROPERTY MANAGER®. A CERTIFIED PROPERTY MANAGER® shall not exaggerate or misrepresent the services offered as compared with the services offered by other property managers. Nothing in this Code, however, shall restrict legal and reasonable business competition by and among property managers.

Article 6. Contract
Any written contract between a CERTIFIED PROPERTY MANAGER® and a client shall be in clear and understandable terms, and shall set forth the specific terms agreed upon between the parties, including a general description of the services to be provided by and the responsibilities of the CERTIFIED PROPERTY MANAGER®.

Article 7. Duty to Firm or Employer
A CERTIFIED PROPERTY MANAGER® shall at all times exercise loyalty to the interests of the employer or firm with whom the CPM® is affiliated and shall be diligent in the maintenance and protection of the interests and property of the employer or firm. A CERTIFIED PROPERTY MANAGER® shall not engage in any activity which could be reasonably construed as contrary to this obligation of loyalty and diligence and shall not accept, directly or indirectly, any rebate, fee, commission, discount, or other benefit, monetary or otherwise, which could reasonably be seen as a conflict with the interests of the employer or firm. A CERTIFIED PROPERTY MANAGER® shall at all times exercise due diligence for the protection of the funds of the employer or firm against all reasonably foreseeable contingencies and losses.

Article 8. Managing the Property of the Client
A CERTIFIED PROPERTY MANAGER® shall not exaggerate, misrepresent or conceal material facts concerning the client's property or any related transaction. A CERTIFIED PROPERTY MANAGER® shall exercise due diligence in the maintenance and management of the client's property and shall make all reasonable efforts to protect it against all reasonable foreseeable contingencies and losses.

Article 9. Duty to Former Clients and Former Firms or Employers
All obligations and duties of a CERTIFIED PROPERTY MANAGER® to clients, firms, and employers as specified in this Code shall also apply to relationships with former clients and former firms and employers. A CERTIFIED PROPERTY MANAGER® shall act in a professional manner when, for whatever reason, relationships are terminated between a CERTIFIED PROPERTY MANAGER® and clients and firm or employer. Nothing in this section, however, shall be construed to cause a CERTIFIED PROPERTY MANAGER® to breach obligations and duties to current clients and firm or employer.

Article 10. Compliance with Laws and Regulations
A CERTIFIED PROPERTY MANAGER® shall at all times conduct business and personal activities with knowledge of and in compliance with applicable federal, state, and local laws and regulations, and shall

maintain the highest moral and ethical standards consistent with the membership in and the purposes of the Institute of Real Estate Management.

Article 11. Equal Opportunity

A CERTIFIED PROPERTY MANAGER® shall not deny equal employment opportunity or equal professional services to any person for reasons of race, color, religion, sex, familial status, national origin, age, or handicap.

Article 12. Duty to Tenants and Others

A CERTIFIED PROPERTY MANAGER® shall competently manage the property of the client with due regard for the rights, responsibilities, and benefits of the tenant and others lawfully on the property. A CERTIFIED PROPERTY MANAGER® shall not engage in any conduct which is in conscious disregard for the safety and health of those persons lawfully on the premises of the client's property.

Article 13. Enforcement

Any violation by a CERTIFIED PROPERTY MANAGER® of the obligations of this Code shall be determined in accordance with and pursuant to the terms of the bylaws and rules and regulations of the Institute of Real Estate Management. Disciplinary action for violation of any portion of this Code shall be carried out by the Institute of Real Estate Management in accordance with the bylaws and rules and regulations established by the Governing Council of the Institute. The result of such disciplinary action shall be final and binding upon the affected CERTIFIED PROPERTY MANAGER®, and without recourse to the Institute, its officers, councillors, members, employees, or agents.

INTERNATIONAL ASSOCIATION FOR FINANCIAL PLANNING

Address: 5775 Glenridge Drive NE, Suite B-300
Atlanta, GA 30328-5364
Telephone: 404/845-0011

WWW: www.iafp.org
Document: The Code of Professional Ethics (1976)

(The Ethics Committee has also developed *Ethics Policies and Procedures* to guide in the application and enforcement of the *Code*. That document is not reprinted here.—Eds.)

The reliance of the public and the business community on sound financial planning and advice imposes on financial planning professionals an obligation to maintain high standards of technical competence, morality, and integrity. To this end, the following Code of Professional Ethics serves as the guiding document.

CANON 1

Members should endeavor as professionals to place the public interest above their own.

Rules of Professional Conduct:

R1.1   A member has a duty to understand and abide by all Rules of Professional Conduct which are prescribed in the Code of Professional Ethics of the Association.

R1.2   A member shall not directly or indirectly condone any act which the member is prohibited from performing by the Rules of this Code.

CANON 2

Members should seek continually to maintain and improve their professional knowledge, skills, and competence.

Rules of Professional Conduct:

R2.1   A member shall keep informed on all matters that are essential to the maintenance of the member's professional competence in the area in which he/she specializes and/or claims expertise.

CANON 3

Members should obey all laws and regulations and avoid any conduct or activity which would cause unjust harm to those who rely upon the professional judgment and skill of the members.

Rules of Professional Conduct:

R3.1   A member shall be subject to disciplinary action for professional misconduct and has the duty to know and abide by the laws and regulations and all legal limitations pertaining to the member's professional activities.

R3.2 A member shall place the needs and best interest of the client above the needs and interests of the member, the member's employees or business associates in all cases; and shall not allow the pursuit of financial gain or other personal benefit to interfere with the exercise of sound professional judgment and skills.

R3.3 In the conduct of business or professional activities, a member shall not engage in any act or omission of a dishonest, deceitful or fraudulent nature.

R3.4 A member shall not knowingly misrepresent or conceal any material limitation on the member's ability to provide the quantity or quality of service that will adequately meet the financial planning needs of the client.

R3.5 In marketing a product, a member shall not knowingly misrepresent or conceal any material limitations on the product's ability to meet the financial needs of the client, and shall scrupulously avoid any statements which are likely to mislead the client regarding to future results of any recommendation.

R3.6 A member has the duty to disclose fully and accurately the material facts representing the true costs, benefits, and limitations of any service or product recommended; and disclose any actual or potential conflict of interest that could impair objectivity.

R3.7 A member shall not disclose to another person any confidential information entrusted to or obtained by the member in the course of the member's business or professional activities, unless a disclosure of such information is required by law or is made to a person who necessarily must have the information in order to discharge legitimate occupational or professional duties.

R3.8 In the rendering of a professional service to a client, a member has the duty to maintain the type and degree of professional independence that (a) is required of practitioners in the member's occupation, or (b) is otherwise in the public interest, given the specific nature of the service being rendered.

CANON 4

Members should be diligent in the performance of their occupational duties.

Rules of Professional Conduct:

R4.1 A member shall competently and consistently discharge the member's occupational duties to every employer, client, purchaser, or user of the member's services, so long as those duties are consistent with what is in the client's best interests.

R4.2 In the making of oral or written recommendations to clients, a member shall (a) distinguish clearly between fact and opinion, (b) base the recommendations on sound professional evaluation of the client's needs, and (c) support the recommendations with appropriate research and adequate documentation of facts.

CANON 5

Members should assist in improving the public understanding of financial planning.

Rules of Professional Conduct:

R5.1 A member shall support efforts to provide lay persons with objective information concerning their financial planning needs, as well as the resources which are available to meet their needs.

R5.2 A member shall not misrepresent the benefits, costs, or limitations of any financial planning service or product, whether the product or service is offered by the member or by another individual or firm.

CANON 6

Members should use the fact of membership in a manner consistent with the Association's Rules of Professional Conduct.

Rules of Professional Conduct:

R6.1 A member shall not misrepresent the criteria for admission to Association membership, which criteria are (1) active participation in the financial services industry; and (2) a written commitment to abide by the Bylaws and the Code of Professional Ethics of the Association.

R6.2 A member shall not misstate his/her authority to represent the Association. Specifically, a member shall not write, speak, or act in such a way as to lead another to believe that the member is officially representing the Association, unless the member has been duly authorized to do so by the officers, directors or Bylaws of the national Association.

R6.3 A member shall not use the fact of general membership in the Association for commercial purposes. A member may use the fact of general membership for the following non-commercial purposes: in resumes, prospectus, and in introductions if the speaker clearly states that the opinions and ideas presented are his/her own and not necessarily those of the Association. Fact of Division membership may be used by an individual in the Practitioner Division[1], or by a company in the Corporate or Broker-Dealer Divisions[2].

R6.4 A member or prospective member applying for Association membership shall not misrepresent any credentials or affiliations with other organizations.

CANON 7

Members should assist in maintaining the integrity of the Code of Professional Ethics of the Association.

Rules of Professional Conduct:

R7.1 A member shall not sponsor as a candidate for Association membership any person who is known by the member to engage in business or professional practices which violate the Rules of this Code.

R7.2 A member possessing unprivileged information concerning an alleged violation of this Code shall, upon request, reveal such information to the body or other authority empowered by the Association to investigate or act upon the alleged violation.

---

1. Individual members in the Practitioner Division (those who have met the necessary requirements of the Division and have signed the Practitioner Division Certificate) may use fact of membership in the following manner:

Member, Practitioner Division
International Association for Financial Planning

Members of the Practitioner Division should contact the compliance department of their broker-dealer to make sure any state or NASD regulatory concerns are addressed before using fact of membership for commercial purposes.

2. Companies in the Corporate and Broker-Dealer Divisions may use fact of membership as follows:

Member, Corporate Division
International Association for Financial Planning;
Member, Broker-Dealer Division
International Association for Financial Planning

© International Association for Financial Planning. Reprinted with permission.

INTERNATIONAL ASSOCIATION OF ADMINISTRATIVE PROFESSIONALS

Address: 10502 Northwest Ambassador Drive, PO Box 20404
Kansas City, MO 64195-0404
Telephone: 816/891-6600
WWW: www.iaap-hq.org
Document: Code of Ethics for Administrative Professionals (1980. Most recently revised 1998.)

(In 1998, The Professional Secretaries International changed its name to the International Association of Administrative Professionals. The PSI code of ethics was amended to reflect this name change in August of that year.—Eds.)

(Preface note: The International Association of Administrative Professionals™ defines an administrative professional as "an individual who possesses a mastery of office skills, demonstrates the ability to assume responsibility without direct supervision, exercises initiative and judgment, and makes decisions within the scope of assigned authority.")

Recognizing that a position of trust imposes ethical obligations upon administrative assistants, office coordinators, executive secretaries and other types of administrative professionals to act for benefit of employers, clients, and the public, members of Professional Secretaries International, now known as the International Association of Administrative Professionals (IAAP) established and promulgated four standards of professional conduct and resolve to be guided by them as embodying the ethical ideals of their profession.

The development of a Code of Ethics demonstrates that the administrative support profession accepts the obligation to engage in self-discipline and accepts the responsibility and trust earned by administrative professionals throughout past generations.

Each administrative professional has a personal obligation to support and follow the Code, recognizing that the greatest penalty possible for its violation is loss of the respect of professional colleagues and the trust of employers, clients, and society.

Ethical behavior is encouraged by both the Code and the profession. An administrative professional's personal ethical behavior may often exceed the requirements of the Code, which do not demand less than the law, and often exceed those of the law. Persons found guilty of violating laws will be considered in prima facie violation of the Code and may be censured or otherwise penalized by the association or profession.

1. The administrative professional shall act as a trusted agent in professional relations, implementing responsibilities in the most competent manner and exercising knowledge and skill to promote the interests of the immediate and corporate employer.

The immediate employer shall be considered to be the person or persons who, by an established and predetermined arrangement, receive directly the agreed upon services of the administrative professional. The corporate employer shall be considered the entity (company or organization) providing the administrative professional's compensation. In cases where the immediate employer does not provide compensation for the administrative professional, the administrative professional's principal obligation shall be to serve the corporate employer. In serving the immediate employer, however, the administrative professional shall not act contrary to interests of the corporate employer or to public safety and welfare or in such a way as to impair the dignity and status of the profession.

The administrative professional shall strive to avoid conflicts of interest with the immediate employer whenever possible, but if such conflicts cannot be avoided or resolved, the administrative professional shall fully disclose to the immediate employer and all interested parties the relevant reasons and circumstances.

Communications and information either given in confidence or such that confidentiality is required to serve the best interests of the immediate employer shall not be revealed by an administrative professional unless permission to do so is granted by the immediate employer or continued confidentiality is harmful to the corporate employer, client, public, or profession. Testimony in a court of law regarding confidential matters should be given only under the immediate or corporate employer's authorization, under legal compulsion, or to protect the public from harm.

The administrative professional will assume responsibilities only when qualified by training and experience and shall inform the immediate or corporate employer concerning any lack of qualification which might harm the interests of the employer or impair the administrative professional's capacity to serve such interests.

In acting as agent for an immediate employer, the administrative professional shall strive to accurately and honestly represent the views and interests of the immediate employer as well as the views and interests of those who seek to contact or influence the immediate employer, and shall not distort or misrepresent such views and interests, whether for personal advantage or to protect the employer from unwelcome information.

The administrative professional shall respond to those seeking the immediate employer's professional attention with impartial courtesy and consistent good will, recognizing that by the administrative professional's demeanor the immediate employer will be judged.

When entrusted with funds or material goods essential to serve the employer, an administrative professional shall never appropriate or use such funds or goods for personal or nonprofessional purposes, and an administrative professional shall never use the employer's facilities or time for the pursuit of such purposes without the express consent of the immediate employer.

The administrative professional shall not accept outside employment or accept any form of compensation from outside sources which would impair the efficiency and effectiveness of the administrative professional or which would be in conflict with the employer's welfare.

2. The administrative professional shall strive to maintain and enhance the dignity, status, competence, and standards of the profession and its practitioners.

The administrative professional, when applying for or being listed for employment, shall not make exaggerated, misleading, or false claims concerning training or qualifications. When judging the qualifications of other persons, whether in providing references, assisting with assignments, or evaluating performances, the administrative professional shall strive to provide fair and objective appraisals and shall attempt to avoid any false, malicious, or indiscriminate injury to or criticism of the professional reputation or work of others.

The administrative professional will cooperate with other administrative professionals in extending public knowledge and appreciation of the profession and its achievements and will strive to protect it from misrepresentation and misunderstanding.

The administrative professional shall strive to improve the standards of the profession by belonging to a professional association, attending and encouraging others to attend professional meetings, exchanging knowledge and information with other administrative professionals, and by achieving and encouraging others to achieve the Certified Professional Secretary® rating.

3. The administrative professional shall insist that judgments concerning continued employment, compensation, and promotion be based upon professional knowledge, ability, experience, and performance.

The administrative professional shall strive to improve working conditions and to ensure equal employment opportunities within the profession and throughout the organization by which employed.

The administrative professional shall refuse to cooperate with or condone by silence the actions of coworkers or employers who misuse their positions for personal, nonprofessional advantage.

The administrative professional shall resist, and if necessary report to the proper authorities, instances in the workplace of harassment for reasons of sex, creed, race, or age.

The administrative professional shall inform the employer concerning any changes in conditions of employment, including fringe benefits, which encourage inefficiency or make difficult the proper performance of prescribed assignments.

4. The administrative professional must consider the promotion and preservation of the safety and welfare of the public to be the paramount duty.

The administrative professional, in addition to sharing with all concerned citizens an obligation to promote the general welfare and safety, has a special obligation to cooperate with and promote the interests of other allied professions and to exercise particular concern for those directly affected by the actions of employers served.

If requested or required by an employer to engage in or passively condone activities which are contrary to the public safety or welfare, the administrative professional shall indicate clearly to the employer the possible harmful consequences and, if such activities continue, the administrative professional must either resign or notify the proper authorities.

The administrative professional is obliged, before reporting to the proper authorities actions contrary to the public interest, to determine that the factual evidence is correct, to be motivated by no desire or personal benefit or vindication, and to inform the employer of such an intention unless doing so will be harmful to the public.

© International Association of Administrative Professionals. Reprinted with permission.

INTERNATIONAL ASSOCIATION OF ASSESSING OFFICERS

Address: 130 East Randolph Street, Suite 850 Chicago, IL 60601
Telephone: 312/819-6100
WWW: www.iaao.org
Document: Code of Ethics and Standards of Professional Conduct (1995)

Preamble

The purposes of this *Code of Ethics and Standards of Professional Conduct* are to establish professional guidelines for assessing officials and all members of the International Association of Assessing Officers (IAAO) and set forth standards by which to judge an IAAO member whose conduct is in question.

Members of IAAO shall conduct themselves in a manner that will reflect favorably upon themselves, the appraisal profession, the property tax system, and IAAO, and avoid any action that could discredit themselves or these entities.

Definitions

As used in this *Code:*

Appraisal refers to an opinion of the value of specified interests in, or aspects of, identified real estate or personal property.

Appraisal assignment refers to those appraisal services in which the appraiser is employed or retained to act (or would be perceived by third parties or the public as acting) as a third disinterested party in rendering an unbiased estimate or opinion of the value of specified interests in or aspects of identified real estate or personal property. (Property tax consultants are not usually considered to be acting as disinterested third parties; therefore, property tax consulting assignments are not considered to be appraisal assignments within the meaning of the *Code*, unless an appraisal as defined by the *Uniform Standards of Professional Appraisal Practice* is made and expressed.)

Appraisal report means any communication, written or oral, of an opinion as to the value of specified interests in or aspects of identified real or personal property. In this context, the purpose of the appraisal of real estate is immaterial; therefore, valuation reports, real estate counseling reports, real estate tax counseling, real estate offering report memoranda, mortgage banking offers, highest and best use studies, market demand and economic feasibility studies, and all other reports communicating an opinion of value are appraisal reports, regardless of their title. The same is true with identified personal property; therefore, all valuation reports, financial statements, stockholders' equity statements, highest and best use studies, supply and demand studies, and all reports communicating an appraisal opinion are appraisal reports, regardless of their title.

Assessment-related assignment refers to the preparation of the assessed value of a single parcel or of an item of real or personal property, the total assessed value of all properties within the boundaries of the tax jurisdiction, or the assessed value of any group of properties. Although appraisal is an important aspect of ad valorem tax administration, other important aspects, including satisfying a variety of information needs, result in appraiser-client relationships that are unique.

A **file memorandum** is a record in the file of the appraiser setting forth the data, reasoning, and conclusions upon which an appraisal is based. Several of the *Code*'s Canons and Ethical Rules require either the preparation of a written appraisal report containing data, reasoning, and conclusions, or the inclusion of a file memorandum in the appraiser's file. The file memorandum shall include a statement, outline or reference form, with work sheets, data sheets, and related material, containing sufficient information to demonstrate substantial compliance with the *Uniform Standards of Professional Appraisal Practice*. In most cases sufficient information should include:

identification/brief description of real estate or personal property; real or personal property interest being appraised; purpose of the appraisal; definition of value being estimated; effective date of the appraisal; scope of the appraisal; all assumptions and limiting conditions; information considered, procedures followed, and reasoning in support of the analyses, opinion, and conclusion of any of the valuation approaches; any additional information required to demonstrate compliance with the *Uniform Standards of Professional Appraisal Practice*; and appraisal conclusions.

Personal property means identifiable, movable, and tangible and intangible items or objects that are not classified as real estate.

Real estate means an identified parcel or tract of land, including improvements, if any.

Real property refers to one or more defined rights, interests, and benefits in a parcel of real estate, whether the unencumbered fee or a lesser estate.

Since a clear understanding of defined terms is essential to a proper understanding of the *Code of Ethics and Standards of Professional Conduct*, it is the responsibility of each IAAO member to be familiar with and understand each defined term in the *Code* when following and applying the Canons and Ethical Rules set forth in the *Code*.

Exceptions
If compliance with or adherence to any Canon or Ethical Rule set forth in the IAAO *Code of Ethics and Standards of Professional Conduct* would constitute a violation of the law of any jurisdiction, such Canon or Ethical Rule shall be void and of no force or effect in such jurisdiction.

In stating each individual Canon or Ethical Rule, no attempt has been made to enumerate all of the various circumstances and conditions that will excuse an IAAO member from strict observance; however, the IAAO recognizes that illness, acts of God, and various other events beyond the control of an IAAO member may make it inequitable to insist upon a strict observance in a particular case. When an IAAO member, in the exercise of reasonable care, commits a violation due to illness, acts of God, or other circumstances beyond his or her control, it is expected that the Ethics Committee will act in a manner that will avoid an inequitable result.

Inasmuch as there are other remedies under applicable federal, state/provincial, and local laws, nothing in this *Code* shall apply to the conduct of a member toward his or her employees and other workers in the member's assessment office or appraisal business, including, but not limited to, employment discrimination.

Canon 1
Members shall conduct their professional duties and activities in a manner that reflects credit upon themselves and their profession.

Ethical Rules
E.R. 1-1 It is unethical for members to conduct their professional duties in a manner that could reasonably be expected to create the appearance of impropriety.

E.R. 1-2 It is unethical for members to accept an appraisal or assessment-related assignment which they are not qualified to perform.

E.R. 1-3 It is unethical for members knowingly to fail in performance of their duties according to applicable laws and regulations or in the uniform application of such laws and regulations.

E.R. 1-4 It is unethical for members not to make available all public records in their custody for public review, unless access to such records is specifically limited or prohibited by law, or the information has been obtained on a confidential basis and the law permits such information to be treated confidentially. Assessing officers must make every reasonable effort to inform the public about their rights and responsibilities under the law and the property tax system.

E.R. 1-5 It is unethical for members not to cooperate with public officials to improve the efficiency and effectiveness of the property tax in particular and public administration in general.

E.R. 1-6 It is unethical to engage in misconduct of any kind that leads to a conviction for a crime involving fraud, dishonesty, false statements, or moral turpitude.

E.R. 1-7 It is unethical to perform any appraisal, assessment, or consulting service that is not in compliance with the IAAO Constitution or the *Uniform Standards of Professional Appraisal Practice*.

Canon 2
Members shall not make public statements, written or oral, that are untrue or tend to mislead or deceive the public in the course of performing their professional duties.

Ethical Rules
E.R. 2-1 It is unethical to use advertising or promotions that are not totally accurate and truthful to solicit assessment-related assignments or to use misleading claims or promises of relief that could lead to loss of confidence in appraisal or assessment professionals by the public.

E.R. 2-2 It is unethical to claim an IAAO professional designation unless authorized, whether the claim is verbal or written, or to claim qualifications that are not factual or may be misleading.

E.R. 2-3 It is unethical not to give full credit to the source(s) of any materials quoted or cited in writings or speeches.

Canon 3
Members shall not engage in appraisal or assessment-related assignments in which they have, or may reasonably be considered by the public as having, a conflict of interest.

Ethical Rules
E.R. 3-1 It is unethical for members to accept an appraisal or assessment-related assignment that can reasonably be construed as being in conflict with their responsibility to their jurisdiction, employer, or client, or in which they have an unrevealed personal interest or bias.

E.R. 3-2 It is unethical for assessment personnel to perform private appraisal assignments (moonlight) in their assessment jurisdictions.

Comment A. It is not unethical for assessment personnel to perform special appraisal assignments for other government agencies when such assignments are part of their duties as assessment professionals.

Comment B. It is not unethical for assessment personnel to perform private appraisal assignments (moonlight) outside of their assessment jurisdictions.

Canon 4
Members shall accept no appraisal or assessment-related assignment which is contingent upon or in-

fluenced by any condition that could impair their objectivity.

Ethical Rules

E.R. 4-1   It is unethical, in the performance of an appraisal or assessment-related assignment, to develop an appraisal, analysis, or opinion that is biased or to prepare, orally present, sign, or deliver an appraisal report that contains any biased analysis or opinion.

Further, it is unethical for a member knowingly to permit a business entity that is wholly owned, or wholly or partially controlled by such member, to prepare, orally present, sign, or deliver a biased report or an appraisal report that contains any biased analysis or opinion.

E.R. 4-2   It is unethical to accept or perform an appraisal assignment if the compensation to be paid for the assignment is contingent upon a reduction or increase in assessed value or taxes, or the consequences of such assignment.

Comment. Property tax consulting assignments are not considered to be appraisal assignments within the meaning of the *Code*, unless an appraisal as defined by the *Uniform Standards of Professional Appraisal Practice* is made. Therefore, unless an appraisal as defined by the *Uniform Standards of Professional Appraisal Practice* is made and expressed, it is not a violation of this E.R. for a member to accept or perform a property tax consulting assignment for which compensation is contingent upon a reduction or increase in assessed value or taxes. For further explanation, see Standards 4 and 5 of the *Uniform Standards of Professional Appraisal Practice.*

E.R. 4-3   It is unethical to accept or perform an appraisal assignment where the member has a personal interest in the subject property or personal bias toward the parties, unless certain conditions are met. Such conditions are:

(a) The member shall disclose such personal interest or bias to the client or employer prior to acceptance of the appraisal assignment, and

(b) The member shall disclose such personal interest or bias in each written or oral appraisal report resulting from such appraisal assignment.

E.R. 4-4   It is unethical to perform appraisal assignments without clear and full disclosure of

the form of compensation as required by the *Uniform Standards of Professional Appraisal Practice*.

Canon 5

Members shall abide by and support the provisions of the IAAO Constitution, Bylaws, and Procedural Rules.

Ethical Rules

E.R. 5-1   It is unethical for an IAAO member:

(a) Knowingly to make false statements or submit misleading information when completing a membership application, or to refrain from promptly submitting any significant information in the possession of such member when requested to do so as part of an IAAO membership application.

(b) Knowingly to submit misleading information to the duly authorized Ethics Committee or subcommittee; to refrain from promptly submitting any significant information in the possession of the member as requested by the committee or subcommittee; to refuse to appear for a personal interview or participate in an interview conducted by telephone as scheduled by the committee or subcommittee; or to refuse to answer promptly all relevant questions concerning an appraisal or assessment-related assignment or related testimony being investigated by the committee or subcommittee. Any member who has submitted misleading information to the Ethics Committee may be subject to ethical charges filed by the committee.

(c) To fail or refuse to submit promptly to an authorized IAAO committee a written appraisal report or file memorandum containing data, reasoning, and conclusions, or to fail or refuse to permit an authorized committee to review an appraisal report, assessment-related assignment, or file memorandum when requested to do so by a person or persons authorized to review such material.

(d) To fail or refuse to submit promptly any significant information in the possession of a member concerning the status of litigation related to an ethics matter when requested to do so by the chair of the Ethics Committee; or knowingly to submit misleading information to the chair of the Ethics Committee concerning the status of litigation.

E.R. 5-2 It is unethical to fail to comply with the terms of a summons issued by the Ethics Committee.

E.R. 5-3 It is unethical not to cooperate fully with the IAAO Executive Board, Ethics Committee, and the staff of IAAO in all matters related to the enforcement of this *Code*, as set forth in the Ethics Committee's Rules and Procedures, as amended from time to time.

E.R. 5-4 It is unethical to violate the IAAO Constitution, Bylaws, or Procedural Rules.

Canon 6
Members shall comply with the requirements of the *Uniform Standards of Professional Appraisal Practice*.

Ethical Rules
E.R. 6-1 It is unethical to fail to observe the requirements of the *Uniform Standards of Professional Appraisal Practice*.

SINCE 1893

INTERNATIONAL ASSOCIATION OF CHIEFS OF POLICE

Address: 515 North Washington Street
Alexandria, VA 22314-2357

Telephone: 703/836-6767
WWW: www.theiacp.org
Documents: Law Enforcement Code of Ethics
Police Code of Conduct

Law Enforcement Code of Ethics
As a law enforcement officer, my fundamental duty is to serve the community; to safeguard lives and property; to protect the innocent against deception, the weak against oppression or intimidation and the peaceful against violence or disorder; and to respect the constitutional rights of all to liberty, equality and justice.

I will keep my private life unsullied as an example to all and will behave in a manner that does not bring discredit to me or to my agency. I will maintain courageous calm in the face of danger, scorn or ridicule; develop self-restraint; and be constantly mindful of the welfare of others. Honest in thought and deed both in my personal and official life, I will be exemplary in obeying the law and the regulations of my department. Whatever I see or hear of a confidential nature or that is confided to me in my official capacity will be kept ever secret unless revelation is necessary in the performance of my duty.

I will never act officiously or permit personal feelings, prejudices, political beliefs, aspirations, animosities or friendships to influence my decisions. With no compromise for crime and with relentless prosecution of criminals, I will enforce the law courteously and appropriately without fear or favor, malice or ill will, never employing unnecessary force or violence and never accepting gratuities.

I recognize the badge of my office as a symbol of public faith, and I accept it as a public trust to be held so long as I am true to the ethics of police service. I will never engage in acts of corruption or bribery, nor will I condone such acts by other police officers. I will cooperate with all legally authorized agencies and their representatives in the pursuit of justice.

I know that I alone am responsible for my own standard of professional performance and will take every reasonable opportunity to enhance and improve my level of knowledge and competence.

I will constantly strive to achieve these objectives and ideals, dedicating myself before God to my chosen profession . . . law enforcement.

Police Code of Conduct
All law enforcement officers must be fully aware of the ethical responsibilities of their position and must strive constantly to live up to the highest possible ethical standards of professional policing.

The International Association of Chiefs of Police believes it important that police officers have clear advice and counsel available to assist them in performing their duties consistent with these standards, and has adopted the following ethical mandates as guidelines to meet these ends.

Primary Responsibilities of a Police Officer

A police officer acts as an official representative of government who is required and trusted to work within the law. The officer's powers and duties are conferred by statute. The fundamental duties of a police officer include serving the community, safeguarding lives and property, protecting the innocent, keeping the peace and ensuring the right of all to liberty, equality and justice.

Performance of the Duties of a Police Officer

A police officer shall perform all duties impartially, without favor or affection or ill will and without regard to status, sex, race, religion, political belief or aspiration. All citizens will be treated equally with courtesy, consideration and dignity.

Officers will never allow personal feeling, animosities or friendships to influence official conduct. Laws will be enforced appropriately and courteously and, in carrying out their responsibilities, officers will strive to obtain maximum cooperation from the public. They will conduct themselves in appearance and deportment in such a manner as to inspire confidence and respect for the position of public trust they hold.

Discretion

A police officer will use responsibly the discretion vested in his position and exercise it within the law. The principle of reasonableness will guide the officer's determinations, and the officer will consider all surrounding circumstances in determining whether any legal action shall be taken.

Consistent and wise use of discretion, based on professional policing competence, will do much to preserve good relationships and retain the confidence of the public. There can be difficulty in choosing between conflicting courses of action. It is important to remember that a timely word of advice rather than arrest—which may be correct in appropriate circumstances—can be a more effective means of achieving a desired end.

Use of Force

A police officer will never employ unnecessary force or violence and will use only such force in the discharge of duty as is reasonable in all circumstances.

The use of force should be used only with the greatest restraint and only after discussion, negotiation and persuasion have been found to be inappropriate or ineffective. While the use of force is occasionally unavoidable, every police officer will refrain from unnecessary infliction of pain or suffering and will never engage in cruel, degrading or inhuman treatment of any person.

Confidentiality

Whatever a police officer sees, hears or learns of that is of a confidential nature will be kept secret unless the performance of duty or legal provision requires otherwise.

Members of the public have a right to security and privacy, and information obtained about them must not be improperly divulged.

Integrity

A police officer will not engage in acts of corruption or bribery, nor will an officer condone such acts by other police officers.

The public demands that the integrity of police officers be above reproach. Police officers must, therefore, avoid any conduct that might compromise integrity and thus undercut the public confidence in a law enforcement agency. Officers will refuse to accept any gifts, presents, subscriptions, favors, gratuities or promises that could be interpreted as seeking to cause the officer to refrain from performing official responsibilities honestly and within the law. Police officers must not receive private or special advantage from their official status. Respect from the public cannot be bought; it can only be earned and cultivated.

Cooperation with Other Police Officers and Agencies

Police officers will cooperate with all legally authorized agencies and their representatives in the pursuit of justice.

An officer or agency may be one among many organizations that may provide law enforcement services to a jurisdiction. It is imperative that a police officer assist colleagues fully and completely with respect and consideration at all times.

Personal-Professional Capabilities

Police officers will be responsible for their own standard of professional performance and will take every reasonable opportunity to enhance and improve their level of knowledge and competence.

Through study and experience, a police officer can acquire the high level of knowledge and competence that is essential for the efficient and effective performance of duty. The acquisition of knowledge is a never-ending process of personal and professional development that should be pursued constantly.

Private Life

Police officers will behave in a manner that does not bring discredit to their agencies or themselves.

A police officer's character and conduct while off duty must always be exemplary, thus maintaining a position of respect in the community in which he or she lives and serves. The officer's personal behavior must be beyond reproach.

© International Association of Chiefs of Police. Reprinted with permission.

INTERNATIONAL ASSOCIATION OF CLOTHING DESIGNERS AND EXECUTIVES

Address: 475 Park Avenue South, 9th Floor
             New York, NY 10016
Telephone: 212/685-6602
WWW: www.iacde.com
Document: The Code of Ethics and Standards of
             Fair Practice

The International Association of Clothing Designers and Executives, in adopting this Code of Ethics and Standards of Fair Practice, desires to set forth principles for the guidance of each member, believing that the foundation of all business relations is confidence, which springs from integrity, fair dealing, efficient service and mutual benefit.

1. We shall keep ourselves informed, maintain an active and open mind toward new and progressive ideas and endeavor to serve the best interests of our profession by a willing exchange of ideas, thus benefiting by the experience of others and contributing to the development of the apparel industry.

2. We shall not speak disparagingly of any Member's ability or product, but shall accord all the same courtesy we expect from others.

3. Unjust and dishonest practices shall be condemned and opposed by concerted action.

4. In our relations with our employers, we shall manifest an interest in the business equal to their own. A spirit of cooperation shall characterize all of our relations for the mutual benefit of both.

5. We shall be accurate in our written or oral statements, thus developing confidence and respect for integrity and character.

6. The direct or indirect sale of patterns by Designer members, their assistants or associates is hereby designated unfair competition and no Designer Member of this Association shall in any manner indulge in such practice.

© International Association of Clothing Designers and Executives. Reprinted with permission.

INTERNATIONAL ASSOCIATION OF CORRECTIONAL OFFICERS

Address: PO Box 81826
             Lincoln, NE 68501-1826

Telephone: 800/255-2382
WWW: n/a
Document: Correctional Officers' Creed (1982)

(The IACO Creed was written by the late Professor Robert Barrington, Northern Michigan University, in 1979, and adopted by IACO in 1982.—Eds.)

To speak sparingly . . . to act, not to argue . . . to be in authority through personal presence . . . to correct without nagging . . . to speak with the calm voice of certainty . . . to see everything, and to know what is significant and what not to notice . . . to be neither insensitive to distress nor so distracted by pity as to miss what must elsewhere be seen . . .

To do neither that which is unkind nor self-indulgent in its misplaced charity . . . never to obey the impulse to tongue lash that silent insolence which in times past could receive the lash . . . to be both firm and fair . . . to know I cannot be fair simply by being firm, nor firm simply by being fair . . .

To support the reputations of associates and confront them without anger should they stand short of professional conduct . . . to reach for knowledge of the continuing mysteries of human motivation . . . to think; always to think . . . to be dependable . . . to be dependable first to my charges and associates, and thereafter to my duty as employee and citizen . . . to keep fit . . . to keep forever alert . . . to listen to what is meant as well as what is said with words and with silences . . .

To expect respect from my charges and my superiors yet never to abuse the one for abuses from the other . . . for eight hours each working day to be an example of the person I could be at all times . . . to acquiesce in no dishonest act . . . to cultivate patience under boredom and calm during confusion . . . to understand the why of every order I take or give . . .

To hold freedom among the highest values though I deny it to those I guard . . . to deny it with dignity that in my example they find no reason to lose their dignity . . . to be prompt . . . to be honest with all who practice deceit that they not find in me excuse for themselves . . . to privately face down my fear that I not signal it . . . to privately cool my anger that I not displace it on others . . . to hold in confidence what I see and hear, which by the telling could harm or humiliate to no good purpose . . . to keep my outside problems outside . . . to leave inside that which should stay inside . . . to do my duty.

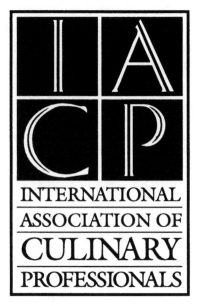

INTERNATIONAL ASSOCIATION OF CULINARY PROFESSIONALS

Address: 304 West Liberty Street, Suite 201
              Louisville, KY 40202
Telephone: 502/581-9786
WWW: www.iacp-online.org
Document: Code of Professional Ethics

As a member of the International Association of Culinary Professionals, I pledge myself to:

Support the growth of knowledge and the free interchange of ideas within the profession, and respect the views and opinions of my colleagues and honor their right to express them.

Strive to achieve and maintain excellence in the preparation for and the presentation of culinary instruction.

Constantly strive to improve and expand my culinary knowledge.

Accurately represent my professional training and qualifications and not knowingly permit, aid, abet or suffer the misstatement of my training and qualifications by others.

Maintain the highest standards of accuracy and honesty in my dealings with colleagues and students, and zealously safeguard any monies or property which may be entrusted to me for safekeeping.

Not publish, or knowingly permit to be published on my behalf, any advertising or promotional material which contains false, deceptive or misleading statements.

Respect the intellectual property rights of others and not knowingly use or appropriate to my own financial or professional advantage any recipe or other intellectual property belonging to another without the proper recognition.

Respect my students and my colleagues, and strive always to ensure that professional comment and criticism of their work is both constructive and appropriate.

Dedicate myself to support and assist the association in serving the profession and the public.

Refrain from any act or omission, and not permit or suffer any act or omission, which would discredit or bring dishonor to the association or any member thereof.

This CODE OF ETHICS for members of the International Association of Culinary Professionals has been adopted to promote and maintain the highest standards of association service and personal conduct among its members. Adherence to these standards is required for membership in the Association, and serves to assure public confidence in the integrity and service of Culinary Professionals.

© International Association of Culinary Professionals. Reprinted with permission.

INTERNATIONAL ASSOCIATION OF FIRE CHIEFS

Address: 4025 Fair Ridge Drive
            Fairfax, VA 22033-2868

Telephone: 703/273-0911
WWW: www.iafc.org
Document: International Association of Fire
            Chiefs Code of Ethics for Fire Chiefs
            (1997)

The purpose of the International Association of Fire Chiefs is to actively support the advancement of the fire service which is dedicated solely to the protection and preservation of life and property against fire and other emergencies coming under the jurisdiction of the fire service. Towards this endeavor, every member of the International Association of Fire Chiefs shall with due deliberation live according to ethical principles consistent with professional conduct and shall:

- Recognize that we serve in a position of public trust that imposes responsibility to use publicly owned resources effectively and judiciously.
- Keep in mind our obligation not to seek advantages or favors for ourselves, friends or family.
- Use information gained by virtue of our position only for the benefit of those we are entrusted to serve.
- Conduct our personal affairs in such a manner that we cannot be improperly influenced in the performance of our duties.
- Recognize and avoid situations wherein our decisions or recommendations may have an impact on our personal financial interests.
- Seek no favor and accept no form of personal reward for influence or official action. Engage in no outside employment or professional activities that may impair or appear to be in conflict with our primary responsibilities as fire officials.
- Handle all personnel matters on the basis of merit.
- Carry out policies established by elected officials and policy makers to the best of our ability, even when they are contrary to our recommendations.
- Refrain from financial investments or business that conflicts with, or is enhanced by, our official positions.

© International Association of Fire Chiefs. Reprinted with permission.

INTERNATIONAL CITY/ COUNTY MANAGEMENT ASSOCIATION

Address: 777 North Capitol Street NE,
                Suite 500
                Washington, DC 20002-4201
Telephone: 202/289-4262
WWW: www.icma.org
Document: ICMA Code of Ethics (1924. Most
                recently revised 1995.)

(The ICMA also publishes *ICMA Code of Ethics with Guidelines*, adopted in 1972 and most recently revised in 1995, which expands on the basic principles and provides practical advice to the members about specific issues. The *Guidelines* are not reprinted here.—Eds.)

The purposes of ICMA are to enhance the quality of local government and to support and assist professional local administrators in the United States and other countries. To further these objectives, certain principles, as enforced by the Rules of Procedure, shall govern the conduct of every member of ICMA, who shall:

1. Be dedicated to the concepts of effective and democratic local government by responsible elected officials and believe that professional general management is essential to the achievement of this objective.

2. Affirm the dignity and worth of the services rendered by government and maintain a constructive, creative, and practical attitude toward local government affairs and a deep sense of social responsibility as a trusted public servant.

3. Be dedicated to the highest ideals of honor and integrity in all public and personal relationships in order that the member may merit the respect and confidence of the elected officials, of other officials and employees, and of the public.

4. Recognize that the chief function of local government at all times is to serve the best interests of all the people.

5. Submit policy proposals to elected officials; provide them with facts and advice on matters of policy as a basis for making decisions and setting community goals; and uphold and implement local government policies adopted by elected officials.

6. Recognize that elected representatives of the people are entitled to the credit for the establishment of local government policies; responsibility for policy execution rests with the members.

7. Refrain from participation in the election of the members of the employing legislative body, and from all partisan political activities which would impair performance as a professional administrator.

8. Make it a duty continually to improve the member's professional ability and to develop the competence of associates in the use of management techniques.

9. Keep the community informed on local government affairs; encourage communication between the citizens and all local government officers; emphasize friendly and courteous service to the public; and seek to improve the quality and image of public service.

10. Resist any encroachment on professional responsibilities, believing the member should be free to carry out official policies without interference, and handle each problem without discrimination on the basis of principle and justice.

11. Handle all matters of personnel on the basis of merit so that fairness and impartiality govern a member's decisions pertaining to appointments, pay adjustments, promotions, and discipline.

12. Seek no favor; believe that personal aggrandizement or profit secured by confidential information or by misuse of public time is dishonest.

INTERNATIONAL FACILITY MANAGEMENT ASSOCIATION

Address: 1 East Greenway Plaza, Suite 1100
                Houston, TX 77046-0194

Telephone: 713/623-4362
WWW: www.ifma.org
Document: IFMA Code of Ethics (1995)

(The IFMA also publishes the *Code of Ethics Issue Resolution Procedure*, which defines responsibilities in the event of ethical conflict. The *Procedure* is not reprinted here.—Eds.)

All IFMA members are expected to comply with the IFMA Code of Ethics. When in doubt, members have the responsibility to seek clarification from IFMA.

1. IFMA members shall treat each other with respect when dealing with matters which could affect their professional reputations. All members shall recognize that the profession will be judged by the conduct of individual members.
2. IFMA members shall maintain the highest professional standards and ethical behavior in their Association relationships. This includes, but is not limited to, the use of mail lists, membership information and resources, or any calls, contacts or working relationship outside of IFMA.
3. IFMA members shall use IFMA membership as a means of professional development for themselves and not for personal aggrandizement.
4. IFMA members shall be responsible for providing educational and professional development information to the membership.
5. IFMA members shall not buy or sell products or services at IFMA functions, except at trade shows or displays established for that purpose.
6. IFMA members shall not discriminate because of race, sex, creed, age, disability or national origin as it relates to their Association relationships.
7. IFMA members shall abide by the Constitution and Bylaws of the Association and shall support the objectives of its Strategic Plan and the interests of the Association stakeholders (members' business entity and leadership, government regulatory agencies and IFMA staff).
8. IFMA members are responsible for reporting to IFMA the actions of individuals or member companies which are considered contrary to the Code of Ethics. These actions may include, but are not limited to, cases of professional malfeasance, discrimination or incompetence. The IFMA Ethics Committee shall investigate complaints received and may issue sanctions for code violations.

This document is a guideline and does not represent the entire breadth of what constitutes good conduct
and ethical behavior. Acceptance of and adherence to this code is a condition of membership in IFMA.

INTERNATIONAL FIRE MARSHALS ASSOCIATION

Address: NFPA, 1 Batterymarch Park
              Quincy, MA 02269-9101
Telephone: 617/984-7424
WWW: www.nfpa.org/members/member_
              sections/International_Fire_Marshals_
              As/international_fire_marshals_as.html
Document: Code of Ethics for Fire Marshals
              (1966)

Foreword

Honesty, justice and courtesy form a moral philosophy which, associated with interest among men, constitutes the foundation of ethics. The fire marshal recognizes such a standard, not in passive observance, but as a set of dynamic principles guiding his conduct and way of life. It is his duty to practice his profession according to this Code.

A keystone of professional conduct is integrity, the fire marshal will discharge his duties with fidelity to the public and to his associates, and with fairness and impartiality to all. It is his duty to interest himself in public welfare and to be ready to apply his special knowledge for the benefit of mankind. He should uphold the honor and dignity of his profession and also avoid association with any enterprise of questionable character. In his dealings with fellow fire marshals, he should be fair and tolerant.

Professional Life

Section 1.   The fire marshal will cooperate in extending the effectiveness of his profession by interchanging information and experience with other fire marshals and by contributing to the work of other persons, professions, schools and the press.

Section 2.   He will not advertise his work or merit in a self-laudatory manner, and he will avoid all conduct or practice likely to discredit or do injury to the dignity and honor of his profession.

Section 3. He will recognize his badge of office as a symbol of public faith and accept it as a public trust to be held as long as he is true to the ethics of his office.

Section 4. He will enforce the law courteously and appropriately without fear or favor, malice or ill will, never implying unnecessary force and never accepting gratuities.

Relations with the Public

Section 5. The fire marshal will endeavor to extend public knowledge of fire protection and will discourage the spreading of untrue, unfair and exaggerated statements regarding fire protection.

Section 6. He will avoid any endorsement of any specific product, trade name or company.

Section 7. He will have due regard for the safety of life and health of the public and employees who may be affected by the work for which he is responsible.

Section 8. He will express an opinion only when it is founded on adequate knowledge and honest conviction while he is serving as a witness before a court, commission or other tribunal.

Section 9. He will not issue ex-parte statements, criticisms or arguments on matters connected with public policy which are inspired or paid for by private interests, unless he indicates on whose behalf he is making the statement.

Section 10. He will refrain from expressing publicly an opinion on a fire protection subject unless he is informed as to the facts relating thereto.

Section 11. He will act with fairness and justice with the public when dealing with fire protection. He will never act officiously or permit personal feelings, prejudices, animosities or friendship to influence his decisions.

Section 12. He will disclose no information concerning the business affairs or technical processes of the public without their consent.

Relations with Employers

Section 13. The fire marshal will act in professional matters for his employer as a faithful agent or trustee.

Section 14. He will make his status clear to his employer before undertaking an engagement if he may be called upon to decide on the use of inventions, apparatus or any other thing in which he may have a financial interest.

Section 15. He will guard against conditions that are dangerous or threatening to life, limb or property on work for which he is responsible or, if he is not responsible, will promptly call such conditions to the attention of those who are responsible.

Section 16. He will present clearly the consequences to be expected from deviations proposed if his judgment is overruled by non-technical authority in cases where he is responsible for the adequacy of fire protection work.

Section 17. He will engage, or advise his employer to engage, and he will cooperate with other experts and specialists whenever the employer's interests are best served by such service.

Section 18. He will not accept compensation, commissions or allowances, directly or indirectly, from contractors or other parties dealing with his employer in connection with work for which he is responsible.

Section 19. He will not allow an interest in any business to affect his decision regarding work for which he is employed or which he may be called upon to perform.

Relations with other Fire Marshals

Section 20. The fire marshal will endeavor to protect all members of the fire protection profession collectively and individually from misrepresentation and misunderstanding.

Section 21. He will take care that credit for fire protection work is given to those to whom credit is properly due.

Section 22. He will uphold the principle of appropriate and adequate compensation for those engaged in fire protection, including those in subordinate capacities, as being in the public interest and maintaining the standards of the profession.

Section 23.   He will endeavor to provide opportunity for the professional development and advancement of those in his employ.

Section 24.   He will not injure, directly or indirectly, the professional reputation, prospects or practice of another fire marshal. However, if he considers that a fire marshal is guilty of unethical, illegal or unfair practice, he will present the information to the proper authority for action.

Section 25.   He will exercise due restraint in criticizing another fire marshal's work in public, recognizing the fact that the societies, the associations and the technical press provide the proper forum for technical discussions and criticisms.

Section 26.   He will not become associated in responsibility for work with persons who do not conform to ethical practices.

© International Fire Marshals Association. Reprinted with permisssion.

INTERNATIONAL HEARING SOCIETY

Address: 16880 Middlebelt Road
              Livonia, MI 48154
Telephone: 734/522-7200
WWW: www.hearingihs.org
Document: Code of Ethics of the International Hearing Society (1983. Most recently revised 1996.)

FOREWORD

This Code of Ethics for Hearing Instrument Specialists® has been prepared and subscribed to by members of the International Hearing Society. These principles of professional conduct are a voluntary effort to provide the best service for the hearing impaired and to guide hearing health professionals in their relations with each other and the public in general.

PREAMBLE

This is a Code of Ethics for those engaged in the testing of human hearing, and in the selection, counseling, fitting, dispensing and servicing of hearing instruments. This Code sets standards of professional integrity and practice, including relationships with patients/clients, colleagues and the general public.

Ethical principles are standards by which the profession and the individual hearing aid specialist determines the propriety of their conduct. Adherence to these standards is required for membership in the International Hearing Society, and further serves to assure public confidence in the integrity of the services of hearing aid specialists in this profession. The International Hearing Society verifies the competence of its members through a qualification program and mandatory continuing education. It is incumbent on all hearing health professionals to abide by all laws, or rules and regulations applicable to the dispensing of hearing instruments.

The basic principle is an accepted Code of Ethical Conduct for hearing aid specialists and dispensers of hearing instruments.

In order that we can best serve hearing impaired persons and contribute toward their participation in the world of sound and speech, we, the members of the International Hearing Society, pledge ourselves to abide with this Code of Ethics:

(A) We shall state only the true facts in our public announcements and advertising of hearing aids and related products, and we shall not, in any way, mislead or misrepresent in regard to their performance, appearance, benefits, elements, and use.

(B) We shall provide thorough and ethical consulting services when we dispense instruments, including the appropriate testing and fitting suitable for the patient/client's particular type of hearing loss.

(C) We shall, at all times, provide the best possible service to the hearing impaired, offering counsel, understanding and technical assistance contributing toward their deriving the maximum benefit from their hearing instruments.

(D) We shall constantly encourage and support research, cooperating with medical and other hearing health professionals and societies to employ the maximum accumulation of scientific knowledge and technical skills in the testing of human hearing for the selection, fitting and maintenance of hearing instruments.

SECTION I: CONDUCT AND RELATIONSHIP WITH PATIENT/CLIENT

Hearing Instrument Specialists engaged in the practice of testing human hearing, and in the selection, counseling, fitting, dispensing and servicing of hearing instruments, shall hold paramount the welfare of the patient/client.

A. Continuing Education

It is in the best interest of the patient/client that the Hearing Instrument Specialist engage and participate in continuing education during each year of active practice.

B. Referral

The Hearing Instrument Specialist shall utilize all resources available, including referral to other specialists as needed.

C. Services Rendered

The Hearing Instrument Specialist shall accept and seek full responsibility for the exercise of judgement within the areas of his expertise. These services include the testing of human hearing, and the selection, counseling, fitting, dispensing and servicing of hearing instruments.

The Hearing Instrument Specialist shall not guarantee outstanding results from the use of hearing instruments, products, services or counseling when such is not the case. He shall exercise caution not to mislead persons to expect results that cannot be predicted.

D. Confidential Aspects of Patient/Client Relations

The Hearing Instrument Specialist shall hold in professional confidence all information and professional records concerning a patient/client and use such data only for the benefit of the patient/client or as the law demands.

E. Conduct in Regard to Colleagues and Hearing Health Care Professions

The Hearing Instrument Specialist must keep the welfare of the patient/client uppermost at all times. He shall avoid personal invective directed toward professional colleagues or members of the hearing health care professions. He shall conduct himself at all times in a manner which will enhance the status of the profession. He shall be supportive to individuals and organizations with whom he is associated to their mutual benefit. He shall not agree to practice under terms or conditions which tend to interfere with or impair the proper exercise of his professional judgement and skill, which tend to cause a deterioration of the quality of his service, or which require him to consent to unethical conduct.

F. Maintenance of Records

The Hearing Instrument Specialist shall initiate and maintain records of services provided to patients/clients. All laws, or rules and regulations pertaining to keeping of records must be carefully observed.

G. Fees and Compensation

The Hearing Instrument Specialist shall not participate with other health professionals or any other person in agreements to divide fees or to cause financial or other exploitation when rendering his professional services.

H. Delay in Providing Services

The Hearing Instrument Specialist shall not delay furnishing care to patients/clients served professionally, without just cause.

I. Discontinuance of Services

The Hearing Instrument Specialist shall not discontinue services to patients/clients without providing reasonable notice of withdrawal, providing all contractual agreements have been satisfied.

SECTION II: RESPONSIBILITY TO THE PROFESSION AND COLLEAGUES

The Hearing Instrument Specialist has the duty to observe all laws, rules and regulations, applicable to the dispensing of hearing instruments, to uphold the dignity and honor of the profession and to accept its ethical principles. He shall not engage in any activity that will bring discredit to the profession and shall expose, without fear or favor, illegal or unethical conduct in the profession.

A. In the event it appears that a Hearing Instrument Specialist is in violation of this Code, fellow Hearing Instrument Specialists are encouraged to report circumstances to the Ethics Committee of the International Hearing Society.

B. The Hearing Instrument Specialist holding an official or elective position in the International Hearing Society or State or Provincial Chapter, shall not use such a position for self-aggrandizement.

SECTION III: ADVERTISING

The Hearing Instrument Specialist who chooses to advertise his services shall use only material considered ethical and complying with laws, or rules and regulations governing advertising.

The Hearing Instrument Specialist shall endorse the following statement of principles that assures protection of the hearing impaired and the public in general.

TRUTH—Advertising shall tell the truth, and shall reveal significant facts, the concealment of which would mislead the public, and shall not dispense any product, or part hereof, representing that it is new, unused, or rebuilt, when such is not the fact.

RESPONSIBILITY—Advertisers shall be willing and able to provide substantiation of claims made.

TASTE AND DECENCY—Advertising shall be free of statements, illustrations, or implications which are offensive to good taste or public decency.

DISPARAGEMENT—Advertising shall offer merchandise or service on its merits, and shall refrain from attacking competitors or disparaging their products, services or methods of doing business.

BAIT ADVERTISEMENT—Advertising shall offer only merchandise or services which are readily available for purchase during the advertised period at the advertised price; e.g., it is unethical for any Hearing Instrument Specialist to advertise a particular model or kind of instrument to obtain prospects for the sale of a different model or kind of instrument than that advertised, or to imply a relationship with a manufacturer and trade names that does not exist.

GUARANTEES AND WARRANTIES—Advertising of guarantees and warranties shall be explicit. Advertising of any guarantee or warranty shall clearly and conspicuously disclose its nature and extent, the manner in which the guarantor or warrantor will perform, and the identity of the guarantor or warrantor. It is unethical to use or cause to be used, any guarantee or warranty which is false, misleading, deceptive, or unfair, whether in respect to the quality, construction, serviceability, performance, or method of manufacture of any industry product, or in respect to the terms and conditions of refund of purchase price thereof, or in any other respect.

SECTION IV: STANDARDS

Maintenance of high standards by all Hearing Instrument Specialists is in the best interest of persons served professionally, Hearing Instrument Specialists and the profession.

A. It shall be unethical for Hearing Instrument Specialists to willfully and knowingly violate any law or rule or regulation applicable to the dispensing of hearing instruments.
B. It shall be unethical to use such terms or to use any abbreviation of such terms as doctor, physician, otologist, Board Certified Hearing Instrument Specialist, certified hearing aid audiologist, clinical audiologist, medical audiologist, research audiologist, industrial audiologist, when such is not the fact.
C. It shall be unethical to use any symbol or depiction which connotes the medical profession.
D. It shall be unethical to use any terms that may reasonably be said to confuse the public that a private business practice has some relationship to a governmental or non-profit medical, educational or research institution.

SECTION V: DISCRIMINATION

The Hearing Instrument Specialist shall not discriminate in the delivery of professional services on the basis of race, national origin, religion, sex, age or marital status.

SECTION VI: ASSOCIATION

The Hearing Instrument Specialist shall associate with groups and organizations having for their objectives the betterment of the profession. Hearing Instrument Specialists shall contribute of their time and funds to further the work of these organizations and the profession.

All members of the International Hearing Society and Hearing Instrument Specialists of this profession pledge themselves to observe and support this Code of Ethics. By violating any part, a member of the International Hearing Society is subject to removal from membership in the International Hearing Society. This Code is interpreted by the Ethics Committee, and enforced by the Grievance Committee of the International Hearing Society. Upon violation of this Code, the Grievance Committee may discipline members, after investigation and hearing.

INTERNATIONAL
READING ASSOCIATION

Address: 800 Barksdale Road, PO Box 8139
              Newark, DE 19714-8139
Telephone: 302/731-1600
WWW: www.reading.org
Document: International Reading Association
              Code of Ethics

The members of the International Reading Association who are concerned with the teaching of reading form a group of professional persons obligated to society and devoted to the service and welfare of individuals through teaching, clinical services, research, and publication. The members of this group are committed to values which are the foundation of a democratic society—freedom to teach, write, and study in an atmosphere conducive to the best interests of the profession. The welfare of the public, the profession, and the individuals concerned should be of primary consideration in recommending candidates for degrees, positions, advancements, the recognition of professional activity, and for certification in those areas where certification exists.

Ethical standards in professional relationships:

1. It is the obligation of all members of the International Reading Association to observe the Code of Ethics of the organization and to act accordingly so as to advance the status and prestige of the Association and of the profession as a whole. Members should assist in establishing the highest professional standards for reading programs and services, and should enlist support for these through dissemination of pertinent information to the public.
2. It is the obligation of all members to maintain relationships with other professional persons, striving for harmony, avoiding personal controversy, encouraging cooperative effort, and making known the obligations and services rendered by professionals in reading.
3. It is the obligation of members to report results of research and other developments in reading.

4. Members should not claim nor advertise affiliation with the **International Reading Association** as evidence of their competence in reading.

Ethical standards in reading services:

1. Professionals in reading must possess suitable qualifications for engaging in consulting, clinical, or remedial work. Unqualified persons should not engage in such activities except under the direct supervision of one who is properly qualified. Professional intent and the welfare of the person seeking services should govern all consulting or clinical activities such as counseling, administering diagnostic tests, or providing remediation. It is the duty of the professional in reading to keep relationships with clients and interested persons on a professional level.
2. Information derived from consulting and/or clinical services should be regarded as confidential. Expressed consent of persons involved should be secured before releasing information to outside agencies.
3. Professionals in reading should recognize the boundaries of their competence and should not offer services which fail to meet professional standards established by other disciplines. They should be free, however, to give assistance in other areas in which they are qualified.
4. Referral should be made to specialists in allied fields as needed. When such referral is made, pertinent information should be made available to consulting specialists.
5. Reading clinics and/or reading professionals offering services should refrain from guaranteeing easy solutions or favorable outcomes as a result of their work, and their advertising should be consistent with that of allied professions. They should not accept for remediation any persons who are unlikely to benefit from their instruction, and they should work to accomplish the greatest possible improvement in the shortest time. Fees, if charged, should be agreed on in advance and should be charged in accordance with an established set of rates commensurate with that of other professions.

Breaches of the Code of Ethics should be reported to Association Headquarters for referral to the Committee on Professional Standards and Ethics for an impartial investigation.

MANA

MANUFACTURERS' AGENTS NATIONAL ASSOCIATION

Address: 23016 Mill Creek Road, PO Box 3467
               Laguna Hills, CA 92654-3467
Telephone: 949/859-4040 or 877/626-2776
WWW: www.MANAonline.org
Document: MANA Code of Ethics

ALL MEMBERS ARE EXPECTED TO ABIDE BY THE FOLLOWING CODE OF CONDUCT

I. THE SALES AGENCY'S RESPONSIBILITIES TO THE MANUFACTURER/PRINCIPAL:

- To comply with the Manufacturer's established policies.
- To conscientiously cover the assigned territory.
- To avoid any form of misrepresentation.
- To agree to take on only those lines or accounts which you have reason to believe will be well represented by your Agency.
- To refrain from representing lines, products and goods which compete with the lines, products and goods you already represent.
- To provide your Manufacturers/Principals with the same loyal service you would expect from your own employees.

II. THE MANUFACTURER'S/PRINCIPAL'S RESPONSIBILITES TO THE SALES AGENCY:

- To enter into a fair, clearly worded written Sales Representative (independent contractor) Agreement which addresses the needs, concerns, expectations and objectives of both parties.
- To refrain from modifying the terms of this agreement, except by mutual written consent after full and friendly discussion.
- To refrain from absorbing, refusing or cutting the Agency's established commissions, territory or accounts, except by mutual consent.
- To agree to practical and dignified means for friendly negotiation of all controversial points that may arise between you and the Sales Agency.

III. RESPONSIBILITIES OF ONE SALES AGENCY TO ANOTHER:

- To exchange mutually beneficial trade information.
- To avoid any suggestion or agreement to divide commissions with those agencies or others representing Principals competitive to my Agency.
- To refrain from using unfair methods to solicit from Manufacturers the known lines or accounts of other established Sales Agencies.
- To act in good faith and deal fairly so as not to deprive another Agency of the fruits of its performance.
- To cooperate to enhance the professional relationship of the Sales Agency and its Principal by supporting MANA, which was established for that purpose; subscribing to its aims and objectives, and in every practical way working to advance the marketing interests of all Sales Agencies and their Principals.

MINERALS, METALS & MATERIALS SOCIETY

Address: 184 Thorn Hill Road
              Warrendale, PA 15086
Telephone: 724/776-9000
WWW: www.tms.org

Minerals, Metals & Materials Society, also known as TMS, subscribes to the same code as the National Society of Professional Engineers. See p.00.

MODERN LANGUAGE ASSOCIATION

Address: 10 Astor Place
             New York, NY 10003
Telephone: 212/475-9500
WWW: www.mla.org
Document: Statement of Professional Ethics

Preamble

As the members of the MLA, we constitute a community of teachers and scholars joined together to serve the larger society by promoting the study and teaching of the modern languages and literatures. At the heart of this enterprise is freedom of inquiry, which we ask of the society we serve. This freedom carries with it the responsibilities of professional conduct. We intend this statement to embody reasonable norms for ethical conduct in teaching, research, and related public service activities in the modern languages and literatures. The statement's governing premises are as follows:

1. *The responsibility for protecting free inquiry lies first with tenured faculty members, who may be called on to speak out against unethical behavior or to defend the academic freedom of colleagues at any rank.*
2. *Tenured and nontenured faculty members alike have ethical obligations to students, colleagues, staff members, their institutions, their local communities, the profession at large, and society. Therefore, in the continuing evaluation of faculty members by their colleagues, the way in which those obligations are fulfilled is an appropriate area for review.[1]*
3. *Our integrity as teachers and scholars implies a commitment to be responsible in using evidence and developing arguments and to be fair in hearing and reading the arguments of both colleagues and students.*
4. *Free inquiry respects the diversity of the modes and objects of investigation, whether they are traditional or innovative. We should defend scholarly practices against unfounded attacks from within or outside our community.*
5. *Our teaching and inquiry must respect simultaneously the diversity of our own culture and that of the cultures we study.*

6. *Judgments of whether a line of inquiry is ultimately useful to society, colleagues, or students should not be used to limit the freedom of the scholar pursuing it.*
7. *As a community valuing free inquiry, we must be able to rely on the integrity and the good judgment of our members. For this reason, we should not*

- *exploit or discriminate against others on any grounds, including race, ethnic origin, religious creed, age, gender, and sexual preference*
- *plagiarize the work of others[2]*
- *sexually harass students, colleagues, or staff members[3]*
- *misuse confidential information*
- *use language that is prejudicial or gratuitously derogatory*
- *make capricious or arbitrary decisions affecting working conditions, professional status, or academic freedom*
- *practice deceit or fraud on the academic community or the public*

Ethical Conduct in Academic Relationships

A. Obligations to Students[4]

1. Faculty members should represent to their students the values of free inquiry.
2. At the outset of each course, faculty members should provide the students with a statement on approaches to the course materials, on the goals of the course, and on the standards by which the students will be evaluated.
3. Faculty members should offer constructive and timely evaluation of students' work and specify the times and places when they are available to consult with students.
4. Student-teacher collaboration entails the same obligation as other kinds of research: faculty members should acknowledge appropriately any intellectual indebtedness.
5. Faculty members whose research in any way includes students as subjects must make clear the obligations, rewards, and consequences of participation. Such relationships also impose on researchers a special responsibility to guard the students involved from any form of abuse, such as betrayal of confidentiality, and to protect them from research-related harm or discomfort.
6. In as much as the teaching of language, writing, and literature not only involves comprehension of the course material but may also draw, more directly than some other subjects do, on students'

intellectual and emotional experiences, faculty members, in devising requirements for written work and oral discussion, have an ethical responsibility to respect both students' privacy and their emotional and intellectual dignity.

7. Faculty members should keep confidential what they know about students' academic standing, personal lives, and political or religious views and should not exploit such personal knowledge.

8. Faculty members should provide unbiased, professional evaluation of students seeking admission to graduate study or applying for financial support.

9. Faculty members should provide direction to graduate students, should respect their scholarly interests, and should not exploit them for personal or professional ends. Faculty members should not expect graduate students to perform unremunerated or uncredited teaching, research, or personal duties.

10. Faculty members working with teaching assistants have a special responsibility to provide them with adequate preparation, continuing guidance, and informed evaluation.

11. Faculty members must weigh the academic performance of each graduate student on its merits.

12. In overseeing and responding to the work of graduate students, whether they are in courses or at the thesis or dissertation stage, advisers should periodically inform them of their standing in the programs.

13. Before graduate students begin searching for jobs, faculty members should provide them with adequate and timely counseling and should be prepared to write honest and constructive letters of recommendation. Under certain circumstances, a faculty member who entertains basic doubts either about a student's competence or about his or her own ability to evaluate the student fairly may wish to decline the task of furnishing such a letter.

B. Obligations to Colleagues

1. Faculty members should evaluate candidates for appointment, reappointment, promotion, or tenure on professional grounds and in appropriate forums.[5] Likewise, such candidates should submit accurate credentials and represent themselves honestly.

2. Tenured faculty members should participate in the institutional processes by which tenure-track faculty members are evaluated and apprised of their

standing. Similarly, the appropriate faculty members should periodically and fairly evaluate all other categories of nontenured faculty members.[6]

3. The appropriate faculty members should inform candidates for promotion or tenure of their rights, of the criteria germane to the evaluation, and of the methods by which the evaluation will be undertaken.

4. Faculty members on committees reviewing colleagues should keep confidential all information about persons under evaluation, not only in promotion and tenure reviews but also in reviews of chairs, searches for departmental administrators, and other such processes.

5. Faculty members in positions of leadership should assist their institutions in devising and implementing policies and procedures that promote a positive working environment. These policies and procedures should, for example, protect tenured and nontenured faculty members alike from any form of exploitation and provide all faculty members with a system for orderly and dignified retirement from full-time academic duties.

6. Faculty members should encourage the development of departmental and institutional policies that extend courtesies and specified privileges to independent scholars.

C. Obligations to Staff Members

1. Faculty members should value staff members as coworkers and, accordingly, should not require them to do inappropriate, unreasonable, unhealthy, or hazardous work.

2. Faculty members should recognize that the use of sexist or racist epithets or the repeated refusal to name a staff member according to his or her wishes constitutes a form of harassment.

3. Faculty members who supervise staff members should work to ensure that other faculty members and graduate students treat those staff members appropriately.

D. Obligations to the Institution and to the Local Community

1. Faculty members should support ethical behavior and protect academic freedom within their institutions.

2. Faculty members should be aware of how the policies, programs, and expansions of their institutions may affect local communities, particularly in matters in which modern language professionals may have a special competence, such as literacy.

3. Faculty members should ensure that their personal activities in politics and in their local communities remain distinct from any positions taken by their universities or colleges. They should avoid appearing to speak for their institutions when acting privately.

4. A faculty member planning to resign should give timely, written notice of this intention in accordance with university regulations. Until the existing appointment ends, he or she should not accept another appointment involving concurrent obligations without the permission of the appropriate administrator.

E. Obligations to the Profession at Large and to Society

1. In contributing to the profession at large, scholars should not accept assignments that they know they cannot carry out responsibly.

2. As referees for presses, journals, and promotion and tenure committees, scholars should judge the work of others fairly and in an informed way and should avoid any conflict of interest. A reader who is so out of sympathy with the author, topic, or critical stance of a work as to be unable to judge its merits without prejudice should decline to review it. Likewise, any referee with a personal relationship that prevents an unbiased evaluation should turn down the invitation to serve.[7]

3. A scholar asked by an editor to evaluate a manuscript or book that the scholar has previously reviewed should inform the editor of the coincidence.

4. Referees should be fully informed of the evaluation procedures and should be allowed anonymity unless there are legal requirements of disclosure.

5. The timetable for publication review should be made clear to both referees and authors. Referees should discharge their tasks in a timely manner; they should decline invitations whose deadlines they cannot meet. Editors should not use referees who habitually prolong the evaluation process. Any changes in a publication schedule should be conveyed promptly to the author involved. Undue delay in review or publication justifies the author to submit the manuscript to another outlet, provided the first editor is informed in writing.

6. A scholar who feels it necessary to submit work to more than one outlet simultaneously should so inform the editors receiving the submission.

7. A scholar who borrows from the works and ideas of others, including those of students, should acknowledge the debt, whether or not the sources are published. Unpublished scholarly material—which may be encountered when it is read aloud, circulated in manuscript, or discussed—is especially vulnerable to unacknowledged appropriation, since the lack of a printed text makes originality hard to establish.

8. In communicating the principles and findings of their research to the public, scholars are obliged to be as accurate in their utterances as they are in addressing the academic community.

Conclusion

Our focus in this document is on the affirmative obligations of the modern language profession. Accountable as we are to the various groups and individuals listed here, we hold the view that a common understanding of our obligations to them will enable us both to exert appropriate restraints in exercising our responsibilities as scholars and teachers and to promote ethical behavior among our colleagues and among those who will follow us in the profession.

Notes

1. When a faculty member's fulfillment of ethical obligations is reviewed, care should be taken that it, like other subjects of evaluation, is not arbitrarily or capriciously judged. Any actions that may lead to the nonrenewal of an appointment, to the dismissal of a tenured faculty member, or to other such sanctions should be pursued in accordance with generally accepted procedural standards. See especially the "1940 Statement of Principles on Academic Freedom and Tenure" of the American Association of University Professors, endorsed by the MLA in 1962 and augmented with interpretive comments in 1970, and the related AAUP "Recommended Institutional Regulations on Academic Freedom and Tenure."

2. In this statement we adopt the definition of plagiarism given in *The MLA Style Manual*: "Plagiarism is the use of another person's ideas or expressions in your writing without acknowledging the source. . . .The most blatant form of plagiarism is reproducing someone else's sentences, more or less verbatim, and presenting them as your own. Other forms include repeating another's particularly apt phrase without appropriate acknowledgment, paraphrasing someone else's argument as your own, introducing another's line of thinking as your own development of an idea, and failing to cite the source for a borrowed thesis or approach" (Achtert and Gibaldi 1.4; cf. "What to Document," 5.1). It is important to note that this definition does not distinguish between published and unpublished sources, between ideas derived from colleagues and those offered by students, or between written and oral presentations.

3. In defining sexual harassment, we drew on statements such as the following: (1) "Sexual harassment is defined by law and includes any unwanted sexual gesture, physical

contact, or statement which is offensive, humiliating, or an interference with required tasks or career opportunities" ("Sexual Harassment"). (2) "Sexual harassment may be broadly defined as any unsolicited or objectionable emphasis on the sexuality or sexual identity of another person (whether student, colleague or employee) that might limit that individual's full participation in the academic community. This includes not only sexual advances, requests for sexual favors, or sexual assault, but also sexist remarks or jokes" (American Philological Association). (3) Conduct that is sexually harassing "interferes with an individual's work or academic performance [or] creates an intimidating, hostile or offensive working or academic environment" (Canadian Association 25-7).

4. For further development of some of the issues treated in this section, see the "Joint Statement on Rights and Freedoms of Students," prepared in 1967 by the AAUP and four other associations representing both students and student personnel administrators.

5. For more detailed recommendations on hiring, see Showalter.

6. We allude here both to part-time faculty members and to non-tenure-track full-time faculty members. For further policy on the first group, see the guidelines set forth in the MLA's "Statement on the Use of Part-Time Faculty," adopted in 1982.

7. For a related statement on journal publications, see *Guidelines for Journal Editors and Contributors*, by the Conference of Editors of Learned Journals.

Works Cited

Achtert, Walter S., and Joseph Gibaldi. *The MLA Style Manual*. New York: MLA, 1985.

American Association of University Professors. *Policy Documents and Reports*. Washington: AAUP, 1990.

American Philological Association. "Statement on Professional Ethics." *Directory of Membership*. 8th ed. Atlanta: Scholars, 1991. N. pag.

Canadian Association of University Teachers. "Policy Statement on Professional Rights, Responsibilities and Relationships." *CAUT Information Service*. Ottawa: CAUT, n.d. 25-1–25-10.

Conference of Editors of Learned Journals. *Guidelines for Journal Editors and Contributors*. New York: MLA, 1984.

"Joint Statement on Rights and Freedoms of Students." American Association, *Policy Documents* 153-58.

Modern Language Association. "Statement on the Use of Part-Time Faculty." *ADE Bulletin* 74 (1983): 65. Rpt. annually in Oct. issues of *Job Information List*, English and foreign lang. eds., beginning 1982.

"1940 Statement of Principles on Academic Freedom and Tenure. With 1970 Interpretive Comments." American Association, *Policy Documents* 3-7.

"Recommended Institutional Regulations on Academic Freedom and Tenure." American Association, *Policy Documents* 21-30.

"Sexual Harassment." *The Faculty/Staff Handbook of the University of Illinois at Chicago, 1990-1992*. Chicago: U of Illinois, Chicago, n.d. 105.

Showalter, English. *A Career Guide for PhDs and PhD Candidates in English and Foreign Languages*. New York: MLA, 1985.

MTNA

MUSIC TEACHERS NATIONAL ASSOCIATION

Address:	The Carew Tower, 441 Vine Street, Suite 505 Cincinnati, OH 45202-2814
Telephone:	513/421-1420
WWW:	www.mtna.org
Document:	MTNA Code of Ethics

We, the members of Music Teachers National Association, having dedicated ourselves to the advancement of musical knowledge and education, recommend the following principles of ethical practice as standards of professional conduct.

Responsibilities to Our Public

- Members shall maintain the highest standard of moral conduct, professional conduct and personal integrity.
- Members shall exhibit the highest standard of expertise by maintaining their professional abilities in their fields of teaching and performing.
- Members shall maintain and increase the prestige of the art of teaching and shall promote the teaching of music as a culturally enriching profession.
- When asked, members shall assist those seeking guidance in selecting an independent teacher by suggesting the names of two or more teachers in the community. The final choice shall be made by the parent and the student.
- Members shall refrain from making exaggerated claims or misleading statements concerning their teaching qualifications. Advertising copy shall be dignified, strictly truthful and representative of the art of music and its responsibility to the community.

Responsibilities to Our Students

- The relationship between teacher and student shall be established, maintained and terminated in a professional manner.
- Members are responsible for encouraging, guiding and developing the musical potential of each student.
- Members shall encourage students to participate in community music activities.

Responsibilities to Our Colleagues

- Members shall maintain a professional attitude and shall act with integrity in regard to colleagues in their profession.
- Members shall participate as fully as possible in activities of Music Teachers National Association.
- Members shall provide professional assistance to one another when such assistance is requested.
- Members shall respect the rights of colleagues when speaking of other teachers' work and/or students and shall avoid conflict with the instruction of a student's regular teacher when serving as an interim instructor.

© Music Teachers National Association. Reprinted with permission.

NATIONAL ASSOCIATION FOR COLLEGE ADMISSION COUNSELING

Address: 1631 Prince Street
            Alexandria, VA 22314-2818
Telephone: 703/836-2222
WWW: www.nacac.com

Document: NACAC Statement of Principles of Good Practice (1937. Most recently revised 1996.)

Ethics in recruiting students and awarding scholarships provided the impetus for creating NACAC in 1937. As a reflection of that major purpose, one of the first actions taken by the founders was the creation of a Code of Ethics. After many years of reviewing, updating, and rewriting, this Code is today's *Statement of Principles of Good Practice*.

While the Code originally applied only to NACAC members, the importance of ethical practices in the admission process for all institutions was recognized by those in the profession. As a result, a joint statement utilizing the basic philosophy of NACAC's Code of Ethics was developed in tandem with the American Association of Collegiate Registrars and Admission Officers and The College Board, and was endorsed by the American Council on Education, the National Association of Secondary School Principals, the National Student Association, and the American School Counselor Association.

The *Statement of Principles of Good Practice* is reviewed annually and revised to reflect new concerns for ethical admission practices and policies.

High schools, colleges, universities, other institutions and organizations, and individuals dedicated to the promotion of formal education believe in the dignity, the worth, and the potentialities of every human being. They cooperate in the development of programs and services in postsecondary counseling, admission, and financial aid to eliminate bias related to race, creed, gender, sexual orientation, age, political affiliation, national origin, and disabling conditions. Believing that institutions of learning are only as strong ultimately as their human resources, they look upon counseling individual students about their educational plans as a fundamental aspect of their responsibilities.

They support, therefore, the following *Statement of Principles of Good Practice* for members of the National Association for College Admission Counseling:

I. ADMISSION PROMOTION AND RECRUITMENT

A. College and University Members agree that they

1. will ensure that admission counselors are viewed as professional members of their institutions'

staffs. As professionals, their compensation shall take the form of a fixed salary rather than commissions or bonuses based on the number of students recruited.

2. will be responsible for the development of publications, written communications, and presentations, i.e., college nights, college days, and college fairs, used for their institution's promotional and recruitment activity. They

a) will state clearly and precisely the requirements for secondary school preparation, admission tests, and transfer student admission.

b) will include a current and accurate admission calendar. If the institution offers special admission options such as early admission, early action, early decision, or waiting list, the publication should define these programs and state deadline dates, notification dates, required deposits, refund policies, and the date when the candidates must reply. If students are placed on wait lists or alternate lists, the letter which notifies the students of the placement should provide a history that describes the number of students placed on the wait lists, the number offered admission, and the availability of financial aid and housing. Finally, if summer admission or mid-year admission is available, students should be made aware of the possibility in official communication from the institutions.

c) will provide precise information about costs, opportunities, and requirements for all types of financial aid, and state the specific relationship between admission practices and policies and financial aid practices and policies.

d) will describe in detail any special programs, including overseas study, credit by examination, or advanced placement.

e) will include pictures and descriptions of the campus and community which are current and realistic.

f) will provide accurate information about the opportunities/selection for institutional housing, deadline dates for housing deposits, housing deposit refunds, and describe policies for renewal availability of such institutional housing.

g) will provide accurate and specific descriptions of any special programs or support services available to students with handicapping conditions, learning disabilities, and/or other special needs.

h) will identify the source and year of study when institutional publications and/or media communications cite published ratings of academic programs, academic rigor or reputations, or athletic rankings.

i) should indicate that the institution is a NACAC member and has endorsed the principles contained in this *Statement*.

3. will exercise appropriate responsibility for all people whom the institution involves in admission, promotional, and recruitment activities (including their alumni, coaches, students, faculty, and other institutional representatives), and educate them about the principles outlined in this *Statement*. Colleges and universities which engage the services of admission management or consulting firms shall be responsible for assuring that such firms adhere to this *Statement*.

4. will speak forthrightly, accurately, and comprehensively in presenting their institutions to counseling personnel, prospective students, and their families. They

a) will state clearly the admission requirements of their institutions, and inform students and counselors about changed admission requirements so that candidates will not be adversely affected in the admission process.

b) will state clearly all deadlines for application, notification, housing, and candidates' reply requirements for both admission and financial aid.

c) will furnish data describing the currently enrolled freshman class and will describe in published profiles all members of the enrolling freshman class. Subgroups within the profile may be presented separately because of their unique character or special circumstances.

d) will not use disparaging comparisons of secondary or postsecondary institutions.

e) will provide accurate information about the use/role of standardized testing in their institutions' admission process.

5. will not use unprofessional promotional tactics by admission counselors and other institutional representatives. They

a) will not contract with secondary school personnel for remuneration for referred students.

b) will not offer to pay a per capita premium to any individual or agency for the recruitment or enrollment of students, international as well as domestic.

c) will not encourage students to transfer if they have shown no interest in doing so.

d) will not compromise the goals and principles of this *Statement*.

6. will refrain from recruiting students who are enrolled, registered, or have declared their intent or submitted contractual deposit with other institutions unless the students initiate inquiries themselves or unless cooperation is sought from institutions which provide transfer programs.

7. will understand the nature and intent of all admission referral services utilized by their institutions (including their alumni, coaches, students, faculty, and other institutional representatives) and seek to ensure the validity and professional competency of such services.

B. Secondary School Members agree that they

1. will provide a program of counseling which introduces a broad range of postsecondary opportunities to students.

2. will encourage students and their families to take the initiative in learning about colleges and universities.

3. will not use disparaging comparisons of secondary or postsecondary institutions.

4. will establish a policy with respect to secondary school representatives for the release of students' names. Any policy which authorizes the release of students' names should provide that the release be made only with the students' permission consistent with applicable laws and regulations. That permission may be a general consent to any release of the students' names. Secondary school representatives shall, in releasing students' names, be sensitive to the students' academic, athletic, or other abilities.

5. will refuse any reward or remuneration from a college, university, or private counseling service for placement of their school's students.

6. will be responsible for all personnel who may become involved in counseling students on postsecondary options available and educate them about the principles in this *Statement*.

7. will be responsible for compliance with applicable laws and regulations with respect to the students' rights to privacy.

8. will not guarantee specific college placement.

9. should provide information about opportunities and requirements for financial aid.

10. should indicate that the institution is a NACAC member and has endorsed the principles in this *Statement*.

C. Independent Counselor Members agree that they

1. will provide a program of counseling which introduces a broad range of postsecondary opportunities to students.

2. will encourage students and their families to take initiative in learning about colleges and universities.

3. will not use disparaging comparisons of secondary or postsecondary institutions.

4. will refuse unethical or unprofessional requests (e.g., for names of top students, names of athletes) from college or university representatives (e.g., alumni, coaches, or other agencies or organizations).

5. will refuse any reward or remuneration from a college, university, agency, or organization for placement of their clients.

6. will be responsible for all personnel who may become involved in counseling students on postsecondary options and educate them about the principles in this *Statement*.

7. will be responsible for compliance with applicable laws and regulations with respect to the students' rights to privacy.

8. will not guarantee specific college placement.

9. will provide advertisements or promotional materials which are truthful and do not include any false, misleading, or exaggerated claims with respect to services offered.

10. will communicate with the secondary school counselor about the college admission process, after obtaining student and parental consent.

11. should provide information about opportunities and requirements for financial aid.

12. should consider donating time to students who need the services of an independent counselor but who are unable to pay.

13. should indicate that the NACAC member has endorsed the principles in this *Statement*.

D. All other members providing college admission counseling services to students agree to adhere to the principles in this Statement.

E. College fairs, clearinghouses, and matching services that provide liaison between colleges and universities and students shall be considered a positive part of the admission process if they effectively supplement other secondary school guidance activities and adhere to this Statement.

II. ADMISSION PROCEDURES

A. College and University Members agree that they

1. will accept full responsibility for admission decisions and for proper notification of those decisions to candidates and, when possible, to their secondary schools.

2. will receive information about candidates in confidence and respect completely, consistent with applicable laws and regulations, the confidential nature of such data.

3. will not apply newly-revised requirements to the disadvantage of a candidate whose secondary school courses were established in accordance with earlier requirements.

4. will not require candidates or the secondary schools to indicate the order of the candidates' college or university preferences, except under early decision plans.

5. will not make offers of admission to students who have not submitted admission applications.

6. will permit first-year candidates for fall admission to choose, without penalty, among offers of admission and financial aid until May 1. Colleges that solicit commitments to offers of admission and/or financial assistance prior to May 1 may do so provided those offers include a clear statement that written requests for extensions until May 1 will be granted, and that such requests will not jeopardize a student's status for admission or financial aid. Candidates admitted under an early decision program are a recognized exception to this provision.

7. will work with their institution's administration to ensure that financial aid and scholarship offers and housing options are not used to manipulate commitments prior to May 1.

8. will, if necessary, establish a wait list that:
   a) is of reasonable length.
   b) is maintained for the shortest possible period and in no case later than August 1.

9. will establish wait list procedures that ensure that no student on any wait list is asked for a deposit in order to remain on the wait list or for a commitment to enroll prior to receiving an official written offer of admission.

10. will state clearly the admission procedures for transfer students by informing candidates of deadlines, documents required, courses accepted, and course equivalency and other relevant policies.

11. will inform students and counselors about new or changed requirements which may adversely affect candidates who have met all required deadlines, deposits, and commitments according to the students' original notification from the institution.

12. will accept, for the purposes of documenting student academic records, only official transcripts in the admission or registration process which come directly from the counseling, guidance, or registrar's offices of the institution(s) the candidate attends or has attended or from other appropriate agencies.

13. will, in the development and administration of their application policies and procedures for early decision programs, abide by the NACAC Guidelines for Admission Decision Options.

14. should admit candidates on the basis of academic and personal criteria rather than financial need. This provision shall not apply to foreign nationals ineligible for federal student assistance.

15. should notify high school personnel when the institution's admission selection committee includes students.

16. should notify candidates as soon as possible if they are clearly inadmissible.

17. should make every effort to provide candidates for financial aid with financial aid decisions as soon as possible following an offer of admission.

B. Secondary School Members agree that they

1. will provide, in a timely manner, for colleges and universities accurate, legible, and complete official transcripts for the school's candidates.

2. will provide colleges and universities with a description of the school's marking system which may include the rank in class and/or grade point average.

3. will in their profiles and other publications provide true and accurate information with regard to test scores for all students in the represented class cohort group who participated in college admission testing.

4. will provide accurate descriptions of the candidates' personal qualities which are relevant to the admission process.

5. will urge candidates to understand and discharge their responsibilities in the admission process. Candidates will be instructed to

a) comply with requests for additional information in a timely manner.

b) respond to institutional deadlines and refrain from stockpiling acceptances.

c) refrain from submitting multiple deposits or making multiple commitments.

d) refrain from submitting more than one application under any early decision plan and, if admitted under such a plan, comply with all institutional guidelines including those regarding the obligations to: enroll, withdraw all other applications, and refrain from submitting subsequent applications.

e) respond to institutional deadlines on housing reservations, financial aid, health records, and course prescheduling, where all or any of these are applicable.

6. will not reveal, unless authorized, candidates' college or university preferences.

7. will sign only one early decision agreement for any student.

8. will counsel students and their families to notify other institutions when they have accepted an admission offer.

9. will encourage students to be the sole authors of their applications and essays and will counsel against inappropriate assistance on the part of others.

10. should report any significant change in candidates' academic status or qualifications, including *personal conduct record*, between the time of recommendation and graduation, where permitted by applicable laws and regulations and if requested by an institution's application.

11. should provide a school profile which clearly describes special curricular opportunities (e.g., honors, Advanced Placement courses, seminars) and a comprehensive listing of all courses with an explanation of unusual abbreviations and any information required for proper understanding.

12. should advise students and their families not to sign any contractual agreement with an institution without examining the provisions of the contract.

13. should counsel students and their families to file a reasonable number of applications.

C. Independent Counselor Members agree that they

1. will urge candidates to recognize and discharge their responsibilities in the admission process. Candidates will be instructed to

a) comply with requests for additional information in a timely manner.

b) respond to institutional deadlines and refrain from stockpiling acceptances.

c) refrain from submitting multiple deposits or making multiple commitments.

d) refrain from submitting more than one application under any early decision plan and, if admitted under such a plan, comply with all institutional guidelines including those regarding the obligations to: enroll, withdraw all other applications, and refrain from submitting subsequent applications.

e) respond to institutional deadlines on housing reservations, financial aid, health records, and course prescheduling, where all or any of these are applicable.

2. will not reveal, unless authorized, candidates' college or university preferences.

3. will follow the process recommended by the candidates' high school for filing college applications.

4. will encourage students to be the sole authors of their applications and essays, and counsel against inappropriate assistance on the part of others.

5. should advise students and their families not to sign any contractual agreement with an institution without examining the provisions of the contract.

6. should counsel students and their families to file a reasonable number of applications.

D. All other members providing college admission counseling services to students agree to adhere to the principles in this Statement.

III. STANDARDIZED COLLEGE ADMISSION TESTING

Members accept the principle that fairness in testing practices should govern all institutional policies. Because test results can never be a precise measurement of human potential, members commit themselves to practices that eliminate bias of any kind, provide equal access, and consider tests as only one measure in admission/counseling practices.

A. College and University Members agree that they

1. will use test scores and related data discreetly and for purposes that are appropriate and validated.

2. will provide prospective students with accurate and complete information about the use of test scores in the admission process.

3. will refrain from using minimum test scores as the sole criterion for admission, thereby denying certain students because of small differences in scores.

4. will use test scores in conjunction with other data such as school record, recommendations, and other relevant information in making decisions.

5. will educate staff in understanding the concepts of test measurement, test interpretation, and test use so they may make informed admission decisions from the test data.

6. will maintain the confidentiality of test scores.

7. will publicize clearly policies relating to placement by tests, awarding of credit, and other policies based on test results.

8. will, in the reporting of test scores, report first on all first-year admitted or enrolled students, or both, including special subgroups (e.g., athletes, nonnative speakers) and then, if they wish, may present separately the score characteristics of special subgroup populations. Universities with more than one undergraduate division may report first by division and then by special subgroups within divisions. Clear explanations of who is included in the subgroup population should be made. Those institutions that do not require tests or for which tests are optional will only report scores if the institution clearly and emphatically states the limits of the group being reported.

9. should conduct institutional research to inquire into the most appropriate use of tests for admission decisions.

10. should counsel students to take only a reasonable number of tests and only those necessary for their postsecondary plans.

11. should refrain from the public reporting of mean and median admission test scores and instead, depending upon the requested information, report scores by any or all of the following methods
   a) middle 50 percent of the scores of all first-year applicants.
   b) middle 50 percent of the scores of all first-year students admitted.
   c) middle 50 percent of the scores of all first-year students enrolled.
   d) appropriate score bands for all first-year students applied, admitted, and enrolled.

B. Secondary School Members agree that they

1. will release and report test scores only with students' consent.

2. will avoid comparing colleges and universities solely on the basis of test scores.

3. will work with other school officials and other groups to keep test results confidential and in perspective.

4. will, in the reporting of test scores, report on *all* students within a discrete class (e.g., freshman, sophomore, junior, senior) who participated in college admission testing.

5. should avoid undue emphasis on test scores as a measure of students' potential and ability when representing students to colleges and universities.

6. should inform students about what tests they need for admission, where they may take them, and how to interpret the results in their own contexts.

7. should be knowledgeable about the limitations of standardized tests and counsel students with these limitations in mind.

8. should inform students about the use and validity of test scores, both for admission and as measures of potential and ability.

9. should counsel students and families on how test scores may be used in the admission process by colleges and universities.

10. should counsel students to take only a reasonable number of those tests necessary for their postsecondary plans, without regard to the impact the test results may have on the school profile report.

11. should counsel students and families about data, other than test results, that may be submitted as part of the application process.

12. should counsel students about test preparation programs and inform them about alternative programs and/or approaches.

13. should refrain from the public reporting of mean and median admission test scores and instead, report scores by either or both of the following:
   a) middle 50 percent of *all* students tested by discrete grade level.
   b) appropriate score bands of *all* students tested by discrete grade level.

C. Independent Counselor Members agree that they

1. will release and report test scores only with students' consent.

2. will avoid comparing colleges and universities solely on the basis of test scores.

3. will avoid undue emphasis on test scores as a measure of students' potential and ability when

representing students to colleges and universities.

4. will work with other school officials and other groups to keep test results confidential and in perspective.

5. should inform students about what tests they need for admission, where they may take them, and how to interpret the results in their own contexts.

6. should be knowledgeable about the limitations of standardized tests and counsel students with these limitations in mind.

7. should inform students about the use and validity of test scores, both for admission and as measures of potential and ability.

8. should counsel students and families on how test scores may be used in the admission process by colleges and universities.

9. should counsel students to take only a reasonable number of tests and only those necessary for their postsecondary plans.

10. should counsel students and families about data, other than test results, that may be submitted as part of the application process.

11. should counsel students about test preparation programs and inform them about alternative programs and/or approaches.

D. All other members providing college admission counseling and/or testing services to students agree to adhere to the principles in this Statement.

IV. FINANCIAL AID

Member institutions are encouraged to support the principle of distributing financial aid funds on the basis of proven financial need. Members agree that financial aid should be offered to candidates in the forms of scholarships, grants, loans, or employment, either alone or in combination. Members agree that financial aid should be viewed as supplementary to the efforts of students' families when students are not self-supporting. No-need scholarship funds should not reduce the total amount of funds available to students with demonstrated need.

A. College and University Members agree that they

1. will, through their publications and communications, provide students, families, and schools with factual and comprehensive information about their institutions' costs, aid opportunities, and practices including practices for foreign nationals.

2. will employ methods in determining the financial contribution of candidates' families and ability to pay, in a consistent and equitable manner.

3. will notify accepted aid applicants of institutional financial aid decisions before the date by which a reply must be made to the offer of admission, assuming all forms are in on time.

4. will make awards to students who apply for renewal of financial aid by reviewing their current financial circumstances and establishing the amount of aid needed.

5. will permit first-year candidates for fall admission to choose, without penalty, among offers of financial aid until May 1. Colleges that solicit commitments to offers of need-based and/or merit-based financial aid prior to May 1 may do so provided those offers include a clear statement that written requests for extensions until May 1 will be granted, and that such requests will not jeopardize a student's status for housing and/or financial aid. Candidates admitted under an early decision program are a recognized exception to this provision.

6. will state clearly policies on renewal of financial aid.

7. will not publicly announce the amount of need-based aid awarded to candidates; however, amounts of no-need scholarship awards may be a matter of public record.

8. will not make financial aid awards to students who have committed to attend other institutions unless the students initiate such inquiries.

9. will not make financial aid awards to students who have not submitted admission applications.

10. will refrain from withholding financial aid awards until the awards from the students' other college choices have been announced.

11. should refrain from using financial need as a consideration in selecting students. This provision shall not apply to foreign nationals ineligible for federal student assistance.

12. should, to the extent possible, within the institutions' capabilities, meet the full need of accepted students.

B. Secondary School Members agree that they

1. will refrain, in public announcements, from giving the amounts of financial aid received by individual students; however, amounts of no-need scholarship awards may be a matter of public record.

2. will not guarantee financial aid or scholarship awards.

3. should not encourage students to apply to particular colleges and universities to enhance their high schools' statistical records regarding number or amount of scholarship awards received.
4. should advise students who have been awarded financial aid by non-collegiate sources that they have the responsibility to notify the college of the type and amount of such outside aid.

C. Independent Counselor Members agree that they

1. will refrain, in public announcements, from giving the amounts of financial aid received by individual students; however, amounts of no-need scholarship awards may be a matter of public record.
2. will not guarantee financial aid or scholarship awards.
3. should advise students who have been awarded financial aid by non-collegiate sources that they have the responsibility to notify the college of the type and amount of such outside aid.

D. All other members providing college admission counseling services to students agree to adhere to the principles in this Statement.

V. ADVANCED STANDING STUDENTS AND THE AWARDING OF CREDIT

A. College and University Members agree that they

1. will design placement, credit, and exemption policies to augment educational placement opportunities, not to recruit students.
2. will evaluate student competency through the use of validated methods and techniques.
3. will define and publish in the institutions' preadmission information the policies and procedures for granting credit.
4. will evaluate previously earned credit, published by the admitting college or university, in a manner which ensures the integrity of academic standards as well as the principle of fairness to the students.

B. Secondary School Members agree that they

1. will alert students to the full implications of college and university placement, credit, and exemption policies with regard to their educational planning and goals.
2. will make students aware of the importance of accreditation.
3. will make students aware of the possibilities of earning credit through both nontraditional educational experiences and examinations and alternative methods of instruction.

C. Independent Counselor Members agree that they

1. will alert students to the full implications of college and university placement, credit, and exemption policies with regard to their educational planning and goals.
2. will make students aware of the importance of accreditation.
3. will make students aware of the possibilities of earning credit through both nontraditional educational experiences and examinations and alternative methods of instruction.

D. All other members providing admission counseling services to students agree to adhere to the principles in this Statement.

NATIONAL ASSOCIATION FOR HOME CARE

Address: 228 Seventh Street SE
Washington, DC 20003
Telephone: 202/547-7424
WWW: www.nahc.org
Document: Code of Ethics (1982)

PREAMBLE

The National Association for Home Care (NAHC) was founded with the intention of encouraging the development and the delivery of the highest quality of medical, social, and supportive services to the aged, infirm, and disabled.

In the process of bringing these essential services to the needy, the Association and its members seek to establish and retain the highest possible level of public confidence.

This Code of Ethics, adopted by the NAHC Board of Directors in September 1982, serves as a statement to the general public that the Association and its individual members stand for integrity and the highest ethical standards.

This Code of Ethics serves to inform members and the general public as to what are acceptable guidelines for ethical conduct for home care agencies and their employees.

It is inherent in the declaration of this Code of Ethics that the Association and its members pledge to protect and preserve the basic rights of their patients and to deal with them in an honest and ethical manner.

Finally, the Code of Ethics serves as notice to government officials that the Association expects its members to abide by all applicable laws and regulations. It is a precondition of membership in the Association that they do so and that failure to comply will result in expulsion from membership in the Association in addition to other penalties prescribed by law.

The Code of Ethics is intended to serve as a guideline to agencies in the following areas:

A. Patient Rights and Responsibilities
B. Relationships to Other Provider Agencies
C. Responsibility to the National Association for Home Care
D. Fiscal Responsibilities
E. Marketing and Public Relations
F. Personnel
G. Legislative
H. Hearing Process

A. PATIENT RIGHTS AND RESPONSIBILITIES

It is anticipated that observance of these rights and responsibilities will contribute to more effective patient care and greater satisfaction for the patient as well as the agency. The rights will be respected by all agency personnel and integrated into all home care agency programs. A copy of these rights will be prominently displayed within the agency and made available to patients upon request.

1. The patient is fully informed of all his/her rights and responsibilities.
2. The patient has the right to appropriate and professional care relating to physician orders.
3. The patient has the right of choice of care providers.
4. The patient has the right to receive information necessary to give informed consent prior to the start of any procedure or treatment.
5. The patient has the right to refuse treatment within the confines of the law and to be informed of the consequences of his action.
6. The patient has the right to privacy.
7. The patient has the right to receive a timely response to his request for service from the agency.
8. A patient will be admitted for service only if the agency has the ability to provide safe professional care at the level of intensity needed. The patient has the right to reasonable continuity of care.
9. The patient has the right to be informed within reasonable time of anticipated termination of service or plans for transfer to another agency.
10. The patient has the right to voice grievances and suggest changes in service or staff without fear of restraint or discrimination.

A fair hearing shall be available to any individual to whom service has been denied, reduced, or terminated or who is otherwise aggrieved by agency action. The fair hearing procedure shall be set forth by each agency as appropriate to the unique patient situation (e.g., funding source, level of care, diagnosis).
11. The patient has the right to be fully informed of agency policies and charges for services, including eligibility for third-party reimbursements.
12. A patient denied service solely on his/her inability to pay shall have the right of referral.
13. The patient and the public have the right to honest, accurate forthright information regarding the home care industry in general and his/her chosen agency in particular (e.g., cost/visit, employee qualifications).

B. RELATIONSHIPS TO OTHER PROVIDER AGENCIES

1. The principle objective of Home Care Agencies is to provide the best possible service to patients. Agencies shall honestly and conscientiously cooperate in providing information about referrals and shall work together to assure comprehensive services to patients and their families.
2. Members shall engage in ethical conduct of their affairs so that maximum fair trade occurs.

C. RESPONSIBILITY TO NAHC

1. The Bylaws and policies of NAHC reflect mutual cooperation among members in attaining goals that assure quality care for the patient and family. The members of NAHC shall abide by those Bylaws and policies. Adjudication or arbitration procedures of the Association shall be used to resolve ethical complaints between members as provided in Section "H" of this document.

2. Members shall promptly pay all membership dues and shall participate and contribute talent to foster a dynamic, progressive organization from which all members can benefit professionally.

D. FISCAL RESPONSIBILITIES

1. The amount of service billed is consistent with amount and type of service provided.
2. The cost per visit includes only legitimate expenses.
3. The medical equipment sold or rented to patients is provided at the lowest possible cost consistent with quality, quantity, and timeliness.
4. The salaries and benefits of the provider and administrative staff shall be consistent with the size of the agency, responsibility, and geographical location.
5. The provider shall not engage in kickbacks and payoffs.
6. The provider shall submit dues to NAHC based on the actual revenues received from all home care activities for the previous year.

E. MARKETING AND PUBLIC RELATIONS

1. Oral and written statements will fairly represent service, benefits, cost, and agency capability.
2. Agencies which promote their service in the public media shall include information descriptive of home care in general, as well as agency-specific information.

F. PERSONNEL

1. The agency shall be an equal opportunity employer and comply with all applicable laws, rules, and regulations.
2. The Agency shall have written personnel policies available to all employees and uniformly applied to all employees.
3. The agency shall provide an ongoing evaluation process for all employees.
4. The agency shall hire qualified employees and utilize them at the level of their competency.
5. The agency shall provide supervision to all employees.
6. The agency shall provide continuing education and inservice training for all employees to update knowledge and skills needed to give competent patient care.
7. The agency shall hire adequate staffing to meet the needs of the patients to whom they render care.
8. The agency shall have a pay scale that is consistent with the geographical location and pay only

for those travel and business expenses that are within a reasonable norm.

G. LEGISLATIVE

Members determined under the provisions of Section "H" to be in violation of this Code shall be subject to disciplinary action, suspension, and/or expulsion from the National Association for Home Care.

H. HEARING PROCESS

In the event of an apparent breach of conduct reflected in this Code or any dispute arising out of allegations of misconduct, redress will be provided in the form of a hearing before an Ethics Committee composed of at least three disinterested parties.

The Committee shall be appointed by the Chairman of the Board and approved by the Board of Directors to hear specific disputes. The Committee shall be noncontinuous, dissolving at the conclusion of its appointed task. Service on the Committee shall be restricted to representatives of NAHC member agencies in good standing.

The Committee by majority vote may suspend or expel a member from the National Association for Home Care or fashion other forms of disciplinary action which are less severe if justified by the Committee's finding of fact.

Judgements of the Committee shall be final and binding with respect to the provisions of this Code. The Committee shall be bound by all the common requirements of due process including, but not limited to, giving the accused a statement of the charges against him/her, an opportunity to appear on his/her own behalf, proper notice of the time and place for any hearing to be conducted by the Committee, the right to suggest witnesses to be heard by the Committee, and the right to representation by counsel with the understanding that counsel may appear to advise his/her client but may not actually testify on behalf of his/her client.

The Committee may require the testimony of individuals under oath administered by a duly qualified notary public. However, if the Committee elects to proceed in this manner, the entire proceeding must be transcribed and retained in the files of the Association.

An accused faced with disciplinary action may appeal the Committee's ruling to the full NAHC Board of Directors. The Committee's decision will be sustained unless two-thirds of the members of the Board, a quorum being present, vote to overturn the decision.

NATIONAL ASSOCIATION OF ALCOHOLISM AND DRUG ABUSE COUNSELORS

Address: 1911 North Fort Myer Drive, Suite 900
              Arlington, VA 22209
Telephone: 703/741-7686 or 800/548-0497
WWW: www.naadac.org
Document: NAADAC Code of Ethics (1987.
              Most recently revised 1995.)

Principle 1: Non-Discrimination

The NAADAC member shall not discriminate against clients or professionals based on race, religion, age, gender, disability, national ancestry, sexual orientation or economic condition.

a. The NAADAC member shall avoid bringing personal or professional issues into the counseling relationship. Through an awareness of the impact of stereotyping and discrimination, the member guards the individual rights and personal dignity of clients.

b. The NAADAC member shall be knowledgeable about disabling conditions, demonstrate empathy and personal emotional comfort in interactions with clients with disabilities, and make available physical, sensory and cognitive accommodations that allow clients with disabilities to receive services.

Principle 2: Responsibility

The NAADAC member shall espouse objectivity and integrity, and maintain the highest standards in the services the member offers.

a. The NAADAC member shall maintain respect for institutional policies and management functions of the agencies and institutions within which the services are being performed, but will take initiative toward improving such policies when it will better serve the interest of the client.

b. The NAADAC member, as educator, has a primary obligation to help others acquire knowledge and skills in dealing with the disease of alcoholism and drug abuse.

c. The NAADAC member who supervises others accepts the obligation to facilitate further professional development of these individuals by providing accurate and current information, timely evaluations and constructive consultation.

d. The NAADAC member who is aware of unethical conduct or of unprofessional modes of practice shall report such inappropriate behavior to the appropriate authority.

Principle 3: Competence

The NAADAC member shall recognize that the profession is founded on national standards of competency which promote the best interests of society, of the client, of the member and of the profession as a whole. The NAADAC member shall recognize the need for ongoing education as a component of professional competency.

a. The NAADAC member shall recognize boundaries and limitations of the member's competencies and not offer services or use techniques outside of these professional competencies.

b. The NAADAC member shall recognize the effect of impairment on professional performance and shall be willing to seek appropriate treatment for oneself or for a colleague. The member shall support peer assistance programs in this respect.

Principle 4: Legal and Moral Standards

The NAADAC member shall uphold the legal and accepted moral codes which pertain to professional conduct.

a. The NAADAC member shall be fully cognizant of all federal laws and laws of the member's respective state governing the practice of alcoholism and drug abuse counseling.

b. The NAADAC member shall not claim either directly or by implication, professional qualifications/affiliations that the member does not possess.

c. The NAADAC member shall ensure that products or services associated with or provided by the member by means of teaching, demonstration, publications or other types of media meet the ethical standards of this code.

Principle 5: Public Statements

The NAADAC member shall honestly respect the limits of present knowledge in public statements concerning alcoholism and drug abuse.

a. The NAADAC member, in making statements to clients, other professionals, and the general public shall state as fact only those matters which have been empirically validated as fact. All other opinions, speculations, and conjecture concerning the nature of alcoholism and drug abuse, its natural history, its treatment or any other matters which touch on the subject of alcoholism and drug abuse shall be represented as less than scientifically validated.

b. The NAADAC member shall acknowledge and accurately report the substantiation and support for statements made concerning the nature of alcoholism and drug abuse, its natural history, and its treatment. Such acknowledgment should extend to the source of the information and reliability of the method by which it was derived.

Principle 6: Publication Credit

The NAADAC member shall assign credit to all who have contributed to the published material and for the work upon which the publication is based.

a. The NAADAC member shall recognize joint authorship and major contributions of a professional nature made by one or more persons to a common project. The author who has made the principal contribution to a publication must be identified as first author.

b. The NAADAC member shall acknowledge in footnotes or in an introductory statement minor contributions of a professional nature, extensive clerical or similar assistance and other minor contributions.

c. The NAADAC member shall in no way violate the copyright of anyone by reproducing material in any form whatsoever, except in those ways which are allowed under the copyright laws. This involves direct violation of copyright as well as the passive assent to the violation of copyright by others.

Principle 7: Client Welfare

The NAADAC member shall promote the protection of the public health, safety and welfare and the best interest of the client as a primary guide in determining the conduct of all NAADAC members.

a. The NAADAC member shall disclose the member's code of ethics, professional loyalties and responsibilities to all clients.

b. The NAADAC member shall terminate a counseling or consulting relationship when it is reasonably clear to the member that the client is not benefiting from the relationship.

c. The NAADAC member shall hold the welfare of the client paramount when making any decisions or recommendations concerning referral, treatment procedures or termination of treatment.

d. The NAADAC member shall not use or encourage a client's participation in any demonstration, research or other non-treatment activities when such participation would have potential harmful consequences for the client or when the client is not fully informed. (See Principle 9)

e. The NAADAC member shall take care to provide services in an environment which will ensure the privacy and safety of the client at all times and ensure the appropriateness of service delivery.

Principle 8: Confidentiality

The NAADAC member working in the best interest of the client shall embrace, as a primary obligation, the duty of protecting client's rights under confidentiality and shall not disclose confidential information acquired in teaching, practice or investigation without appropriately executed consent.

a. The NAADAC member must provide the client his/ her rights regarding confidentiality, in writing, as part of informing the client in any areas likely to affect the client's confidentiality. This includes the recording of the clinical interview, the use of material for insurance purposes, the use of material for training or observation by another party.

b. The NAADAC member shall make appropriate provisions for the maintenance of confidentiality and the ultimate disposition of confidential records. The member shall ensure that data obtained, including any form of electronic communication, are secured by the available security methodology. Data shall be limited to information that is necessary and appropriate to the services being provided and be accessible only to appropriate personnel.

c. The NAADAC member shall adhere to all federal and state laws regarding confidentiality and the member's responsibility to report clinical information in specific circumstances to the appropriate authorities.

d. The NAADAC member shall discuss the information obtained in clinical, consulting, or observational relationships only in the appropriate settings for professional purposes that are in the client's best interest. Written and oral reports must present only data germane and pursuant to the purpose of evaluation, diagnosis, progress, and compliance. Every effort shall be made to avoid undue invasion of privacy.

e. The NAADAC member shall use clinical and other material in teaching and/or writing only when there is no identifying information used about the parties involved.

Principle 9: Client Relationships

It is the responsibility of the NAADAC member to safeguard the integrity of the counseling relationship and to ensure that the client has reasonable access to effective treatment.

The NAADAC member shall provide the client and/or guardian with accurate and complete information regarding the extent of the potential professional relationship.

a. The NAADAC member shall inform the client and obtain the client's agreement in areas likely to affect the client's participation including the recording of an interview, the use of interview material for training purposes, and/or observation of an interview by another person.

b. The NAADAC member shall not engage in professional relationships or commitments that conflict with family members, friends, close associates, or others whose welfare might be jeopardized by such a dual relationship.

c. The NAADAC member shall not exploit relationships with current or former clients for personal gain, including social or business relationships.

d. The NAADAC member shall not under any circumstances engage in sexual behavior with current or former clients.

e. The NAADAC member shall not accept as clients anyone with whom they have engaged in sexual behavior.

Principle 10: Interprofessional Relationships

The NAADAC member shall treat colleagues with respect, courtesy, fairness, and good faith and shall afford the same to other professionals.

a. The NAADAC member shall refrain from offering professional services to a client in counseling with another professional except with the knowledge of the other professional or after the termination of the client's relationship with the other professional.

b. The NAADAC member shall cooperate with duly constituted professional ethics committees and promptly supply necessary information unless constrained by the demands of confidentiality.

c. The NAADAC member shall not in any way exploit relationships with supervisees, employees, students, research participants or volunteers.

Principle 11: Remuneration

The NAADAC member shall establish financial arrangements in professional practice and in accord with the professional standards that safeguard the best interests of the client first, and then of the counselor, the agency, and the profession.

a. The NAADAC member shall inform the client of all financial policies. In circumstances where an agency dictates explicit provisions with its staff for private consultations, clients shall be made fully aware of these policies.

b. The NAADAC member shall consider the ability of a client to meet the financial cost in establishing rates for professional services.

c. The NAADAC member shall not engage in fee splitting. The member shall not send or receive any commission or rebate or any other form of remuneration for referral of clients for professional services.

d. The NAADAC member, in the practice of counseling, shall not at any time use one's relationship with clients for personal gain or for the profit of an agency or any commercial enterprise of any kind.

e. The NAADAC member shall not accept a private fee for professional work with a person who is entitled to such services through an institution or agency unless the client is informed of such services and still requests private services.

Principle 12: Societal Obligations

The NAADAC member shall to the best of his/her ability actively engage the legislative processes, educational institutions, and the general public to change public policy and legislation to make possible opportunities and choice of service for all human beings of any ethnic or social background whose lives are impaired by alcoholism and drug abuse.

NATIONAL ASSOCIATION OF COLLEGES AND EMPLOYERS

Address: 62 Highland Avenue
              Bethlehem, PA 18017-9085
Telephone: 610/868-1421 or 800/544-5272
WWW: www.jobweb.org/nace/
Document: Principles for Professional Conduct
              for Career Services & Employment
              Professionals (1994)

(The National Association of Colleges and Employers, formerly called the College Placement Council, Inc., also publishes *Principles for Third-Party Recruiters* and *A Faculty Guide to Ethical and Legal Standards in Student Hiring* which are not reprinted here.—Eds.)

Career services and employment professionals are involved in an important process—helping students choose and attain personally rewarding careers, and helping employers develop effective college relations programs which contribute to effective candidate selections for their organizations. The impact of this process upon individuals and organizations requires commitment by practitioners to principles for professional conduct.

Career services and employment professionals are involved in this process in a partnership effort, with a common goal of achieving the best match between the individual student and the employing organiza-

tion. The National Association of Colleges and Employers (NACE, formerly the College Placement Council, Inc.), as the national professional association for career planning, placement, and recruitment, is also concerned with this process. The concern led NACE to the development and adoption of the *Principles for Professional Conduct*. The principles presented here are designed to provide practitioners with three basic precepts for career planning, placement, and recruitment:

• Maintain an open and free selection of employment opportunities in an atmosphere conducive to objective thought, where job candidates can choose optimum long-term uses of their talents that are consistent with personal objectives and all relevant facts;

• Maintain a recruitment process that is fair and equitable to candidates and employing organizations;

• Support informed and responsible decision making by candidates.

Adherence to the guidelines will support the collaborative effort of career planning, placement, and recruitment professionals while reducing the potential for abuses. The guidelines also apply to new technology or third-party recruiting relationships which may be substituted for the traditional personal interaction among career services professionals, employer professionals, and students.

These principles are not all-inclusive; they are intended to serve as a framework within which the career planning, placement, and recruitment processes should function, and as a foundation upon which professionalism can be promoted.

As part of NACE's commitment to provide leadership in the ethics area and to facilitate the ongoing dialogue on ethics-related issues, the NACE Principles for Professional Conduct Committee was established. The committee, made up of representatives of each of the six regions—Western Association of Colleges and Employers (WACE), Rocky Mountain Association of Colleges and Employers (RMACE), Southwest Association of Colleges & Employers (SWACE), Southeastern Association of Colleges and Employers (SACE), Midwest Association of Colleges and Employers (Midwest ACE), and Eastern Association of Colleges and Employers (EACE)—will provide advisory opinions to members on the application of the *Principles*, act as an informational clearinghouse for various ethical issues arising within the regions, periodically review and recommend changes to this document, and resolve problems which may arise.

It is important to keep in mind one final point. The *Principles* do not address certain professional obligations to support state and regional associations, professional development programs, salary surveys, and other demographic trend surveys. Obligations such as these are recognized as vital to the continuing growth of our profession, but since they do not relate directly to the recruitment process, they are not addressed specifically in this document. However, the National Association of Colleges and Employers Board of Governors strongly encourages career services and employment professionals to support and participate in these activities.

Principles for Career Services Professionals

1. Career services professionals, without imposing personal values or biases, will assist individuals in developing a career plan or making a career decision.

2. Career services professionals will know the career services field and the educational institution and students they represent, and will have appropriate counseling skills.

3. Career services professionals will provide students with information on a range of career opportunities and types of employing organizations. They will inform students of the means and resources to gain access to information which may influence their decisions about an employing organization. Career services professionals will also provide employing organizations with accurate information about the educational institution and its students and about the recruitment policies of the career services office.

4. Career services professionals will provide generally comparable services to all employers, regardless of whether the employers contribute services, gifts, or financial support to the educational institution or office and regardless of the level of such support.

5. Career services professionals will establish reasonable and fair guidelines for access to services by employers. When guidelines permit access to organizations recruiting on behalf of an employer and to international employers, the following principles will apply:
   a) Organizations providing recruiting services for a fee will be required to inform career services of the specific employer they represent and the specific jobs for which they are recruiting, and will permit verification of the

information. Third-party recruiters that charge fees to students will not be permitted access to career services;
   b) Employers recruiting for work outside of the United States are expected to adhere to the equal employment opportunity (EEO) policy of the career services office. They will advise the career services office and the students of the realities of working in that country and of any cultural and foreign law differences.

6. Career services professionals will maintain EEO compliance and follow affirmative action principles in career services activities in a manner that includes the following:
   a) Referring all interested students for employment opportunities without regard to race, color, national origin, religion, age, gender, sexual orientation, or disability, and providing reasonable accommodations upon request;
   b) Notifying employing organizations of any selection procedures that appear to have an adverse impact based upon the student's race, color, national origin, religion, age, gender, sexual orientation, or disability;
   c) Assisting recruiters in accessing certain groups on campus to provide a more inclusive applicant pool;
   d) Informing all students about employment opportunities, with particular emphasis on those employment opportunities in occupational areas where certain groups of students are underrepresented;
   e) Developing awareness of, and sensitivity to, cultural differences and the diversity of students, and providing responsive services;
   f) Responding to complaints of EEO noncompliance, working to resolve such complaints with the recruiter or employing organization, and, if necessary, referring such complaints to the appropriate campus department or agency.

7. Any disclosure of student information outside of the educational institution will be with prior consent of the student unless health and/or safety considerations necessitate the dissemination of such information. Career services professionals will exercise sound judgment and fairness in maintaining the confidentiality of student information, regardless of the source, including written records, reports, and computer data bases.

8. Only qualified personnel will evaluate or interpret tests of a career planning and placement na-

ture. Students will be informed of the availability of testing, the purpose of such tests, and the disclosure policies regarding test results.

9. If the charging of fees for career services becomes necessary, such fees will be appropriate to the budgetary needs of the office and will not hinder student or employer access to services. Career services professionals are encouraged to counsel student and university organizations engaged in recruitment activities to follow this principle.

10. Career services professionals will advise students about their obligations in the recruitment process and establish mechanisms to encourage their compliance. Students' obligations include providing accurate information; adhering to schedules; accepting an offer of employment in good faith; notifying employers on a timely basis of an acceptance or nonacceptance and withdrawing from the recruiting process after accepting an offer of employment; interviewing only with employers for whom students are interested in working and whose eligibility requirements they meet; and requesting reimbursement of only reasonable and legitimate expenses incurred in the recruitment process.

11. Career services professionals will provide services to international students consistent with U.S. immigration laws; inform those students about these laws; represent the reality of the available job market in the United States; encourage pursuit of only those employment opportunities in the United States that meet the individual's work authorization; and encourage pursuit of eligible international employment opportunities.

12. Career services professionals will promote and encourage acceptance of these principles throughout their educational institution, and will respond to reports of noncompliance.

Principles for Employment Professionals

1. Employment professionals will refrain from any practice that improperly influences and affects job acceptances. Such practices may include undue time pressure for acceptance of employment offers and encouragement of revocation of another employment offer. Employment professionals will strive to communicate decisions to candidates within the agreed-upon time frame.

2. Employment professionals will know the recruitment and career development field as well as the industry and the employing organization that they represent, and work within a framework of professionally accepted recruiting, interviewing, and selection techniques.

3. Employment professionals will supply accurate information on their organization and employment opportunities. Employing organizations are responsible for information supplied and commitments made by their representatives. If conditions change and require the employing organization to revoke its commitment, the employing organization will pursue a course of action for the affected candidate that is fair and equitable.

4. Neither employment professionals nor their organizations will expect, or seek to extract, special favors or treatment which would influence the recruitment process as a result of support, or the level of support, to the educational institution or career services office in the form of contributed services, gifts, or other financial support.

5. Employment professionals are strongly discouraged from serving alcohol as part of the recruitment process. However, if alcohol is served, it will be limited and handled in a responsible manner in accordance with the law and the institution's and employer's policies.

6. Employment professionals will maintain equal employment opportunity (EEO) compliance and follow affirmative action principles in recruiting activities in a manner that includes the following:
   a) Recruiting, interviewing, and hiring individuals without regard to race, color, national origin, religion, age, gender, sexual orientation, or disability, and providing reasonable accommodations upon request;
   b) Reviewing selection criteria for adverse impact based upon the student's race, color, national origin, religion, age, gender, sexual orientation, or disability;
   c) Avoiding use of inquiries that are considered unacceptable by EEO standards during the recruiting process;
   d) Developing a sensitivity to, and awareness of, cultural differences and the diversity of the work force;
   e) Informing campus constituencies of special activities that have been developed to achieve the employer's affirmative action goals;
   f) Investigating complaints forwarded by the career services office regarding EEO noncompliance and seeking resolution of such complaints.

7. Employment professionals will maintain the confidentiality of student information, regardless of the source, including personal knowledge, written records/reports, and computer data bases. There will be no disclosure of student information to another organization without the prior written consent of the student, unless necessitated by health and/or safety considerations.

8. Those engaged in administering, evaluating, and interpreting assessment tools, tests, and technology used in selection will be trained and qualified to do so. Employment professionals must advise the career services office of any test conducted on campus and eliminate such a test if it violates campus policies. Employment professionals must advise students in a timely fashion of the type and purpose of any test that students will be required to take as part of the recruitment process and to whom the test results will be disclosed. All tests will be reviewed by the employing organization for disparate impact and job-relatedness.

9. When using organizations that provide recruiting services for a fee, employment professionals will respond to inquiries by the career services office regarding this relationship and the positions the organization was contracted to fill. This principle applies equally to any other form of recruiting that is used as a substitute for the traditional employer/student interaction.

10. When employment professionals conduct recruitment activities through student associations or academic departments, such activities will be conducted in accordance with the policies of the career services office.

11. Employment professionals will cooperate with the policies and procedures of the career services office, including certification of EEO compliance or exempt status under the Immigration Reform and Control Act, and will honor scheduling arrangements and recruitment commitments.

12. Employment professionals recruiting for international operations will do so according to EEO standards. Employment professionals will advise the career services office and students of the realities of working in that country and of any cultural or foreign law differences.

13. Employment professionals will educate and encourage acceptance of these principles throughout their employing institution and by third parties representing their employing organization on

campus, and will respond to reports of noncompliance.

NATIONAL ASSOCIATION OF COUNTIES

Address: 440 First Street NW
              Washington, DC 20001-2080
Telephone: 202/393-6226
WWW: www.naco.org
Document: Code of Ethics for County Officials
              (1991)

Preamble

The National Association of Counties (NACo) is committed to the highest standards of conduct by and among county officials in the performance of their public duties. Individual and collective adherence to high ethical standards by public officials is central to the maintenance of public trust and confidence in government.

While county officials agree on the need for proper conduct, they may experience personal conflict or differing views of values or loyalties.

In such cases the principles contained in this Code of Ethics provide valuable guidance in reaching decisions which are governed, ultimately, by the dictates of the individual conscience of the public official and his or her commitment to the public good.

Certain of these ethical principles are best expressed as positive statements: actions which should be taken; courses which should be followed; goals which should permeate both public and private conduct. Other principles are expressed as negative statements: actions to be avoided and conduct to be condemned.

The Code of Ethics for County Officials has been created by and for elected county officials. However, these principles apply to the day to day conduct of both elected and appointed officials and employees of county government.

NACo recognizes that this Code of Ethics should serve as a valuable reference guide for all those in whom the public has placed its trust.

Ethical Principles

The ethical county official should:

- Properly administer the affairs of the county.
- Promote decisions which only benefit the public interest.
- Actively promote public confidence in county government.
- Keep safe all funds and other properties of the county.
- Conduct and perform the duties of the office diligently and promptly dispose of the business of the county.
- Maintain a positive image to pass constant public scrutiny.
- Evaluate all decisions so that the best service or product is obtained at a minimal cost without sacrificing quality and fiscal responsibility.
- Inject the prestige of the office into everyday dealings with the public, employees and associates.
- Maintain a respectful attitude toward employees, other public officials, colleagues and associates.
- Effectively and efficiently work with governmental agencies, political subdivisions and other organizations in order to further the interest of the county.
- Faithfully comply with all laws and regulations applicable to the county and impartially apply them to everyone.

The ethical county official should not:

- Engage in outside interests that are not compatible with the impartial and objective performance of his or her duties.
- Improperly influence or attempt to influence other officials to act in his or her own benefit.
- Accept anything of value from any source which is offered to influence his or her action as a public official.

The ethical county official accepts the responsibility that his or her mission is that of servant and steward to the public.

National Association of Credit Management

NATIONAL ASSOCIATION OF CREDIT MANAGEMENT

Address: 8840 Columbia 100 Parkway
              Columbia, MD 21045-2158
Telephone: 410/740-5560
WWW: www.nacm.org
Document: Canons of Business Credit Ethics

    I. Justice, equity and confidence constitute the foundation of credit administration.

   II. Agreements and contracts reflect integrity and should never be breached by either party.

 III. The interchange of credit information must be based upon confidence, cooperation, reciprocity and confidentiality.

 IV. It is deemed unethical to be a party to unwarranted assignments or transfers of an insolvent debtor's assets nor should creditors participate in secret arrangements.

  V. Creditors should cooperate for the benefit of all in adjustment or liquidation of insolvent estates or companies.

 VI. Creditors must render all possible assistance to honest debtors who become insolvent.

 VII. Dishonest debtors must be exposed and referred to the authorities.

VIII. Cooperation, fairness and honesty must dominate in all insolvent debtor proceedings.

 IX. Costly administrative procedures in the rehabilitation or liquidation of an insolvent debtor shall be avoided at all times.

  X. Members pledge themselves to uphold the integrity, dignity and honor of the credit professional in all of their business dealings.

NATIONAL ASSOCIATION OF EMERGENCY MEDICAL TECHNICIANS

Address: 408 Monroe Street
              Clinton, MS 39056-4210
Telephone: 601/924-7744 or 800/346-2368
WWW: www.naemt.org
Document: The EMT Code of Ethics (1978)

Professional status as an Emergency Medical Technician and Emergency Medical Technician-Paramedic is maintained and enriched by the willingness of the individual practitioner to accept and fulfill obligations to society, other medical professionals and the profession of Emergency Medical Technician. As an Emergency Medical Technician at the basic level or an Emergency Medical Technician-Paramedic, I solemnly pledge myself to the following code of professional ethics:

A fundamental responsibility of the Emergency Medical Technician is to conserve life, to alleviate suffering, to promote health, to do no harm, and to encourage the quality and equal availability of emergency medical care.

The Emergency Medical Technician provides services based on human need, with respect for human dignity, unrestricted by consideration of nationality, race, creed, color or status.

The Emergency Medical Technician does not use professional knowledge and skills in any enterprise detrimental to the public well-being.

The Emergency Medical Technician respects and holds in confidence all information of a confidential nature obtained in the course of professional work unless required by law to divulge such information.

The Emergency Medical Technician, as a citizen, understands and upholds the law and performs the duties of citizenship; as a professional, the Emergency Medical Technician has the never-ending responsibility to work with concerned citizens and other health care professionals in promoting a high standard of emergency medical care to all people.

The Emergency Medical Technician shall maintain professional competence and demonstrate concern for the competence of other members of the Emergency Medical Services health care team.

An Emergency Medical Technician assumes responsibility in defining and upholding standards of professional practice and education.

The Emergency Medical Technician assumes responsibility for individual professional actions and judgment, both in dependent and independent emergency functions, and knows and upholds the laws which affect the practice of the Emergency Medical Technician.

An Emergency Medical Technician has the responsibility to be aware of and participate in matters of legislation affecting the Emergency Medical Technician and the Emergency Medical Services System.

The Emergency Medical Technician adheres to standards of personal ethics which reflect credit upon the profession.

Emergency Medical Technicians, or groups of Emergency Medical Technicians, who advertise professional services, do so in conformity with the dignity of the profession.

The Emergency Medical Technician has an obligation to protect the public by not delegating to a person less qualified any service which requires the professional competence of an Emergency Medical Technician.

The Emergency Medical Technician will work harmoniously with, and sustain confidence in, Emergency Medical Technician associates, the nurse, the physician and other members of the emergency medical services health care team.

The Emergency Medical Technician refuses to participate in unethical procedures, and assumes the responsibility to expose incompetence or unethical conduct of others to the appropriate authority in a proper and professional manner.

NATIONAL ASSOCIATION OF ENVIRONMENTAL PROFESSIONALS

Address: Three Adams Street
              South Portland, ME 04106-1606
Telephone: 207/767-1505 or 888/251-9902
WWW: www.naep.org
Document: Code of Ethics and Standards of
              Practice for Environmental
              Professionals

The objectives of Environmental Professionals are to conduct their personal and professional lives and activities in an ethical manner. Honesty, justice and courtesy form moral philosophy which, associated with a mutual interest among people, constitute the foundation of ethics. Environmental Professionals should recognize such a standard, not in passive observance, but as a set of dynamic principles guiding their conduct and way of life. It is their duty to practice their profession according to this **Code of Ethics**.

As the keystone of professional conduct is integrity, Environmental Professionals will discharge their duties with fidelity to the public, their employers, clients, and with fairness and impartiality to all. It is their duty to interest themselves in public welfare, and to be ready to apply their special knowledge for the benefit of mankind and their environment.

Creed

The objectives of an Environmental Professional are:

1. to recognize and attempt to reconcile societal and individual human needs with responsibility for physical, natural, and cultural systems.

2. to promote and develop policies, plans, activities and projects that achieve complementary and mutual support between natural and man-made, and present and future components of the physical, natural and cultural environment.

Ethics

As an Environmental Professional I will:

1. be personally responsible for the validity of all data collected, analyses performed, or plans developed by me or under my direction. I will be responsible and ethical in my professional activities.

2. encourage research, planning, design, management and review of activities in a scientifically and technically objective manner. I will incorporate the best principles of the environmental sciences for the mitigation of environmental harm and enhancement of environmental quality.

3. not condone misrepresentation of work I have performed or that was performed under my direction.

4. examine all of my relationships or actions which could be legitimately interpreted as a conflict of interest by clients, officials, the public or peers. In any instance where I have a financial or personal interest in the activities with which they are directly or indirectly involved, I will make a full disclosure of that interest to my employer, client, or other affected parties.

5. not engage in conduct involving dishonesty, fraud, deceit or misrepresentation or discrimination.

6. not accept fees wholly or partially contingent on the client's desired result where that desired result conflicts with my professional judgement.

Guidance for Practice as an Environmental Professional

As an Environmental Professional I will:

1. encourage environmental planning to begin in the earliest stages of project conceptualization.

2. recognize that total environmental management involves the consideration of all environmental factors including: technical, economic, ecological, and sociopolitical and their relationships.

3. incorporate the best principle of design and environmental planning when recommending measures to reduce environmental harm and enhance environmental quality.

4. conduct my analysis, planning, design and review my activities primarily in subject areas for which

I am qualified, and shall encourage and recognize the participation of other professionals in subject areas where I am less experienced. I shall utilize and participate in interdisciplinary teams wherever practical to determine impacts, define and evaluate all reasonable alternatives to proposed actions, and assess short-term versus long-term productivity with and without the project or action.

5. seek common, adequate, and sound technical grounds for communication with and respect for the contributions of other professionals in developing and reviewing policies, plans, activities, and projects.
6. determine that the policies, plans, activities or projects in which I am involved are consistent with all governing laws, ordinances, guidelines, plans, and policies, to the best of my knowledge and ability.
7. encourage public participation at the earliest feasible time in an open and productive atmosphere.
8. conduct my professional activities in a manner that ensures consideration of technically and economically feasible alternatives.

Encourage Development of the Profession
As an Environmental Professional I will:
1. assist in maintaining the integrity and competence of my profession.
2. encourage education and research, and the development of useful technical information relating to the environmental field.
3. be prohibited from lobbying in the name of the National Association of Environmental Professionals.
4. advertise and present my services in a manner that avoids the use of material and methods that may bring discredit to the profession.

© National Association of Environmental Professionals. Reprinted with permission.

NATIONAL ASSOCIATION OF FIRE INVESTIGATORS

Address: PO Box 957257
             Hoffman Estates, IL 60195

Telephone: 312/427-6320
WWW: www.nafi.org
Document: Code of Ethics (1961)

PREAMBLE: Fire investigation is an honorable profession based on service, research, knowledge, preparation, experience, technical know-how and ethical standards. In recognition of the dedicated professional men who serve the world as Fire Investigators under the American system of "Justice Under the Law," the National Association of Fire Investigators has established a Creed and Code of Ethics, which is binding upon all of its members. Each member agrees as follows:

1. As a Fire Investigator, I will at all times conduct myself according to this CODE OF ETHICS, which I have signed.
2. I will deal justly and impartially with all individuals, regardless of their physical, mental, emotional, political, economic, social, racial or religious characteristics.
3. I do, as a Fire Investigator, regard myself as a member of an important and honorable profession, and will strive to serve fairly in all other respects not specifically covered by this CODE.
4. I will conduct myself in such a manner as to inspire others within the profession and to retain the confidence of the general public.
5. I will continue to work for the goals of NAFI in fostering better understanding and a closer spirit of cooperation between the various public and private law enforcement agencies and the general public throughout the United States of America.
6. I will not use any information that might come to me during the conduct of a fire investigation for personal advantage or profit or in any way reveal confidential information in violation of the trust imposed upon me.
7. I will strive toward continuing education in my work. I will avail myself of every opportunity to improve my techniques and enlarge my experience in the field of Fire Investigation.
8. I will not work with or provide information to persons whose goals are inconsistent with the Fire Investigator's Creed, which requires an honest and unbiased investigation.
9. I will make no claims to professional qualifications which I do not possess.
10. I will at all times strive to be a fact finder, seeking for the truth and attempting to determine the

true and accurate cause of all fires and explosions or other occurrences which I investigate.

I accept these principles and pledge to abide by them.

© National Association of Fire Investigators. Reprinted with permission.

NATIONAL ASSOCIATION OF HEALTH UNDERWRITERS

Address: 2000 North Fourteenth Street,
            Suite 450
            Arlington, VA 22201
Telephone: 703/276-0220
WWW: www.nahu.org
Document: NAHU Code of Ethics (1997)

- To hold the selling, servicing, and distribution of disability and health insurance plans as a professional and a public trust and to do all in my power to maintain its prestige.
- To keep paramount the needs of those whom I serve.
- To respect my clients' trust in me, and to never do anything which would betray their trust or confidence.
- To give all service possible when service is needed.
- To present policies factually and accurately, providing all information necessary for the issuance of sound insurance coverage to the public I serve.
- To use no advertising which may be false or misleading.

- To consider the sale of disability income and health insurance plans as a career, to know and abide by the insurance laws of my state, and to seek to constantly increase my knowledge and improve my ability to meet the needs of my clients.
- To be fair and just to my competitors, and to engage in no practices which may reflect unfavorably on myself or my industry.
- To treat prospects, clients and companies fairly by submitting applications which reveal all available information pertinent to underwriting a policy.
- To be loyal to my clients, associates, fellow agents and brokers, and the company or companies whose products I represent.

© National Association of Health Underwriters. Reprinted with permission.

NATIONAL ASSOCIATION OF HOME BUILDERS

Address: 1201 Fifteenth Street NW
            Washington, DC 20005-2800
Telephone: 202/822-0200 or 800/368-5242
WWW: www.nahb.com
Document: Suggested Model Code of Ethics for
            Local Builders Associations (1993)

As members in good standing of the (*name of local builders association*), we believe in, and accept, the responsibilities and obligations inherent in our provision of housing, light commercial construction and any other services. Consistent with NAHB's Code of Ethics contained in its constitution, we support the following objectives:

1. To conduct business affairs with professionalism and skill.
2. To provide the best housing value possible.

3. To protect the consumer through the use of quality materials and construction practices backed by integrity and service.
4. To provide housing with high standards of safety, sanitation and livability.
5. To meet all financial obligations in a responsible manner.
6. To comply with the spirit and letter of business contracts, and manage employees, subcontractors and suppliers with fairness and honor.
7. To keep informed regarding public policies and other essential information which affect our business interests and those of the building industry as a whole.
8. To comply with the rules and regulations prescribed by law and government agencies for the health, safety and welfare of the community.
9. To keep honesty as our guiding business policy.
10. To provide timely response to items covered under warranty.
11. To seek to resolve controversies through a non-litigation dispute resolution mechanism.
12. To support and abide by the decisions of the association in promoting and enforcing this Code of Ethics.

Members assume the responsibilities in this Code of Ethics freely and solemnly and are mindful that these responsibilities are a part of their obligation as members of the (*name of local builders association*).

We also believe that homeownership should be within reach of all Americans.

Finally, because we hold inviolate the free enterprise system and American way of life, we pledge our support to our associates, our local, state and national associations, and all related industries concerned with the preservation of inalienable rights and freedoms.

NATIONAL ASSOCIATION OF LEGAL ASSISTANTS

Address: 1516 South Boston Avenue, Suite 200
Tulsa, OK 74119-4464
Telephone: 918/587-6828

WWW: www.nala.org
Document: Code of Ethics and Professional Responsibility (1975. Most recently revised 1995.)

(NALA also publishes *NALA Model Standards and Guidelines for Utilization of Legal Assistants*, which is not reprinted here.—Eds.)

Preamble

A legal assistant must adhere strictly to the accepted standards of legal ethics and to the general principles of proper conduct. The performance of the duties of the legal assistant shall be governed by specific canons as defined herein so that justice will be served and goals of the profession attained. (See NALA Model Standards and Guidelines for Utilization of Legal Assistants, Section II.)

The canons of ethics set forth hereafter are adopted by the National Association of Legal Assistants, Inc., as a general guide intended to aid legal assistants and attorneys. The enumeration of these rules does not mean there are not others of equal importance although not specifically mentioned. Court rules, agency rules and statutes must be taken into consideration when interpreting the canons.

Definition

Legal assistants, also known as paralegals, are a distinguishable group of persons who assist attorneys in the delivery of legal services. Through formal education, training and experience, legal assistants have knowledge and expertise regarding the legal system and substantive and procedural law which qualify them to do work of a legal nature under the supervision of an attorney.

Canon 1— A legal assistant must not perform any of the duties that attorneys only may perform nor take any actions that attorneys may not take.

Canon 2—A legal assistant may perform any task which is properly delegated and supervised by an attorney, as long as the attorney is ultimately responsible to the client, maintains a direct relationship with the client, and assumes professional responsibility for the work product. (See NALA Model Standards and Guidelines for Utilization of Legal Assistants, Sections IV and VII.)

Canon 3—A legal assistant must not: (See NALA Model Standards and Guidelines for Utilization of Legal Assistants, Sections VI.)

a) engage in, encourage, or contribute to any act which could constitute the unauthorized practice of law; and

b) establish attorney-client relationships, set fees, give legal opinions or advice or represent a client before a court or agency unless so authorized by that court or agency; and

c) engage in conduct or take any action which would assist or involve the attorney in a violation of professional ethics or give the appearance of professional impropriety.

Canon 4—A legal assistant must use discretion and professional judgment commensurate with knowledge and experience but must not render independent legal judgment in place of an attorney. The services of an attorney are essential in the public interest whenever such legal judgment is required. (See NALA Model Standards and Guidelines for Utilization of Legal Assistants, Section VII.)

Canon 5—A legal assistant must disclose his or her status as a legal assistant at the outset of any professional relationship with a client, attorney, a court or administrative agency or personnel thereof, or a member of the general public. A legal assistant must act prudently in determining the extent to which a client may be assisted without the presence of an attorney. (See NALA Model Standards and Guidelines for Utilization of Legal Assistants, Section V.)

Canon 6—A legal assistant must strive to maintain integrity and a high degree of competency through education and training with respect to professional responsibility, local rules and practice, and through continuing education in substantive areas of law to better assist the legal profession in fulfilling its duty to provide legal service.

Canon 7—A legal assistant must protect the confidences of a client and must not violate any rule or statute now in effect or hereafter enacted controlling the doctrine of privileged communications between a client and an attorney. (See NALA Model Standards and Guidelines for Utilization of Legal Assistants, Section V.)

Canon 8—A legal assistant must do all other things incidental, necessary, or expedient for the attainment of the ethics and responsibilities as defined by statute or rule of court.

Canon 9—A legal assistant's conduct is guided by bar associations' codes of professional responsibility and rules of professional conduct.

NATIONAL ASSOCIATION OF LEGAL SECRETARIES

Address: 314 East Third Street, Suite 210
              Tulsa, OK 74120
Telephone: 918/582-5188
WWW: www.nals.org
Document: NALS Code of Ethics and
              Professional Responsibility

Members of the National Association of Legal Secretaries are bound by the objectives of this association and the standards of conduct required of the legal profession.

Every member shall:
Encourage respect for the law and the administration of justice;

Observe rules governing privileged communications and confidential information;

Promote and exemplify high standards of loyalty, cooperation, and courtesy;

Perform all duties of the profession with integrity and competence; and

Pursue a high order of professional attainment.

Integrity and high standards of conduct are fundamental to the success of our professional association. This Code is promulgated by the National Association of Legal Secretaries and accepted by its members to accomplish these ends.

Canon 1.   Members of this association shall maintain a high degree of competency and integrity through continuing education to better assist the legal profession in fulfilling its duty to provide quality legal services to the public.

Canon 2. Members of this association shall maintain a high standard of ethical conduct and shall contribute to the integrity of this association and the legal profession.

Canon 3. Members of this association shall avoid conflict of interest pertaining to a client matter.

Canon 4. Members of this association shall preserve and protect the confidences and privileged communications of a client.

Canon 5. Members of this association shall exercise care in using independent professional judgment and in determining the extent to which a client may be assisted without the presence of a lawyer and shall not act in matters involving professional legal judgment.

Canon 6. Members of this association shall not solicit legal business on behalf of a lawyer.

Canon 7. Members of this association, unless permitted by law, shall not perform paralegal functions except under the direct supervision of a lawyer and shall not advertise or contract with members of the general public for the performance of paralegal functions.

Canon 8. Members of this association, unless permitted by law, shall not perform any duties restricted to lawyers or do things which lawyers themselves may not do and shall assist in preventing the unauthorized practice of law.

Canon 9. Members of this association not licensed to practice law shall not engage in the practice of law as defined by statutes or court decisions.

Canon 10. Members of this association shall do all other things incidental, necessary, or expedient to enhance professional responsibility and participation in the administration of justice and public service in cooperation with the legal profession.

NATIONAL ASSOCIATION OF LIFE UNDERWRITERS

Address: 1922 F Street NW
             Washington, DC 20006-4387
Telephone: 202/331-6000
WWW: www.nalu.org
Document: Code of Ethics (1986)

PREAMBLE: Those engaged in life underwriting occupy the unique position of liaison between the purchasers and the suppliers of life and health insurance and closely related financial products. Inherent in this role is the combination of professional duty to the client and to the company, as well. Ethical balance is required to avoid any conflict between these two obligations. Therefore,

I Believe It To Be My Responsibility

To hold my profession in high esteem and strive to enhance its prestige.

To fulfill the needs of my clients to the best of my ability.

To maintain my clients' confidences.

To render exemplary service to my clients and their beneficiaries.

To adhere to professional standards of conduct in helping my clients to protect insurable obligations and attain their financial security objectives.

To present accurately and honestly all facts essential to my clients' decisions.

To perfect my skills and increase my knowledge through continuing education.

To conduct my business in such a way that my example might help raise the professional standards of life underwriting.

To keep informed with respect to applicable laws and regulations and to observe them in the practice of my profession.

To cooperate with others whose services are constructively related to meeting the needs of my clients.

NATIONAL ASSOCIATION OF PERFORMING ARTS MANAGERS AND AGENTS

Address: 459 Columbus Avenue #133
              New York, NY 10024
Telephone: 212/799-5308
WWW: www.napama.org
Document: NAPAMA Guidelines for Ethical
              Behavior

The performing arts represent the highest level of communication. NAPAMA's purpose is to facilitate that communication in an effective, responsible manner. Therefore, these Guidelines for Ethical Behavior have been formulated by the NAPAMA membership to govern our relationship with artists, presenters and other managers. Each of these areas involves mutual obligations, some contractual in nature and others in the domain of professional courtesy and good business practice. We wish to focus on the essence, which is to be forthright and clear in all dealings with our colleagues.

NAPAMA's greatest obligation is to foster the development of and access to performing arts of the highest quality. We propose that the cultivation of excellence is the best means of maximizing the public appetite for live performance, which will in turn increase the opportunities available to talented artists. The principles of professional conduct described in these guidelines assume a condition of ample opportunity which may or may not exist at the moment and a standard of ethics which is painless only if it does.

I. Manager-Artist Relations
By virtue of their positions of leadership, managers have responsibilities to all performing artists.

1. Managers and agents are often besieged by artists seeking representation. If their work merits attention, one must ascertain their freedom to enter into a management agreement and be prepared to honor, and to encourage them to honor, any existing obligations to previous management. Man-

agers should not entice artists from other managements' rosters, especially with unreasonable optimistic predictions about engagement and fees which might be procured for them.

2. The terms of a management agreement should be stated clearly, comprehensively and in writing. It is not reasonable to assume, just because mutual obligations and responsibilities are detailed in a contract, that these details, and their consequences are understood and remembered by the artist. He or she should be informed, in particular, and before the contract is signed, of the probable eventual costs of promotional and publicity materials, travel, long-distance phone calls, etc., the mechanisms to be used for reimbursement of these expenses as well as the provisions made for contract renewal or termination.

3. Artists fees should be remitted to the artist within a clearly specified time period, and expenses should be itemized and invoiced periodically. If any misunderstanding occurs concerning expense reimbursements, remedy the situation by improving communication with the artist involved.

4. Momentum can be crucial in the development of an artist's career. If a manager feels he or she has reached the end of his of her effectiveness for a particular artist, he or she should be frank about this and offer the artist the option of going elsewhere.

5. Artists have corresponding responsibilities toward managers. In particular, they must be clear about their own needs, priorities and expectations, and, having assumed any contractual obligations toward a manager or presenter, they must fulfill them. Failure to do so impairs not only the reputation and effectiveness of the manager but, by extension, the opportunities available to fellow artists on the roster. In addition, failure to honor obligations for reasons not enumerated in Act of God clauses will entail financial obligations of the artist to managers and presenters involved.

II. Manager-Presenter Relations
The manager-presenter relationship is the crux of our profession. Both represent entities beyond themselves—performing artists on the one hand and the concert-going public on the other. As such, it involves mutual trust and a commitment to the perpetuation of the performing arts.

1. Managers are expected to be accurate, efficient and timely sources of information about perform-

ing artists. This precludes any willful misrepresentation of the needs, capabilities and availabilities of the artists one is authorized to represent and also any corresponding misrepresentation of artists one is not authorized to represent.

2. During the booking and contracting process, managers should be mindful of their leadership role: every instance of booking activity should be a model of the process for both sides of the bargaining table. This involves being frank and forceful with presenters about the effects on artists' careers of potential abuses, such as unreasonable holds, premature requests for contracts, and other restrictions, such as exaggerated exclusivity clauses. Conversely, managers, especially when dealing with less experienced presenters, must not abuse any rights or expectations to which the imprecise use of language may seem to entitle them. No enticements, such as gifts of value or monetary kickbacks, may be offered to presenters for booking artists. Not only is this illegal, it is a particularly loathsome violation of our trust.

3. Both managements and presenting organizations are responsible for the actions and commitments of their staffs.

4. Holds. It is recognized, given the committee structure governing many presenting organizations and the complicated and delicate process involved in putting a season together, that the requesting and granting of "holds" may be a necessary step in the booking process. All parties involved must recognize and respect the good faith aspect of holds and not abuse the process. In particular, holds should only be requested and granted with the understanding that a response, positive or negative, must be made within an agreed time-frame, generally less than thirty days.

5. Contracts should only be requested and supplied when all parties can confirm their intention to sign it. It should then be completely, accurately and promptly executed, including any and all riders, except when specific retarding circumstances (government grants, etc.) are clearly defined. All parties, including the artist(s), should be fully aware of all conditions and be ready and willing to fulfill them. Any subsequent impairments should be fully, frankly and promptly communicated to all concerned. All parties should remember that verbal agreements are legally binding.

6. Cancellations. The manager-presenter relationship is a partnership in the service of a larger cause—

the bond between artists and audiences. The contract is a crucial link in that chain. If it is broken, far more is lost than what can be entered on a balance sheet. In the event a cancellation threatens, be it willful or not on any part, the important thing is to save the bond. The process will be painful and difficult no matter what. The best preventive medicine is a thoughtfully designed and realistic contract. The only palliative is the frankness and good will of the parties.

Artists must realize that willful cancellation of a commitment can damage a career, impair the reputation of management and damage the credibility of a presenter in the eyes of the public. It is especially reprehensible when the desire to cancel stems from a more lucrative or prestigious engagement elsewhere. This indicates a short-sighted view of what constitutes career advancement. Such cancellations will involve reimbursements to both presenters and management for out-of-pocket expenses, promotional costs and lost commissions.

Presenters must realize how much is at stake when they request a hold or a contract. Based on these commitments, itineraries and budgets are set. Failure to honor a commitment can adversely affect the viability of an entire tour, with consequences not only for management and artists but also for other presenters. It is especially reprehensible when the desire to cancel stems from problematic ticket sales. The solution is to devote more energy to promotion. Presenters will find managements and artists willing to assist in marketing efforts. Such cancellations will involve reimbursements to management and artists. NAPAMA members are advised not to sign contracts which contain cancellation at will clauses.

If, despite all efforts to prevent it, a cancellation does occur, all sides must use their best efforts to either find a suitable replacement artist or to reschedule the date.

III. Manager-Manager Relations

Relations among managers are the only ones addressed in these guidelines which are not the object of contractual agreements and are perhaps the least public bonds in the complex web of our professional interactions with others. Yet, the way we deal with each other is emblematic of the way we can be expected to deal with our artists and presenters.

1. Managers should respect the integrity of one another's rosters. This precludes claiming to represent an artist one is not authorized to represent.

2. Managers should be circumspect, judicious, fair-minded and diplomatic when tempted to discuss a colleague's putative shortcomings with artists, presenters or other managers. Confusing the good of the field with one's personal or professional advantage is as reprehensible a shortcoming as any other.

3. No guidelines can deal adequately with the problem of artists and managers shopping for each other while allied elsewhere. The men and women of our profession should obey the ancient laws of chivalry and act like "gentlemen" at all times. A manager should not approach an artist on another management's roster. If approached by an artist, a manager should discuss the current situation fairly and then proceed from there with tact.

IV. Manager-Employee Relations

Given the unique nature of the performing arts management industry—lack of recognized training programs, small offices, entrepreneurial focus co-existing with not-for-profit structures—a fair degree of "musical chairs" is to be expected. This can lead to delicate situations regarding both the engagement and separation of personnel.

1. One facet of managers' professionalism is that we are educators, and should expect to instruct employees in both the nuts and bolts aspects of our business and its wider, perhaps philosophical aspects. Some of our best "students" will inevitably go off on their own, either to work with competitors or to start their own organizations. This fact should not, in and of itself, be a cause for recrimination.

2. The conditions of employment should be clearly stated in writing. It is particularly important to be clear about the disposition of monies which may be payable after the employee in question has left the organization. Any severance conditions, such as provisions which preclude working with artists on the roster for a specified time period, should be made explicit, in writing, from the beginning.

3. Employees are expected to respect the confidentiality of the internal communications, procedures, pricing structures and contacts of their current and former employers.

V. Conventions

Crowded convention schedules and problematic management-presenter ratios create a condition of scarcity as far as contacts with presenters are concerned, a situation which offers possibilities for abuse and offense. The best method of avoiding

these is for all concerned to observe the basic rules of politeness and decency which pertain everywhere in civilized life, and in particular, to respect a notion of territoriality in the exhibit hall. Manager colleagues have purchased exhibit space and, with it, a zone of influence which should extend only as far as necessary for two or three people to stand and converse comfortably.

1. Exhibits should not impinge on neighboring spaces nor should they block or obstruct the view of another booth.

2. Audio-visual equipment should be oriented so as to be viewed from within the exhibit space, not from outside.

3. The aisles should be considered a neutral space in which presenters may circulate freely without being accosted.

4. Presenters should never be approached in front of another manager's space.

5. Conversations among presenters or presenters and other managers should not be interrupted.

6. At educational sessions, showcases and hospitality events, presenters should not be importuned with sales-oriented conversations which distract from the business at hand.

Infractions of these guidelines make the exhibit hall a distasteful experience for many presenters. Adherence to them helps assure that all concerned will be better able to profit from what is an expensive investment in our artists' careers.

VI. Complaints Procedures

Honest differences of opinion will develop concerning the applicability and interpretation of these Guidelines. In the interest of facilitating the resolution of conflicts which may occur among the parties involved, NAPAMA has instituted an Ethics Advisory Committee. Any party to a dispute involving a manager who is a member of NAPAMA may call on the committee as follows: An informal call may be made to one of the designated Committee members, who will attempt to clarify the dispute without involving the committee as a whole or any other parties.

The National Association of Performing Managers and Agents (NAPAMA) is a national trade association dedicated to promoting the professionalism of its members and the vitality of the performing arts.

NATIONAL ASSOCIATION OF PROFESSIONAL EDUCATORS

Address: PO Box 2206
            Reston, VA 22090
Telephone: 623/584-4920
WWW: www.teacherspet.com/napeindx.htm
Document: A Code of Ethics for Professional
            Educators (1975)

The Professional Educator strives to create an atmosphere that nurtures to fulfillment the potential of each student.

The Professional Educator acts with conscientious concern in order to exemplify the highest standards of professional commitment.

The Professional Educator accepts the responsibility to guarantee every child the right to a continuous quality education.

The Professional Educator is responsible for ethical conduct toward students, professional colleagues, parents and the community.

PRINCIPLE I: Ethical Conduct Toward Students

The Professional Educator accepts personal responsibility for helping the students develop basic criteria so that the students will be able to evaluate the consequences of and accept the responsibility for their actions.

The Professional Educator, in accepting a position of public trust, measures success by the progress of each student toward realization of one's potential as an effective citizen.

1. The educator deals considerately and justly with each student and seeks to resolve problems, including discipline, according to law and school policy.
2. The educator does not intentionally expose the student to disparagement.
3. The educator does not reveal confidential information concerning students, unless required by law.
4. The educator makes a reasonable effort to protect the student from conditions detrimental to learning, health, or safety.
5. The educator endeavors to present facts without distortion, bias or personal prejudice.

PRINCIPLE II: Ethical Conduct Toward Practices and Performance

The Professional Educator assumes responsibility for professional teaching practices and professional performance and continually strives to demonstrate competence.

The Professional Educator endeavors to maintain the dignity of the profession by respecting and obeying the law, demonstrating personal integrity, and exemplifying honesty.

1. The educator applies for, accepts, or assigns a position or a responsibility on the basis of professional qualifications and adheres to the terms of a contract or appointment.
2. The educator maintains sound mental health, physical stamina, and social prudence necessary to perform the duties of any professional assignment.
3. The educator organizes instruction in a manner that seeks to accomplish objectives clearly related to learning.
4. The educator continues professional growth.
5. The educator complies with written local school policies and applicable laws and regulations which are not in conflict with this code of ethics.
6. The educator does not intentionally misrepresent official policies of the school or educational organizations and clearly distinguishes those views from one's own personal opinions.
7. The educator honestly accounts for all funds committed to one's charge.
8. The educator does not use institutional or professional privileges for personal or partisan advantage.

PRINCIPLE III: Ethical Conduct Toward Professional Colleagues

The Professional Educator, in exemplifying ethical relations with colleagues, accords just and equitable treatment to all members of the profession.

1. The educator does not reveal confidential information concerning colleagues unless required by law.
2. The educator does not willfully make false statements about a colleague or the school system.
3. The educator does not interfere with a colleague's freedom of choice and works to eliminate coercion that forces educators to support actions and ideologies that violate individual professional integrity.
4. The educator does not interfere with a colleague's exercise of political and citizenship rights and responsibilities.

PRINCIPLE IV: Ethical Conduct Toward Parents and Community

The Professional Educator pledges to protect public sovereignty over public education and private control of private education.

The Professional Educator recognizes that quality education is the common goal of the public, boards of education and educators, and that a cooperative effort is essential among these groups to attain that goal.

1. The educator makes reasonable efforts to communicate to parents all information which should be revealed in the interest of the student.
2. The educator endeavors to understand community cultures and relate the home environment of students to the school.
3. The educator manifests a positive role in school public relations.

© National Association of Professional Educators. Reprinted with permission.

NATIONAL ASSOCIATION OF PURCHASING MANAGEMENT

Address: 2055 East Centennial Circle, PO Box 22160 Tempe, AZ 85285-2160
Telephone: 800/888-6276
WWW: www.napm.org
Document: Principles and Standards of Purchasing Practice (1923. Most recently revised 1992.)

(NAPM's Ethical Standards Committee has also developed a model set of guidelines to heighten awareness and acceptance of appropriate conduct. These guidelines are intended to accompany the principles below, but are not reprinted here.—Eds.)

LOYALTY TO YOUR ORGANIZATION
JUSTICE TO THOSE WITH WHOM YOU DEAL
FAITH IN YOUR PROFESSION

From these principles are derived the NAPM standards of purchasing practice. (Domestic and International)

1. Avoid the intent and appearance of unethical or compromising practice in relationships, actions, and communications.
2. Demonstrate loyalty to the employer by diligently following the lawful instructions of the employer, using reasonable care and only authority granted.
3. Refrain from any private business or professional activity that would create a conflict between personal interests and the interests of the employer.
4. Refrain from soliciting or accepting money, loans, credits, or prejudicial discounts, and the acceptance of gifts, entertainment, favors, or services from present or potential suppliers that might influence, or appear to influence, purchasing decisions.
5. Handle confidential or proprietary information belonging to employers or suppliers with due care and proper consideration of ethical and legal ramifications and governmental regulations.
6. Promote positive supplier relationships through courtesy and impartiality in all phases of the purchasing cycle.
7. Refrain from reciprocal agreements that restrain competition.
8. Know and obey the letter and spirit of laws governing the purchasing function and remain alert to the legal ramifications of purchasing decisions.
9. Encourage all segments of society to participate by demonstrating support for small, disadvantaged, and minority-owned businesses.
10. Discourage purchasing's involvement in employer-sponsored programs of personal purchases that are not business related.
11. Enhance the proficiency and stature of the purchasing profession by acquiring and maintaining current technical knowledge and the highest standards of ethical behavior.
12. Conduct international purchasing in accordance with the laws, customs, and practices of foreign countries, consistent with United States laws, your organization policies, and these Ethical Standards and Guidelines.

NATIONAL ASSOCIATION OF REALTORS®

Address:	430 North Michigan Avenue Chicago, IL 60611-4087
Telephone:	800/874-6500
WWW:	nar.REALOR.com
Document:	Code of Ethics and Standards of Practice of the NATIONAL ASSOCIATION OF REALTORS® (1913. Most recently revised 1999.)

Where the word REALTORS® is used in this Code and Preamble, it shall be deemed to include REALTOR-ASSOCIATE®s .

While the Code of Ethics establishes obligations that may be higher than those mandated by law, in any instance where the Code of Ethics and the law conflict, the obligations of the law must take precedence.

Preamble. . .

Under all is the land. Upon its wise utilization and widely allocated ownership depend the survival and growth of free institutions and of our civilization. REALTORS® should recognize that the interests of the nation and its citizens require the highest and best use of the land and the widest distribution of land ownership. They require the creation of adequate housing, the building of functioning cities, the development of productive industries and farms, and the preservation of a healthful environment.

Such interests impose obligations beyond those of ordinary commerce. They impose grave social responsibility and a patriotic duty to which REALTORS® should dedicate themselves, and for which they should be diligent in preparing themselves. REALTORS® , therefore, are zealous to maintain and improve the standards of their calling and share with their fellow REALTORS® a common responsibility for its integrity and honor.

In recognition and appreciation of their obligations to clients, customers, the public, and each other, RE-ALTORS® continuously strive to become and remain informed on issues affecting real estate and, as knowledgeable professionals, they willingly share the fruit of their experience and study with others. They identify and take steps, through enforcement of this Code of Ethics and by assisting appropriate regulatory bodies, to eliminate practices which may damage the public or which might discredit or bring dishonor to the real estate profession.

Realizing that cooperation with other real estate professionals promotes the best interests of those who utilize their services, REALTORS® urge exclusive representation of clients; do not attempt to gain any unfair advantage over their competitors; and they refrain from making unsolicited comments about other practitioners. In instances where their opinion is sought, or where REALTORS® believe that comment is necessary, their opinion is offered in an objective, professional manner, uninfluenced by any personal motivation or potential advantage or gain.

The term REALTOR® has come to connote competency, fairness, and high integrity resulting from adherence to a lofty ideal of moral conduct in business relations. No inducement of profit and no instruction from clients ever can justify departure from this ideal.

In the interpretation of this obligation, REALTORS® can take no safer guide than that which has been handed down through the centuries, embodied in the Golden Rule, "Whatsoever ye would that others should do to you, do ye even so to them."

Accepting this standard as their own, REALTORS® pledge to observe its spirit in all of their activities and to conduct their business in accordance with the tenets set forth below.

Duties to Clients and Customers
Article 1
When representing a buyer, seller, landlord, tenant, or other client as an agent, REALTORS® pledge themselves to protect and promote the interests of their client. This obligation of absolute fidelity to the client's interests is primary, but it does not relieve REALTORS® of their obligation to treat all parties honestly. When serving a buyer, seller, landlord, tenant or other party in a non-agency capacity, REALTORS® remain obligated to treat all parties honestly. *(Amended 1/93)*

- **Standard of Practice 1-1**
  REALTORS®, when acting as principals in a real estate transaction, remain obligated by the duties imposed by the Code of Ethics. *(Amended 1/93)*

- **Standard of Practice 1-2**

The duties the Code of Ethics imposes are applicable whether REALTORS® are acting as agents or in legally recognized non-agency capacities except that any duty imposed exclusively on agents by law or regulation shall not be imposed by this Code of Ethics on REALTORS® acting in non-agency capacities.

As used in this Code of Ethics, "client" means the person(s) or entity(ies) with whom a REALTOR® or a REALTOR®'s firm has an agency or legally recognized non-agency relationship; "customer" means a party to a real estate transaction who receives information, services, or benefits but has no contractual relationship with the REALTOR® or the REALTOR®'s firm; "agent" means a real estate licensee (including brokers and sales associates) acting in an agency relationship as defined by state law or regulation; and "broker" means a real estate licensee (including brokers and sales associates) acting as an agent or in a legally recognized non-agency capacity. *(Adopted 1/95, Amended 1/99)*

- **Standard of Practice 1-3**

REALTORS®, in attempting to secure a listing, shall not deliberately mislead the owner as to market value.

- **Standard of Practice 1-4**

REALTORS®, when seeking to become a buyer/tenant representative, shall not mislead buyers or tenants as to savings or other benefits that might be realized through use of the REALTOR®'s services. *(Amended 1/93)*

- **Standard of Practice 1-5**

REALTORS® may represent the seller/landlord and buyer/tenant in the same transaction only after full disclosure to and with informed consent of both parties. *(Adopted 1/93)*

- **Standard of Practice 1-6**

REALTORS® shall submit offers and counter-offers objectively and as quickly as possible. *(Adopted 1/93, Amended 1/95)*

- **Standard of Practice 1-7**

When acting as listing brokers, REALTORS® shall continue to submit to the seller/landlord all offers and counter-offers until closing or execution of a lease unless the seller/landlord has waived this obligation in writing. REALTORS® shall not be obligated to continue to market the property after an offer has been accepted by the seller/landlord. REALTORS® shall recommend that sellers/landlords

obtain the advice of legal counsel prior to acceptance of a subsequent offer except where the acceptance is contingent on the termination of the pre-existing purchase contract or lease. *(Amended 1/93)*

- **Standard of Practice 1-8**

REALTORS® acting as agents or brokers of buyers/tenants shall submit to buyers/tenants all offers and counter-offers until acceptance but have no obligation to continue to show properties to their clients after an offer has been accepted unless otherwise agreed in writing. REALTORS® acting as agents or brokers of buyers/tenants shall recommend that buyers/tenants obtain the advice of legal counsel if there is a question as to whether a pre-existing contract has been terminated. *(Adopted 1/93, Amended 1/99)*

- **Standard of Practice 1-9**

The obligation of REALTORS® to preserve confidential information (as defined by state law) provided by their clients in the course of any agency relationship or non-agency relationship recognized by law continues after termination of agency relationships or any non-agency relationships recognized by law. REALTORS® shall not knowingly, during or following the termination of professional relationships with their clients:

1) reveal confidential information of clients; or
2) use confidential information of clients to the disadvantage of clients; or
3) use confidential information of clients for the REALTOR®'s advantage or the advantage of third parties unless:
   a) clients consent after full disclosure; or
   b) REALTORS® are required by court order; or
   c) it is the intention of a client to commit a crime and the information is necessary to prevent the crime; or
   d) it is necessary to defend a REALTOR® or the REALTOR®'s employees or associates against an accusation of wrongful conduct. *(Adopted 1/93, Amended 1/99)*

- **Standard of Practice 1-10**

REALTORS® shall, consistent with the terms and conditions of their property management agreement, competently manage the property of clients with due regard for the rights, responsibilities, benefits, safety and health of tenants and others lawfully on the premises. *(Adopted 1/95)*

- **Standard of Practice 1-11**

REALTORS® who are employed to maintain or manage a client's property shall exercise due diligence and make reasonable efforts to protect it against reasonably foreseeable contingencies and losses. *(Adopted 1/95)*

- **Standard of Practice 1-12**

When entering into listing contracts, REALTORS® must advise sellers/landlords of:

1) the REALTOR®'s general company policies regarding cooperation with and compensation to subagents, buyer/tenant agents and/or brokers acting in legally recognized non-agency capacities;

2) the fact that buyer/tenant agents or brokers, even if compensated by listing brokers, or by sellers/landlords may represent the interests of buyers/tenants; and

3) any potential for listing brokers to act as disclosed dual agents, e.g., buyer/tenant agents. *(Adopted 1/93, Renumbered 1/98, Amended 1/99)*

- **Standard of Practice 1-13**

When entering into buyer/tenant agreements, REALTORS® must advise potential clients of:

1) the REALTOR®'s general company policies regarding cooperation and compensation; and

2) any potential for the buyer/tenant representative to act as a disclosed dual agent, e.g., listing broker, subagent, landlord's agent, etc. *(Adopted 1/93, Renumbered 1/98, Amended 1/99)*

Article 2

REALTORS® shall avoid exaggeration, misrepresentation, or concealment of pertinent facts relating to the property or the transaction. REALTORS® shall not, however, be obligated to discover latent defects in the property, to advise on matters outside the scope of their real estate license, or to disclose facts which are confidential under the scope of agency duties owed to their clients. *(Amended 1/93)*

- **Standard of Practice 2-1**

REALTORS® shall only be obligated to discover and disclose adverse factors reasonably apparent to someone with expertise in those areas required by their real estate licensing authority. Article 2 does not impose upon the REALTOR® the obligation of expertise in other professional or technical disciplines. *(Amended 1/96)*

- **Standard of Practice 2-2** *(Renumbered as Standard of Practice 1-12 1/98)*
- **Standard of Practice 2-3** *(Renumbered as Standard of Practice 1-13 1/98)*

- **Standard of Practice 2-4**

REALTORS® shall not be parties to the naming of a false consideration in any document, unless it be the naming of an obviously nominal consideration.

- **Standard of Practice 2-5**

Factors defined as "non-material" by law or regulation or which are expressly referenced in law or regulation as not being subject to disclosure are considered not "pertinent" for purposes of Article 2. *(Adopted 1/93)*

Article 3

REALTORS® shall cooperate with other brokers except when cooperation is not in the client's best interest. The obligation to cooperate does not include the obligation to share commissions, fees, or to otherwise compensate another broker. *(Amended 1/95)*

- **Standard of Practice 3-1**

REALTORS®, acting as exclusive agents or brokers of sellers/landlords, establish the terms and conditions of offers to cooperate. Unless expressly indicated in offers to cooperate, cooperating brokers may not assume that the offer of cooperation includes an offer of compensation. Terms of compensation, if any, shall be ascertained by cooperating brokers before beginning efforts to accept the offer of cooperation. *(Amended 1/99)*

- **Standard of Practice 3-2**

REALTORS® shall, with respect to offers of compensation to another REALTOR®, timely communicate any change of compensation for cooperative services to the other REALTOR® prior to the time such REALTOR® produces an offer to purchase/lease the property. *(Amended 1/94)*

- **Standard of Practice 3-3**

Standard of Practice 3-2 does not preclude the listing broker and cooperating broker from entering into an agreement to change cooperative compensation. *(Adopted 1/94)*

- **Standard of Practice 3-4**

REALTORS®, acting as listing brokers, have an affirmative obligation to disclose the existence of dual or variable rate commission arrangements (i.e., listings where one amount of commission is payable if the listing broker's firm is the procuring cause of sale/lease and a different amount of commission is payable if the sale/lease results through the efforts of the seller/landlord or a cooperating broker). The listing broker shall, as soon as practical, disclose the existence of such arrangements to potential cooperating brokers and shall, in response to inquiries from cooperating brokers, disclose the differential that would result in a cooperative transaction or in a sale/lease that results through the efforts of the seller/landlord. If the cooperating broker is a buyer/tenant representative, the buyer/tenant representative must disclose such information to their client. *(Amended 1/94)*

- **Standard of Practice 3-5**
  It is the obligation of subagents to promptly disclose all pertinent facts to the principal's agent prior to as well as after a purchase or lease agreement is executed. *(Amended 1/93)*

- **Standard of Practice 3-6**
  REALTORS® shall disclose the existence of an accepted offer to any broker seeking cooperation. *(Adopted 5/86)*

- **Standard of Practice 3-7**
  When seeking information from another REALTOR® concerning property under a management or listing agreement, REALTORS® shall disclose their REALTOR® status and whether their interest is personal or on behalf of a client and, if on behalf of a client, their representational status. *(Amended 1/95)*

- **Standard of Practice 3-8**
  REALTORS® shall not misrepresent the availability of access to show or inspect a listed property. *(Amended 11/87)*

Article 4

REALTORS® shall not acquire an interest in or buy or present offers from themselves, any member of their immediate families, their firms or any member thereof, or any entities in which they have any ownership interest, any real property without making their true position known to the owner or the owner's agent. In selling property they own, or in which they have any interest, REALTORS® shall reveal their ownership or interest in writing to the purchaser or the purchaser's representative. *(Amended 1/91)*

- **Standard of Practice 4-1**
  For the protection of all parties, the disclosures required by Article 4 shall be in writing and provided by REALTORS® prior to the signing of any contract. *(Adopted 2/86)*

Article 5

REALTORS® shall not undertake to provide professional services concerning a property or its value

where they have a present or contemplated interest unless such interest is specifically disclosed to all affected parties.

Article 6

REALTORS® shall not accept any commission, rebate, or profit on expenditures made for their client, without the client's knowledge and consent.

When recommending real estate products or services (e.g., homeowner's insurance, warranty programs, mortgage financing, title insurance, etc.), REALTORS® shall disclose to the client or customer to whom the recommendation is made any financial benefits or fees, other than real estate referral fees, the REALTOR® or REALTOR®'s firm may receive as a direct result of such recommendation. *(Amended 1/99)*

- **Standard of Practice 6-1**
  REALTORS® shall not recommend or suggest to a client or a customer the use of services of another organization or business entity in which they have a direct interest without disclosing such interest at the time of the recommendation or suggestion. *(Amended 5/88)*

Article 7

In a transaction, REALTORS® shall not accept compensation from more than one party, even if permitted by law, without disclosure to all parties and the informed consent of the REALTOR®'s client or clients. *(Amended 1/93)*

Article 8

REALTORS® shall keep in a special account in an appropriate financial institution, separated from their own funds, monies coming into their possession in trust for other persons, such as escrows, trust funds, clients' monies, and other like items.

Article 9

REALTORS®, for the protection of all parties, shall assure whenever possible that agreements shall be in writing, and shall be in clear and understandable language expressing the specific terms, conditions, obligations and commitments of the parties. A copy of each agreement shall be furnished to each party upon their signing or initialing. *(Amended 1/95)*

- **Standard of Practice 9-1**
  For the protection of all parties, REALTORS® shall use reasonable care to ensure that documents pertaining to the purchase, sale, or lease of real estate

are kept current through the use of written extensions or amendments. *(Amended 1/93)*

Duties to the Public

Article 10

REALTORS® shall not deny equal professional services to any person for reasons of race, color, religion, sex, handicap, familial status, or national origin. REALTORS® shall not be parties to any plan or agreement to discriminate against a person or persons on the basis of race, color, religion, sex, handicap, familial status, or national origin. *(Amended 1/90)*

• **Standard of Practice 10-1**
REALTORS® shall not volunteer information regarding the racial, religious or ethnic composition of any neighborhood and shall not engage in any activity which may result in panic selling. REALTORS® shall not print, display or circulate any statement or advertisement with respect to the selling or renting of a property that indicates any preference, limitations or discrimination based on race, color, religion, sex, handicap, familial status or national origin. *(Adopted 1/94)*

Article 11

The services which REALTORS® provide to their clients and customers shall conform to the standards of practice and competence which are reasonably expected in the specific real estate disciplines in which they engage; specifically, residential real estate brokerage, real property management, commercial and industrial real estate brokerage, real estate appraisal, real estate counseling, real estate syndication, real estate auction, and international real estate.

REALTORS® shall not undertake to provide specialized professional services concerning a type of property or service that is outside their field of competence unless they engage the assistance of one who is competent on such types of property or service, or unless the facts are fully disclosed to the client. Any persons engaged to provide such assistance shall be so identified to the client and their contribution to the assignment should be set forth. *(Amended 1/95)*

• **Standard of Practice 11-1**
The obligations of the Code of Ethics shall be supplemented by and construed in a manner consistent with the Uniform Standards of Professional Appraisal Practice (USPAP) promulgated by the Appraisal Standards Board of the Appraisal Foundation.

The obligations of the Code of Ethics shall not be supplemented by the USPAP where an opinion or recommendation of price or pricing is provided in pursuit of a listing, to assist a potential purchaser in formulating a purchase offer, or to provide a broker's price opinion, whether for a fee or not. *(Amended 1/96)*

• **Standard of Practice 11-2**
The obligations of the Code of Ethics in respect of real estate disciplines other than appraisal shall be interpreted and applied in accordance with the standards of competence and practice which clients and the public reasonably require to protect their rights and interests considering the complexity of the transaction, the availability of expert assistance, and, where the REALTOR® is an agent or subagent, the obligations of a fiduciary. *(Adopted 1/95)*

• **Standard of Practice 11-3**
When REALTORS® provide consultive services to clients which involve advice or counsel for a fee (not a commission), such advice shall be rendered in an objective manner and the fee shall not be contingent on the substance of the advice or counsel given. If brokerage or transaction services are to be provided in addition to consultive services, a separate compensation may be paid with prior agreement between the client and REALTOR®. *(Adopted 1/96)*

Article 12

REALTORS® shall be careful at all times to present a true picture in their advertising and representations to the public. REALTORS® shall also ensure that their professional status (e.g., broker, appraiser, property manager, etc.) or status as REALTORS® is clearly identifiable in any such advertising. *(Amended 1/93)*

• **Standard of Practice 12-1**
REALTORS® may use the term "free" and similar terms in their advertising and in other representations provided that all terms governing availability of the offered product or service are clearly disclosed at the same time. *(Amended 1/97)*

• **Standard of Practice 12-2**
REALTORS® may represent their services as "free" or without cost even if they expect to receive compensation from a source other than their client provided that the potential for the REALTOR® to obtain a benefit from a third party is clearly disclosed at the same time. *(Amended 1/97)*

• **Standard of Practice 12-3**
The offering of premiums, prizes, merchandise discounts or other inducements to list, sell, purchase, or lease is not, in itself, unethical even if receipt of the benefit is contingent on listing, selling, pur-

chasing, or leasing through the REALTOR® making the offer. However, REALTORS® must exercise care and candor in any such advertising or other public or private representations so that any party interested in receiving or otherwise benefiting from the REALTOR®'s offer will have clear, thorough, advance understanding of all the terms and conditions of the offer. The offering of any inducements to do business is subject to the limitations and restrictions of state law and the ethical obligations established by any applicable Standard of Practice. *(Amended 1/95)*

- **Standard of Practice 12-4**
  REALTORS® shall not offer for sale/lease or advertise property without authority. When acting as listing brokers or as subagents, REALTORS® shall not quote a price different from that agreed upon with the seller/landlord. *(Amended 1/93)*

- **Standard of Practice 12-5**
  REALTORS® shall not advertise nor permit any person employed by or affiliated with them to advertise listed property without disclosing the name of the firm. *(Adopted 11/86)*

- **Standard of Practice 12-6**
  REALTORS®, when advertising unlisted real property for sale/lease in which they have an ownership interest, shall disclose their status as both owners/landlords and as REALTORS® or real estate licensees. *(Amended 1/93)*

- **Standard of Practice 12-7**
  Only REALTORS® who participated in the transaction as the listing broker or cooperating broker (selling broker) may claim to have "sold" the property. Prior to closing, a cooperating broker may post a "sold" sign only with the consent of the listing broker. *(Amended 1/96)*

Article 13

REALTORS® shall not engage in activities that constitute the unauthorized practice of law and shall recommend that legal counsel be obtained when the interest of any party to the transaction requires it.

Article 14

If charged with unethical practice or asked to present evidence or to cooperate in any other way, in any professional standards proceeding or investigation, REALTORS® shall place all pertinent facts before the proper tribunals of the Member Board or affiliated institute, society, or council in which membership is held and shall take no action to disrupt or obstruct such processes. *(Amended 1/99)*

- **Standard of Practice 14-1**
  REALTORS® shall not be subject to disciplinary proceedings in more than one Board of REALTORS® or affiliated institute, society or council in which they hold membership with respect to alleged violations of the Code of Ethics relating to the same transaction or event. *(Amended 1/95)*

- **Standard of Practice 14-2**
  REALTORS® shall not make any unauthorized disclosure or dissemination of the allegations, findings, or decision developed in connection with an ethics hearing or appeal or in connection with an arbitration hearing or procedural review. *(Amended 1/92)*

- **Standard of Practice 14-3**
  REALTORS® shall not obstruct the Board's investigative or professional standards proceedings by instituting or threatening to institute actions for libel, slander or defamation against any party to a professional standards proceeding or their witnesses based on the filing of an arbitration request, an ethics complaint, or testimony given before any tribunal. *(Adopted 11/87, Amended 1/99)*

- **Standard of Practice 14-4**
  REALTORS® shall not intentionally impede the Board's investigative or disciplinary proceedings by filing multiple ethics complaints based on the same event or transaction. *(Adopted 11/88)*

Duties to REALTORS®

Article 15

REALTORS® shall not knowingly or recklessly make false or misleading statements about competitors, their businesses, or their business practices. *(Amended 1/92)*

Article 16

REALTORS® shall not engage in any practice or take any action inconsistent with the agency or other exclusive relationship recognized by law that other REALTORS® have with clients. *(Amended 1/98)*

- **Standard of Practice 16-1**
  Article 16 is not intended to prohibit aggressive or innovative business practices which are otherwise ethical and does not prohibit disagreements with other REALTORS® involving commission, fees, compensation or other forms of payment or expenses. *(Adopted 1/93, Amended 1/95)*

- **Standard of Practice 16-2**
  Article 16 does not preclude REALTORS® from making general announcements to prospective clients describing their services and the terms of

their availability even though some recipients may have entered into agency agreements or other exclusive relationships with another REALTOR®. A general telephone canvass, general mailing or distribution addressed to all prospective clients in a given geographical area or in a given profession, business, club, or organization, or other classification or group is deemed "general" for purposes of this standard. *(Amended 1/98)*

Article 16 is intended to recognize as unethical two basic types of solicitations:

First, telephone or personal solicitations of property owners who have been identified by a real estate sign, multiple listing compilation, or other information service as having exclusively listed their property with another REALTOR®; and

Second, mail or other forms of written solicitations of prospective clients whose properties are exclusively listed with another REALTOR® when such solicitations are not part of a general mailing but are directed specifically to property owners identified through compilations of current listings, "for sale" or "for rent" signs, or other sources of information required by Article 3 and Multiple Listing Service rules to be made available to other REALTORS® under offers of subagency or cooperation. *(Amended 1/93)*

- **Standard of Practice 16-3**

Article 16 does not preclude REALTORS® from contacting the client of another broker for the purpose of offering to provide, or entering into a contract to provide, a different type of real estate service unrelated to the type of service currently being provided (e.g., property management as opposed to brokerage). However, information received through a Multiple Listing Service or any other offer of cooperation may not be used to target clients of other REALTORS® to whom such offers to provide services may be made. *(Amended 1/93)*

- **Standard of Practice 16-4**

REALTORS® shall not solicit a listing which is currently listed exclusively with another broker. However, if the listing broker, when asked by the REALTOR®, refuses to disclose the expiration date and nature of such listing; i.e., an exclusive right to sell, an exclusive agency, open listing, or other form of contractual agreement between the listing broker and the client, the REALTOR® may contact the owner to secure such information and may discuss the terms upon which the REALTOR® might take a future listing or, alternatively, may take a

listing to become effective upon expiration of any existing exclusive listing. *(Amended 1/94)*

- **Standard of Practice 16-5**

REALTORS® shall not solicit buyer/tenant agreements from buyers/tenants who are subject to exclusive buyer/tenant agreements. However, if asked by a REALTOR®, the broker refuses to disclose the expiration date of the exclusive buyer/tenant agreement, the REALTOR® may contact the buyer/tenant to secure such information and may discuss the terms upon which the REALTOR® might enter into a future buyer/tenant agreement or, alternatively, may enter into a buyer/tenant agreement to become effective upon the expiration of any existing exclusive buyer/tenant agreement. *(Adopted 1/94, Amended 1/98)*

- **Standard of Practice 16-6**

When REALTORS® are contacted by the client of another REALTOR® regarding the creation of an exclusive relationship to provide the same type of service, and REALTORS® have not directly or indirectly initiated such discussions, they may discuss the terms upon which they might enter into a future agreement or, alternatively, may enter into an agreement which becomes effective upon expiration of any existing exclusive agreement. *(Amended 1/98)*

- **Standard of Practice 16-7**

The fact that a client has retained a REALTOR® as an agent or in another exclusive relationship in one or more past transactions does not preclude other REALTORS® from seeking such former client's future business. *(Amended 1/98)*

- **Standard of Practice 16-8**

The fact that an exclusive agreement has been entered into with a REALTOR® shall not preclude or inhibit any other REALTOR® from entering into a similar agreement after the expiration of the prior agreement. *(Amended 1/98)*

- **Standard of Practice 16-9**

REALTORS®, prior to entering into an agency agreement or other exclusive relationship, have an affirmative obligation to make reasonable efforts to determine whether the client is subject to a current, valid exclusive agreement to provide the same type of real estate service. *(Amended 1/98)*

- **Standard of Practice 16-10**

REALTORS®, acting as agents of, or in another relationship with, buyers or tenants, shall disclose that relationship to the seller/landlord's agent or broker at first contact and shall provide written confirmation of that disclosure to the seller/landlord's agent or broker not later than execution of a purchase agreement or lease. *(Amended 1/98)*

• **Standard of Practice 16-11**

On unlisted property, REALTORS® acting as buyer/tenant agents or brokers shall disclose that relationship to the seller/landlord at first contact for that client and shall provide written confirmation of such disclosure to the seller/landlord not later than execution of any purchase or lease agreement.

REALTORS® shall make any request for anticipated compensation from the seller/landlord at first contact. *(Amended 1/98)*

• **Standard of Practice 16-12**

REALTORS®, acting as agents or brokers of sellers/landlords or as subagents of listing brokers, shall disclose that relationship to buyers/tenants as soon as practicable and shall provide written confirmation of such disclosure to buyers/tenants not later than execution of any purchase or lease agreement. *(Amended 1/98)*

• **Standard of Practice 16-13**

All dealings concerning property exclusively listed, or with buyer/tenants who are subject to an exclusive agreement shall be carried on with the client's agent or broker, and not with the client, except with the consent of the client's agent or broker or except where such dealings are initiated by the client. *(Adopted 1/93, Amended 1/98)*

• **Standard of Practice 16-14**

REALTORS® are free to enter into contractual relationships or to negotiate with sellers/landlords, buyers/tenants or others who are not subject to an exclusive agreement but shall not knowingly obligate them to pay more than one commission except with their informed consent. *(Amended 1/98)*

• **Standard of Practice 16-15**

In cooperative transactions REALTORS® shall compensate cooperating REALTORS® (principal brokers) and shall not compensate nor offer to compensate, directly or indirectly, any of the sales licensees employed by or affiliated with other REALTORS® without the prior express knowledge and consent of the cooperating broker.

• **Standard of Practice 16-16**

REALTORS®, acting as subagents or buyer/tenant agents or brokers, shall not use the terms of an offer to purchase/lease to attempt to modify the listing broker's offer of compensation to subagents or buyer's agents or brokers nor make the submission of an executed offer to purchase/lease contingent on the listing broker's agreement to modify the offer of compensation. *(Amended 1/98)*

• **Standard of Practice 16-17**

REALTORS® acting as subagents or as buyer/tenant agents or brokers, shall not attempt to extend a listing broker's offer of cooperation and/or compensation to other brokers without the consent of the listing broker. *(Amended 1/98)*

• **Standard of Practice 16-18**

REALTORS® shall not use information obtained by them from the listing broker, through offers to cooperate received through Multiple Listing Services or other sources authorized by the listing broker, for the purpose of creating a referral prospect to a third broker, or for creating a buyer/tenant prospect unless such use is authorized by the listing broker. *(Amended 1/93)*

• **Standard of Practice 16-19**

Signs giving notice of property for sale, rent, lease, or exchange shall not be placed on property without consent of the seller/landlord. *(Amended 1/93)*

• **Standard of Practice 16-20**

REALTORS®, prior to or after terminating their relationship with their current firm, shall not induce clients of their current firm to cancel exclusive contractual agreements between the client and that firm. This does not preclude REALTORS® (principals) from establishing agreements with their associated licensees governing assignability of exclusive agreements. *(Adopted 1/98)*

Article 17

In the event of contractual disputes or specific non-contractual disputes as defined in Standard of Practice 17-4 between REALTORS® associated with different firms, arising out of their relationship as REALTORS®, the REALTORS® shall submit the dispute to arbitration in accordance with the regulations of their Board or Boards rather than litigate the matter.

In the event clients of REALTORS® wish to arbitrate contractual disputes arising out of real estate transactions, REALTORS® shall arbitrate those disputes in accordance with the regulations of their Board, provided the clients agree to be bound by the decision. *(Amended 1/97)*

• **Standard of Practice 17-1**

The filing of litigation and refusal to withdraw from it by REALTORS® in an arbitrable matter constitutes a refusal to arbitrate. *(Adopted 2/86)*

- **Standard of Practice 17-2**

  Article 17 does not require REALTORS® to arbitrate in those circumstances when all parties to the dispute advise the Board in writing that they choose not to arbitrate before the Board. *(Amended 1/93)*

- **Standard of Practice 17-3**

  REALTORS®, when acting solely as principals in a real estate transaction, are not obligated to arbitrate disputes with other REALTORS® absent a specific written agreement to the contrary. *(Adopted 1/96)*

- **Standard of Practice 17-4**

  Specific non-contractual disputes that are subject to arbitration pursuant to Article 17 are:

  1) Where a listing broker has compensated a cooperating broker and another cooperating broker subsequently claims to be the procuring cause of the sale or lease. In such cases the complainant may name the first cooperating broker as respondent and arbitration may proceed without the listing broker being named as a respondent. Alternatively, if the complaint is brought against the listing broker, the listing broker may name the first cooperating broker as a third-party respondent. In either instance the decision of the hearing panel as to procuring cause shall be conclusive with respect to all current or subsequent claims of the parties for compensation arising out of the underlying cooperative transaction. *(Adopted 1/97)*

  2) Where a buyer or tenant representative is compensated by the seller or landlord, and not by the listing broker, and the listing broker, as a result, reduces the commission owed by the seller or landlord and, subsequent to such actions, another cooperating broker claims to be the procuring cause of sale or lease. In such cases the complainant may name the first cooperating broker as respondent and arbitration may proceed without the listing broker being named as a respondent. Alternatively, if the complaint is brought against the listing broker, the listing broker may name the first cooperating broker as a third-party respondent. In either instance the decision of the hearing panel as to procuring cause shall be conclusive with respect to all current or subsequent claims of the parties for compensation arising out of the underlying cooperative transaction. *(Adopted 1/97)*

  3) Where a buyer or tenant representative is compensated by the buyer or tenant and, as a result, the listing broker reduces the commission owed by the seller or landlord and, subsequent to such actions, another cooperating broker claims to be the procuring cause of sale or lease. In such cases the complainant may name the first cooperating broker as respondent and arbitration may proceed without the listing broker being named as a respondent. Alternatively, if the complaint is brought against the listing broker, the listing broker may name the first cooperating broker as a third-party respondent. In either instance the decision of the hearing panel as to procuring cause shall be conclusive with respect to all current or subsequent claims of the parties for compensation arising out of the underlying cooperative transaction. *(Adopted 1/97)*

  4) Where two or more listing brokers claim entitlement to compensation pursuant to open listings with a seller or landlord who agrees to participate in arbitration (or who requests arbitration) and who agrees to be bound by the decision. In cases where one of the listing brokers has been compensated by the seller or landlord, the other listing broker, as complainant, may name the first listing broker as respondent and arbitration may proceed between the brokers. *(Adopted 1/97)*

The Code of Ethics was adopted in 1913. Amended at the Annual Convention in 1924, 1928, 1950, 1951, 1952, 1955, 1956, 1961, 1962, 1974, 1982, 1986, 1987, 1989, 1990, 1991, 1992, 1993, 1994, 1995, 1996, 1997 and 1998.

Explanatory Notes

The reader should be aware of the following policies which have been approved by the Board of Directors of the National Association:

In filing a charge of an alleged violation of the Code of Ethics by a REALTOR®, the charge must read as an alleged violation of one or more Articles of the Code. Standards of Practice may be cited in support of the charge.

The Standards of Practice serve to clarify the ethical obligations imposed by the various Articles and supplement, and do not substitute for, the Case Interpretations in *Interpretations of the Code of Ethics*.

Modifications to existing Standards of Practice and additional new Standards of Practice are approved from time to time. Readers are cautioned to ensure that the most recent publications are utilized.

NATIONAL ASSOCIATION OF SOCIAL WORKERS

Address: 750 First Street NE, Suite 700
                Washington, DC 20002-4241
Telephone: 202/408-8600 or 800/638-8799
WWW: www.naswdc.org
Document: NASW Code of Ethics (1996)

(Below is an extract of the *NASW Code of Ethics*. The complete text, available from the Association, expands on each principle stated here and establishes a set of specific standards detailing the ethical responsibilities of the social worker to clients, colleagues, the profession, and the broader society.—Eds.)

Preamble

The primary mission of the social work profession is to enhance human well-being and help meet basic human needs, with particular attention to the needs of people who are vulnerable, oppressed, and living in poverty. A historic and defining feature of social work is the profession's focus on individual well-being in a social context and the well-being of society. Fundamental to social work is attention to the environmental forces that create, contribute to, and address problems in living.

The mission of the social work profession is rooted in a set of core values. These core values, embraced by social workers throughout the profession's history, are the foundation of social work's unique purpose and perspective. Core values, and the ethical principles that flow from them, must be balanced within the context and complexity of the human experience.

Core Values and Ethical Principles

Value: *Service*
Ethical Principle: *Social workers' primary goal is to help people in need and to address social problems.*

Value: *Social Justice*
Ethical Principle: *Social workers challenge social injustice.*

Value: *Dignity and Worth of the Person*
Ethical Principle: *Social workers respect the inherent dignity and worth of the person.*

Value: *Importance of Human Relationships*
Ethical Principle: *Social workers recognize the central importance of human relationships.*

Value: *Integrity*
Ethical Principle: *Social workers behave in a trustworthy manner.*

Value: *Competence*
Ethical Principle: *Social workers practice within their areas of competence and develop and enhance their professional expertise.*

© National Association of Social Workers. Reprinted with permission.

NATIONAL AUCTIONEERS ASSOCIATION

Address: 8880 Ballentine
                Overland Park, KS 66214
Telephone: 913/541-8084
WWW: www.auctioneers.org
Document: Code of Ethics (Most recently revised 1997.)

PREAMBLE

The public auction subjects all possessions to equitable public appraisal and competitive offer and thereby determines fair and current value of all personal goods and estates.

Auctioneers are masters of procedure and conduct of the public auction. Auctioneers are confidants of the public and instrumentalities of community progress and development. Such functions impose grave responsibilities and duties beyond ordinary business policy to which members must dedicate themselves. Members must strive to maintain the highest standards of the profession and share with fellow Auctioneers a common responsibility for integrity and honor.

Auctioneers will conduct business in accordance with the following Code of Ethics adopted by National Auctioneers Association.

PART I—PROFESSIONAL RELATIONSHIPS

Article 1. In the best interest of the public, of fellow Auctioneers and of their own business, Auctioneers should be loyal to National Auctioneers Association.

Article 2. The Auctioneer should so conduct their business as to avoid disputes with fellow Auctioneers, but in the event of a controversy between two Auctioneers who are members of National Auctioneers Association, they should not resort to a lawsuit, but submit their differences to arbitration by National Auctioneers Association, and the decision of such arbitration should be accepted as final and binding. If the dispute should be with non-members, the members should offer the services of this Board to arbitrate.

Article 3. Where members are charged with unethical practice, they should promptly and voluntarily place all the pertinent facts before the proper committee for investigation and report.

Article 4. Members should never publicly criticize a competitor, and where an opinion is especially requested, it should be rendered in conformity with strict professional courtesy and dignity.

Article 5. Members should not solicit the services of an employee of a fellow Auctioneer without the fellow Auctioneer's knowledge and consent.

Article 6. In the best interest of society, of the members' associates, and of the members' own business, Auctioneers should at all times be loyal to National Auctioneers Association and active in its works; and should willingly share with fellow members the lessons of their experience.

PART II—RELATION TO CLIENTS

Article 7. In justice of those who place their interests in the members' hands, Auctioneers should endeavor to keep abreast of business conditions, to keep informed in matters of law and proposed legislation affecting such interests, so as to give intelligent business advice and effective service.

Article 8. In accepting the sale of real or personal property, members pledge to be fair to both seller and buyer, and to protect the owners' interest as they would their own.

Article 9. When consulted for an appraisal of value or liquidation problem, members should give a well considered opinion, reflecting expert knowledge and sound judgment, taking requisite time for study, inquiry and deliberation. The members' counsel represents a professional service which they should render in writing and for which they should make a reasonable charge. Members should not undertake to give an appraisal or offer an opinion on any proposition on which they have a direct or even indirect interests, without a full disclosure of such interest.

Article 10. Before accepting a sale it is the duty of Auctioneers to advise the owner intelligently and honestly regarding the market value of the business or proposition and the reasonable chance of selling at value or above.

PART III—RELATIONS TO THE PUBLIC

Article 11. It is the duty of every member to protect the public against fraud, misrepresentation or unethical practices in connection with the sale, disposal or liquidation of any real or personal property Auctioneers are called upon to dispose of at public auction.

Article 12. It is the duty of members to ascertain all pertinent facts concerning every sale for which they are engaged, so that in offering members may avoid error, exaggeration and misrepresentation.

Article 13. Auctioneers are confidential trustees of the information given by the seller or gained by them through relationship, and Auctioneers must never disclose the gross receipts of a sale or any other information that would tend to be a violation of the profession.

Article 14. No special conditions, real or assumed, or inducements or directions from anyone relieve the member from responsibility strictly to observe the Code of Ethics in this letter and spirit.

NATIONAL DANCE ASSOCIATION'S NATIONAL REGISTRY OF DANCE EDUCATORS

Address: 1900 Association Drive
            Reston, VA 20191-1599
Telephone: 703/476-3436
WWW: www.aahperd.org/nda/nda.html
Document: Code of Ethics for Dance Educators
            in the Private Sector (1996)

(The NDA Registry offers dance educators a *Code of Safety* as well as a *Code of Ethics*. The NDA has published additional standards in *Guidelines for the Safe Practice of Teaching Dance* and *Opportunity-to-Learn Standards for Dance Education*. Only the *Code of Ethics* is reprinted here.—Eds.)

Preface

The following National Registry of Dance Educators Code of Ethics sets forth ethical guidelines for the Registered Dance Educator teaching dance in the private sector or school environment. The intent of this Code of Ethics is to: (1) suggest responsible professional behavior for dance educators, henceforth designated as responsibilities; (2) make these responsibilities known to the community at large; and (3) enable registrants to voluntarily pledge adherence to these responsibilities through registration.

The responsibilities set forth recommend professional behavior to individuals seeking registration in the National Registry of Dance Educators. The intent is that by adhering to these standards of professional conduct the public will be well served, the profession will be advanced and individual integrity will be promoted. The individual signing this agreement does so voluntarily, assuming full responsibility for its contents.

CODE OF ETHICS

A Registered Dance Educator:

1) Teaches only those forms of dance in which he/she has received quality professional educa-

tion and training. *Quality professional education* and *training* may include:

a) Dance training begun during childhood and continued more intensely through adolescence into young adulthood with the result that the dancer and educator is highly skilled and knowledgeable of syllabi (in some genres), curricula, and terminology within the chosen dance form; proficient in the execution of the chosen genre; and possesses verbal and nonverbal communication skills comparable to or surpassing those of recognized professional dancers and educators.

b) Education in aesthetic, scientific, social, historic and cultural constructs of dance as a part of past and present civilizations. This includes knowledge of current educational theories and reform movements within dance education and arts education.

c) State certification for teaching dance where applicable.

d) Degrees in dance education, choreography and/or performance from accredited institutions such as genre specific academies, dance or arts institutions, and colleges and universities supporting programs for dance majors and minors.

e) Nondance degrees mutually supported by extensive training in dance as defined in a) through d) above.

2) Accurately represents his/her credentials in education, performance, and teaching experience to the public.

3) Utilizes current pedagogical knowledge, methods, and techniques known through research and literature, and adheres to safe practices in the teaching of dance to others, as further defined by the National Registry of Dance Educators with reference to the *Guidelines for the Safe Practice of Teaching Dance*.

a) It is understood that injuries may occur from one's participation in dance instruction and dance activity; however, it is further understood that the Registered Dance Educator takes reasonable precautions to minimize their occurrence through prudent teaching practices.

b) Recommended precautions, which are further defined in the *Guidelines for the Safe Practice of Teaching Dance* include age appropriate curricula, teaching scientifically sound movement techniques, teaching to the ability of the student and following recommended class periods for age and ability of the student.

4) Practices in approved environments and under conditions safe for the practice of dance as further defined by the National Registry of Dance Educators with reference to the "Facilities" Section of the National Dance Association's *Opportunity-to-Learn Standards for Dance Education*.

   a) It is understood that injuries may occur from one's participation in dance instruction and dance activity; however, it is further understood that the Registered Dance Educator takes reasonable precautions to minimize their occurrence through the prudent choice of teaching site.

   b) Recommended precautions, which are further defined in the *Opportunities-to-Learn Standards for Dance Education* section of "Facilities" include safe floor surface and construction requirements, adequate space, lighting, ventilation and room temperature in the studio and in dressing room and bathroom facilities.

5) Respects the uniqueness of the individual student so that the dance program is directed toward being a positive experience for age-appropriate learning to take place in a safe environment that is free from abusive language, undue intimidation, stress and unhealthy competition.

6) Encourages the total development of the student regardless of age, gender, ability or ethnicity.

7) Practices professional conduct at all times without sexual harassment, inappropriate or sexually-suggestive touching, or romantic involvement with students.

8) Conducts all business and professional activities with honesty and integrity and projects a professional image in all aspects of practicing dance education.

9) Actively supports the dance education profession whenever possible through participation in community, state, and national organizations to promote high standards in practice, research and development of dance education, and continues their education in progressive educational practices.

10) Actively supports professional dance performers and performances in their communities whenever possible.

11) Accepts responsibility to one's self, students, and colleagues to maintain personal physical, mental and emotional good health.

© National Dance Association's National Registry of Dance Educators, Inc. Reprinted with permission.

nea

NATIONAL EDUCATION ASSOCIATION

Address: 1201 Sixteenth Street NW
Washington, DC 20036-3290
Telephone: 202/833-4000
WWW: www.nea.org
Document: Code of Ethics of the Education Profession (1975)

Preamble
The educator, believing in the worth and dignity of each human being, recognizes the supreme importance of the pursuit of truth, devotion to excellence, and the nurture of democratic principles. Essential to these goals is the protection of freedom to learn and to teach and the guarantee of equal education opportunity for all. The educator accepts the responsibility to adhere to the highest ethical standards.

The educator recognizes the magnitude of the responsibility inherent in the teaching process. The desire for the respect and confidence of one's colleagues, of students, of parents, and of the members of the community provides the incentive to attain and maintain the highest possible degree of ethical conduct. The Code of Ethics of the Education Profession *indicates the aspiration of all educators and provides standards by which to judge conduct.*

The remedies specified by the NEA and/or its affiliates for the violation of any provision of the Code shall be exclusive and no such provision shall be enforceable in any form other than one specifically designated by the NEA or its affiliates.

PRINCIPLE I

Commitment to the Student
The educator strives to help each student realize his or her potential as a worthy and effective member of

society. The educator therefore works to stimulate the spirit of inquiry, the acquisition of knowledge and understanding, and the thoughtful formulation of worthy goals.

In fulfillment of the obligation to the student, the educator—

1. Shall not unreasonably restrain the student from independent action in the pursuit of learning.
2. Shall not unreasonably deny the student access to varying points of view.
3. Shall not deliberately suppress or distort subject matter relevant to the student's progress.
4. Shall make reasonable effort to protect the student from conditions harmful to learning or to health and safety.
5. Shall not intentionally expose the student to embarrassment or disparagement.
6. Shall not on the basis of race, color, creed, sex, national origin, marital status, political or religious beliefs, family, social or cultural background or sexual orientation, unfairly—
   a) Exclude any student from participation in any program
   b) Deny benefits to any student
   c) Grant any advantage to any student.
7. Shall not use professional relationships with students for private advantage.
8. Shall not disclose information about students obtained in the course of professional service unless disclosure serves a compelling professional purpose or is required by law.

PRINCIPLE II

Commitment to the Profession

The education profession is vested by the public with a trust and responsibility requiring the highest ideals of professional service.

In the belief that the quality of the services of the education profession directly influences the nation and its citizens, the educator shall exert every effort to raise professional standards, to promote a climate that encourages the exercise of professional judgment, to achieve conditions that attract persons worthy of the trust to careers in education, and to assist in preventing the practice of the profession by unqualified persons.

In fulfillment of the obligation to the profession, the educator—

1. Shall not in an application for a professional position deliberately make a false statement or fail to disclose a material fact related to competency and qualifications.
2. Shall not misrepresent his/her professional qualifications.
3. Shall not assist any entry into the profession of a person known to be unqualified in respect to character, education, or other relevant attribute.
4. Shall not knowingly make a false statement concerning the qualifications of a candidate for a professional position.
5. Shall not assist a noneducator in the unauthorized practice of teaching.
6. Shall not disclose information about colleagues obtained in the course of professional service unless disclosure serves a compelling professional purpose or is required by law.
7. Shall not knowingly make false or malicious statements about a colleague.
8. Shall not accept a gratuity, gift, or favor that might impair or appear to influence professional decisions or action.

© National Education Association. Reprinted with permission.

NATIONAL ENVIRONMENTAL HEALTH ASSOCIATION

Address:	720 South Colorado Boulevard, South Tower, Suite 970 Denver, CO 80246-1925
Telephone:	303/756-9090
WWW:	www.neha.org
Document:	Code of Ethics for NEHA Credentialed Professionals (1992)

As an environmental professional, credentialed by the National Environmental Health Association, I hereby acknowledge, accept, and profess to abide by the following code of conduct and ethics:

- As long as my credential is in an active status, I shall endeavor to keep myself current and informed and satisfy any continuing education requirements that may be in effect for my credential.
- I will proudly represent my credentialed status and the credential itself to my professional peers, and to the public I serve.
- In the course of performing my duties, I will conduct myself in a professional manner befitting of my credentialed status.
- For the sake of elevating the recognition and status of my field, I will actively encourage my professional colleagues to consider earning this credential for themselves.
- I will do nothing to undermine, detract from, or otherwise cause to develop any damaging associations with respect to this credential. I accept that any activity on my part that will cause this credential any measure of injury serves as a breach and a failure on my part to uphold this code of ethics. Moreover, I accept that such action for which I might be responsible, could result in the revocation of my credential.
- I commit that my professional goal is to serve humankind by doing whatever I am able to do in the course of carrying out my professional responsibilities to maintain and provide a healthful environment for all.

NATIONAL FEDERATION OF INTERSCHOLASTIC COACHES ASSOCIATION

Address: PO Box 20626,
            11724 Northwest Plaza Circle
            Kansas City, MO 64153-1158
Telephone: 816/464-5400
WWW: n/a
Document: Coaches Code of Ethics

The function of a coach is to educate students through participation in interscholastic competition. An interscholastic program should be designed to enhance academic achievement and should never interfere with opportunities for academic success. Each student-athlete should be treated as though he or she were the coaches' own, and his or her welfare should be uppermost at all times. Accordingly, the following guidelines for coaches have been adopted by the NFICA Board of Directors.

The coach shall be aware that he or she has a tremendous influence, for either good or ill, on the education of the student athlete and, thus, shall never place the value of winning above the value of instilling the highest ideals of character.

The coach shall uphold the honor and dignity of the profession. In all personal contact with student-athletes, officials, athletic directors, school administrators, the state high school athletic association, the media, and the public, the coach shall strive to set an example of the highest ethical and moral conduct.

The coach shall take an active role in the prevention of drug, alcohol and tobacco abuse.

The coach shall avoid the use of alcohol and tobacco products when in contact with players.

The coach shall promote the entire interscholastic program of the school and direct his or her program in harmony with the total school program.

The coach shall master the contest rules and shall teach them to his or her team members. The coach shall not seek an advantage by circumvention of the spirit or letter of the rules.

The coach shall exert his or her influence to enhance sportsmanship by spectators, both directly and by working closely with cheerleaders, pep club sponsors, booster clubs, and administrators.

The coach shall respect and support contest officials. The coach shall not indulge in conduct which would incite players or spectators against the officials. Public criticism of officials or players is unethical.

Before and after contests, coaches for the competing teams should meet and exchange cordial greetings to set the correct tone for the event.

A coach shall not exert pressure on faculty members to give student-athletes special consideration.

A coach shall not scout opponents by any means other than those adopted by the league and/or state high school athletic association.

NATIONAL GENEALOGICAL SOCIETY

Address: 4527 Seventeenth Street North
Arlington, VA 22207-2399
Telephone: 703/525-0050 or 800/473-0060
WWW: www.ngsgenealogy.org
Documents: Standards for Sound Genealogical Research (1997)
Standards for Use of Technology in Genealogical Research (1997)
Standards for Using Records Repositories and Libraries (1997)

Standards for Sound Genealogical Research

Recommended by the National Genealogical Society

Remembering always that they are engaged in a quest for truth, family history researchers consistently—

- record the source for each item of information they collect.
- test every hypothesis or theory against credible evidence, and reject those that are not supported by the evidence.
- seek original records, or reproduced images of them when there is reasonable assurance they have not been altered, as the basis for their research conclusions.
- use compilations, communications and published works, whether paper or electronic, primarily for their value as guides to locating the original records.
- state something as a fact only when it is supported by convincing evidence, and identify the evidence when communicating the fact to others.
- limit with words like "probable" or "possible" any statement that is based on less than convincing evidence, and state the reasons for concluding that it is probable or possible.
- avoid misleading other researchers by either intentionally or carelessly distributing or publishing inaccurate information.
- state carefully and honestly the results of their own research, and acknowledge all use of other researchers' work.
- recognize the collegial nature of genealogical research by making their work available to others through publication, or by placing copies in appro-

priate libraries or repositories, and by welcoming critical comment.
- consider with open minds new evidence or the comments of others on their work and the conclusions they have reached.

Standards for Use of Technology in Genealogical Research

Recommended by the National Genealogical Society

Mindful that computers are tools, genealogists take full responsibility for their work, and therefore they—

- learn the capabilities and limits of their equipment and software, and use them only when they are the most appropriate tools for a purpose.
- refuse to let computer software automatically embellish their work.
- treat compiled information from on-line sources or digital databases like that from other published sources, useful primarily as a guide to locating original records, but not as evidence for a conclusion or assertion.
- accept digital images or enhancements of an original record as a satisfactory substitute for the original only when there is reasonable assurance that the image accurately reproduces the unaltered original.
- cite sources for data obtained on-line or from digital media with the same care that is appropriate for sources on paper and other traditional media, and enter data into a digital database only when its source can remain associated with it.
- always cite the sources for information or data posted on-line or sent to others, naming the author of a digital file as its immediate source, while crediting original sources cited within the file.
- preserve the integrity of their own databases by evaluating the reliability of downloaded data before incorporating it into their own files.
- provide, whenever they alter data received in digital form, a description of the change that will accompany the altered data whenever it is shared with others.
- actively oppose the proliferation of error, rumor and fraud by personally verifying or correcting information, or noting it as unverified, before passing it on to others.
- treat people on-line as courteously and civilly as they would treat them face-to-face, not separated by networks and anonymity.
- accept that technology has not changed the principles of genealogical research, only some of the procedures.

Standards for Using Records Repositories and Libraries

Recommended by the National Genealogical Society

Recognizing that how they use unique original records and fragile publications will affect other users, both current and future, family history researchers habitually—

- are courteous to research facility personnel and other researchers, and respect the staff's other daily tasks, not expecting the records custodian to listen to their family histories nor provide constant or immediate attention.
- dress appropriately, converse with others in a low voice, and supervise children appropriately.
- do their homework in advance, know what is available and what they need, and avoid ever asking for "everything" on their ancestors.
- use only designated work space areas, respect off-limits areas, and request permission before using photocopy or microform equipment, asking for assistance if needed.
- treat original records at all times with great respect and work with only a few records at a time, recognizing that they are irreplaceable and that each user must help preserve them for future use.
- treat books with care, never forcing their spines, and handle photographs properly, preferably wearing archival gloves.
- *never* mark, mutilate, rearrange, relocate, or remove from the repository any original, printed, microform, or electronic document or artifact.
- use only procedures prescribed by the repository for noting corrections to any errors or omissions found in published works, never marking the work itself.
- keep note-taking paper or other objects from covering records or books, and avoid placing any pressure upon them, particularly with a pencil or pen.
- use only the method specifically designated for identifying records for duplication, avoiding use of paper clips, adhesive notes, or other means not approved by the facility.
- unless instructed otherwise, replace volumes and files in their proper locations.
- before departure, thank the records custodians for their courtesy in making the materials available.
- follow the rules of the records repository without protest, even if they have changed since a previous visit or differ from those of another facility.

NATIONAL GUILD OF HYPNOTISTS

Address:	PO Box 308
	Merrimack, NH 03054-0308
Telephone:	603/429-9438
WWW:	www.ngh.net
Document:	Code of Ethics and Standards of the National Guild of Hypnotists

When the National Guild of Hypnotists (N.G.H.) was established, it was conceived by the charter members that the organization would provide an open forum for a free exchange of ideas concerning hypnotism. Their goal was to promote harmony, mutual trust and cooperation among practitioners and to protect and promote the art, science and philosophy of hypnotism. It was further decided that members of the National Guild of Hypnotists should constantly strive to establish and maintain a high code of ethics and encourage continuing education and high standards for all individuals and organizations in the field of hypnotism.

In keeping with the Constitution of the United States it was felt that N.G.H. rules and regulations should express high standards without infringing on the personal freedom of hypnotists or their clients.

The N.G.H. Code of Ethics and Standards presents principles and regulations intended to be a guide for the individual member.

I. GENERAL PRINCIPLES:

A. The physical and mental well-being of each client shall always be a prime consideration.

B. The rights and desires of the client shall always be respected.

C. Members shall avoid any conduct which could be construed as moral impropriety or sexual misconduct with a client.

D. Members shall use hypnosis strictly within the limits of their training and competence.

E. Members shall be honest and ethical in their advertising and business dealings.

F. Hypnosis shall be employed in accordance with established laws and regulations.

G. Members shall be aware of their limitations and always avoid infringement on other professions.

H. Professional behavior and respect should be extended to all fellow hypnotists.

II. PRACTICE OF HYPNOSIS:

A. Members shall establish and maintain proper records necessary to a professional practice.

B. Members shall use hypnosis with clients to motivate them to eliminate negative or unwanted habits, facilitate the learning process, improve memory and concentration, develop self-confidence, eliminate stage fright, improve athletic abilities, and for other social, educational and cultural endeavors of a non-medical nature, unless within the limits of their training and competence to do otherwise.

C. Induction methods that are not harmful to the client shall always be used.

D. Demonstrational hypnosis shall always be presented in a tasteful manner which is considerate of the fact that individuals have volunteered to participate in a public demonstration and shall be treated with courtesy and respect.

E. De-hypnotization:
1. Positive suggestions of well-being shall always be given prior to de-hypnotization.
2. No sudden or shocking methods of awakening shall be used.
3. All unnecessary suggestions shall be removed prior to de-hypnotization.

F. Age-regression and forensic hypnosis:
Age-regression and forensic hypnosis shall be used only by those who have had additional training in these specific fields of study.

G. Hallucinations:
1. Frightening, shocking, obscene, sexually suggestive, degrading or humiliating suggestions shall never be used with a hypnotized client.
2. Sudden changes of emotion shall be avoided when working with the hypnotized client.

H. Posthypnotic Suggestions:
1. Positive posthypnotic suggestions shall be employed to meet the needs of the client.
2. Posthypnotic suggestions to a client blocking the induction of hypnosis by other persons are considered an infringement on the rights of that client and shall not be used.

I. Responsibility of Members:
It shall be the responsibility of members of the National Guild of Hypnotists to conduct themselves in a professional and ethical manner, always cognizant of their professional responsibilities to the clients, colleagues and society.

Members shall not disseminate false or exaggerated claims regarding hypnosis, but shall attempt whenever possible to inform and educate the public with a true perspective of hypnosis.

Members shall publicly maintain a professional demeanor toward other professions expressing divergent views on hypnosis.

J. Nonacademic Titles or Degrees:
Recognized degrees are those which are awarded by institutions of higher learning, recognized by state, regional, national boards and/or accrediting agencies.

K. Advertising:
All advertising shall be factually presented in a professional and ethical way consistent with accepted standards of the profession. Members shall advertise services and capabilities as hypnotists in conjunction with other specialties, occupations, vocations, arts or professions only if duly trained, properly qualified and professionally recognized in those fields.

L. Education:
1. Schools of instruction now existing and those to be established in the future shall provide a full curriculum consisting of the following:
    a. Theory, practice and applications of hypnosis.
    b. Complete instruction and supervised practice in methodology.
    c. Possibilities and limitations of hypnosis.
    d. An elementary knowledge of normal and abnormal psychology.

2. Curricula and schools shall be approved and certified by the N.G.H.
3. Individual instructors shall be approved and certified by the N.G.H.

M. Members in good standing:

Members who maintain the required number of continuing-education hours, are of high moral character, conduct themselves and their practice of hypnosis in a professional and ethical manner and meet their financial dues obligation shall be considered and recommended as members in good standing of the National Guild of Hypnotists.

© National Guild of Hypnotists. Reprinted with permission.

NATIONAL PRESS PHOTOGRAPHERS ASSOCIATION

Address: 3200 Croasdaile Drive, Suite 306
             Durham, NC 27705
Telephone: 919/383-7246
WWW: metalab.unc.edu/nppa
Document: Code of Ethics

The National Press Photographers Association, a professional society dedicated to the advancement of photojournalism, acknowledges concern and respect for the public's natural-law right to freedom in searching for the truth and the right to be informed truthfully and completely about public events and the world in which we live.

We believe that no report can be complete if it is not possible to enhance and clarify the meaning of words. We believe that pictures, whether used to depict news events as they actually happen, illustrate news that has happened or to help explain anything of public interest, are an indispensable means of keeping people accurately informed; that they help all people, young and old, to better understand any subject in the public domain.

Believing the foregoing we recognize and acknowledge that photojournalists should at all times maintain the highest standards of ethical conduct in serving the public interest. To that end the National Press Photographers Association sets forth the following Code of Ethics which is subscribed to by all of its members:

1. The practice of photojournalism, both as a science and art, is worthy of the very best thought and effort of those who enter into it as a profession.

2. Photojournalism affords an opportunity to serve the public that is equalled by few other vocations and all members of the profession should strive by example and influence to maintain high standards of ethical conduct free of mercenary considerations of any kind.

3. It is the individual responsibility of every photojournalist at all times to strive for pictures that report truthfully, honestly and objectively.

4. Business promotion in its many forms is essential, but untrue statements of any nature are not worthy of a professional photojournalist and we severely condemn any such practice.

5. It is our duty to encourage and assist all members of our profession, individually and collectively, so that the quality of photojournalism may constantly be raised to higher standards.

6. It is the duty of every photojournalist to work to preserve all freedom-of-the-press rights recognized by law and to work to protect and expand freedom-of-access to all sources of news and visual information.

7. Our standards of business dealings, ambitions and relations shall have in them a note of sympathy for our common humanity and shall always require us to take into consideration our highest duties as members of society. In every situation in our business life, in every responsibility that comes before us, our chief thought shall be to fulfill that responsibility and discharge that duty so that when each of us is finished we shall have endeavored to lift the level of human ideals and achievement higher than we found it.

8. No Code of Ethics can prejudge every situation, thus common sense and good judgment are required in applying ethical principles.

© National Press Photographers Association. Reprinted with permission.

NATIONAL PROPERTY MANAGEMENT ASSOCIATION

Address: 1108 Pinehurst Road
             Dunedin, FL 34698
Telephone: 727/736-3788
WWW: www.npma.org
Document: NPMA Code of Ethics (1970)

I will recognize that all individuals inherently desire to practice their occupations to the best of their ability. I will assume that all individuals want to do their best.

I will maintain a broad and balanced outlook and will recognize the value in the ideas and opinions of others.

I will be guided in all my activities by truth, accuracy, fair dealing, and good taste.

I will keep informed of the latest developments in techniques, equipment, and processes.

I will recommend or initiate methods to increase productivity and efficiency.

I will support efforts to strengthen the property management profession through training and education.

I will help my associates reach personal and professional fulfillment.

I will earn and carefully guard my reputation for good moral character and good citizenship.

I will recognize that leadership is a call to service.

NATIONAL RECREATION AND PARK ASSOCIATION

Address: 22377 Belmont Ridge Road
             Ashburn, VA 20148
Telephone: 703/858-0784
WWW: www.nrpa.org
Documents: NRPA Professional Code of Ethics
             NRPA Code of Ethics on the
             Environment (1996)

NRPA Professional Code of Ethics
The National Recreation and Park Association has provided leadership to the nation in fostering the expansion of recreation and parks. NRPA has stressed the value of recreation, both active and passive, for individual growth and development. Its members are dedicated to the common cause of assuring that people of all ages and abilities have the opportunity to find the most satisfying use of their leisure time and enjoy an improved quality of life.

The Association has consistently affirmed the importance of well informed and professionally trained personnel to continually improve the administration of recreation and park programs. Members of NRPA are encouraged to support the efforts of the Association and profession by supporting state affiliate and national activities and participating in continuing education opportunities, certification, and accreditation.

Membership in NRPA carries with it special responsibilities to the public at large, and to the specific communities and agencies in which recreation and park services are offered. As a member of the National Recreation and Park Association, I accept and agree to abide by this Code of Ethics and pledge myself to:

- Adhere to the highest standards of integrity and honesty in all public and personal activities to inspire public confidence and trust.
- Strive for personal and professional excellence and encourage the professional development of associates and students.
- Strive for the highest standards of professional competence, fairness, impartiality, efficiency, effectiveness, and fiscal responsibility.
- Avoid any interest or activity which is in conflict with the performance of job responsibilities.
- Promote the public interest and avoid personal gain or profit from the performance of job duties and responsibilities.
- Support equal employment opportunities.

NRPA Code of Ethics on the Environment

PREAMBLE

The National Recreation and Park Association believes that park and recreation citizen and professional advocates, whether at the local, state and national level, have an environmental responsibility to assume a leadership role in conserving the quality of the natural environment. This belief originates from the recognition that the critical relationship between human activity and the natural environment includes our urban parks, greenways, open spaces, historic and cultural sites and our vast wildland and marine reserves.

Park and recreation advocates can carry out this responsibility by the creation and implementation of policies and practices which promote environmentally sensitive planning, management, and development and by integrating environmental education into the quality recreation opportunities made available to their constituents. In doing so, they provide an example and promote sound environmental practices and life-styles among the constituents that they serve. Through high quality recreation experiences, the public will nurture a sense of reverence, connectedness and stewardship for the natural environment, and develop its own environmental ethic.

CODE OF ETHICS

All park and recreation advocates, because of their special responsibility to assure resource accessibility for today, resource protection for tomorrow and high quality environmental experiences for all, subscribe to the following basic tenets of conduct:

- Purchase and use environmentally safe and sensitive products for use in facility and park operations, taking into consideration the effects of product production, use, storage and disposal.

- Implement management practices and programs which help to conserve and protect water and soil, enhance air quality and protect wildlife.
- Investigate, implement and promote the use of "state of the art" energy conserving technologies as they are able to be applied to ongoing operations.
- Reduce waste production, reuse and recycle materials from facility and park operations, use recycled products and handle hazardous and all other wastes according to lawful and safe procedures.
- Use planning and design techniques which will recognize the unique environmental characteristics of the site and will emphasize those characteristics through the site's proposed development, management and interpretation.
- Provide innovative and creative programs which increase appreciation for the natural world, promote environmentally conscious lifestyles, emphasize selective consumption and low-impact resource and transcend the boundaries of our own agencies.
- Implement maintenance management practices which recognize the natural attributes and sensitivity of the sites being maintained and support the mission of the profession to promote the value and integrity of our park assets.
- Cooperate with allied organizations and individuals by forming partnerships, sharing resources, assisting in conflict resolution, and advocating the values of the environment to ensure proper stewardship for the descendants that follow us.

In endorsing these basic precepts, the park and recreation advocate expresses the belief that he or she has an obligation to set an example and assume a leadership position in the development and use of policies, practices and programs which promote a healthy environment.

© National Recreation and Park Association. Reprinted with permission.

NATIONAL REGISTRY OF ENVIRONMENTAL PROFESSIONALS

Address: PO Box 2099
             Glenview, IL 60025-6099
Telephone: 847/724-6631
WWW: www.nrep.org
Document: Code of Ethical Practice (Most
             recently revised 1996.)

(All registrants of the National Registry of Environmental Professionals are provided with the *Code of Ethical Practice* upon receiving their credentials. The *Code of Ethical Practice* serves to summarize many of the significant *Canons of the Code of Professional Practice*, which is comprised of a general code for all registrants and specific codes for different registrations and certifications. The entire *Canons* are not reprinted here.—Eds.)

WHEREAS, the goal of an Environmental Professional or Manager is to be of the highest moral principles in providing knowledgeable decisions relating to the planning and management of environmental activities in which industry, government and the public may place their complete confidence.

THEREFORE, this Code of Ethical Practice shall govern the professional activities of National Registry of Environmental Professionals (NREP) registrants:

- To practice only in those areas of environmental science, safety, health or technology in which professional competence has been attained;
- To emblaze documents with the NREP seal, name or initials only when such documents are complete and contain only your work or work done under your personal, direct supervision and for which you can attest that all information is true and complete;
- To take all appropriate measures to prevent any conflict of interest that could compromise the planning and management of environmental activities;
- To perform assigned or contracted environmental planning and management duties always in a professional manner respectful of laws and regulations and the needs and concerns of others;
- To use the best principles of environmental science, health, safety and technology in planning and management to protect and enhance environmental quality;
- To cooperate with all levels of government in the furtherance and development of appropriate public policies supportive of environmental quality, occupational health and safety;
- To comply with applicable environmental quality, occupational health and safety, and product safety laws and regulations;
- To manage facilities in a manner to protect health and safety of employees and of individuals in surrounding communities;
- To fully disclose in writing to employers/clients all known positive and negative impacts to the environment of assigned activities, duties and/or responsibilities;
- To refrain from using the name of the National Registry of Environmental Professionals or its seal in any activity not previously approved by the Board of Directors.

Knowingly violating the Code of Ethical Practice shall be grounds for revocation of NREP professional registration.

NATIONAL SHERIFFS' ASSOCIATION

Address: 1450 Duke Street
             Alexandria, VA 22314-3490
Telephone: 703/836-7827
WWW: www.sheriffs.org
Document: Code of Ethics of the Office of the
             Sheriff

As a constitutionally elected sheriff, I recognize and accept that I am given a special trust and confidence by the citizens and employees whom I have been elected to serve, represent and manage. This trust and confidence is my bond to ensure that I shall behave and act according to the highest personal and professional standards. In furtherance of this pledge. I will abide by the following Code of Ethics.

I SHALL ENSURE that I and my employees, in the performance of our duties, will enforce and administer the law according to the standards of the U.S. Constitution and applicable State Constitutions and statutes so that equal protection of the law is guaranteed to everyone. To that end I shall not permit personal opinions, party affiliations, or consideration of the status of others to alter or lessen this standard of treatment of others.

I SHALL ESTABLISH, PROMULGATE AND ENFORCE a set of standards of behavior of my employees which will govern the overall management and operation of the law enforcement functions, court related activities, and corrections operations of my agency.

I SHALL NOT TOLERATE NOR CONDONE brutal or inhumane treatment of others by my employees nor shall I permit or condone inhumane or brutal treatment of inmates in my care and custody.

I STRICTLY ADHERE to standards of fairness and integrity in the conduct of campaigns for election and I shall conform to all applicable statutory standards of election financing and reporting so that the Office of the Sheriff is not harmed by the actions of myself or others.

I SHALL ROUTINELY CONDUCT or have conducted an internal and external audit of the public funds entrusted to my care and publish this information so that citizens can be informed about my stewardship of these funds.

I SHALL FOLLOW the accepted principles of efficient and effective administration and management as the principle criteria for my judgments and decisions in the allocation of resources and services in law enforcement, court related and corrections functions of my office.

I SHALL HIRE AND PROMOTE only those employees or others who are the very best candidates for a position according to accepted standards of objectivity and merit. I shall not permit other factors to influence hiring or promoting practices.

I SHALL ENSURE that all employees are granted and receive relevant training supervision in the performance of their duties so that competent and excellent service is provided by the Office of the Sheriff.

I SHALL ENSURE that during my tenure as Sheriff, I shall not use the Office of Sheriff for private gain.

I SHALL ACCEPT AND WILL ADHERE TO THIS CODE OF ETHICS. In so doing, I also accept responsibility for encouraging others in my profession to abide by this Code.

© National Sheriffs' Association. Reprinted with permission.

NATIONAL SOCIETY OF ACCOUNTANTS

Address:	1010 North Fairfax Street
	Alexandria, VA 22314
Telephone:	703/549-6400 or 800/966-6679
WWW:	www.nsacct.org

This organization is also known as National Society of Public Accountants. The code of ethics for this organization is entered under that name. See p. 00.

NATIONAL SOCIETY OF FUND RAISING EXECUTIVES

Address:	1101 King Street, Suite 700
	Alexandria, VA 22314-2967
Telephone:	703/684-0410 or 800/666-FUND
WWW:	www.nsfre.org
Document:	NSFRE Code of Ethical Principles and Standards of Professional Practice (1960. Most recently revised 1994.)

Statements of Ethical Principles (1991. Most recently revised 1994)

The National Society of Fund Raising Executives exists to foster the development and growth of fund-raising professionals and the profession, to preserve and enhance philanthropy and volunteerism, and to promote high ethical standards in the fund-raising profession.

To these ends, this code declares the ethical values and standards of professional practice that NSFRE members embrace and that they strive to uphold in their responsibilities for generating philanthropic support.

Members of the National Society of Fund Raising Executives are motivated by an inner drive to improve the quality of life through the causes they serve. They seek to inspire others through their own sense of dedication and high purpose. They are committed to the improvement of their professional knowledge and skills in order that their performance will better serve others. They recognize their stewardship responsibility to ensure that needed resources are vigorously and ethically sought and that the intent of the donor is honestly fulfilled. Such individuals practice their profession with integrity, honesty, truthfulness and adherence to the absolute obligation to safeguard the public trust.

Furthermore, NSFRE members:

- serve the ideal of philanthropy, are committed to the preservation and enhancement of volunteerism, and hold stewardship of these concepts as the overriding principle of professional life;
- put charitable mission above personal gain, accepting compensation by salary or set fee only;
- foster cultural diversity and pluralistic value, and treat all people with dignity and respect;
- affirm, through personal giving, a commitment to philanthropy and its role in society;
- adhere to the spirit as well as the letter of all applicable laws and regulations;
- bring credit to the fund-raising profession by their public demeanor;
- recognize their individual boundaries of competence and are forthcoming about their professional qualifications and credentials;
- value the privacy, freedom of choice and interests of all those affected by their actions;
- disclose all relationships that might constitute, or appear to constitute, conflicts of interest;
- actively encourage all their colleagues to embrace and practice these ethical principles;
- adhere to the following standards of professional practice in their responsibilities for generating philanthropic support.

Standards of Professional Practice (Adopted and incorporated into the NSFRE Code of Ethical Principles in 1992.)

1. Members shall act according to the highest standards and visions of their institution, profession and conscience.
2. Members shall avoid even the appearance of any criminal offense or professional misconduct.
3. Members shall be responsible for advocating, within their own organizations, adherence to all applicable laws and regulations.
4. Members shall work for a salary or fee, not percentage-based compensation or a commission.
5. Members may accept performance-based compensation such as bonuses provided that such bonuses are in accord with prevailing practices within the members' own organizations and are not based on a percentage of philanthropic funds raised.
6. Members shall not pay, seek or accept finder's fees, commissions or percentage-based compensation for obtaining philanthropic funds and shall, to the best of their ability, discourage their organizations from making such payments.
7. Members shall effectively disclose all conflicts of interest; such disclosure does not preclude or imply ethical impropriety.
8. Members shall accurately state their professional experience, qualifications and expertise.
9. Members shall adhere to the principle that all donor and prospect information created by, or on behalf of, an institution is the property of that institution and shall not be transferred or utilized except on behalf of that institution.
10. Members shall, on a scheduled basis, give donors the opportunity to have their names removed from lists that are sold to, rented to, or exchanged with other organizations.
11. Members shall not disclose privileged information to unauthorized parties.
12. Members shall keep constituent information confidential.
13. Members shall take care to ensure that all solicitation materials are accurate and correctly reflect the organization's mission and use of solicited funds.
14. Members shall, to the best of their ability, ensure that contributions are used in accordance with donors' intentions.
15. Members shall ensure, to the best of their ability, proper stewardship of charitable contributions, including timely reporting on the use and management of funds and explicit consent by the donor before altering the conditions of a gift.
16. Members shall ensure, to the best of their ability, that donors receive informed and ethical advice about the value and tax implications of potential gifts.
17. Members' actions shall reflect concern for the interests and well-being of individuals affected by those actions. Members shall not exploit any relationship with a donor, prospect, volunteer or employee to the benefit of the member or the member's organization.
18. In stating fund-raising results, members shall use accurate and consistent accounting methods that conform to the appropriate guidelines adopted by

the American Institute of Certified Public Accountants (AICPA)* for the type of institution involved. (* In countries outside of the United States, comparable authority should be utilized.)

19. All of the above notwithstanding, members shall comply with all applicable local, state, provincial and federal civil and criminal laws.

© National Society of Fund Raising Executives. Reprinted with permission.

NATIONAL SOCIETY OF PROFESSIONAL ENGINEERS

Address:	1420 King Street
	Alexandria, VA 22314-2794
Telephone:	703/684-2800
WWW:	www.nspe.org
Document:	Code of Ethics for Engineers (Most
	recently revised 1996.)

(The *Code of Ethics of Engineers* was formulated for the engineering profession in 1946 by the Committee on Engineering Ethics of the Engineers' Council for Professional Development, now the Accreditation Board for Engineering Technology (ABET). It is used as the basis of the codes for this and other engineering organizations.—Eds.)

Preamble

Engineering is an important and learned profession. As members of this profession, engineers are expected to exhibit the highest standards of honesty and integrity. Engineering has a direct and vital impact on the quality of life for all people. Accordingly, the services provided by engineers require honesty, impartiality, fairness and equity, and must be dedicated to the protection of the public health, safety, and welfare. Engineers must perform under a standard of professional behavior that requires adherence to the highest principles of ethical conduct.

I. Fundamental Canons

Engineers, in the fulfillment of their professional duties, shall:

1. Hold paramount the safety, health and welfare of the public.
2. Perform services only in areas of their competence.
3. Issue public statements only in an objective and truthful manner.
4. Act for each employer or client as faithful agents or trustees.
5. Avoid deceptive acts.
6. Conduct themselves honorably, responsibly, ethically, and lawfully so as to enhance the honor, reputation, and usefulness of the profession.

II. Rules of Practice

1. Engineers shall hold paramount the safety, health, and welfare of the public.
   a. If engineers' judgment is overruled under circumstances that endanger life or property, they shall notify their employer or client and such other authority as may be appropriate.
   b. Engineers shall approve only those engineering documents that are in conformity with applicable standards.
   c. Engineers shall not reveal facts, data or information without the prior consent of the client or employer except as authorized or required by law or this Code.
   d. Engineers shall not permit the use of their name or associate in business ventures with any person or firm that they believe is engaged in fraudulent or dishonest enterprise.
   e. Engineers having knowledge of any alleged violation of this Code shall report thereon to appropriate professional bodies and, when relevant, also to public authorities, and cooperate with the proper authorities in furnishing such information or assistance as may be required.
2. Engineers shall perform services only in the areas of their competence.
   a. Engineers shall undertake assignments only when qualified by education or experience in the specific technical fields involved.
   b. Engineers shall not affix their signatures to any plans or documents dealing with subject matter in which they lack competence, nor to any plan or document not prepared under their direction and control.
   c. Engineers may accept assignments and assume responsibility for coordination of an entire

project and sign and seal the engineering documents for the entire project, provided that each technical segment is signed and sealed only by the qualified engineers who prepared the segment.

3. Engineers shall issue public statements only in an objective and truthful manner.
   a. Engineers shall be objective and truthful in professional reports, statements, or testimony. They shall include all relevant and pertinent information in such reports, statements, or testimony, which should bear the date indicating when it was current.
   b. Engineers may express publicly technical opinions that are founded upon knowledge of the facts and competence in the subject matter.
   c. Engineers shall issue no statements, criticisms, or arguments on technical matters that are inspired or paid for by interested parties, unless they have prefaced their comments by explicitly identifying the interested parties on whose behalf they are speaking, and by revealing the existence of any interest the engineers may have in the matters.

4. Engineers shall act for each employer or client as faithful agents or trustees.
   a. Engineers shall disclose all known or potential conflicts of interest that could influence or appear to influence their judgment or the quality of their services.
   b. Engineers shall not accept compensation, financial or otherwise, from more than one party for services on the same project, or for services pertaining to the same project, unless the circumstances are fully disclosed and agreed to by all interested parties.
   c. Engineers shall not solicit or accept financial or other valuable consideration, directly or indirectly, from outside agents in connection with the work for which they are responsible.
   d. Engineers in public service as members, advisors, or employees of a governmental or quasi-governmental body or department shall not participate in decisions with respect to services solicited or provided by them or their organizations in private or public engineering practice.
   e. Engineers shall not solicit or accept a contract from a governmental body on which a principal or officer of their organization serves as a member.

5. Engineers shall avoid deceptive acts.
   a. Engineers shall not falsify their qualifications or permit misrepresentation of their or their associates' qualifications. They shall not misrepresent or exaggerate their responsibility in or for the subject matter of prior assignments. Brochures or other presentations incident to the solicitation of employment shall not misrepresent pertinent facts concerning employers, employees, associates, joint venturers, or past accomplishments.
   b. Engineers shall not offer, give, solicit or receive, either directly or indirectly, any contribution to influence the award of a contract by public authority, or which may be reasonably construed by the public as having the effect of intent to influencing the awarding of a contract. They shall not offer any gift or other valuable consideration in order to secure work. They shall not pay a commission, percentage, or brokerage fee in order to secure work, except to a bona fide employee or bona fide established commercial or marketing agencies retained by them.

III. Professional Obligations

1. Engineers shall be guided in all their relations by the highest standards of honesty and integrity.
   a. Engineers shall acknowledge their errors and shall not distort or alter the facts.
   b. Engineers shall advise their clients or employers when they believe a project will not be successful.
   c. Engineers shall not accept outside employment to the detriment of their regular work or interest. Before accepting any outside engineering employment, they will notify their employers.
   d. Engineers shall not attempt to attract an engineer from another employer by false or misleading pretenses.
   e. Engineers shall not actively participate in strikes, picket lines, or other collective coercive action.
   f. Engineers shall not promote their own interest at the expense of the dignity and integrity of the profession.

2. Engineers shall at all times strive to serve the public interest.
   a. Engineers shall seek opportunities to participate in civic affairs; career guidance for youths; and work for the advancement of the safety, health and well-being of their community.

b. Engineers shall not complete, sign, or seal plans and/or specifications that are not in conformity with applicable engineering standards. If the client or employer insists on such unprofessional conduct, they shall notify the proper authorities and withdraw from further service on the project.

c. Engineers shall endeavor to extend public knowledge and appreciation of engineering and its achievements.

3. Engineers shall avoid all conduct or practice that deceives the public.

a. Engineers shall avoid the use of statements containing a material misrepresentation of fact or omitting a material fact.

b. Consistent with the foregoing, Engineers may advertise for recruitment of personnel.

c. Consistent with the foregoing, Engineers may prepare articles for the lay or technical press, but such articles shall not imply credit to the author for work performed by others.

4. Engineers shall not disclose, without consent, confidential information concerning the business affairs or technical processes of any present or former client or employer, or public body on which they serve.

a. Engineers shall not, without the consent of all interested parties, promote or arrange for new employment or practice in connection with a specific project for which the Engineer has gained particular and specialized knowledge.

b. Engineers shall not, without the consent of all interested parties, participate in or represent an adversary interest in connection with a specific project or proceeding in which the Engineer has gained particular specialized knowledge on behalf of a former client or employer.

5. Engineers shall not be influenced in their professional duties by conflicting interests.

a. Engineers shall not accept financial or other considerations, including free engineering designs, from material or equipment suppliers for specifying their product.

b. Engineers shall not accept commissions or allowances, directly or indirectly, from contractors or other parties dealing with clients or employers of the Engineer in connection with work for which the Engineer is responsible.

6. Engineers shall not attempt to obtain employment or advancement or professional engagements by untruthfully criticizing other engineers, or by other improper or questionable methods.

a. Engineers shall not request, propose, or accept a commission on a contingent basis under circumstances in which their judgment may be compromised.

b. Engineers in salaried positions shall accept part-time engineering work only to the extent consistent with policies of the employer and in accordance with ethical considerations.

c. Engineers shall not, without consent, use equipment, supplies, laboratory, or office facilities of an employer to carry on outside private practice.

7. Engineers shall not attempt to injure, maliciously or falsely, directly or indirectly, the professional reputation, prospects, practice, or employment of other engineers. Engineers who believe others are guilty of unethical or illegal practice shall present such information to the proper authority for action.

a. Engineers in private practice shall not review the work of another engineer for the same client, except with the knowledge of such engineer, or unless the connection of such engineer with the work has been terminated.

b. Engineers in governmental, industrial, or educational employ are entitled to review and evaluate the work of other engineers when so required by their employment duties.

c. Engineers in sales or industrial employ are entitled to make engineering comparisons of represented products with products of other suppliers.

8. Engineers shall accept personal responsibility for their professional activities, provided, however, that Engineers may seek indemnification for services arising out of their practice for other than gross negligence, where the Engineer's interests cannot otherwise be protected.

a. Engineers shall conform with state registration laws in the practice of engineering.

b. Engineers shall not use association with a nonengineer, a corporation, or partnership as a "cloak" for unethical acts.

9. Engineers shall give credit for engineering work to those to whom credit is due, and will recognize the proprietary interests of others.

a. Engineers shall, whenever possible, name the person or persons who may be individually responsible for designs, inventions, writings, or other accomplishments.

b. Engineers using designs supplied by a client recognize that the designs remain the property of the client and may not be duplicated by the Engineer for others without express permission.

c. Engineers, before undertaking work for others in connection with which the Engineer may make improvements, plans, designs, inventions, or other records that may justify copyrights or patents, should enter into a positive agreement regarding ownership.

d. Engineers' designs, data, records, and notes referring exclusively to an employer's work are the employer's property. Employer should indemnify the Engineer for use of the information for any purpose other than the original purpose.

"By order of the United States District Court for the District of Columbia, former Section 11c of the NSPE Code of Ethics prohibiting competitive bidding, and all policy statements, opinions, rulings or other guidelines interpreting its scope, have been rescinded as unlawfully interfering with the legal right of engineers, protected under the antitrust laws, to provide price information to prospective clients; accordingly, nothing contained in the NSPE Code of Ethics, policy statements, opinions, rulings or other guidelines prohibits the submission of price quotations or competitive bids for engineering services at any time or in any amount."

Statement by NSPE Executive Committee

In order to correct misunderstandings which have been indicated in some instances since the issuance of the Supreme Court decision and the entry of the Final Judgment, it is noted that in its decision of April 25, 1978, the Supreme Court of the United States declared: "The Sherman Act does not require competitive bidding."

It is further noted that as made clear in the Supreme Court decision:

1. Engineers and firms may individually refuse to bid for engineering services.
2. Clients are not required to seek bids for engineering services.
3. Federal, state, and local laws governing procedures to procure engineering services are not affected, and remain in full force and effect.
4. State societies and local chapters are free to actively and aggressively seek legislation for professional selection and negotiation procedures by public agencies.
5. State registration board rules of professional conduct, including rules prohibiting competitive bidding for engineering services, are not affected and remain in full force and effect. State registration boards with authority to adopt rules of professional conduct may adopt rules governing procedures to obtain engineering services.
6. As noted by the Supreme Court, "nothing in the judgment prevents NSPE and its members from attempting to influence governmental action . . ."

NOTE:

In regard to the question of application of the Code to corporations vis-à-vis real persons, business form or type should not negate nor influence conformance of individuals to the Code. The Code deals with professional services, which services must be performed by real persons. Real persons in turn establish and implement policies within business structures. The Code is clearly written to apply to the Engineer and items incumbent on members of NSPE to endeavor to live up to its provisions. This applies to all pertinent sections of the Code.

© National Society of Professional Engineers. Reprinted with permission.

NATIONAL SOCIETY OF PUBLIC ACCOUNTANTS

Address:	1010 North Fairfax Street
	Alexandria, VA 22314
Telephone:	703/549-6400 or 800/966-6679
WWW:	www.nsacct.org
Document:	Code of Ethics for Members of the
	National Society of Public Accountants
	(Most recently revised 1990.)

(The National Society of Public Accountants is also known as The National Society of Accountants. This *Code of Ethics* is an official condensation of the principles contained in the Society's *Rules of Professional Conduct and Official Interpretations* which are binding in detail on all members. The complete *Rules* are not reprinted here.—Eds.)

I. MEMBERS OF THIS SOCIETY shall not violate the confidential relationship between themselves and their clients or former clients.

II. MEMBERS OF THIS SOCIETY shall not offer or render a professional service for a contingent fee during any period where the professional service consists of an audit engagement, a review engagement or a compilation engagement, including the period of time covered by any historical financial statements involved while performing an audit, a review or a compilation engagement; further, a member shall not offer to accept or accept a contingent fee for the preparation of original or amended tax returns or claims for tax refunds.

III. MEMBERS OF THIS SOCIETY or a firm of which they are a partner or shareholder shall not express an opinion on financial statements of an enterprise unless they and their firm are independent of such enterprise. Accordingly, members shall not express an opinion nor perform a review or compilation of financial statements of an enterprise financed in whole, or in part, by public distribution of securities or on financial statements for use as a basis of credit if they or members of their immediate family own or are committed to acquire a substantial financial interest in the enterprise, or during the period covered by an audit, review or compilation, they have been a director, officer or employee of the enterprise unless such interest or relationship is disclosed in the report.

IV. MEMBERS OF THIS SOCIETY shall not allow any person(s) to practice in their corporate, partnership or individual name who is not a partner, professional corporation co-shareholder or in their employ.

V. MEMBERS OF THIS SOCIETY who render professional services including an audit engagement, a review engagement or a compilation engagement shall not at the same time engage in any business or occupation which would create a conflict of interest while performing the aforementioned professional services.

VI. MEMBERS OF THIS SOCIETY shall be diligent, thorough and completely candid in expressing an opinion or other assurance on financial statements they have audited, reviewed or compiled.

VII. MEMBERS OF THIS SOCIETY shall not sign an audit report purporting to express their opinion as a result of an audit or examination of financial statements, unless they, or members or employees of their firm, have audited or examined the financial statements.

VIII. MEMBERS OF THIS SOCIETY shall not permit their names to be used in conjunction with any special purpose statement prepared for their clients that anticipates results of future operations, unless they disclose the source of the information used and what assumptions they have made, and unless they indicate they do not vouch for the accuracy of the forecast.

IX. MEMBERS OF THIS SOCIETY shall not accept a commission from any person or client for whom the member offers or renders concurrently a professional service, where the professional service consists of an audit engagement or a review engagement (including the period of time covered by any historical financial statements involved while performing an audit or review engagement), nor accept a commission where the member performs a compilation of a financial statement when the member expects or reasonably might expect that a third party will use the financial statement and the member's compilation report or transmittal does not disclose a lack of independence.

X. MEMBERS OF THIS SOCIETY shall not seek to obtain clients by advertising or other forms of solicitation in a manner that is false, misleading or deceptive.

XI. MEMBERS OF THIS SOCIETY who engage in the practice of accounting as a sole proprietor shall not use a plural term in the name of their firm, as "and company" or "and associates" or any other terms which would indicate anything other than individual ownership.

XII. MEMBERS OF THIS SOCIETY who receive an engagement for services by referral from another accountant shall not discuss or accept an extension of their services beyond the specific engagement without first consulting with the referring practitioner.

NATIONAL THERAPEUTIC RECREATION SOCIETY

Address: 22377 Belmont Ridge Road
               Ashburn, VA 20148
Telephone: 703/858-0784
WWW: www.nrpa.org/branches/ntrs.htm
Document: Code of Ethics (Most recently revised
               1990.)

(The Society also publishes *Interpretive Guidelines*, approved in 1994, which are intended to expand on and help clarify the *Code of Ethics*. The *Guidelines* are not reprinted here.—Eds.)

PREAMBLE

Leisure, recreation, and play are inherent aspects of the human experience, and are essential to health and well-being. All people, therefore, have an inalienable right to leisure and the opportunities it affords for play and recreation. Some human beings have disabilities, illnesses, or social conditions which may limit their participation in the normative structure of society. These persons have the same need for and right to leisure, recreation, and play.

Accordingly, the purpose of therapeutic recreation is to facilitate leisure, recreation, and play for persons with physical, mental, emotional or social limitations in order to promote their health and well-being. This goal is accomplished through professional services delivered in clinical and community settings. Services are intended to develop skills and knowledge, to foster values and attitudes, and to maximize independence by decreasing barriers and by increasing ability and opportunity.

The National Therapeutic Recreation Society exists to promote the development of therapeutic recreation in order to ensure quality services and to protect and promote the rights of persons receiving services.

The National Therapeutic Recreation Society and its members are morally obligated to contribute to the health and well-being of the people they serve. In order to meet this important social responsibility, the National Therapeutic Recreation Society and its members endorse and practice the following ethical principles.

I. The Obligation of Professional Virtue

Professionals possess and practice the virtues of integrity, honesty, fairness, competence, diligence, and self-awareness.

A. *Integrity:* Professionals act in ways that protect, preserve and promote the soundness and completeness of their commitment to service. Professionals do not forsake nor arbitrarily compromise their principles. They strive for unity, firmness, and consistency of character. Professionals exhibit personal and professional qualities conducive to the highest ideals of human service.

B. *Honesty:* Professionals are truthful. They do not misrepresent themselves, their knowledge, their abilities, or their profession. Their communications are sufficiently complete, accurate, and clear in order for individuals to understand the intent and implications of services.

C. *Fairness:* Professionals are just. They do not place individuals at unwarranted advantage or disadvantage. They distribute resources and services according to principles of equity.

D. *Competence:* Professionals function to the best of their knowledge and skill. They only render services and employ techniques of which they are qualified by training and experience. They recognize their limitations, and seek to reduce them by expanding their expertise. Professionals continuously enhance their knowledge and skills through education and by remaining informed of professional and social trends, issues and developments.

E. *Diligence:* Professionals are earnest and conscientious. Their time, energy, and professional resources are efficiently used to meet the needs of the persons they serve.

F. *Awareness:* Professionals are aware of how their personal needs, desires, values, and interests may influence their professional actions. They are especially cognizant of where their personal needs may interfere with the needs of the persons they serve.

II. The Obligation of the Professional to the Individual

A. *Well-Being:* Professionals' foremost concern is the well-being of the people they serve. They do everything reasonable in their power and within the scope of professional practice to benefit them. Above all, professionals cause no harm.

B. *Loyalty:* Professionals' first loyalty is to the well-being of the individuals they serve. In instances of multiple loyalties, professionals make the nature and the priority of their loyalties explicit to everyone concerned, especially where they may be in question or in conflict.

C. *Respect:* Professionals respect the people they serve. They show regard for their intrinsic worth and for their potential to grow and change. The following areas of respect merit special attention:

1. *Freedom, Autonomy, and Self-Determination:* Professionals respect the ability of people to make, execute, and take responsibility for their own choices. Individuals are given adequate opportunity for self-determination in the least restrictive environment possible. Individuals have the right of informed consent. They may refuse participation in any program except where their welfare is clearly and immediately threatened and where they are unable to make rational decisions on their own due to temporary or permanent incapacity. Professionals promote independence and avoid fostering dependence. In particular, sexual relations and other manipulative behaviors intended to control individuals for the personal needs of the professional are expressly unethical.

2. *Privacy:* Professionals respect the privacy of individuals. Communications are kept confidential except with the explicit consent of the individual or where the welfare of the individual or others is clearly imperiled. Individuals are informed of the nature and the scope of confidentiality.

D. *Professional Practices:* Professionals provide quality services based on the highest professional standards. Professionals abide by standards set by the profession, deviating only when justified by the needs of the individual. Care is used in administering tests and other measurement instruments. They are used only for their express purposes. Instruments should conform to accepted psychometric standards. The nature of all practices, including tests and measurements, are explained to individuals. Individuals are also debriefed on the results and implications of professional practices. All professional practices are conducted with the safety and well-being of the individual in mind.

III. The Obligation of the Professional to Other Individuals and to Society

A. *General Welfare:* Professionals make certain that their actions do not harm others. They also seek to promote the general welfare of society by advocating the importance of leisure, recreation and play.

B. *Fairness:* Professionals are fair to other individuals and to the general public. They seek to balance the needs of the individuals they serve with the needs of other persons according to principles of equity.

IV. The Obligation of the Professional to Colleagues

A. *Respect:* Professionals show respect for colleagues and their respective professions. They take no action that undermines the integrity of their colleagues.

B. *Cooperation and Support:* Professionals cooperate with and support their colleagues for the benefit of the persons they serve. Professionals demand the highest professional and moral conduct of each other. They approach and offer help to colleagues who require assistance with an ethical problem. Professionals take appropriate action toward colleagues who behave unethically.

V. The Obligation of the Professional to the Profession

A. *Knowledge:* Professionals work to increase and improve the profession's body of knowledge by supporting and/or by conducting research. Research is practiced according to accepted canons and ethics of scientific inquiry. Where subjects are involved, their welfare is paramount. Prior permission is gained from subjects to participate in research. They are informed of the general nature of the research and any specific risks that may be involved. Subjects are debriefed at the conclusion of the research, and are provided with results of the study upon request.

B. *Respect:* Professionals treat the profession with critical respect. They strive to protect, preserve, and promote the integrity of the profession and its commitment to public service.

C. *Reform:* Professionals are committed to regular and continuous evaluation of the profession. Changes are implemented that improve the profession's ability to serve society.

VI. The Obligation of the Profession to Society

A. *Service:* The profession exists to serve society. All of its activities and resources are devoted to the principle of service.

B. *Equality:* The profession is committed to equality of opportunity. No person shall be refused service because of social status, ethnic background, sexual orientation, or inability to pay. The profession neither conducts nor condones discriminatory practices. It actively seeks to correct inequities that unjustly discriminate.

C. *Advocacy:* The profession advocates for the people it is entrusted to serve. It protects and promotes their health and well-being and inalienable right to leisure, recreation, and play in clinical and community settings.

© National Therapeutic Recreation Society. Reprinted with permission.

NATIONAL WEATHER ASSOCIATION

Address: 6704 Wolke Court
             Montgomery, AL 36116-2134
Telephone: 334/213-0388
WWW: www.nwas.org

The National Weather Association subscribes to the same code of ethics as the American Meteorological Society. See p. 00.

NATIONAL WRITERS ASSOCIATION

Address: 3140 South Peoria Street, #295PMB
             Aurora, CO 80014
Telephone: 303/841-0246

WWW: www.nationalwriters.com
Document: Code of Ethics (1994)

1. The Writer shall recognize that the constitutional guarantees of expression and freedom of the press imply a responsibility not to abuse these freedoms.
2. The Writer shall check carefully for accuracy and verification of all facts used when writing both fiction and nonfiction.
3. The Writer shall not knowingly include in factual material any false or misleading statements without pointing out valid reasons for doing so.
4. The Writer shall not use ideas or material belonging to others except in observance of the 'fair use' doctrine, or if the material is in the public domain, or unless permission from the rightful owners as been obtained and proper credit is given.
5. The Writer shall not use the writing profession for the purpose of defaming, libeling, or maligning others.
6. The Writer shall avoid using the writing profession to undermine or overthrow the ideals of justice, freedom, democracy, and humanity.

STANDARDS OF PRACTICE

1. The Writer will professionally prepare every manuscript submitted, using clean type, dark ribbon, heavy white paper with ample margins, name and address in the upper left-hand corner of the first page, double-spacing throughout. The Writer will carefully revise to correct any errors in typing, spelling, punctuation, or grammar.
2. The Writer will become familiar with any publication's editorial needs, slant, and readership before submission.
3. The Writer will enclose a self-addressed stamped envelope (SASE) with each query or submission, except in the case of a book manuscript, in which case enclosure of adequate postage for return will suffice.
4. The Writer will exercise patience in waiting for a report on a manuscript or query and refrain from troubling an editor with unnecessary correspondence. A prompt and earnest compliance should follow any request by an editor for a re-write or revision unless such request is contrary to the Writer's ideals or convictions. Notification shall be given an editor at once if it is impossible to carry out an assignment by required deadline dates.

5. Once a Writer accepts an assignment, he shall abide by the provisions of that assignment in all respects, including the meeting of deadlines, rate and method of payment, and expenses.

6. The Writer will submit a complete manuscript to one publication at a time only, unless the publication will accept simultaneous submissions, in which case the Writer will advise the editor that this is a multiple submission.

7. The Writer may type his/her copyright notice in the upper-right hand corner of the manuscript's first page and make every endeavor to offer first rights only for sale, unless adequate compensation is offered for additional rights.

8. The Writer shall understand that should he/she agree to do 'work for hire,' he/she loses all rights to the material, including the copyright.

9. The Writer will be familiar with the copyright laws, the rights and powers for writers contained therein, and the ways in which the law may be used as a method of obtaining better contracts and letters of agreement.

10. The Writer will carefully study any contract before signing, making sure that all clauses and wordings are understood. Impartial professional help and advice will be sought if any portion of the contract is questionable.

© National Writers Association. Reprinted with permission.

PROFESSIONAL NUMISMATISTS GUILD, INC.

Address: 3950 Concordia Lane
             Fallbrook, CA 92028
Telephone: 760/728-1300
WWW: www.pngdealers.com
Document: PNG Code of Ethics

As a coin dealer, I recognize my obligation towards the public and towards my fellow members of the PNG and my industry. It is my intention to be worthy of the confidence and respect of those with whom I come in contact in the numismatic trade. For this purpose I have pledged myself as follows:

In my relations with the public:

1. To furnish my clientele advice on numismatic matters to the best of my ability.

2. To sell at prices that commensurate with a reasonable return on my investment and then prevailing market conditions.

3. To purchase coins from the public at reasonable prices with due allowance for buyer's risk and prevailing market conditions.

4. To neither broadcast, publish, nor advertise, in any manner, any representation or any implication with intent to create a false or incorrect conclusion with regard to my own goods, prices, or services, or those of a competitor or to make false claims to a policy, or to make any false representation as to my prices or those of my competitors.

5. To assist recognized governmental authorities in the prosecution of violators of the law in numismatic matters.

6. To refrain from knowingly dealing in stolen coins, medals or other numismatic material or publications or offering counterfeits or altered specimens, that are legal to own, to furnish the buyer with an invoice showing in detail, the nature of such coins sold and when selling a processed coin or a treated coin, where known, to furnish the buyer with an invoice showing in detail the nature of such coin sold.

7. To accurately grade merchandise, giving cognizance to the fact that grading is inherently subjective and a matter of personal opinion, yet utilize recognized industry standards.

8. To disclose to my customers materials sufficient to allow my customers to properly understand the risks associated with the purchase and sale of coins in either oral or written form as the circumstances may dictate. A written disclosure policy, which may appear on the invoice utilized by a member or in other form, shall contain the following language: "The coin market is speculative and unregulated. Many areas of numismatics lend themselves to third party grading and authentication. Certification does not eliminate all risks associated with the grading of coins."

9. Each member of the PNG shall notify their employer in writing of the provisions of the bylaws and furnish a copy of such notice to the Executive Director. Complaint against a member for violating the Code of Ethics may be brought by any member or non-member of the PNG. A PNG member against whom a complaint is filed, by virtue of membership in the PNG, agrees to resolve the dispute by binding arbitration under the rules of the Professional Numismatists Guild, Inc.

10. The following constitute unfair or deceptive acts which a PNG member pledges they will not do in their dealings with consumers and the general public:

    a. Representing to a consumer that a coin that has been graded by a captive grading service is of equal fungibility (salability) to that of an independent grading service, unless that statement is factual.

    b. Representing to a consumer that grade of a numismatic item that is encapsulated by an independent grading service is equal to the value quoted for a similarly dated and similarly described coin of a different independent grading service, unless that statement is factual.

    c. Offering any misleading price comparison.

    d. Misleading use of the survey of any financial institution or other institution or investment guide or use of examples in a way calculated to create an inaccurate impression.

    e. Misrepresenting the origin of a coin, its provenance, pedigree or deceptively stating a source of a coin. Representing that a coin is from a hoard, an estate or of a particular provenance unless such statement is true.

    f. Misrepresenting the grade of a coin, giving cognizance to the fact that grading is inherently subjective and a matter of personal opinion, yet utilizing recognized industry standards.

    g. Misrepresenting the value of a coin.

    h. Misrepresenting the weight of a coin. It is deceptive to state the weight of a coin or medal in pounds or ounces without making it clear whether the weight is in troy ounces or avoirdupois ounces.

    i. Failing to identify whizzed coins.

    j. Using high pressure sales techniques.

    k. Reporting or utilizing price realized at any auction sale unless such use is of a coin that actually sold at the price and circumstances represented.

    l. Repairing any coin without disclosure.

    m. Representing that holding coins for a specific period insures profitability.

    n. Representing affiliation with any government agency unless such representation is true.

    o. Failing to take cognizance of and compliance with the blue sky laws of various jurisdictions and the Federal securities laws, as may be applicable.

    p. Promising immediate delivery of goods where the same is not possible, and not disclosing in a deferred delivery the reasons therefore in a manner consistent with all local, state and federal requirements.

    q. That each member comply with the law and regulations under the Hobby Protection Act.

11. Each auctioneer member of the PNG shall in his dealing with the public, make full, complete and conspicuous disclosure of all terms necessary and material for a consumer to make an informed judgment concerning bidding, consigning and conduct associated with an auction sale. The PNG Board shall from time to time issue regulations which shall evidence industry practices and be binding upon auctioneer-members.

In my relations with my fellow members of this Association, I have pledged to:

1. Refrain from the voluntary public expressions of adverse criticism of other members or their merchandise.

2. To recognize my own contracts and undertakings as well as those of fellow members.

3. To freely exchange information with other members when requested.

4. To avoid making false statements or representations in my relations with my competitors and to cooperate generally towards the betterment of our industry and the hobby in my relations with fellow members.

5. To obey this code of ethics and the terms and conditions of these bylaws and membership in the Guild.

Registered PNG Numismatist

1. Any non-member employee or a member of a firm that a member is affiliated with that utilizes the PNG logo or trademark, or who seeks a bourse table at any convention at which PNG membership is a requisite for entitlement to such table, and who actively buys, sells or deals with the public shall be required to register with the Professional

Numismatists Guild, Inc. and agree to abide by its Code of Ethics.

2. Such non-member or his employer or affiliated company shall file a Registered PNG Numismatist application and pay an annual assessment to be determined by the Board from time to time, and sign a copy of the Code of Ethics acknowledging receipt thereof. Such document, or in the failure of the PNG member or non-member to supply it, the use of the PNG logo or any other privileges of membership, shall bear the employee and employer's signature and shall indicate that the employee agrees to be bound by the Code of Ethics as now or hereafter adopted. The employer shall also agree to be bound thereby, including the provisions in the PNG Bylaw for mandatory and binding arbitration. Such document shall thereupon be returned to the PNG.

3. By executing such document, such non-member or the employer understands that they shall have personal liability for any transaction undertaken, with member or non-member without regard to the actual legal identity or personae of the seller.

4. Each member shall be required to notify the PNG within three days of such time when such non-member employee is no longer in their employ, and each member shall promptly notify the PNG of a new non-member employee which is added, in which case such notice shall be accompanied by the application and the registration fee.

Professional Photographers of America
THE WORLD'S GREAT STORYTELLERS ℠

PROFESSIONAL PHOTOGRAPHERS OF AMERICA

Address: 229 Peachtree Street, Suite 2200
             Atlanta, GA 30303

Telephone: 404/522-8600
WWW: www.ppa-world.org
Document: Code of Ethics

I, as a requirement for admission to and retention of membership and participation in Professional Photographers of America, Inc., agree to strive at all times to upgrade and improve my knowledge and skill of professional photography, marketing and related areas. In all my dealings with the users of photography and the general public, I will:

I. Strive to present all photographic services in surroundings and in a manner which reflects the highest levels of professionalism.

II. Deal with all users of photography and the general public with honesty and integrity.

III. Not use any marketing or competitive practice which violates any Federal Trade Commission, or other Federal or State regulatory agency rule or regulation, or Federal or State statute or any decision of any Federal or State Court.

IV. Strive to produce photography and photographic services in accordance with the highest levels of professionalism at all times.

V. In all dealings with fellow professional photographers, students and others who aspire to be professional photographers, I shall share the knowledge and skill of professional photography.

VI. Support efforts for and assist in the education of all interested persons and the general public in the art and science of professional photography.

 Public Relations Society of America

PUBLIC RELATIONS SOCIETY OF AMERICA

Address: 33 Irving Place
             New York, NY 10003-2376
Telephone: 212/995-2230 or 800-937-7772
WWW: www.prsa.org
Document: Code of Professional Standards for the Practice of Public Relations (1988)

(This *Code* was adopted by the PRSA Assembly in 1988. It replaces a code of ethics in force since 1950 and revised in 1954, 1959, 1963, 1977, and 1983. The *Code* includes sections entitled "Official Interpretations of the Code" which are not reprinted here. Additional information on the *Code* and enforcement procedures may be obtained from the chair of the Board of Ethics through PRSA Headquarters.—Eds.)

Declaration of Principles

Members of the Public Relations Society of America base their professional principles on the fundamental value and dignity of the individual, holding that the free exercise of human rights, especially freedom of speech, freedom of assembly, and freedom of the press, is essential to the practice of public relations.

In serving the interests of clients and employers, we dedicate ourselves to the goals of better communication, understanding, and cooperation among the diverse individuals, groups, and institutions of society, and of equal opportunity of employment in the public relations profession.

We pledge:

To conduct ourselves professionally, with truth, accuracy, fairness, and responsibility to the public;

To improve our individual competence and advance the knowledge and proficiency of the profession through continuing research and education;

And to adhere to the articles of the Code of Professional Standards for the Practice of Public Relations as adopted by the governing Assembly of the Society.

Code of Professional Standards for the Practice of Public Relations

These articles have been adopted by the Public Relations Society of America to promote and maintain high standards of public service and ethical conduct among its members.

1. A member shall conduct his or her professional life in accord with the **public interest**.
2. A member shall exemplify high standards of **honesty and integrity** while carrying out dual obligations to a client or employer and to the democratic process.
3. A member shall **deal fairly** with the public, with past or present clients or employers, and with fellow practitioners, giving due respect to the ideal of free inquiry and to the opinions of others.
4. A member shall adhere to the highest standards of **accuracy and truth**, avoiding extravagant claims or unfair comparisons and giving credit for ideas and words borrowed from others.
5. A member shall not knowingly disseminate **false or misleading information** and shall act promptly to correct erroneous communications for which he or she is responsible.
6. A member shall not engage in any practice which has the purpose of **corrupting** the integrity of channels of communications or the processes of government.
7. A member shall be prepared to **identify publicly** the name of the client or employer on whose behalf any public communication is made.
8. A member shall not use any individual or organization professing to serve or represent an announced cause, or professing to be independent or unbiased, but actually serving another or **undisclosed interest**.
9. A member shall **not guarantee the achievement** of specified results beyond the member's direct control.
10. A member shall **not represent conflicting** or competing interests without the express consent of those concerned, given after a full disclosure of the facts.
11. A member shall not place himself or herself in a position where the member's **personal interest is or may be in conflict** with an obligation to an employer or client, or others, without full disclosure of such interests to all involved.
12. A member shall **not accept fees, commissions, gifts or any other consideration** from anyone except clients or employers for whom services are performed without their express consent, given after full disclosure of the facts.
13. A member shall scrupulously safeguard the **confidences and privacy rights** of present, former, and prospective clients or employers.
14. A member shall not intentionally **damage the professional reputation** or practice of another practitioner.
15. If a member has evidence that another member has been guilty of unethical, illegal, or unfair practices, including those in violation of this Code, the member is obligated to present the information promptly to the proper authorities of the Society for action in accordance with the procedure set forth in Article XII of the Bylaws.
16. A member called as a witness in a proceeding for enforcement of this Code is obligated to appear,

unless excused for sufficient reason by the judicial panel.

17. A member shall, as soon as possible, sever relations with any organization or individual if such relationship requires conduct contrary to the articles of this Code.

■ THE ASSOCIATION OF ■
RTNDA·
ELECTRONIC JOURNALISTS

RADIO-TELEVISION NEWS DIRECTORS ASSOCIATION

Address: 1000 Connecticut Avenue NW,
             Suite 615
             Washington, DC 20036-5302
Telephone: 202/659-6510
WWW: www.rtnda.org
Document: Code of Ethics (1987)

The responsibility of radio and television journalists is to gather and report information of importance and interest to the public accurately, honestly and impartially.

The members of the Radio-Television News Directors Association accept these standards and will:

1. Strive to present the source or nature of broadcast news material in a way that is balanced, accurate and fair.
    A. They will evaluate information solely on its merits as news, rejecting sensationalism or misleading emphasis in any form.
    B. They will guard against using audio or video material in a way that deceives the audience.
    C. They will not mislead the public by presenting as spontaneous news any material which is staged or rehearsed.
    D. They will identify people by race, creed, nationality or prior status only when it is relevant.
    E. They will clearly label opinion and commentary.
    F. They will promptly acknowledge and correct errors.
2. Strive to conduct themselves in a manner that protects them from conflicts of interest, real or per-

ceived. They will decline gifts or favors which would influence or appear to influence their judgments.
3. Respect the dignity, privacy and well-being of people with whom they deal.
4. Recognize the need to protect confidential sources. They will promise confidentiality only with the intention of keeping that promise.
5. Respect everyone's right to a fair trial.
6. Broadcast the private transmissions of other broadcasters only with permission.
7. Actively encourage observance of this Code by all journalists, whether members of the Radio-Television News Directors Association or not.

RADIOLOGICAL SOCIETY OF NORTH AMERICA

Address: 820 Jorie Boulevard
             Oak Brook, IL 60523-2251
Telephone: 630/571-2670
WWW: www.rsna.org

The Radiological Society of North America subscribes to the same code of ethics as the American Medical Association. See p. 00.

Society for Human Resource Management
Partners in the Workplace

SOCIETY FOR HUMAN RESOURCE MANAGEMENT

Address: 1800 Duke Street
             Alexandria, VA 22314-3499

Telephone: 703/548-3440
WWW: www.shrm.org
Document: Code of Ethics

As a member of the Society for Human Resource Management, I pledge myself to:

- Maintain the highest standards of professional and personal conduct.
- Strive for personal growth in the field of human resource management.
- Support the Society's goals and objectives for developing the human resource management profession.
- Encourage my employer to make the fair and equitable treatment of all employees a primary concern.
- Strive to make my employer profitable both in monetary terms and through the support and encouragement of effective employment practices.
- Instill in the employees and the public a sense of confidence about the conduct and intentions of my employer.
- Maintain loyalty to my employer and pursue its objectives in ways that are consistent with the public interest.
- Uphold all laws and regulations relating to my employer's activities.
- Refrain from using my official positions, either regular or volunteer, to secure special privilege, gain or benefit for myself.
- Maintain the confidentiality of privileged information.
- Improve public understanding of the role of human resource management.

This Code of Ethics for members of the Society for Human Resource Management has been adopted to promote and maintain the highest standards of personal conduct and professional standards among its members. By joining the Society, a member espouses this Code, thereby assuring public confidence in the integrity and service of human resource management professionals.

© Society for Human Resource Management. Reprinted with permission.

SOCIETY FOR TECHNICAL COMMUNICATION

Address: 901 North Stuart Street, Suite 904
Arlington, VA 22203-1822

Telephone: 703/522-4114
WWW: www.stc-va.org
Document: STC Ethical Guidelines for Technical Communicators

As technical communicators, we observe the following guidelines in our professional activities. Their purpose is to help us maintain ethical practices.

Legality—

We observe the laws and regulations governing our professional activities in the workplace. We meet the terms and obligations of contracts that we undertake. We ensure that all terms of our contractual agreements are consistent with the STC Ethical Guidelines.

Honesty—

We seek to promote the public good in our activities. To the best of our ability, we provide truthful and accurate communications. We dedicate ourselves to conciseness, clarity, coherence, and creativity, striving to address the needs of those who use our products. We alert our clients and employers when we believe material is ambiguous. Before using another person's work, we obtain permission. In cases where individuals are credited, we attribute authorship only to those who have made an original, substantive contribution. We do not perform work outside our job scope during hours compensated by clients or employers, except with their permission; nor do we use their facilities, equipment, or supplies without their approval. When we advertise our services, we do so truthfully.

Confidentiality—

Respecting the confidentiality of our clients, employers, and professional organizations, we disclose business-sensitive information only with their consent or when legally required. We acquire releases from clients and employers before including their business-sensitive information in our portfolios or before using such material for a different client or employer or for demo purposes.

Quality—

With the goal of producing high quality work, we negotiate realistic, candid agreements on the schedule, budget, and deliverables with clients and employers in the initial project planning stage. When working on the project, we fulfill our negotiated roles in a timely, responsible manner and meet the stated expectations.

Fairness—

We respect cultural variety and other aspects of diversity in our clients, employers, development teams, and audiences. We serve the business interests of our clients and employers, as long as such loyalty does not require us to violate the public good. We avoid conflicts of interest in the fulfillment of our professional responsibilities and activities. If we are aware of a conflict of interest, we disclose it to those concerned and obtain their approval before proceeding.

Professionalism—

We seek candid evaluations of our professional performance from clients and employers. We also provide candid evaluations of communication products and services. We advance the technical communication profession through our integrity, standards, and performance.

© Society for Technical Communication. Used with permission from the Society for Technical Communication, Arlington, Virginia.

THE SOCIETY *of*
AMERICAN ARCHIVISTS

SOCIETY OF AMERICAN ARCHIVISTS

Address:	527 South Wells Street, Fifth Floor
	Chicago, IL 60607-3922
Telephone:	312/922-0140
WWW:	www.archivists.org
Document:	Code of Ethics for Archivists (1992)

(The Society of American Archivists also publishes *Code of Ethics for Archivists and Commentary*, a summary of the principal guidelines in the *Code* followed by commentary that "explains the reasons for some of the statements and provides a basis for discussion of the points raised." It is not reprinted here.—Eds.)

Archivists select, preserve, and make available documentary materials of long-term value that have lasting value to the organization or public that the archivist serves. Archivists perform their responsibilities in accordance with statutory authorization or institutional policy. They subscribe to a code of ethics based on sound archival principles and promote institutional and professional observance of these ethical and archival standards.

Archivists arrange transfers of records and acquire documentary materials of long-term value in accordance with their institutions' purposes, stated policies, and resources. They do not compete for acquisitions when competition would endanger the integrity or safety of documentary materials of long-term value, or solicit the records of an institution that has an established archives. They cooperate to ensure the preservation of materials in repositories where they will be adequately processed and effectively utilized.

Archivists negotiating with transferring officials or owners of documentary materials of long-term value seek fair decisions based on full consideration of authority to transfer, donate, or sell; financial arrangements and benefits; copyright; plans for processing; and conditions of access. Archivists discourage unreasonable restrictions on access or use, but may accept as a condition of acquisition clearly stated restrictions of limited duration and may occasionally suggest such restrictions to protect privacy. Archivists observe faithfully all agreements made at the time of transfer or acquisition.

Archivists establish intellectual control over their holdings by describing them in finding aids and guides to facilitate internal controls and access by users of the archives.

Archivists appraise documentary materials of long-term value with impartial judgment based on thorough knowledge of their institutions' administrative requirements or acquisitions policies. They maintain and protect the arrangement of documents and information transferred to their custody to protect its authenticity. Archivists protect the integrity of documentary materials of long-term value in their custody, guarding them against defacement, alteration, theft, and physical damage, and ensure that their evidentiary value is not impaired in the archival work of arrangement, description, preservation, and use. They cooperate with other archivists and law enforcement agencies in the apprehension and prosecution of thieves.

Archivists respect the privacy of individuals who created, or are the subjects of, documentary materials of long-term value, especially those who had no voice in the disposition of the materials. They neither reveal nor profit from information gained through work with restricted holdings.

Archivists answer courteously and with a spirit of helpfulness all reasonable inquiries about their holdings, and encourage use of them to the greatest extent compatible with institutional policies, preservation of holdings, legal considerations, individual rights, donor agreements, and judicious use of archival resources. They explain pertinent restrictions to potential users, and apply them equitably.

Archivists endeavor to inform users of parallel research by others using the same materials, and, if the individuals concerned agree, supply each name to the other party.

As members of a community of scholars, archivists may engage in research, publication, and review of the writings of other scholars. If archivists use their institutions holdings for personal research and publication, such practices should be approved by their employers and made known to others using the same holdings. Archivists who buy and sell manuscripts personally should not compete for acquisitions with their own repositories, should inform their employers of their collecting activities, and should preserve complete records of personal acquisitions and sales.

Archivists avoid irresponsible criticism of other archivists or institutions and address complaints about professional or ethical conduct to the individual or institution concerned, or to a professional archival organization.

Archivists share knowledge and experience with other archivists through professional associations and cooperative activities and assist the professional growth of others with less training or experience. They are obligated by professional ethics to keep informed about standards of good practice and to follow the highest level possible in the administration of their institutions and collections. They have a professional responsibility to recognize the need for cooperative efforts and support the development and dissemination of professional standards and practices.

Archivists work for the best interests of their institutions and their profession and endeavor to reconcile any conflicts by encouraging adherence to archival standards and ethics.

SOCIETY OF AMERICAN FORESTERS

Address: 5400 Grosvenor Lane
              Bethesda, MD 20814-2198
Telephone: 301/897-8720
WWW: www.safnet.org
Document: Code of Ethics for Members of the
              Society of American Foresters (1976.
              Most recently revised 1992.)

(The Society's original code of ethics was adopted on November 12, 1948, and amended on December 4, 1971. The present code was adopted by member referendum on June 23, 1976, and revised in 1986 and 1992.—Eds.)

PREAMBLE

Stewardship of the land is the cornerstone of the forestry profession. The purpose of these canons is to govern the professional conduct of members of the Society of American Foresters in their relations with the land, the public, their employers, including clients, and each other as provided in article VIII of the Society's Constitution. Compliance with these canons demonstrates our respect for the land and our commitment to the wise management of ecosystems, and ensures just and honorable professional and human relationships, mutual confidence and respect, and competent service to society.

These canons have been adopted by the membership of the Society and can only be amended by the membership. Procedures for processing charges of violation of these canons are contained in Bylaws established by the Council. The canons and procedures apply to all membership categories in all forestry-related disciplines, except Honorary Members.

All members upon joining the Society agree to abide by this Code as a condition of membership.

CANONS

1. A member will advocate and practice land management consistent with ecologically sound principles.
2. A member's knowledge and skills will be utilized for the benefit of society. A member will strive for accurate, current, and increasing knowledge of forestry, will communicate such knowledge when not confidential, and will challenge and correct untrue statements about forestry.
3. A member will advertise only in a dignified and truthful manner, stating the services the member is qualified and prepared to perform. Such advertisements may include references to fees charged.
4. A member will base public comment on forestry matters on accurate knowledge and will not distort or withhold pertinent information to substantiate a point of view. Prior to making public statements on forest policies and practices, a member will indicate on whose behalf the statements are made.
5. A member will perform services consistent with the highest standards of quality and with loyalty to the employer.
6. A member will perform only those services for which the member is qualified by education or experience.
7. A member who is asked to participate in forestry operations which deviate from accepted professional standards must advise the employer in advance of the consequences of such deviation.
8. A member will not voluntarily disclose information concerning the affairs of the member's employer without the employer's express permission.
9. A member must avoid conflicts of interest or even the appearance of such conflicts. If, despite such precaution, a conflict of interest is discovered, it must be promptly and fully disclosed to the member's employer and the member must be prepared to act immediately to resolve the conflict.
10. A member will not accept compensation or expenses from more than one employer for the same service, unless the parties involved are informed and consent.
11. A member will engage, or advise the member's employer to engage, other experts and specialists in forestry or related fields whenever the employer's interest would be best served by such action, and a member will work cooperatively with other professionals.
12. A member will not by false statement or dishonest action injure the reputation or professional associations of another member.
13. A member will give credit for the methods, ideas, or assistance obtained from others.
14. A member in competition for supplying forestry services will encourage the prospective employer to base selection on comparison of qualifications and negotiation of fee or salary.
15. Information submitted by a member about a candidate for a prospective position, award, or elected office will be accurate, factual, and objective.
16. A member having evidence of violation of these canons by another member will present the information and charges to the Council in accordance with the Bylaws.

© Society of American Foresters. Reprinted with permission.

SOCIETY OF FINANCIAL SERVICE PROFESSIONALS

Address: 270 South Bryn Mawr Avenue
                Bryn Mawr, PA 19010
Telephone: 610/526-2500
WWW: www.financialpro.org
Document: Code of Ethics of the Society of
                Financial Service Professionals
                (1978)

(Historical background to this code may be found in *In Pursuit of Professionalism: A New History of the*

Society of Chartered Property & Casualty Under-writers 1943-1983 (Malvern, PA, 1984).—Eds.)

INTRODUCTION

- Men and women who have chosen to enter into membership in the Society voluntarily bind themselves to this the Code of Ethics of their professional organization.

- The purpose of the Code is to give further force to the pledge taken by all holders of the CLU and ChFC designations and to provide a series of standards by which those involved in providing insurance and financial planning and economic security may conduct themselves in a professional manner. The Code is founded upon the two ethical imperatives of competent advice and service to the client and enhancement of the public regard for the CLU and ChFC designations.

- Competent advice and service to the client is at the very essence of any professional calling. Enhancement of the public regard for professional designations gives voice to the concept that in accepting Society membership an obligation is also accepted to all other holders of similar and allied professional designations and degrees.

- In its design, the Code presents the two ethical Imperatives, supported by Guides which give specificity to the Imperatives, and interpretive comment which is intended to aid in a uniform understanding of the Guides.

- A violation of the Code would expose a member to sanctions which range from reprimand to revocation of membership in the Society. A member is in violation of the Code when a final judgment is made that the member has breached an ethical imperative through failure to adhere to one or more of the Guides.

- For ease of drafting and reading, the masculine gender and singular number have been used. When appropriate, masculine is to be read as feminine and singular as plural. The word "client" is used under the First Imperative since standards concerning advice and service have greatest applicability to the relationship of client to professional insurance and financial services practitioner.

FIRST IMPERATIVE: To competently advise and serve the client. . .

Guide 1.1: A member shall provide advice and service which are in the client's best interest.
Interpretive Comment.

A. A member possessing a specific body of knowledge which is not possessed by the general public has an obligation to use that knowledge for the benefit of the client and to avoid taking advantage of that knowledge to the detriment of the client.

B. In a conflict of interest situation the interest of the client must be paramount.

C. The member must make a conscientious effort to ascertain and to understand all relevant circumstances surrounding the client.

D. The member is to accord due courtesy and consideration to those engaged in related professions who are also serving the client.

E. A member is to give due regard to any agent-principal relationship which may exist between the member and such companies as he may represent.

Guide 1.2: A member shall respect the confidential relationship existing between client and member.
Interpretive Comment.

A. Competent advice and service may necessitate the client sharing personal and confidential information with the member. Such information is to be held in confidence by the member unless released from the obligation by the client.

Guide 1.3: A member shall continue his education throughout his professional life.
Interpretive Comment.

A. To advise and serve competently, a member must continue to maintain and to improve his professional abilities.

B. Continuing education includes both the member adding to his knowledge of the practice of his profession, and the member keeping abreast of changing economic and legislative conditions which may affect the financial plans of the insuring public.

C. A member may continue his education through formal or informal programs of study or through other professional experiences.

Guide 1.4: A member shall render continuing advice and service.
Interpretive Comment.

A. Advice and service, to be competent, must be ongoing as the client's circumstances change and as these changes are made known to the member.

B. A client with whom a member has an active professional relationship is to be informed of economic and legislative changes which relate to the client-member relationship.

SECOND IMPERATIVE: To enhance the public regard for professional designations and allied professional degrees held by members. . .

Guide 2.1: A member shall obey all laws governing his business or professional activities.
Interpretive Comment.

A. Business activities are non-personal activities carried on outside the life insurance community; professional activities are non-personal activities carried on within the life insurance community.

B. A member has a legal obligation to obey all laws applicable to his business and professional activities. The placement of this Guide within the Code raises this obligation to the level of an ethical obligation.

Guide 2.2: A member shall avoid all activities which detract from the integrity and professionalism of the Chartered Life Underwriter designation, the Chartered Financial Consultant designation, or any other allied professional degree or designation held by members.
Interpretive Comment.

A. Personal, business, and professional activities are encompassed within the scope of this Guide.

B. Activities which could present a violation of this Guide might include:

1. A member's failure to obey a law unrelated to the member's business or professional activities.

2. A member impairing the reputation of another practitioner.

3. A member unfairly competing with another practitioner.

4. Actions which result in the member discrediting his own reputation.

5. A member discrediting life underwriting as a profession, the institution of life insurance or the Society of CLU & ChFC.

6. A member advertising the Chartered Life Underwriter or Chartered Financial Consultant designation or membership in the Society in an undignified manner, or in a manner prohibited by the bylaws of the Society.

Guide 2.3: A member shall encourage others to attain the Chartered Life Underwriter and/or the Chartered Financial Consultant designations.
Interpretive Comment.

A. Enhancement of the public regard for the CLU and ChFC designations depends upon a continuing increase in the number of holders of the designations who are available to advise and serve the public.

B. Encouraging others who might be qualified to enter into a practice is one hallmark of a professional.

Guide 2.4: A member shall avoid using the Chartered Life Underwriter or Chartered Financial Consultant designation in a false or misleading manner.
Interpretive Comment.

A. The CLU and ChFC designations are granted by the American College to specified individuals. Acts which directly or indirectly extend the member's personal designation to others would present a violation of this Guide.

B. Chartered Life Underwriter (CLU) or Chartered Financial Consultant (ChFC) may not be used in a name of a business in a manner which would reasonably lead others to conclude that someone other than the named member held the designation. Example:

1. John Jones, CLU & Associates is permissible.

2. John Jones & Associates, Chartered Financial Consultants is not permissible.

© Society of Financial Service Professionals. Reprinted with permission.

SOCIETY OF FIRE PROTECTION ENGINEERS

Address:	7315 Wisconsin Avenue, Suite 1225W Bethesda, MD 20814
Telephone:	301/718-2910
WWW:	www.sfpe.org
Document:	Canons of Ethics for Protection Engineers (1984. Most recently revised 1992)

Preamble

Fire protection engineering is an important learned profession. The members of the profession recognize that their work has a direct and vital impact on the quality of life for all people. Accordingly, the services provided by fire protection engineers require honesty, impartiality, fairness and equity, and must be dedicated to the protection and enhancement of the public safety, health and welfare. In the practice of their profession, fire protection engineers must maintain and constantly improve their competence and perform under a standard of professional behavior which requires adherence to the highest principles of ethical conduct with balanced regard for the interests of the public, clients, employers, colleagues and the profession. Fire protection engineers are expected to act in accordance with this Code and all applicable laws and actively encourage others to do so.

Fundamental Principles

Fire protection engineers uphold and advance the honor and integrity of their profession by:

I. Using their knowledge and skill for the enhancement of human welfare;

II. Being honest and impartial, and serving with fidelity the public, their employers and clients;

III. Striving to increase the competence and prestige of the fire protection engineering profession.

Knowledge and Skill

Canon 1

Fire protection engineers shall be dedicated to the safety, health and welfare of the public in the performance of their professional duties. If fire protection engineers become knowledgeable of hazardous conditions that threaten the present or future safety, health or welfare of the public, then they shall so advise their employers or clients. Should knowledge of such conditions not be properly acted upon, then fire protection engineers shall notify the appropriate public authority.

Canon 2

Fire protection engineers shall consider the consequences of their work and societal issues pertinent to it and shall seek to extend public understanding of those relationships.

Canon 3

Fire protection engineers shall be encouraged to contribute services for the advancement of the safety, health and welfare of the community and support worthy causes.

Honesty and Impartiality

Canon 4

Fire protection engineers shall perform professional services only in the areas of their competence and after full disclosure of their pertinent qualifications.

Canon 5

Fire protection engineers shall be honest and truthful in presenting data and estimates, professional opinions and conclusions, and in their public statements dealing with professional matters and shall not engage in improper solicitation of professional employment or contracts.

Canon 6

Fire protection engineers shall act in professional matters for each employer or client as faithful agents or trustees and shall not disclose confidential information concerning the business affairs or technical processes of any present or former client or employer without consent.

Canon 7

Fire protection engineers shall be made and actions taken without bias because of race, religion, sex, age, national origin or physical handicaps.

Canon 8

Fire protection engineers shall make prior disclosure to all interested parties of all known or potential conflicts of interest or other circumstances which could influence or appear to influence their judgement or the quality of their service.

Competence and Prestige

Canon 9

Fire protection engineers shall perform services and associate with others only in such a manner as to uphold and enhance the honor and integrity of the profession.

Canon 10

Fire protection engineers shall continue their professional development throughout their careers and shall provide opportunities for the professional development of those engineers under their supervision.

Canon 11

Fire protection engineers having knowledge of any alleged violation of this Code shall cooperate with the proper authorities in furnishing such information or assistance as may be required.

Canon 12

Fire protection engineers shall accept responsibility for their actions, seek, accept and offer honest criticism of work, properly credit the contributions of others, and shall not accept credit for the work of others.

Canon 13

Fire protection engineers shall strive to advance the knowledge and skills of the profession and to make these advancement available to colleagues, clients and the public.

Canon 14 (adopted 9/17/92)

Fire protection engineers shall perform professional services using only those engineering methods and tools for which they have an adequate understanding of the correct use and limitations.

© Society of Fire Protection Engineers. Reprinted with permission.

SOCIETY OF PETROLEUM ENGINEERS

Address: P.O. Box 833836
              Richardson, TX 75083-3836
Telephone: 972/952-9393
WWW: www.spe.org
Document: Guide for Professional Conduct (1985)

Preamble

Engineers recognize that the practice of engineering has a direct and vital influence on the quality of life for all people. Therefore, engineers should exhibit high standards of competency, honesty, and impartiality; be fair and equitable; and accept a personal responsibility for adherence to applicable laws, the protection of the public health, and maintenance of safety in their professional actions and behavior. These principles govern professional conduct in serving the interests of the public, clients, employers, colleagues, and the profession.

The Fundamental Principle

The engineer as a professional is dedicated to improving competence, service, fairness, and the exercise of well-founded judgment in the practice of engineering for the public, employers, and clients with fundamental concern for the public health and safety in the pursuit of this practice.

Canons of Professional Conduct

1. Engineers offer services in the areas of their competence and experience affording full disclosure of their qualifications.
2. Engineers consider the consequences of their work and societal issues pertinent to it and seek to extend public understanding of those relationships.
3. Engineers are honest, truthful, and fair in presenting information and in making public statements reflecting on professional matters and their professional role.
4. Engineers engage in professional relationships without bias because of race, religion, sex, age, national origin, or handicap.
5. Engineers act in professional matters for each employer or client as faithful agents or trustees disclosing nothing of a proprietary nature concerning the business affairs or technical processes of any present or former client or employer without specific consent.
6. Engineers disclose to affected parties known or potential conflicts of interest or other circumstances which might influence—or appear to influence—judgment or impair the fairness or quality of their performance.
7. Engineers are responsible for enhancing their professional competence throughout their careers and for encouraging similar actions by their colleagues.
8. Engineers accept responsibility for their actions; seek and acknowledge criticism of their work; offer honest criticism of the work of others; properly credit the contributions of others; and do not accept credit for work not theirs.
9. Engineers, perceiving a consequence of their professional duties to adversely affect the present or future public health and safety, shall formally advise their employers or clients and, if warranted, consider further disclosure.
10. Engineers act in accordance with all applicable laws and the canons of ethics as applicable to the practice of engineering as stated in the laws and regulations governing the practice of engineering

in their country, territory, or state, and lend support to others who strive to do likewise.

SOCIETY OF PROFESSIONAL JOURNALISTS

Address: 16 South Jackson Street
             Greencastle, IN 46135-1514
Telephone: 765/653-3333
WWW: spj.org
Document: Code of Ethics (1996)

(The Society of Professional Journalists' first code of ethics was adopted in 1926, when the organization was called Sigma Delta Chi. That code was borrowed from the American Society of Newspaper Editors. In 1973, Sigma Delta Chi wrote its own code, which was revised in 1984 and 1987. The present version of the Society of Professional Journalists' *Code of Ethics* was adopted in September 1996.—Eds.)

Preamble
Members of the Society of Professional Journalists believe that public enlightenment is the forerunner of justice and the foundation of democracy. The duty of the journalist is to further those ends by seeking truth and providing a fair and comprehensive account of events and issues. Conscientious journalists from all media and specialties strive to serve the public with thoroughness and honesty. Professional integrity is the cornerstone of a journalist's credibility.

Members of the Society share a dedication to ethical behavior and adopt this code to declare the Society's principles and standards of practice.

Seek Truth and Report It
Journalists should be honest, fair and courageous in gathering, reporting and interpreting information.

Journalists should:
- Test the accuracy of information from all sources and exercise care to avoid inadvertent error. Deliberate distortion is never permissible.
- Diligently seek out subjects of news stories to give them the opportunity to respond to allegations of wrongdoing.
- Identify sources whenever feasible. The public is entitled to as much information as possible on sources' reliability.
- Always question sources' motives before promising anonymity. Clarify conditions attached to any promise made in exchange for information. Keep promises.
- Make certain that headlines, news teases and promotional material, photos, video, audio, graphics, sound bites and quotations do not misrepresent. They should not oversimplify or highlight incidents out of context.
- Never distort the content of news photos or video. Image enhancement for technical clarity is always permissible. Label montages and photo illustrations.
- Avoid misleading re-enactments or staged news events. If re-enactment is necessary to tell a story, label it.
- Avoid undercover or other surreptitious methods of gathering information except when traditional open methods will not yield information vital to the public. Use of such methods should be explained as part of the story.
- Never plagiarize.
- Tell the story of the diversity and magnitude of the human experience boldly, even when it is unpopular to do so.
- Examine their own cultural values and avoid imposing those values on others.
- Avoid stereotyping by race, gender, age, religion, ethnicity, geography, sexual orientation, disability, physical appearance or social status.
- Support the open exchange of views, even views they find repugnant.
- Give voice to the voiceless; official and unofficial sources of information can be equally valid.

- Distinguish between advocacy and news reporting. Analysis and commentary should be labeled and not misrepresent fact or context.
- Distinguish news from advertising and shun hybrids that blur the lines between the two.
- Recognize a special obligation to ensure that the public's business is conducted in the open and that government records are open to inspection.

Minimize Harm
Ethical journalists treat sources, subjects and colleagues as human beings deserving of respect.

Journalists should:

- Show compassion for those who may be affected adversely by news coverage. Use special sensitivity when dealing with children and inexperienced sources or subjects. Be sensitive when seeking or using interviews or photographs of those affected by tragedy or grief.
- Recognize that gathering and reporting information may cause harm or discomfort. Pursuit of the news is not a license for arrogance.
- Recognize that private people have a greater right to control information about themselves than do public officials and others who seek power, influence or attention. Only an overriding public need can justify intrusion into anyone's privacy.
- Show good taste. Avoid pandering to lurid curiosity.
- Be cautious about identifying juvenile suspects or victims of sex crimes.
- Be judicious about naming criminal suspects before the formal filing of charges.
- Balance a criminal suspect's fair trial rights with the public's right to be informed.

Act Independently
Journalists should be free of obligation to any interest other than the public's right to know.

Journalists should:

- Avoid conflicts of interest, real or perceived.
- Remain free of associations and activities that may compromise integrity or damage credibility.
- Refuse gifts, favors, fees, free travel and special treatment, and shun secondary employment, political involvement, public office and service in community organizations if they compromise journalistic integrity.
- Disclose unavoidable conflicts.
- Be vigilant and courageous about holding those with power accountable.

- Deny favored treatment to advertisers and special interests and resist their pressure to influence news coverage.
- Be wary of sources offering information for favors or money; avoid bidding for news.

Be Accountable
Journalists are accountable to their readers, listeners, viewers and each other.

Journalists should:

- Clarify and explain news coverage and invite dialogue with the public over journalistic conduct.
- Encourage the public to voice grievances against the news media.
- Admit mistakes and correct them promptly.
- Expose unethical practices of journalists and the news media.
- Abide by the same high standards to which they hold others.

SOCIETY OF PROFESSIONALS IN DISPUTE RESOLUTION

Address: 1527 New Hampshire Avenue NW, Third Floor Washington, DC 20036
Telephone: 202/667-9700
WWW: www.spidr.org
Document: Ethical Standards of Professional Responsibility (1986)

Introduction
The Society of Professionals in Dispute Resolution (SPIDR) was established in 1972 to promote the peaceful resolution of disputes. Members of the Soci-

ety believe that resolving disputes through negotiation, mediation, arbitration and other neutral interventions can be of great benefit to disputing parties and to society. In 1983, the SPIDR Board of Directors charged the SPIDR Ethics Committee with the task of developing ethical standards of professional responsibility. The Committee membership represented all the various sectors and disciplines within SPIDR. This document, adopted by the Board on June 2, 1986, is the result of that charge.

The purpose of this document is to promote among SPIDR Members and Associates ethical conduct and a high level of competency among SPIDR members, including honesty, integrity, impartiality and the exercise of good judgement in their dispute resolution efforts. It is hoped that this document also will help to (1) define the profession of dispute resolution, (2) educate the public, and (3) inform users of dispute resolution services.

Application of Standards
Adherence to these ethical standards by SPIDR Members and Associates is basic to professional responsibility. SPIDR Members and Associates commit themselves to be guided in their professional conduct by these standards. The SPIDR Board of Directors or its designee is available to advise Members and Associates about the interpretation of these standards. Other neutral practitioners and organizations are welcome to follow these standards.

Scope
It is recognized that SPIDR Members and Associates resolve disputes in various sectors within the disciplines of dispute resolution and have their own codes of professional conduct. These standards have been developed as general guidelines of practice for neutral disciplines represented in the SPIDR membership. Ethical considerations relevant to some, but not to all, of these disciplines are not covered by these standards.

General Responsibilities
Neutrals have a duty to the parties, to the professions, and to themselves. They should be honest and unbiased, act in good faith, be diligent, and not seek to advance their own interests at the expense of their parties'.

Neutrals must act fairly in dealing with the parties, have no personal interest in the terms of the settlement, show no bias towards individuals and institutions involved in the dispute, be reasonably available as requested by the parties, and be certain that the parties are informed of the process in which they are involved.

Responsibilities to the Parties
1. **Impartiality.** The neutral must maintain impartiality toward all parties. Impartiality means freedom from favoritism or bias either by word or by action, and a commitment to serve all parties as opposed to a single party.
2. **Informed Consent**. The neutral has an obligation to assure that all parties understand the nature of the process, the procedures, the particular role of the neutral, and the parties' relationship to the neutral.
3. **Confidentiality.** Maintaining confidentiality is critical to the dispute resolution process. Confidentiality encourages candor, a full exploration of the issues, and a neutral's acceptability. There may be some types of cases, however, in which confidentiality is not protected. In such cases, the neutral must advise the parties, when appropriate in the dispute resolution process, that the confidentiality of the proceedings cannot necessarily be maintained. Except in such instances, the neutral must resist all attempts to cause him or her to reveal any information outside the process. A commitment by the neutral to hold information in confidence within the process also must be honored.
4. **Conflict of Interest**. The neutral must refrain from entering or continuing in any dispute if he or she believes or perceives that participation as a neutral would be a clear conflict of interest and any circumstances that may reasonably raise a question as to the neutral's impartiality. The duty to disclose is a continuing obligation throughout the process.
5. **Promptness**. The neutral shall exert every reasonable effort to expedite the process.
6. **The Settlement and its Consequences**. The dispute resolution process belongs to the parties. The neutral has no vested interested in the terms of a settlement, but must be satisfied that agreements in which he or she has participated will not impugn the integrity of the process. The neutral has a responsibility to see that the parties consider the terms of a settlement. If the neutral is concerned about the possible consequences of a proposed agreement, and the needs of the parties dictate, the neutral must inform the parties of that concern. In adhering to this standard, the neutral may find it advisable to educate the parties,

to refer one or more parties for specialized advice, or to withdraw from the case. In no case, however, shall the neutral violate section 3, Confidentiality, of these standards.

Unrepresented Interests

The neutral must consider circumstances where interests are not represented in the process. The neutral has an obligation, where in his or her judgement the needs of parties dictate, to assure that such interests have been considered by the principal parties.

Use of Multiple Procedures

The use of more than one dispute resolution procedure by the same neutral involves additional responsibilities. Where the use of more than one procedure is initially contemplated, the neutral must take care at the outset to advise the parties of the nature of the procedures and the consequences of revealing information during any one procedure which the neutral may later use for decision making or share with another decision maker. Where the use of more than one procedure is contemplated after the initiation of the dispute resolution process, the neutral must explain the consequences and afford the parties an opportunity to select another neutral for the subsequent procedures. It is also incumbent upon the neutral to advise the parties of the transition from one dispute resolution process to another.

Background and Qualifications

A neutral should accept responsibility only in cases where the neutral has sufficient knowledge regarding the appropriate process and subject matter to be effective. A neutral has a responsibility to maintain and improve his or her professional skills.

Disclosure of Fees

It is the duty of the neutral to explain to the parties at the outset of the process the basis of compensation, fees, and charges, if any.

Support of the Profession

The experienced neutral should participate in the development of new practitioners in the field and engage in efforts to educate the public about the value and use of neutral dispute resolution procedures. The neutral should provide pro bono services, where appropriate.

Responsibilities of Neutrals Working on the Same Case

In the event that more than one neutral is involved in the resolution of a dispute, each has an obligation to inform the others regarding his or her entry in the case. Neutrals working with the same parties should maintain an open and professional relationship with each other.

Advertising and Solicitation

A neutral must be aware that some forms of advertising and solicitations are inappropriate and in some conflict resolution disciplines, such as labor arbitration, are impermissible. All advertising must honestly represent the services to be rendered. No claims of specific results or promises which imply favor of one side over another for the purpose of obtaining business should be made. No commissions, rebates, or other similar forms of remuneration should be given or received by a neutral for the referral of clients.

© Society of Professionals in Dispute Resolution. Reprinted with permission.

SOIL SCIENCE SOCIETY OF AMERICA

Address: 677 South Segoe Road
                Madison, WI 53711-1086
Telephone: 608/273-8095
WWW: www.soils.org

The Soil Science Society of America subscribes to the code of ethics of the American Society of Agronomy. See p. 00.

SPECIAL LIBRARIES ASSOCIATION

Address: 1700 Eighteenth Street NW
                Washington, DC 20009-2514
Telephone: 202/234-4700
WWW: www.sla.org

The Special Libraries Association subscribes to the code of ethics of the American Library Association. See p. 00.

WEDDING AND PORTRAIT PHOTOGRAPHERS INTERNATIONAL

Address: PO Box 2003
             1312 Lincoln Boulevard
             Santa Monica, CA 90406-2003
Telephone: 310/451-0090
WWW: www.wppi-online.com
Document: Code of Ethics (1995)

1. I will conform to the highest ethical and technical standards in the practice of my profession, striving constantly to improve my artistic abilities as a professional photographer.
2. I will make no misleading promises or advertisements concerning services offered, and will be prompt in meeting all photographic schedules.
3. I will use only high quality, dependable equipment, film and accessories, which I will test regularly and maintain in good working condition.
4. I will always have spare equipment available to use in case of emergencies.
5. I will attend each event neatly dressed and groomed in attire appropriated for the occasion, photographing the occasion in a dignified, professional and unobtrusive manner.
6. My role as a photographer will be conducted, at all times, in accordance with WPPI standards, in keeping with the dignity of the occasion, and in harmony with the environment.
7. I will build rapport both personally and professionally with my clientele to make the photographic experience as meaningful as possible.
8. I will always honor my promise as an honest business person and will make every effort to satisfy my imaging clientele with excellent service.
9. When conducting wedding photography services, I will make every effort to provide each bride and groom with a photographic record of their wedding which meets these standards.
10. At weddings, I will conduct myself in accordance with the doctrines and customs of each particular House of Worship, and will conform to prevailing regulations pertaining to taking of photographs before, during and after the wedding ceremony.

© Wedding and Portrait Photographers International. Reprinted with permission.

THE WILDLIFE SOCIETY

Address: 5410 Grosvenor Lane
             Bethesda, MD 20814-2197
Telephone: 301/897-9770
WWW: wildlife.org
Document: Ethics and Professional Conduct for Wildlife Biologists

Associate and Certified Wildlife Biologists shall conduct their activities in accordance with the Code of Ethics and the Standards for Professional Conduct as prescribed by The Wildlife Society outlined below.

A. Code of Ethics

Associate and Certified Wildlife Biologists have a responsibility for contributing to an understanding of mankind's proper relationship with natural resources, and in particular for determining the role of wildlife in satisfying human needs. Certified wildlife biologists will strive to meet this obligation through the following professional goals: They will subscribe to the highest standards of integrity and conduct. They will recognize research and scientific management of wildlife and their environments as primary goals. They will disseminate information to promote understanding of, and appreciation for, values of wildlife and their habitats. They will strive to increase knowledge and skills to advance the practice of wildlife management. They will promote competence in the field of wildlife management by supporting high standards of education, employment, and performance. They will encourage the use of sound biological information in management decisions. They will support fair and uniform standards of employment and treatment of those professionally engaged in the practice of wildlife management.

B. Standards for Professional Conduct

The following tenets express the intent of the Code of Ethics as prescribed by The Wildlife Society and traditional norms for professional service. **Wildlife biologists shall at all times**:

1. Recognize and inform prospective clients or employers of their prime responsibility to the public interest, conservation of the wildlife resource, and the environment. They shall act with the authority of professional judgment, and avoid actions or omissions that may compromise these broad responsibilities. They shall respect the competence, judgment, and authority of the professional community.

2. Avoid performing professional services for any client or employer when such service is judged to be contrary to the Code of Ethics or Standards for Professional Conduct or detrimental to the well-being of the wildlife resource and its environment.

3. Provide maximum possible effort in the best interest of each client/employer accepted, regardless of the degree of remuneration. They shall be mindful of their responsibility to society, and seek to meet the needs of the disadvantaged for advice in wildlife-related matters. They should studiously avoid discrimination in any form, or the abuse of professional authority for personal satisfaction.

4. Accept employment to perform professional services only in areas of their own competence, and consistent with the Code of Ethics and Standards for Professional Conduct described herein. They shall seek to refer clients or employers to other natural resource professionals when the expertise of such professionals shall best serve the interests of the public, wildlife, and the client/employer. They shall cooperate fully with other professionals in the best interest of the wildlife resource.

5. Maintain a confidential professional-client/employer relationship except when specifically authorized by the client/employer or required by due process of law or this Code of Ethics and Standards to disclose pertinent information. They shall not use such confidence to their personal advantage or to the advantage of other parties, nor shall they permit personal interests or other client/employer relationships to interfere with their professional judgment.

6. Refrain from advertising in a self-laudatory manner, beyond statements intended to inform prospective clients/employers of qualifications, or in a manner detrimental to fellow professionals and the wildlife resource.

7. Refuse compensation or rewards of any kind intended to influence their professional judgment or advice. They shall not permit a person who recommends or employs them, directly or indirectly, to regulate their professional judgment. They shall not accept compensation for the same professional services from any source other than the client/employer without the prior consent of all the clients or employers involved. Similarly, they shall not offer a reward of any kind or promise of service in order to secure a recommendation, a client, or preferential treatment from public officials.

8. Uphold the dignity and integrity of the wildlife profession. They shall endeavor to avoid even the suspicion of dishonesty, fraud, deceit, misrepresentation, or unprofessional demeanor.

Appendix

Cross-Index of Represented Professions

ACCOUNTANTS
American Institute of Certified Public
   Accountants
Institute of Certified Management Accountants
Institute of Internal Auditors
Institute of Management Accountants
National Society of Accountants
National Society of Public Accountants

ACTUARIES
American Academy of Actuaries

ACUPUNCTURISTS
American Association of Oriental Medicine

ADMINISTRATORS
American Association of Airport Executives
American Association of Homes and Services for
   the Aging
American Association of School Administrators
American College of Health Care Administrators
American College of Healthcare Executives
American Judicature Society
American Health Care Association
American Hospital Association
American Society for Public Administration
American Society of Association Executives
Community Associations Institute
General Agents and Managers Association
Institute of Real Estate Management
International Association of Fire Chiefs
International City/County Management
   Association
International Facility Management Association
National Association of Counties
National Association of Credit Management
National Association of Purchasing Management
National Property Management Association
National Society of Fund Raising Executives
Society for Human Resource Management

ADMISSIONS COUNSELORS
National Association for College Admission
   Counseling

ADVERTISING PROFESSIONALS
American Advertising Federation
American Association of Advertising Agencies

AEROSPACE ENGINEERS
American Institute of Aeronautics and Astronautics

AGENTS
National Association of Performing Arts
   Managers and Agents

AGRONOMISTS
American Society of Agronomy
Soil Science Society of America

AIR QUALITY ENGINEERS
Air and Waste Management Association

AIR TRAFFIC CONTROLLERS
Air Traffic Control Association

AIRPORT MANAGERS
American Association of Airport Executives

ALTERNATIVE MEDICINE PRACTITIONERS
American Association of Oriental Medicine
National Guild of Hypnotists

ANESTHESIOLOGISTS
American Society of Anesthesiologists

ANESTHETISTS
American Association of Nurse Anesthetists

ANTHROPOLOGISTS
American Anthropological Association

APPRAISERS
American Society of Appraisers
Appraisal Institute
International Association of Assessing Officers

ARBITRATORS
American Arbitration Association
Society of Professionals in Dispute Resolution

ARCHAEOLOGISTS
Archaeological Institute of America

ARCHITECTS
American Institute of Architects
American Society of Landscape Architects

ARCHIVISTS
Society of American Archivists

ARTISTS' MANAGERS *see* AGENTS

ASSESSORS *see* APPRAISERS

ASSOCIATION EXECUTIVES
American Society of Association Executives

ATTORNEYS
American Bar Association
Association of Trial Lawyers of America
Federal Bar Association

AUCTIONEERS
National Auctioneers Association

AUDIOLOGISTS
American Speech-Language-Hearing Association
International Hearing Society

AUDITORS
Institute of Internal Auditors

AUTHORS *see* WRITERS

BIOANALYSTS
American Association of Bioanalysts

BIOLOGISTS
American Society for Microbiology
The Wildlife Society

BOTANISTS
Botanical Society of America

BROADCASTERS
Radio-Television News Directors Association

BUILDERS *see* CONTRACTORS

CAREER PLANNERS
Association for Career and Technical Education
National Association of Colleges and Employers

CARTOGRAPHERS
American Congress on Surveying and Mapping

CHEFS
International Association of Culinary
Professionals

CHEMICAL ENGINEERS
American Chemical Society
American Institute of Chemical Engineers
Association of Consulting Chemists & Chemical
Engineers

CHEMISTS
American Chemical Society
American Institute of Chemists
Association of Consulting Chemists & Chemical
Engineers

CHILD WELFARE WORKERS
Child Welfare League of America

CITY/COUNTY MANAGERS
International City/County Management
Association
National Association of Counties

CITY PLANNERS *see* PLANNERS

CIVIL ENGINEERS
American Society of Civil Engineers

CLERGY
American Association of Pastoral Counselors

CLINICAL RESEARCHERS
Association of Clinical Research Professionals

CLINICAL SOCIAL WORKERS
Clinical Social Work Federation

CLOTHING DESIGNERS
International Association of Clothing Designers
and Executives

COACHES
National Federation of Interscholastic Coaches
Association

COLLEGE/UNIVERSITY TEACHERS
see EDUCATORS

COMMUNITY DEVELOPERS *see* PLANNERS

COMMUNITY MANAGERS
Community Associations Institute

COMPUTER SCIENTISTS
Association for Computing Machinery
Institute for Certification of Computing
Professionals

CONSERVATIONISTS *see*
ENVIRONMENTALISTS

CONSULTANTS
American Consulting Engineers Council
Association of Consulting Chemists & Chemical
Engineers
Association of Management Consulting Firms
Institute of Management Consultants

CONTRACTORS
Associated Builders and Contractors
National Association of Home Builders

COOKS *see* CHEFS

CORRECTIONAL OFFICERS
American Correctional Association
International Association of Correctional Officers

COST ENGINEERS
AACE International

COUNSELORS
American Association for Marriage and Family
Therapy
American Association of Pastoral Counselors
American Counseling Association
American Mental Health Counselors Association
National Association of Alcoholism and Drug
Abuse Counselors

COUNTY OFFICIALS *see* CITY/COUNTY
MANAGERS

COURT MANAGERS
American Judicature Society

CREDIT MANAGERS
National Association of Credit Management

DANCE EDUCATORS
National Dance Association's National Registry
of Dance Educators

DANCE/MOVEMENT THERAPISTS
American Dance Therapy Association

DATA MANAGERS *see* INFORMATION
TECHNOLOGISTS

DENTAL ASSISTANTS
American Dental Assistants Association

DENTAL HYGIENISTS
American Dental Hygienists' Association

DENTISTS
American Dental Association

DERMATOLOGISTS
American Academy of Dermatology

DESIGNERS
American Society of Interior Designers
Industrial Designers Society of America
International Association of Clothing Designers
and Executives

DIETITIANS
American Dietetic Association

DOCTORS *see* PHYSICIANS

ECOLOGISTS *see* ENVIRONMENTALISTS

EDITORS
American Society of Newspaper Editors
Society for Technical Communication

EDUCATORS
Academy of Management
American Association of School Administrators

American Association of University Professors
American Federation of Musicians of the United
States and Canada
American Federation of Teachers
American Historical Association
American Political Science Association
Association for Career and Technical Education
International Reading Association
Modern Language Association
Music Teachers National Association
National Association of Professional Educators
National Dance Association's National Registry
of Dance Educators
National Education Association
National Federation of Interscholastic Coaches
Association

ELECTRICAL ENGINEERS
Institute of Electrical and Electronics Engineers

EMERGENCY MEDICAL TECHNICIANS
National Association of Emergency Medical
Technicians

EMERGENCY SERVICES ADMINISTRATORS
International Association of Fire Chiefs

ENGINEERS
AACE International
Air and Waste Management Association
American Chemical Society
American Consulting Engineers Council
American Institute of Chemical Engineers
American Nuclear Society
American Society of Civil Engineers
American Society of Heating, Refrigerating, and
Air-Conditioning Engineers
American Society of Mechanical Engineers
American Society of Safety Engineers
Association of Consulting Chemists & Chemical
Engineers
Board of Certified Safety Professionals
Institute of Electrical and Electronics
Engineers
Institute of Industrial Engineers
Minerals, Metals & Materials Society
National Society of Professional Engineers
Society of Fire Protection Engineers
Society of Petroleum Engineers

ENGLISH PROFESSORS
Modern Language Association

ENTOMOLOGISTS
Entomological Society of America

ENVIRONMENTALISTS
Air and Waste Management Association
Ecological Society of America
National Association of Environmental
Professionals
National Environmental Health Association
National Registry of Environmental Professionals
Society of American Foresters
The Wildlife Society

ERGONOMICS
Human Factors and Ergonomics Society

EXECUTIVES *see* ADMINISTRATORS

FACILITY MANAGERS *see* PROPERTY/
FACILITY MANAGERS

FAMILY AND CONSUMER SCIENTISTS
American Association of Family and Consumer
Sciences

FAMILY PHYSICIANS
American Academy of Family Physicians

FAMILY THERAPISTS *see* COUNSELORS

FARMERS *see* AGRONOMISTS

FASHION DESIGNERS *see* CLOTHING
DESIGNERS

FINANCE PROFESSIONALS
Association for Investment Management &
Research
Certified Financial Planner Board of Standards
International Association for Financial Planning
Financial Executives Institute
National Association of Credit Management
Society of Financial Service Professionals

FIRE PROFESSIONALS
International Association of Fire Chiefs
International Fire Marshals Association
National Association of Fire Investigators
Society of Fire Protection Engineers

FOREIGN LANGUAGE PROFESSORS
Modern Language Association

FORESTERS *see* ENVIRONMENTALISTS

FUNDRAISERS
National Society of Fund Raising Executives

GENEALOGISTS
Association of Professional Genealogists
Board for Certification of Genealogists
National Genealogical Society

GENETICISTS
Genetics Society of America

GEOLOGISTS
American Institute of Professional Geologists

GYNECOLOGISTS
American College of Obstetricians and
Gynecologists

HEALTH CARE ADMINISTRATORS
American Association of Homes and Services for
the Aging
American College of Health Care Administrators
American College of Healthcare Executives
American Health Care Association
American Hospital Association

HEALTH INFORMATION MANAGERS *see*
MEDICAL RECORDS ADMINISTRATORS

HEARING INSTRUMENT SPECIALISTS *see*
AUDIOLOGISTS

**HEATING, REFRIGERATING & A/C
ENGINEERS**
American Society of Heating, Refrigerating, and
Air-Conditioning Engineers

HISTORIANS
American Historical Association

HOME CARE PROVIDERS
National Association for Home Care

HOME ECONOMISTS *see* FAMILY AND
CONSUMER SCIENTISTS

HOSPITAL ADMINISTRATORS *see* HEALTH
CARE ADMINISTRATORS

HOTEL/HOSPITALITY MANAGERS
American Bed and Breakfast Association

HUMAN RESOURCE MANAGERS
Society for Human Resource Management

HYPNOTISTS/HYPNOTHERAPISTS
National Guild of Hypnotists

INDUSTRIAL DESIGNERS
Industrial Designers Society of America

INDUSTRIAL ENGINEERS
Institute of Industrial Engineers

INFORMATION TECHNOLOGISTS
Association of Information Technology
Professionals
Institute for Certification of Computing
Professionals

INSURANCE PROFESSIONALS
American Academy of Actuaries
Chartered Property Casualty Underwriter Society
General Agents and Managers Association

National Association of Health Underwriters
National Association of Life Underwriters
Society of Financial Service Professionals

INTERIOR DESIGNERS
American Society of Interior Designers

INTERNISTS
American Society of Internal Medicine

INVESTMENT PROFESSIONALS *see* FINANCE
PROFESSIONALS

JOURNALISTS
American Society of Journalists and Authors
American Society of Newspaper Editors
National Press Photographers Association
Radio-Television News Directors Association
Society of Professional Journalists

JUDGES
American Bar Association

LABORATORY MANAGERS
American Association of Bioanalysts

LANDSCAPE ARCHITECTS
American Society of Landscape Architects

LAW ENFORCEMENT OFFICERS
American Correctional Association
American Federation of Police
International Association of Chiefs of Police
International Association of Correctional Officers
National Sheriffs' Association

LAWYERS *see* ATTORNEYS

LEGAL ASSISTANTS
American Judicature Society
National Association of Legal Assistants

LEGAL SECRETARIES
National Association of Legal Secretaries

LIBRARIANS
American Library Association
Special Libraries Association

LOBBYISTS
American League of Lobbyists

MANAGEMENT ACCOUNTANTS *see*
ACCOUNTANTS

MANAGEMENT CONSULTANTS *see*
CONSULTANTS

MANAGEMENT PROFESSORS
Academy of Management

MANAGERS *see* ADMINISTRATORS

MANUFACTURER AGENTS
Manufacturers' Agents National Association

MARKETING PROFESSIONALS
American Marketing Association
Direct Marketing Association

MARRIAGE COUNSELORS
American Association for Marriage and Family
Therapy

MATERIALS ENGINEERS
Minerals, Metals & Materials Society

MATHEMATICIANS
American Mathematical Society

MECHANICAL ENGINEERS
American Society of Mechanical Engineers

MEDIATORS *see* ARBITRATORS

MEDICAL RECORDS ADMINISTRATORS
American Health Information Management
Association

MEDICAL TECHNOLOGISTS
American Association of Bioanalysts
American Medical Technologists

METEOROLOGISTS
American Meteorological Society
National Weather Association

MICROBIOLOGISTS
American Society for Microbiology

MIDWIVES
American College of Nurse-Midwives

MUSIC TEACHERS
American Federation of Musicians of the United
States and Canada
Music Teachers National Association

MUSICIANS
American Federation of Musicians of the United
States and Canada
Music Teachers National Association

NEWS PROFESSIONALS *see* JOURNALISTS

NUCLEAR SCIENTISTS
American Nuclear Society

NUMISMATISTS
Professional Numismatists Guild

NURSES
American Association of Nurse Anesthetists
American College of Nurse-Midwives
American Nurses Association

NURSING HOME ADMINISTRATORS
American Association of Homes and Services for
the Aging

American College of Health Care Administrators
American Health Care Association

NUTRITIONISTS
American Dietetic Association

OBSTETRICIANS
American College of Obstetricians and
Gynecologists

OCCUPATIONAL THERAPISTS
American Occupational Therapy Association

OPHTHALMOLOGISTS
American Academy of Ophthalmology

OPTICIANS
American Board of Opticianry / National Contact
Lens Examiners
Guild of Prescription Opticians of America

OPTOMETRISTS
American Academy of Optometry
American Optometric Association

ORTHOPAEDIC SURGEONS
American Academy of Orthopaedic Surgeons

OSTEOPATHS
American Osteopathic Association

OTOLARYNGOLOGISTS
American Academy of Otolaryngology — Head
and Neck Surgery Foundation

PARALEGALS *see* LEGAL ASSISTANTS

PARAMEDICS *see* EMERGENCY MEDICAL
TECHNICIANS

PASTORAL COUNSELORS
American Association of Pastoral Counselors

PATHOLOGISTS
College of American Pathologists

PERSONNEL MANAGERS *see* HUMAN
RESOURCE MANAGERS

PETROLEUM ENGINEERS
Society of Petroleum Engineers

PHARMACISTS
American Pharmaceutical Association —
Academy of Pharmacy Practice and
Management
American Society of Health-System Pharmacists

PHOTOGRAPHERS
National Press Photographers Association
Professional Photographers of America
Wedding and Portrait Photographers International

PHYSICAL THERAPISTS
American Physical Therapy Association

PHYSICIAN ASSISTANTS
American Academy of Physician Assistants

PHYSICIANS
American Academy of Dermatology
American Academy of Family Physicians
American Academy of Ophthalmology
American Academy of Orthopaedic Surgeons
American Academy of Otolaryngology — Head
and Neck Surgery Foundation
American College of Obstetricians and
Gynecologists
American College of Surgeons
American Medical Association
American Osteopathic Association
American Psychiatric Association
American Psychoanalytic Association
American Society of Internal Medicine
American Society of Plastic and Reconstructive
Surgeons
American Urological Association
College of American Pathologists
Radiological Society of North America

PHYSICISTS
American Physical Society

PHYSIOLOGISTS
American Physiological Society

PLACEMENT OFFICERS
National Association of Colleges and Employers

PLANNERS
American Institute of Certified Planners
American Planning Association
American Society of Transportation and Logistics

PLASTIC SURGEONS
American Society of Plastic and Reconstructive
Surgeons

PODIATRISTS
American Podiatric Medical Association

POLICE *see* LAW ENFORCEMENT OFFICERS

POLITICAL SCIENTISTS
American Political Science Association

POLLSTERS *see* PUBLIC OPINION
RESEARCHERS

PROFESSORS *see* EDUCATORS

PROPERTY/FACILITY MANAGERS
American Association of Airport Executives
Community Associations Institute
International Facility Management Association
Institute of Real Estate Management
National Association of REALTORS®
National Property Management Association

PSYCHIATRISTS
American Psychiatric Association

PSYCHOANALYSTS
American Psychoanalytic Association

PSYCHOLOGISTS
American Psychological Association
American Psychological Society

PUBLIC ACCOUNTANTS *see* ACCOUNTANTS

PUBLIC ADMINISTRATORS
American Society for Public Administration
International City/County Management
Association
National Association of Counties

PUBLIC OPINION RESEARCHERS
American Association for Public Opinion
Research

PUBLIC RELATIONS PROFESSIONALS
Public Relations Society of America

PURCHASING PROFESSIONALS
American Purchasing Society
National Association of Purchasing Management

QUALITY CONTROLLERS
American Society for Quality

RADIOLOGISTS
Radiological Society of North America

READING SPECIALISTS
International Reading Association

REAL ESTATE AGENTS/BROKERS
National Association of REALTORS®

RECREATION PROFESSIONALS
National Recreation and Park Association

RECREATIONAL THERAPISTS
National Therapeutic Recreation Society

REPORTERS *see* JOURNALISTS

RESPIRATORY CARE PROFESSIONALS
American Association for Respiratory Care

SAFETY PROFESSIONALS
American Society of Safety Engineers
Board of Certified Safety Professionals

SALES REPRESENTATIVES *see*
MANUFACTURER AGENTS

SCHOOL ADMINISTRATORS
American Association of School
Administrators

SECRETARIES
International Association of Administrative
Professionals
National Association of Legal Secretaries

SHERIFFS *see* LAW ENFORCEMENT OFFICERS

SOCIAL WORKERS
Child Welfare League of America
Clinical Social Work Federation
National Association of Social Workers

SOCIOLOGISTS
American Sociological Association

SPEECH-LANGUAGE PATHOLOGISTS
American Speech-Language-Hearing Association

STATISTICIANS
American Academy of Actuaries
American Statistical Association

SURGEONS *see* PHYSICIANS

SURVEYORS
American Congress on Surveying and Mapping

TAXATION PROFESSIONALS
International Association of Assessing Officers
National Society of Public Accountants

TEACHERS *see* EDUCATORS

TECHNICAL WRITERS
Society for Technical Communication

THERAPISTS
American Association for Respiratory Care
American Dance Therapy Association
American Occupational Therapy Association
American Physical Therapy Association
National Therapeutic Recreation Society

TRANSPORTATION PROFESSIONALS
American Society of Transportation and Logistics

TRAVEL AGENTS
American Society of Travel Agents

UNDERWRITERS
Chartered Property Casualty Underwriter Society
National Association of Health Underwriters
National Association of Life Underwriters
Society of Financial Service Professionals

URBAN PLANNERS *see* PLANNERS

UROLOGISTS
American Urological Association

WEATHER FORECASTERS *see*
METEOROLOGISTS

WRITERS
American Society of Journalists and Authors
National Writers Association
Society for Technical Communication

About the Editors

John P. Stierman is an associate professor in the reference unit of the Western Illinois University library, Macomb, Illinois. He received both his B.A. and an M.A. in history from the University of Northern Iowa, and an M.A. in library and information science from the University of Iowa.

Kathleen E. Joswick is a professor at Western Illinois University in Macomb, Illinois, and serves as the reference unit coordinator at the university's library. Ms. Joswick holds an M.A. in English from State University College of New York at Buffalo and an M.A. in library and information science from Northern Illinois University.

Jeanne Koekkoek Stierman is an associate professor in the reference unit of the Western Illinois University library in Macomb, Illinois. She received a B.A. from Dordt College, an M.B.A. from the University of Iowa, and an M.A. in library and information science from the University of Iowa.

Roderick Sharpe is the access services librarian at the Western Illinois University library, Macomb, Illinois. He graduated from the Royal Academy of Music in London, received an M.M. from Drake University, and was awarded an M.A. in library and information science from the University of Iowa.